LEVEL SIX

SCOPE ENGLISH ANTHOLOGY

Literature and Reading Program

Edited by
Katherine Robinson
Editorial Director, Scope Magazine

SCHOLASTIC INC.

The Scope English Story

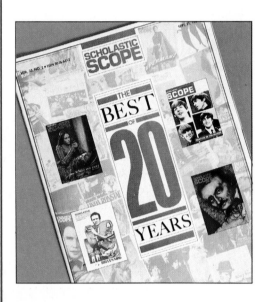

In 1964, when Scholastic first published it, SCOPE Magazine was a near-revolutionary publication: a magazine designed to bring good literature and reading, and useful skills, to young people. Now, after more than twenty years, SCOPE is the most widely used magazine in junior and senior high school Reading and English programs—reaching nearly 40 percent of all secondary schools in the United States.

Teachers have found SCOPE Magazine so useful in motivating readers that they have asked for a more permanent resource containing the high quality reading selections and activities found in every issue of SCOPE. So we developed SCOPE ENGLISH—a complete English program including both reading and literature as well as a comprehensive writing and language program. Teachers all over America are finding in SCOPE ENGLISH precisely those qualities that made SCOPE Magazine so popular: It makes English easier to learn, more motivating, more teachable. We've included selections from the magazine that are of high interest to students—stories, poems, plays, TV scripts, articles and more—as well as tried-and-true teacher favorites that create a basic curriculum framework. The reading levels of these selections are accessible to all junior and senior high school students, grades 6–12, yet the ideas are challenging and provocative. SCOPE ENGLISH includes an *Anthology* at each grade level, organized by themes, authors, or genres, and a *Writing and Language* text, written in clear, conversational style.

SCOPE ENGLISH contains eye-catching photos and illustrations that actually aid in students' understanding of the important events in a selection. An illustration is provided every three to five pages of text, to make the reading experience less threatening for the students. All the materials motivate secondary students to read more and write better.

More than twenty years after SCOPE Magazine first brought the SCOPE philosophy to the English classroom, we're proud to be able to reach you with the SCOPE ENGLISH program. We hope you will find these materials just as useful and helpful as you've found SCOPE Magazine to be in making English learning easier and more satisfying.

LITERATURE CONSULTANTS

Jane Yolen
Author

Theodore Hipple, Ph.D.
Department Chair
Curriculum and Instruction
University of Tennessee
Knoxville, Tennessee

READING CONSULTANT

Virginia B. Modla, Ph.D.
Reading Curriculum Associate
School District of Cheltenham Township
Elkins Park, Pennsylvania

LEVEL SIX READERS

Cynthia Imes
Teacher
Appleton High School West
Appleton, Wisconsin

Ann Miller
Coordinator, Learning Resource Center
Aptos High School
Aptos, California

John Russell
Teacher
Blue Springs High School
Blue Springs, Missouri

CURRICULUM CONSULTANTS

Barbara Coulter
Director of Language Education
Detroit Public Schools
Detroit, Michigan

Nora Forester
Reading Coordinator
North Side School District
San Antonio, Texas

William Horst
Secondary Section Committee
National Council of Teachers of English

Barbara Krysiak, Ed.D.
Principal
North Hampton Elementary School
North Hampton, New Hampshire

Nancy McHugh
Teacher
Grant High School
Van Nuys, California

COVER: THE SADNESS OF THE KING (1952, detail), by Henri Matisse. Courtesy of the National Museum of Modern Art, Paris, France.

Editorial, Design, and Art Production: Kirchoff/Wohlberg, Inc.

ISBN 0-590-34693-8

12 11 10 9 8 7 6 5 4 3   9/8 0 1 2/9

Printed in the U.S.A.

LEVEL SIX
Contents

SECTION 3 Relationships

SECTION 4 Artists at Work

SECTION 5   Discovery

SECTION 11   Shakespeare's Macbeth

LEVEL SIX
Skills Lessons

UNDERSTANDING LITERATURE

Reading Various Types of Literature

Plot

Setting and Mood

Characterization

Theme

Imagery

Style

Irony and Satire

READING COMPREHENSION

VOCABULARY/WORD ATTACK

ORAL LANGUAGE DEVELOPMENT

PROCESS WRITING

WRITING ABOUT THE SELECTION

RESEARCH AND STUDY SKILLS

APPEARANCE AND REALITY

It was a geography of dreams,
a history of magic.
I know by memory the islands and faces
that I saw or perhaps dreamed.

— Jorge Carrera Andrade
Ecuador

The Sleeping Gypsy
Henri Rousseau (1844-1910)
Museum of Modern Art
Gift of Mrs. Simon Guggenheim

Appearance and Reality

Which is more real—what reason tells you or what you imagine? Is beauty something you can see, or something that is inside? Is real life always truer than dreams? Writers all over the world have tried to answer these questions. Using many forms, writers show us that things are not always what they appear to be.

Imaginary Worlds

In his famous novel *Don Quixote*, the Spanish writer Miguel de Cervantes tells about a man who lives in an imaginary world, convincing everyone he meets that he is crazy. During his many adventures, Quixote bumps into the realities of everyday life over and over again. But he remains convinced that he is a knight, that windmills are giants, and that life is more exciting than other people think. Maybe there is something to be said for living in a dream world. Quixote's story has made people laugh ever since it was published in 1605. When you read it, you'll see that it's still funny today.

Outward Appearances

Isaac Bashevis Singer grew up in Poland and later moved to the United States. In his writing, Singer often uses the simple form of the folktales he heard when he was a boy. The tale you will read is about a family so poor they can't afford a mirror, so no one in the family is too sure what he or she looks like. Then one day a mirror arrives, and everyone finds out "the truth." But is the image in a mirror always a true one? As in many folktales, the moral of this story is clearly stated.

Writers often tell us that what a person looks like does not always show what is *really* there. *The Elephant Man* by Sir Frederick Treves is a true story of a man who was so deformed that most people screamed and panicked when they saw him. But one person recognized that inside the "monster" was a gentle, intelligent man.

Like many biographies, this story is written in the *first person*—it is told by someone who was there. The author, who became the Elephant Man's friend and protector, can give us a close look at someone he knew well. We meet a man who, trapped in a grotesque body, escapes to a dream world. The Elephant Man reads stories and longs to be a romantic hero. He loves the glittering fantasies of the theater. In his imagination, he is a dashing, attractive man-about-town. And Treves tries never to let a mirror remind his friend of his outward appearance.

But is the Elephant Man really ugly? Through Frederick Treves's words, we see the Elephant Man, not as a hideous mon-

Pandora's Box, *René Magritte, 1951*

ster, but as a sensitive, romantic soul.

The French writer Edmond Rostand wrote a play about another ugly man who had a romantic soul. Cyrano de Bergerac is in love with the beautiful Roxanne, but fears she will laugh at the attentions of such an unattractive admirer. So he writes eloquent love letters to her—and signs them "Christian," the name of his handsome friend. Roxanne falls madly in love with her suitor. But is it Christian she loves? Or is it Cyrano, whose words stir her soul? Like the story of the Elephant Man, Rostand's play forces us to ask how important beauty really is.

Entering New Worlds

The British poet Alfred, Lord Tennyson lived in the late 19th century, an age of factories and commerce. But his imagina-tion often turned to earlier, more glorious days. Tennyson's poem "Lady Clare" is about true love between a lady and a knight of olden times. The poem tells that a person's birth is not as important as what the person becomes. But the poem also transports you, the reader, to a distant world of romance.

The celebrated master of deduction, Sherlock Holmes, and his faithful companion, Dr. Watson, match wits with an ingenious villain in Sir Arthur Conan Doyle's "The Speckled Band." Holmes demonstrates an understanding of the difference between appearance and reality that enables him to save a young woman from a horrible fate.

Through poems, plays, stories, or true accounts, writers take you to places you have never been. So, to leave everyday life behind, just turn the page.

Don Quixote

based on the novel by Miguel de Cervantes

Miguel de Cervantes was born in 1547 in Spain. He was an adventurous youth who fought in the Spanish navy and later was captured by pirates. When Cervantes was finally free, after five years of imprisonment and several daring attempts to escape, he began to write plays and stories of romance and adventure. But not until he published Don Quixote, *which made fun of romance and adventure stories, did he become popular and successful.*

"There he goes again!" screeched the housekeeper.

Quijada had pulled yet another book off the shelf and was settling into a corner of the room to devour it.

The housekeeper shook her head and raised her eyes to the ceiling. With outstretched arms, she demanded that someone tell her why she bothered to keep house for a gentleman who no longer cared to live in it. "It's those books!" she blustered. "He lives in those moldy old books about knights and damsels and castles!" She twirled a finger beside her temple. "Making him loopy, that's what it's doing," she said to Quijada's niece.

Quijada didn't move a muscle except to turn a page. There was pretty fiery stuff going on in his book, and he was much too busy to deal with insults. A brave and valiant knight had just knocked someone on the helmet, and the clang of steel on steel resounded in Quijada's head. Quijada read on, his eyes widening with pleasure.

Fair maidens were in distress all over the place. Knaves were being run through the middle with lances. Horses were snorting and charging and kicking up mushrooms of dust.

"Go to it!" Quijada shouted.

The battle raged. Gleaming swords clashed in the early morning light. Heads rolled. Blood stained the ground. Quijada flailed his arms and stabbed the air with an imaginary sword.

"Submit or be killed!" he thundered, and rode off into the next chapter.

Quite obviously, Quijada was not on speaking terms with reality. He had forsaken the here and now for the there and then — the "then" being about a hundred years earlier, when Spain had produced knights like bakery muffins.

"How grand and noble they are," thought Quijada between paragraphs. "Questing for truth and purity, righting wrongs, winning the love of fair maidens." He sighed deeply, shaken to the very roots.

And then suddenly, his eyes widened and his nostrils flared with courage and resolution. Quivering with excitement, he rose to his feet and placed his hand upon his wildly beating heart.

"I shall become a knight," he whispered. "A glorious knight errant in the service of Spain."

When the tables and chairs rose up in protest, Quijada silenced them with a freezing stare. "Don't try to stop me. My mind is made up. Now, sirs, I take my leave. I must prepare myself for the battles I am to fight!" He then swaggered out to find a suit of armor.

Quijada banged around in the murky half-light of the cellar until he came upon a rusting metal mound covered with sticky cobwebs.

"Egad!" he exclaimed. "Great granddaddy's armor! And it's practically brand new!"

By late afternoon, Quijada had the suit oiled and shined, and he set about trying to climb inside it. But this was not as easy as he had thought it would be. Without a squire to assist him, he struggled like an overturned beetle trying to right itself. Figuring that a few heart-felt grunts just might do the trick, Quijada grunted for all he was worth. His grunting was so good, in fact, that it reached the ears of his housekeeper, who flew to the cellar stairs in alarm. She peered into the depths below, and her eyes popped with horror at the sight that she saw. There before her was a strange metal man creaking across the floor like a device in a torture chamber.

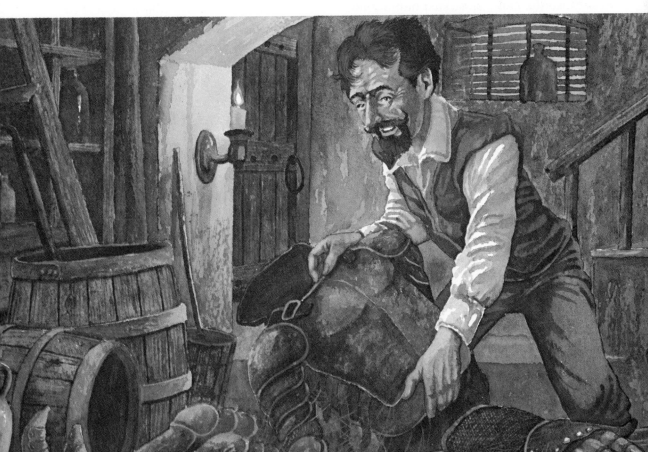

"Pretty snappy!" came a muffled voice from inside the helmet.

The housekeeper reeled, and a series of squeaks escaped her lips.

"Hmmm," said Quijada thoughtfully, "Sounds like I missed a spot with the oil can."

Quijada next turned his attention to a trusty steed. The books had said that knights rode the finest horses in all the kingdom, a goal that was totally out of reach for Quijada, considering what he had to work with. His horse bore a rather striking resemblance to a dead tree branch with ears. On a good day, the animal could manage a sort of hobbling walk, although it was generally agreed that his best gait was lying down.

Quijada renamed his horse Rozinante because the name suggested nobility and breeding. It was a name his horse could carry with pride as long as he didn't have to carry Quijada as well.

The final detail was, of course, a proper name for himself. A bold and daring knight could hardly be expected to go around as Sir Jawbone, which is what Quijada means in Spanish. So the days slipped by while Quijada hatched courtly names of all shapes and sizes, none of which fit him even half as well as his armor.

At the end of a week, Quijada was still nameless and beginning to wish he hadn't been so quick to give up Rozinante to an old horse. The outlook seemed grim; but then, suddenly, the mists cleared, and the grandest of all names burst into his brain:

Don Quixote de la Mancha!

Quijada cocked his head. Yes, there was a certain loftiness about it. It inspired

confidence. It suggested bravery. It was a name truly fit for a knight.

And so the following morning, Don Quixote de la Mancha rode off into the dawn to begin his adventures.

The first order of business was to be properly knighted. Don Quixote scanned the bleak and barren landscape around him. Just over the crest of a little hill stood a ramshackle inn, its thatched roof a yellow dot against the sky.

"Behold!" cried Don Quixote to his horse. "A sprawling manor house wherein lives a gentleman of great wealth and position. What luck! I shall be knighted there. Onward, Rozinante. Destiny awaits me!"

The sky was a deep twilight purple when Don Quixote at last reached the inn.

"You want me to do what?" squeaked the innkeeper in disbelief.

"Your lordship," said Don Quixote, "pray, do me the honor of bestowing upon this humble being the sacred order of knighthood." He bowed his head solemnly and his visor clanged shut.

The innkeeper bit into a dirty fingernail and eyed Don Quixote's metal suit. "Listen, mister, we don't do knighterizing here." He spat the fingernail fragment into the dust. "This is an inn. You want food, I got food. You want lodging, I can give you a couple of square feet in the stable. That's all I got left."

"I most humbly thank you, your lordship," Don Quixote replied from behind his visor, which was now stuck in the down position.

"Hey, Tolosa!" shouted the innkeeper. "Set this guy up in the barn!"

Tolosa appeared, wiping her hands on a stained apron. Her hair was in disarray, her dress hem frayed and uneven, and her shoes on the verge of complete collapse.

Don Quixote, peeping through his visor grille, gasped at this vision of refinement and virtue. "Your ladyship," he breathed, bowing deeply and nearly toppling from his horse.

Tolosa burst out laughing. "Your ladyship?" she squealed. "Well, I like that!" and she roared even louder.

"Knock it off," said the innkeeper. "You can see the guy's a little buggy in the head. He thinks I'm a lord."

Tolosa was now wracked with hysteria. "You?" she exploded, snorting behind her hands. "Who is this weirdo, anyway?"

"Don Quixote at your service," replied the visor grille.

"He wants me to make him a knight," said the innkeeper. "Can you beat that?"

Tolosa was now down to an occasional giggle. "That's cute," she said. "I think you ought to do it for him."

"Oh, your lordship," cooed Don Quixote, "I am wholly dedicated to the ideals of truth, purity, and valor. I assure you I will do my best to be worthy of this great appointment."

The innkeeper raised an eyebrow. "You will, huh?" He shrugged. "OK. Why not? I'll make you a knight. Get your stuff together."

Don Quixote was knighted in the stable that very evening as Tolosa and Rozinante looked on. The ceremony might have been a pile of nonsense, but it was very solemn, so when it was over, Don Quixote glowed with pride.

"What did you think of that?" the innkeeper asked Tolosa as they watched Don Quixote ride off into the distance.

"Not bad," she replied. "I kind of liked being called a lady."

"You did, eh? Well, get a move on, your ladyship. You've got customers."

Don Quixote carried on alone through two adventures and made a mess of them both. As he lay in bed recovering from battle wounds that had forced him to return home, he got to thinking that he might do better with a squire. A squire could help him over the rough spots, carry his shield, and get him in and out of his armor.

Meanwhile his housekeeper and niece moaned pathetically, overcome with worry that he might not survive. They begged him to stop playing knight and behave himself. But Don Quixote waved them off, muttering that they must be crazy to make such a suggestion. As soon as he was well enough to travel, he was out the door.

At the edge of town, Don Quixote came across a poor farmer named Sancho Panza. "Hi there!" he called. "I bid you join me, good sir, for I am in need of a squire."

"Yeah?" said Sancho, wiping his nose on a dirty sleeve. "What's a squire?"

Don Quixote sniffed. "Surely, sir, you have read books of knight errantry."

"I must have missed those," said Sancho.

"Ah, well," replied Don Quixote, "I'll fill you in. Come along now. It's likely we shall soon do battle for an island of which you will naturally be made governor — "

"Governor?" croaked Sancho. "Me?"

"Certainly. It's the least I could do for my own squire."

Sancho's eyes bulged. "Wait right there!" he cried. "Don't give that island to anyone else! I'm coming! I'm coming!" and he scrambled off to find his donkey.

Don Quixote and Sancho had traveled only a short way when suddenly Don Quixote pulled back on his reins and ordered Sancho to hold up. Then he rose on his stirrups, withdrew his sword, and cut furious zigzag patterns in the air. "Giants!" he thundered. "Fearsome giants!"

Sancho blinked. "Where, sir?"

"Yonder!" roared Don Quixote, pointing to a row of windmills in the distance.

"If you'll excuse me, sir," said Sancho meekly, "but those appear to be — "

"Terrible monsters!" cried Don Quixote. "With long, powerful arms. See how they wave at us. It is a challenge, Sancho, a great challenge; but I, Don Quixote de la Mancha, am prepared to slay them!"

In breathless excitement, Don Quixote fumbled with his battle gear. "Shield . . . I need my shield . . . this sword's no good . . . that goes back in, oof! There, and . . . hold this a minute, will you, Sancho?"

"Sir!" wailed Sancho. "Listen to me! You can't go around attacking windmills. If anybody saw you . . ."

Don Quixote's visor clanged shut. "Gimme that lance, Sancho. I'm ready. FALL, YOU KNAVES!" he shouted to the windmills, and he was off at a furious gallop.

Clods of dirt shot from Rozinante's flying hooves. The rushing wind whistled through chinks in Don Quixote's armor.

25

"Faster, Rozinante! We shall use the element of surprise!"

Sancho was stiff with shock as he watched Don Quixote steadily narrowing the distance between himself and the whirling windmill blades.

"Behold, you miserable giants!" screeched Don Quixote.

Closer and closer he came, his jaw set, his teeth clenched, his eyes ablaze with the glory of battle.

And then there was a terrible clang as the steel of Don Quixote's lance met the wood of the descending blades. Suddenly he was hoisted out of his saddle and lifted high into the air. His fingers still clutching his lance, he hung from the turning windmill like an overripe apple. A great gust of wind spun the blades around, flinging Don Quixote across the meadow in a wide arc and depositing him in a clump of prickly bushes.

When Sancho reached him, he was struggling to a sitting position and pulling twigs out of his eyebrows.

"Why didn't you listen to me?" moaned Sancho. "I told you they were windmills."

"Ah," said Don Quixote, "but only at the very last second when an evil magician changed them into windmills."

Sancho gurgled as though he were being choked. "You can't be serious!"

Don Quixote narrowed his eyes. "Serious?" he cried. "Of course I'm serious! What do you take me for — some kind of nut?" And then, addressing the magician, he hissed, "So that's the way it's to be, is it? Ah ha! Well! You have met your match in Don Quixote!" He scrambled to his feet.

"Arm yourself, you dastardly swine! The battle, sir, has just begun!"

Thus it was that Don Quixote went into the knight errant business. He concocted adventures like an aspiring soda jerk who suddenly finds he has the run of the ice-cream counter.

His effects on people certainly would have made headlines if the towns and villages had had newspapers to put headlines in. The people considered him a cross between a comic-opera hero and a large mosquito. He charged forward trying to save them from imagined disasters, and the general reaction was to swat at him.

Eventually Don Quixote began to lose a little of his enthusiasm. The roar of battle seemed to fade. The blood and sweat no longer filled his nose like sweet perfume. The time had come, he judged, to hang up his suit of armor and retire.

"I think I'm going to get out of the knight game," he told Sancho one day. "I'd kind of like to be a shepherd. Grass and trees and meadows are nice to be around. Sheep are nice to be around. I like to listen to them baa. A few baas in the morning, a couple of lunchtime baas, and at night, a lullaby of baas. Peaceful, don't you think, Sancho? Not like horse snorts. Horses aren't peaceful. Sheep are peaceful."

So Don Quixote and Sancho headed home across the fields and dirt roads and back through the gates of the present.

When Don Quixote announced to his niece and housekeeper that chivalry and knights and charging steeds were nonsense, they immediately concluded he had gone off his rocker. The truth of the matter

was, of course, that he had climbed back onto his rocker, so it just goes to show that being crazy is relative.

Dying, however, is not relative, and it was plain to everyone that Don Quixote was about to meet his final adventure. They put him to bed and called for the doctor, who could do nothing, for the end was very near.

Don Quixote picked at his covers and smiled feebly. "I will soon be in the meadows," he said, "under the warmth of a greater sun. I leave my worldly possessions to you, dear friends and family."

"Oh, sir!" said Sancho, choking back the tears. "We have so many battles left to fight! Stop this silliness at once!"

Don Quixote patted Sancho's hand. "A good try, my friend, but Death cannot be tricked. I take my leave now."

And as the gentle bleeting of sheep reached Don Quixote's ears, he smiled peacefully and went to meet them.

READING COMPREHENSION

Summarizing. Choose the best phrase to complete each sentence. Then write the complete statements on your paper.

1. The books Quijada read were about _____ (life in 18th-century Spain, the troubles of an innkeeper, the adventures of knights).

2. As time went on, Don Quixote _____ (was successful in his battles, decided that he needed a squire, became fearful of death).

3. Before Don Quixote died, he admitted that _____ (chivalry and knights were nonsense, he was upset by people laughing at him, he was not ready to die).

Interpreting. Write the answer to each question on your paper.

1. Why did Don Quixote name his horse Rozinante?

2. Why did the ceremony in which Don Quixote was knighted turn out to be a solemn one?

3. When Don Quixote was dying, why did Sancho tell him to stop the silliness and that they had many battles to fight?

For Thinking and Discussing. What did people think of Don Quixote while he was a knight errant? How did they react when he gave up chivalry? What do you think caused the change in their attitude?

UNDERSTANDING LITERATURE

Fiction. *Fiction* is a story that is made up or imagined by the author.

As fiction, *Don Quixote* must have a plot, a setting, and characters. Plot is the series of events that occur in the story. Setting is the place and time in which the story happens. The characters are the people in the story.

Answer the questions about plot, setting, and characters in *Don Quixote*.

1. When does *Don Quixote* take place? Could the story have happened recently? Explain your answer.

2. What motivated the main character to become a knight?

3. Here are four events from the plot. Write them on your paper in the order in which they happened.
   a. Don Quixote attacks the windmills.
   b. The innkeeper knights the Don.
   c. Sancho Panza becomes Don Quixote's squire.
   d. Quijada reads books about knights.

4. The theme of a story is its message— the author's comment on life or human nature. Explain how *Don Quixote* illustrates the theme "Anything can happen if you believe that it will."

WRITING

Write one or two beginning paragraphs for an original story about a person who wants to change the world. Include setting, characters, and one event.

The Cat Who Thought She Was a Dog and the Dog Who Thought He Was a Cat

Isaac Bashevis Singer

Although Isaac Bashevis Singer has lived in the United States since 1935, his work is usually set in Poland, where he was born in 1904. Singer writes in Yiddish, the traditional language of European Jews, but he helps translate his works into English. His ideas often have roots in Jewish tradition. In 1978, he was awarded the Nobel Prize for literature.

Once there was a poor peasant, Jan Skiba by name. He lived with his wife and three daughters in a one-room hut with a straw roof, far from the village. The house had a bed, a bench bed, and a stove, but no mirror. A mirror was a luxury for a poor peasant. And why would a peasant need a mirror? Peasants aren't curious about their appearance.

But this peasant did have a dog and a cat in his hut. The dog was named Burek and the cat, Kot. They had both been born within the same week. As little food as the peasant had for himself and his family, he still wouldn't let his dog and cat go hungry. Since the dog had never seen another dog and the cat had never seen another cat and they saw only each other, the dog thought he was a cat and the cat thought she was a dog. True, they were far from being alike by nature. The dog barked and the cat meowed. The dog

chased rabbits and the cat lurked after mice. But must all creatures be exactly like their own kind? The peasant's children weren't exactly alike either. Burek and Kot lived on good terms, often ate from the same dish, and tried to mimic each other. When Burek barked, Kot tried to bark along, and when Kot meowed, Burek tried to meow, too. Kot occasionally chased rabbits and Burek made an effort to catch a mouse.

The peddlers who bought groats, chickens, eggs, honey, calves, and whatever was available from the peasants in the village never came to Jan Skiba's poor hut. They knew that Jan was so poor he had nothing to sell. But one day a peddler happened to stray there. When he came inside and began to lay out his wares, Jan Skiba's wife and daughters were bedazzled by all the pretty doodads. From his sack, the peddler drew yellow beads, false pearls,

tin earrings, rings, brooches, colored kerchiefs, garters, and other such trinkets. But what enthralled the women of the house most was a mirror set in a wooden frame. They asked the peddler its price and he said a half gulden, which was a lot of money for poor peasants.

After a while, Jan Skiba's wife, Marianna, made a proposition to the peddler. She would pay him five groshen a month for the mirror. The peddler hesitated a moment. The mirror took up too much space in his sack and there was always the danger it might break. He, therefore, decided to go along, took the first payment of five groshen from Marianna, and left the mirror with the family. He visited the region often, and he knew the Skibas to be honest people. He would gradually get his money back and a profit besides.

The mirror created a commotion in the hut. Until then, Marianna and the children had seldom seen themselves. Before they had the mirror, they had only seen their reflections in the barrel of water that stood by the door. Now they could see themselves clearly and they began to find defects in their faces, defects they had never noticed before. Marianna was pretty but she had a tooth missing in front and she felt that this made her ugly. One daughter discovered that her nose was too snub and too broad; a second, that her chin was too narrow and too long; a third, that her face was sprinkled with freckles. Jan Skiba too caught a glimpse of himself in the mirror and grew displeased by his thick lips and his teeth, which protruded like a buck's.

That day, the women of the house

became so absorbed in the mirror they didn't cook supper, didn't make up the bed, and neglected all the other household tasks. Marianna had heard of a dentist in the big city who could replace a missing tooth, but such things were expensive. The girls tried to console each other that they were pretty enough and that they would find suitors, but they no longer felt as jolly as before. They had been afflicted with the vanity of city girls. The one with the broad nose kept trying to pinch it together with her fingers to make it narrower; the one with the too-long chin pushed it up with her fist to make it shorter; the one with the freckles wondered if there was a salve in the city that could remove freckles. But where would the money come from for the fare to the city? And what about the money to buy this salve? For the first time, the Skiba family deeply felt its poverty and envied the rich.

But the human members of the household were not the only ones affected. The dog and the cat also grew disturbed by the mirror. The hut was low and the mirror had been hung just above a bench. The first time the cat sprang up on the bench and saw her image in the mirror, she became terribly perplexed. She had never before seen such a creature. Kot's whiskers bristled, she began to meow at her reflection and raised a paw to it, but the other creature meowed back and raised her paw too. Soon the dog jumped up on the bench, and when he saw the other dog he became wild with rage and shock. He barked at the other dog and showed him his teeth, but the other barked back and bared his fangs, too.

So great was the distress of Burek and Kot that for the first time in their lives they turned on each other. Burek took a bite out of Kot's throat and Kot hissed and spat at him and clawed his muzzle. They both started to bleed and the sight of blood aroused them so that they nearly killed or crippled each other. The members of the household barely managed to separate them. Because a dog is stronger than a cat, Burek had to be tied outside, and he howled all day and all night. In their anguish, both the dog and the cat stopped eating.

When Jan Skiba saw the disruption the mirror had created in his household, he decided a mirror wasn't what his family needed. "Why look at yourself," he said, "when you can see and admire the sky, the sun, the moon, the stars, and the earth, with all its forests, meadows, rivers, and plants?" He took the mirror down from the wall and put it away in the woodshed. When the peddler came for his monthly installment, Jan Skiba gave him back the mirror and in its stead, bought kerchiefs and slippers for the women. After the mirror disappeared, Burek and Kot returned to normal. Again Burek thought he was a cat and Kot was sure she was a dog. Despite all the defects the girls had found in themselves, they made good marriages. The village priest heard what had happened at Jan Skiba's house and he said, "A glass mirror shows only the skin of the body. The real image of a person is in his willingness to help himself and his family and, as far as possible, all those he comes in contact with. This kind of mirror reveals the very soul of the person."

Summarizing. Choose the best phrase to complete each sentence. Then write the complete statements on your paper.

1. Burek and Kot thought they were alike because _____ (they were similar in nature, they had never seen another dog and cat, they had been born in the same week).

2. The mirror upset the household because the family _____ (found defects in their faces, went into debt to pay for it, became jealous of each other).

3. When Jan Skiba decided to return the mirror, he told the others that _____ (the mirror was too expensive, the peddler had insisted on taking it back, they should look at the wonders of nature rather than at themselves).

Interpreting. Write the answer to each question on your paper.

1. Why did the peddler go along with Marianna's plan to pay for the mirror?

2. After getting the mirror, why did the family feel poor and inferior to others?

3. What did the village priest mean when he said that a person's willingness to help himself and others is the kind of mirror that "reveals the very soul of the person"?

For Thinking and Discussing. Do you think it would have been better if the family had never had a mirror? Explain.

Theme. *Theme* is the author's message about an aspect of life or human nature. Often, the reader must infer the theme from events in the story. Sometimes, however, the theme is presented directly, perhaps by one of the characters.

In "The Cat Who Thought She Was a Dog . . . ," the theme is easy for the reader to find. The following exercise will help you find the theme in this story.

Read each of the following statements. On your paper, write the statements that tell about the story's theme. Omit those that do not.

1. "The house had a bed, a bench bed, and a stove. . . ."

2. "'Why look at yourself . . . when you can see and admire the sky . . . ?'"

3. "'A glass mirror shows only the skin of the body.'"

4. ". . . he said a half gulden, which was a lot of money for poor peasants."

5. "'The real image of a person is in his willingness to help himself and his family. . . .'"

At the end of the story, whose words express the author's theme directly?

WRITING

Write a paragraph explaining one of the themes stated above. In your closing sentence, include a statement about what this theme teaches you about life.

The Elephant Man

based on the biography by Sir Frederick Treves

John Merrick, a deformed but extremely brave man, became famous during his lifetime in 19th-century England. And recently, a play and a movie were based on his life. Here you will read Merrick's real story. It is told by the doctor who helped him and became his friend.

In the Mile End Road, across from London Hospital, stood a row of small shops. One of them was vacant and for rent. The front of the shop, except for the door, was hidden by a hanging sheet of canvas. Pinned to the canvas was a notice that the Elephant Man was inside. He could be seen for the price of twopence.

Painted on the canvas in bright colors was a life-size picture of the Elephant Man. It showed a frightful creature that could only have come out of a nightmare. It was a man — but a man with the skin, face, and body of an elephant. Yet it was clear that it was still more man than beast. Somehow that made it more disgusting — the creature was still human. For some strange reason, it was impossible to pity a man who was changing into an animal. Palm trees were painted in the background, which seemed to suggest that the sickening object had roamed in the wild.

Before I learned of the exhibit, it had closed. But a boy I knew hunted up the man who ran the show, and I was granted a private view for the price of a shilling.

The shop was empty and gray with dust. Some old tin cans and a few dried-up vegetables were heaped on a shelf. The light in the place was dim, being shut out by the painted canvas outside. A red tablecloth made into a curtain hid the far end of the shop. The room was cold and damp, for the month was November. The year, I might add, was 1884.

The showman pulled back the curtain, and I saw a bent figure sitting on a stool, covered by a brown blanket. The figure was huddled over a gas burner to warm itself. It did not move when the curtain was drawn back. Loneliness seemed to hang in the air around it. It might have been a captive in a cave, or a witch watching for something unholy in the flame. Outside, the sun was shining, and one could hear the footsteps of the people passing by. A boy whistled a tune, and there was a friendly hum of traffic in the street.

The showman — speaking as if to a

dog — called out harshly, "Stand up!" The thing arose slowly and let the blanket that covered it fall.

There stood the most disgusting object called human that I have ever seen. As a doctor, I had observed every kind of defect and injury. But never had I seen such a twisted and unnatural being as this lonely figure.

He was naked to the waist, and his feet were bare. He wore a pair of worn-out trousers that had once belonged to some fat gentleman. From the painting in the street, I had thought the Elephant Man would be a giant. But this was a little man, below the average height, and made to look even shorter by his curved back.

The most striking thing about him was his huge, strangely shaped head. From the brow came a huge bony mass like a loaf. From the back of the head hung a bag of spongy-looking skin. It had the look of brown cauliflower. On top of the skull were a few long, limp hairs. The bony growth on the forehead almost covered one eye. The head was as big around as a man's waist.

From the upper jaw stuck out another mass of bone. It came out of the mouth like a pink stump, turning the upper lip inside out. In the painting, this had been made to look like the beginning of an elephant's trunk, or a tusk. The nose was just a lump of flesh. The face had no more expression than a block of wood. From the back hung sacklike masses of flesh, covered with the same cauliflower skin. The right arm was huge and without shape. It too was covered with hanging clumps of the rough skin. The hand was large and clumsy, more like a paddle than a hand.

The other arm was completely different. It was not only normal, but well-shaped, covered with fine skin. The hand was beautiful — a woman would have envied it. But from the chest hung a bag of the same deformed flesh. And the lower limbs were like the bad arm. They were clumsy and grossly out of shape.

To add a further burden, the poor man had had a disease that left him lame. He could only walk with a stick. As he told me later, this meant that he could never run away. From the showman, I learned nothing about the Elephant Man other than that he was English, that his name was John Merrick, and that he was 21 years old.

At the time I discovered the Elephant Man, I taught anatomy at the Medical College across the street. I wanted to examine him in detail and write an account of his many problems. The showman agreed to let me see him in my office at the college. But I knew it would not be easy. The Elephant Man could not show himself in the street. He would have been mobbed by the crowd and seized by the police.

But he had a disguise. It was a long black cape that reached to the ground. Where he got it, I cannot imagine. It looked like something worn on the stage. On his head, he wore a big black cap with a large bill. When you remember that his head was as big around as a man's waist, you can imagine the size of the hat. From the

bill hung a gray flannel curtain that covered the Elephant Man's face. A slit was cut in it so he could look out. This costume, worn by a man bent over and hobbling on a stick, was one of the strangest ever designed. I arranged that Merrick should ride across the street in a cab, and gave him a card so he would be allowed into the college. This card was to play an important part in Merrick's future.

I made a careful examination of my visitor. He was shy, mixed-up, and frightened. It was almost impossible to understand his speech. The great bony mass that stuck out from his mouth blurred his words. He went back in the cab to the shop, and I thought I had seen the last of him. Next day I found that the show had been closed by the police, and that the shop was empty.

I supposed that Merrick was retarded, and had been retarded from birth. The fact that his face could show no expression, that his speech was a mere sputter, and that he seemed to have no emotions at all gave grounds for this belief. I suppose I really hoped that his mind was the blank I thought it to be. I could not bear to think that he understood what he was. Here was a man only 21, who was so deformed that everyone he met fell back in horror and disgust. He was taken around the country to be shown off as a monster. He was lame, could use only one arm, and could not make himself understood. Later I learned that Merrick was highly intelligent. Even worse, he had a romantic imagination. It was then that I realized the terrible tragedy of his life.

For I was fated to meet the Elephant Man again, two years later. In England, the showman and Merrick had been moved from place to place by the police. The law considered the public display of Merrick as indecent.

At last, the showman took his charge to Europe. Where they went at first I do not know, but they finally went to Brussels. In Belgium too, the show was closed, as brutal and indecent. John Merrick was no longer of value. He was a burden. He must be got rid of. There was nothing Merrick could do. The showman, having robbed Merrick of the little money he had saved, gave him a ticket to London.

He was bound for Liverpool Station. The journey can be imagined. Merrick was dressed in his cloak and cap with the gray flannel curtain. A mob hooted at him as he hobbled along. People ran ahead to get a look at him. They lifted the hem of his cape to peer at his body. He tried to hide in the train or some dark corner of the boat. But he could never be free from that ring of curious eyes, and the whispers of fear and disgust. He had so little money that he had nothing either to eat or drink on the way. A dog would have been shown some kindness. Merrick got none.

In London, he was saved from the crowd by the police and taken to a waiting room. There he sank on the floor in the darkest corner. The police did not know what to do with him. They had never dealt with an object like this. He could not explain himself. No one could understand his speech. But he had something that gave him a ray of hope. It was my card.

The card proved that this odd creature knew someone in London. A messenger was sent to the London Hospital, which is quite near the station. Luckily I was in the building. I went back to the station with the messenger. In the waiting room, I had some trouble getting through the crowd. There on the floor, in a corner, was Merrick. He looked like a heap of old clothes. It seemed as if he had been thrown there like a bundle. He seemed pleased to see me, but he was nearly dead from the journey and the lack of food. The police helped him into a cab, and I drove with him to the hospital. He fell asleep almost as soon as he sat down.

In the attic of the hospital was a ward with a single bed. It was used for emergency cases — a patient with an unknown fever, or a man who suddenly went insane. Here the Elephant Man was put to bed, made comfortable, and given food. The kind director of the hospital agreed with me that Merrick must not be turned out again into the world.

The director wrote a letter to the London *Times,* telling about Merrick's plight and asking for money to support him. The English public is generous. In a week, we had enough money to keep Merrick for life.

There were two empty rooms at the back of the hospital, on the ground floor, looking out on a large courtyard called Bedstead Square. This was because the iron beds were brought there for cleaning and painting. The front room was made into a bedroom, and the smaller one into a bathroom. The state of Merrick's skin made a bath at least once a day necessary. Once he began to bathe, the unpleasant odor he had was gone. Merrick took up his life in the hospital in December, 1886.

Now Merrick had something he had never dreamed of — a home of his own for life. I began to get to know him. I soon learned his speech, so that I could talk freely with him. He enjoyed this greatly, for he loved to talk, and had never in his life had anyone to talk to. I was not busy at the time, so I saw him almost every day.

I found Merrick, as I have said, very intelligent. Somehow he had learned to read, and read hungrily. He had not read many books. The Bible and the Church of England Prayer Book he knew very well, but he had read mostly newspapers and such bits of old magazines as he could pick up. But he found most delight in love stories. These tales were very real to him. He would tell me about the lives of the people in them. His view of the world was that of a child, but a child with some of the strong feelings of a man.

Of his early days, I could learn but little. He did not like to talk about the past. It had been a nightmare, and he still shuddered to think of it. He was born, he believed, in or near Leicester. Of his father, he knew nothing. Of his mother, he had some memory. It was very faint, and I think had been largely built up in his mind. There were mothers in the stories he read, and he wanted his mother to be one of those lovable, lullaby-singing women.

Once, he remembered, someone had been kind to him. He clung to this dream, and made it more real in imagination, for no one else had been kind to him since the day he could toddle.

It was a favorite belief of his that his mother was beautiful. It was a story of his own making, but it was a great joy to him. His mother may have been lovely, but she had left him when he was very small. His earliest memories were of the workhouse to which he had been taken. Whatever his mother was really like, he spoke of her with pride and even respect. Once, talking about his own appearance, he said, "It is very strange, for mother was so beautiful."

The rest of Merrick's life up to the time I met him was one dull record of shame and shabbiness. He was dragged from town to town and from fair to fair as if he were a strange beast in a cage. A dozen times a day, he would have to expose his body to a crowd that greeted him with "Oh! What a horror! What a beast!" He had had no childhood. He had had no boyhood. He had never known pleasure. He knew nothing of fun or the joy of living. His sole idea of happiness was to creep into the dark and hide. Shut up alone, waiting for the next show, how must he have felt to hear the laughter of boys and girls outside, enjoying the fair? At the age of 20, he was a creature without hope.

How did this brutish life affect a sensitive and intelligent man? It would be a good guess that he would become a bitter and angry hater of people, filled with spite. Or he might have become a person so full of sadness that it drove him mad. Merrick,

however, had done neither. He had passed through the fire and come out whole. His troubles had made him noble. He was a gentle, loving, lovable being, pleasant, without a sour thought or unkind word for anyone. I never heard him complain. I never heard him moan about his ruined life or resent the treatment he had received. His journey through life had been dark and uphill all the way. Now he suddenly found himself in a bright light, warm and full of welcome. He was grateful, and expressed his feelings with childlike openness.

Yet he was afraid of his fellow men, of the fear in people's eyes, of always being stared at, of the cruel words of the crowd. In his home in Bedstead Square, he was hidden from them. But now and then, a thoughtless porter or maid would open his door to let friends have a peep at the Elephant Man. It seemed to him that the eyes of the world still followed him. And he could not believe that he really had a home for life.

Once he said to me, "When I am next moved, can I go to a home for the blind or to a lighthouse?" He liked the thought of being with people who could not see him. And, in a lighthouse, no one could open a door and peep at him. He had never seen a lighthouse, but he had seen a picture of one. There he could forget that he had once been the Elephant Man. A lonely column of stone in the sea was the home he longed for.

I set out to rid his mind of these ideas. I wanted him to get used to other people, to get to know his own kind. He needed to meet men and women who would treat him like a normal and intelligent young man, not a monster.

I thought women would be most important in helping him to believe in himself. Merrick admired women to the point of worship. Of course, they were not real women, only dreams. Among them was his beautiful mother, in a circle of women from the books he had read.

His first day at the hospital had been spoiled by a mistake. A nurse had been sent to bring him food, but not told what he looked like. When she came into the room and saw him, she screamed, dropped the tray she was carrying, and ran. From then on, he was looked after by volunteer nurses. But he knew that they were merely doing their work. They were like machines rather than women.

I asked a friend of mine, a young and pretty widow, if she thought she could go into Merrick's room with a smile, wish him good morning, and shake him by the hand. She said she could, and she did. I did not expect its effect upon Merrick. As he let go her hand, he bent his head and sobbed until I thought he would never stop. He told me afterward that she was the only woman who had ever smiled at him. She was the first woman, in his whole life, who had shaken hands with him.

From that day, Merrick began to change. He was no longer a hunted thing, but a man.

Merrick's case attracted much attention in the papers, so that he had a constant flow of visitors. Everybody wanted to see him. Every lady in the social world came

to see him. They were all good enough to greet him with a smile, and to shake hands with him.

The Merrick whom I had found hiding behind a rag of a curtain in an empty shop was now talking to duchesses and

countesses. They brought him presents, made his room bright with pictures, and supplied him with books. He soon had a large library, and most of his day was spent reading.

None of this spoiled him or puffed him up. He never asked for anything or made demands. He was always humble and thankful. But he lost his shyness. He liked to see his door open and people look in. His speech improved, although to the end it was hard for strangers to understand.

He was also beginning to be less aware of his ugliness, to think it might not be so bad after all. The fact that I would not allow a mirror of any kind in his room helped him to feel this way.

One exciting day, the future Queen Alexandra, then Princess of Wales, came to see John Merrick. She entered the room and shook him warmly by the hand. It was a delight beyond Merrick's wildest dream. No other gracious act of the princess ever caused such happiness as she brought into that room.

Merrick was now one of the most contented creatures I had ever met. More than once, he said to me, "I am happy every hour of the day." It was good to hear that — from the half-dead heap of misery I had seen in the corner of the waiting room at Liverpool Station.

But as happy as he was, Merrick could not whistle, nor sing. His face could show no expression. He could weep, but he could not smile.

The princess paid Merrick many visits. She sent him a Christmas card every year, with a message in her own handwriting. Once she sent him a signed picture of herself. To Merrick, it was a sacred object. He would hardly let me touch it. He cried over it and wrote her a letter of thanks in words that anyone at court would have been proud of.

Other ladies did as the princess had done — sent pictures to Merrick. His table was so covered with photos of beautiful ladies and the gifts they gave him that he might have been a star of the stage.

Yet, in many ways, Merrick stayed a child. He loved make-believe, pretending to be a hero. One Christmas, he told me that, as a present, he would like a dressing case, with silver fittings. A comb edged in silver. Brushes with silver backs. Razors with ivory handles. A toothbrush with a silver handle. A silver shoehorn. A silver cigarette case. Merrick had no hair to comb. He could not smoke, or put a toothbrush in his twisted mouth. He wore only shapeless slippers on his poor feet. His skin could not be shaved. Yet every day he put out the brushes and shoehorn and cigarette case, as if a young man-about-town were getting ready for a round of social events. It gave him pleasure to imagine that he was that kind of man.

There was one shadow in Merrick's life. He was romantic. He would have liked to be a dashing lover, meeting a girl in a lovely garden to tell her how he adored her. Yet he had never seen anything but horror in the eyes of young women who had looked at him. I think that when he talked of life among the blind, he had a half-formed idea that a woman who could not see him might fall in love with him.

One of his ambitions was to go to the theater. It was not an easy wish to satisfy. How could the Elephant Man be taken there? Where could he sit without causing a panic in the audience? At last, a famous actress, Mrs. Kendal, took charge. A box was reserved. Merrick was brought to the theater in a carriage with drawn curtains. He used a private entrance. I had asked some nurses from the hospital to put on evening dresses and sit in the front row of the box. They formed a screen for Merrick, who sat in shadow at the back.

Merrick was awed and amazed by the show. It left him speechless. Often it seemed to take his breath away. I looked at a yawning, bored young man of the same age in a nearby seat and compared him to Merrick, thrilled almost beyond belief.

He talked of the show for weeks and weeks. To him, it had all been real. It was a vision of another world.

Later on, Merrick told me of another longing. He wanted to see the country, to live in some green, private place and learn something about flowers, animals, and birds. He had never seen the country, except from a wagon on a dusty road. He had never walked in fields or climbed a hill. But he had read of the country and yearned to see it.

This was harder to arrange than the visit to the theater. But another lady — Lady Knightley — offered him a cottage on her estate. Merrick was taken to the railroad station in the usual way. The railroad gave him a private car, with drawn curtains.

But the housekeeper at the cottage had not been told what he really looked like. When he stepped inside, she threw her apron over her face and ran into the fields.

So Merrick was taken to the cottage of the gamekeeper. It was hidden from view and close to the edge of a wood. The gamekeeper and his wife were able to stand his presence. They treated him kindly, and he spent the one great holiday of his life. He could roam where he pleased. He met no one, for the wood was on a private estate. It was the happiest time he had ever known. The breath of the country passed over him like a healing wind. No one could peep at him, no one could laugh at him. It seemed as if all the stain had been wiped away from his past.

He wrote me about the violets he picked, the sound of birds, the hare he startled, the dog he made friends with. He came back to London, healthier, happy to be home again among his books and his many friends.

Six months later, Merrick was found dead in bed. This was in April, 1890. He was lying on his back as if asleep, and seemed to have died suddenly, with no struggle. The way he died was strange. So large and heavy was his head that he could not sleep lying down. If he tried, the huge skull fell backward, causing great discomfort. So he slept sitting up, his back supported by pillows.

He had often told me he wished he could lie down and sleep "like other people." I think on this last night he decided to try. The pillow was soft. His head, placed on it, must have fallen back and dislocated his neck. So his death was due to the desire that was always in his life — the hopeless desire to be "like other people."

Merrick's body was horrible. But the spirit of Merrick, if it could be seen, would seem a handsome and heroic man, with strong limbs and eyes that flashed courage.

He had borne on his back a burden almost too heavy to bear. He had been ill-treated and shamed. Now his burden was loosed from his back, and he carried it no more.

READING COMPREHENSION

Summarizing. Choose the best phrase to complete each sentence. Then write the complete statements on your paper.

1. The narrator _____ (was interested in making a profit from the Elephant Man's deformity, was a doctor and friend of Merrick's, had known Merrick from birth).

2. The police closed down the public display of the Elephant Man because _____ (it was brutal and indecent, it was difficult to control the crowds, they feared for Merrick's safety).

3. Toward the end of his life, Merrick became _____ (bitter and angry, less afraid of people, cured of his deformity).

Interpreting. Write the answer to each question on your paper.

1. What caused Merrick's death?

2. Why did Dr. Treves call Merrick's life a "terrible tragedy" after learning about his intelligence and imagination?

3. Why was Merrick's holiday in the country the happiest time he had ever known?

For Thinking and Discussing. Despite his horrible physical handicap, the Elephant Man described himself as "happy every hour of the day." How do you think this could be so?

UNDERSTANDING LITERATURE

Nonfiction. Not all works of literature are made up or imagined by their authors. Some stories are factual, not fictional. Factual, or true, stories are *nonfiction*. A biography is an example of nonfiction. It is the true account of a person's life.

In a biography, the writer can choose events in a person's life and use them to present the theme, a comment about life or human nature. In *The Elephant Man*, Treves showed the contrast between outer appearance and inner reality.

Read each of the following details from *The Elephant Man*. Which ones show the author's message? Write them on your paper. Leave out the insignificant details.

1. "Once he said, 'When I am next moved, can I go to a home for the blind? . . .' He liked the thought of being with people who could not see him."

2. "He needed to meet men and women who would treat him like a normal and intelligent young man, not a monster."

3. "Merrick's case attracted much attention in the papers, so that he had a constant flow of visitors."

4. "So his death was due to the desire that was always in his life—the hopeless desire to be 'like other people.'"

WRITING

Write a paragraph about your reaction to the friendship of Treves and Merrick. What did Treves admire about his friend?

Cyrano de Bergerac

based on the play by Edmond Rostand

Edmond Rostand was born in 1868 in France. He became a famous author instantly when his play Cyrano de Bergerac *was performed in 1897. The play was inspired by the life of an actual 17th-century writer. Through Rostand, Cyrano de Bergerac, the poetic soldier with the big nose, has become a romantic hero.*

CHARACTERS

Lignière (Lin **YAIR**)
Christian (Cris tee **on**)
Montfleury (Mont floor ē)
Cyrano (See ran o)
Young Man
Le Bret
Servant

Roxanne
Sentry
First Soldier
Second Soldier
Third Soldier
First Nun
Second Nun

Act I

The courtyard of a hotel decorated like a theater. The time is 1640; the place is Paris, France. A crowd of soldiers, noblemen, ladies, and peasants is waiting for a play to begin.

Lignière: So where is this lady you are looking for? I must be going.
Christian: Please, wait a little longer. Ah! There she is! You must tell me what her name is.

Lignière: That is Roxanne — a fine young woman — intelligent — unmarried —
Christian: Oh, how can I talk to such a woman? I who have no wit, no way with words. (*He stares at Roxanne. Roxanne turns and their eyes meet.*)
The Crowd: The play begins!
Montfleury: "Thrice happy he who hides — "
Cyrano: Stop!
Montfleury: "Thrice happy he — "

Cyrano: Have I not forbidden you to appear on stage?

Montfleury: When you insult me, you insult the name of poetry as well.

Cyrano: Alas! Poetry never knew your name, Mount Fury. Now listen carefully, you well of bad acting. At the count of three, you are going to disappear down that well. One — two — three! Shoo, goose! Before I add your feathers to my cap! *(He draws his sword, and Montfleury runs off. The crowd laughs.)*

A Young Man: Who are you to dislike this actor so?

Cyrano: He is no actor. Words beg to fly, and his fall into the mud. And why do you stare so at my nose?

A Young Man: But I —

Cyrano: Do you think it a stone, a hill-top, a mountain?

A Young Man: Please —

Cyrano: Do you think it gives the singing birds a perch to rest their weary feet?

A Young Man: No —

Cyrano: When I blow it, do you think sailors stand on ships and shout, "Thar she blows"?

A Young Man: I have not been looking at your nose.

Cyrano: And why not? Do you find it so awful? Too large for anything less than an elephant?

A Young Man: No — as a matter of fact, I find it rather small.

Cyrano: Small, man! Your eyes fail you. Yours is small. A button the size of your wit. No, this is a great nose. And a great nose indicates a great man. Now, be off! *(The Young Man exits.)*

Le Bret: But why, Cyrano? Why do you do these things?

Cyrano: Because, my friend, I am in love.

Le Bret: You? In love?

Cyrano: Does that strike you as strange? I find it strange that you think that.

Le Bret: Well, you never mentioned this before. But tell me — who is it?

Cyrano: Who do you think it would be? If I am a man whom no woman would look upon, who would it be? Why the fairest flower of all, of course.

Le Bret: Roxanne?

Cyrano: Yes, Roxanne.

Le Bret: Then, why don't you tell her?

Cyrano: What? My nose would only get in the way.

Le Bret: But you are a man of great wit, of great courage.

Cyrano: But she would only laugh at me. And more than anything else in the world, I fear her laughing at me.

(A Servant enters.)

Servant: Excuse me, monsieur. Roxanne would like to know when she might meet you?

Cyrano: Me? She wants to see me?

Servant: Yes, she has a secret to tell you. She would like to see you alone.

Cyrano: A secret? She would like to see me alone?

Servant: It's most important.

Cyrano: Yes, well, the pastry shop on Honor Street?

Servant: Agreed. First thing in the morning?

Cyrano: I will be there before the rooster crows. If need be, I shall wait forever.

(The Servant exits.)

Le Bret: Well, my friend, you seem happy enough now.

Cyrano: Happy? Happy is too poor a word. It is the first day of spring. Bells ring out, and the sun breaks through the clouds. My heart has never known such joy!

Act II

The pastry shop on Honor Street.

Roxanne: I want to thank you for what you did yesterday. That young man you talked circles around thinks he is in love with me.

Cyrano: Then I did it not for my nose but your eyes.

Roxanne: Ah — what I have to say now is not going to be easy. I am in love with someone.

Cyrano: Oh?

Roxanne: Someone who does not know it.

Cyrano: Oh?

Roxanne: Not yet anyway.

Cyrano: Oh?

Roxanne: But he will know today.

Cyrano: Oh!

Roxanne: Someone who loves me too, I think, but has never said a word about it.

Cyrano: Oh?

Roxanne: Give me your hand a moment. Ah — how warm it is.

Cyrano: Oh.

Roxanne: This someone is a soldier: proud — and brave — and handsome —

Cyrano: Handsome!

Roxanne: Cyrano! What is it?

Cyrano: Oh — nothing.

Roxanne: I love him very much. But I have only seen him once. At the theater yesterday.

Cyrano: Did you speak?

Roxanne: Only with our eyes. But they said everything.

Cyrano: But how do you know?

Roxanne: I know what I know.

Cyrano: Oh. What is his name?

Roxanne: Christian.

Cyrano: But I do not understand why you are telling me all this.

Roxanne: Because he is a soldier, and I am afraid for him.

Cyrano: But what would you have me do?

Roxanne: He is new in your company. Will you look out for him and be his friend?

Cyrano: If you wish it.

Roxanne: And have him write me a letter?

Cyrano: Yes, I will see to that.

Roxanne: We shall always be the best of friends — you and I, no?

Cyrano: Yes. Certainly. Always.

(Roxanne exits. Soon after, Christian enters.)

Cyrano: I know a friend of yours.

Christian: Whose?

Cyrano: Yours. A certain Roxanne.

Christian: She talked to you? What did she say?

Cyrano: Everything.

Christian: She cares for me?

Cyrano: Maybe — well, I must admit you are a handsome devil. She is expecting a letter from you.

Christian: Oh — no!

Cyrano: Now there's a singularly peculiar response.

Christian: It's impossible for me to tell her what is in my heart.

Cyrano: Why, man, take it out and look at it. Copy down exactly what it says.

Christian: But I am hopeless at such things. I can barely follow one word with another. If only I had your wit —

Cyrano: If only I had your looks. Together we could make quite a hero.

Christian: What?

Cyrano: Would you take the words that I give you and speak them to her?

Christian: Yes. But — the letter — I don't even know how to start.

Cyrano: Start with this. *(He takes a letter from his pocket.)*

Christian: But doesn't it need any changes?

Cyrano: Only your signature. The rest is letter-perfect.

Christian: But tell me: Why are you doing all this?

Cyrano: Let's just say it's for the poet within me.

Act III

The garden in front of Roxanne's house. Over the door is a balcony. It is early evening.

Cyrano: And how do you find Christian?
Roxanne: He writes such wonderful letters.
Cyrano: These letters — are they poetic?
Roxanne: They are absolutely brilliant. I think he may be a better poet than you even. Does that make you jealous?
Cyrano: Should it? What are they about?
Roxanne: Full of dreams, the scent of flowers in spring, the roar of a mountain waterfall, the still beauty of winter snow, sunshine, moonshine.
Cyrano: Really!
Roxanne: Yes, it just goes to show that a handsome face need not have an empty head.
Cyrano: And tonight is your first meeting face-to-face?
Roxanne: Since the moment our eyes first met.
Cyrano: So what will you talk about?
Roxanne: Why love, of course. The poetry of love. You won't tell him, will you?
Cyrano: My tongue is heavy as a stone. Well, I'll be off. Good night. *(Roxanne enters her house.)*

(Christian enters.)

Cyrano: Oh, Christian. Are you ready to learn your lines?
Christian: No.
Cyrano: What? Are you crazy?
Christian: I needed your help in the be-

ginning. But she loves me now. From here on, my words will be my own.
Cyrano: Suit yourself. *(He exits.)*
Roxanne: *(opening the door):* Christian, are you there? Come sit here in the garden and tell me of the poetry of love.
Christian: The what?
Roxanne: Tell me how you love me. *(Silence.)* Yes?
Christian: I — love — you.
Roxanne: Yes, of course. How much?
Christian: I love you very much.
Roxanne: But tell me how you feel?
Christian: I LOVE YOU VERY MUCH!
Roxanne: Is that all?
Christian: I don't love you.
Roxanne: Oh — now that's interesting.
Christian: Roxanne, I don't know what I'm saying.
Roxanne: Well, as soon as you do, drop by.
Christian: Don't go! Let me just say —
Roxanne: That you love me. Yes, you told me that already. Good night, Christian! *(She enters the house.)*
Christian: But —

(Cyrano steps from behind a tree.)

Cyrano: So, how did it go?
Christian: I need your help!
Cyrano: Mine?
Christian: Yes, now! I can't leave her like this!
Cyrano: But there isn't time.
Christian: Look! A light in the upstairs window!
Cyrano: Perhaps it's a possibility.

Christian: Would you?

Cyrano: Stand over there. I'll stay here and tell you what to say.

Christian: Roxanne!

Roxanne: Who's there?

Christian: It's me again.

Roxanne: It's late, Christian.

Christian: I have things to tell you.

Roxanne: Besides you don't love me anymore?

Christian (*Cyrano whispers the words for Christian to repeat.*): Besides you . . . there is no one to love.

Roxanne: That's better.

Christian: At the sweet sight of you . . . my words sometimes stick together like honey . . . stuck in the hive of my heart.

Roxanne: Better yet. But why do you pause between words? Is your tongue stuck too?

Cyrano *(trying to sound like Christian):* My words must fly up heavy with sweetness. Yours simply fall down.

Roxanne: I shall come down to you as swiftly as my words.

Cyrano: No!

Roxanne: No?

Cyrano: You are framed in the light like an angel. And I am clothed in darkness like a beast. As it should be.

Roxanne: A beast with a silver tongue. Is that why you sound different?

Cyrano: Different or the same. Tonight you hear me for the first time. Tonight you hear my soul.

Roxanne: And the other times?

Cyrano: My letters are filled with poetry of my love for you. But standing here amid the scent of beautiful flowers, underneath the starry heavens — those rhymes seem so artificial. It is no contest compared to the beauty of nature. No contest compared to the beauty of you.

Roxanne: Yes, that is love.

Cyrano: So let us not compete with the universe but join it. And breathe in the warm air of evening and speak in silence. For after an evening like this, I am now able to die a happy man.

Roxanne: Oh, Christian! Forgive me for what happened before. I do love you so.

Cyrano: Before I go, there is one thing more —

Christian *(softly):* A kiss!

Cyrano: What? For that you must ask her yourself.

Roxanne: What did you say?

Christian: A kiss, Roxanne? Would you honor me with a kiss?

Roxanne: My arms will surround you like the flowers around your feet.

Cyrano: So, climb up!

Christian: What? How?

Cyrano: Hand over hand up this vine. You are a soldier, no?

(Christian climbs up to the balcony.)

Cyrano: *(after a few moments):* Is Christian there?

Christian: Cyrano!

Roxanne: Yes, he's right here where he belongs.

Cyrano: I bring alarming news. We are marching off to war.

Roxanne: No — no! This can't be! When?

Cyrano: In an hour.

Christian: What?

Cyrano: The orders came through this evening.

Roxanne: Well, shall we?

Christian: Shall we what?

Roxanne: Get married before you leave?

Christian: Married? Now? Yes — How?

Roxanne: I know a priest who lives on the way to your barracks. *(Pause.)* And another thing.

Christian: Yes?

Roxanne: Cyrano?

Cyrano: Yes?

Roxanne: Will you see to it that he writes often?

Cyrano: That I can promise you.

Act IV

A French fort surrounded by countryside. Dawn. Le Bret enters.

Sentry *(offstage):* Halt! Who goes there?
Cyrano *(offstage):* Bergerac!
Sentry: Advance and be recognized!
Cyrano *(enters):* Bergerac, you knuckle-head!
Le Bret: Welcome! Are you all right?
Cyrano: Not a scratch. It's really quite easy.
Le Bret: Yes, go on risking your life crossing Spanish lines every night to post a letter. Easy you say? It would be — for you to get killed.
Cyrano: But I cannot break my promise that he should write every day.
(The camp stirs. Soldiers enter.)
First Soldier: I'm so hungry I could eat a horse.
Second Soldier: Save me the saddle.
Third Soldier: How can we fight on empty stomachs?
Cyrano: Is your stomach the only thing you have on your mind?
Christian: Cyrano, I think it might be a good idea to have a letter ready for Roxanne in case anything should happen to me.
Cyrano: I agree. It's such a good idea, in fact, that I have already written one.
Christian: Let me read it. *(He takes the letter.)* What is this spot? Is it a tear?
Cyrano: A tear? Yes. I was so carried away by the sadness of the occasion — by putting myself in your situation — that I cried.

Christian: You cried?
Sentry *(offstage):* Halt! Who goes there?
Le Bret: What is it?
Sentry *(offstage):* A coach!
Le Bret: A coach! Through enemy lines? Make sure it is not a trap.

(The soldiers, with their swords drawn, gather around the coach and open the door.)

Roxanne: Good morning, gentlemen. *(She hugs Christian.)*
Christian: What the —
Cyrano: How did you get through?
Roxanne: Whenever a Spanish soldier stopped the coach, I said I was going to visit my lover. We were then allowed to pass.
Christian: But —
Roxanne: If I had said my husband, who would have believed that?
La Bret: It is not safe for you to stay here.
Roxanne: But why not?
Christian: Because —
Roxanne: You are waiting for an attack? No, I shall stay here and suffer your fate.
Third Soldier: Suddenly I'm not so hungry anymore. I am prepared to fight!
Roxanne: Well, I'm starving. Will all of you join me for breakfast?
All: What?
Roxanne: Go into the coach. Those baskets are not empty, you know.
Second Soldier: Madame, you are truly a feast for our eyes.
Cyrano *(low to Christian):* If she should

mention the number of letters, do not act surprised.

Christian: What do you mean?

Cyrano: You have written more often than you know about.

Christian: How often *have* I written?

Cyrano: Often.

Christian: Once a week?

Cyrano: More.

Christian: Twice? Three times? *(Silence.)* Every day?

Cyrano: Yes.

Christian: But how? We have been unable to move from here for a month.

Cyrano: Through enemy lines at night.

Christian: You risked your life every night to send a letter!

Cyrano: Sh-h-h! Or she will hear us.

Christian: Roxanne, I must know. Why did you come here?

Roxanne: I knew you loved me. But until your letters — each one more beautiful than the last — I had no idea how much. And — I want to ask your apology.

Christian: For what?

Roxanne: For loving you because you were so handsome and dashing. For not loving you for your inner beauty. Knowing you as I do now, I would love you even if you were ugly.

Christian: Ugly? Really?

Roxanne: Of course. You are so much more than I ever imagined.

Christian: Please go to the soldiers now. They won't start the feast without you. *(Roxanne exits; he motions to Cyrano.)*

Cyrano: Yes?

Christian: She loves me for my inner beauty.

Cyrano: What's wrong with that?

Christian: Because that means she loves you. *(Cyrano looks startled.)* And you love her.

Cyrano: I love her?

Christian: Yes. Admit it. *(Cyrano nods his head.)* She said she would love me even if I were ugly.

Cyrano: She told you that?

Christian: You must tell her everything.

Cyrano: No.

Christian: She must choose between us.

Cyrano: That makes no sense. You are married to her.

Christian: That's no problem. There were no witnesses. Cyrano, she must choose between us. She must love me for who I am, not for what she thinks I am.

Cyrano: Don't worry. There is no contest. You will win.

Christian: Roxanne!

Cyrano: Christian, don't do it!

Christian: Roxanne! *(She hurries to him.)* Cyrano has something to tell you. *(Christian leaves.)*

Cyrano: It's just something that Christian thinks you should know.

(Shots are heard nearby.)

Roxanne: I already do. He still doesn't believe what I just told him.

Cyrano: You told him that you would love him —

Roxanne: Even if he were ugly.

Cyrano: Roxanne, I —

Roxanne: Yes?

Le Bret: Cyrano —

Cyrano: Oh, nothing.

(Several soldiers enter, carrying a still form underneath a cloak.)

Roxanne: Christian! *(She bends over Christian's body.)*

Cyrano: She knows, Christian. She loves you. *(Christian closes his eyes.)*

Roxanne: Is he?

First Soldier: Yes.

Second Soldier: We found this letter in his pocket. *(He hands it to Roxanne.)*

Le Bret: The enemy approaches! Gather your muskets! Spread out!

Cyrano: I fight in honor of two deaths — Christian's and mine.

Act V

Fifteen years later. The scene is a park in a convent. It is autumn.

First Nun: Cyrano should be arriving soon. He hasn't missed a Saturday in ten years, has he?

Second Nun: No, and it's more than ten years. Ever since Roxanne joined us.

Roxanne *(dressed completely in black)*: Ah, there's the strike of the hour. He is usually here by — *(Cyrano appears at the top of the stairs. He walks slowly and uses a cane.)* There you are! I thought you were going to be late for the first time in fourteen years.

Cyrano: I was visited by a stranger. He was most difficult to get rid of, until I told him I was on my way to meet you.

First Nun: Good evening, Cyrano.

Cyrano: Tonight I will let you pray for my soul, sister. You look surprised. Well, the devil has paid much too much attention to me over the years. *(He faints.)*

Roxanne: What is it? *(They place Cyrano on a chair and open his collar.)*

Cyrano: An old war wound. Nothing really.

Roxanne: I have my letter here. *(She pulls out the letter.)*

Cyrano: Didn't you say that one day I could read his last letter?

Roxanne: Yes.

Cyrano: Let's let today be that day.

Roxanne: Here.

Cyrano *(unfolding the crumbling pages)*: "Dearest Roxanne, By the time you read this letter — "

Roxanne: You're going to read it out loud?

Cyrano: " — have left the only woman I ever loved behind. If there could be any thought I would like you to have at this moment" *(Roxanne looks over at him and sees that the letter has dropped to the ground)* "it would be that you would not dwell on the sadness, but on those bright moments — "

Roxanne: Cyrano!

Cyrano *(opening his eyes as if awakened)*: What?

Roxanne: It was you!

Cyrano: No.

Roxanne: The letters —

Cyrano: No.

Roxanne: The voice under the balcony —

Cyrano: No.

Roxanne: It was you who loved me!

Cyrano: No, he loved you.

Roxanne: All these years — all these years you kept silent. Even the tear on that letter was yours.

Cyrano: The blood was his.

Roxanne: Why is it only today that you are letting the real you surface?

Cyrano: Because when you mourn the death of Christian, perhaps you could also shed a tear for another who loved you almost as well. And certainly for longer.

Roxanne: Dear — dear Cyrano. I love you too.

Cyrano: Will you help me to my feet? *(She steadies him.)* I must draw my sword for one last fight with the stranger who visited me earlier today. He said he was going to see me again soon, but I had no idea he meant while I was with you. Bah! Bad timing, but then, when are these things anything else but? So I fight on in the spirit of the soldier who can no longer hold his sword, the poet who can no longer speak his words, the lover who can no longer see his beloved. I fight on knowing that the odds are against me, that the hands on yonder clock are slowing to a halt, that the leaves are drifting down, that all is in vain; but yet, I am standing for one last surge into the unknown that will take away everything I am, everything that I have ever been. *(Cyrano sinks to his knees. He falls over backward, but Roxanne catches him and kneels down with his head cradled in her lap.)* I have lost all. But one thing remains.

Roxanne *(kisses him on the forehead)*: Yes?

Cyrano *(smiling)*: The white feather in my cap.

(He dies then, in Roxanne's arms.)

READING COMPREHENSION

Summarizing. Choose the best phrase to complete each sentence. Then write the complete statements on your paper.

1. Cyrano did not tell Christian of his love for Roxanne because _____ (he was afraid Christian would laugh at him, Christian might tell Roxanne, he knew Christian loved Roxanne).

2. Cyrano spoke for Christian in the garden after Christian _____ (ran out of words of love, had to go to war, fell off the balcony and injured himself).

3. Roxanne realized Cyrano loved her when _____ (he kissed her before he died, he recited the letter she thought Christian had written, Christian revealed the truth before he died).

Interpreting. Write the answer to each question on your paper.

1. Why did Christian want Roxanne to choose between Cyrano and himself?

2. Cyrano was able to keep his love for Roxanne secret for many years. Why was he afraid to tell her about it?

3. What did Cyrano mean when he said, "I must draw my sword for one last fight with the stranger who visited me earlier today"?

For Thinking and Discussing. Should Cyrano have spoken to Roxanne about his feelings? How would their lives have been changed if he had?

UNDERSTANDING LITERATURE

Drama. Another way to tell a story is to act it out in a play, or drama. *Drama* comes from the Greek word meaning "to perform." Although there is a written script that can be read for enjoyment, a drama is created to be performed.

A drama features dialogue to be spoken by the characters. Set descriptions provide the setting. Stage directions help the actors move about on stage. The plot develops from one act to the next.

The central idea present throughout a drama is its *theme*. Action revolves around this underlying idea, and the acts are held together by it. The movement of a drama is an acting out of this theme.

Find examples of dialogue from the play that show the following points. Write each example on your paper.

1. Cyrano makes fun of his own nose.

2. Christian cannot express his love.

3. Roxanne admires the combination of looks and wit.

4. Roxanne loves the poetic soul that shows in the letters.

5. Cyrano expresses his love for Roxanne through Christian.

6. Roxanne realizes she loves Cyrano.

WRITING

Write a short outline of the events of the plot in the five acts of the play. Then list the characters that appear in each act.

Lady Clare

Alfred, Lord Tennyson

Alfred, Lord Tennyson, born in 1809, was an English baron. His poetry drew more from history and the imagination than from the changing world of the 19th century. Few poets are very successful during their lifetimes. Tennyson was an exception. Highly popular, he was made poet laureate of Britain in 1850.

It was the time when lilies blow,
  And clouds are highest up in air,
Lord Ronald brought a lily-white doe
  To give his cousin, Lady Clare.

I trow they did not part in scorn:
  Lovers long-betrothed were they:
They two will wed the morrow morn, —
  God's blessing on the day!

"He does not love me for my birth,
  Nor for my lands so broad and fair;
He loves me for my own true worth,
  And that is well," said Lady Clare.

In there came old Alice the nurse,
  Said, "Who was this that went from thee?"
"It was my cousin," said Lady Clare,
  "Tomorrow he weds with me."

"O God be thanked!" said Alice the nurse,
  "That all comes round so just and fair:
Lord Ronald is heir of all your lands,
  And you are *not* the Lady Clare."

"Are ye out of your mind, my nurse, my nurse,"
  Said Lady Clare, "that ye speak so wild?"
"As God's above," said Alice the nurse,
  "I speak the truth: You are my child."

"The old earl's daughter died at my breast;
  I speak the truth, as I live by bread!
I buried her like my own sweet child,
  And put my child in her stead."

"Falsely, falsely have ye done,
  O Mother," she said, "if this be true,
To keep the best man under the sun
  So many years from his due."

"Nay now, my child," said Alice the nurse,
  "But keep the secret for your life,
And all you have will be Lord Ronald's,
  When you are man and wife."

"If I'm a beggar born," she said,
  "I will speak out, for I dare not lie.
Pull off, pull off, the brooch of gold,
  And fling the diamond necklace by."

"Nay now, my child," said Alice the nurse,
  "But keep the secret all you can."
She said, "Not so: but I will know
  If there be any faith in man."

"Nay now, what faith?" said Alice the
    nurse,
  "The man will cleave unto his right."
"And he shall have it," the lady replied,
  "Though I should die tonight."

"Yet give one kiss to your mother dear.
  Alas, my child, I sinned for thee."
"O Mother, Mother, Mother," she said,
  "So strange it seems to me."

"Yet here's a kiss for my mother dear,
  My mother dear, if this be so,
And lay your hand upon my head,
  And bless me, Mother, ere I go."

She clad herself in a russet gown,
  She was no longer Lady Clare:
She went by dale, and she went by down,
  With a single rose in her hair.

The lily-white doe Lord Ronald had brought
  Leaped up from where she lay,
Dropped her head in the maiden's hand,
  And followed her all the way.

Down stepped Lord Ronald from his tower:
  "O Lady Clare, you shame your worth!
Why come you dressed like a village maid,
  That are the flower of the earth?"

"I come dressed like a village maid,
  I am but as my fortunes are:
I am a beggar born," she said,
  "And not the Lady Clare."

"Play me no tricks," said Lord Ronald,
  "For I am yours in word and in deed;
Play me no tricks," said Lord Ronald,
  "Your riddle is hard to read."

O, and proudly stood she up!
  Her heart within her did not fail;
She looked into Lord Ronald's eyes,
  And told him all her nurse's tale.

He laughed a laugh of merry scorn:
  He turned and kissed her where she
    stood:
"If you are not the heiress born,
  And I," said he, "the next in blood—"

"If you are not the heiress born,
  And I," said he, "the lawful heir,
We two will wed tomorrow morn,
  And you shall still be Lady Clare."

READING COMPREHENSION

Summarizing. Choose the best phrase to complete each sentence. Then write the complete statements on your paper.

1. Lord Ronald and Lady Clare _____ (had just met, had been engaged for a long time, did not really love each other).

2. Alice wanted Lady Clare to _____ (keep the secret of her birth, break her engagement, give up her title).

3. Lady Clare felt that Lord Ronald loved her for _____ (her noble position, the lands she owned, her true worth as a person).

Interpreting. Write the answer to each question on your paper.

1. What did Alice tell Lady Clare about her birth?

2. Why did Lady Clare decide to tell Lord Ronald the truth?

3. Why did Lady Clare visit Lord Ronald dressed like a village maid?

For Thinking and Discussing

1. If you had been Lady Clare, would you have told Lord Ronald the truth about your birth?

2. Were you surprised at the way the poem ended? Were you pleased with it? If you had been the poet, would you have ended it differently?

UNDERSTANDING LITERATURE

Narrative Poem. Like a short story, a *narrative poem* has a plot, a setting, and characters. Unlike prose, however, a narrative poem is written to be read aloud so that the reader can appreciate the sound of the language and the rhyming lines. The theme in a narrative poem is its message to the reader about an aspect of life or human nature. In "Lady Clare," Tennyson makes a statement about the worth of the individual.

Answer the following questions about "Lady Clare." Write your answers on your paper.

1. In what order did the following events happen in "Lady Clare"?
   a. Lady Clare finds out that her real mother is Alice the nurse.
   b. Lord Ronald gives Lady Clare a lily-white doe.
   c. Lord Ronald decides to marry Lady Clare even if she isn't the true heir.
   d. Lady Clare reveals the truth about her birth.

2. What was the setting of the story?

3. Who are the three characters?

4. Which four lines in "Lady Clare" state the theme of the poem?

WRITING

Write a new ending for the poem, in which Lady Clare answers Lord Ronald. Write your ideas in a four-line stanza or in a prose paragraph.

The Adventure of the Speckled Band

by Sir Arthur Conan Doyle
adapted by Catherine Edwards Sadler

Detective stories such as those about the famous Sherlock Holmes delight and challenge the mind. Pay attention to the clues as you read and see if you can solve the mystery along with the great master.

The strange adventure of the speckled band occurred when I was still a bachelor, sharing rooms with my friend, Mr. Sherlock Holmes. It is the most fantastic of all the cases I have written.

It all began in April of 1883. I awoke one morning to find Sherlock Holmes standing fully dressed by my bed. I blinked up at him in surprise. The clock on the mantelpiece showed that it was only quarter past seven.

"Very sorry to wake you, Watson," he said.

"What is it then," I asked. "A fire?"

"No, a client. It seems a young lady has arrived and is quite upset. She insists on seeing me. She is waiting in the sitting room now. When young ladies wander about the city at this hour, and wake sleepy people from their beds, it is usually for some urgent reason. I know you like to follow interesting cases from the beginning. So I thought I should wake you and give you that chance."

"My dear fellow," I said, excitedly, "I would not miss it for anything." There was nothing I enjoyed more than observing Holmes during an investigation. I greatly admired his rapid deductions which were swift as intuition, but always based on logic. I quickly threw on my clothes. A few minutes later Holmes and I walked into the sitting room. A darkly dressed lady rose as we entered the room. She wore a heavy veil.

"Good morning, madam," Holmes said cheerfully. "My name is Sherlock Holmes. This is my intimate friend and associate, Dr. Watson. You can speak freely in front of him. Ha, I see that our housekeeper, Mrs. Hudson, has lighted a fire. Please draw your chair up to it. I shall order you a cup of hot coffee, for I observe that you are shivering."

"It is not the cold that makes me shiver," she said in a low voice.

"What then?" asked Holmes.

"It is fear, Mr. Holmes. It is terror!"

She raised her veil as she spoke. Her face was drawn and gray and her eyes were frightened and restless like those of a hunted animal. Her features and figure were young, but her hair was streaked with gray.

"You must not fear," Sherlock said soothingly. "We shall soon set matters right. You have come by train, I see."

"You know me then?" she asked nervously.

"No, but I observe the second half of a return ticket in the palm of your left glove. You must have started early and yet you had a long drive in a carriage before you reached the train station."

The lady gave a violent start and stared at my friend in confusion.

"There is no mystery, my dear madam," said he, smiling. "The left arm of your jacket is spattered with mud in at least seven places. The marks are fresh. An open carriage is the only vehicle that throws up mud in that way."

"You are perfectly correct," she said. "I started from home before six, reached the train depot at twenty past, and came by the first train. Sir, I can stand this strain no longer. I shall go mad if it continues. I have no one to turn to. There is one man who cares for me, but he can be of little help. Oh, sir, do you think that you can help me? At present I can't reward you for your services, but in a month or six weeks I shall be married and in control of my own money. At that time, you will not find me ungrateful."

"My profession is its own reward," said Holmes. "But you can pay for my ex-penses. Now please tell us what is troubling you."

"My name is Helen Stoner. I live with my stepfather, who is the last survivor of one of the oldest Saxon families in England — the Roylotts of Stoke Moran.

"The family was once among the richest in England. Over the years the riches were spent foolishly. Eventually nothing was left but a few acres of land and a two-hundred-year-old house with a heavy mortgage. The last squire lived there as a pauper. His son — my stepfather — realized that he must do something to help himself. He borrowed money from a relative and studied medicine. Then he went to India where he set up a large practice. There was a series of robberies involving his native butler. In a fit of anger he beat the butler to death. He was arrested and remained in prison a long time. He returned to England a disappointed and bitter man.

"When Dr. Roylott was in India he married my mother, Mrs. Stoner. She was a widow with twin daughters, Julia and myself. We were only two years old at the time of her remarriage. She had a small fortune which she turned over to Dr. Roylott. There was one provision, however. We were to be given a yearly sum should we marry. Shortly after our return to England, my mother died. She was killed eight years ago in a railway accident. Dr. Roylott gave up efforts to start a medical practice in London and took us to live with him in the old house in Surrey. The money my mother had left was enough for all our wants. There now

seemed to be no obstacle to our happiness.

"But a terrible change came over my stepfather at that time. He shut himself up in the house and quarreled with anyone who crossed his path. His temper was so violent and his strength so immense that people would flee when he approached.

"Last week he hurled the local blacksmith into a stream. It was only by paying him off that I stopped a public scandal. He has no friends except the wandering gypsies. He lets them camp out on the land and sometimes wanders away with them for weeks. He has a passion for Indian animals. At this moment a cheetah and a baboon wander freely over the grounds. They are feared by the villagers as much as their master.

"My sister Julia and I had little pleasure in our lives. No servant would stay with us. For a long time we did all the housework ourselves. Julia was only thirty when she died, but her hair had already begun to whiten, as has mine."

"Your sister is dead, then?"

"She died two years ago. It is of her death that I wish to speak to you. As you can imagine, we had little opportunity to meet anyone our own age. We had, however, an aunt — our mother's sister, who lived nearby. Occasionally, we were allowed to pay her short visits. Julia went there at Christmas two years ago. She met a major to whom she became engaged. My stepfather learned of the engagement and did not object. But within two weeks a terrible event happened which took away my only companion."

Sherlock Holmes had been leaning back in his chair, his eyes closed. He now half-opened them and glanced at Miss Stoner.

"Please be precise with the details," he said.

"It is easy for me to be so. Every event of that dreadful time is seared into my memory. As I have already said, the manor house is very old. Only one wing is now lived in. The bedrooms in this wing are on the ground floor. The first is Dr. Roylott's, the second is my sister's, and the third is mine. They all open out onto the same corridor. Do I make myself clear?"

"Precisely so."

"The windows of the three rooms open out onto the lawn. That fatal night, Dr. Roylott had gone to his room early. We knew that he had not gone to sleep as my sister was bothered by the smell of the strong Indian cigars he smokes. She left her room because of it, and came to mine. She remained for some time chatting about her approaching wedding. At eleven o'clock she rose to leave, but paused at the door.

"'Tell me, Helen,' she said, 'have you ever heard anyone whistle in the dead of night?'

"'Never,' said I.

"'I suppose that you couldn't whistle in your sleep?'

"'Certainly not. But why?'

"'Because during the past few nights at about three in the morning I have heard a low, clear whistle. I am a light sleeper and it has awakened me. I cannot tell where it comes from, perhaps from the next room, perhaps from the lawn. Have you heard it?'

"'No, I have not,' I said. 'It must be those wretched gypsies.'

"'Very likely. And yet you would have heard it had it come from the lawn.'

"'Ah, but I sleep more heavily than you.'

"'Well, it isn't important,' she said. She smiled back at me, closed my door, and a few minutes later I heard her key turn in the lock."

"Indeed," said Holmes. "Do you always lock yourselves in at night?"

"Always."

"And why?"

"I think I mentioned to you that the Doctor kept a cheetah and a baboon. We felt more secure with the doors locked."

"Quite so. Proceed with your statement."

"I could not sleep that night. I felt uneasy. It was a wild night. The wind was howling outside. The rain was beating and splashing against the windows. Suddenly, I heard the wild scream of a terrified woman. I knew it was my sister's voice. I sprang from my bed, wrapped a shawl around me, and rushed into the corridor. As I opened my door, I heard a low whistle. It was soon followed by a clanging sound, as if something metal had fallen. As I ran toward my sister's door, it slowly opened. I stared at it, horror-stricken, not knowing what would come forth. By the light of the hall lamp I saw my sister standing in the doorway. Her face white with terror, her hands groped for help, she swayed back and forth. I ran to her and threw my arms around her. But at that moment her legs gave way. She fell to the ground. She writhed as though in terrible pain. At first I thought that she hadn't recognized me. But as I bent over her she suddenly shrieked, 'Oh my God! Helen! It was the band. The speckled band!' She was about to speak again and pointed to the Doctor's room, but a fresh wave of pain seized her. I called loudly for my stepfather. He rushed from his room in his dressing gown. When he reached my sister's side she was unconscious. He poured brandy down her throat and sent for medical aid from the village. But it was no use. She died without regaining consciousness. Such was the dreadful end of my beloved sister."

"One moment," said Holmes. "Are you sure about this whistle and the metallic sound? Could you swear to it?"

"It is my strong impression that I heard it. But with the crash of the winds outside and the creaking of an old house, it is possible I was mistaken."

"Was your sister dressed?" Holmes asked.

"No, she was in her nightdress. In her right hand was a charred matchstick and in her left hand was a matchbox."

"Showing that she had struck a light and looked around her. That is important. And what conclusions did the coroner come to?"

"He investigated the case with great care. He did not find any satisfactory cause of death. The door had been closed from within. The windows were barred by shutters with iron bars which were locked each night. The walls of her room were solid, as was the floor. It is certain, therefore, that my sister was quite alone. Besides, there were no marks of violence upon her."

"How about poison?"

"The doctors found none."

"What do you think she died of?" Sherlock asked.

"It is my belief she died of pure fear and nervous shock. But I can't imagine what frightened her so," Miss Stoner answered.

"Were the gypsies on the land at the time?"

"Yes, there are nearly always some there."

"Ah, and what do you think she meant by 'speckled band'?"

"Sometimes I think it was merely the wild talk of fear. Other times I think it referred to some band of people . . . perhaps to the gypsies — perhaps to the spotted handkerchiefs so many wear around their heads."

Holmes shook his head. He looked far from satisfied.

"Two years have passed since then," continued the lady. "Until recently my life was lonelier than ever. But a month ago a dear friend asked my hand in marriage. My stepfather did not oppose the match. We are to be married in the spring. Two days ago some repairs were started on the house. A hole was made in my bedroom wall. I have had to move to the room where my sister died. I have had to sleep in the very bed where she slept. Imagine my terror last night when I heard the same whistle that she had heard before she died.

I jumped out of bed and lit the lamp, but there was nothing to see. I was too shaken to go to bed again. So I dressed and as soon as it was daylight, I slipped out of the house and made my way to you."

"You have done wisely," said my friend. "But have you told me all?"

"Yes, all."

"Miss Stoner, you have not. You are screening your stepfather."

"Why? What do you mean?" she asked.

Holmes pushed back the frill of lace that decorated her sleeve. Five little bruises — the marks of four fingers and a thumb — were printed on her white wrist.

"You have been cruelly treated," said Sherlock Holmes.

The lady blushed and covered up her injured wrist. "He is a hard man," she said, "and perhaps he does not know his own strength."

Holmes leaned his chin on his hands and stared silently into the fire for some minutes.

"This is serious business," he said at last. "There are a thousand details I must know before I decide what to do. But we haven't a moment to lose. If we come to Stoke Moran today can we look over the bedrooms without your stepfather knowing?"

"He spoke of coming into town today on important business. He will probably be away all day. We have a housekeeper, but she is old and foolish. I can easily keep her out of the way."

"Excellent. Will you join me, Watson?"

"By all means," I answered at once.

"Then we shall both come. What are you going to do, Miss Stoner?"

"I have one or two things to do in town. But I shall return by the twelve o'clock train. I will be there in time for your arrival."

"You may expect us early in the afternoon," said Holmes. "I have myself some small business matters to attend to. Will you join us for breakfast?"

"No, I must go. My heart is lighter now that I have confided in you. I shall look forward to seeing you again this afternoon." She dropped her thick veil back over her face and glided from the room.

"And what do you think of it all, Watson?" Sherlock asked me after she had left.

"It seems to me to be a most dark and sinister business," I said.

"Yes, both dark and sinister," agreed Sherlock.

"If the walls and floors are solid and the windows were barred and the door was locked, then her sister must have been alone when she met her mysterious end."

"What about the nightly whistles and the very peculiar words of the dying woman?" added Sherlock.

"I cannot think."

"When you combine whistles at night with the presence of a band of gypsies, a stepfather who has much to lose by his stepdaughter's marriage, her strange dying words, and the metallic clang her sister heard, it does seem to point to the gypsies."

"But what did the gypsies do?" I asked.

"I cannot imagine," Holmes answered seriously.

"I see many objections to such a theory."

"And so do I. It is precisely for that reason that we are going to Stoke Moran today. But what the devil?!"

The door flung open. A huge man now stood in the doorway. He wore a black top hat, a long frock coat, and a pair of tall boots. He held a whip in his hand. He was so tall that his hat brushed the crossbar of the doorway. He was so wide that he seemed to fill it from side to side. His face was tanned and wrinkled and his deep-set eyes and high, thin nose made him look like a fierce old bird of prey.

"Which of you is Holmes?" he demanded.

"I am," said Holmes quietly.

"I am Dr. Grimesby Roylott, of Stoke Moran."

"Indeed, Doctor," said Holmes blandly. "Please take a seat."

"I will do nothing of the kind. My stepdaughter has been here. I have traced her. What has she been saying to you?" screamed the old man furiously.

"I hear the spring flowers are blooming in the country," Sherlock commented.

"Ha! You put me off, do you?" said our new visitor. He took a step forward and shook his hunting crop. "I know you, you scoundrel. I have heard of you before. You are Holmes the meddler!"

My friend smiled.

"Holmes the busybody!"

His smile broadened.

"Holmes the snoop."

Holmes chuckled heartily. "Your conversation is most entertaining," he said. "When you go out, close the door . . . there is a draught."

"I will go when I have had my say.

Don't you dare meddle in my affairs. I know Miss Stoner has been here — I traced her! I am a dangerous man to cross! See here!" He stepped forward swiftly and seized the steel firepoker and bent it into a curve with his huge brown hands.

"See that you keep yourself out of my way," he snarled and hurled the twisted poker into the fireplace. Then he strode out of the room.

"He seems a very pleasant person, no?" said Holmes, laughing. "If he had remained, I could have shown him my own strength." As he spoke he picked up the steel poker. With a sudden effort he straightened it out again.

"This incident with the Doctor adds interest to the case. But I do hope our little friend will not suffer because of her visit to us. And now, Watson, we shall order breakfast and afterward I shall take a walk."

It was nearly one o'clock when Sherlock Holmes returned from his walk. He held a sheet of blue paper in his hand. Notes and figures were scrawled on it.

"I have seen the will of the dead wife," he said. "It seems her fortune is not worth that much anymore. If both girls were married, their stepfather would be left with very little. If even one married, his lifestyle would have to change drastically. My morning's work has not been wasted. It proves that he has a very strong reason for stopping his stepdaughters' marriages. We must hurry to the train. Please, slip your revolver into your pocket. A gun can be an excellent argument against a man who can twist steel pokers into knots!

That and a toothbrush are all that we need."

We drove by cab to the train station and from there traveled by train to Leatherhead, the nearest train depot to Miss Stoner's home. We hired a carriage and driver to take us to the Roylott mansion in Stoke Moran. During the drive, Sherlock sat deep in thought. His arms were folded, his hat was pulled down over his eyes, and his chin was sunk down upon his chest. Suddenly, however, he tapped me on the shoulder and pointed over the meadows.

"Look there!" said he.

In the distance I could see the wooded grounds and gray gables of a very old mansion.

"Stoke Moran?" he asked the driver.

"Yes, sir, that's the house of Dr. Grimesby Roylott."

"There is some building going on there," said Holmes. "That is where we are going."

"There's the village," said the driver. He pointed to a cluster of rooftops some distance to the left. "But if you want to get to the house, you'll find it shorter to get out and walk by footpath over the fields. There it is, where the lady is walking."

"And the lady, I fancy, is Miss Stoner," observed Holmes, shading his eyes. "Yes, I think we had better do what you suggest."

We got off, paid our fare, and the carriage rattled back down the road.

"I thought it best for that fellow to think we came here on business," commented Holmes. "Good afternoon, Miss Stoner."

Our client had hurried to meet us. "I have been waiting so eagerly for you," she said happily. "All has turned out splendidly. Dr. Roylott has gone to town, and it is unlikely he will be back before evening."

"We have had the pleasure of making the Doctor's acquaintance," said Holmes. In a few words he sketched out what had occurred. Miss Stoner turned white to the lips.

"Good heavens!" she cried. "He followed me then."

"So it appears."

"He is so cunning. I never know when I am safe from him. What will he say when he returns?"

"He may find that someone even more cunning than he is on his track. You must lock yourself up from him tonight. If he is violent, we will take you to your aunt's tomorrow. Let us examine the bedrooms immediately."

The building was built of gray stone. There were three distinct wings to the house. The left wing had broken and boarded-up windows and the roof was caving in. The central portion was in a little better repair but obviously was not in use. The right-hand building seemed modern. There were blinds in the windows and blue smoke curled from one of the chimneys. This was where the family lived. A scaffold leaned against the end wall although there were no signs of workmen about. Holmes walked up and down the ill-trimmed lawn. He examined the outside of the windows carefully.

"I take it, this is the window to your old bedroom," he said, pointing to the farthest window. "The center one is to your sister's room, and the one next to the main building is to Dr. Roylott's room. Is that right?"

"Exactly so. But I am now sleeping in the middle room," said Miss Stoner.

"Because of the repairs. By the way, there doesn't seem to be any real need for repairs to that end wall."

"No, there isn't. I believe it was an excuse to move me from my room."

"Ah! I see," said Holmes. "Would you please go into your room and bar your shutters?"

Miss Stoner did so. Holmes tried in every way to force the shutters open, but they would not budge. He tested the hinges as well, but they were solid iron and attached firmly to the stone wall. "Hum!" said he, scratching his head. "My theory presents some difficulties. No one could pass through these shutters if they were bolted. Well, let us go within and see if we learn anything there."

A small side door led to a white-washed corridor. Three bedrooms opened off it. Holmes would not examine the third room. We went immediately to the middle room where Miss Stoner now slept. It was a cozy little room with a low ceiling and a gaping fireplace. There was little furniture in the room. The floorboards were old and worn as was the wood paneling which covered the wall. Holmes drew one of the chairs into the corner and sat down. His eyes traveled around and around and up and down, taking in every detail of the room.

"To what room does that bell connect?" he asked at last. He pointed to a thick bell-rope which hung beside the bed. The tassel at its end lay upon the pillow.

"It goes to the housekeeper's room."

"It looks newer than the other objects in the room."

"Yes, it was only put there a couple of years ago," Miss Stoner answered.

"Your sister asked for it, I suppose?" asked Holmes.

"No, I never heard of her using it. We used to get what we wanted for ourselves."

"Indeed, it seemed unnecessary to put so nice a bell-pull there. You will excuse me for a few minutes while I examine this floor." He held his magnifying glass in his hand and crawled backward and forward, examining the cracks between the boards. Then he examined the wood paneling. He walked over to the bed. He spent some time staring at it and running his eye up and down the wall. Finally he took the bell-rope in his hand and gave it a good pull.

"Why, it's a fake," he said.

"Won't it ring?" she asked.

"No, it isn't even attached to a wire. This is very interesting. It is attached to a hook in the ventilator shaft."

"How very absurd! I never noticed that before."

"Very strange!" muttered Holmes and pulled at the rope. "There are a few curious things about this room. For example, what fool builder would put a ventilator between two rooms when he could have connected it directly to the outside air?!"

"That is also quite new," said Miss Stoner.

"Done about the same time as the bell-rope?" asked Holmes.

"Yes, there were several little changes made at that time."

"They seem to be of a particularly odd nature — fake bell-ropes and ventilators which do not ventilate! With your permission, Miss Stoner, I would now like to examine your stepfather's room."

Dr. Grimesby Roylott's bedroom was large and plainly furnished. There was a camp bed, a wooden shelf full of books, an armchair beside the bed, a plain wooden chair against the wall, a round table, and a large iron safe. Holmes walked slowly around the room and examined each item.

"What's in here?" he asked, tapping the safe.

"My stepfather's business papers," Miss Stoner answered.

"Oh! You have seen inside then?" asked Holmes.

"Only once, years ago. I remember it was full of papers."

"There isn't a cat in it, is there?" Holmes asked.

"No. What a strange idea."

"Well, look at this!" He picked up a small saucer of milk which was on top.

"No, we don't keep a cat. But there is a cheetah and a baboon."

"Ah, yes, of course! Well, a cheetah is just a big cat, and yet a saucer of milk seems a bit small for its great thirst. There is one more thing I want to see." He squatted down in front of the wooden chair and examined the seat of it carefully.

"Thank you. That is quite settled," said he. He rose and put his lens into his pocket. "Hullo! Here is something interesting!"

A whip hung on one corner of the bed. The end of it was knotted into a nooselike loop.

"What do you make of that, Watson?"

"It's a common enough whip," I answered. "But I don't know why it's knotted like that."

"That is not quite so common, is it? Ah, me! It is a wicked world when a clever man turns his brains to crime. I think that I have seen enough now, Miss Stoner. With your permission we shall walk on the lawn."

I had never seen my friend's face look so grim. We walked several times up and down the lawn and neither Miss Stoner nor myself said a word. Sherlock was the first to speak. "It is very essential, Miss Stoner, that you follow my advice in every way."

"I shall most certainly do so," she said.

"Your life may depend on it!" he added.

"I will follow your directions exactly."

"In the first place, my friend and I must spend the night in your room."

Both Miss Stoner and I gazed at him in astonishment.

"Yes," he said, "it must be so. Let me explain. I believe that is the village inn over there?" He pointed to a large building in the distance.

"Yes, that is The Crown," she answered.

"Very good. Your windows can be seen from there?"

"Certainly."

"On your stepfather's return you must say that you have a headache and go to your room. When he retires for the night, you must open your shutters, put your lamp in the window as a signal to us, and then quietly go into your old room. In spite of the repairs, can you stay there for one night?"

"Oh, yes, easily."

"The rest you will leave in our hands," said Holmes.

"But what will you do?" asked Miss Stoner.

"We shall spend the night in your room, and investigate the noise which has disturbed you."

"I believe, Mr. Holmes, that you have already made up your mind as to this case," said Miss Stoner.

"Perhaps I have."

"Then for pity's sake tell me what was the cause of my sister's death."

"I should prefer to have more proof before I speak," he answered.

"You can at least tell me whether my own idea was correct. Did she die from sudden fright?"

"No, I do not think so. I think the cause of death was more definite. And now, Miss Stoner, we must leave you. If Dr. Roylott returned and saw us, everything would be ruined. Be brave. If you follow my directions, I believe we can end this nightmare."

Sherlock Holmes and I had no trouble renting a room at the local inn, The Crown. It was on the upper floor and had a view of the right wing of the manor house. At dusk, we saw Dr. Grimesby Roylott drive past. His huge form loomed above the lad who drove him. The boy had some difficulty undoing the heavy iron gates. We heard the hoarse roar of the Doctor's voice. We saw the fury with which he clenched his fists at him. The carriage drove on. A few minutes later we saw a light spring up among the trees. A lamp was lit in one of the sitting rooms.

"Do you know, Watson," said Holmes as we sat together in the darkness, "I have some hesitation about taking you with me tonight. This is a dangerous case."

"Can I be of assistance?" I asked.

"Your presence might be most necessary."

"Then I shall certainly come," I said.

"It is very kind of you," Holmes said.

"You speak of danger," I commented. "You have certainly seen more in these bedrooms than I have."

"No, I imagine you saw all I did. But I have deduced more."

"I saw nothing remarkable except a bell-rope, but what that could mean I do not know."

"You saw the ventilator too?"

"Yes, but it is not unusual to have an opening between two rooms. It was so small that a rat could hardly pass through."

"I knew that we should find such a ventilator even before we came to Stoke Moran."

"My dear Holmes!" I exclaimed.

"Oh, yes, I did. You remember that Miss Stoner's sister complained that she could smell her stepfather's cigar. That suggested to me that there was some sort of opening between the two rooms. It had to have been a small one or the coroner would have noticed it. I deduced therefore that it was an air vent."

"But what harm can there be in that?" I asked.

"Well, there is at least a curious coincidence of dates. A ventilator is made, a bell-rope is hung, and a young lady dies. Doesn't that strike you as odd?"

"I cannot see any connection between the three things."

"Did you observe anything peculiar about the bed?" Sherlock asked.

"No."

"It was clamped to the floor. Did you ever see a bed fastened to the floor before?"

"I cannot say that I have," I answered.

"That lady could not move her bed. It obviously had to remain a certain distance away from the ventilator and the rope. I call it a rope because that is actually what it is, since no bell is attached."

"Holmes, I begin to see what you are hinting at. We are only just in time to prevent some horrible crime."

"Yes, when a doctor goes wrong he is the worst of criminals. He has nerve and he has knowledge. We shall see horrors before this night is through. For goodness sake let us smoke a quiet pipe and turn our minds to something cheerful."

At nine o'clock the light among the trees was turned out. All was dark in the direction of the Manor house. Two hours passed slowly. Then at the stroke of eleven, a single light shone out in front of us.

"That is our signal," said Holmes, springing to his feet. "It comes from the middle window."

We left the inn and went out into the dark night. A chill blew in our faces. The yellow light guided us through the gloom.

We walked across the grounds, and onto the lawn. We were just about to climb into the middle window when we saw a strange creature. It looked like some hideous child. It threw itself onto the lawn and then ran swiftly into the darkness.

"My God!" I whispered. "Did you see that?"

Holmes was as startled as I. Then he broke into a low laugh and said into my ear:

"That's the baboon!"

I had forgotten the strange pets the Doctor kept. There was a cheetah too. Perhaps we might find it on our shoulders any moment. We took off our shoes and climbed into the room. My friend noiselessly closed the shutters, moved the lamp onto the table, and cast his eyes around the room. All was as it had been during the day. Then he creeped up to me and whispered, "The least sound would ruin our plans."

I nodded to show that I had heard.

"We must sit without light. He would see it through the ventilator. Do not fall asleep," he whispered. "Your very life depends on it. Have your pistol ready in case we need it. I will sit on the side of the bed. You sit in that chair."

I took out my revolver and laid it on the corner of the table.

Holmes had brought a long thin cane. This he placed on the bed beside him. By it he laid a box of matches and a stump of candle. Then he turned down the lamp.

I shall never forget that night. I could not hear a sound, but I knew my friend sat wide-eyed waiting for something to happen. The shutters cut off all outside light. We were in absolute darkness. Once in a while we heard a catlike whine. It was the cheetah on the prowl. Far away we could hear the parish clock. It boomed out every quarter of an hour. Twelve struck, then one, and two, and three, and still we sat waiting.

Suddenly there was a fleeting gleam from the room next door. It vanished immediately. In its place came the smell of burning oil and heated metal. Someone in the next room had lit a lantern. I heard some movement and then all was silent once more. For half an hour I sat straining my ears. Then suddenly I heard another sound . . . a gentle, soothing sound like steam escaping a tea kettle. The instant we heard it Holmes sprang from the bed, struck a match and lashed furiously with his cane at the bell-pull.

"Did you see it, Watson?" he yelled. "Did you see it?"

But I saw nothing. At the moment when Holmes struck the match I heard a low clear whistle. The sudden glare made it impossible for me to see what my friend was lashing out at. Sherlock's face had turned deathly pale. It was filled with horror and hate.

He had stopped striking the bell-pull and was now staring at the ventilator. Suddenly there was a horrible cry. It grew louder and louder. It was a yell of fear, pain, and anger. It struck cold in our hearts. I stood gazing at Holmes and he at me, until the last echoes of it had died away into the silence.

"What can it mean?" I gasped.

"It means that it is all over," answered Holmes. "And perhaps, it is for the best. Take your pistol and we shall enter Dr. Roylott's room."

He lit the lamp and led the way down the corridor. He knocked at the door twice. There came no reply. Then he turned the handle and entered. I followed with the cocked pistol in my hand.

On the table stood a lantern. Its shutter was half open. Beside the table on a wooden chair sat Dr. Grimesby Roylott. He was dressed in a long gray dressing gown. His whip lay across his lap. His chin was cocked upward and his eyes were fixed in a dreadful stare. Around his brow he had a peculiar yellow band with brownish speckles. It seemed tightly bound around his head. Roylott made neither sound nor motion as we entered the room.

"The band! The speckled band!" whispered Holmes.

I took a step forward. In an instant his strange headgear began to move. The diamond-shaped head and puffed neck of a snake appeared.

"It's a swamp adder!" cried Holmes. "The deadliest snake in India. It has turned on its master. Let us thrust this creature back into its den. We can then take Miss Stoner to a place of shelter and let the county police know what has happened."

He took the whip swiftly from the dead man's lap and threw the noose around the reptile's neck. He lifted it from its horrid perch and carried it at arm's length to the iron safe. He threw it into the safe and closed the door firmly upon it.

Such are the true facts of Dr. Grimesby Roylott's death. The next morning we sent Miss Stoner by train to her aunt's and turned the entire matter into the hands of the local police.

"I had," said Holmes on the way back to London, "come to an entirely wrong conclusion about this case. It just goes to show that one must never make judgments without enough information. The presence of the gypsies and the use of the word 'band,' which could refer to a group of people, put me on the wrong scent. But I soon saw the error of my reasoning. There was simply no way that a human being could enter that room by the window or door. Then I spotted the fake bell-pull and the ventilator. The discovery that the bed was clamped to the floor was of key importance. It made me suspect that the rope was used as a bridge for something to pass from the ventilator opening to the bed. The idea of a snake instantly came to me. The fact that the Doctor kept creatures from India made me believe that I was on the right track. Furthermore, snake poison is very difficult to discover by chemical testing . . . and it works quickly. This would appeal to the Doctor. Two little fang marks would be very hard to detect. Then I thought of the whistle. He had obviously trained it, probably by the use of the milk we saw, to return to him when he whistled. He would put the snake through the ventilator at the hour that he thought best. It would then crawl

through the ventilator, along the bell-pull rope and down onto the bed. It might or might not bite the occupant. Perhaps she would escape its bite every night for a week. But sooner or later it would attack.

"I had come to these conclusions before we entered his room. An inspection of his chair confirmed my thought. It showed that he had been standing on it — which, of course, he would have to do to reach the ventilator. The sight of the safe, the saucer of milk, and the loop in the whip decided the matter. The metallic clang that Miss Stoner heard was caused by her stepfather hastily closing the door of his safe upon the deadly snake. Once I had made up my mind, I arranged for Miss Stoner to leave her room and for us to be there in her place. When I heard the creature hiss, I instantly lit the light and attacked it."

"Which made it return through the ventilator," I added.

"Yes, and caused it to turn upon its master on the other side. You see, my blows roused its snakish temper. It flew upon the first person it saw. In a way, I am responsible for Dr. Roylott's death. In all honesty, I doubt that I shall lose much sleep because of it."

READING COMPREHENSION

Summarizing. Choose the best phrase to complete each sentence. Then write the complete statements on your paper.

1. Helen Stoner was afraid for her life because _____ (Dr. Roylott had threatened her, she heard the same whistle that her sister had heard before her death, she had seen the speckled band).

2. In order to prove his case and protect Miss Stoner, Holmes decided that he and Watson would _____ (stay in Dr. Roylott's room, call the police, spend the night in the middle room).

3. The cause of Julia Stoner's death turned out to be _____ (gas fumes, strangulation, a poisonous snake bite).

Interpreting. Write the answer to each question on your paper.

1. What was Dr. Roylott's motive for wanting to stop his stepdaughters' marriages?

2. Why did Holmes rule out that a person had been in the room with Helen Stoner's sister when she died?

3. Based on what you learned, why was Miss Stoner particularly lucky that she came to Holmes when she did?

For Thinking and Discussing. How do you think Miss Stoner reacted when she found out what happened? Do you think she had mixed feelings?

UNDERSTANDING LITERATURE

Mystery. Writers of mystery stories plan their plots very carefully. They reveal the details of the plot in a way that will keep the reader in suspense. Often, they present a series of incidents and clues that at first seem unconnected or unimportant. Little by little, the reader discovers how the pieces of the puzzle fit together. It is only at the end of the story, however, that the reader understands the entire picture.

Throughout "The Adventure of the Speckled Band," the reader is presented with clues that tie in directly with other clues and incidents in the story. Only at the end, however, when Sherlock Holmes explains how he solved the case, do all the connections become clear.

Look at the pairs of clues below. On your paper, write one or two sentences explaining how each pair of clues is connected.

1. The whistle and the saucer of milk

2. The clanging sound and the safe

3. The bell-rope and the ventilator

4. The chair and the whip

5. The speckled band and the fact that no cause of death was found

WRITING

Imagine that you are Helen Stoner. Write a letter to Sherlock Holmes thanking him for solving the case. Discuss the clues and remark on Holmes's deductive powers.

Section Review

Context Clues. Sometimes you come across a word you do not know. You might figure out the meaning of the word by its *context* — the way the word is used.

Example: The photographer *focused* the lens of the camera and took a picture.

Even if you did not know the word *focused*, you still know something about taking a picture. Your knowledge gives you a clue that the photographer did something to the camera lens in order to produce a clear picture. The photographer adjusted the lens. The word *focused* means "adjusted."

What is the meaning of each word in heavy type below? Try to figure it out from its context. Write the word and its meaning on your paper.

1. "Don Quixote . . . got to thinking that he might do better with a **squire**. A squire could help him over the rough spots, carry his shield, and get him in and out of his armor."

2. "Burek and Kot . . . tried to **mimic** each other. When Burek barked, Kot tried to bark along, and when Kot meowed, Burek tried to meow, too."

3. "It would be a good guess that he would become a bitter and angry hater of people, filled with **spite**."

Main Ideas and Details. Stories are usually written in paragraphs. Each paragraph is a group of sentences that tells about one main idea. One sentence in the paragraph may state the main idea. Other sentences in the paragraph give details that tell more about the main idea. Read this paragraph:

> The battle raged. Gleaming swords clashed in the morning light. Heads rolled. Blood stained the ground. Quijada flailed his arms and stabbed the air with an imaginary sword.

In this example, the first sentence states the main idea of the paragraph. The other sentences give details that tell more about the main idea.

Read each of the following paragraphs. Then, in your own words, write the main idea on a piece of paper.

1. "A glass mirror shows only the skin of the body. The real image of a person is in his willingness to help himself and his family and, as far as possible, all those he comes in contact with. This kind of mirror reveals the very soul of the person."

2. "Of his early days, I could learn but little. He did not like to talk about the past. It had been a nightmare, and he still shuddered to think of it."

3. "Happy? Happy is too poor a word. It is the first day of spring. Bells ring out, and the sun breaks through the clouds. My heart has never known such joy!"

WRITING

The Writing Process. As any professional writer can tell you, writing well is not easy. However, writing can be made less difficult if you follow a process, or series of steps: (1) Set your goal by choosing a topic and deciding on the purpose of your writing; (2) Make a plan for carrying out your goal by gathering and organizing your ideas; (3) Write a first draft, or rough version, of your composition; and (4) Revise your first draft by looking for ways to improve your writing, and by editing and proofreading. You will follow these steps to complete the writing assignment in each Section Review.

Step 1: Set Your Goal

In setting a goal, you choose a topic and decide on your purpose. You also identify your audience so that you can communicate effectively.

Consider which story in Section 1 interests you most, and choose one of the following general topics for a composition:

1. Don Quixote in "Don Quixote"
2. The mirror in "The Cat Who Thought She Was a Dog and The Dog Who Thought He Was a Cat"
3. John Merrick in "The Elephant Man"
4. The theme of love in "Cyrano de Bergerac"
5. Sherlock Holmes's powers of detection in "The Adventure of the Speckled Band"

After you have chosen your general topic, you need to narrow it down and define your purpose, or decide how you want to focus your writing. Do you want to describe a character or an event? Do you want to express an opinion or prove a point? The purpose you choose will guide you as you write.

Suppose, for example, you had narrowed your topic down to the people who saw John Merrick in "The Elephant Man." You might choose to describe, compare, or interpret the other characters' reactions to his looks. You might state your purpose in this way:

PURPOSE: To show how people reacted differently to seeing the Elephant Man.

Write down a statement of purpose for the topic you have chosen.

Finally, identify your audience, or your readers. You will want to keep your readers in mind as you write. Try to respond to any questions or reactions that you think they may have. In this case, assume that the audience will be your teacher and your classmates. Remember that they already know something about your topic.

Step 2: Make a Plan

With your topic and purpose in mind, you can begin to write down thoughts and details that you might include in your paper. Look through the story for events and statements that relate to your topic and take notes. Organize your notes in a way that clearly develops your purpose. You might number them in the order in which you want to present them. Or you might arrange your ideas in groups that relate to the same subtopic, and make a rough outline.

Step 3: Write a First Draft

Remember, the first draft is a *rough* draft. It is not supposed to be a finished piece of writing. Don't worry about making mistakes. You will be able to change and correct your work later.

Refer to your notes or outline as you write, but feel free to make changes. You can add new ideas, discard old ones, or change their order as you go along.

Step 4: Revise

When you revise, you make changes and corrections that turn your first draft into a finished piece of writing. If possible, put your work aside for a day or two before you begin to revise. That way you will be able to look at it with a fresh eye. As you revise, ask yourself these questions:

☐ Does every idea relate to your purpose?
☐ Is the meaning of each sentence clear?
☐ Does each paragraph contain a main-idea sentence?
☐ Do all the details in each paragraph support the main idea?
☐ Should any words or sentences be deleted or added?
☐ Are the ideas in a clear, logical order?

When you have finished revising your paper, proofread it for mistakes. Then type your paper or copy it over neatly.

QUIZ

The following is a quiz for Section 1. Write the answers in complete sentences on your paper.

Reading Comprehension

1. Why did Don Quixote act and talk differently from everyone else?

2. What effect did the removal of the mirror have on the Skiba household in "The Cat Who Thought She Was a Dog and the Dog Who Thought He Was a Cat"?

3. How did the Elephant Man change during his stay at the hospital?

4. How did Lady Clare find out that Lord Ronald truly loved her?

5. Why did Holmes wake Dr. Watson up so early in the morning at the beginning of "The Adventure of the Speckled Band"?

Understanding Literature

6. Write four events from "The Cat Who Thought She Was a Dog and the Dog Who Thought He Was a Cat" that summarize the story's plot.

7. Could the story of the Elephant Man have happened at any other place and time? Why or why not?

8. What point did Rostand want to make about appearances by telling the story of Cyrano de Bergerac?

9. What elements of a short story are found in the poem "Lady Clare"?

10. What was the relationship between Helen Stoner and her stepfather in "The Adventure of the Speckled Band"? Support your point of view.

ACTIVITIES

Word Attack. Words that are made up of two or more words are called *compound words*. Compound words that are written as one word, such as *showman*, are called closed compound words. Compound words written as two words, such as *walking cane*, are called open compound words. Some compound words, such as *mix-up*, are hyphenated.

The compound words below are from the story "The Elephant Man." Write each word on your paper. Tell whether it is a closed compound, open compound, or hyphenated compound. Then use each word in a sentence.

gamekeeper	lighthouse
half-dead	worn-out
shoehorn	man-about-town
waiting room	make-believe

Speaking and Listening

1. The scene of Don Quixote attacking windmills is quite famous and has become a symbol for someone who persists in fighting an imaginary enemy. Find a partner to take the part of Sancho Panza, and practice acting out the scene. Use the dialogue in the story. Be prepared to present the scene for your classmates.

2. "Lady Clare" is a narrative poem. Practice reading it aloud as though you were telling a story in verse. You might try using different voices for the words of Lady Clare, Alice the nurse, and Lord Ronald. Be prepared to present the poem, or part of it, to your class.

Researching

1. Knights were a special social class in England, France, and Spain between 1100 and 1300. Do some research on knights and knighthood, and try to answer these questions: How did knighthood evolve as a social class? How did a person become a knight? What did knights do? What were the duties of pages and squires? What special privileges did a knight have? What was chivalry? What were tournaments and what purpose did they serve? What were the parts of a knight's armor? Present your facts to the class.

2. In "The Adventure of the Speckled Band," you read that Dr. Roylott allowed gypsies to camp out on the manor grounds. Do some research about gypsies. Find out about their origin, language, life-style, customs, and where they can be found today. Report your findings to the class.

Creating

1. In Don Quixote's imagination, windmills were fearsome giants waving long powerful arms. What would Don Quixote think of a train or a sports car? Write a paragraph describing what he might imagine either one to be and why.

2. Suppose a bird thinks it is a squirrel and a squirrel thinks it is a bird. Write one or two paragraphs describing how they would mimic each other. Include a statement of main idea and supporting details in each paragraph.

JUSTICE

Every truth has two sides.

—Aesop
Greece

Three Judges
Georges Rouault (1871-1958)
Museum of Modern Art
Sam A. Lewisohn Bequest

Justice

Life isn't always fair. But a writer has the power to create a world in which bad people are always punished and justice is always done.

People have written about justice since literature began. The ancient Greek philosophers devoted much of their writing to deciding what was right and what was wrong. Writers ever since have followed their example. In some stories, you know from the beginning that a bad person will be punished or taught a lesson. In other stories, you are surprised by the way justice is done. And some writers remind you that life can be unjust, that sometimes the innocent are punished unfairly, and that right and wrong are not always easy to tell apart.

Punishing Evil

Geoffrey Chaucer, who is considered to be the greatest English writer of the Middle Ages, wrote many stories like "The Pardoner's Tale" in which evil people are punished. In his stories, it is usually easy to tell the "bad guys" from the "good guys." The three troublemakers of "The Pardoner's Tale" are bad in just about every possible way. They are stupid, disrespectful, and disloyal; they brag, they drink, and they gamble. But most of all, the three are selfish and greedy. Many writers show that the love of money is a bad thing. In Chaucer's story, a bag of gold leads directly to death.

Death, in this story, appears as a person. In many old stories from around the world, a mysterious character turns out to be more, or less, than human. These characters often seem to be in control of the strings of justice. In "The Pardoner's Tale," the character Death makes sure the greedy young men get what they deserve.

Greed, again, is the subject of Guy de Maupassant's short story "The Necklace." Mathilde, because she longs to be rich, is unkind to her penniless husband. But in this story, there are no mysterious characters who have the power to punish Mathilde for her greed. Everything seems to happen purely by chance. Yet Mathilde gets what she deserves—but in a way that will surprise you. You will never guess the ending of this story.

Teaching a Lesson

Some stories are told over and over for generations, until no one remembers who invented them. These stories are called "folktales." Because people everywhere are alike in certain ways, similar folktales are found in many lands. And many folktales are about a wise person who teaches a bad person a lesson.

In this section, you will read two folktales from opposite sides of the world. But the stories are surprisingly alike. In both, a person is so greedy that he accuses someone of "stealing" something that can't be stolen—a smell! And in both, a clever judge finds a "punishment" to fit this unusual "crime." As you will see, justice does not always mean that a wrongdoer is punished. Sometimes it is enough just to have someone taught a lesson.

Solving a Problem

In a mystery story, a crime has been committed. Someone must be brought to justice—but who? It is often not clear at first who killed the victim or stole the jewels. The fun of a mystery is in figuring out who did it. No one is better at fooling the reader than Agatha Christie. As you will see when you read "Sanctuary," it is always exciting to read her stories and try to answer the riddle.

But sometimes there are other questions to answer. Is someone who breaks the law always a bad person? Is it always the bad person who is punished?

In "Billy Budd," a young, popular sailor is sentenced to hang for a murder he never meant to commit. Everyone wonders if justice has been served. In books, as in real life, justice is not simple.

The Pardoner's Tale

based on The Canterbury Tales *by Geoffrey Chaucer*

*"The Pardoner's Tale" is one part of a very long poem,
called* The Canterbury Tales, *that contains many different
stories. Geoffrey Chaucer began writing this long poem in
1387. The English language that people spoke then is different from the language we speak today. For example, Chaucer's own words for the last two lines of the selection are:*

> *Thus ended been thise homicydes two,*
> *And eek the false empoysoner also.*

*"The Pardoner's Tale" is retold here as a story in modern
English. The more modern English version is:*

> *Thus these two murderers received their due,*
> *So did the treacherous young poisoner, too!*

My story is, in fact, a warning:
Three villains met one early morning
In a tavern, plotting and drinking.
And as they sat, a bell was clinking
On a coffin, lonely and gray.
They asked a man: Who died that day?
He said, "Before you came here, I was
    told
He was a friend of yours in days of old.
Suddenly, last night, your friend was
    slain.
He was at his house, dead drunk again,

When Death crept in to steal his life.
Stabbed through the heart he was, as
    with a knife
And never moved a muscle. Then
Death crept back out to kill again.
The plague is this accursed Black
    Death.
He snuffs out thousands with a single
    breath.
This very year in a town near by
This same Death caused two hundred
    people to die.

If you should meet him, you'd best be
      wary
Of this awesome adversary!"
One villain bragged, "He's not so rough!
I've beaten men ten times as tough.
Come on now friends, let's find this rat.
We'll knock him down, we'll lay him
      flat!"
They took an oath to kill the man
And out into the town they ran.
They swore to fight and die for one
      another,
To defend each man as if he were a
      brother.
The villains stumbled down the street
And a poor, old man they chanced to
      meet.
"Greetings to you lords," the old man
      said,
Wrapped by his cloak except around his
      head.
The drunkards laughed in wicked glee,
And teased the old man nastily.
"Old man," they said, "show us your
      face,
You stupid fool, run from this place.
You should be dead, you ancient old
      crone!
You're just a bag of skin and bone.
You're old and bent, your eyes are
      weak!"
The old man turned to them to speak:
"Not even Death will take my life;
So, like a wretched prisoner at strife

Within himself, I walk alone and wait
For Death to open up his gate.
But Death refuses to take me home.
To younger men his gazes roam.
And now, dear gentlemen, take heed,
Do not indulge in lust and greed.
Be kind to those as old as I.
I've done nothing to you, please let me
      by."
"Oh, no you don't," said one villain,
      "Not so fast.
I heard you mention, a moment past,
A certain traitor, Death, who singles out
And kills the fine young fellows
      hereabout.
You are his spy. Wait here a bit.
Say where he is or you shall pay for it."
"Well, brave sirs" the old man said, "I'll
      tell you three:
Death is in the grove, beneath a tree.
I saw him there. He's waiting for you."
Then up the path, the villains flew.
They reached an oak tree, and there they
      found
A pile of money heaped on the ground.
Golden coins, a treasure, so they
      thought.
No longer was it Death those fellows
      sought.
For they were all so thrilled to see the
      sight,
The money was so beautiful and bright.
That down they sat by the precious pile.
The wickedest spoke first, after a while.

"Brothers," he said, "listen to what I
say.
Who knew this would be our lucky day?
It's clear that Fortune has given us this
treasure
To allow us to live in prosperity and
pleasure.
Now we must bring this money back at
night,
And find a place to hide it well out of
sight.
So people won't accuse us all of stealing
Or robbery and other dirty dealing.
Now one of us should go back for
supplies
And the others guard the place where
the treasure lies."
The youngest one ran quickly back to
town.
As soon as he had gone, the other two
sat down.
Then one man turned to face the other
And said, "You can trust me as a
brother.
Now there's a lot of gold to be
Divided up among us three.
But I think there is a better plan —
To share the gold between us with one
less man."
The other said, "I like your style.
Now quick, he will be back in a little
while.
Tell me, how should we carry out this
wrong?
That lad is tall and awfully strong."

"Well," said his friend, "that may be
right and true,
But one man is not quite as powerful as
two.
When he comes back, get up to play
And while you're wrestling, it will go
this way:
I'll run a dagger through his back,
And then it's your turn to attack.
Then all this money will be ours to
spend,
Divided equally, of course, my friend."
Now, on the way to town the youngest
lad
Thought the same thought the others
had.
If they were dead, then he alone
Would soon that golden treasure own.
So on he ran, no thought to tarry
Right to the town's apothecary.
And said, "Sell me some poison, if you
will.
I have a lot of rats I want to kill."
The druggist said, "I've a deadly
brew
That will surely kill a rat or two.
If any living thing should this stuff eat,
It will fall down and die right at your
feet."
The fellow took the poison brew and
ran
To the next street down, and found a
man
Who gave him three large bottles. He
withdrew

90

Villagers Merrymaking at an Inn, *Adriaen van Ostade, 1652*

And poured the poison mix in only two,
Then filled three bottles with wine to the
 brim.
Back to his friends, he took the wine
 with him.
When he rejoined his friends at the
 treasure tree,
Their numbers soon were counted less
 than three.
His "brothers" killed this fellow, two on
 one.
Then said the first of them, when it was
 done,

"Now for a drink, let's sit and be
 merry,
For later there'll be a corpse to bury."
And each one, reaching for a quenching
 sip,
Put a poisoned bottle to his lip.
And so the villains died beside the gold.
Their bodies lay there lifeless, stiff and
 cold.
Thus these two murderers received their
 due,
So did the treacherous young poisoner,
 too!

READING COMPREHENSION

Summarizing. Choose the best phrase to complete each sentence. Then write the complete statements on your paper.

1. The three villains left the town in search of _____ (gold that would make them rich, Death in order to kill him, an old man to rob).

2. After one villain had returned to town, the others _____ (counted the money, plotted his murder, ran away).

3. The youngest villain bought poison to _____ (kill his companions, kill the rats, murder the old man).

Interpreting. Write the answer to each question on your paper.

1. Why did the youngest villain go back to town instead of staying with the others?

2. The first sentence of the poem is, "My story is, in fact, a warning." What is the author's warning to the reader?

3. Why didn't the two remaining villains get the treasure after they had killed their friend?

For Thinking and Discussing

1. The villains went back on their oath to fight and die for each other. Why do you suppose they did that?

2. Did you suspect that the old man was more than just a traveler? Who did you think he was?

UNDERSTANDING LITERATURE

Plot. The *plot* is the series of events that takes place in the story or tale. All the action that occurs is part of the plot.

The plot has a beginning, a middle, and an end. You may find clues in the beginning or middle that help you guess the ending. Clues that help you figure out the ending are called *foreshadowing*.

"The Pardoner's Tale" ends with the death of the three villains. Foreshadowing hints at this ending. You may have guessed the outcome if you realized that the old man was Death in disguise.

Read the following facts from the tale. Write down those facts that hint that the old man was really Death.

1. The old man was wrapped in a cloak.

2. The three villains liked to drink and plot.

3. The old man said, "But Death refuses to take me home. To younger men his gazes roam."

4. The old man showed up just after the villains bragged about finding Death.

5. Two of the villains agreed to split the gold two ways.

WRITING

Now that you know the ending of "The Pardoner's Tale," go back to the selection and find other foreshadowing clues. You may either outline them or write about them in a paragraph.

The Necklace

by Guy de Maupassant

Guy de Maupassant lived in France in the second half of the 19th century. He is especially famous for his short stories, and he wrote over 300 of them. These stories became popular as soon as he began to publish them, and for a good reason. When you read "The Necklace," you will see that no one is better than de Maupassant at surprising the reader.

She was one of those pretty and charming girls born, as though by mistake, into a family of laborers. There was no way for her to meet and marry a man of wealth and importance, so she let herself be married off to a little clerk in the Ministry of Education.

Her tastes were simple because she had never been able to afford any other. She was unhappy, however, for she felt that she had married beneath her. Her natural beauty, grace, and intelligence put her on the same level as the highest lady in the land.

She suffered endlessly. She suffered from the poorness and ugliness of her surroundings. All the things that other women of her class never noticed, tormented and insulted her. She imagined herself in an elegant home filled with beautiful furnishings — silk draperies, crystal, chandeliers, expensive furniture — and waited on by dozens of servants to satisfy her every whim. She dreamed of being sought after by famous and powerful men, of being the envy of every other woman.

When she sat down to dinner at her humble table, her husband exclaimed with delight, "Aha! Soup! There's nothing better." She imagined, instead, delicate food served in lovely china dishes.

She had no fancy clothes, no jewels, nothing. She yearned for such things; she felt that she was made for them.

An old school friend was very wealthy. She refused to visit her friend because she suffered so deeply when she returned home. She would weep whole days with grief, regret, despair, and misery.

One evening her husband came home with a joyful air, holding a large envelope in his hand.

"Here's something for you," he said.

Swiftly she tore the paper and drew out a card on which were printed these words:

The Minister of Education and Madame Ramponneau request the pleasure of the company of Monsieur and Madame Loisel at the Ministry on the evening of Monday, January the 18th.

Instead of being delighted, as her husband hoped, she flung the invitation rudely across the table, asking, "What do you want me to do with this?"

"Why, darling, I thought you'd be pleased. You never go out, and this is a great occasion. I went to a great deal of trouble to get an invitation. Everyone wants one. It's for the select few. All the really important people will be there."

She looked at him out of furious eyes, and asked impatiently, "And what do you suppose I am to wear to such an affair?"

He had not thought about it; he stammered, "Why, the dress you go to the theater in. It looks very nice, to me. . . ."

He stopped, confused, when he saw that his wife was beginning to cry. Two large tears ran slowly down from the corners of her eyes toward the corners of her mouth.

"What's the matter with you? What's the matter with you?" he asked anxiously.

With a great effort, she overcame her grief and replied in a calm voice, wiping her wet cheeks, "Nothing. Only I haven't a dress and so I can't go to this party. Give your invitation to some friend of yours whose wife will be dressed better than I would."

He was heartbroken.

"Look here, Mathilde," he persisted. "What would be the cost of a suitable dress, which you could use on other occasions as well, something very simple?"

She thought for several seconds, counting up prices and also wondering carefully how much money she could ask from her husband without him immediately refusing.

At last, she replied with some hesitation,

"I don't know exactly, but I think I could buy one with four hundred francs."

He grew slightly pale, but he said, "Very well. I'll give you four hundred francs. But please try and get a really nice dress with the money."

The day of the party drew near, and Madame Loisel seemed sad and uneasy. One evening, her husband said to her, "What's the matter with you? You've been acting strange for the last three days."

"I'm utterly miserable at not having any jewels, not a single stone, to wear," she replied. "I would almost rather not go to the party."

"Wear flowers," he said. "They're very fashionable at this time of year. For ten francs, you could get two or three gorgeous roses."

She was not convinced.

"No . . . there's nothing so humiliating as looking poor in the middle of a lot of rich women."

"How stupid you are!" exclaimed her husband. "Go and see your friend, Madame Forestier, and ask her to lend you some jewels. You know her quite well enough for that."

She uttered a cry of delight. "That's true. I never thought of it."

Next day, she went to see her friend and told her about her trouble.

Madame Forestier went to her dressing table, picked up a large box, brought it to Madame Loisel, opened it, and said, "Choose, my dear."

First she saw some bracelets, then a pearl necklace, then a cross in gold and gems of exquisite workmanship. She tried the effect of the jewels before the mirror, hesitating, unable to make up her mind.

Suddenly she discovered, in a black satin case, a superb diamond necklace. Her heart beat rapidly. Her hands trembled as she lifted the necklace. She fastened it around her neck, and was filled with joy at the sight of herself.

Then, with hesitation, she asked anxiously, "Could you lend me this, just this alone?"

"Yes, of course."

She threw herself into her friend's arms, embraced her warmly, and went away with her treasure.

The day of the party arrived. Madame Loisel was a success. She was the prettiest woman present — elegant, graceful, smiling, and beside herself with happiness. All the men stared at her, asked her name, and wanted to be introduced to her.

She danced madly, ecstatically, drunk with pleasure, with no thought of anything, in the triumph of her beauty, in the pride of her success.

She left about four o'clock in the morning. Since midnight, her husband had been dozing in a deserted little room, in company with three other men whose wives were having a good time.

He threw over her shoulders the cloaks he had brought for them to go home in, modest everyday garments, whose poorness clashed with the beauty of the ball dress. She was conscious of this and was anxious to hurry away, so she would not be noticed by the other women putting on their costly furs.

Loisel restrained her. "Wait a little. You'll catch cold in the open. I'm going to get a cab."

She would not wait, but instead walked with him until they found a cab. When the cab brought them to their door, they sadly walked up to their own apartment. It was the end, for her. As for him, he was thinking that he must be at the office at ten in the morning.

She took off the garments in which she had wrapped her shoulders, to see herself in all her glory before the mirror. But suddenly she uttered a cry. The necklace was no longer around her neck!

"What's the matter with you?" asked her husband, already half-undressed.

She turned toward him, very upset. "I . . . I . . . I've no longer got Madame Forestier's necklace. . . ."

He stared with astonishment. "What! . . . Impossible!"

They searched in the folds of her dress, in the folds of the coat, in the pockets, everywhere. They could not find it.

"Are you sure that you still had it on when you came away from the ball?" he asked.

"Yes, I touched it in the hall at the ministry."

"But if you had lost it in the street, we should have heard it fall."

"Yes. Probably we should. Did you take the number of the cab?"

"No. You didn't notice it, did you?"

"No."

Loisel put on his clothes again. "I'll go over all the ground we walked," he said, "and see if I can't find it."

He went out. She remained in her evening clothes, huddled in a chair, lacking strength to get into bed.

Her husband returned about seven. He had found nothing.

He went to the police station, to the newspapers, to the cab companies, everywhere that a ray of hope took him.

She waited all day long, in a state of anguish at this fearful catastrophe.

Loisel came home at night, his face lined and pale; he had discovered nothing.

"You must write to your friend," he said, "and tell her that you've broken the clasp of her necklace and are getting it mended. That will give us time to look about us."

By the end of a week, they had lost all hope.

Loisel, who had aged five years, declared, "We must see about replacing the diamonds."

In a shop at the Palais-Royal, they found a string of diamonds that seemed to them exactly like the one they were looking for. It was worth 40,000 francs. They were allowed to have it for 36,000.

Loisel had 18,000 francs left to him by his father. He borrowed the rest by taking out loans without knowing if he could pay them back, entering into ruinous business deals — mortgaging the remaining years of his life. He went to get the necklace, putting down 36,000 francs on the jeweler's counter.

Madame Loisel took back the necklace to Madame Forestier. "You could have brought it back sooner," she said coldly. "I might have needed it."

She did not, as her friend had feared,

open the case. If she had noticed the substitution, what would she have thought? What would she have said? Would she not have called her a thief?

Madame Loisel came to know the ghastly life of terrible poverty. Right from the start, she played her part heroically. This fearful debt must be paid off. She would pay it. The servant was dismissed. They changed their apartment; they took a garret under the roof.

She came to know the heavy work of the house, the hateful duties of the kitchen. She washed the plates, wearing out her pink nails on the coarse pottery and the bottoms of pans. She washed the dirty linen, the shirts, and the dishcloths, and hung them out to dry on a string; every morning, she took the dustbin down into the street and carried up the water, stopping on each landing to catch her breath. And, clad like a poor woman, she went to the fruiterer, to the grocer, to the butcher, a basket on her arm, haggling, insulted, fighting for every wretched halfpenny of her money.

Every month, loans had to be paid off, others had to be renewed.

Her husband worked in the evenings as a bookkeeper for a few pennies a page.

And this life lasted ten years.

At the end of ten years everything was paid off.

Madame Loisel looked old now. She had become like all the other strong, hard, coarse women of poor households. Her hair was badly done, her skirts were messy, her hands were red. She spoke in a shrill voice, and the water slopped all over the floor when she scrubbed it. But sometimes, when her husband was at the office, she sat down by the window and thought of that evening long ago, of the ball at which she had been so beautiful and so much admired.

What would have happened if she had never lost those jewels? Who knows? Who knows? How strange life is, how fickle! How little is needed to ruin or to save!

One Sunday, as she had gone for a walk to freshen herself after the labors of the week, she saw a woman taking a child out for a walk. It was Madame Forestier, still young, still beautiful, still attractive.

Madame Loisel for a moment didn't know what to do. Should she speak to her? Yes, certainly. And now that the necklace was paid for, she would tell her all. Why not?

She went up to her. "Good morning, Jeanne."

The other did not recognize her, and was surprised at being spoken to by a poor woman.

"But . . . madame . . ." she stammered. "I don't know . . . you must be making a mistake."

"No . . . I am Mathilde Loisel."

Her friend uttered a cry. "Oh! . . . My poor Mathilde, how you have changed! . . ."

"Yes, I've had some hard times since I saw you last, and many sorrows . . . and all on your account."

"On my account! . . . How was that?"

"You remember the diamond necklace you lent me for the ball at the ministry?"

"Yes. Well?"

"Well, I lost it."

"How could you? You brought it back."

"I brought you another one just like it. And for the last ten years we have been paying for it. You realize it wasn't easy for us. We had no money. . . . Well, it's paid for at last, and I'm glad."

Madame Forestier had stopped. "You say you bought a diamond necklace to replace mine?"

"Yes. You hadn't noticed it? They were very much alike." And she smiled in proud and innocent happiness.

"Oh, my poor Mathilde! But mine was imitation. It was worth at the very most only five hundred francs! . . ."

READING COMPREHENSION

Summarizing. Choose the best phrase to complete each sentence. Then write the complete statements on your paper.

1. Mathilde suffered endlessly because _____ (her husband was a lazy spendthrift, she was beautiful but poor, she had to work for a living).

2. The Loisels discovered the loss of the necklace _____ (at the party, in the cab, when they returned home).

3. At the end of the story, Mathilde _____ (found out that the lost necklace was not real diamonds, was accused of theft by Madame Forestier, was divorced by her husband).

Interpreting. Write the answer to each question on your paper.

1. Why did Monsieur Loisel suggest that his wife visit Madame Forestier?

2. Why did Monsieur Loisel age five years in the week that followed the loss of the necklace?

3. Why didn't Mathilde immediately tell Madame Forestier that she had lost the necklace?

For Thinking and Discussing

1. If you had been Mathilde, how would you have handled the loss of the necklace?

2. How do you think Mathilde Loisel felt after learning the truth about the necklace? Did you feel sorry for her?

UNDERSTANDING LITERATURE

Plot. Before authors write a story, they plan out the events in the plot. They decide what things to tell first, second, and so on. They also decide what *not* to tell the reader until the very end of the story.

Sometimes, readers may guess the ending if the story contains foreshadowing. However, some authors do not provide any clues that might give away the ending of the story. Instead, they provide a *surprise ending*.

"The Necklace" has a surprise ending. Until the end, most readers probably do not suspect that the first necklace was an imitation. The author made sure of this by avoiding any clues that might have given away the surprise.

The sentences below could have been in "The Necklace." On your paper, write those that might have given away the surprise ending.

1. Mathilde dreamed of impressing the entire party with her necklace.

2. Madame Forestier said, "Don't choose that. It's practically worthless!"

3. Mathilde's husband thought the necklace looked cheap, but said nothing.

4. Mathilde knew the diamond necklace would be impossible to replace.

WRITING

Write a different ending to the story that would not be a surprise, but one that the reader might expect.

Two Folktales About Justice

All over the world, stories called "folktales" are handed down from generation to generation. Folktales are usually simple and have a moral, or message, at the end. Here are two folktales: The first is a story from Japan; the second is from Peru, retold in play form. You may be surprised at how stories from different countries can be so alike.

Ooka and the Stolen Smell

a Japanese folktale retold by I. G. Edmonds

Japanese legends tell of a great judge called Ooka the Wise. Ooka was as clever as Sherlock Holmes in identifying clues to crimes, and he was especially skilled in finding just the right punishment to fit every crime. Here is the story of one of Ooka's most unusual cases.

Now it so happened in the days of old Yedo, as Tokyo was once called, that the storytellers told marvelous tales of the wit and wisdom of His Honorable Honor, Ooka Tadasuke.

This famous judge never refused to hear a complaint, even if it seemed strange or unreasonable. People sometimes came to his court with the most unusual cases, but Ooka always agreed to listen. And the strangest case of all was the famous "Case of the Stolen Smell."

It all began when a poor student rented a room over a tempura shop — a shop where fried food could be bought. The student was a most likable young man, but the shopkeeper was a miser who suspected everyone of trying to get the better of him. One day, he heard the student talking with one of his friends.

"It is sad to be so poor that one can only afford to eat plain rice," the friend complained.

"Oh," said the student, "I have found a very satisfactory answer to the problem. I eat my rice each day while the shopkeeper downstairs fries his fish. The smell comes up, and my humble rice seems to have much more flavor. It is really the smell, you know, that makes things taste so good."

The shopkeeper was furious. To think that someone was enjoying the smell of his fish for nothing! "Thief!" he shouted. "I demand that you pay me for the smells you have stolen."

"A smell is a smell," the young man replied. "Anyone can smell what he wants to. I will pay you nothing!"

Scarlet with rage, the shopkeeper rushed to Ooka's court and charged the student with theft. Of course, everyone laughed

Gravely, Ooka sat on the dais and heard the evidence. Then he delivered his verdict.

"The student is obviously guilty," he said severely. "Taking another person's property is theft, and I cannot see that a smell is different from any other property."

The shopkeeper was delighted, but the student was horrified. He was very poor, and he owed the shopkeeper for three months' smelling. He would surely be thrown into prison.

"How much money have you?" Ooka asked him.

"Only five mon, Honorable Honor," the boy replied. "I need that to pay my rent, or I will be thrown out into the street."

"Let me see the money," said the judge.

The young man held out his hand. Ooka nodded and told him to drop the coins from one hand to the other.

The judge listened to the pleasant clink of the money and said to the shopkeeper, "You have now been paid. If you have any other complaints in the future, please bring them to the court. It is our wish that all injustices be punished and all virtue rewarded."

"But, most Honorable Honor," the shopkeeper protested, "I did not get the money! The thief dropped it from one hand to the other. See! I have nothing." He held up his empty hands.

Ooka stared at him gravely. "It is the court's judgment that the punishment should fit the crime. I have decided that the price of the *smell* of food shall be the *sound* of money. Justice has prevailed as usual in my court."

at him, for how could anyone steal a smell? Ooka would surely send the man about his business. But to everyone's astonishment, the judge agreed to hear the case.

"Every man is entitled to his hour in court," he explained. "If this man feels strongly enough about his smells to make a complaint, it is only right that I, as city magistrate, should hear the case." He frowned at the amused spectators.

The Baker's Neighbor

by Adele Thane

Here is another folktale in which a greedy person learns a lesson. This traditional story from Peru is told here in the form of a play.

CHARACTERS

Manuel Gonzales, a baker
Pablo Perez, his neighbor
Carlos, a boy
Ramona
Inez } Carlos' sisters
Isabel
Judge
Three Women
Three Villagers

A street in an old town in Peru. Manuel's Bakery is at right. There is an outdoor counter with shelves for the display of pastries in front of the bakery, and a wooden table and stool near the counter. Across the street, at left, is the patio of Pablo's house, with a bench and chairs on it. At the rear of the stage, there is a flowering tree with a circular seat around the trunk.

It is early morning. Manuel comes out of the bakery with a tray of pies, which he carries to the counter. As he is putting the pies on a shelf, Pablo steps out onto his patio, sniffs the air, and smiles with delight.

Pablo: Good morning, Baker Manuel. Your pies smell especially delicious this morning. How many did you bake last night?

Manuel *(sullenly):* What's it to you, Pablo? You never buy any; you just smell them. Every day you stand there and fill your nostrils with the fragrance of my pastries. It's a miracle there's any flavor left in them when my customers come to buy.

Pablo: But it makes me happy to smell your pastries. You are the best baker in Peru. Everyone says so.

Manuel: Well, why don't you buy a pie or a cake and take it home? Then you could smell it all you want.

Pablo: Oh, but if I bought it and ate it, I couldn't smell it anymore.

Manuel *(snorting in disgust):* Bah! *(When he finishes setting out the pies, he goes into the bakery with the empty tray.)*

(Pablo crosses to the counter and inhales deeply, closing his eyes in delight. Manuel returns with a tray of cakes and a cash box.)

Manuel *(pushing Pablo away from the counter):* Hey! Take your big nose away from there! I can't sell those pies if you sniff them all over!

(Pablo saunters back to his patio. Manuel places a tray of cakes on the counter, then carries the cash box to the table and sits down.)

Pablo: Are you going to count your money, Manuel? *(Manuel ignores Pablo but empties coins from the cash box onto the table. Pablo then sits in a chair and watches Manuel with an amused smile.)* How much did you take in yesterday?

Manuel: None of your business! *(He inspects each coin carefully, then writes in a small notebook, adds figures, scowling and mumbling to himself.)*

(Carlos and his sisters enter left. They stop when they see Manuel counting his money and talk quietly together.)

Ramona: Gracious, what a lot of money!

Carlos: Papa says the bakery has made Manuel the richest man in town.

Inez: If he's that rich, why doesn't he smile? He looks so cross and unfriendly.

Carlos: That's because he's a miser. A miser doesn't like people — only money. The more money he has, the more he wants. And he keeps it all to himself — he never shares it with anyone.

Isabel *(catching sight of Pablo):* There's Pablo!

Carlos and His Sisters *(enthusiastically; ad lib):* Hello, Pablo! How are you? Good to see you! *(etc.)*

Pablo *(beaming at them as he gets up):* Hello, my young friends, hello! You're up bright and early.

Isabel: We're going to the bakery.

Ramona: Carlos is going to treat us.

Carlos: I helped Papa pick beans, and he gave me this. *(He holds up a silver coin.)*

Pablo: You're a good boy, Carlos.

Inez *(starting across to the bakery):* Come on! Let's see what there is. *(Children crowd around the counter.)*

Ramona: Look at those coconut patties!

Isabel: And the jelly roll! Yummy!

Inez: Carlos, why don't you buy a pie and cut it into quarters? Then we'd each have a piece.

Carlos: I don't know. I'd sort of like a cake.

Manuel *(impatiently):* Well, young fellow, what do you want? *(To Inez)* Keep your fingers off that pie!

Inez *(indignantly):* I didn't touch it!

Manuel: Come now, hurry up and decide. This isn't a waiting room. I have to make a living. What with rent and taxes, it's as much as I can do.

Carlos: How much is that cake with the pink frosting?

Manuel: You can't afford that. How much money do you have? *(Carlos holds out his hand to show him.)* Not enough. That cake costs three times what you can pay.

Carlos: What *can* I buy with my money? I want something for all of us.

Manuel: You can have four tapioca tarts — and I'm giving them away at that price. *(He hands the tarts to Carlos.)* Here you are. Now take your tarts over to Pablo and let him smell them. *(He puts Carlos' coin with the others on the table, sits down, and makes an entry in his notebook.)*

(Carlos passes out the tarts to his sisters as they cross to the patio.)

Carlos *(offering a tart to Pablo):* Have a bite?

Pablo: No, thank you, Carlos. You earned it — you eat it.

Isabel: Pablo, why did Manuel say we should let you smell our tarts?

Pablo: Oh, he's annoyed, because every morning I stand here and enjoy the smell of his freshly baked pies and cakes when they are right out of the oven. Ah, what fragrance! It's as if the bakery has burst into bloom.

Ramona: If you could be a beautiful smell, Pablo, instead of a man — would you like to be a beautiful bakery smell?

Pablo *(laughing):* Well, that's a new one on me! If I were a *smell* instead of a man — of all the comical ideas!

Inez *(explaining):* It's a game we play among ourselves. We ask each other what thing we'd like to be if we weren't a person — what color, what sight, what sound —

Ramona: What sound would *you* like to be, Pablo, if you weren't a person?

Pablo: This minute?

Ramona: Any minute.

Pablo: Let me think. *(Suddenly he slaps his knee.)* I have it! If I were a sound instead of a man, I'd choose to be a song! A happy little song in children's hearts. Or turning up in a boy's whistle — like this! *(He whistles a merry tune.)*

Isabel: What sound do you think Manuel would like to be?

Carlos: That's easy. He'd be the sound of gold pieces jingling in his own pocket.

Isabel: I'm going to ask him. *(She goes to the table where Manuel is putting his money back into the cash box.)* Manuel, may I ask you a question?

Manuel *(scowling):* What is it?

Isabel: If you were a sound instead of a baker, what sound in the whole wide world would you choose to be?

Manuel: Well, of all the idiotic nonsense! Clear out of here and stop bothering me!

I have better things to do than to answer stupid questions.

(Isabel returns to the patio, and Pablo goes center.)

Pablo: It has taken you a long time to count your money, Manuel.

Manuel (*sneering*): It wouldn't take *you* long to count yours.

Pablo: That's right. I don't care much for money.

Manuel: You're too lazy to earn it.

Pablo (*good-naturedly*): Oh, I work when I have to. But I'd rather sit in the sun and take advantage of all the small everyday pleasures that life has to offer.

Manuel: Like smelling my pastries, I suppose — without charge?

Pablo (*shrugging*): The air is free.

Manuel: It's not as free as you think.

Pablo: What do you mean?

Manuel: I'm going to make you pay for all the pastry smells I've supplied you with for many years.

Pablo (*smiling in disbelief*): You can't mean that!

Manuel: But I do! You stand outside my bakery every day and smell my pies and cakes. To my mind, that is the same as taking them without paying for them. You are no better than a thief, Pablo Perez!

Pablo (*mildly*): I never took anything that didn't belong to me, and you know it. What's more, I haven't done your business any harm. Why, I've even helped it. People often stop when they see me standing here and go in to buy something.

(*The children giggle, then begin to taunt Manuel and run around him, sniffing.*)

Isabel: I smell raisins!

Ramona: I smell spice!

Inez: How much does it cost to smell the flour on your apron?

Carlos: May I smell your cap for a penny? (*He snatches the baker's cap from Manuel's head and sniffs it, laughing.*)

Manuel (*angrily, snatching it back*): You'll laugh on the other side of your face when I get the judge!

Pablo: When you get *who*?

Manuel: The judge. I'm going to tell him the whole story. I'll show you I'm not joking. The judge will make you pay me. (*He grabs his cash box from the table and exits left.*)

(*Three women enter right. They come downstage and question the children.*)

1st Woman: What's the matter with Manuel?

2nd Woman: Will he be back soon? I want to buy a cake.

3rd Woman: So do I. What happened?

1st Woman: He looked so angry. Where's he gone?

Girls (*excitedly, ad lib*): He's gone to get the judge! He is angry! He is furious! (*etc.*)

1st Woman: The judge! What for?

Carlos: He says Pablo will have to pay for smelling his cakes and pies.

2nd Woman (*to Pablo*): He wants you to pay him for doing *that*?

3rd Woman: He can't be serious!

Pablo Oh, yes, he is! But I think it's very funny. (*He laughs, and the women join in.*)

1st Woman: It's ridiculous! Everyone who goes by the shop smells his pastry.

2nd Woman: Is he going to take everyone in town to court?

(*They are all in gales of laughter when Manuel returns with the judge, followed by several villagers.*)

Manuel (*to the judge*): There he is! (*He points to Pablo.*) There's the thief!

Judge: Calm yourself, Manuel. It has not

yet been proved that Pablo is a thief. First he must have a fair trial.

(The judge sits down at the table and motions for two chairs to be placed facing him. Villagers and the three women gather under the tree and on the patio with the children. They whisper and talk together as they seat themselves.)

1st Villager: In all my days, I've never heard of a case like this before.

2nd Villager: How can a man steal the *smell* of anything?

3rd Villager: I'm surprised the judge would even listen to the baker's story. Money for smelling his cakes! How absurd!

2nd Woman: He sells as much bread and pastry as he can bake. What more does he want?

3rd Villager: Manuel loves money and he figures this is a way to get more of it.

Judge (rapping table with his gavel): Quiet, everyone! Court is in session. I am ready to hear Manuel Gonzales, baker, against Pablo Perez, neighbor. I will hear the baker first. Manuel, tell your story.

Manuel (rising): This man, Pablo Perez, comes and stands outside my bakery every day.

Judge: Does he block the way?

Manuel: Not exactly.

Judge: Does he keep other people from going into your bakery?

Manuel: No, sir, but —

Judge: Then what *does* he do?

Manuel: He stands there, looking at my pies and cakes *and smelling them.*

Judge: That pleases you, doesn't it?

Manuel: Pleases me! Far from it! Look here, Your Honor — every night, I mix the flour and knead the dough and slave over a hot oven while that shiftless, good-for-nothing Pablo sleeps. Then he gets up in the morning, fresh as a daisy, and comes out here to smell the fine, sweet pastry I've baked. He takes full value of this free daily luxury. He acts as if it's his privilege. Now I ask you, Judge — is it right that I should work so hard to provide him with this luxury, without charge? No! He should pay for it!

Judge: I see. You may sit down, Manuel. Now, Pablo Perez, it is your turn. (Pablo stands.) Is it true that you stand in front of Manuel's bakery and smell his cakes and pies?

Pablo: I can't help smelling them, Your Honor. Their spicy fragrance fills the air.

Judge: Would you say you *enjoy* it?

Pablo: Oh, yes, sir. I am a man of simple pleasures. Just the smell of a bakery makes me happy.

Judge: But did you ever pay the baker for this pleasure?

Pablo: Well, no, sir. It never occurred to me that I had to pay him.

Judge: Pablo Perez, you will now put ten gold pieces on this table — for Manuel Gonzales.

(The villagers gasp. Manuel looks surprised and delighted.)

Pablo (stunned): Ten gold pieces! For smelling the air near my own house?

Judge: Do you have that amount?

Pablo: I — I guess so, but it's my life's savings.

Judge: Where is it?

Pablo: In my house.

Judge: Get it and bring it here.

(Slowly Pablo crosses patio and exits left. The villagers talk to each other disapprovingly.)

1st Villager: The judge shouldn't make Pablo pay.

1st Woman: Pablo is an honest man.

2nd Villager: I don't see how the judge could rule in the baker's favor.

3rd Villager: Why, he's richer than the judge himself.

2nd Woman: And now he's going to get poor Pablo's savings.

3rd Woman: It's not fair!

Judge *(rapping with his gavel)*: Silence in the court!

(Pablo returns sadly with a purse and puts it on the table before the judge. Manuel, elated, rubs his hands together greedily.)

Manuel *(to the judge)*: I knew Your Honor would do the right thing by me. Thank you, Judge. *(He picks up the purse and starts to put it into his cash box.)*

Judge *(rising)*: Not so fast, Manuel! Empty that purse on the table and count the gold pieces, one by one.

Manuel *(grinning craftily)*: Ah, yes, Your Honor. I must make sure I haven't been cheated. How kind of you to remind me!

(He empties the purse and begins to count, excitedly. The judge watches Manuel as he lovingly fingers each coin.)

Judge: It gives you great pleasure to touch that gold, doesn't it, Manuel? You *enjoy* it.

Manuel: Oh, I do, I do! . . . Eight . . . nine . . . ten. It's all here, your honor, and none of it false.

Judge: Please put it back in the purse.

(Manuel does so.) Now return it to Pablo.

Manuel *(in disbelief)*: Return it! But — but you just told Pablo to pay it to me.

Judge: No, I did not tell him to pay it to you. I told him to put it on this table. Then I instructed you to count the money, which you did. In doing so, you enjoyed Pablo's money — the way he has enjoyed your cakes and pies. In other words, he has smelled your pastry and you have touched his gold. Therefore, I hereby declare that the case is now settled. *(He raps twice with his gavel. Manuel shamefacedly shoves the purse across the table to Pablo and turns to leave. The judge stops him.)* Just a moment, Manuel! I hope this has been a lesson to you. In the future, think less about making money and more about making friends. Good friends and neighbors are better than gold. And now, if you please — my fee!

Manuel: Yes, Your Honor. *(He opens his cash box willingly, but the judge closes the lid.)*

Judge: Put away your money. There's been enough fuss over money already today. The fee I am asking is this — pies and cakes for everyone here — free of charge!

(Manuel nods his head vigorously in assent. The villagers and children cheer; then they rush to the pastry counter and help themselves. Manuel goes into the bakery and reappears with more pastry piled high on a tray. Pablo and the judge hold a whole pie between them and start to eat from opposite edges toward the center of the pie. Fade out.)

READING COMPREHENSION

Summarizing. Choose the best phrase to complete each sentence. Then write the complete statements on your paper.

1. In "Ooka and the Stolen Smell," the restaurant owner took the student to court because the student _____ (enjoyed the smell of the fried fish, stole some fish, did not pay his rent).

2. The judge sentenced the student to _____ (pay the shopkeeper, drop his coins from one hand to the other, go to prison for three months).

3. In "The Baker's Neighbor," Manuel was allowed to _____ (count Pablo's money, keep Pablo's money, charge Pablo for smelling his pies).

4. After the judge gave his verdict, Manuel _____ (collected money from Pablo, went out of business, had to give free pies to all).

Interpreting. Write the answer to each question on your paper.

1. Why was the shopkeeper unhappy with Ooka's decision?

2. When Pablo put his money on the table, why was Manuel happy?

3. Why did the judges side against the shopkeeper and Manuel?

For Thinking and Discussing. What was the moral, or message, of the two folktales? How did the judges' decisions reflect the moral and serve as a lesson?

UNDERSTANDING LITERATURE

Plot. The plot of a story or play can be divided into four parts:

1. *The problem.* Usually a problem arises soon after the story or play begins.

2. *The rising action.* The characters try to solve their problem. The story action builds, or rises.

3. *The turning point or climax.* The action builds to its highest point.

4. *The resolution.* Even after the problem is settled, there may be some action remaining in the story. When this action is over, the story is ended.

Below are some events from "The Baker's Neighbor." Write whether each event is part of the *problem, rising action, turning point* or *climax,* or *resolution.*

1. Manuel takes Pablo to court.

2. The villagers receive free pastries.

3. Pablo smells the pastries every day.

4. The judge tells Pablo to put ten gold pieces on the table.

5. Both men answer the judge.

6. The judge settles the case by letting Manuel touch Pablo's money.

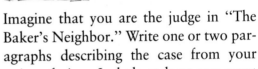

WRITING

Imagine that you are the judge in "The Baker's Neighbor." Write one or two paragraphs describing the case from your point of view. Include at least one event from each of the four parts of a plot.

111

Sanctuary

by Agatha Christie

Agatha Christie began writing mysteries when she heard her sister say it was impossible to find a detective story where she didn't know who had committed the crime. As you will see, Agatha Christie soon changed that. Her books have baffled millions of readers. If you have never read a mystery by Agatha Christie, you are about to discover why she is one of the most popular authors in the world today.

The vicar's wife came round the corner of the vicarage with her arms full of chrysanthemums. A good deal of rich garden soil was attached to her strong brogue shoes and a few fragments of earth were adhering to her nose, but of that fact she was perfectly unconscious.

She had a slight struggle in opening the vicarage gate which hung, rustily, half off its hinges. A puff of wind caught at her battered felt hat, causing it to sit even more rakishly than it had done before. "Bother!" said Bunch.

Christened Diana by her optimistic parents, Mrs. Harmon had become Bunch at an early age for somewhat obvious reasons and the name had stuck to her ever since. Clutching the chrysanthemums, she made her way through the gate to the churchyard and so to the church door.

The November air was mild and damp. Clouds scudded across the sky with patches of blue here and there. Inside, the church was dark and cold; it was unheated except at service times.

"Brrrrrh!" said Bunch expressively. "I'd better get on with this quickly. I don't want to die of cold."

With the quickness born of practice she collected the necessary paraphernalia: vases, water, flower holders. "I wish we had lilies," thought Bunch to herself. "I get so tired of these scraggy chrysanthemums." Her nimble fingers arranged the blooms in their holders.

There was nothing particularly original or artistic about the decorations, for Bunch Harmon herself was neither original nor artistic, but it was a homely and pleasant arrangement. Carrying the vases carefully, Bunch stepped up the aisle and made her way toward the altar. As she did so the sun came out.

It shone through the east window of somewhat crude colored glass, mostly blue and red — the gift of a wealthy Victorian

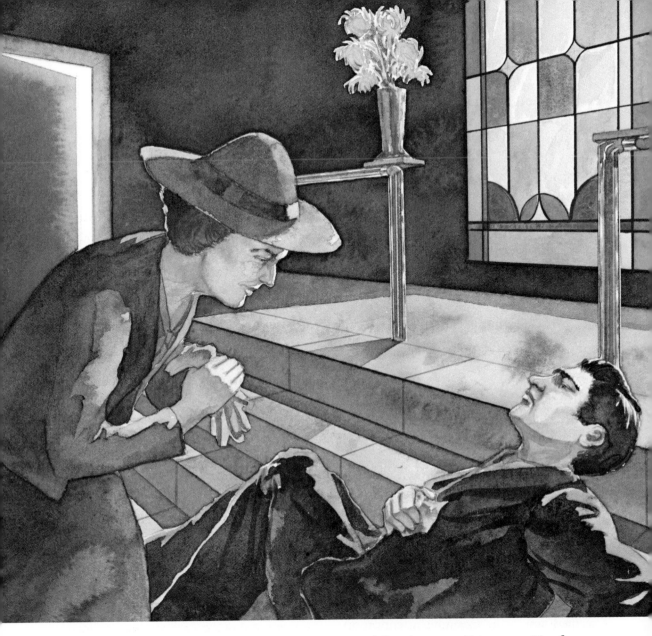

churchgoer. The effect was almost startling in its sudden opulence. "Like jewels," thought Bunch. Suddenly she stopped, staring ahead of her. On the chancel steps was a huddled dark form.

Putting down the flowers carefully, Bunch went up to it and bent over it. It was a man lying there, huddled over on himself. Bunch knelt down by him and slowly, carefully, she turned him over. Her fingers went to his pulse — a pulse so feeble and fluttering that it told its own story, as did the almost greenish pallor of his face. There was no doubt, Bunch thought, that the man was dying.

He was a man of about 45, dressed in a dark, shabby suit. She laid down the limp hand she had picked up and looked at his other hand. This seemed clenched like a fist on his breast. Looking more closely, she saw that the fingers were closed over what seemed to be a large wad or handkerchief, which he was holding tightly to his chest. All round the clenched hand there were splashes of a dry, brown fluid which, Bunch guessed, was dry blood. Bunch sat back on her heels, frowning.

Up till now the man's eyes had been closed, but at this point they suddenly opened and fixed themselves on Bunch's face. They seemed fully alive and intelligent. His lips moved, and Bunch bent forward to catch the words, or rather the word. It was only one word that he said:

"Sanctuary."

There was, she thought, just a very faint smile as he breathed out this word. There was no mistaking it, for after a moment he said it again, "Sanctuary. . . ."

Then, with a faint, long-drawn-out sigh, his eyes closed again. Once more Bunch's fingers went to his pulse. It was still there, but fainter now and more intermittent. She got up with decision.

"Don't move," she said, "or try to move. I'm going for help."

The man's eyes opened again, but he seemed now to be fixing his attention on the colored light that came through the east window. He murmured something that Bunch could not quite catch. She thought, startled, that it might have been her husband's name.

"Julian?" she said. "Did you come here to find Julian?" But there was no answer. The man lay with eyes closed, his breathing coming in slow, shallow fashion.

Bunch turned and left the church rapidly. She glanced at her watch and nodded with some satisfaction. Dr. Griffiths would still be in his surgery. It was only a couple of minutes' walk from the church. She went in, without waiting to knock or ring, passing through the waiting room and into the doctor's surgery.

"You must come at once," said Bunch. "There's a man dying in the church."

Some minutes later, Dr. Griffiths rose from his knees after a brief examination.

"Can we move him from here into the vicarage? I can attend to him better there — not that it's any use."

"Of course," said Bunch. "I'll go along and get things ready. I'll get Harper and Jones, shall I? To help you carry him."

"Thanks. I can telephone from the vicarage for an ambulance, but I'm afraid — by the time it comes . . ." He left the remark unfinished.

Bunch said, "Internal bleeding?"

Dr. Griffiths nodded. He said, "How on earth did he come here?"

"I think he must have been here all night," said Bunch, considering. "Harper unlocks the church in the morning as he goes to work, but he doesn't usually come in."

It was about five minutes later when Dr. Griffiths put down the telephone receiver and came back into the morning room where the injured man was lying on quickly arranged blankets on the sofa. Bunch was moving a basin of water and clearing up after the doctor's examination.

"Well, that's that," said Griffiths. "I've sent for an ambulance and I've notified the police." He stood, frowning, looking down on the patient who lay with closed eyes. His left hand was plucking in a nervous, spasmodic way at his side.

"He was shot," said Griffiths. "Shot at fairly close quarters. He rolled his handkerchief up into a ball and plugged the wound with it so as to stop the bleeding."

"Could he have gone far after that happened?" Bunch asked.

"Oh yes, it's quite possible. A mortally wounded man has been known to pick himself up and walk along a street as though nothing had happened and then suddenly collapse five or ten minutes later. So he needn't have been shot in the church. Oh no. He may have been shot some distance away. Of course, he may have shot himself and then dropped the revolver and staggered blindly toward the church. I don't quite know why he made for the church and not for the vicarage."

"Oh, I know that," said Bunch. "He said it: 'Sanctuary.'"

The doctor stared at her. "Sanctuary?"

"Here's Julian," said Bunch, turning her head as she heard her husband's steps in the hall. "Julian! Come here."

The Reverend Julian Harmon entered the room. His vague, scholarly manner always made him appear much older than he really was. "Dear me!" said Julian Harmon, staring in a mild, puzzled manner at the surgical appliances and the prone figure on the sofa.

Bunch explained with her usual economy of words. "He was in the church, dying. He'd been shot. Do you know him, Julian? I thought he said your name."

The vicar came up to the sofa and looked down at the dying man. "Poor fellow," he said, and shook his head. "No, I don't know him. I'm almost sure I've never seen him before."

At that moment the dying man's eyes opened once more. They went from the doctor to Julian Harmon and from him to his wife. The eyes stayed there, staring into Bunch's face. Griffiths stepped forward.

"If you could tell us," he said urgently.

But with his eyes fixed on Bunch, the man said in a weak voice, "Please — please — " And then, with a slight tremor, he died. . . .

Sergeant Hayes licked his pencil and turned the page of his notebook.

"So that's all you can tell me, Mrs. Harmon?"

"That's all," said Bunch. "These are the things out of his coat pockets."

On a table at Sergeant Hayes's elbow was a wallet, a rather battered old watch with the initials W.S., and the return half of a ticket to London. Nothing more.

"You've found out who he is?" asked Bunch.

"A Mr. and Mrs. Eccles phoned up the station. He's her brother, it seems. Name of Sandbourne. Been in a low state of health and nerves for some time. He's been getting worse lately. The day before yesterday he walked out and didn't come back. He took a revolver with him."

"And he came out here and shot himself with it?" said Bunch. "Why?"

"Well, you see, he'd been depressed."

Bunch interrupted him. "I don't mean that. I mean, why here?"

Since Sergeant Hayes obviously did not know the answer to that one he replied in an oblique fashion, "Come out here, he did, on the five-ten bus."

"Yes," said Bunch again. "But why?"

"I don't know, Mrs. Harmon," said Sergeant Hayes. "There's no accounting. If the balance of a mind is disturbed — "

Bunch finished for him. "They may do it anywhere. But it still seems to me unnecessary to take a bus out to a small country place like this. He didn't know anyone here, did he?"

"Not so far as can be ascertained," said Sergeant Hayes. He coughed in an apologetic manner and said, as he rose to his feet, "It may be as Mr. and Mrs. Eccles will come out and see you, ma'am — if you don't mind, that is."

"Of course I don't mind," said Bunch. "It's very natural. I only wish I had something to tell them."

"I'll be getting along," said Sergeant Hayes.

"I'm only so thankful," said Bunch, going with him to the front door, "that it wasn't murder."

A car had drawn up at the vicarage gate. Sergeant Hayes, glancing at it, remarked, "Looks as though that's Mr. and Mrs. Eccles come here now, ma'am, to talk with you."

Bunch braced herself to endure what, she felt, might be rather a difficult ordeal. "However," she thought, "I can always call Julian in to help me. A clergyman's a great help when people are bereaved."

Exactly what she had expected Mr. and Mrs. Eccles to be like, Bunch could not have said, but she was conscious, as she greeted them, of a feeling of surprise. Mr. Eccles was a stout and florid man whose natural manner would have been cheerful and facetious. Mrs. Eccles had a vaguely flashy look about her. She had a small, mean, pursed-up mouth. Her voice was thin and reedy.

"It's been a terrible shock, Mrs. Harmon, as you can imagine," she said.

"Oh, I know," said Bunch. "It must have been. Do sit down. Can I offer you — well, it's a bit early for tea — "

Mr. Eccles waved a pudgy hand. "No, no, nothing for us," he said. "It's very kind of you, I'm sure. Just wanted to . . . well . . . what poor William said and all that, you know?"

"He's been abroad a long time," said Mrs. Eccles, "and I think he must have had some very nasty experiences. Very quiet and depressed he's been, ever since he came home. Said the world wasn't fit to live in and there was nothing to look forward to. Poor Bill, he was always moody."

Bunch stared at them both for a moment or two without speaking.

"Pinched my husband's revolver, he did," went on Mrs. Eccles. "Without our knowing. Then it seems he come out here by bus. I suppose that was nice feeling on his part. He wouldn't have liked to do it in our house."

"Poor fellow, poor fellow," said Mr. Eccles, with a sigh. "It doesn't do to judge."

There was another short pause, and Mr. Eccles said, "Did he leave a message? Any last words, nothing like that?"

His bright, rather piglike eyes watched Bunch closely. Mrs. Eccles, too, leaned forward as though anxious for the reply.

"No," said Bunch quietly. "He came into the church when he was dying, for sanctuary."

Mrs. Eccles said in a puzzled voice, "Sanctuary? I don't think I quite — "

Mr. Eccles interrupted. "Holy place, my dear," he said impatiently. "That's what the vicar's wife means. It's a sin — suicide, you know. I expect he wanted to make amends."

"He tried to say something just before he died," said Bunch. "He began, 'Please,' but that's as far as he got." Mrs. Eccles put her handkerchief to her eyes and sniffed.

"Oh, dear," she said. "It's terribly upsetting, isn't it?"

"There, there, Pam," said her husband. "Don't take on. These things can't be helped. Poor Willie. Still, he's at peace now. Well, thank you very much, Mrs. Harmon. I hope we haven't interrupted you. A vicar's wife is a busy lady, we know that."

They shook hands with her. Then Eccles turned back suddenly to say, "Oh yes, there's just one other thing. I think you've got his coat here, haven't you?"

"His coat?" Bunch frowned.

Mrs. Eccles said, "We'd like all his things, you know. Sentimental like."

"He had a watch and a wallet and a railway ticket in the pockets," said Bunch. "I gave them to Sergeant Hayes."

"That's all right, then," said Mr. Eccles. "He'll hand them over to us, I expect. His private papers would be in the wallet."

"There was a pound note in the wallet," said Bunch. "Nothing else."

"No letters? Nothing like that?"

Bunch shook her head.

"Well, thank you again, Mrs. Harmon. The coat he was wearing — perhaps the sergeant's got that too, has he?"

Bunch frowned in an effort of remembrance.

"No," she said. "I don't think . . . let me see. The doctor and I took his coat off to examine his wound." She looked round the room vaguely. "I must have taken it upstairs with the towels and basin."

"I wonder now, Mrs. Harmon, if you don't mind . . . We'd like his coat, you know, the last thing he wore. Well, the wife feels rather sentimental about it."

"Of course," said Bunch. "Would you like me to have it cleaned first? I'm afraid it's rather — well — stained."

"Oh no, no, no, that doesn't matter."

Bunch frowned. "Now I wonder where . . . Excuse me a moment." She went upstairs and it was some few minutes before she returned.

"I'm so sorry," she said breathlessly. "My daily woman must have put it aside with other clothes that were going to the cleaners. It's taken me quite a long time to find it. Here it is. I'll do it up for you in brown paper."

Disclaiming their protests, she did so; then once more effusively bidding her farewell, the Eccles departed.

Bunch went slowly back across the hall and entered the study. The Reverend Julian

Harmon looked up and his brow cleared. He was composing a sermon and was fearing that he'd been led astray by the interest of the political relations between Judaea and Persia, in the reign of Cyrus.

"Yes, dear?" he said hopefully.

"Julian," said Bunch, "what's *sanctuary* exactly?"

Julian Harmon gratefully put aside his sermon paper.

"Well," he said, "sanctuary in Roman and Greek temples applied to the *cella* in which stood the statue of a god. The Latin word for altar, *ara,* also means protection." He continued learnedly: "In A.D. 399 the right of sanctuary in Christian churches was finally and definitely recognized. The earliest mention of the right of sanctuary in England is in the Code of Laws issued by Ethelbert in A.D. 600 . . ."

He continued for some time with his exposition but was, as often, disconcerted by his wife's reception of his erudite pronouncement.

"Darling," she said, "you are sweet."

Bending over, she kissed him on the tip of his nose. Julian felt rather like a dog who has been congratulated on performing a clever trick.

"The Eccles have been here," said Bunch.

The vicar frowned. "The Eccles? I don't seem to remember . . ."

"You don't know them. They're the sister and her husband of the man in the church."

"My dear, you ought to have called me."

"There wasn't any need," said Bunch. "They were not in need of consolation. I wonder now." She frowned. "If I put a casserole in the oven tomorrow, can you manage, Julian? I think I shall have to go up to London for the sales."

"The sails?" Her husband looked at her blankly. "Do you mean a yacht or a boat or something?"

Bunch laughed.

"No, darling. There's a special white sale at Burrows and Portman's. You know, sheets, tablecloths, and towels and glass cloths. I don't know what we do with our glass cloths, the way they wear through. Besides," she added thoughtfully, "I think I ought to go and see Aunt Jane."

That sweet old lady, Miss Jane Marple, was enjoying the delights of the metropolis for a fortnight, comfortably installed in her nephew's studio flat.

"So kind of dear Raymond," she murmured. "He and Joan have gone to America for a fortnight and they insisted I should come up here and enjoy myself. And now, dear Bunch, do tell me what it is that's worrying you."

Bunch was Miss Marple's favorite godchild, and the old lady looked at her with great affection as Bunch, thrusting her best felt hat further on the back of her head, started on her story.

Bunch's recital was concise and clear. Miss Marple nodded her head as Bunch finished. "I see," she said. "Yes, I see."

"That's why I felt I had to see you," said Bunch. "You see, not being a clever person — "

"But you are clever, my dear."

"No, I'm not. Not clever like Julian."

"Julian, of course, has a very solid intellect," said Miss Marple.

"That's it," said Bunch. "Julian's got the intellect, but on the other hand, I've got the sense."

"You have a lot of common sense, Bunch, and you're very intelligent."

"You see, I don't really know what I ought to do. I can't ask Julian because — well, Julian's so full of rectitude . . ."

This statement appeared to be perfectly understood by Miss Marple, who said, "I know what you mean, dear. We women — well, it's different." She went on, "You told me what happened, Bunch, but I'd like to know first exactly what you think."

"It's all wrong," said Bunch. "The man who was there in the church, dying, knew all about sanctuary. He said it just the way Julian would have said it. I mean, he was a well-read, educated man. And if he'd shot himself, he wouldn't drag himself into a church afterward and say 'sanctuary.' Sanctuary means that you're pursued, and when you get into a church you're safe. Your pursuers can't touch you. At one time even the law couldn't get at you."

She looked questioningly at Miss Marple. The latter nodded. Bunch went on, "Those people, the Eccles, were quite different. Ignorant and coarse. And there's another thing. That watch — the dead man's watch. It has the initials W.S. on the back of it. But inside — I opened it — in very small lettering there was 'To Walter from his father' and a date. Walter. But the Eccles kept talking of him as William or Bill."

Miss Marple seemed about to speak, but Bunch rushed on, "Oh, I know you're not always called the name you're baptized by. I mean, I can understand that you might be christened William and called 'Porky' or 'Carrots' or something. But your sister wouldn't call you William or Bill if your name was Walter."

"You mean that she wasn't his sister?"

"I'm quite sure she wasn't his sister. They were horrid — both of them. They came to the vicarage to get his things and to find out if he'd said anything before he died. When I said he hadn't, I saw it in their faces — relief. I think, myself," finished Bunch, "it was Eccles who shot him."

"Murder?" said Miss Marple.

"Yes," said Bunch, "murder. That's why I came to you, darling."

Bunch's remark might have seemed incongruous to an ignorant listener, but in certain spheres Miss Marple had a reputation for dealing with murder.

"He said 'please' to me before he died," said Bunch. "He wanted me to do something for him. The awful thing is I've no idea what."

Miss Marple considered for a moment or two and then pounced on the point that had already occurred to Bunch. "But why was he there at all?" she asked.

"You mean," said Bunch, "if you wanted sanctuary, you might pop into a church anywhere. There's no need to take a bus that only goes four times a day and come out to a lonely spot like ours for it."

"He must have come there for a purpose," Miss Marple thought out loud. "He must have come to see someone. Chipping Cleghorn's not a big place, Bunch. Surely you must have some idea of who it was he came to see?"

Bunch reviewed the inhabitants of her village in her mind before rather doubtfully shaking her head. "In a way," she said, "it could be anybody."

"He never mentioned a name?"

"He said Julian, or I thought he said Julian. It might have been Julia, I suppose. As far as I know, there isn't any Julia living in Chipping Cleghorn."

She screwed up her eyes as she thought back to the scene. The man lying there on the chancel steps, the light coming through the window with its jewels of red and blue light.

"Jewels," said Bunch suddenly. "Perhaps that's what he said. The light coming through the east window did look like jewels."

"Jewels," said Miss Marple thoughtfully.

"I'm coming now," said Bunch, "to the most important thing of all. The reason why I've really come here today. You see, the Eccles made a great fuss about having his coat. We took it off when the doctor was seeing to him. It was an old, shabby sort of coat — there was no reason they should have wanted it. They pretended it was sentimental, but that was nonsense.

"Anyway, I went up to find it, and as I was going up the stairs I remembered how he'd made a kind of picking gesture with his hand, as though he was fumbling with the coat. So when I got hold of the coat I looked at it very carefully and I saw that in once place the lining had been sewn up again with a different thread. So I unpicked it and I found a little piece of paper inside. I took it out and I sewed it up again properly with thread that matched. I was careful and I don't really think that the Eccles would know I've done it. I don't think so, but I can't be sure. And I took the coat down to them and made some excuse for the delay."

"The piece of paper?" asked Miss Marple.

Bunch opened her handbag. "I didn't show it to Julian," she said, "because he would have said that I ought to have given it to the Eccles. But I thought I'd rather bring it to you instead."

"A cloakroom ticket," said Miss Marple, looking at it. "Paddington Station."

"He had a return ticket to Paddington in his pocket," said Bunch.

The eyes of the two women met. "This calls for action," said Miss Marple briskly. "But it would be advisable, I think, to be careful. Would you have noticed at all, Bunch dear, whether you were followed when you came to London today?"

"Followed!" exclaimed Bunch. "You don't think — "

"Well, I think it's possible," said Miss Marple. "When anything is possible, I think we ought to take precautions." She rose with a brisk movement. "You came up here ostensibly, my dear, to go to the sales. I think the right thing to do, therefore, would be for us to go to the sales. But before we set out, we might put one or two little arrangements in hand. I don't suppose," Miss Marple added obscurely, "that I shall need the old speckled tweed with the beaver collar just at present . . ."

It was about an hour-and-a-half later that the two ladies, rather the worse for wear and battered in appearance, and both clasping parcels of hard-won household linen, sat down at a small and sequestered hostelry called the Apple Bough to restore their forces with steak-and-kidney pudding followed by apple tart and custard.

"Really a prewar-quality face towel," gasped Miss Marple, slightly out of breath. "With a J on it, too. So fortunate that Raymond's wife's name is Joan. I shall put them aside until I really need them and then they will do for her if I pass on sooner than I expect."

"I really did need the glass cloths," said Bunch. "And they were very cheap, though not as cheap as the ones that woman with the ginger hair managed to snatch from me."

A smart young woman with a lavish application of rouge and lipstick entered the Apple Bough at that moment. After

looking round vaguely for a moment or two, she hurried to their table. She laid down an envelope by Miss Marple's elbow.

"There you are, miss," she said briskly.

"Oh, thank you, Gladys," said Miss Marple. "Thank you very much. So kind of you."

"Always pleased to oblige, I'm sure," said Gladys. "Ernie always says to me, 'Everything what's good you learned from that Miss Marple of yours that you were in service with,' and I'm sure I'm always glad to oblige you, miss."

"Such a dear girl," said Miss Marple as Gladys departed again. "Always so willing and so kind."

She looked inside the envelope and then passed it on to Bunch. "Now be very careful, dear," she said. "By the way, is there still that nice young inspector at Melchester that I remember?"

"I don't know," said Bunch. "I expect so."

"Well, if not," said Miss Marple thoughtfully, "I can always ring up the chief constable. I think he would remember me."

"Of course he'd remember you," said Bunch. "Everybody would remember you. You're quite unique." She rose.

Arrived at Paddington, Bunch went to the Parcels Office and produced the cloakroom ticket. A moment or two later a rather shabby old suitcase was passed across to her, and carrying this, she made her way to the platform.

The journey home was uneventful. Bunch rose as the train approached Chipping Cleghorn and picked up the old suitcase. She had just left her carriage when a man, sprinting along the platform, suddenly seized the suitcase from her hand and rushed off with it.

"Stop!" Bunch yelled. "Stop him, stop him. He's taken my suitcase."

The ticket collector who, at this rural station, was a man of somewhat slow processes had just begun to say, "Now, look here, you can't do that — " when a smart blow in the chest pushed him aside, and the man with the suitcase rushed out from the station. He made his way toward a waiting car. Tossing the suitcase in, he was about to climb after it, but before he could move, a hand fell on his shoulder, and the voice of Police Constable Abel said, "Now then, what's all this?"

Bunch arrived, panting, from the station. "He snatched my suitcase," she said.

"Nonsense," said the man. "I don't know what this lady means. It's my suitcase. I just got out of the train with it."

"Now, let's get this clear," said Police Constable Abel.

He looked at Bunch with a bovine and impartial stare. Nobody would have guessed that Police Constable Abel and Mrs. Harmon spent long half-hours in Police Constable Abel's off time discussing the respective merits of manure and bone meal for rose bushes.

"You say, madam, that this is your suitcase?" said Police Constable Abel.

"Yes," said Bunch. "Definitely."

"And you, sir?"

"I say this suitcase is mine."

The man was tall, dark, and well dressed, with a drawling voice and a superior manner. A feminine voice from inside the car said, "Of course it's your suitcase, Edwin. I don't know what this woman means."

"We'll have to get this clear," said Police Constable Abel. "If it's your suitcase, madam, what do you say is inside it?"

"Clothes," said Bunch. "A long speckled coat with a beaver collar, two wool jumpers, and a pair of shoes."

"Well, that's clear enough," said Police Constable Abel. He turned to the other.

"I am a theatrical costumer," said the dark man importantly. "This suitcase contains theatrical properties which I brought down here for an amateur performance."

"Right, sir," said Police Constable Abel. "Well, we'll just look inside, shall we, and see? We can go along to the police station, or if you're in a hurry, we'll take the suitcase back to the train station and open it there."

"It'll suit me," said the dark man. "My name is Moss, by the way. Edwin Moss."

The police constable, holding the suitcase, went back into the station. "Just taking this into the Parcels Office, George," he said to the ticket collector.

Police Constable Abel laid the suitcase on the counter of the Parcels Office and pushed back the clasp. The case was not locked. Bunch and Mr. Edwin Moss stood on either side of him, their eyes regarding each other vengefully.

"Ah!" said Police Constable Abel, as he pushed up the lid.

Inside, neatly folded, was a long, rather shabby tweed coat with a beaver fur collar. There were also two wool jumpers and a pair of country shoes.

"Exactly as you say, madam," said Police Constable Abel, turning to Bunch.

Nobody could have said that Mr. Edwin Moss underdid things. His dismay and compunction were magnificent.

"I do apologize," he said. "I really do apologize. Please believe me, dear lady, when I tell you how very, very sorry I am. Unpardonable — quite unpardonable — my behavior has been." He looked at his watch. "I must rush now. Probably my suitcase has gone on the train." Raising his hat once more, he said meltingly to Bunch, "Do, do forgive me," and rushed hurriedly out of the Parcels Office.

"Are you going to let him get away?" asked Bunch in a conspiratorial whisper of Police Constable Abel.

The latter slowly closed a bovine eye in a wink.

"He won't get too far, ma'am," he said. "That's to say, he won't get far unobserved, if you take my meaning."

"Oh," said Bunch, relieved.

"That old lady's been on the phone," said Police Constable Abel, "the one as was down here a few years ago. Bright she is, isn't she? But there's been a lot cooking up all today. Shouldn't wonder if the inspector or sergeant was out to see you about it tomorrow morning."

It was the inspector who came, the Inspector Craddock who Miss Marple remembered. He greeted Bunch with a smile as an old friend.

"Crime in Chipping Cleghorn again," he said cheerfully. "You certainly don't lack for sensation here, do you, Mrs. Harmon?"

"I could do with rather less," said Bunch. "Have you come to ask me questions or are you going to tell me things for a change?"

"I'll tell you some things first," said the inspector. "To begin with, Mr. and Mrs. Eccles have been having an eye kept on them for some time. There's reason to believe they've been connected with several robberies in this part of the world. For another thing, although Mrs. Eccles has a brother called Sandbourne who has recently come back from abroad, the man you found dying in the church yesterday was definitely not Sandbourne."

"I knew that he wasn't," said Bunch. "His name was Walter, to begin with, not William."

The inspector nodded. "His name was Walter St. John, and he escaped forty-eight hours ago from Charrington Prison."

"Of course," said Bunch softly to herself, "he was being hunted down by the law, and he took sanctuary." Then she asked, "What had he done?"

"I'll have to go back rather a long way. It's a complicated story. Several years ago there was a certain dancer doing turns at the music halls. I don't expect you'll have ever heard of her, but she specialized in an Arabian Nights'turn. 'Aladdin in the Cave of Jewels,' it was called."

"She wasn't much of a dancer, I believe, but she was — well — attractive. Anyway, a certain Asiatic royalty fell for her in a big way. Among other things, he gave her a very magnificent emerald necklace."

"The historic jewels of a rajah?" murmured Bunch ecstatically.

Inspector Craddock coughed. "Well, a rather more modern version, Mrs. Harmon. The affair didn't last very long, broke up when our potentate's attention was captured by a certain film star whose demands were not quite so modest.

"Zobeida, to give the dancer her stage name, hung onto the necklace, and in due course it was stolen. It disappeared from her dressing room at the theater, and there was a lingering suspicion in the minds of the authorities that she herself might have engineered its disappearance. Such things have been known as a publicity stunt, or indeed from more dishonest motives.

"The necklace was never recovered, but during the course of the investigation the attention of the police was drawn to this man, Walter St. John. He was a man of education and breeding who had come down in the world and who was employed as a working jeweler with a rather obscure firm which was suspected as acting as a fence for jewel robberies.

"There was evidence that this necklace had passed through his hands. It was, however, in connection with the theft of some other jewelry that he was finally brought to trial and convicted and sent to prison. He had not very much longer to serve, so his escape was rather a surprise."

"But why did he come here?" asked Bunch.

"We'd like to know that very much, Mrs. Harmon. Following up his trail, it seems that he went first to London. He didn't visit any of his old associates, but he visited an elderly woman, a Mrs. Jacobs, who had formerly been a theatrical dresser. She won't say a word of what he came for, but according to other lodgers in the house, he left carrying a suitcase."

"I see," said Bunch. "He left it in the cloakroom at Paddington and then he came down here."

"By that time," said Inspector Craddock, "Eccles and the man who calls himself Edwin Moss were on his trail. They wanted that suitcase. They saw him get on the bus. They must have driven out in a car ahead of him and been waiting for him when he left the bus."

"And he was murdered?" said Bunch.

"Yes," said Craddock. "He was shot. It was Eccles's revolver, but I rather fancy it was Moss who did the shooting. Now, Mrs. Harmon, what we want to know is, where is the suitcase that Walter St. John actually deposited at Paddington Station?"

Bunch grinned. "I expect Aunt Jane's got it by now," she said. "Miss Marple, I mean. That was her plan. She sent a former maid of hers with a suitcase packed with her things to the cloakroom at Paddington and we exchanged tickets. I collected her suitcase and brought it down by train. She seemed to expect that an attempt would be made to get it from me."

It was Inspector Craddock's turn to grin. "So she said when she rang up. I'm driving up to London to see her. Do you want to come too, Mrs. Harmon?"

"Wel-l," said Bunch, thinking. "Wel-l, as a matter of fact, it's very fortunate. I had a toothache last night so I ought to go to London to see the dentist, oughtn't I?"

"Definitely," said Inspector Craddock.

Miss Marple looked from Inspector Craddock's face to the eager face of Bunch Harmon. The suitcase lay on the table. "Of course, I haven't opened it," the old lady said. "I wouldn't dream of doing such a thing till somebody official arrived. Besides," she added, with a demurely mischievous Victorian smile, "it's locked."

"Like to make a guess at what's inside, Miss Marple?" asked the inspector.

"I should imagine, you know," said Miss Marple, "that it would be Zobeida's theatrical costumes. Would you like a chisel, Inspector?"

The chisel soon did its work. Both women gave a slight gasp as the lid flew up. The sunlight coming through the window lit up what seemed like an inexhaustible treasure of sparkling jewels, red, blue, green, orange.

"Aladdin's Cave," said Miss Marple. "The flashing jewels the girl wore to dance."

"Ah," said Inspector Craddock. "Now, what's so precious about it, do you think, that a man was murdered to get hold of it?"

"She was a shrewd girl, I expect," said Miss Marple thoughtfully. "She's dead, isn't she, Inspector?"

"Yes, died three years ago."

"She had this valuable emerald necklace," said Miss Marple musingly. "Had the stones taken out of their setting and fastened here and there on her theatrical costume, where everyone would take them for merely colored rhinestones. Then she

128

had a replica made of the real necklace, and that, of course, was what was stolen. No wonder it never came on the market. The thief soon discovered the stones were false."

"Here is an envelope," said Bunch, pulling aside some of the glittering stones.

Inspector Craddock took it from her and extracted two official-looking papers from it. He read aloud, " 'Marriage certificate between Walter Edmund St. John and Mary Moss.' That was Zobeida's real name."

"So they were married," said Miss Marple. "I see."

"What's the other?" asked Bunch.

"A birth certificate of a daughter, Jewel."

"Jewel?" cried Bunch. "Why, of course. Jewel! Jill! That's it. I see now why he came to Chipping Cleghorn. That's what he was trying to say to me. Jewel. The Mundys, you know. Laburnam Cottage. They look after a little girl for someone. They're devoted to her. She's been like their own granddaughter. Yes, I remember now, her name was Jewel, only, of course, they call her Jill.

"Mrs. Mundy had a stroke about a week ago, and the old man's been very ill with pneumonia. They were both going to go to the infirmary. I've been trying hard to find a good home for Jill somewhere. I didn't want her taken away to an institution.

"I suppose her father heard about it in prison and he managed to break away and get hold of this suitcase from the old dresser he or his wife left it with. I suppose if the jewels really belonged to her mother, they can be used for the child now."

"I should imagine so, Mrs. Harmon. If they're really here."

"Oh, they'll be here all right," said Miss Marple cheerfully. . . .

"Thank goodness you're back, dear," said the Reverend Julian Harmon, greeting his wife with affection and a sigh of content. "Mrs. Burt always tries to do her best when you're away, but she really gave me some very peculiar fish cakes for lunch. I didn't want to hurt her feelings so I gave them to Tiglash Pileser, but even he wouldn't eat them, so I had to throw them out of the window."

"Tiglash Pileser," said Bunch, stroking the vicarage cat, who was purring against her knee, "is very particular about what fish he eats. I often tell him he's got a proud stomach!"

"And your tooth, dear? Did you have it seen to?"

"Yes," said Bunch. "It didn't hurt much, and I went to see Aunt Jane again, too . . ."

"Dear old thing," said Julian. "I hope she's not failing at all."

"Not a bit," said Bunch, with a grin.

The following morning Bunch took a fresh supply of chrysanthemums to the church. The sun was once more pouring through the east window, and Bunch stood in the jeweled light on the chancel steps. She said very softly under her breath, "Your little girl will be all right. I'll see that she is. I promise."

Then she tidied up the church, slipped into a pew, and knelt for a few moments to say her prayers before returning to the vicarage to attack the piled-up chores of two neglected days.

READING COMPREHENSION

Summarizing. Choose the best phrase to complete each sentence. Then write the complete statements on your paper.

1. The man who was dying inside the church _____ (said something Bunch could not understand, named the person who shot him, was known to Bunch).

2. When Mr. and Mrs. Eccles arrived, they said that the dead man _____ (was not related to them, had worked for them, had been depressed).

3. An important piece of evidence in the case was _____ (an old tweed coat, a gun, a cloakroom ticket).

Interpreting. Write the answer to each question on your paper.

1. Why did Walter St. John get the suitcase back from the old dresser who was holding it?

2. For what reason did Miss Marple put her old tweed coat and other belongings into a suitcase?

3. Why did Zobeida sew her jewels on her costume?

For Thinking and Discussing. Walter's escape from prison was a surprise because he had only a short time left to serve. What was he trying to do? Do you think his reason for escaping was foolish or understandable? Explain.

UNDERSTANDING LITERATURE

Plot. The *plot* of a story may contain many events. Often, the author presents events in the order in which they happened in time. However, in some stories, the present-time focus of the action stops for a *flashback.*

A flashback interrupts the present focus of the action and takes it back to a previous time. Flashbacks provide important plot information. In "Sanctuary," a flashback starts as the inspector begins to tell the history of the jewels and of Walter St. John's involvement with Zobeida. It ends as he asks Bunch about the present location of the suitcase.

Read these events from "Sanctuary." Write the events in the order in which they actually occurred in time.

1. Bunch spoke with the Eccles.

2. The police opened Walter's suitcase.

3. Zobeida got a necklace as a gift.

4. Walter was shot.

5. Bunch met with Miss Marple.

6. Walter went to prison.

WRITING

Suppose that Walter St. John is hiding in the church, thinking about what has happened to him. Write two paragraphs describing the scene. In the first paragraph, tell what is happening at present. In the second paragraph, write a flashback that tells about some of the past events in Walter's life.

Billy Budd

a radio play based on Herman Melville's novel

A naval court explores the events that led to the execution of Billy Budd, a sailor on the warship Indomitable. *Attorneys Willett and Smythe-Wilkins attempt to answer the question: Why was a man, whom almost everyone admired, sent to his death?*

Commentator: It is March 4, 1798. A naval court is being called to order in London, England.

Farnworth *(banging a gavel):* This court is now in session. We are here to investigate the execution of Billy Budd on the warship *Indomitable,* on September 4, 1797. Are all the witnesses here?

Willett: Yes, sir.

Smythe-Wilkins: Excuse me, sir. I am an attorney hired by the family of Captain Edward Vere.

Farnworth: Vere has died, sir. He is not on trial here.

Smythe-Wilkins: His family feels that his name is. Why has this case been re-opened?

Farnworth: Mr. Mordant, one of the ship's officers, asked that it be.

Smythe-Wilkins: Wasn't he a member of the court-martial that voted unanimously to convict Billy Budd?

Farnworth: Yes.

Smythe-Wilkins: That is strange. *(Pause.)* Sir, I am here to defend Captain Vere's good name. May I cross-examine witnesses?

Farnworth: You may. We have nothing to hide. Our aim is to find out exactly why Billy Budd was executed. Call the first witness.

Willett: Lieutenant Ratcliffe.

(We hear footsteps. Then Willett swears Ratcliffe in.)

Willett: Was it your duty to force merchant sailors to join the navy when you needed men to fight?

Ratcliffe: It was.

Willett: What happened when you boarded the ship *Rights of Man,* looking for sailors for the navy?

Ratcliffe: That was where I drafted Billy Budd.

Willett: Did you draft any others?

Ratcliffe: No.

Willett: Why not?

Ratcliffe: The other men didn't look very good next to Budd.

Willett: Did he object when you drafted him?

Ratcliffe: No.

Willett: What made you think he was able?

Ratcliffe: The best men under fire are not the biggest or the fiercest. They are the ones who move with grace. They carry out orders well.

Willett: Was Budd like that?

Ratcliffe: He was all strength and grace. He moved in tune with nature. He was innocence itself.

Smythe-Wilkins: I object! Ratcliffe has not been asked whether Budd was innocent or not.

Farnworth: Witnesses are not to judge innocence or guilt, Mr. Ratcliffe.

Ratcliffe: I am sorry, sir. When I said "innocent," I meant "simple," in the way that children are.

Willett: Describe Budd's behavior when he joined your crew.

Ratcliffe: Most of the drafted sailors were angry, but not Billy. He did everything with gusto. He ate, worked, and sang with gusto. Just about everyone liked him.

Willett: Are you suggesting that he had no faults?

Ratcliffe *(after a pause):* Sometimes he stuttered.

Willett: When?

Ratcliffe: When someone made him very angry. But that's only what I *heard*. I once saw Billy when he was upset, though. A sailor was whipped for being away from his post. Since it was wartime, that was a serious offense. So Captain Vere had him whipped. As Billy watched this, he looked horrified.

Willett: Did he try to stop the whipping?

Ratcliffe: No.

Willett: What was your opinion of Captain Vere and Mr. Claggart, the master-at-arms?

Ratcliffe: Both men were able and did their jobs. Otherwise, they were different. Captain Vere always spoke to the point. Mr. Claggart was a tricky man. Captain Vere was strict, but he treated everyone the same. Mr. Claggart did everything to please the officers above him. But he pushed around the men who were below him in rank. He also was secretive. Some of the officers thought he had spies working for him.

Smythe-Wilkins: Sir, may I ask this witness a question?

Farnworth: Go ahead.

Smythe-Wilkins: You talk about secrecy. But don't forget that we were at war. There had been mutinies on two other ships just before Budd's execution. And most of the sailors who had been forced to join your crew were angry. You said so yourself.

Ratcliffe: That is true.

Smythe-Wilkins: No further questions.

Willett: Mr. Ratcliffe, was there any talk or sign of mutiny among your crew?

Ratcliffe: No.

Willett: No further questions.

Farnworth: Lieutenant Ratcliffe, you are dismissed.

(We hear Ratcliffe leave the stand. Then Dansker takes the stand and is sworn in.)

Willett: What was Billy Budd to you?

Dansker: He was my friend.

Willett: When did this friendship begin?

Dansker: It was the day after a sailor was whipped. Billy and I were sitting on the upper deck.

(*Music comes up and fades out — to suggest a change in time and place. Then we hear Billy Budd and Dansker talking on the upper deck.*)

Budd: Dansker, would they whip a man for little things?

Dansker: What do you mean?

Budd: The way you stow your bags.

Dansker: No. What's up?

Budd: The corporals have called me on this twice. Why?

Dansker: Jemmy Legs is down on you.

Budd: Jemmy Legs?

Dansker: That's what we call Claggart. He's in charge of those corporals. (*He lowers his voice.*) Watch it. Here he comes.

(*We hear footsteps approach.*)

Claggart (*pretending to be friendly*): Ho, Dansker. The new man is a pleasant young fellow, isn't he? Are you teaching him all about what goes on here?

Dansker: We're just talking.

Claggart: Well, talk away.

(*We hear his footsteps leave.*)

Budd (*innocently*): Well, you heard him call me a pleasant young fellow.

Dansker: Yes. Jemmy Legs has a sweet voice.

Budd: To me he has. When I pass him, he usually says a pleasant word.

Dansker: That's because he's down on you.

Budd: I don't understand.

(*Music comes up and fades out. We are now back in the courtroom. Dansker continues his story.*)

Dansker: He wanted me to explain. But I knew that if I tried, he'd be even more confused. So I didn't.

Willett: What *did* you mean?

Dansker: Claggart was jealous of Billy because Billy was popular with the men. He hated Billy because Billy was good and innocent, and Claggart could never be like that. Billy told me about some more trouble later. He was sleeping on the upper deck, when he heard a voice. It belonged to one of the corporals, a spy we call "Squeak."

(*Music comes up and fades out. Then we hear Squeak whispering to Billy Budd.*)

Squeak (*whispering*): Billy, you were forced to serve on this ship, weren't you?

Budd: Yes.

Squeak: Well, so was I. And we're not the only ones. There's a gang of us. We could do something about our situation. Won't you help us?

Budd: What do you mean?

Squeak: If you help us, these two gold coins are yours.

Budd (*stuttering in anger*): I don't know what you're driving at. But you'd better go where you belong. If you don't, I'll toss you over the rail!

(*Music comes up and fades out. We are back in the courtroom. Dansker continues to speak.*)

Dansker: Billy told me about this. I told him that Jemmy Legs was down on him.

But Billy couldn't believe that Jemmy Legs and his men would set a trap for him.

Willett: Didn't you tell him to report this to the authorities?

Dansker: The authorities were the ones who were setting the trap!

(We hear people in the courtroom clearing their throats.)

Willett: Did you have anything else to do with Billy Budd?

Dansker: I was with him the day Captain Vere sent for him. He had no idea he was going to his death. He thought maybe the captain was going to promote him. Billy gave his best, and he expected the best. That's not what he got, though.

Willett: No further questions.

Smythe-Wilkins: May I question the witness?

Farnworth: Go ahead.

Smythe-Wilkins: What was your opinion of Captain Vere?

Dansker: He was fair enough.

Smythe-Wilkins: No further questions.

(We hear Dansker leave the stand. Commander Hastings takes the stand and is sworn in.)

Willett: What did you know about Billy's conduct?

Hastings: Very little. I was the ship's surgeon, and Billy was very healthy. He never reported in sick.

Willett: What do you know about the events leading up to his execution?

Hastings: Captain Vere and I were on deck one day, talking about the health of the crew.

(Music comes up and fades out. Then we hear Hastings talking with Captain Vere.)

Hastings: Isn't that Claggart over there in the shadows?

Vere *(in a low voice):* That man *belongs* in the shadows. I can't say why, but I don't like him. Let's walk away.

Hastings: You can't avoid him. He's coming this way.

(We hear footsteps approach.)

Claggart: Captain, I've heard something serious. I'd like to speak to you privately.

Hastings: I must go now, anyway. Good day, sir.

(We hear him walk away.)

Claggart: Sir, I have learned that at least one man aboard is dangerous. He is one of the drafted sailors, and he could stir up trouble—

Vere: Name him.

Claggart: William Budd.

Vere: I am astonished. Billy seems so innocent, and he's popular with the men.

Claggart: In spite of his youth and good looks, he's a clever one. He has reasons for trying to win over his shipmates.

Vere: I find this hard to believe. In fact, I've been thinking of promoting Budd. Can you prove that what you say is true? *(He lowers his voice.)* Remember, you can be hanged for lying.

(Music comes up and fades out. We are back in the courtroom. Hastings continues to speak.)

Hastings: Claggart mentioned some things that Budd had said and done—so he had *heard*.

Willett: Was there any *proof* that Budd was planning a mutiny?

Hastings: No. Captain Vere thought about having a hearing to find out if the charges were true. Then he thought this might upset the crew. So he met with Claggart and Budd in his cabin.

Willett: Do you know what happened there?

Hastings: Yes. Captain Vere told me about it later. Claggart repeated his accusation. Budd's face turned deathly white. Captain Vere asked him to speak in his own defense. Budd tried to speak, but he was too choked up with anger. Suddenly his arm shot out and hit Claggart's forehead. Claggart fell down and didn't move. Captain Vere sent Billy away and called me to the cabin.

(Music comes up and fades out. We hear Hastings enter Captain Vere's cabin.)

Vere: Examine this man on the floor. Is he dead?

Hastings *(after a pause):* Yes, he is.

Vere *(very upset):* He was struck dead by an angel of God! Yet the angel must hang! *(Pause.)* Help me move the body to the next cabin. *(We hear them moving the body.)* I will call a court-martial right away. Tell the lieutenants what happened. Warn them not to say a word about it.

(Music comes up and fades out. We are back in the courtroom.)

Willett: Is there anything you wish to add?

Hastings: Yes. I saw an extraordinary thing at the execution. Budd's body did not move during the hanging. It didn't even twitch. Later, one of the men asked me if Billy had willed himself not to move. But I knew that was impossible.

Willett: Are you suggesting that there was something supernatural about Billy Budd?

Hastings: No. I simply don't have a scientific explanation for it.

Willett: Before this happened, what did you think of Mr. Claggart?

Hastings: I did not know him very well. But there was something strange about him. Everything he did was thought out first.

Willett: No further questions.

Smythe-Wilkins: May I question the witness?

Farnworth: Go ahead.

Smythe-Wilkins: You say that Captain Vere said, "The angel of God must hang." What did he mean?

Hastings: I'm not sure. I thought he might be mad.

Smythe-Wilkins *(furious):* What? How dare you sir?

Hastings: Also, his decision to call a secret trial right away made me wonder. He should have notified Admiral Farnworth.

Smythe-Wilkins: Where were you trained as a doctor?

Hastings: At Cambridge.

Smythe-Wilkins: Were you trained to identify mental illness?

Hastings: No.

Smythe-Wilkins: Then how can you say that Captain Vere was mad?

Hastings: I am not saying that he definitely was. I do not know for sure.

Smythe-Wilkins: What did you think of Captain Vere before all this happened?

Hastings: I thought he was just. He was not brilliant, but he was able.

Smythe-Wilkins: After this event, did you ever see a hint of madness in him?

Hastings: No.

Smythe-Wilkins: No further questions.

(We hear Hastings leave the stand. Then Lieutenant Mordant takes the stand and is sworn in.)

Willett: Were you a member of the court-martial called by Captain Vere?

Mordant: Yes, I was. There were two other lieutenants besides me.

Willett: How did you learn what had happened?

Mordant: The surgeon told us.

Willett: How did you react?

Mordant: The other two felt Captain Vere

was being too secretive. That was not my own view. But I became annoyed with Captain Vere during the court-martial. I had heard the surgeon repeat the captain's words: "The angel of God must hang." I felt he had judged Billy before the trial began.

Willett: Tell us about the court-martial.

Mordant: It began with Captain Vere telling the whole story. Then the first lieutenant spoke.

(Music comes up and fades out. Then we hear the first lieutenant speaking at the court-martial.)

First Lieutenant: William Budd, is it as Captain Vere says?

Budd: Captain Vere tells the truth. But Mr. Claggart did not. I am true to the King's Navy.

Vere: I believe you.

Budd: God will bless you for that, sir.

First Lieutenant: Was there hatred between you and Mr. Claggart?

Budd: No. I did not mean to kill him. If I could have spoken up, I would not have hit him. But he lied to my face in front of my captain. I had to protest. The only way I could was with a fist. I am sorry for that.

Mordant: You say that Mr. Claggart lied about you. But why would he have lied if there was no hatred between you?

Budd *(unable to answer this)*: Captain?

Vere: Lieutenant Mordant, your question is a natural one. But *why* Claggart said what he did is not our business here. We must deal only with the result of the prisoner's deed.

First Lieutenant: Budd, if you have any-

thing else to say for yourself, say it now.

Budd: I have said it all.

First Lieutenant: Guard, take this man away.

(We hear Billy Budd being taken away. Then there is silence.)

Vere: Your military duty seems to clash with the compassion you feel for Billy Budd. . . . Is this true?

First Lieutenant: Yes.

Vere: I share your compassion for him. But we are officers in the King's Navy. We must uphold martial law. A sailor strikes an officer in wartime, and the blow kills. That is a crime punishable by death.

Mordant *(upset)*: But Budd never meant to murder — or to mutiny.

Vere: That plea might make this a lesser crime in another court. But we are at war, and we must consider the Mutiny Act.

First Lieutenant: Can we convict Billy Budd, but give him a penalty less than death?

Vere: If we did, we'd look like cowards to the other sailors. They would think we were afraid of them. That would be the end of law and order on this ship. I feel as you do for this unlucky boy. I also feel we have no choice in the matter.

(Music comes up and fades out. We are now back in the courtroom. Mordant is still on the stand.)

Willett: What happened next?

Mordant: We were stunned. We voted to convict Billy Budd to death.

Willett: How did Captain Vere react to the execution?

Mordant: He kept his feelings to himself. Later, he was wounded in combat. Before he died, his last words were, "Billy Budd. Billy Budd."

Willett: No further questions.

Smythe-Wilkins: Mr. Mordant, the vote to convict Billy Budd was unanimous. Did Captain Vere stop you from speaking out?

Mordant: No.

Smythe-Wilkins: Why *didn't* you speak out?

Mordant: I have often asked myself that. Perhaps I was overwhelmed by Captain Vere. Perhaps I could not put my argument into words. The case needed compassion and courage, not caution.

Smythe-Wilkins: Courage? Did Captain Vere ever show fear in combat?

Mordant: I mean another kind of courage.

Smythe-Wilkins: If you were even half as courageous as Captain Vere, you would be a credit to the King. No further questions.

Farnworth: Mr. Mordant, you are dismissed.

(We hear Mordant leave the stand. Reverend Cavendish, the ship's chaplain, takes the stand and is sworn in.)

Willett: When did you learn of Mr. Claggart's death?

Cavendish: Captain Vere announced it to the whole crew.

Willett: How did the crew take the news?

Cavendish: They were shocked into

silence. Then there was a confused murmuring.

Willett: Did you then visit the prisoner?

Cavendish: Yes. I was the only person allowed to talk to him.

Willett: Didn't Captain Vere visit him?

Cavendish: Once — right after the court-martial.

Willett: How did Billy take the news from Captain Vere?

Cavendish: I don't know. Captain Vere kept things to himself. But he looked as if he was suffering.

Willett: Tell us about *your* visit with the prisoner.

Cavendish: I found I had nothing to offer him that would make him any more peaceful than he already was.

Willett: Did he understand that he was to die at dawn?

Cavendish: Yes, but he didn't fear death at all.

Willett: Did you try to stop the execution from taking place?

Cavendish: No. That would have been acting beyond my duties. Besides, it would have been useless.

Willett: Describe the execution.

Cavendish: At 4:00 A.M., I led Billy to the upper deck. His last words were loud and clear. He said, "God bless Captain Vere!"

Willett: Was he being sarcastic?

Cavendish: No. He didn't know how to be sarcastic.

Willett: What did Captain Vere do?

Cavendish: He stood as stiff as a musket. Then they hanged Billy Budd. At that moment, the sun broke through the clouds. It was as if it were a sign from God.

Willett: We want only the facts, please.

Cavendish: Those are *my* facts.

Willett: Did you notice that Budd did not move at the moment of death?

Cavendish: Yes.

Willett: Did this surprise you?

Cavendish: No. Perhaps God spared him the agony of death. The sailors seem to think that something special happened. They still speak of Billy with awe.

Willett: There's an account of what happened in the navy's newspaper. It blames Budd and excuses Claggart. Have you read it?

Cavendish: Yes. It's filled with lies. I trust the sailors' opinions. Perhaps Captain Vere should have trusted them, too.

Smythe-Wilkins: Sailors aboard two other ships started mutinies. Should they have been trusted?

Cavendish: There was no sign of mutiny aboard our ship. The only mutinies were make-believe. One was made up by Mr. Claggart. The other one was in Captain Vere's fearful mind.

Smythe-Wilkins: Are you saying there was not even the possibility of a mutiny?

Cavendish: All things are possible.

Smythe-Wilkins: What do you mean?

Cavendish: Beneath the hatred and lying that is all around us, there is a core of truth and love. Once in a lifetime, if we are lucky, someone like Billy Budd comes along to show us what we can be.

Smythe-Wilkins: No further questions.

Farnworth: Mr. Willett?

Willett: No further questions, and there are no more witnesses.

Farnworth: The court will recess and meet again to make a decision.

READING COMPREHENSION

Summarizing. Choose the best phrase to complete each sentence. Then write the complete statements on your paper.

1. A naval court was called to order in 1798 to _____ (try Billy Budd, investigate the execution of Billy Budd, try Captain Vere).

2. Ratcliffe said that Mr. Claggart _____ (pushed around the men who were below him, treated everyone the same, was incapable of doing his job).

3. Claggart accused Billy Budd of _____ (fighting with the other men, ignoring his duties, planning a mutiny).

4. Billy Budd was convicted of _____ (killing Claggart, disobeying an officer, suspicion of mutiny).

Interpreting. Write the answer to each question on your paper.

1. According to Dansker, why did Claggart set a trap for Budd?

2. Why did Captain Vere have doubts about Claggart's accusations against Budd?

3. Why did Captain Vere feel that he had no choice but to execute Billy Budd?

For Thinking and Discussing. Do you think Billy Budd's execution was just? Why or why not? What do you think should have been done? What do you think the naval court investigating his execution will do?

UNDERSTANDING LITERATURE

Plot. Some stories and plays do not present all the events of the plot in the order in which they happened in time. A story or play may begin in the present and then flash back to tell what happened earlier. In "Billy Budd," there are several *flashbacks* that interrupt the present action and go back to a time in the past.

Below are some events from the play. Write the list of events in the order that they actually occurred in time. Then identify the events that were told about in one of the flashback scenes.

☐ The naval court was called to order.

☐ Billy Budd struck Claggart down.

☐ Billy Budd was hanged.

☐ Billy Budd asked Dansker about being whipped.

☐ Claggart accused Billy Budd of mutiny.

☐ Captain Vere said Claggart had been struck dead by an angel of God.

☐ Reverend Cavendish described Billy Budd's execution.

WRITING

Reverend Cavendish said that Captain Vere had visited Billy Budd right after the court-martial. Write a scene between Captain Vere and Billy Budd in which Captain Vere tells Billy that he is to be executed. Write the scene as a flashback that might have been included in the play.

Section Review

Predicting Outcomes. You have learned how the plot of a story is structured. The plot has a beginning, a middle, and an end. In the beginning, a problem usually develops. In the middle, the action rises as characters try to solve the problem. Eventually, the story reaches a turning point, or climax. Finally, the problem is solved, and a resolution is reached. By the end of a story, you should understand why all events happened as they did.

VOCABULARY

Synonyms/Antonyms. *Synonyms* are two or more words that have the same or similar meanings. For example, *easy* and *simple* are synonyms.

Antonyms are words that have opposite meanings. *Easy* and *difficult* are antonyms.

Read the sentences below. In the list below the sentences, find one synonym and one antonym for each italicized word. On your paper, write (a) the italicized word, (b) its synonym, and (c) its antonym.

1. "If you should meet him, you'd best be wary
Of this awesome *adversary*!"
2. "If I were a smell instead of a man — of all the *comical* ideas!"
3. "Every night, I . . . slave over a hot oven while that *shiftless*, good-for-nothing Pablo sleeps."
4. "She imagined herself in an *elegant* home filled with beautiful furnishings — . . ."
5. ". . . bidding her farewell, the Eccles *departed*."
6. "But I became *annoyed* with Captain Vere during the court-martial."

energetic	plain	left
irritated	funny	friend
enemy	fancy	pleased
arrived	serious	lazy

Read each paragraph below. Select the best choice to complete each statement. Then write the entire sentence on your paper.

1. In "The Pardoner's Tale," Death took many lives, including the three villains who wanted to kill him. In the future, Death will probably _____.
   a. be killed by someone else
   b. take even more lives
   c. stop killing people

2. In "The Necklace," Mathilde learned she had worked hard unnecessarily for ten years. Now Mathilde will probably _____.
   a. stay upset about the incident
   b. ask for the necklace back
   c. forget the whole thing

3. In "Sanctuary," Walter wanted his daughter to get the jewels. Now the jewels will probably be _____.
   a. kept by the police
   b. returned to the Eccles
   c. given to Jewel

WRITING

A Story. In your reading, you have learned about the different elements of a story. A story has a setting, a plot, and characters, all of which revolve around a conflict or problem that is eventually resolved. These elements are organized into a beginning, a middle, and an end. The beginning establishes the setting, introduces the characters, and sets up the conflict. The middle describes the incidents that complicate the conflict and move it along. The end tells the outcome of the story. Most stories are told by a narrator and contain dialogue that brings the characters to life.

Step 1: Set Your Goal

Anything that stirs your imagination can make a good topic for a story. If you feel excited about your story idea, chances are your readers will like it, too. Think of a topic for a story you would like to write. It might be something that actually happened to you or to someone you know. It might be something from your imagination. Or, it might be an idea that came from something you read, such as a newspaper article or another story.

Once you have decided on a topic, think about your purpose in telling the story. Your main purpose, of course, is to tell it well and make it interesting. But you may have another purpose as well. For example, Agatha Christie's purpose in writing "Sanctuary" was to write a detective story that would stump her readers. The two folktales about justice had a message for readers. Think about your topic. Decide on a purpose for your story and state your purpose in a sentence.

Step 2: Make a Plan

Once you have decided on a topic and a purpose, you need to plan your story. Begin by jotting down a description of each major character. Imagine that you know each one personally. Describe what the character looks like, how he or she behaves, and his or her personality traits. Include each character's job and interests, and tell how the characters are related to one another.

Next, describe the setting in which your story takes place. Include details that appeal to the five senses. By referring to your description as you write, you can keep the details about the setting consistent throughout the story.

Now, make a plot outline by listing all the events that might be part of your story. Be sure to include events for each of the four basic elements of a plot: *action, conflict, climax, resolution*. The *action* includes what the characters do and what happens to them. The *conflict* is the struggle between two opposing forces in the story. It is the conflict in a story that keeps readers wondering what will happen next. Readers become involved in how the characters will solve their problems. The *climax* is the point at which the conflict reaches its highest point — the turning point — and the outcome seems inevitable. The *resolution* shows what happens to the characters after the action is over. It brings the story to a close.

Finally, decide who is telling the story, or the point of view. If you are telling the story through your own eyes or the eyes of one character, you may use the first person. If you want your narrator to tell about the thoughts and experiences of many characters, you will want to use the third person. Whichever point of view you choose, maintain it throughout the story.

Step 3: Write a First Draft

A story is more than a list of events. The language you use and the details you include should make it come alive for the reader. As you write your first draft, use your plot outline as a guide. Begin your story in a way that will attract your readers' attention and make them want to read on. Give clear and vivid descriptions of your setting and characters. Include dialogue to give your readers the feeling that what they are reading is actually happening. Remember, this is a rough draft. Concentrate on telling an interesting story, not a perfect one.

Step 4: Revise

As you revise your first draft, try to put yourself in your readers' place. Check to see if you included all the information they need to follow the plot. Try reading the story aloud. If you stumble over a phrase, reword it to make it clearer.

Once you are satisfied with your story, proofread it and make a final copy.

QUIZ

The following is a quiz for Section 2. Write the answers in complete sentences on your paper.

Reading Comprehension

1. In "The Pardoner's Tale," how did the greediness of the three villains lead to their deaths?

2. In "Ooka and the Stolen Smell" and "The Baker's Neighbor," why did the judges feel that hearing or touching — but not keeping — the money was fair payment?

3. In "The Necklace," how did Mathilde act toward her husband because they were not wealthy?

4. In "Sanctuary," how had the real jewels been kept safe from thieves?

5. In "Billy Budd," why did Dansker think Claggart was down on Billy?

Understanding Literature

6. In "The Pardoner's Tale," what problem were the three villains trying to solve in the beginning?

7. In either "Ooka and the Stolen Smell" or "The Baker's Neighbor," would you call the ending of the story a surprise ending? Defend your answer.

8. In "The Necklace," why might the last sentence be the climax of the story? Explain.

9. In "Sanctuary," what foreshadowing gives you clues about the ending of the story? What references to jewels are in the first paragraphs of the story?

10. In "Billy Budd," Ratcliffe compares Captain Vere and Mr. Claggart. What image do you get of them?

ACTIVITIES

Word Attack

1. In "The Necklace," Mathilde was described as suffering "endlessly" and "deeply." The words *endlessly* and *deeply* both end in the suffix *-ly*. The suffix *-ly* often signals that the word is being used as an adverb. (An adverb modifies a verb, adjective, or another adverb.) Add the suffix *-ly* to each of the words below. Use the new word as an adverb in a sentence of your own. Check a dictionary if you are not sure of the spelling.

careful	anxious	swift
warm	impatient	joyous
immediate	exact	utter

2. In "Sanctuary," we learned that Zobeida's necklace may have vanished for dishonest reasons. The word *dishonest* is made up of the prefix *dis-* and the base word *honest*. The prefix *dis-* in this case means "not." Therefore, *dishonest* means "not honest." Add the prefix *dis-* to each of the following words. Then use five of the new words in sentences of your own.

agree	favor	please
approve	honor	quiet
continue	obey	tasteful

Speaking and Listening

1. Folktales were originally handed down orally from one generation to the next. Reread "Ooka and the Stolen Smell" or "The Baker's Neighbor" and practice telling the story orally in your own words. Instead of retelling the folktale, you may wish to make up a tale of your own that expresses the same moral. In either case, be prepared to present the tale to the class.

2. Chaucer wrote in Middle English, the kind of English that was spoken from about 1100 to about 1450. Locate an original version of "The Pardoner's Tale" and try reading it aloud as it is written. Can you read and understand the words? Present a passage for the class.

Researching. Choose one of the following authors as the subject of a short biography: Geoffrey Chaucer, Guy de Maupassant, Agatha Christie, Herman Melville. Find out: when and where the author was born; what his or her early life was like; what kind of education he or she had; if he or she was famous when alive; and for what other works the author is famous. Write your findings as a biography to present to the class.

Creating

1. Pretend that you are one of the villains in "The Pardoner's Tale." Write a paragraph explaining what lesson you learned from the events of the story. Then write a paragraph telling what you might do differently if you had your life to live over.

2. Write a dialogue for the ending of "Billy Budd." Present Admiral Farnworth's decision and the characters' reactions to it.

RELATIONSHIPS

We are not different nor alike
but each strange in his leather body
sealed in skin and reaching out clumsy hands
and loving is an art
that cannot outlive
the open hand
the open eye
the door in the chest standing open.

— Marge Piercy
United States

Hans Tietze and Erica Tietze-Conrat
Oskar Kokoschka (1886-1980)
The Museum of Modern Art, Abby Aldrich Rockefeller Fund

Relationships

Other people play a big part in everyone's life. Reading about relationships in poetry, fiction, and nonfiction can help you understand *your* feelings about experiences that, in some way, everyone has shared.

Communities

Everyone belongs to a community, or group. You probably belong to several— your school, your neighborhood, and the city or town where you live. Your community can affect the way you think and act.

To describe a character's relationship to a community, writers often show how he or she behaves in a conflict with it. In the first story in this section, "Marriage Is a Private Affair" by Chinua Achebe, an older person and a younger person have different relationships to their community. The story is set in Nigeria, a country where, for some people, a person's *tribe* (the people he or she lives with and is related to) is very important. In this story, a young man rejects the tribal custom of marrying the woman his father chooses, and selects his own bride. The tribe is shocked, and a break occurs between father and son. We learn that both of the main characters are strong-willed and stubborn. We also see how important the community values are to the father. And

we see that, although it is not an easy choice, the young man's love for his wife is stronger than his desire to please his father or to obey the customs of his people. Sometimes your relationship with a community can conflict with a relationship to someone else.

Pride is the issue in a tale about a small town in 19th-century France. In "Master Cornille's Secret," all the village's windmills—except one—are driven out of business by a modern mill. What is the secret of Master Cornille's mill? The answer shows how much neighbors' opinions can matter.

Parents and Children

The love of parents for their children can be a powerful protecting force. In a brief essay, "The Sparrow," the Russian writer Ivan Turgenev describes an episode from nature revealing that love can be stronger than the desire to remain alive.

But love can also be a force that prevents a person from growing. The poem "Fear," by Gabriela Mistral, expresses the thoughts of a mother who cannot let her child go.

Anaïs Nin felt that her own mother was like the mother in Mistral's poem. Nin was a daring, unusual woman, and her mother did not like seeing a daughter become so different from herself. Further-

Peasant Wedding, *Peter Brueghel the Elder, ca. 1565*

more, the daughter hated the idea of being like her mother in any way. Only after her mother's death was Nin able to accept the fact that, in some respects, she resembled her mother. In her diary, she expresses this new feeling in a special way.

Two People

Love between a man and a woman can also be powerful. It can make them do things they would ordinarily never do. Sometimes it can even make people give up the one they love most.

A play by Josefina Niggli, "The Ring of General Macías," presents difficult questions. Is it always right to save the life of the one you love? Could honor be more important than life? In this dramatic story of war-torn Mexico, love means being willing to lose the person you live for.

"The Quiet Man," a story from Ireland, also shows that love can lead to unexpected acts. Shawn Kelvin hates to fight. But is the need to save his honor in the eyes of his wife strong enough to make him do something he despises? Maybe there is something about Shawn's character we have yet to discover.

In the last selection, "The Test of Courage," Michael is used to letting Peter tell him what to do. A daring adventure puts them both in danger, and Michael unexpectedly finds himself in the role of leader. He shows Peter the way to safety and passes "the test of courage."

By showing how people behave in relationships, writers can give you a vivid understanding of the characters they create. In this section, you will meet some new characters. And in some of them, you may even recognize yourself.

Marriage Is a Private Affair

by Chinua Achebe

Born in 1930 in Nigeria, Chinua Achebe's writings describe the changing African continent. He often looks at people caught between ancient traditions and the modern world. In this story, a young Nigerian wants to do something that no one in his tribe has ever done. Can he do it?

"**H**ave you written to your dad yet?" asked Nene one afternoon as she sat with Nnaemeka in her room at 16 Kasanga Street, Lagos.

"No, I've been thinking about it. I think it's better to tell him when I get home on leave!"

"But why? Your leave is such a long way off yet — six whole weeks. He should be let into our happiness now."

Nnaemeka was silent for a while, and then began very slowly as if he groped for his words: "I wish I were sure it would be happiness to him."

"Of course it must," replied Nene, a little surprised. "Why shouldn't it?"

"You have lived in Lagos all your life, and you know very little about people in remote parts of the country."

"That's what you always say. But I don't believe anybody will be so unlike other people that they will be unhappy when their sons are engaged to marry."

"Yes. They are most unhappy if the engagement is not arranged by them. In our case, it's worse — you are not even an Ibo."

This was said so seriously and so bluntly that Nene could not find speech immediately. In the cosmopolitan atmosphere of the city, it had always seemed to her something of a joke that a person's tribe could determine whom he married.

At last she said, "You don't really mean that he will object to your marrying me simply on that account? I had always thought you Ibos were kindly disposed to other people."

"So we are. But when it comes to marriage, well, it's not quite so simple. And this," he added, "is not peculiar to the Ibos. If your father were alive and lived in the heart of Ibibio-land, he would be exactly like my father."

"I don't know. But anyway, as your father is so fond of you, I'm sure he will forgive you soon enough. Come on then, be a good boy and send him a nice lovely letter. . . ."

"It would not be wise to break the news to him by writing. A letter will bring it upon him with a shock. I'm quite sure about that."

"All right, honey, suit yourself. You know your father."

As Nnaemeka walked home that evening, he turned over in his mind different ways of overcoming his father's opposition, especially now that his father had gone and found a girl for him. He had a thought of showing his father's letter to Nene but decided on second thought not to, at least for the moment. He read it again when he got home and couldn't help smiling to himself. He remembered Ugoye quite well, an Amazon of a girl who used to beat up all the boys, himself included, on the way to the stream. She was a complete dunce at school.

> I have found a girl who will suit you admirably — Ugoye Nweke, the eldest daughter of our neighbor, Jacob Nweke. She has a proper Christian upbringing. When she stopped schooling some years ago, her father (a man of sound judgment) sent her to live in the house of a pastor where she has received all the training a wife could need. Her Sunday school teacher has told me that she reads her Bible very fluently. I hope we shall begin negotiations when you come home in December.

On the second evening of his return from Lagos, Nnaemeka sat with his father under a cassia tree. This was the old man's retreat where he went to read his Bible when the parching December sun had set and a fresh, reviving wind blew on the leaves.

"Father," began Nnaemeka suddenly, "I have come to ask for forgiveness."

"Forgiveness? For what, my son?" he asked in amazement.

"It's about this marriage question."

"Which marriage question?"

"I can't — we must — I mean it is impossible for me to marry Nweke's daughter."

"Impossible? Why?" asked his father.

"I don't love her."

"Nobody said you did. Why should you?" he asked.

"Marriage today is different — "

"Look here, my son," interrupted his father, "nothing is different. What one looks for in a wife are a good character and a Christian background."

Nnaemeka saw there was no hope along the present line of argument.

"Moreover," he said, "I am engaged to marry another girl who has all of Ugoye's good qualities, and who — "

His father did not believe his ears. "What did you say?" he asked slowly.

"She is a good Christian," his son went on, "and a teacher in a girls' school in Lagos."

"Teacher, did you say? If you consider that a qualification for a good wife, I should like to point out to you, Emeka, that no Christian woman should teach. St. Paul in his letter to the Corinthians says that women should keep silence." He rose slowly from his seat and paced forward and backward. This was his pet subject, and he condemned those church leaders who encouraged women to teach in their schools.

"Whose daughter is she, anyway?"

"She is Nene Atang."

"What!" All the mildness was gone again. "Did you say Neneataga, what does that mean?"

"Nene Atang from Calabar. She is the only girl I can marry." This was a very rash reply, and Nnaemeka expected the storm to burst. But it did not. His father merely walked away into his room. This was most unexpected and puzzled Nnaemeka. His father's silence was infinitely more menacing than a flood of threatening speech. That night the old man did not eat.

When he sent for Nnaemeka a day later, he applied all possible ways of dissuasion. But the young man's heart was hardened, and his father eventually gave him up as lost.

"I owe it to you, my son, as a duty to show you what is right and what is wrong. Whoever put this idea into your head might as well have cut your throat. It is Satan's work." He waved his son away.

"You will change your mind, Father, when you know Nene."

"I shall never see her," was the reply. From that night, the father scarcely spoke to his son. He did not, however, cease hoping that he would realize how serious was the danger he was heading for. Day and night, he put him in his prayers.

Nnaemeka, for his own part, was very deeply affected by his father's grief. But he kept hoping that it would pass away.

If it had occurred to him that never in the history of his people had a man married a woman who spoke a different tongue, he might have been less optimistic.

"It has never been heard," was the verdict of an old man speaking a few

weeks later. In that short sentence, he spoke for all of his people. This man had come with others to sympathize with Okeke when news went round about his son's behavior. By that time, the son had gone back to Lagos.

"What did Our Lord say?" asked another gentleman. "Sons shall rise against their fathers; it is there in the Holy Book."

"It is the beginning of the end," said another.

Six months later, Nnaemeka was showing his young wife a short letter from his father:

It amazes me that you could be so unfeeling as to send me your wedding picture. I would have sent it back. But on further thought, I decided just to cut off your wife and send it back to you because I have nothing to do with her. How I wish that I had nothing to do with you either.

When Nene read through this letter and looked at the cut picture, her eyes filled with tears, and she began to sob.

"Don't cry, my darling," said her husband. "He is essentially good-natured and will one day look more kindly on our marriage." But years passed and that one day did not come.

For eight years, Okeke would have nothing to do with his son, Nnaemeka. Only three times (when Nnaemeka asked to come home and spend his leave) did he write to him.

"I can't have you in my house," he replied on one occasion. "It can be of no interest to me where or how you spend your leave — or your life, for that matter."

The story eventually got to the little village in the heart of the Ibo country that Nnaemeka and his young wife were a most happy couple. But his father was one of the few people in the village who knew nothing about this. He always displayed so much temper whenever his son's name was mentioned that everyone avoided it in his presence. By a tremendous effort of will, he had succeeded in pushing his son to the back of his mind. The strain had nearly killed him but he had persevered, and won.

Then one day, he received a letter from Nene, and in spite of himself he began to glance through it until all of a sudden the expression on his face changed and he began to read more carefully.

. . . Our two sons, from the day they learned that they have a grandfather, have insisted on being taken to him. I find it impossible to tell them that you will not see them. I beg you to allow Nnaemeka to bring them home for a short time during his leave next month. I shall remain here in Lagos.

The old man at once felt the resolution he had built up over so many years falling in. He was telling himself that he must not give in. He tried to steel his heart against all emotional appeals. He leaned against a window and looked out. The sky was overcast with heavy black clouds and a high wind began to blow, filling the air with dust and dry leaves. It was one of those rare occasions when even Nature takes a hand in a human fight. Very soon it began to rain, the first rain in the year. It came down in large sharp drops and was accompanied by the lightning and thunder that mark a change of season.

Okeke was trying hard not to think of his two grandsons. But he knew he was now fighting a losing battle. He tried to hum a favorite hymn but the pattering of large raindrops on the roof broke up the tune. His mind immediately returned to the children. How could he shut his door against them? By a curious mental process, he imagined them standing, sad and forsaken, under the harsh angry weather — shut out from his house.

That night he hardly slept, from remorse — and a vague fear that he might die without making it up to them.

Summarizing. Choose the best phrase to complete each sentence. Then write the complete statements on your paper.

1. Nnaemeka's father disapproved of Nene because she _____ (did not teach school, refused to meet him, was not an Ibo).

2. After Nnaemeka married Nene, his father _____ (became friendlier to Nene, largely ignored his son, never left the house).

3. Nene wrote a letter to Okeke asking him to _____ (let his grandchildren visit him, let her visit him, come to her house for a visit).

Interpreting. Write the answer to each question on your paper.

1. What was Okeke's idea of a proper marriage for his son?

2. Why did the villagers side with the father against the son?

3. Why did the father falter in sticking to his decision when he learned about his two grandsons?

For Thinking and Discussing.

1. How do you feel about Okeke's attitudes about marriage and his behavior concerning his son's marriage?

2. Do you think Okeke will finally let his grandchildren visit? What might happen if he does?

Character. The *characters* in a story are the people who take part in the action of the story. There are several ways to learn what each character is like.

1. *by their actions:* The things that characters do tell you much about them.

2. *by their speech:* You can learn about characters by the things they say.

3. *by their thoughts:* You may learn about characters by what they think.

Each statement below tells you something you know about a character in "Marriage Is a Private Affair." Write whether the statement describes the character's *actions, speech,* or *thoughts.*

You know:

1. Nnaemeka wanted Okeke's approval because he thought of how to get it.

2. Okeke disapproved of Nene because he said so directly to his son.

3. Nnaemeka loved Nene because he went ahead and married her.

4. Okeke was very upset because he refused to visit his son.

5. Nene was concerned about her children because she wrote to Okeke.

WRITING

If Okeke wrote a letter in reply to Nene, what would he say? Write a letter you feel Okeke would write, based on what you know of his character.

Master Cornille's Secret

by Alphonse Daudet

Alphonse Daudet lived in the second half of the 19th century. He wrote many stories about life in the countryside and small towns of southern France. In this story, a miller has a whole town mystified. Can you guess his secret?

Frances Mamai is an old musician who comes sometimes to pass the evening with me in the old mill where I live. He told me the other evening of a little village drama that happened some 20 years ago. The good man's story impressed me, and I will try to tell it to you as I heard it.

Imagine for a moment that you are seated before a jar of sweet-smelling wine, and it is an old musician who is speaking.

Our province, my dear monsieur, has not always been a dead place, entirely unknown to fame, as it is today. Long ago, there was a big business done here in grinding grain. The people from all the farms within 20 miles brought us their grain to grind. The hills all around the village were covered with windmills. To right and left, one could see nothing but the sails turning about in the wind above the pines, and long strings of little donkeys loaded with bags climbing the hills and stretching out along the roads. It was pleasant to hear all through the week the cracking of the whips on the hilltops, the creaking of the windmills, and the voices of the millers' men.

On Sundays, we went to the mills in groups. The millers treated us to wine. The millers' wives were as lovely as queens, with their lace collars and their gold crosses. I used to carry my fife, and we danced until it was pitch-dark. Those mills, you see, were the pleasure and wealth of our province.

Unluckily, some Frenchmen from Paris got the idea of setting up a steam flour mill on the road to Tarascon. Very fine and new it was; the people fell into the habit of sending their grain there, and the poor windmills were left without work. For some time, they tried to keep up the struggle, but steam was the stronger. One after another, they were all obliged to close. We saw no more strings of little donkeys. The millers' pretty wives sold their gold crosses. No more wine! No more dancing! No matter how hard the wind might blow, the sails did not move. Then, one fine day, all those shanties were torn down, and vines and olive trees were planted where they stood.

But one little mill held out and continued to turn bravely on its hill. That was Master Cornille's mill, the same one in which we are passing the evening at this moment.

Master Cornille was an old miller who had lived for 60 years in flour and was crazy over his trade. The setting up of the steam mills made him act like a madman. For a week, he ran about the village, collecting people round him and shouting at the top of his lungs that the flour from the steam mills was poison.

"Don't go there," he would say. "Those villains use steam to make bread — steam, which is an invention of the devil!" And he would spout a lot of fine words in praise of windmills, but no one listened to them.

Then, in a towering rage, the old man shut himself up in his mill, and lived alone like a wild beast. He wouldn't even keep with him his granddaughter Vivette, a child of 15. Since the death of her parents, she had no one but her grandfather in the world. The poor child had to hire herself out among the farms for the harvest, the silk-worm season, or the olive picking. And yet, her grandfather seemed to love the child dearly. He often traveled eight miles on foot in the heat of the sun to see her at the farm where she was working. When he was with her, he would pass hours at a time gazing at her and weeping.

People thought that the old miller had been led by greed to send Vivette away. It did not do him credit to allow his grandchild to travel about that way from one farm to another, exposed to coarse laborers, and to all the problems of young working women. People thought it very wrong too that a man of Master Cornille's reputation should go through the streets barefooted, with cap all holes and a shirt all in rags.

The fact is that on Sunday, when we saw him come in to mass, we were ashamed for him, we old men. Cornille felt it so keenly that he didn't dare to come and sit in a front pew. He always remained at the back of the church, near the holy-water vessel.

There was something in Master Cornille's life we couldn't understand. For a long time, no one in the village had brought him any grain, and yet the sails of his windmill were always in motion as before. In the evening, people met the old miller on the roads, driving before him his donkey loaded with fat bags of flour.

"Good evening, Master Cornille," the peasants would call out to him. "Is business still good?"

"Still good, my children," the old man would reply, with a cheerful air. "Thank God, we have no lack of work."

Then, if any one asked where so much work could come from, he would put a finger to his lips and answer gravely: "Hush! I am working for export."

No one could get anything more from him.

Grainfields, *Jacob Isaadesz van Ruisdael, 1628*

As for putting your nose inside his mill, it wasn't to be thought of. Even little Vivette herself never went in there.

When people passed in front of it, they always found the door closed, and the huge sails moving. The old donkey was browsing on the platform; and a large, thin cat was taking a sunbath on the windowsill, and glaring at them with a wicked look.

All this smelled of mystery, and made people talk a great deal. Everyone had his own explanation of Master Cornille's secret. But the general report was that there

fallen in love with each other. At heart, I was not displeased, because, after all, the name of Cornille was held in honor among us. It would have pleased me to see that pretty little bird of a Vivette trotting about my house. I decided to settle the business at once. I went up to the mill to say a word to the grandfather.

Ah! You should have seen how he received me! It was impossible for me to get him to open his door. I explained my reasons through the keyhole. All the time I was talking, there was that lean villain of a cat snorting like a devil over my head.

The old man didn't give me time to finish, but shouted at me to go back to my fife. He said that if I was in such a hurry to get my boy married, I could go and look for a girl at the steam mill. The blood went to my head when I heard such rough talk. But I was wise enough to control myself.

Leaving the old fool in his mill, I returned to inform the children of my treatment. The poor lambs couldn't believe it; they asked me as a favor to allow them to go up together to the mill and speak to the grandfather. I hadn't the courage to refuse, and off my lovers went.

When they reached the mill, Master Cornille had gone out. The door was securely locked, but the old fellow, when he went away, had left his ladder outside. Suddenly it occurred to the children to go in by the window and see what there might be inside that famous mill.

What a strange thing! The main room of the mill was empty. Not a sack, not a particle of grain, not the slightest trace of flour on the walls or on the spiderwebs.

were even more bags of silver in the mill than bags of grain.

After a while, however, everything came to light. This is how it happened:

One fine day, as I was playing on my fife for the young people to dance, I noticed that my eldest boy and little Vivette had

They couldn't even smell that pleasant, warm odor of ground wheat that makes the air of a mill so fragrant.

The lower room had the same look of poverty and neglect: a few rags, a crust of bread, and in a corner three or four sacks, which had burst, with rubbish and plaster sticking out.

That was Master Cornille's secret! It was that plaster that he paraded at night on the roads, to save the honor of the mill and to make people think that he made flour there. Poor mill! Poor Cornille! Long ago, the steam millers had robbed him of his last customer. The sails still turned, but the mill ground nothing.

The children returned to me in tears, and told me what they had seen. It tore my heart to listen to them. Without a moment's loss of time, I ran to the neighbors. I told them the story, and we agreed instantly that we must carry to Cornille's mill all the wheat there was in our houses.

No sooner said than done. The whole village started off, and we arrived at the top of the hill with a procession of donkeys loaded with grain — and real grain, too!

The mill was wide-open. In front of the door, Master Cornille sat on a bag of plaster, weeping, with his face in his hands. He had found on returning home that someone had entered his mill and discovered his sad secret.

"Poor me!" he said. "Now there's nothing left for me to do but to die. The mill is dishonored."

And he sobbed as if his heart would break, calling his mill by all sorts of names, speaking to it as if it was a living person.

At that moment, the donkeys arrived on the platform, and we all began to shout as we did in the palmy days of the millers: "Holla! Mill there! Holla! Master Cornille!"

And the bags were piled up before the door, and the fine red grain strewed the earth in all directions.

Master Cornille stared. He took up some grain in the hollow of his old hand, and said, laughing and weeping at once: "It is grain! Lord God! Real grain! Leave me; let me look at it."

Then, turning to us, he said, "Ah! I knew that you'd come back to me. All those steam millers are thieves."

We offered to carry him in triumph to the village.

"No, no, my children," he said. "First of all, I must give my mill something to eat. Just think! It's so long since he has had anything between his teeth!"

And it brought tears to the eyes of us all to see the poor old man rush about, emptying the sacks, looking after the millstones, while the grain was crushed and the fine floury dust rose to the ceiling.

I must do our people justice: From that day, we never allowed the old miller to lack work. Then one morning Master Cornille died, and the sails of our last mill ceased to turn — this time forever. When Cornille was dead, no one followed in his footsteps.

What can you expect, monsieur? Everything has an end in this world, and we must believe that the day of windmills has passed.

READING COMPREHENSION

Summarizing. Choose the best phrase to complete each sentence. Then write the complete statements on your paper.

1. The windmills closed because _____ (a storm damaged them, a steam mill took away their business, the workers moved away).

2. Eventually, the town learned that Master Cornille's mill had _____ (bags of stolen wheat, no wheat, changed wheat to plaster).

3. The town decided to _____ (buy the mill from Master Cornille, have Master Cornille arrested, bring their grain to Master Cornille's windmill).

Interpreting. Write the answer to each question on your paper.

1. Who was telling the story?

2. Why wouldn't Master Cornille let his granddaughter live with him?

3. How did Master Cornille hide the fact that his mill was not getting any grain?

4. What feelings probably made Master Cornille act as he did?

For Thinking and Discussing

1. Do you feel people were wrong for using the steam mill? Explain.

2. How would you describe Master Cornille's behavior? Did you feel sorry for him? Why or why not?

UNDERSTANDING LITERATURE

Character. Sometimes you form opinions of people based on what you hear about them. In a story, your opinions of the characters will depend partly on who is telling you about the characters.

Most stories are told by someone who is not part of the action. The narrator is not a character in the story. These stories are written in the *third person*.

Other stories, however, may be written in the *first person*. This means that the narrator is a character in the story who actually takes part in the action. All descriptions of other characters come from this particular person. If another person in the story were narrator, you might form a different opinion of the characters.

"Marriage Is a Private Affair" was written in the third person. The narrator did not take part in the action. But "Master Cornille's Secret" was written in the first person. The narrator was a citizen of the town. He started the story by saying the musician passes the evening "with me in the old mill where I live." If a story is told in the first person, the narrator uses words such as *I, me, my, we, us,* and *our*.

Write five sentences from the story indicating that it is written in the first person.

WRITING

Write a description of Master Cornille as his granddaughter might describe him. Then write a description of Master Cornille as he might describe himself.

The Sparrow

by Ivan Turgenev

Nature doesn't have to be shocking or spectacular to influence us. A small event can make us aware of our feelings about life. In this essay, a 19th-century Russian novelist tells how something that he witnessed in nature affected him.

I was returning from a day's hunting and was walking toward the house along an alley in my garden. My dog was running ahead of me.

Suddenly she slowed her pace and began to advance stealthily, as though she had caught scent of game.

I looked down the path and saw a young sparrow with a streak of yellow near its beak and a bit of puff on its head. It had fallen out of the nest. (A strong wind was swaying the birch trees.) The tiny bird sat there trying helplessly to use its barely grown wings.

My dog was stealing up to the infant sparrow when, abruptly, an old black-chested bird fell like a stone right in front of the dog's face, and with all its feathers standing on end, misshapen, uttering a desperate and pitiful chirp, it hopped once and then again in the direction of the dog's open jaw.

The bird had thrown itself in front of the dog to shield its young one, but its own small body was trembling with terror, its little voice was frenzied and hoarse, and it was numb with fright — it was sacrificing itself!

What a huge monster the dog must have seemed to the mother sparrow! Nevertheless, it could not bear to stay on its high, safe perch in the tree. A force stronger than its will to remain alive made it hurl itself to the rescue.

My Treasure, the dog, stopped still and then backed up. Evidently he too recognized that force. . . .

I hastened to call off the puzzled dog and went on my way, awed.

Yes, do not laugh. I was awed by that small, heroic bird — by its impulse of love.

Love, I felt more than ever, is stronger than death and the fear of death. Only through love is life sustained and nourished.

1. Why had the black-chested bird fallen in front of the dog? Why was this a particularly brave act on the bird's part?

2. Do you agree with the author's opinion of love? Or do you feel it is foolish to endanger yourself for someone else? Explain.

3. Animals have a strong instinct to protect their young. Do you think humans share this instinct?

4. Would you risk your life for someone you loved? For a casual friend? For a total stranger? Explain.

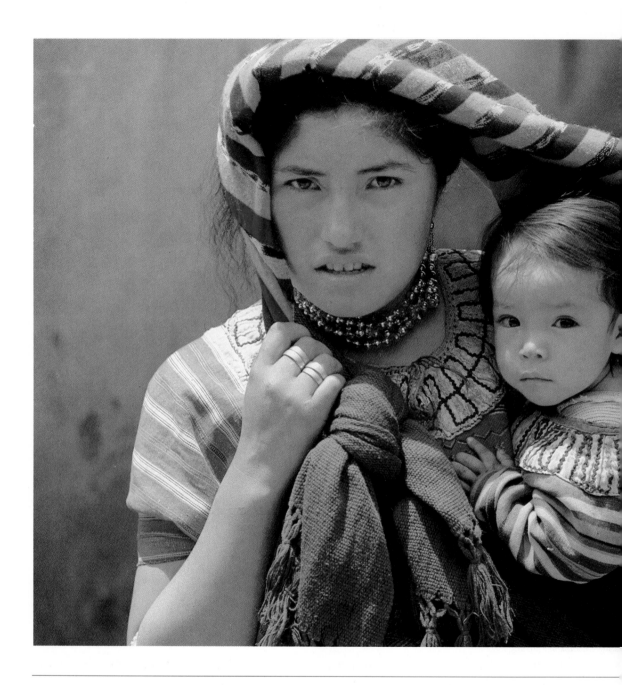

1. How old do you think the author and her child are?

2. What things does the author fear about her daughter? Do you think she is afraid to see her child grow up? How might that affect their relationship?

3. Would you say the mother loves her child? Or is the mother selfish?

Fear

by Gabriela Mistral
(translated by Doris Dana)

I don't want them to turn
my little girl into a swallow.
She would fly far away into the sky
and never fly again to my straw bed,
or she would nest in the eaves
where I could not comb her hair.
I don't want them to turn
my little girl into a swallow.

I don't want them to make
my little girl a princess.
In tiny golden slippers
how could she play in the meadow?
And when night came, no longer
would she sleep at my side.
I don't want them to make
my little girl a princess.

And even less do I want them
one day to make her queen.
They would put her on a throne
where I could not go to see her.
And when nighttime came
I could never rock her . . .
I don't want them to make
my little girl a queen!

4. Who is "them" that the author refers to throughout the poem? Why doesn't the author give "them" a name? What is the author's opinion of "them"? Do you agree?

The Diary of Anaïs Nin

by Anaïs Nin

Anaïs Nin wrote "to unmask the self that lies hidden behind the self that we present to the world." Her stories, about a woman's relationships, reveal truths about all people.

My mother wanted me to be someone other than the woman I was. She disliked my artist friends. She wanted me to be as she had been, essentially maternal. While she was alive, she threatened my aspiration to escape the servitudes of women. Very early I was determined not to be like her, but like the women who had enchanted my father . . . who lured him away from us.

During her life, she condemned my freedom. She often harked back to the lovely, submissive child I once was, and frowned upon what I had become.

It was not the loss of my mother which reawakened my love for her, it was because my mother's disappearance removed the stigma of her judgments, the dangers and guilt brought about by her influence, and left me a simple human being no longer concerned with my own survival, but able to recognize her qualities.

During her life, I fought her influence, and she fought in me the kind of women who had displaced her.

As soon as she died, my rebellion collapsed. She left me a sewing machine, a gold thimble, the diaries she had bound by hand in France. I became "possessed" by the spirit of my mother. It was my only way to maintain her alive within myself. Death of a loved one is like a mutilation, a part of your body is torn from you, you die a little. And then following that, the spirit of the dead one enters into you, as if in this way you sustain his life, assure his continuity. I, who had refused to iron and wash clothes long ago, washed and ironed Joaquin's shirts and felt myself becoming my mother. I took on her maternal virtues.

Better than the keeping of physical reminders is this moment when we cease to struggle against the parent's own image of us and accept our resemblances as part of our being.

In ancient mystic beliefs, the spirit of the dead entered a newborn child. Surely our parents give birth to us twice, the second time when they die, and as they die, in rebellion against death, we accept the legacy of their character traits.

The Music Room: Harmony in Green and Rose, *James McNeill Whistler, 1860*

1. While her mother was alive, what things did the author dislike about her? What things did the mother dislike about her daughter? Do you agree with their opinions? Explain.

2. How did the daughter's attitude change after her mother's death?

3. Do you feel the mother loved her daughter? Should parents try to mold their children a certain way? Explain.

4. Do you agree with Nin's conclusion that "we accept the legacy of [our parents'] character traits" after their deaths?

The Ring of General Macías

by Josefina Niggli

Josefina Niggli, born in Mexico, now lives in North Carolina. But many of her plays, filmscripts, and TV scripts are based on people and events from Mexican history. In this exciting play, war forces a woman to make the hardest decision anyone could make.

CHARACTERS

Marica, the sister of General Macías
Raquel, the wife of General Macías
Andrés de la O, a captain in the Revolutionary Army
Cleto, a private in the Revolutionary Army
Basilio Flores, a captain in the Federal Army
Time: A night in April, 1912
Place: Just outside Mexico City

The living room of General Macías's home is luxuriously furnished. The room is dark except for moonlight coming through the windows. A young girl enters the room carrying a candle. She waits for a moment and listens, then moves quickly to a bookcase. She places the candle on top of the bookcase and begins searching behind the books. She finally finds what she wants: a small bottle. While she is searching, a woman enters the room. As the girl turns with the bottle, the woman switches on the light. *The girl gives a half scream, and tries to hide the bottle behind her back. The light reveals her to be about 20 years old. The woman has a queenly air. She is about 32.*

Marica: Raquel! What are you doing here?
Raquel: What did you have hidden behind the books, Marica?
Marica: I? Nothing. Why do you think I have anything?
Raquel: Give it to me.
Marica: No. No, I won't.
Raquel: I demand that you give it to me.
Marica: You have no right to order me about. I'm a married woman. I . . . I . . . *(She begins to sob.)*
Raquel *(gently):* You shouldn't be up. The doctor told you to stay in bed. *(She takes the bottle out of the girl's hand.)* It was poison. I thought so.
Marica: Oh, Raquel, why do we have to have wars? Why do men have to go to war and be killed?

170

Raquel: Men must fight for what they believe is right. It is an honorable thing to die for your country as a soldier.

Marica: But how about the women? What becomes of us?

Raquel: We can pray.

Marica *(bitterly):* Yes, we can pray. And then comes the terrible news, and it's no use praying any more. All the reason for our praying is dead. Why should I go on living with Tomas dead?

Raquel: Living is a duty.

Marica: How can you be so cold, so hard? Your husband is out there fighting, too. My brother worships you. He has never even looked at another woman since the first day he saw you. Does he know how cold and hard you are?

Raquel: Domingo is my — honored husband.

Marica: You've been married for ten years. And I've been married for three months. If Domingo is killed, it won't be the same for you. You've had ten years. *(She is crying wildly.)* I haven't anything . . . anything at all.

Raquel: You've had three months . . . three months of laughter. And now perhaps five months of tears. Not more. You're only twenty. And in five months, Tomas will become just a lovely memory.

Marica: I'll remember Tomas all my life.

Raquel: Of course. But you're young . . . and the young need laughter. And one day in Paris, or Rome, or even Mexico City, you'll meet another man. You'll marry again. There will be children in your house. How lucky you are.

Marica: I'll never marry again.

Raquel: You're only twenty. You'll think differently when you're a little older.

Marica: What will you do if Domingo is killed?

Raquel: I shall be very proud that he died in all his courage . . . in all the greatness of a hero.

Marica: But you would not weep, would you?

Raquel: No, I'd not weep. I'd sit here in this empty house and wait.

Marica: Wait for what?

Raquel: For the jingle of his spurs as he walks across the tiled hall. For the sound of his laughter in the patio. For the feel of his hand —

Marica *(screams):* Stop it!

Raquel: I'm sorry.

Marica: You do love him, don't you?

Raquel: I don't think even he knows how much.

Marica: I thought after ten years people slid away from love. But you and Domingo — why, you're all he thinks about. When he's away from you, he talks about you all the time. I heard him say once that when you were out of his sight he was like a man without eyes or ears or hands.

Raquel: I know. I, too, know that feeling.

Marica: Then how could you let him go to war? Perhaps to be killed? How could you?

Raquel *(sharply):* Marica, you are of the family Macías. Your family is a family of great warriors.

Marica: But Domingo loves you enough to forget that. If you had asked him, he wouldn't have gone to war. He would have stayed here with you.

Raquel: No, he would not have stayed. Your brother is a man of honor.

Marica *(beginning to cry again):* I begged Tomas not to go. I begged him.

Raquel: Would you have loved him if he had stayed?

Marica: I don't know. I don't know.

Raquel: There is your answer. You'd have despised him. Loved and despised him. Now come, Marica, it's time for you to go to bed.

Marica: Aren't you coming upstairs, too?

Raquel: No . . . I haven't been sleeping very well lately. I think I'll read for a little while.

Marica: Good night, Raquel. And thank you.

Raquel: Good night, little one.

(Marica leaves. Raquel stares down at the bottle of poison in her hand, then puts it away. She selects a book, gets a blanket, and sits down on the sofa. Suddenly she hears a noise in the patio. She goes to the patio door and peers out.)

Raquel: Who's there? Who's there? Oh! *(She backs into the room. A man and young boy, dressed in the clothing and hats of peasants, come into the room. Raquel draws herself up regally. Her voice is cold and commanding.)* Who are you, and what do you want here?

Andrés: We are hunting for the wife of General Macías.

Raquel: I am Raquel Rivera de Macías.

Andrés: Cleto, stand guard in the patio.

Cleto: Yes, my captain. *(Cleto leaves.)*

(The man strolls around the room, looking it over. He finds a bottle of wine and pours himself a glass and drains it.)

Raquel: How very interesting.

Andrés: What?

Raquel: To be able to drink wine with that hat on.

Andrés: The hat? Oh, forgive me, señora. In military camp, one forgets one's polite manners. Would you care to join me in another glass?

Raquel (sitting): Why not? It's my wine.

Andrés: And very excellent wine. (He pours two glasses, and pulls over a chair.) You don't mind, do you?

Raquel: Would it make any difference if I did?

Andrés: No. The Federals are searching the streets for us and we have to stay somewhere.

Raquel: Of course, I suppose I could scream.

Andrés: Naturally.

Raquel: My sister-in-law is upstairs asleep. And there are several servants in the back of the house. Mostly men servants. Very big men.

Andrés: Very interesting.

Raquel: What would you do if I screamed?

Andrés: Nothing.

Raquel: I am afraid you are lying to me. You are one of the fighting peasants, aren't you?

Andrés: I am a captain in the Revolutionary Army.

Raquel: This house is completely loyal to the Federal government.

Andrés: I know. That's why I'm here.

Raquel: And now that you are here, just what do you expect me to do?

Andrés: I expect you to offer sanctuary to myself and Cleto.

Raquel: Cleto? (She looks toward the patio.) Oh, your army. What a magnificent army you have. I'm sure you must win many victories.

Andrés: We do. And we will win the greatest victory, remember that.

Raquel: This has gone on long enough. Will you please take your army and climb over the patio wall with it?

Andrés: I told you that we came here so that you could give us sanctuary.

Raquel: My dear captain — captain without a name . . .

Andrés: Andrés de la O, your servant.

Raquel (startled): Andrés de la O!

Andrés: I am flattered. You have heard of me.

Raquel: Naturally. Everyone in the city has heard of you. You have a reputation for politeness — especially to women.

Andrés: I see that the tales about me have lost nothing in the telling.

Raquel: I can't say. I'm not interested in gossip about your type of soldier.

Andrés: Then let me give you something to heighten your interest. (He suddenly takes her in his arms and kisses her. She stiffens for a moment, then remains perfectly still. He moves away.)

Raquel (rage forcing her to whisper): Get out of here — at once!

Andrés: I can understand why Macías loves you. I couldn't before, but now I can understand it.

Raquel: Get out of my house.

Andrés: So cruel, señora, and I with a present for you? A very nice present — from your husband.

Raquel: A present! From Domingo?

Andrés: I don't know him that well. I call him General Macías.

Raquel: Is he well? How does he look? He's a prisoner . . . your prisoner!

Andrés: Naturally. That's why I know so much about you. He talks about you constantly.

Raquel: You know nothing about him. You're lying to me.

(Cleto comes to the window.)

Andrés: I assure you, señora —

Cleto: My captain . . .

Andrés: What is it, Cleto?

Cleto: There are soldiers at the end of the street. They are searching all the houses. They will be here soon.

Andrés: Don't worry. We are quite safe here. Stay in the patio until I call you.

Cleto: Yes, my captain.

Raquel: You are not safe here. When those soldiers come I shall turn you over to them.

Andrés: I think not.

Raquel: You can't escape from them.

Andrés: Look at this ring. *(He takes a gold ring from out of his shirt and holds it out to her.)*

Raquel: Why, it's — a wedding ring.

Andrés: Read the inscription inside of it. Read it! *(She reluctantly takes the ring.)*

Raquel: "D.M. — R.R. — June 2, 1902." Where did you get this?

Andrés: General Macías gave it to me.

Raquel: Not this ring. He'd never give you this ring. *(with dawning horror)* He's dead! You stole it from his dead finger. He's dead.

Andrés: Not yet. But he will be dead if I don't return by sunset tomorrow.

Raquel: I don't believe you. I don't believe you. You're lying to me.

Andrés: You will hide me until those soldiers get out of this district. When it is safe enough, Cleto and I will leave. But if you betray me to them, your husband will be shot tomorrow evening at sunset. Do you understand?

Cleto *(at the patio door):* The soldiers are coming closer, my captain. They are at the next house.

Andrés *(to Raquel):* Where shall we hide? Think, woman! If you love your husband at all — think!

Raquel: I don't know. Marica upstairs — the servants in the rest of the house — I don't know.

Andrés: The general has bragged to us about you. He says you are braver than most men. He says you are very clever. This is a time to be both brave and clever.

Cleto *(pointing to the closet):* What door is that?

Raquel: It's a closet . . . a storage closet.

Andrés: We'll hide in there.

Raquel: It's very small. It's not big enough for both of you.

Andrés: Cleto, hide yourself in there.

Cleto: But, my captain —

Andrés: That's an order! Hide yourself.

Cleto: Yes, sir. *(Cleto steps into the closet.)*

Andrés: Now, señora, where are you going to hide me?

Raquel: How did you persuade my husband to give you this ring?

Andrés: That's a very long story, señora, for which we have no time just now. Later I will be glad to give you all the details.

But at present it is only necessary for you to remember that his life depends upon mine.

Raquel: Yes — yes, of course. Give me your hat. *(She takes his hat to the closet and hands it to Cleto.)* There is a smoking jacket hanging up in there. Hand it to me.

(Cleto hands her the jacket. She brings it to Andrés.) Put this on.

Andrés: Such a pity my shoes are not comfortable slippers.

Raquel: Sit in that chair.

Andrés: My dear lady —

Raquel: If I must save your life, allow me

to do it in my own way. Sit down. (*Andrés sits. She covers his legs and feet with a blanket.*) If anyone speaks to you, don't answer. Don't turn your head. As far as you are concerned, there is no one in this room — not even me. (*There is the sound of men's voices in the patio.*) The Federal soldiers are here. If you pray, ask God to keep Marica upstairs. She is very young and very stupid. She'll betray you before I can shut her mouth.

Andrés: I'll —

Raquel: Silence! Stare straight ahead of you and pray. (*She goes to the window and speaks loudly to the soldiers.*) Really! What is the meaning of this uproar?

Flores (*at the patio door*): Do not alarm yourself, señora. I am Captain Basilio Flores, at your service, señora.

Raquel: What do you mean, invading my house and making so much noise at this hour of the night?

Flores: We are hunting for two spies. One of them is the notorious Andrés de la O. You may have heard of him, señora.

Raquel (*looking at Andrés*): Considering what he did to my cousin — yes, I've heard of him.

Flores: Your cousin, señora?

Raquel (*goes to Andrés and puts her hand on his shoulder. He stares woodenly in front of him.*): Felipe was his prisoner before the poor boy managed to escape.

Flores (*crosses over to Andrés*): Captain Basilio Flores, at your service. (*He salutes.*)

Raquel: Felipe doesn't hear you. He doesn't even know you are in the room.

Flores: It is a sad thing.

Raquel: Must your men make so much noise?

Flores: The hunt must be thorough, señora. And now if some of my men can go through here to the rest of the house —

Raquel: Why?

Flores: But I told you, señora. We are hunting for two spies —

Raquel (*speaking quickly from controlled nervousness*): And do you think I have them hidden some place, and I the wife of General Macías?

Flores: The wife of General Macías! But I didn't know . . .

Raquel: Now that you do know, I suggest you remove your men and their noise at once.

Flores: But, señora, I regret — I still have to search this house.

Raquel: I can assure you, Captain, that I have been sitting here all evening, and no peasant spy has passed me and gone into the rest of the house.

Flores: They needn't have come through here, señora.

Raquel: So . . . you do think I conceal spies in this house. Then search it! Look under the sofa . . . under the table. And don't miss that closet, Captain.

Flores: Please, señora . . . I am only doing my duty. You are making it very difficult.

Raquel: I'm sorry. My sister-in-law is upstairs. She has just received word that her husband has been killed. They were married three months ago. She's only twenty. I didn't want —

Marica (*from upstairs*): Raquel, what is all the noise downstairs?

Raquel (*calling back*): It is nothing. Go back to bed.

Marica: But I can hear men's voices in the patio.

Raquel: It is only some Federal soldiers hunting for two peasant spies. *(She turns and speaks rapidly to Flores.)* If she comes down here, she must not see my cousin. Felipe escaped, but her husband was killed. The doctor thinks the sight of my poor cousin might affect her mind. You understand?

Flores: Certainly, señora. What a sad thing.

Marica: Raquel, I'm afraid! *(She tries to push past Raquel into the room. Raquel and Flores stand between her and Andrés.)* Spies! In this house. Oh, Raquel!

Raquel: The doctor will be very angry if you don't return to bed at once.

Marica: But those terrible men will kill us. What is the matter with you two? Why are you standing there like that? *(She tries again to look past them.)*

Flores: It is better that you go back to your room, señora.

Marica: But why? Upstairs I am alone. Those terrible men will kill me. I know they will.

Flores: Don't be afraid, señora. There are no spies in this house.

Marica: Are you sure?

Flores *(laughing):* Of course.

Raquel: Now go back to bed, Marica. Please, for my sake.

Marica: You are both acting very strangely. I think you have something hidden in this room you don't want me to see.

Raquel *(sharply):* You are quite right. Captain Flores has captured one of the spies. He is sitting in the chair behind me. He is dead. Now will you please go upstairs!

Marica: Oh! That such a terrible thing could happen in this house. *(She runs out of the room.)*

Flores *(worried):* Was it wise to tell her such a story, señora?

Raquel: Better that than the truth. Good night, Captain, and thank you.

Flores: Good night, señora. And don't worry. Those spies won't bother you. If they were anywhere in this district, my men would have found them.

Raquel: I'm sure of it.

(The captain salutes her, then goes into the patio. Neither Andrés nor Raquel moves until the voices outside die away. Then Raquel staggers and nearly falls, but Andrés catches her in time.)

Andrés: They've gone, Cleto. Bring a glass of wine. Quickly.

Cleto: What happened?

Andrés: Nothing. Just a faint. *(He holds the wine to her lips.)*

Cleto: She's a great lady, that one. When she told him to look in the closet, my knees were trembling, I can tell you.

Andrés: My own bones were playing a pretty tune.

Cleto: Why do you think she married Macías?

Andrés: Love is a peculiar thing, Cleto.

Raquel *(moans and sits up):* Are they — are they gone?

Andrés: Yes, they've gone. I've never known a braver lady.

Raquel: Will you go now, please?

Andrés: We'll have to wait until the district is free of them — but if you'd like to write a letter to your husband while we're waiting —

Raquel: You'd take it to him? You'd really give it to him?

Andrés: Of course.

Raquel: Thank you. *(She goes to the desk and sits down.)*

Andrés *(to Cleto):* You stay here with the señora. I'm going to find out how much of the district has been cleared.

Cleto: Yes, my captain.

(Andrés leaves. Cleto stares at Raquel as she starts to write. After a moment, she turns to him.)

Raquel: Why do you keep staring at me?

Cleto: Why did you marry a man like that one, señora?

Raquel: You're very impertinent.

Cleto: I'm sorry, señora.

Raquel *(after a brief pause):* What do you mean: "a man like that one"?

Cleto: Well, you're very brave, señora.

Raquel: And don't you think the general is very brave?

Cleto: No, señora. Not very.

Raquel: What are you trying to tell me?

Cleto: Nothing, señora. It is none of my affair.

Raquel: Tell me what is in your mind.

Cleto: I don't understand it. The captain says love is a peculiar thing, but I don't understand it.

Raquel: Cleto, did the general willingly give that ring to your captain?

Cleto: Yes, señora.

Raquel: Why?

Cleto: The general wanted to save his own life. He said he loved you and he wanted to save his life.

Raquel: How would giving that ring to your captain save the general's life?

Cleto: The general's supposed to be shot tomorrow afternoon. But he's talked about you a lot, and when my captain knew we had to come into the city, he thought perhaps we might take refuge here if the Federals got on our trail. So he went to the general and said that if he fixed it so we'd be safe here, my captain would save him from the firing squad.

Raquel: Was your trip here to the city very important — to your cause, I mean?

Cleto: Indeed yes, señora. The captain got a lot of fine information. It means we'll win the next big battle. My captain is a very clever man, señora.

Raquel: Did the general know about this information when he gave his ring to your captain?

Cleto: I don't see how he could help knowing it, señora. He heard us talking about it enough.

Raquel: Who knows about that bargain to save the general's life beside you and your captain?

Cleto: No one, señora. The captain isn't one to talk, and I didn't have time to.

Raquel *(While the boy has been talking, the life seems to have drained completely out of her.):* How old are you, Cleto?

Cleto: I don't know, señora. I think I'm twenty, but I don't know.

Raquel *(speaking to herself):* Tomas was twenty.

Cleto: Who is Tomas?

Raquel: He was married to my sister-in-law. Cleto, you think my husband is a coward, don't you?

Cleto: Yes, señora.

Raquel: You don't think any woman is worth it, do you? Worth the price of a great battle, I mean?

Cleto: No, señora. But as the captain says, love is a very peculiar thing.

Raquel: If your captain loved a woman as much as the general loves me, would he have given an enemy his ring?

Cleto: Ah, but the captain is a great man, señora.

Raquel: And so is my husband a great

man. He is of the family Macías. All of that family have been great men. All of them — brave and honorable men. They have always held their honor to be greater than their lives. That is a tradition of their family.

Cleto: Perhaps none of them loved a woman like you, señora.

Raquel: How strange you are. I saved you from the Federals because I want to save my husband's life. You call me brave and yet you call him a coward. There is no difference in what we have done.

Cleto: But you are a woman, señora.

Raquel: Has a woman less honor than a man, then?

Cleto: No, señora. The general is a soldier. He has a duty to his own cause. You are a woman. You have a duty to your husband. It is right that you should try to save him. It is not right that he should try to save himself.

Raquel: Yes, of course. It is right that I should save him. Your captain has been gone some time, Cleto. You'd better find out if he is still safe.

Cleto: Yes, señora. (*As he reaches the door she stops him.*)

Raquel: Are you afraid of death, Cleto?

Cleto: No, señora. It's like the captain says . . . dying for what you believe in — that's the finest death of all.

Raquel: And you believe in the Revolutionary cause?

Cleto: Yes, señora. I am a poor peasant, that's true. But still I have a right to live like a man, with my own ground, and my own family, and my own future. (*He goes out.*)

Raquel: He's so young. But Tomas was no older. And he's not afraid. He said so. Oh, Domingo — Domingo!

(*She straightens abruptly, takes the bottle of poison from the desk, and stares at it. Then she crosses to the wine bottle and laces it with the poison. She hurries back to the desk and is busy writing when Andrés and Cleto return.)*

Andrés: You'll have to hurry that letter. The district is clear now.
Raquel: I'll be through in just a moment. You might as well finish the wine while you're waiting.
Andrés: Thank you. A most excellent idea.
Raquel: Why don't you give some to — Cleto?
Andrés: This is too fine a wine to waste on that boy.
Raquel: He'll probably never have another chance to taste such wine.
Andrés: Very well. Pour yourself a glass, Cleto.
Cleto: Thank you. Your health, my captain.
Raquel: Drink it outside, Cleto. I want to speak to your captain. *(Andrés nods and Cleto goes out.)* I want you to give my husband a message for me. I can't write it. You'll have to remember it. But first, give me a glass of wine too.
Andrés *(pouring the wine)*: It might be easier for him if you wrote it.
Raquel: I think not. *(She takes the glass.)* I want you to tell him that I never knew how much I loved him until tonight.
Andrés: Is that all?
Raquel: Yes. Tell me, Captain, do you think it possible to love a person too much?
Andrés: Yes, señora. I do.
Raquel: So do I. Let us drink a toast, Captain — to honor. To bright and shining honor.

Andrés *(raises his glass)*: To honor. *(He drains his glass. She lifts hers almost to her lips and then puts it down. From the patio comes a faint cry.)*
Cleto: Captain. Captain.

(Andrés brushes his hand across his face as if to clear his sight. When he hears Cleto, he tries to go to the patio but stumbles and falls. He looks accusingly at Raquel.)

Andrés: Why?
Raquel: Because I love him. Can you understand that?
Andrés: We'll win. The Revolution will win. You can't stop that.
Raquel: Yes, you'll win. I know that now.

(Andrés looks at her and tries to smile. He manages to pull the ring from his shirt and extend it to her. But it drops from his hand.)

Raquel *(runs to the window and calls)*: Cleto. Cleto! *(She comes back to Andrés. She kneels beside him and picks up the ring and puts it on her finger. Then she walks to the sofa and sinks down on it.)*

Marica *(calling)*: Raquel! Raquel! *(Raquel snaps off the light, leaving the room in darkness. Marica comes into the room carrying a candle. The light is too dim to reveal the dead Andrés.)* What are you doing down here in the dark? Why don't you come to bed?
Raquel: I'll come in just a moment.
Marica: But what are you doing, Raquel?
Raquel: Nothing. Just listening . . . listening to an empty house.

READING COMPREHENSION

Summarizing. Choose the best phrase to complete each sentence. Then write the complete statements on your paper.

1. Raquel felt that to die for one's country was _____ (an honorable act, a foolish act, a lucky event).

2. If Andrés failed to return, _____ (Cleto would take his place, General Macías would be killed, his army would lose the battle).

3. Cleto told Raquel that General Macías wanted to _____ (die for his country, kill Andrés, save his life for her).

Interpreting. Write the answer to each question on your paper.

1. Why did Raquel hide Andrés and Cleto?

2. How did Raquel's and Marica's attitudes toward a soldier dying for his country differ?

3. Why did General Macías give his ring to his enemy?

4. Why did Raquel poison the spies?

5. What were Raquel's feelings at the end of the story?

For Thinking and Discussing.

1. Do you agree with General Macías' actions? Why or why not?

2. Do you think Raquel did the right thing when she caused her husband's death? Explain your answer.

UNDERSTANDING LITERATURE

Character. Each character in a story behaves in a particular way. By the end of the story, you should be able to understand why characters acted as they did. Their *motivation*, or reason for the action, should be clear to you.

For example, in "Master Cornille's Secret," Master Cornille tried to keep everyone out of his mill. His motivation was to save the honor of the mill.

Read the following actions taken by characters in "The Ring of General Macías." Write each character's motivation.

1. Marica tried to take poison at the beginning of the story.

2. General Macías gave Andrés his ring.

3. Andrés and Cleto hid in Raquel's house.

4. Raquel hid Andrés from Flores.

5. Raquel and Flores shielded Andrés from Marica.

6. Cleto told Raquel about the agreement to save the General's life.

7. Raquel poisoned Andrés and Cleto.

WRITING

At the end of the play, Raquel started to write her husband a letter. Compose the letter Raquel might have written, describing her love for her husband. Also, have her explain her motivation for poisoning Andrés and Cleto.

The Quiet Man

based on the story by Maurice Walsh

Shawn Kelvin hates to fight. But he loves his wife. Which feeling is stronger? In a different kind of love story, set in Ireland, everyone gets a surprise.

Shawn Kelvin, at the age of 20, went to the States to seek his fortune. After 15 years, he returned to his home in Ireland. Whether he had made his fortune, or had not, no one could know for certain. For he was a quiet man, not given to talking about himself and the things he had done.

A quiet man, under middle size, with strong shoulders and deep-set blue eyes — that was Shawn Kelvin. One shoulder had a trick of hunching slightly higher than the other. Some folks said this came from a habit he had of protecting his eyes from the glare of steel furnaces in a place called Pittsburgh. Others said it used to be a way he had of guarding his chin that time he was a sort of sparring-partner punching bag at a boxing camp.

Shawn Kelvin came home and found that he was the last of the Kelvins, and that the farm he had been born on now belonged to Big Liam O'Grady. Shawn took no action to recover the land, although O'Grady had got it meanly. Shawn had had enough of fighting, and all he wanted now was peace. He quietly went and looked about him for the place, and peace, he wanted. When he had found it, he quietly produced the money for a neat,

small farm on Knockanore Hill. It was not a big place but it was good in heart, and it got all the sun that was going. Best of all, it suited Shawn, for it held the peace that tuned to his own quietness.

There, in a four-roomed thatched cottage, Shawn made his life, and no thought came to him of bringing a wife into the place.

"Shawn, old son," one of his friends might hint, "aren't you sometimes terrible lonely?"

"Never!" might say Shawn. "Why?"

And then they would laugh.

Yet Fate had the thought and the dream in her loom for him. On Sundays, Shawn used to go to church. There Fate laid her lure for him.

Sitting quietly on his wooden bench, he would fix his eyes on the priest and say his prayers. But after a time, Shawn's eyes no longer fixed themselves on the priest. They went no farther than two seats ahead. A girl sat there. Sunday after Sunday she sat in front of him. And Sunday after Sunday his casual admiration grew warmer.

She had short red hair, and Shawn liked the color and wave of that flame. And he liked the set of her shoulders and the way

184

she had of leaning forward at her prayers. And the service over, Shawn used to stay in his seat so that he might get one quick but sure look at her face as she passed. He liked her face, too. And he smiled sadly at himself because she was an O'Grady.

One person, only, noted Shawn's look and the thought behind the look. Not the girl. Her brother, Big Liam O'Grady, the very man who as good as stole the old Kelvin farm. And that man smiled too — an ugly smile. And he put away his bit of knowledge in his mind for a day when it might come in useful for his own purposes.

The girl's name was Ellen — Ellen O'Grady. She was past her first youth, into that second one that had no sure ending. She might be 30 — but was no less. Though she had been sought in marriage more than once, she had accepted no one, or rather, had not been allowed to encourage anyone. Her brother saw to that.

Liam O'Grady was a big man, with the strength of an ox and a heart no bigger than a sour apple. He was an overbearing man who often went into wild rages. He and his sister Ellen lived on a big ranch. Ellen was his housekeeper and maid of all work. She was a careful housekeeper, a good cook, and she demanded no wage. All this suited Big Liam, and so she remained single.

Big Liam himself was not a marrying man. There were not many women with a dowry big enough to tempt him. But in due time, the dowry, and the woman that came with it, came under his nose. His neighbor, James Carey, died and left his fine farm and all on it to his widow. Big Liam looked once at Kathy Carey and looked many times at her farm. Both pleased him. He took the steps required by tradition. He sent a messenger to open talks between them. The messenger came back within the hour.

"My soul," said he, "but she is the quick one! I hadn't ten words out of me when she was down my throat. 'I am in no hurry,' says she, 'to come wife to a house with another woman at the fire corner. When Ellen is in a place of her own, I will listen to what Liam O'Grady has to say.' "

"She will, I say!" Big Liam said. "She will so."

Now was the right time to remember Shawn Kelvin and the look in his eyes. He smiled knowingly and with contempt. Shawn Kelvin daring to cast sheep's eyes at an O'Grady! That undersized chicken heart, who took the loss of his father's farm lying down! But what of it? The required dowry would be small, and the girl would never go hungry.

The very next market day at Listowel, he sought out Shawn Kelvin and placed a huge hand on his shoulder.

"Shawn Kelvin, a word with you! Come and have a drink."

Shawn hesitated. "Very well," he said then. He did not care for O'Grady, but he would hurt no man's feelings.

They went across to Sullivan's bar and had a drink, and Shawn paid for it. Big Liam came directly to his subject, as if he were doing Shawn a favor.

"I want to see Ellen settled in a place of her own," said he.

Shawn's heart lifted into his throat and stayed there.

"Your place is small," went on the big man, "but it is handy, and you don't owe on it. But not much of a dowry can I be giving with Ellen. Say two hundred pounds at the end of harvest. What do you say, Shawn Kelvin?"

Shawn swallowed his heart, and his voice came slow and cool. "What does Ellen say?"

"I haven't asked her," said Big Liam. "But what would she say, blast it?"

"Whatever she says, she will say it herself, not you, Big Liam."

But what could Ellen say? She looked within her own heart and found it empty. She looked at her brother's hard face and saw herself slowly getting old at his fire corner. She looked up at Knockanore Hill and saw the white cottage among the green hills. And finally she looked at Shawn Kelvin, that small man with the clean face. She said a prayer and sank head and shoulders and accepted.

Shawn was far from satisfied with that resigned acceptance, but then was not the time to press for a warmer one. He saw that she was doomed beyond hope to a home bought for her by her brother. Let it be his own home then. There were many worse ones.

So Ellen O'Grady married Shawn Kelvin.

But Big Liam O'Grady did not win Kathy Carey to wife. She took to husband her own farmhand. This made Big Liam the laughingstock of his neighbors. And

to his contempt for Shawn Kelvin he now added an unreasoning dislike.

Shawn Kelvin had his red-haired woman under his own roof now. He had no illusions about her feelings for him. On himself, and on himself only, lay the task of molding her into a wife and lover.

First he turned his attention to material things. He hired a small servant maid to help her with the housework. Then he bought a horse and cart. And on market days, husband and wife would drive down to the village, do their selling and their buying, and drive home again, with their groceries in the cart and a bundle of second-hand magazines on the seat at Ellen's side. And in the nights, they would sit by the fire, and he would read aloud to her out of the high-colored magazines.

Ellen would sit and listen and smile and go on with her knitting or her sewing. And when the reading was done, they would sit and talk quietly in their own quiet way. For they were both quiet. It was Shawn who did most of the talking. He had a patient, vivid way of picturing for her the things he had seen and felt. And often enough, the stories were funny, and Ellen would chuckle, or throw back her lovely red curls in laughter. It was grand to make her laugh.

Shawn's friends, in some hesitation at first, came up the slope in ones and twos to see them. But Ellen welcomed them with her shy, frank smile, and a table loaded with cakes and heather honey. And at the right time, it was she herself who brought out the decanter of whisky and the polished glasses. Shawn was proud of her. She would sit then and listen to their

discussions and be forever surprised at the knowledgeable man her husband was. And sometimes she would put in a word or two and he listened, too, and they would look to see her smile.

When Ellen first came to Knockanore, her heart held only fear and emptiness. But, for reason piled on reason, she now found herself admiring Shawn Kelvin. A quiet liking came to her for this quiet man who was so gentle and considerate. Then, one great heart-stirring dark night, she found herself fallen head and heels in love with her own husband.

A woman, loving her husband, may or may not be proud of him. But she will fight like a tiger if anyone, except herself, makes fun of him. And there was one man who made fun of Shawn Kelvin: her brother, Big Liam O'Grady. At fair or market or church, Big Liam did not try to hide his contempt and dislike. Ellen knew why. He had lost a wife and farm. He had lost in herself a cheap housekeeper, and he had been made the object of sly humor. And for these things, in some twisted way, he blamed Shawn. Big Liam O'Grady felt contempt for him because Shawn dared not say anything about the old Kelvin land, and would not now even ask for the dowry that was his due.

One evening before market day, Ellen spoke to her husband. "Has Big Liam paid you my dowry yet, Shawn?"

"Sure there's no hurry, girl," said Shawn.

"Have you asked him?"

"I have not. I am not looking for your dowry, Ellen."

"And Big Liam could never understand

that," she said. "You will ask him to-morrow."

"Very well so, my love," agreed Shawn easily.

The next day, in that quiet way of his, he asked Big Liam. But Big Liam was blunt. He had no loose money and Kelvin would have to wait until he had. "Ask me again, little Shawn," he finished, his face in a mocking smile.

His voice had been carelessly loud, and people had heard. They laughed and talked. "The devil's own boy — that Big Liam O'Grady! Stealing the land and keeping his grip on the dowry! He would smash little Shawn at the wind of a word!"

A friend of Shawn's, Matt Tobin the thresher, heard this and called out, "I would like to be there the day Shawn Kelvin loses his temper."

"A bad day for poor Shawn!"

"It might be," said Matt Tobin, "but I would come from the other end of town to see what would be in it for someone."

Shawn had moved away with his wife, not listening or not hearing.

"You see, Ellen?" he said. "The times are hard on the big ranchers, and we don't need the money, anyway."

"Do you think Big Liam does?" Her voice had a cut in it. "He could buy you and all Knockanore. Ask him again."

"But, girl dear, I never wanted a dowry with you."

She liked him to say that, but far better would she like to win for him the respect and admiration that was his due. She must do that now at all costs. Shawn, drawing back now, would be the butt of his fellow men.

Shawn asked Big Liam again, unhappy in his asking. And Shawn asked again a third time. The issue was become a famous one now. Men talked about it, and women, too. Bets were made on it.

The day at last came when Big Liam grew tired of being asked. That was the big October cattle fair at Listowel. He had sold 20 cows at a good price. He had, then, a great roll of bills in his pocket when he saw Shawn and Ellen coming across to where he was bargaining with Matt Tobin for a week's worth of thresh-ing. He had had a drink or two more than was good for him and the whiskey had loosened his tongue. He strode to meet Shawn, and people got out of his savage way.

He caught Shawn by the shoulder — and held him — and bent down to grin in his face.

"What is it, little fellow? Don't be ashamed to ask!"

Matt Tobin was probably the only one there to notice how easily Shawn pulled his shoulder free. Matt's eyes brightened. But Shawn did nothing further and said no word.

The big man laughed. "Go on, you chicken! What do you want?"

"You know, O'Grady."

"I do. Listen, little Shawn!" Again he brought his hand down on Shawn's shoul-der. "Listen, little Shawn! If I had a dowry to give my sister, it would not be a shrimp like you to get her!"

His great hand gripped and he flung Shawn backward as if he were only the image of a man.

Shawn went backward, but he did not fall. He gathered himself like a spring, feet under him, arms raised. But as quickly as the spring coiled, as quickly it slackened. He turned away to his wife. She was there facing him, her face pale and set.

"Woman, woman!" he said in his deep voice. "Why would you and I shame ourselves like this?"

"Shawn!" she cried. "Will you let him shame you now?"

"But your own brother, Ellen — before them all?"

"And he cheating you — " she said.

"What is his dirty money to me? Are you an O'Grady, after all?"

This stung her and she stung him back in one final effort. She placed her hand below her stomach and looked close into his face. She said, "I am an O'Grady. It is a pity that the father of my son is a Kelvin and a coward."

Shawn Kelvin's cheekbones were like hard marble, but his voice was as soft as a dove's.

"Is that the way of it? Let us be going home then."

He took her arm, but she shook his hand off. Yet she walked at his side, head up, through the crowd. Her brother laughed loudly at them.

"That fixes the pair of them!" he cried.

There was talk then — plenty of it. "Did you see the way he flung him? I bet he'll give Big Liam a wide road after this. That's a pound you owe me, Matt Tobin."

"I'll pay it," said Matt Tobin. He stood looking at the ground, his hand rubbing the back of his head. His friend had failed him in the face of the people.

Shawn and Ellen went home, without a single word or glance for each other. And all night, they lay side by side, still and quiet. They slept little. Ellen lay on her side, grieving for what she had said and unable to unsay it. Shawn, on his back, thought about things with a cold clarity. He realized that he was at the fork of life and that a finger pointed the way. He must do a thing so final that, once done, it could never again be questioned. Before morning, he came to his decision. He said to himself, "Oh, you fool! You might have known that you should never have taken an O'Grady without breaking the O'Gradys."

He got up early in the morning at his usual hour and went out, as usual, to his morning chores. Then he returned and spoke for the first time.

"Ellen, will you come with me down to see your brother?"

She hesitated, her hands thrown wide in a helpless, hopeless gesture. "Little use you going to see my brother, Shawn. I should go and — and not come back."

"Don't blame me now or later, Ellen. It has been put on me and the thing I am going to do is the only thing to be done. Will you come?"

"Very well," she agreed. "I will be ready in a minute."

They went to Big Liam O'Grady's farmhouse. From behind a barn came the purr and zoom of a threshing machine. Shawn tied the horse to the wheel of a farm cart and, with Ellen, approached the house.

A servant girl leaned over the kitchen half-door and pointed toward the barn.

The master was out back and should she run across for him?

"Never mind!" said Shawn, "I'll get him. Ellen, will you go in and wait?"

"No," said Ellen, "I'll come with you." She knew her brother.

As they went toward the barn, the purr and zoom grew louder. Turning the corner, they walked into the midst of activity. A long double row of cornstacks stretched across the yard. Between them, Matt Tobin's threshing machine was busy. Matt

than 40 men about the place. As was the custom, all of Big Liam's friends and neighbors were giving him a hand with the harvesting.

Big Liam came around the machine. "Look who's here!"

He was in his worst of tempers this morning. He took two slow steps and stopped, feet set wide apart.

"What is it this time?" he shouted. That was the un-Irish welcome he gave his sister and her husband.

Shawn and Ellen came forward. As they came, Matt Tobin slowed down his engine. Big Liam heard the change and looked angrily over his shoulder.

"What do you mean, Tobin? Get on with the threshing!"

"Big Liam, this is my engine, and if you don't like it, you can leave it!" said Matt Tobin.

"We will see in a minute," he said, and turned to the two now near at hand.

"What is it?" he growled.

"A private word with you. I won't keep you long." Shawn was calm and cold.

"You will not — on a busy morning," sneered the big man. "There is no need for private words between me and Shawn Kelvin."

"There is a need," urged Shawn. "It will be best for us all if you hear what I have to say in your own house."

"Or here on my own land. Out with it! I don't care who hears!"

Shawn looked around him. Up on the machine, up on the straw stacks, men leaned idle on fork handles and looked down at him. He was in the middle of Clan O'Grady, for they were mostly

Tobin himself was feeding the firebox with pieces of hard black peat. Up on a platform, men were feeding the machine. As the machine bit at the corn, it made an angry snarl that changed and slowed into a satisfied zoom. There were not fewer

O'Grady men. Matt Tobin was the only man he could call a friend. Very well! Since he had to prove himself, it was fitting that he do it here in front of the O'Grady men.

Shawn brought his eyes back to Big Liam. "O'Grady," said he, "you set a great store by money."

"No harm in that. You do it yourself, little Shawn."

"Take it so! I will play your game. You would bargain your sister and cheat! Listen, you big brute! You owe me two hundred pounds. Will you pay it?" There was an iron ring in his voice.

"I will pay it when I am ready."

"Today."

"No, and not tomorrow."

"Right. If you break your bargain, I break mine."

"What's that?" shouted Big Liam.

"If you keep your two hundred pounds, you keep your sister."

"What is it?" shouted Big Liam again. "What is that you say?"

"You heard me. Here is your sister Ellen! Keep her!"

He was completely astounded. "You can't do that!"

"It is done," said Shawn.

Ellen O'Grady had been quiet as a statue at Shawn's side. But now, slow like doom, she faced him. She leaned forward and looked into his eyes and saw the pain behind the strength.

"You do this to the mother of your son, Shawn Kelvin?" She whispered gently to him.

His face was like stone.

"I know — I know!" That was all she said, and walked quietly to where Matt Tobin stood.

Matt Tobin placed a hand on her arm.

"Give him time," he whispered. "Give him his own time. He's slow but he's deadly as a tiger when he moves."

Big Liam was no fool. He knew how far he could go. Whatever people thought of Kelvin, public opinion would be dead against him. He must change his stance while he had time. He threw up his head and laughed.

"You fool! I was only making fun of you. What are your dirty few pounds to the likes of me? Stay where you are."

He turned and walked angrily into the house.

Shawn Kelvin was left alone in that wide ring of men. Now they looked at one another, looked at Shawn Kelvin, frowned, and shook their heads. They knew Big Liam. They knew that, giving up the money, his savagery would break out. They waited to prevent him from going too far.

Shawn Kelvin did not look at anyone. He stood still as a rock, his face calm.

Big Liam was back in two minutes. He walked straight to Shawn and stopped within a foot of him.

"Look, little Shawn!" In his hand was a crumpled bundle of bank notes. "Here is your money. Take it, and then see what will happen to you. Take it!" He thrust it into Shawn's hand. "Count it. Make sure you have it all — and then I will kick you out of this yard. Count it!"

Shawn did not count it. Instead he crumpled it into a ball in his strong fingers. Then he turned on his heels and walked to the front of the engine. He gestured to Matt Tobin, but it was Ellen, quick as a flash, who obeyed the gesture. Although her hand got scorched, she jerked open the door of the firebox. Then Shawn Kelvin, with one easy sweep, threw the crumpled ball of notes into the heart of the flames.

Big Liam gave one mighty shout. No, it was more an anguished scream than a shout — "My money! My money!"

He gave two furious bounds forward, his great arms raised to crush and kill. But his hands never touched the small man.

"You dumb ox!" said Shawn Kelvin. His shoulder moved a little, but no one there could follow the terrific drive of that right hook. The smack of bone on bone was sharp as a whip crack. Big Liam stopped dead, went back on his heel, and staggered back three steps.

"Now and forever! Man of the Kelvins!" roared Matt Tobin.

But Big Liam was a man of iron. That blow should have laid him out on his back. Blows like that had tied men to the ground for the full count. But Big Liam only shook his head, and drove in at the little man. And the little man, instead of circling away, drove in at him.

The men of the O'Gradys saw then a show that they had not knowledge enough to appreciate fully. Back in the States, thousands had paid as much as $10 each to see the prizefighter, the great Tiger Kelvin, in action. And never was his action more devastating than now.

Big Liam never touched Shawn with clenched fist. He did not know how. Shawn, 40 pounds lighter, drove him across the yard with punches.

Shawn set out to demolish his enemy in the shortest time possible, and it took him five minutes to do it. Five, six, eight times he knocked the big man down. At last, Shawn finished him with his terrible double hit — left below the breastbone and right under the jaw.

Big Liam lifted on his toes and fell flat on his back.

Shawn did not waste a glance at the fallen giant. He swung full circle on the O'Grady men, his iron voice challenging: "I am Shawn Kelvin, of Knockanore Hill. Is there an O'Grady who thinks himself a better man? Come then."

His face was deep-carved stone. His great chest lifted, the air whistled through his nose. His eyes dared them.

No man came.

He swung around then and walked to his wife. He stopped before her.

His face was still of stone.

"Mother of my son, will you come home with me?

She looked in his eyes. "Is it so you ask me, Shawn Kelvin?"

His face of stone softened at last. "As my wife only — Ellen Kelvin!"

"Very well, heart's treasure." She caught his arm in both of hers. "Let us be going home."

And she went with him, proud as the morning.

READING COMPREHENSION

Summarizing. Choose the best phrase to complete each sentence. Then write the complete statements on your paper.

1. Big Liam let Ellen marry Shawn in order to _____ (be free to marry Kathy Carey, get a dowry from Shawn, see Ellen living happily).

2. After being married for a time, Ellen found she had _____ (stopped loving her husband, fallen in love with Shawn, fallen in love with another man).

3. Big Liam showed his contempt for Shawn by _____ (refusing to visit the married couple, not paying Ellen's dowry, asking Shawn for money).

4. In the fight, _____ (Big Liam defeated Shawn, Shawn defeated Big Liam, both men were knocked out).

Interpreting. Write the answer to each question on your paper.

1. Why did Shawn avoid a fight with Liam?

2. How did Shawn's and Liam's personalities differ?

3. Why did Shawn burn the dowry money?

For Thinking and Discussing. Why do you think Shawn was called "the quiet man"? Was this a title of respect or contempt? Explain your answer.

UNDERSTANDING LITERATURE

Character. You know you can learn about characters by their speech, thoughts, and actions. You consider all these things and then draw conclusions about each character's personality. This is called *indirect characterization.*

For example, you could tell that Shawn scorned Big Liam O'Grady's money. His words showed it when he said to Ellen, "What is his dirty money to me?" His actions also showed it when he burned the dowry. These incidents told you about Shawn indirectly.

Sometimes an author also describes a character directly. This is called *direct characterization.*

For example, you learned that Shawn was a quiet man. You did not conclude this from Shawn's actions or speech. Instead, you were told directly: ". . . he was a quiet man, not given to talking about himself and the things he had done."

Choose one character from the story. Write three things that you learn directly about the character. Then write three things that you learn indirectly about the same person. Be sure to include the story sentences that support your conclusions.

WRITING

The story ends with Shawn and Ellen riding home together. Write a dialogue of what they might have said to each other. Base the conversation on the things you have learned about each character.

The Test of Courage

by Liam O'Flaherty

*It is not often that a simple boyhood adventure turns into
an opportunity for a young man to display intelligence,
courage, and leadership—in fact, to grow up almost
overnight. Michael O'Hara has just such an experience.*

At sundown on a summer evening, Michael O'Hara and Peter Cooke left their village with great secrecy. Crouching behind fences, they made a wide circuit and then ran all the way to a little rock-bound harbor that lay a mile to the southwest. They carried their caps in their hands as they ran and they panted with excitement. They were about to execute a plan of adventure which they had devised for weeks. They were going to take Jimmy the weaver's boat out for a night's bream fishing.

Michael O'Hara was twelve years and four months, five months younger than his comrade. He had very intelligent eyes of a deep-blue color and his fair hair stood up on end like close-cropped bristles. He looked slender and rather delicate in his blue jersey and grey flannel trousers that only reached half way down his bare shins. Although it was he who had conceived and planned the adventure, just as he planned all the adventures of the two comrades, he now lagged far behind in the race to the port. This was partly due to his inferior speed. It was also due to a nervous reaction against embarking on an expedition that would cause grave anxiety to his parents.

Peter Cooke looked back after reaching the great mound of boulders that lined the head of the harbor. He frowned and halted when he saw his companion far behind. His sturdy body seemed to be too large for his clothes, which were identical with those worn by O'Hara. His hair was black and curly. His face was freckled. He had the heavy jaws and thick nose of a fighter. His small grey eyes, set close together, lacked the intelligence of Michael O'Hara's eyes.

"Hurry on," he cried in a loud whisper, when Michael came closer. "What ails you? Are you tired already?"

Michael looked back over his shoulder furtively.

"I thought I saw somebody," he said in a nervous tone.

"Who?" said Peter. "Who did you see?"

"Over there," Michael said.

He pointed towards the north in the direction of the village, which was now half hidden by the intervening land. Only the thatched roofs and the smoking chimneys of the houses were visible. The smoke rose straight up from the chimneys in the still twilight. To the west of the village ran a lane, its low fence standing out against the fading horizon of the sky like a curtain full of irregular holes.

"I think it was my mother I saw coming home from milking the cow along the lane," Michael said in a voice that was slightly regretful. "I just saw her head over the fence, but it looked like her shawl. I don't think she saw me, though. Even if she did see me, she wouldn't know who it was."

"Come on," Peter said. "She couldn't see you that far away. We have to hurry or it will be dark before we get the curragh in the water."

As nimbly as goats, the two boys ran down the sloping mound of granite boulders and along the flat stretch of grey limestone that reached out to the limit of the tide. Then they went into a cave beneath a low cliff that bordered the shore. They brought the gear they had hidden in this cave down to the sea's edge and dropped it at the point where they were to launch the boat.

"Do you think we'll be able to carry her down, Peter?" Michael said, as they ran back across the mound of boulders to fetch the boat.

Peter halted suddenly and looked at his comrade. He was irritated by the nervous tone of Michael's voice.

"Are you getting afraid?" he said roughly.

"Who? Me?" said Michael indignantly.

"If you are," said Peter, "say the word and we'll go back home. I don't want to go out with you if you start whinging."

"Who's whinging?" Michael said. "I only thought we mightn't be able to carry her down to the rock. Is there any harm in that?"

"Come on," said Peter, "and stop talking nonsense. Didn't we get under her four times to see could we raise her? We raised her, didn't we? If we could raise her, we can carry her. Jimmy the weaver can rise under her all by himself and he's

an old man. He's such a weak old man, too, that no crew in the village would take him out fishing with them. It would be a shame if the two of us weren't as strong as Jimmy the weaver."

"I hope he won't put a curse on us," Michael said as they walked along, "when he finds out that we took his curragh. He's terrible for cursing when he gets angry. I've seen him go on his two knees and curse when two eggs were stolen from under his goose and she hatching. He pulled up his trousers and cursed on his naked knees."

"He'd be an ungrateful man," Peter said, "if he put a curse on us after all we've done for him during the past week. Four times we drew water from the well for him. We dug potatoes for him in his little garden twice and we gave him a rabbit that we caught. The whole village would throw stones at his house if he put a curse on us after we doing all that for him."

All the village boats usually rested on the flat ground behind the mound of granite boulders. There was a little wall of loose stones around each boat to protect it from the great south winds that sometimes blew in from the ocean. At present only the weaver's boat remained in its stone pen, lying bottom up within its pro-

tecting wall, with stone props under the transoms to keep it from the ground. All the other pens were empty, for it was the height of the bream season and the men were at sea.

"Come on now," Peter said when they reached the boat. "Lift up the bow."

They got on each side of the bow and raised it without difficulty.

"You get under it now and settle yourself," Peter said.

Michael crouched and got under the boat, with his face towards the stern. He rested his shoulders against the front seat and braced his elbows against the frame. Although they had practiced raising the boat, he now began to tremble lest he might not be able to bear the weight when Peter raised the stern.

"Keep your legs well apart," Peter said, "and stand loose same as I told you."

"I'm ready," Michael said nervously. "You go ahead and raise her."

Peter put on his cap with the peak turned backwards. Then he set himself squarely under the stern of the boat. He gritted his teeth and made his strong back rigid. Then he drew in a deep breath and made a sudden effort. He raised the boat and then spread his legs to distribute the weight. Both boys staggered for a few moments, as they received the full weight of the boat on their shoulders.

"Are you balanced?" Peter said.

"Go ahead," said Michael.

Peter led the way, advancing slowly with the rhythmic movement of his body which he had copied from his elders. He held his body rigid above the hips, which swayed as he threw his legs forward

limply in an outward arc. As each foot touched the ground, he lowered his hips and then raised them again with the shifting of weight to the other foot.

Michael tried to imitate this movement, but he was unable to do it well, owing to his nervousness. In practice he had been just as good as Peter. Now, however, the memory of his mother's shawled head kept coming into his mind to disturb him.

"Try to keep in step," Peter called out, "and don't grip the frame. Let your shoulders go dead."

"I'm doing my best," Michael said, "but it keeps shifting on my shoulders."

"That's because you're taking a grip with your hands. Let your shoulders go dead."

They were both exhausted when they finally laid down the boat on the weed-covered rock by the sea's edge. They had to rest a little while. Then they gently pushed the boat into the water over the smooth carpet of red weed. They had to do this very carefully, because the coracle was just a light frame of thin pine lathes covered with tarred canvas. The least contact with a sliver of stone, or even with a limpet cone, would have put a hole in the canvas. Fortunately the sea was dead calm, and they managed the launching without accident.

"Now, in God's name," Peter said, imitating a man's voice, as he dipped his hand in the seawater and made the Sign of the Cross on his forehead according to ritual, "I'll go aboard and put her under way. You hand in the gear when I bring her stern to shore."

He got into the prow seat, unshipped

the oars and dipped them in the water before fixing them on the tholepins. Then he maneuvered the stern of the boat face to the rock. Michael threw aboard the gear, which included a can of half-baited limpets for bait, four lines coiled on small wooden frames, half a loaf of bread rolled up in a piece of cloth, and the anchor rope with a large granite stone attached. Then he also dipped his right hand in the brine water and made the Sign of the Cross on his forehead.

"In God's name," he said reverently, as he put one knee on the stern and pushed against the rock with his foot, "head her out."

As Peter began to row, Michael took his seat on the after transom and unshipped his oars. He dipped them in the water and put the oars in the tholepins.

"Face land, right hand underneath," Peter called out just like a grownup captain giving orders to his crew.

"I'm with you," Michael said. "Head her out."

The two boys rowed well, keeping time perfectly. Soon they had cleared the mouth of the little harbor and they were in the open sea. Night was falling, but they could see the dark cluster of village boats beneath a high cliff to the west. They turned east.

"Take a mark now and keep her straight," Peter said.

Michael brought two points on the dim land to the west into line with the stern and they rowed eastwards until they came abreast of a great pile of rock that had fallen from the cliff. Here they cast anchor. When they had tied the anchor rope to the cross-stick in the bow, the boat swung round and became motionless on the still water.

"Oh! You devil!" Peter said excitedly. "Out with the lines now and let us fish. Wouldn't it be wonderful if we caught a boatload of bream. We'd be the talk of the whole parish."

"Maybe we will," cried Michael, equally excited.

Now he was undisturbed by the memory of his mother's shawled head. Nor was he nervous about his position, out at night on a treacherous ocean in a frail coracle. The wild rapture of adventure had taken full possession of him.

Such was the haste with which they baited and paid out their lines that they almost transfixed their hands with the hooks. Each boy paid out two lines, one on either side of the boat. They had cast anchor right in the midst of a school of bream. Peter was the first to get his lines into water. They had barely sunk when he got a strike on both of them.

"Oh! You devil!" he cried. "I've got two."

In his excitement he tried to haul the two lines simultaneously and lost both of the soft-lipped fish. In the meantime, Michael also got a strike on one of his lines. He swallowed his breath and hauled rapidly. A second fish struck while he was hauling the first line. He also became greedy and grabbed the second line, letting the first fish escape. But he landed the second fish.

"Oh! Peter," he cried, "we'll fill the boat like you said."

He put the fish smartly between his

knees and pulled the hook from its mouth. He dropped it on the bottom of the boat, where it began to beat a tattoo with its tail.

"Oh! You devil!" Peter cried. "The sea is full of them."

He had again thrown his lines into the water and two fish immediately impaled themselves on the hooks. This time he landed both fish, as the lessening of excitement enabled him to use his skill.

"We should have brought more limpets," Michael said. "This lot we brought won't be half enough!"

The fish continued to strike. Despite losing a large percentage, they had caught thirty-five before an accident drove the boat away from the school. A light breeze had come up from the land. It hardly made a ripple on the surface of the sea, yet its impact caused the boat to lean away from the restraint of the anchor rope. The rope went taut. Then the anchor stone slipped from the edge of a reef on which it had dropped. Falling into deeper water, it could not find ground. The boat swung round and began to drift straight out to sea, pressed by the gentle breeze.

The two boys, intent on their fishing, did not notice the accident. Soon, however, the fish ceased to strike. They did not follow the boat into deep water. The lines hung idly over the sides.

"They're gone," Michael said. "Do you think it's time for us to go home?"

"We can't go home yet," Peter said indignantly. "We have only thirty-five fish yet. Wait until they begin to strike again when the tide turns. Then you'll see that we'll fill the boat. In any case, we can't go

back until the moon rises. It's too dark now to make our way past the reef."

"It's dark all right," Michael said in a low voice. "I can't see land, although it's so near."

Now that the fish had gone away, the vision of his mother's shawled head returned to prick his conscience, and the darkness frightened him as it always did. Yet he dared not insist on trying to make port, lest Peter might think he was a coward.

"They'll start biting again," Peter continued eagerly. "You wait and see. We'll fill the boat. Then the moon will be up, and it will be lovely rowing into port. Won't they be surprised when they see all the fish we have? They won't say a word to us when we bring home that awful lot of fish."

Michael shuddered on being reminded of the meeting with his parents after this escapade.

"I'm hungry," he said. "Do you think we should eat our bread? No use bringing it back home again."

"I'm hungry, too," Peter said. "Let's eat the bread while we're waiting for the tide to turn."

They divided the half loaf and began to eat ravenously. When they had finished, Michael felt cold and sleepy.

"We should have brought more clothes to put on us," he said. "The sea gets awful cold at night, doesn't it?"

"Let's lie up in the bow," Peter said, "I feel cold myself. We'll lie together in the shelter of the bow while we're waiting for the tide to turn. That way we won't feel the cold in the shelter of the bow."

They lay down in the bow side by side. There was just room enough for their two bodies stretched close together.

"It's much warmer this way sure enough," Michael said sleepily.

"It's just like being in bed," Peter said. "Oh! You devil! When I grow up I'll be a sailor. Then I can sleep every night out in the middle of the sea."

They fell asleep almost at once. In their sleep they put their arms about one another. The moon rose and its eerie light fell on them, as they lay asleep in the narrow bow, rocked gently by the boat's movement, to the soft music of the lapping water. The moonlight fell on the dark sides of the boat that drifted before the breeze. It shone on the drifting lines that hung from the black sides, like the tentacles of an evil monster that was carrying the sleeping boys out far over the empty ocean. The dead fish were covered with a phosphorescent glow when the boat swayed towards the moon.

Then the moonlight faded and dawn came over the sea. The sun rose in the east and its rays began to dance on the black canvas. Michael was the first to awaken. He uttered a cry of fright when he looked about him and discovered where he was. The land was now at a great distance. It was little more than a dot on the far horizon. He gripped Peter by the head with both hands.

"Wake up, Peter," he cried. "Oh! Wake up. Something terrible has happened."

Thinking he was at home in bed, Peter tried to push Michael away and to turn over on his other side.

"It's not time to get up yet," he muttered.

When he finally was roused and realized what had happened, he was much more frightened than Michael.

"Oh! You devil!" he said. "We pulled anchor. We're lost."

There was a look of ignorant panic in his small eyes. Michael bit his lip in an effort to keep himself from crying out loud. It was a great shock to find that Peter, who had always been the leader of the two comrades and who had never before shown any signs of fear, was now in panic.

"We're not lost," he said angrily.

"Will you look at where the land is?" cried Peter. "Will you look?"

Suddenly Michael felt that he no longer wanted to cry. His eyes got a hard and almost cruel expression in them.

"Stand up, will you?" he said sharply. "Let me pull the rope."

Peter looked at Michael stupidly and got out of the way. He sat on the forward transom, while Michael hauled in the anchor rope.

"What could we do?" he said. "We're lost unless they come and find us. We could never row that far with the wind against us."

"Why don't you give me a hand with the rope and stop whinging?" cried Michael angrily.

Peter was roused by this insult from a boy whom he had until now been able to dominate. He glared at Michael, spat on his hands and jumped to his feet.

"Get out of my way," he said gruffly. "Give me a hold of that rope. Look who's talking about whinging."

With his superior strength, Peter quickly got the rope and anchor stone into the bow. Then the two of them hauled in the lines. They did not trouble to wind them on the frames but left them lying in a tangled heap on the bottom.

"Hurry up," Peter kept saying. "We have to hurry out of here."

Still roused to anger by Michael's insult, he got out his oars and turned the bow towards the dot of land on the horizon. Michael also got out his oars.

"Left hand on top," Peter shouted, "and give it your strength. Stretch to it. Stretch."

"We better take it easy," Michael said. "We have a long way to go."

"Stretch to it, I tell you," Peter shouted still more loudly. "Give it your strength if you have any."

As soon as he found the oars in his hands, as a means of escape from what he feared, he allowed himself again to go into a panic. He rowed wildly, leaping from the transom with each stroke.

"Why can't you keep time?" Michael shouted at him. "Keep time with the stern. You'll only kill yourself that way."

"Row, you devil, and stop talking," cried Peter. "Give length to your stroke and you'll be able to row with me."

"But you're supposed to keep with me," Michael said. "You're supposed to keep with the stern."

Suddenly Peter pulled so hard that he fell right back off the transom into the bow. One of the oars jumped off the thole pin as he fell backwards. It dropped over the side of the boat and began to drift astern. Michael turned the boat and picked up the oar.

"Don't do that again," he said as he gave the oar to Peter. "Listen to what I tell you and row quietly."

Peter looked in astonishment at the cruel eyes of his comrade. He was now completely dominated by them.

"It's no use, Michael," he said dejectedly. "You see the land is as far away as ever. It's no use trying to row."

"We'll make headway if we row quietly," Michael said. "Come on now. Keep time with the stern."

Now that he had surrendered to the will of his comrade, Peter rowed obediently in time with the stern oars. The boat began to make good way.

"That's better," Michael said, when they had been rowing a little while. "They'll soon be out looking for us. All we have to do is keep rowing."

"And where would they be looking for us?" said Peter. "Sure nobody saw us leave the port."

"They'll see the boat is gone," Michael said. "Why can't you have sense? I bet they're out looking for us now. All we have to do is to keep rowing quietly."

"And how would they see us?" Peter said after a pause. "We can hardly see the land from here, even though it's so big. How could they see this curragh from the land and it no bigger than a thimble on the water?"

Michael suddenly raised his voice and said angrily:

"Is it how you want us to lie down and let her drift away until we die of hunger and thirst? Stop talking and row quietly. You'll only tire yourself with your talk."

"Don't you be shouting at me, Michael O'Hara," Peter cried. "You better watch out for yourself. Is it how you think I'm afraid of you?"

They rowed in silence after that for more than two hours. The boat made good way, and the land became much more distinct on the horizon. It kept rising up from the ocean and assuming its normal shape. Then Peter dropped his oars and let his head hang forward on his chest. Michael went forward to him.

"I'm thirsty," Peter said. "I'm dying with the thirst. Is there any sign of anybody coming?"

"There is no sign yet, Peter," Michael said gently. "We have to have courage, though. They'll come all right. Let you lie down in the bow for a while. I'll put your jersey over your face to keep the sun from touching you. That way you won't feel the thirst so much. I heard my father say so."

He had to help Peter into the bow, as the older boy was completely helpless with exhaustion. He pulled off Peter's jersey and put it over his face.

"Lie there for a while," he said, "and I'll keep her from drifting. Then you can spell me."

He returned to his seat and continued to row. He suffered terribly from thirst. He was also beginning to feel the first pangs of sea-hunger. Yet he experienced an exaltation that made him impervious to this torture. Ever since his imagination had begun to develop, he had been plagued by the fear that he would not be able to meet danger with courage. Even though he deliberately sought out little dangers and tested himself against them without flinching, he continued to believe that the nervousness he felt on these occasions was a sign of cowardice and that he would fail when the big test came.

Now that the big test had come, he experienced the first dark rapture of manhood instead of fear. His blue eyes were no longer soft and dreamy. They had a look of somber cruelty in them, the calm arrogance of the fighting male. His mind was at peace, because he was now free from the enemy that had lurked within him. Even the pain in his bowels and in his parched throat only served to excite the triumphant will of his awakening manhood. When his tired muscles could hardly clutch the oars within his blistered palms, he still continued to row mechanically.

In the afternoon, when the village boats finally came to the rescue, Michael was still sitting on his transom, trying to row feebly. By then he was so exhausted that he did not hear the approach of the boats until a man shouted from the nearest one of them. Hearing the shout, he fell from his seat in a faint.

When he recovered consciousness, he was in the bow of his father's boat. His father was holding a bottle of water to his lips. He looked up into his father's rugged face and smiled when he saw there was no anger in it. On the contrary, he had never before seen such tenderness in his father's stern eyes.

"Was it how you dragged anchor?" his father said.

Although his upper lip was twitching with emotion, he spoke in a casual tone, as to a comrade.

"It could happen to the best of men," the father continued thoughtfully after Michael had nodded his head. "There's no harm done though, thank God."

He put some clothes under the boy's head, caressed him roughly and told him to go to sleep. Michael closed his eyes. In another boat, Peter's father was shouting in an angry tone.

Michael opened his eyes again when his father and the other men in the boat had begun to row. He looked at the muscular back of his father, who was rowing in the bow seat. A wave of ardent love for his father swept through his blood, making him feel tender and weak. Tears began to stream from his eyes, but they were tears of joy because his father had looked at him with tenderness and spoken to him as to a comrade.

READING COMPREHENSION

Summarizing. Choose the best phrase to complete each sentence. Then write the complete statements on your paper.

1. Michael and Peter had devised a plan to _____ (run away, steal fish from the other boats, take Jimmy the weaver's boat out for a night of fishing).

2. The boys stopped catching fish because _____ (it was too dark, they ran out of bait, there were no fish in the deep water where they had drifted).

3. When the boys woke up to find that they had drifted far away from land, Peter was the one who _____ (panicked, took charge, was amused).

Interpreting. Write the answer to each question on your paper.

1. Why did Michael and Peter have to sneak out of the village?

2. Which of the two boys had the upper hand at the beginning of the adventure? How do you know?

3. How did Michael show that he had more sense and courage than Peter when they were in danger?

4. Why did Michael feel so much love for his father at the end of the story?

For Thinking and Discussing. How did Michael and Peter change roles from the beginning of the story to the end? What was the author trying to say about outer strength and inner strength?

UNDERSTANDING LITERATURE

Character. When we read a story, we become aware of the personality of each character. Some characters are very simple and show only one trait throughout a story. These are called *flat characters*. Other characters are more complex and show many different and sometimes even opposite personality traits. These are called *round characters*. Round characters are like people in real life. They reveal a variety of traits in response to different events and other people.

Michael O'Hara and Peter Cooke in "The Test of Courage" are round characters. The following statements tell about their personality traits. Write a sentence describing something the character did, thought, or said to support each statement.

1. Michael was nervous about disobeying his parents.

2. Peter was confident and bossy.

3. Both boys loved adventure.

4. Peter became frightened and panicky in the face of danger.

5. Michael had the courage to act sensibly in the face of danger.

WRITING

Write about a personal experience that brought out a personality trait that you don't usually exhibit. Describe how the experience affected your view of yourself.

Section Review

VOCABULARY

Base Words. Sometimes a story has a word you may not know. However, you might recognize a smaller word, or words, within the larger word. The base word can help you understand the meaning of the larger, unfamiliar word.

Example: Nnaemeka was unhappy about his father's *opposition* to Nene.

You may not know the word *opposition*, but you might know the word *opposite*. If you know the word *opposite*, you may figure out that *opposition* means "the act of being against."

Write the best word to complete each sentence.

1. Nnaemeka's marriage left Okeke in *amazement*, meaning Okeke was _____.

   pleased   surprised   shy

2. Master Cornille's cruel *treatment* of his granddaughter meant that he _____ badly toward her.
   looked   smelled   acted

3. Andrés de la O was famous for his *politeness*, meaning he was _____.
   rude   mannerly   brave

4. Liam O'Grady's *acceptance* of Shawn's offer meant he would _____ it.
   take   ignore   consider

READING

Comparison and Contrast. Sometimes you may read two stories that are similar. The stories may have characters who act the same way or think alike. You can *compare* the characters to see how they are similar. You can *contrast* the characters to see how they are different.

For example, both "Marriage Is a Private Affair" and "The Quiet Man" are stories about marriage. You could compare Nnaemeka and Shawn because each loved his wife. You could also contrast them because Shawn was willing to give up his wife, while Nnaemeka was not.

Choose the best phrase to complete each sentence. Then write the entire sentence.

1. Master Cornille and Okeke were similar because both _____.
   a. lived a life of ease
   b. did not want to accept change
   c. disliked the railroad

2. Andrés de la O and Big Liam O'Grady were different because Andrés _____.
   a. was kinder to women
   b. was not afraid to fight
   c. enjoyed having a housekeeper

3. Master Cornille and Raquel were similar because both _____.
   a. disliked grandchildren
   b. thought war was exciting
   c. believed strongly in honor

4. Michael and Peter were different because Michael _____.
   a. liked adventure
   b. was level-headed
   c. was physically stronger

WRITING

A Composition. A composition is made up of several paragraphs on a single topic. It begins with an introductory paragraph and ends with a conclusion. Each of the other paragraphs covers a single aspect of the topic.

Step 1: Set Your Goal

When you choose a topic for a composition, it should be one about which you know something or in which you are especially interested. For this composition assignment, choose one of the countries in which the stories in this section take place — Nigeria, France, Mexico, or Ireland — as your topic.

After you have selected a topic, you will need to narrow it by choosing a certain aspect to write about. For example, if you chose Nigeria as your topic, you might narrow it to some aspect of its geography, history, or the customs and traditions of its people. Your limited topic might be the customs and traditions surrounding marriage. Your composition should be about five paragraphs. Limit your topic until it seems narrow enough to cover in this amount of space.

Next, define your purpose. The main purpose of your composition is to inform your readers about a subject. Your specific purpose is the exact kind of information you are going to present. The following is an example:

PURPOSE: To inform the reader of the various customs and traditions surrounding marriage in different parts of Nigeria.

Write down your statement of purpose so that you can refer to it while you write.

Step 2: Make a Plan

Once you have narrowed your topic and defined your purpose, you need to gather information and ideas for the body of your composition. Begin by writing down the facts and ideas you want to include. You will probably have to do some research to come up with all the facts you need. As you research, take notes on the information you think you might use.

Once you have gathered all the information you want to include in your composition, the next step is to organize the information into groups of similar ideas. Each group should cover one main idea. Try to organize your notes into three groups. Each group will make up one paragraph in the body of your composition.

Step 3: Write a First Draft

Now it is time to write the first draft of your composition. Don't worry about writing perfectly. Later, when you revise, you can add, take out, and change words and sentences to make your composition better. For now, just try to put your facts and ideas into sentences and arrange them into paragraphs.

Write the body of your composition before you write the introduction and conclusion. Using your organized notes as a guide, write one paragraph to cover each group of ideas. Be sure each paragraph has a topic sentence that states the main idea of the paragraph. When you finish writing the body of your composition, read it over to make sure the paragraphs are in the best order.

The introduction serves two purposes: (1) It tells what the composition is about; and (2) it encourages the reader to read on. Write an introductory paragraph of three to five sentences. Then write a brief conclusion to sum up what you have written. Finally, give your composition a title.

Step 4: Revise

After you have finished writing your draft, set it aside for a day. When you return to your work, it will be easier to notice changes you should make. Ask yourself the following questions as you revise:

☐ Does the introduction tell what the composition is about? Does it grab the reader's attention?

☐ Does each paragraph contain a topic sentence? Do the sentences in each paragraph relate to the main idea?

☐ Are the paragraphs arranged so that they flow smoothly?

☐ Does the conclusion summarize the information in the body of the composition?

☐ Does the title relate to the purpose of your composition?

When you have finished revising your composition, read it over for errors in spelling, capitalization, punctuation, and grammar. Then make a final copy.

QUIZ

The following is a quiz on Section 3. Write the answers in complete sentences on your paper.

Reading Comprehension

1. In "Marriage Is a Private Affair," how did Nnaemeka and his father differ on the issue of marriage?

2. In "Master Cornille's Secret," what was the secret Master Cornille managed to keep for so long?

3. In "The Sparrow," why did the sparrow attack the dog?

4. In "The Ring of General Macías," why did Raquel poison Andrés and Cleto?

5. In "The Quiet Man," how did Shawn finally manage to get his dowry from Big Liam?

Understanding Literature

6. Write some of the things you learned about Okeke through direct characterization and through indirect characterization.

7. What conflicts did Master Cornille face? Which, if any, were examples of people against themselves? People against other people?

8. What conflicts does the speaker in "Fear" face? What kind of mother do you think she is?

9. What did you learn about Raquel through her actions? Her speech? Her thoughts?

10. How did Michael and Peter's relationship change at the end of the story?

ACTIVITIES

Word Attack. In "The Diary of Anaïs Nin," you read that Nin had the "aspiration to escape the servitudes of women." The word *servitude* is made up of the base word *serve* and the suffix *-tude*. The suffix *-tude* indicates "a condition or state of being." *Servitude*, therefore, means "a condition or state of being in another's service." Write the meaning of each of the words below. Then use each one in a sentence. Check a dictionary if you need help.

plenitude   multitude   exactitude
fortitude   magnitude   quietude

Speaking and Listening

1. "Fear" is a poem that expresses how a mother feels about the world's changing her daughter and the effect that would have on their relationship. Practice reading the poem aloud. Try to convey the emotion that the poem evokes. Be prepared to read it aloud.

2. With a classmate, act out one of the following scenes. Be prepared to present the scene for your class.
   a. In "Marriage Is a Private Affair," the conversation between Nnaemeka and his father when they discussed the marriage question.
   b. The scene in "The Ring of General Macías" between Andrés and Raquel after Andrés first entered the house.
   c. The scene in "A Test of Courage" when Michael and Peter realized that they had drifted out to sea and began to row back to shore.

Researching

1. The play "The Ring of General Macías" takes place during the Mexican Revolution. Do some research about it. When and why did it begin? How long did it last? Who was fighting whom? Who led the revolutionary forces? Did the United States play any role in the revolution? Present your findings to the class.

2. "The Test of Courage" takes place near a sea village along the coast of Ireland. Some of the words used in the story are typical of that kind of environment and are probably not familiar to you. Look at the list of words below from the story. Find the meaning of each one.

bream   curragh   limpet
transom   coracle   bow
port   stern

Creating

1. Write a short newspaper account of the events of Master Cornille's secret. Tell who, what, where, when, why, and how. Describe Master Cornille's character and the way the town responded to his problem.

2. In "Marriage Is a Private Affair," Okeke and his son Nnaemeka disagreed about how a marriage partner should be chosen. Write a paragraph or two telling about your views on how one should choose a husband or a wife. Tell whether you think your parents would agree or disagree with you.

211

SECTION 4

ARTISTS AT WORK

A piper in the streets today
Set up, and tuned, and started to play
And away, away, away on the tide
Of his music we started; on every side
Doors and windows were opened wide
And men left down their work and came,
And women with petticoats colored like flame,
And little bare feet that were blue with cold
Went dancing back to the age of gold,
and all the world went gay, went gay
For half an hour in the street today.

—Seumas O'Sullivan
Ireland

Paul Helleu Sketching with His Wife
John Singer Sargent (1856-1925)
The Brooklyn Museum, Museum Collection Fund

Artists at Work

A work of art can change our whole idea of the world. How do artists work? Why do they create? Writers have always been fascinated by the artist's special power.

Sources of Inspiration

Where do artists find the subjects that inspire their work? The relationship between artist and subject is the theme of many works of literature. Writers tell us that an artist's energy and inspiration often come from love.

In Lin Yutang's story "The Jade Goddess," a young artist carves a likeness in jade of the beautiful woman he loves. But Chang and his lover must hide from people who want to separate them. If Chang continues to carve his masterpieces, he will be recognized by his style. Can he stifle his creativity for the sake of love? In the end, Lin Yutang reminds us that the person who inspires a work of art is mortal—only art can last forever.

Christina Rossetti's poem, "In the Artist's Studio," describes an artist inspired for a different reason by love. Over and over, a painter creates idealized images of the woman he loves. In real life, she is not as she seems in his paintings. An artist can create a world in which everything is exactly as he or she wants it to be.

The Artist's Experience

Heinrich Böll's story "The Laugher" is a look inside the mind of an unusual type of artist. Could laughing be an art? The narrator of this story can laugh so well, and in so many ways, that he is in demand for his skill. Yet, because he must produce laughter on request, he can no longer laugh naturally on his own. Böll makes you think about art's proper place in our lives. Perhaps art should not be something a person does for money. All art should, perhaps, be as natural a part of life as laughter.

You will also read a famous painter's own words about his art. In Leonardo da Vinci's "The Painter's Hands," you will get a sense of the power and keen excitement of being a great artist.

In the Greek myth "Pygmalion," an artist falls in love with a sculpture he creates. In this ancient story, art inspires love, and not the other way around.

In "The Bedquilt," a shy, insecure woman creates a remarkable quilt, and her whole life changes. People treat her with new respect, and she herself feels a new sense of her own worth. Through her quilting, she is able to express herself in a manner impossible in words.

The last story looks at artists in still another way. Suppose a great writer of the past could somehow be transported

Self Portrait, *Olof Krans, 1908*

through time into our own century. Would anyone recognize his or her genius? Would the writer understand the way we feel today about his or her work? Isaac Asimov's science-fiction tale, "The Immortal Bard," will make you laugh. But it will also make you think.

Finally, Thom Gunn's "Blackie, the Electric Rembrandt" is a clever poem about art in an unusual medium: tattooing.

While you read what writers have to say about artists and their work, remember: You are not just reading *about* art. In reading, you are experiencing it.

215

The Jade Goddess

by Lin Yutang

Lin Yutang, born in 1895, wrote in both English and Chinese. Although he spent 30 years in the United States, he eventually returned to Asia, where he died in 1976 in Hong Kong. He wrote and translated many books that help English-speaking people understand the Chinese way of life. In this story, in which a jade carver's art is the proof and memorial of his love, he combines details about life in ancient China with feelings that transcend all times and places.

It must have been almost a thousand years ago. Meilan was the only daughter of a high official, Commissioner Chang of Kaifeng. She was very pampered, and her father gave her all his affection.

As always happens, a number of relatives came to live at the mansion. One day, a distant nephew arrived. His name was Chang Po. He was an intelligent lad of 16, lively and full of spirit. His hands, with their long, slim fingers, were remarkable for a country lad.

He was a year older than Meilan, and they often met and talked and laughed together. Meilan loved to hear Chang Po tell stories of the country.

Chang Po was one of those original people born to create. He had taught himself to paint without a master. In his spare time, he made wonderful lanterns and molded the most lifelike clay animals.

At the age of 18, Chang Po had grown tall and handsome, and Meilan was attracted to him. As cousins, there was a natural closeness between them. It was clearly understood, however, that since they were relatives, marriage was out of the question.

One day, Chang Po suddenly announced to the honored mother of the house that he was leaving to learn a trade. He had found a jade-worker's shop and had offered himself as an apprentice. The mother thought it just as well, since he was too often with Meilan. But Chang continued to live on at the house, returning every night. He had even more to say to his cousin than before.

"Meilan," the mother said one day, "you are both grown up now, and although Chang Po is your cousin, you shouldn't see each other too often."

Her mother's words made Meilan think. She had never realized that she was in love with the boy Chang.

That night, she met Chang Po in the garden. Sitting on a stone bench in the moonlight, she casually mentioned what her mother had said.

"Cousin Po," she said, blushing, "Mother says I mustn't see you so much."

"Yes, we are grown up now."

The girl hung her head. "What does that mean?" She spoke half to herself.

Chang Po answered quietly. "It means that something in you makes you more charming every day to me, something that makes me want to see you. Something that makes me feel happy when you are near, and lonely and sad when I am away."

The girl sighed and asked, "Are you happy now?"

"Yes. Meilan, we belong to each other," he said softly.

"You know very well that I cannot marry you and that my parents will arrange a marriage for me before long. Please understand."

"I understand only this," Chang said, drawing the girl into his arms. "Since the heaven and earth were created, you were made for me and I was made for you. I will not let you go. It cannot be wrong to love you."

Meilan fled from his embrace and ran to her room.

The awakening of young love was a terrible thing. From that night on, she was completely changed. The more they tried to stop the love that had been awakened, the more they felt themselves in its power.

They tried not to see each other. Their love was increased by secrecy. Those were the days of young passions and tender regrets, temporary separations and renewed pledges, so sweet and so bitter. Both knew that they were in the power of something greater than themselves.

They had no plans. They just loved. According to the customs of the time, Meilan's parents were already suggesting one young man after another for her, but she kept putting them off. Sometimes she said she did not want to marry at all, which greatly shocked her mother. As Meilan was yet young, the parents did not insist. Since she was their only daughter, they were half-willing to keep her with them longer.

Meanwhile Chang was working and learning his trade. In jade work, Chang Po had found his natural element. Like a born artist, he had made himself in a short time a master of his trade. He loved it; he worked tirelessly until every detail was perfect. The master of the shop was amazed by him. The rich gentry began to come to the jade shop with orders.

One day, Meilan's father decided to give a present to the empress on her birthday. He wanted to find something special and located a large piece of jade of very fine quality. The commissioner went to the shop where Chang Po worked. He looked at Chang Po's sculpture, and was impressed by its individuality.

"Son, here is a very special job for you. This is for the empress, and if you do this job well, your fortune is made."

Chang Po examined the jade. His hands traveled slowly over the uncarved stone. He was delighted. It was agreed that he should make it into a goddess of mercy. Chang Po knew that he would make one of such beauty as had never been seen before.

Chang Po permitted no one to see the statue until it was completed.

When it was finished, the statue of the

goddess was in the usual design, but it was a perfect work of art, exquisite in its tender beauty. The goddess's face was like that of the girl he loved.

Naturally the commissioner was greatly pleased. This piece would be special even in the palace.

"The face is like Meilan's," the father remarked.

"Yes," replied Chang Po proudly.

"She is the inspiration." The commissioner paid Chang generously. "Young man," he said, "from now on your success is assured."

Chang Po's name was made. Yet what he wanted most he could not have. The success meant nothing to him without Meilan. He realized that the greatest desire of his heart was beyond his reach. The young man lost interest in his work and could not carve.

Meilan was now approaching the age of 21 and was not yet engaged. A marriage was being arranged with a powerful family. The girl could delay no longer.

Reckless with despair, the girl and the boy planned to elope. The couple began their escape one evening through the back of the garden. As it happened, an old servant saw them at the dark hour of the night. His suspicion was aroused. Thinking it was his duty to protect the family from a scandal, the servant held the girl and would not let her go. Chang had no choice. He pushed the servant aside. The old man tottered, but would not let go. Chang hit him and the poor man fell. His head struck a jagged rock, and he lay limp on the ground. Seeing the servant lifeless, they fled.

The next morning, the family discovered the elopement and the dead servant. While they tried to hush the scandal, efforts to trace the couple proved completely unsuccessful. The commissioner was thrown into a fit of helpless rage. "I shall cover the earth," he vowed, "and bring him back to justice."

After escaping from the capital, the young couple traveled on and on. Avoiding the big towns, they finally crossed the Yangtze River and came down to south China.

"I hear that there is good jade in Kiangse," Chang said to Meilan.

"Do you think you should work at jade again?" she asked hesitantly. "Your work will be recognized and betray you."

"I thought that was what we planned to do all along," Chang replied.

"That was before old Tai died. They think we murdered him. Can't you change your trade — make lanterns or clay dolls as you used to do?"

"Why? I have made a name for myself with jade."

"You have. That is the whole trouble," Meilan said.

"I don't think we have to worry. Kiangse is almost a thousand miles from the capital. Nobody will know us."

"Then you must change your style. Don't do those extraordinary things. Just do well enough to bring in customers."

Chang Po bit his lips and said nothing. Should he content himself with what a thousand ordinary jade workers were doing to remain safely unknown? Should he destroy his art or allow his art to destroy him? He had not thought of this.

With his wife's jewels, Chang Po was able to buy a stock of uncarved stones of various qualities and set up a shop. Meilan watched him work.

"Good enough, darling," she would say. "Nobody carves any better. For my sake, please."

Chang Po began to make a number of common round earrings and necklaces. But occasionally, he made some lovely and original creations. These things were bought up as fast as he could make them, and brought him far greater profits than the ordinary commercial goods.

"Darling, I am worried," Meilan pleaded with him. "You are getting to be too well known. I am expecting a baby. Please be careful."

"A child!" he exclaimed. "Now we are a family!" Chang Po kissed away what he called her womanish fancies.

After a year, the reputation of Paoho jade was established, for that was the name Chang Po had given his shop. The town of Kian itself became known as the city where people could buy delightful jade objects.

One day, a man walked into the shop, and after looking around casually at the display of goods, asked, "Aren't you Chang Po, relative of Commissioner Chang of Kaifeng?"

Chang Po quickly denied it, saying that he had never been to Kaifeng.

Meilan peeped from behind the shop. When the man was gone, she told Chang that the stranger was a secretary from her father's office. Perhaps his jade work had betrayed them.

Hastily they packed their jadeware and belongings, hired a boat, and left after dark, fleeing upriver. Their baby was only three months old.

At Kanshein, they had to stop, for the baby fell ill and they had run out of money after a month on the voyage. Chang Po had to take out one of his finest creations, a crouching dog with one eye closed, and sell it to a jade merchant named Wang.

"Why, this is Paoho jade," said the merchant. "No other shop makes such things."

"You are right. I bought it at Paoho," Chang Po said. He was secretly delighted.

"Why did you do it?" asked Meilan when she heard what Chang Po had done.

"Because we need the money to set up the shop."

"Listen to me this time," Meilan said. "We open a clay shop here."

"Why — " Chang Po stopped short.

"We were nearly caught because you would not listen. Does jade mean so much to you? More than your wife and baby? Later, things may change and you can go back to your art again."

Against his wish, Chang Po set up a shop making baked black-clay figurines. He yearned to handle jade again.

"Mud! Why should I work with this, when I can cut jade?"

Meilan was frightened by the fire in his eyes. "It will be your ruin."

One day, the jade merchant Wang met Chang Po and invited him into his inn, in the hope of getting some more Paoho jade. "I just came back from a trip to Kian," Wang said. He unwrapped a parcel and said, "You see this is the kind of stuff that Paoho shop is turning out now."

"Imitation!" Chang shouted.

"You are quite right," the merchant said softly. "You talk like one who knows."

"I should know," Chang said angrily.

"Yes. I remember you sold me that wonderful crouching dog. Have you any more pieces of that quality?"

"I will show you what real Paoho jade is like."

At his shop, Chang Po showed him jade that he had carved in Kian. The merchant was able to persuade Chang to sell them. On his next trip, Wang told some of his friends at the jade fair about the remarkable things he had been able to buy from the owner of an ordinary clay shop in the south. "It seems strange that such a man should own such lovely jade," he said.

Some six months later, three soldiers came with orders to arrest Chang Po and the commissioner's daughter and bring them to the capital. The secretary from the commissioner's office was with them.

"I will come with you if you will let me pack a few things," Chang said.

"And there are things to bring for the baby," Meilan added. "Don't forget he is the commissioner's grandson. If he becomes ill on the way, you will be responsible."

The men had instructions from the commissioner himself to treat them well on the journey. Chang Po and his wife were allowed to go to the back of the shop while the soldiers waited in front.

It was a hard moment of parting. Chang Po kissed his wife and baby and jumped from the window, knowing that he would never see them again in his life.

"I'll love you always," Meilan whispered softly from the window. "Never touch jade again."

Chang Po took a last look at Meilan as she stood before the window, one arm raised high to bid him good-bye forever.

When he had disappeared, she calmly entered the front of the shop to put down some of her things in a bag as if she were very busy packing. She told the soldiers to hold her baby and chatted with them as she went about packing. When the soldiers grew suspicious and searched the house, Chang Po was already gone.

Meilan returned to her home to find her mother dead and her father an old man. When she greeted him, there was no smile of forgiveness on his face. Only a look at her baby son softened him a little. In a way, the old man was relieved that Chang Po had escaped, for he would not have known what to do with him. Still, he could never forgive the man who had ruined his daughter's life and brought such misery to the whole family.

Years passed and no news had come of Chang Po. Governor Yang from Canton arrived one day, and the commissioner gave a dinner in his honor. In the course of the dinner, the governor said that he had bought a beautiful statue, which rivaled the goddess of mercy the commissioner had given to the empress. In fact, it was far more beautiful. He was going to give it to the empress, for the statues would make a pair.

The dinner guests were doubtful and said that a goddess more beautiful than the one the empress owned was impossible.

The governor had a shining wood case brought in. As the white jade goddess of mercy was removed from its case and placed on the middle of the table, a hush fell upon them all. Here was the tragic goddess of mercy.

A maidservant hurried to tell Meilan. From behind a latticed partition, Meilan looked into the room and paled when she saw the jade figure on the table. "He has done it! I know it is he," she whispered. She pulled herself together to hear whether Chang Po was still alive.

"Who is the artist?" asked a guest.

"That is the most interesting part of the story," the Canton governor replied. "He is not a regular jade worker. I came to know about him through my wife's niece. She was going to a wedding and had borrowed my wife's antique bracelets to wear for the occasion. My niece broke one of them and was horrified. She insisted that she would have the one bracelet copied. She went to many shops but none would take the job. Everyone said that it could not be done these days. She advertised in teahouses. Soon after, a shabbily dressed man appeared and said he had come to answer the advertisement. The bracelet was shown to him. He said he could do it and he did. That is how I first heard about the man.

"When I learned that the empress would like another statue to match the goddess of mercy, I thought of this man. I ordered the finest piece of jade and sent for him. When he was brought in, he looked very frightened, as if he had been caught as a

222

thief. It took me a long time to explain to him that I wanted him to make a goddess of mercy to match the one the empress already had.

"He examined the stone from every angle. 'What is the matter?' I asked. 'Is it not good enough?' Finally he turned and said proudly, 'This piece will do. It is worth trying. All my life, I have been hoping to get white jade of this quality. I will do it, Governor, but only if you do not pay me for it — and leave me in complete freedom to do what I have in mind.'

"I put him in a room with a simple bed and table and gave him all the equipment he asked for. He was rather a strange fellow. He talked to no one, and he worked like one inspired. I was not allowed to see the statue for five months. Another three months passed before he came with the finished work. I was astonished when I saw it. As he looked at his own creation, there was a strange expression on his face.

'There, Governor,' he said. 'I want to thank you. That statue is my life story.'

"He left before I could answer. I went after him, but he was gone. He had completely disappeared."

The guests heard a scream from the next room, a woman's scream so heart-rending that everyone froze in his place. Alone, the old commissioner rushed to Meilan, lying on the floor.

A guest who was a close friend of the family whispered to the startled governor, "That is the daughter of the commissioner. *She is the goddess.* I am sure your artist is no other than her husband, Chang Po."

When Meilan was revived, she walked up to the table. Slowly her hands rose to touch the statue and then rested tightly on it, as if in seeing and feeling the statue she was in touch with her husband once more. Everyone saw that the jade statue and the girl were the same woman.

"Keep the statue, my dear," the governor told her when he had learned what had happened. "I can find some other present for the empress. I hope that it will be some consolation to you. It is yours until you are with your husband again."

From that day, Meilan grew weaker, as if some mysterious disease were eating away her body. The commissioner was ready to forgive everything if his son-in-law could be found. By the following spring, word came back from the Canton governor that all efforts to locate Chang Po had come to nothing.

Two years later, Chang Po's little son died of an epidemic that swept through the city. Meilan then cut off her hair and entered a convent, taking along with her the jade goddess as her only possession. According to the prioress, she seemed to live in a world by herself. She would not permit another nun, not even the prioress, to enter her room.

The prioress told the governor that Meilan had been seen at night writing prayer after prayer and burning it before the statue. She let no one into that secret world of hers, but she was happy and hurt nobody.

Some 20 years after she joined the convent, Meilan died. And so the perishable goddess of mercy passed away, and the jade goddess remained.

READING COMPREHENSION

Summarizing. Choose the best phrase to complete each sentence. Then write the complete statements on your paper.

1. A marriage between Meilan and Chang Po was not encouraged because _____ (Meilan was already engaged, they were cousins, Chang Po was poor).

2. Meilan didn't want Chang Po to work with jade because _____ (she was jealous of his sculpture, he earned more working with clay, she was afraid that his art would betray his real identity).

3. The commissioner was ready to forgive Chang Po when he saw _____ (the new statue, how much Meilan missed him, that everyone loved him).

Interpreting. Write the answer to each question on your paper.

1. What stopped Chang Po from being completely happy with the success of the statue of the goddess?

2. Why was Chang Po unable to create mediocre works in jade?

3. Why did Meilan join a convent at the end of the story?

For Thinking and Discussing.

1. What did Chang Po mean when he said "That statue is my life story"?

2. Why were both Meilan and Chang Po's lives tragic?

UNDERSTANDING LITERATURE

Imagery. *Imagery* is language that appeals to the reader's senses and emotions, and creates a picture in the reader's mind.

Select the best choice to complete each statement below. Then write the entire sentence on your paper.

1. "'Mud! Why should I work with this, when I can cut jade?'" This imagery appeals to the sense of touch, and suggests the feeling of _____.
   a. disgust and frustration
   b. joy
   c. fear

2. "The guests heard a scream from the next room, . . . so heartrending that everyone froze in his place." This imagery appeals to the sense of hearing, and suggests a feeling of _____.
   a. coldness
   b. horror
   c. loneliness

3. "The statue . . . was a perfect work of art, exquisite in its tender beauty." This imagery appeals to the sense of sight, and suggests a feeling of _____.
   a. tragedy
   b. awe or pleasure
   c. softness

WRITING

Imagine that you are Meilan, and that the commissioner has found Chang Po. Describe your reunion, using imagery that expresses joy and relief.

The Painter in His Studio, *Johannes Vermeer, ca. 1632–1675*

In an Artist's Studio

by Christina Rossetti

One face looks out from all his canvases,
    One selfsame figure sits or walks or leans:
    We found her hidden just behind those screens,
That mirror gave back all her loveliness.
A queen in opal or in ruby dress,
    A nameless girl in freshest summer-greens,
    A saint, an angel — every canvas means
The same one meaning, neither more nor less.
He feeds upon her face by day and night,
    And she with true kind eyes looks back on him,
Fair as the moon and joyful as the light:
    Not wan with waiting, not with sorrow dim;
Not as she is, but was when hope shone bright;
    Not as she is, but as she fills his dream.

---

1. What does the poet mean when she says "every canvas means the same one meaning"? What do you think the "one meaning" is?

2. Does the artist paint the model as she really is? Use examples from the poem to explain why or why not.

The Laugher

by Heinrich Böll

Born in 1917, German novelist and short-story writer Heinrich Böll received the Nobel Prize for literature in 1972. In this story, he asks you to think about what art really is. When you think of art, you probably think of painting or sculpting. You may think of music, acting, or writing. But you probably don't think of laughing. Could anything be an art if it is done well enough?

When someone asks me what business I am in, I am seized with embarrassment: I blush and stammer, I who am otherwise known as a man of poise. I envy people who can say: I am a bricklayer. I envy barbers, bookkeepers, and writers. All these professions speak for themselves. They need no lengthy explanation, while I am forced to reply to such questions: I am a laugher. Then I am always asked, "Is that how you make your living?" Truthfully I must say, "Yes." I actually do make a living at my laughing, and a good one, too. My laughing is — commercially speaking — much in demand. I am a good laugher, experienced. No one else laughs as well as I do. No one else has such command of the fine points of my art. For a long time, in order to avoid tiresome explanations, I called myself an actor. My talents in the field of mime and speech are small, so I felt this title to be too far from the truth. I love the truth, and the truth is: I am a laugher. I am neither a clown nor a comedian. I do not make people gay, I portray gaiety: I laugh like a Roman emperor, or like a sensitive schoolboy. I am as much at home in the laughter of the 17th century as in that of the 19th. When occasion demands, I laugh my way through all the centuries, all classes of society, all categories of age. It is simply a skill I have acquired, like the skill of being able to repair shoes. In my breast, I harbor the laughter of America, the laughter of Africa, white, red, yellow

laughter. For the right fee, I let it peal out in accordance with the director's requirements.

I have become indispensable. I laugh on records. I laugh on tape. Television directors treat me with respect, I laugh mournfully, moderately, hysterically. I laugh like a streetcar conductor or like a clerk in the grocery; laughter in the morning, laughter in the evening, nighttime laughter, and the laughter of twilight. In short: Wherever and however laughter is required — I do it.

It need hardly be pointed out that a profession of this kind is tiring, especially as I have also — this is my specialty — mastered the art of infectious laughter. This has also made me indispensable to third- and fourth-rate comedians, who are scared — and with good reason — that their audiences will miss their punch lines. I spend most evenings in nightclubs. My job is to begin to laugh during the weaker parts of the program. It has to be carefully timed. My hearty, loud laughter must not come too soon, but neither must it come too late. It must come just at the right spot. At the pre-arranged moment, I burst out laughing. Then the whole audience roars with me, and the joke is saved.

But as for me, I drag myself exhausted to the checkroom. I put on my overcoat, happy that I can go off duty at last. At home, I usually find telegrams waiting for me: "Urgently require your laughter. Recording Tuesday," and a few hours later I am sitting in an overheated express train bemoaning my fate.

I need scarcely say that when I am off duty or on vacation I have little desire to laugh. The cowhand is glad when he can forget the cow. Carpenters usually have doors at home that don't work or drawers that are hard to open. Candy makers like sour pickles. Butchers like pastry, and the baker prefers sausage to breads. Bullfighters raise pigeons for a hobby. Boxers turn pale when their children have nosebleeds: I find all this quite natural, for I never laugh off duty. I am a very solemn person, and people consider me — perhaps rightly so — a pessimist.

During the first years of our married life, my wife would often say to me: "Do laugh!" Since then, she has come to realize that I cannot grant her this wish. I am happy when I am free to relax my tense face muscles in a solemn expression. Indeed, even other people's laughter gets on my nerves. It reminds me too much of my profession. So our marriage is a quiet, peaceful one. Now my wife has also forgotten how to laugh. Now and again I catch her smiling, and I smile, too. We speak in low tones. I hate the noise of the nightclubs, the noise that sometimes fills the recording studios. People who do not know me think I am taciturn. Perhaps I am, because I have to open my mouth so often to laugh.

I go through life with a calm expression. From time to time, I permit myself a gentle smile. I often wonder whether I have ever laughed. I think not. My brothers and sisters have always known me for a serious boy.

So I laugh in many different ways, but my own laughter I have never heard.

READING COMPREHENSION

Summarizing. Choose the best phrase to complete each sentence. Then write the complete statements on your paper.

1. The laugher was a good professional laugher because he _____ (was skilled and experienced, had a wonderful sense of humor, enjoyed laughing so much).

2. The laugher considered himself _____ (a great comedian, a serious person, very talkative).

3. The laugher could laugh in many different ways, but he wondered _____ (if he could get a job as an actor, if he had ever truly laughed as himself, if his laughter frightened people).

4. One thing the laugher liked to do when he was on vacation was _____ (go to nightclubs, laugh a great deal, talk quietly with his wife).

Interpreting. Write the answer to each question on your paper.

1. Why did the laugher wish he could say he was a barber or a bookkeeper?

2. How would you describe the laugher's real personality?

3. What details in the story show that the laugher was unhappy with his profession?

For Thinking and Discussing. Why do you think the laugher didn't like his profession?

UNDERSTANDING LITERATURE

Imagery. *Imagery* is language that appeals to the reader's senses or emotions. Some images create a complete picture in the reader's mind. Böll's imagery gives a more complete picture of the laugher's life.

Read the following excerpts. Select the best choice to complete each statement. Write the entire sentence on your paper.

1. "Bullfighters raise pigeons for a hobby. Boxers turn pale when their children have nosebleeds. . . ." This image suggests that _____.
   a. at home, people are very unlike their professional selves
   b. boxers panic in emergencies
   c. the laugher wishes that he had become a bullfighter

2. "I laugh like a Roman emperor, or like a sensitive schoolboy. I am as much at home in the laughter of the 17th century as in that of the 19th. When occasion demands, I laugh my way through all the centuries . . ." This image suggests that _____.
   a. the laugher's hobby is reading
   b. at home he laughs like a teenager
   c. the laugher can laugh like anyone of any age from any time in history

WRITING

Write a paragraph describing a hobby or pastime you really enjoy. Use words and imagery that convey how much you like the activity you're describing.

The Painter's Hands

by Leonardo da Vinci

*Painter, sculptor, poet, architect, engineer, scientist, musician
. . . Leonardo da Vinci's career shows that creativity can be
applied to many fields. Born in 1452 in Florence, Italy, he
apprenticed to the painter Verocchio at age 14. Although
Leonardo did do many things brilliantly, he is thought of
first for his painting. He reveals here how a great artist can
have the power of a god.*

If the painter wishes to see enchanting beauties, he has the power to produce them. If he wishes to see monstrosities, he has the power to create them. If he wishes to produce towns or deserts, he can. If in the hot season he wants cool and shady places, or in the cold season warm places, he can make them. If he wants valleys, if from high mountaintops he wants to survey vast stretches of country, if beyond he wants to see the horizon on the sea, he has the power to create all this. Likewise, if from deep valleys he wants to see high mountains, or from high mountains deep valleys and beaches. Indeed, whatever exists in the universe, or in the imagination, the painter has first in his mind and then in his hands.

1. Leonardo da Vinci was one of the greatest painters who ever lived. He was also a fine writer and an inventor. Why do you think he became a painter? Use examples from "The Painter's Hands" to explain your answer.

2. What do you think is a more important quality in the creator of art — imagination or technical skill? How do you think da Vinci would have answered this question? Explain.

Study of hands, *Leonardo da Vinci, ca. 1452–1519*

Pygmalion

a Greek myth retold by Doris Gates

*Pygmalion has no interest in women. Then he falls in love —
with a statue! This ancient Greek legend has been told and
retold for centuries. Its message is about art's power to
change our feelings — and the mysterious forces of love.*

On the island of Cyprus, there lived a sculptor named Pygmalion. The man was a fine artist and his studio was a gathering place for his admirers. They marveled at the way he worked in stone and ivory. His statues seemed so real a visitor would sometimes put out a hand and touch the statue to make sure it was not living flesh.

Now Pygmalion hated women; no one knew exactly why. Some said he had been disappointed in love; others that he had had a cruel mother who had resented his birth. In any case, Pygmalion lived alone in his studio, and no woman ever came there. Nor had he ever fashioned a statue in the form of a woman.

But one day, Pygmalion was seized with a great desire to sculpt a woman. He was shocked and bewildered by the sudden urge.

"Has Aphrodite, the goddess of love, put this spell upon me?" he asked himself. "And, if so, to what purpose?"

He tried to ignore the strange desire, but in vain. It kept him from sleep. It hounded his every waking moment. At last, he gave in to it.

As he started work on the statue, he felt ashamed of what he was doing. He banished all visitors from his studio. No one must ever learn of his self-betrayal. Nor would they. When the sculpture was completed, he would destroy it.

The statue began to take form under his hands. At first, he had thought to fashion an ugly female figure, completely without grace. If this were Aphrodite's trick, it should not succeed, whatever her plan. But as he began to cut away the marble to the point where the figure began to emerge, Pygmalion's hands seemed to act on their own. Day after day, the figure grew more beautiful. Despite his best intentions, Pygmalion was fashioning an object so lovely that even he began to feel an admiration for it. The chiseled face wore an expression so soft and charming, it was hard to imagine it was only stone. The sculptor gazed on it in amazement. He smiled as he had never before smiled upon a woman. But, of course, this was merely a statue!

Then came the final polishing of the marble. Pygmalion smoothed it until it

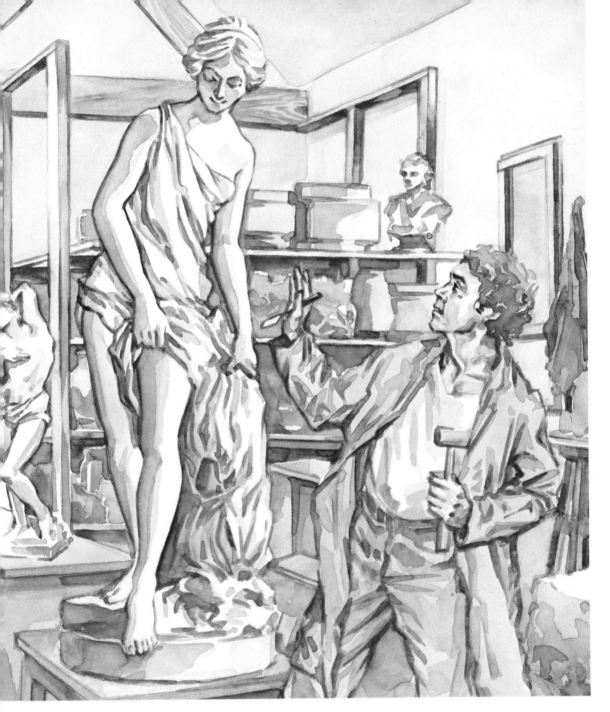

glowed. It even took on the glowing tone of healthy young flesh. His hands moved almost lovingly upon it.

At last, the day came when nothing remained to be done. The life-sized statue stood upon its pedestal complete. Pygmalion walked slowly around it, and when he came to where its face looked sweetly down upon him, a strange feeling gripped him. He fell in love!

Now began a period of perfect misery for Pygmalion. The pangs of unrequited love are torment, especially when the object of that love is there before the sufferer day and night. Pygmalion tried to embrace the lovely figure, but the cold stone repulsed him. For all its realistic appearance, it was only stone.

"Ah, if you could but speak to me," Pgymalion exclaimed to the face bending above him. "Your eyes look into mine. Your lips smile, almost opening to speak. Yet you are ever silent."

He remembered his plan to destroy the statue, but that was unthinkable now. Life would lose all meaning without this lovely creation. Then, in his desperation, Pygmalion began to pretend his marble love was really human. He talked to her. He robed her in silken garments. He even tucked her into bed at night with a pillow beneath her head. He brought her gifts young girls prize — flowers, birds, and jewels. The bare and cluttered studio became a kind of bower for his beloved. His sculptor's tools gathered dust.

Then came the day that was sacred to Aphrodite on the island of Cyprus. Altars everywhere were decked with roses, her favorite flower. All the people were celebrating, Pygmalion among them.

Half fearfully, he approached an altar where incense sent up its sweet fragrance. There he offered a prayer to the great goddess.

"Oh, Aphrodite, protector of lovers, listen to me now. If it be in your power, then send me a wife like the woman I have sculpted. Until now, I have shunned the company of women. But now I acknowledge my fault in this. Only grant me such a wife as I crave, and I will honor you above all immortals."

It so happened that Aphrodite, invisible, was present at that altar to hear Pygmalion's prayer. Perhaps she had indeed made him carve that statue. If so, then she must have watched with amusement his love for it. It would not have pleased the goddess of love that Pygmalion should spurn women. Whatever her reasons, Aphrodite now listened to Pygmalion's prayer. She was moved by its sincerity. Still, she did not reveal her presence. Pygmalion left the altar wondering if his prayer would be answered.

Straight home he went to gaze on his beloved statue. But as he approached the pedestal, he stopped, amazed. Were his eyes playing him tricks, or had he simply gone mad? She was smiling at him as before, only there was a difference in the smile. It was wider, warmer. Her eyes had a sparkle that no marble could produce. As he gazed, a warm color rose into her cheeks. He rushed forward and seized her hand. It was warm within his own. He could feel a pulse beating faintly under his thumb. The statue was alive!

With a glad cry, Pygmalion lifted his arms, and the statue stepped lightly down and into them.

Pygmalion gave his love the name Galatea. Soon their marriage was celebrated. They became the parents of a son called Paphos, for whom an island was later named. And as far as anyone knows, they lived happily ever after.

READING COMPREHENSION

Summarizing. Choose the best phrase to complete each sentence. Then write the complete statements on your paper.

1. Pygmalion never sculpted women because _____ (he hated women, the goddess Aphrodite forbade it, Aphrodite would be jealous).

2. When Pygmalion finished the beautiful statue, he _____ (smashed it to pieces, fell in love with his creation, started to work on other statues).

3. Galatea came to life because _____ (Pygmalion's kiss awoke her from a deep sleep, she was carved from a magical stone, Aphrodite granted Pygmalion's wish).

Interpreting. Write the answer to each question on your paper.

1. Why was Pygmalion ashamed of his desire to create a statue of a woman?

2. Why did Pygmalion decide to sculpt a statue of an ugly woman?

3. How did Pygmalion's attitude toward love change during the story?

For Thinking and Discussing.

1. Do you think Pygmalion would have fallen in love with the statue if someone else had created it? Explain your answer.

2. Do you think that many artists "fall in love" with their own creations? Why or why not?

UNDERSTANDING LITERATURE

Imagery. Writers use language that appeals to the senses to create *imagery*. This retelling of Pygmalion skillfully uses imagery to explain how the statue was like, yet unlike, a human being and to describe the amazing transformation of the statue into a living woman.

Here are some examples of *imagery* from the story. Copy each sentence on your paper and tell which of your senses — sight, hearing, smell, taste, or touch — each image appeals to. (Some images may appeal to more than one sense.)

1. The chiseled face wore a charming expression.

2. ". . . the cold stone repulsed him."

3. "'Your lips smile, almost opening to speak. Yet you are ever silent.'"

4. The "incense sent up its sweet fragrance."

5. Her hand was "warm within his own. He could feel a pulse beating."

6. "Her eyes had a sparkle that no marble could produce."

WRITING

Pretend you are Aphrodite. Write a paragraph in which you describe watching Pygmalion creating his statue and then falling in love with it. Use imagery that shows how you take pity on Pygmalion and grant him his wish.

The Bedquilt

by Dorothy Canfield Fisher

Dorothy Canfield Fisher is well known for her stories about American women. No one pays much attention to Aunt Mehetabel until, at the age of 68, she sews a marvelous quilt. It's never too late to discover your creative powers.

Of all the Elwell family, Aunt Mehetabel was certainly the most unimportant member. It was in the old-time New England days, when an unmarried woman was an old maid at 20. At 40, she was everyone's servant, and by 60, she had gone through so much discipline that she could need no more in the next world. Aunt Mehetabel was 68.

She had never for a moment known the pleasure of being important to anyone. Not that she was useless in her brother's family. She was expected, as a matter of course, to take upon herself the most uninteresting part of the household labors. On Mondays, she accepted as her share the washing of the men's shirts, heavy with sweat and stiff with dirt from the fields and from the their own hardworking bodies. Tuesdays she never dreamed of being allowed to iron anything pretty, like the baby's white dresses or the fancy aprons of her young lady nieces. She stood all day pressing out a succession of dishcloths and towels and sheets.

In preserving-time, she was allowed to have none of the responsibility of deciding when the fruit had cooked long enough.

Nor did she share in the little excitement of pouring the sweet-smelling stuff into the stone jars. She sat in a corner with the children and stoned cherries all the time, or hulled strawberries until her fingers were dyed red.

The Elwells were not consciously unkind to their aunt. They were even, in a vague way, fond of her. But she was so unimportant a figure in their lives that she was almost invisible to them. Aunt Mehetabel did not resent this treatment. She took it quite as naturally as they gave it. It was to be expected when one was an old-maid dependent in a busy family.

In the winter when they all sat before the big hearth, roasted apples, drank mulled cider, and teased the girls and boys about their sweethearts, she shrank into a dusky corner with her knitting. She was happy if the evening passed without her brother saying, "Ask your Aunt Mehetabel about the boys that used to come a-courtin' her!" or, "Mehetabel, how was't when you was in love with Abel Cummings?" As a matter of fact, she had been the same at 20 as at 60, a mouselike little creature, too shy for anyone to notice, or to raise her eyes for

238

a moment and wish for a life of her own.

Her sister-in-law, a big hearty house-wife, was rather kind in an absent, offhand way to the shrunken little old woman, and it was through her that Mehetabel was able to enjoy the one pleasure of her life.

Even as a girl, she had been clever with her needle in the way of patching bed-quilts. In patchwork, she enjoyed a mild importance. She could really do that as well as anyone else. During years of de-votion to this one art, she had accumulated a considerable store of quilting patterns. Sometimes the neighbors would send over and ask "Miss Mehetabel" for the loan of her sheaf-of-wheat design, or the dou-ble-star pattern. It was with an agreeable flutter at being able to help someone that she went to the dresser, in her bare little room under the eaves, and drew out from her crowded portfolio the pattern desired.

She never knew how her great idea came to her. Sometimes she thought she must have dreamed it, sometimes she even wondered reverently if it had not been "sent" to her. She never admitted to her-self that she could have thought of it without other help. It was too great, too ambitious, too lofty a project for her humble mind to have conceived. Even when she finished drawing the design with her own fingers, she gazed at it in amaze-ment, not daring to believe that it could indeed be her handiwork. At first, it seemed to her only like a lovely but unreal dream.

For a long time, she did not once think of putting an actual quilt together follow-ing that pattern, even though she herself had invented it. It was not that she feared the enormous effort that would be needed to get those tiny, oddly shaped pieces of bright-colored material sewed together with the perfection of fine workmanship needed. No, she thought eagerly of such endless effort. Her heart was uplifted by her vision of the beauty of the whole creation as she saw it, when she shut her eyes to dream of it — that complicated, splendidly dif-ficult pattern. It was good enough for the angels in heaven to quilt.

But as she dreamed, her nimble old fingers reached out longingly to turn her dream into reality. She began to think adventurously of trying it out — it would perhaps not be too selfish to make one square — just one unit of her design to see how it would look. She dared do nothing in the household where she was a dependent, without asking permission. With a heart full of hope and fear thump-ing furiously against her old ribs, she approached the mistress of the house.

Sophia listened absently to her sister-in-law's halting request. "Why, yes, Me-hetabel," she said. "Why, yes, start an-other quilt if you want to. I've got a lot of pieces from the spring sewing that will work in real good." Mehetabel tried hon-estly to make her see that this would be no common quilt, but her limited vocab-ulary and her emotion stood between her and expression. At last, Sophia said, with a kindly impatience: "Oh, there! Don't bother me. I never could keep track of your quiltin' patterns, anyhow. I don't care what pattern you go by."

Mehetabel rushed back up the steep attic stairs to her room, and in a joyful state began preparations for the work of

her life. Her very first stitches showed her that it was even better than she hoped. By some heaven-sent inspiration, she had invented a pattern beyond which no patchwork quilt could go.

She had but little time during the daylight hours, which were filled with household drudgery. After dark, she did not dare to sit up late at night lest she burn too much candle. It was weeks before the little square began to show the pattern. Then Mehetabel was in a fever to finish it. She was too conscientious to shirk even the smallest part of her share of the housework, but she rushed through it now so fast that she was panting as she climbed the stairs to her little room.

Every time she opened the door, no matter what weather hung outside the one small window, she always saw the little room flooded with sunshine. She smiled to herself as she bent over the countless scraps of cotton cloth on her work table. Already — to her — they were arranged in orderly, complex, beauty.

Finally she could wait no longer, and one evening ventured to bring her work down beside the fire where the family sat, hoping that good fortune would give her a place near the candles on the mantelpiece. She had reached the last corner of that first square and her needle flew in and out, in and out, with nervous speed. To her relief, no one noticed her. By bedtime, she had only a few more stitches to add.

As she stood up with the others, the square fell from her trembling old hands and fluttered to the table. Sophia glanced at it carelessly. "Is that the new quilt you said you wanted to start?" she asked, yawning. "Looks like a real pretty pattern. Let's see it."

Up to that moment, Mehetabel had labored in the purest spirit of selfless dedication. The emotional shock, given her by Sophia's cry of admiration as she held the work toward the candle to examine it, was as much astonishment as joy to Mehetabel.

"Land's sakes!" cried her sister-in-law. "Why, Mehetabel Elwell, where did you get that pattern?"

"I made it up," said Mehetabel. She spoke quietly but she was trembling.

"No!" exclaimed Sophia. "Did you! Why, I never see such a pattern in my life. Girls, come here and see what your Aunt Mehetabel is doing."

The three tall daughters turned back reluctantly from the stairs. "I never could seem to take much interest in patchwork quilts," said one. Already the oldtime skill born of early pioneer hardship and the craving for beauty had gone out of style.

"No, nor I neither!" answered Sophia. "But a stone image would take an interest in this pattern. Honest, Mehetabel, did you really think of it yourself?" She held it up closer to her eyes and went on, "And how under the sun and stars did you even git your courage up to start in a-making it? Land! Look at all those tiny squinchy little seams! Why, the wrong side ain't a thing but seams! Yet the good side's just like a picture, so smooth you'd think 'twas woven that way. Only nobody could."

The girls looked at it right side, wrong side, and echoed their mother's exclamations. Mr. Elwell himself came over to see what they were discussing. "Well, I declare!" he said, looking at his sister with eyes more approving than she could ever remember. "I don't know a thing about patchwork quilts, but to my eye that beats old Mis' Andrew's quilt that got the blue ribbon so many times at the County Fair."

As she lay that night in her narrow hard bed, too proud, too excited to sleep, Mehetabel's heart swelled and tears of joy ran down from her old eyes.

The next day, her sister-in-law astonished her by taking the huge pan of potatoes out of her lap and setting one of the younger children to peeling them. "Don't you want to go on with that quiltin' pattern?" she said. "I'd kind o'like to see how you're goin' to make the grapevine design come out on the corner."

For the first time in her life, the dependent old maid contradicted her powerful sister-in-law. Quickly and jealously, she said, "It's not a grapevine. It's a sort of curlicue I made up."

"Well, it's nice-looking anyhow," said Sophia pacifyingly. "I never could have made it up."

By the end of the summer, the family interest had risen so high that Mehetabel was given for herself a little round table in the sitting room, for her, where she could keep her pieces and use odd minutes for her work. She almost wept over such kindness and resolved firmly not to take advantage of it. She went on faithfully with her housework, not neglecting a corner. But the atmosphere of her world changed. Now things had a meaning. Through the longest task of washing milk pans, there rose a rainbow of promise. She took her place by the little table and put the thimble on her knotted, hard finger with intense seriousness.

She was even able to bear with some degree of dignity the honor of having the minister and the minister's wife comment admiringly on her great project. The family felt quite proud of Aunt Mehetabel, as Minister Bowman had said it was work as fine as any he had ever seen, "and he didn't know but finer!" The remark was repeated to the neighbors in the following weeks when they dropped in and examined in silence some astonishingly difficult feat that Mehetabel had just finished.

The Elwells especially prided themselves on the slow progress of the quilt. "Mehetabel has been to work on that corner for six weeks, come Tuesday, and she ain't half done yet," they explained to visitors. They fell out of the way of always expecting her to be the one to run on errands, even for the children. "Don't bother your Aunt Mehetabel," Sophia would call. "Can't you see she's got to a ticklish place on the quilt?"

The old woman sat straighter in her chair, held up her head. She was a part of the world at last. She joined in the conversation and her remarks were listened to. The children were even told to mind her when she asked them to do some service for her, although this she dared to do but seldom.

One day, some people from the next town, total strangers, drove up to the Elwell house and asked if they could inspect the wonderful quilt, which they had heard about even down in their end of the valley. After that, Mehetabel's quilt came little by little to be one of the local sights. No visitor to town, whether he knew the Elwells or not, went away without having been to look at it. To make her presentable to strangers, the Elwells saw to it that their aunt was better dressed than she had ever been before. One of the girls made her a pretty little cap to wear on her thin white hair.

A year went by and a quarter of the quilt was finished. A second year passed and half was done. The third year Mehetabel had pneumonia and lay ill for weeks and weeks, horrified by the idea that she might die before her work was completed. A fourth year and one could really see the grandeur of the whole design. In September of the fifth year, the entire family gathered around her to watch eagerly, as Mehetabel quilted the last stitches. The girls held it up by the four corners and they all looked at it in hushed silence.

Then Mr. Elwell cried as one speaking with authority. "By ginger! That's goin' to the County Fair!"

Mehetabel blushed a deep red. She had thought of this herself, but never would have spoken aloud of it.

"Yes, indeed!" cried the family. One of the boys was sent to the house of a neighbor who was chairman of the Fair Committee for their village. He came back beaming, "Of course he'll take it. Like's not it may git a prize, he says. But he's got to have it right off because all the things from our town are going tomorrow morning."

Even in her pride, Mehetabel felt a pang as the bulky package was carried out of the house. As the days went on, she felt lost. For years, it had been her one thought. The little round stand had been heaped with a litter of bright-colored scraps. Now it was terribly bare. One of the neighbors who took the long journey to the Fair reported when he came back that the quilt was hung in a good place in a glass case in "Agricultural Hall." But that meant little to Mehetabel's ignorance of every-thing outside her brother's home. She drooped. The family noticed it. One day, Sophia said kindly, "You feel sort o'lost without the quilt, don't you, Mehetabel?"

"They took it away so quick!" she said wistfully. "I hadn't hardly had one good look at it myself."

The Fair was to last a fortnight. At the beginning of the second week, Mr. Elwell asked his sister how early she could get up in the morning.

"I dunno. Why?" she asked.

"Well, Thomas Ralston has got to drive to West Oldton to see a lawyer. That's four miles beyond the Fair. He says if you can git up so's to leave here at four in the morning he'll drive you to the Fair, leave you there for the day, and bring you back again at night."

Mehetabel's face turned very white. Her eyes filled with tears. It was as though someone had offered her a ride in a golden chariot up to the gates of heaven. "Why, you can't mean it!" she cried wildly. Her brother laughed. He could not meet her eyes. Even to him, this was revelation of the narrowness of her life in his home. "Oh, 'tain't so much — just to go to the Fair," he told her in some confusion, and then, "Yes, sure I mean it. Go git your things ready, for it's tomorrow morning he wants to start."

A trembling, excited old woman stared all that night at the rafters. She who had never been more than six miles from home — it was to her like going into another world. She who had never seen anything more exciting than a church supper was to see the County Fair. She had never dreamed of doing it. She could not at all imagine what it would be like.

The next morning, all the family rose early to see her off. Perhaps her brother had not been the only one to be shocked by her happiness. As she tried to eat her breakfast, they called out advice to her about what to see. Her brother said not to miss inspecting the stock, her nieces said the embroidery was the only thing worth looking at, Sophia told her to be sure to look at the display of preserves. Her nephews asked her to bring home an account of the trotting races.

The buggy drove up to the door, and she was helped in. The family ran to and fro with blankets. Her wraps were tucked about her. They all stood together and waved good-bye as she drove out of the yard. She waved back, but she scarcely saw them.

On her return home that evening she was ashy pale, and so stiff that her brother had to lift her out bodily. But her lips were set in a blissful smile. They crowded around her with questions until Sophia pushed them all aside. She told them Aunt Mehetabel was too tired to speak until she had had her supper. The young people held their tongues while she drank her tea, and absentmindedly ate a scrap of toast with an egg. Then the old woman was helped into an easy chair before the fire. They gathered about her, eager for news of the great world, and Sophia said, "Now, come, Mehetabel, tell us all about it!"

Mehetabel drew a long breath. "It was

just perfect!" she said. "Finer even than I thought. They've got it hanging up in the very middle of a sort o' closet made of glass, and one of the lower corners is ripped and turned back so's to show the seams on the wrong side."

"What?" asked Sophia, a little blankly.

"Why, the quilt!" said Mehetabel in surprise. "There are a whole lot of other ones in that room, but not one that can hold a candle to it, if I do say it who shouldn't. I heard lots of people say the same thing. You ought to have heard what the women said about that corner, Sophia. They said — well, I'd be ashamed to tell you what they said. I declare if I wouldn't!"

Mr. Elwell asked. "What did you think of that big ox we've heard so much about?"

"I didn't look at the stock," returned his sister. She turned to one of her nieces. "That set of pieces you gave me, Maria, from your red dress, come out just lovely! I heard one woman say you could 'most smell the red roses."

"How did Jed Burgess' bay horse place in the mile trot?" asked Thomas.

"I didn't see the races."

"How about the preserves?" asked Sophia.

"I didn't see the preserves," said Mehetabel calmly.

Seeing that they were gazing at her with astonished faces, she went on, to give them a reasonable explanation, "You see, I went right to the room where the quilt was, and then I didn't want to leave it. It had been so long since I'd seen it. I had to look at it first real good myself, and then I looked at the others to see if there was any that could come up to it. Then the people begun comin' in and I got so interested in hearin' what they had to say I couldn't think of goin' anywheres else.

"I ate my lunch right there too, and I'm glad as can be I did, too; for what do you think?" — she gazed about her with kindling eyes. "While I stood there with a sandwich in one hand, didn't the head of the whole concern come in and open the glass door and pin a big bow of blue ribbon right in the middle of the quilt with a label on it, 'First Prize.' "

There was a stir of proud congratulation. Then Sophia returned to questioning, "Didn't you go to see anything else?"

"Why, no," said Mehetabel. "Only the quilt. Why should I?"

She fell into a reverie. As if it hung again before her eyes, she saw the glory that shone around the creation of her hand and brain. She longed to make her listeners share the golden vision with her. She struggled for words. She fumbled blindly for unknown words of praise. "I tell you it looked like — " she began, and paused.

Vague recollections of hymnbook phrases came into her mind. They were the only kind of poetic expression she knew. But they were dismissed as being inappropriate for something in real life. Also as not being nearly striking enough.

Finally, "I tell you, it looked real good," she assured them and sat staring into the fire, on her tired old face the supreme content of an artist who has realized her ideal.

READING COMPREHENSION

Summarizing. Choose the best phrase to complete each sentence. Then write the complete statements on your paper.

1. An unmarried woman in Old New England was an _____ (important member of the family, unimportant dependent of her family, outcast).

2. Aunt Mehetabel's personality could best be described as _____ (shy, confident, angry and bitter).

3. Mehetabel's family encouraged her to work on the quilt because they _____ (felt she was in the way, wanted to sell the quilt, realized it was a work of art).

4. The quilt gave Mehetabel a sense of _____ (sadness, growing old, pride and dignity).

Interpreting. Write the answer to each question on your paper.

1. How did Aunt Mehetabel get the idea for her quilt?

2. How did Aunt Mehetabel's life change after the family saw the first square of the quilt?

3. How does Aunt Mehetabel show herself to be a true artist?

For Thinking and Discussing. Do you think Aunt Mehetabel will retain her place of importance in the family now that the quilt is finished?

UNDERSTANDING LITERATURE

Symbols. A *symbol* is something that has a meaning of its own but also stands for something larger than itself. In this story, the bedquilt symbolizes the change that comes over Aunt Mehetabel when she finally asserts herself as an artist and a human being.

The three statements on the numbered list below describe the quilt. On your paper, match each statement about the quilt with a statement about Mehetabel from the lettered list.

1. The quilt was made of the discarded scraps of the family's clothes.

2. The family took a great deal of interest in the quilt. Everyone who saw it noticed it was special.

3. When the quilt was finished, it won first prize at the fair.

a. Her family began to see Mehetabel as an important and valuable person.

b. Mehetabel was totally content — an artist who had realized her ideal.

c. Mehetabel gathered what crumbs of comfort she could from their occasional caresses of kindness.

WRITING

In a paragraph, tell how the patchwork quilt, made of old, discarded materials, is a symbol of Aunt Mehetabel's life.

The Immortal Bard

by Isaac Asimov

Isaac Asimov has written over two hundred books. Yet he has found time to be a research scientist as well as a writer of nonfiction, fantasy, and science fiction. As this story shows, his work contains ideas about many subjects. People call artists immortal because their work can last forever. But in this tale, immortal *has another meaning.*

"Oh yes," said Dr. Phineas Welch, the famous scientist, "I can bring back the spirits of the dead."

Scott Robertson, the school's young English teacher, smiled and said, "Really, Dr. Welch?"

"I mean it," said the scientist. He looked to the right and to the left to be sure they were not being overheard. "And not just the spirits. I bring back bodies, too."

"I wouldn't have thought it was possible," said the English teacher.

"Why not? It's just a simple matter of temporal transference."

"Oh, you mean time travel," said the English teacher. "But that's quite — uh — unusual."

"Not if you know how."

"Well, tell me how, Dr. Welch."

"I can't tell you that," said the scientist. "But I have brought back quite a few men. Archimedes, Newton, Galileo. Poor fellows."

"Didn't they like it here?" asked the English teacher. "I should think they would have been fascinated by our modern science."

"Oh, they were," said the scientist. "They were. But not for long."

"What was wrong?"

"They couldn't get used to our way of life. They got terribly lonely and frightened. I had to send them back."

"That's too bad."

"Yes," said the scientist. "Great minds, but not flexible minds. Not universal. So I tried Shakespeare."

"WHAT?" yelled Robertson.

"Don't yell, my boy," said Welch. "It's bad manners."

"Did you say you brought back William Shakespeare?"

"I did. I needed someone with a universal mind. Someone who would understand people well enough to be able to live with them centuries after his own

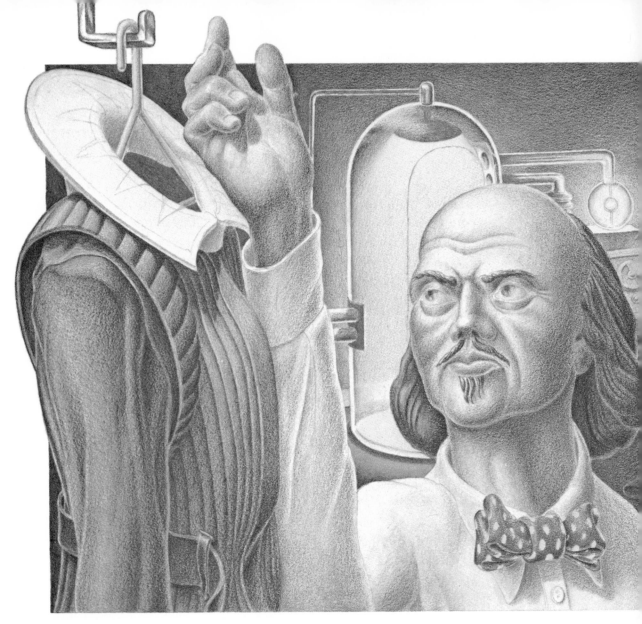

time. Shakespeare was the man. I've even got his signature. As a souvenir, you know."

"Do you have it with you?" asked the English teacher eagerly.

"Right here." The scientist fumbled in one vest pocket after another. "Ah, here it is."

He handed a little piece of cardboard to the English teacher. Printed on one side

was: "L. Klein & Sons, Wholesale Hardware." On the other side, written in straggly script, was:

WILLIAM SHAKESPEARE

"Tell me," Robertson said. "What did he look like?"

"Not like his pictures. Bald and with an ugly mustache. Of course, I did my

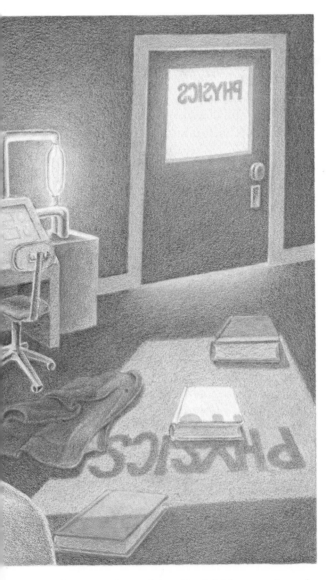

best to please him. I told him we thought highly of his plays and still performed them onstage. In fact, I said we thought they were the greatest examples of literature in the English language, maybe in any language."

"Good. Good!" said the English teacher.

"I said people had written many volumes of commentaries about his plays. Naturally he was eager to see the books, so I got some for him from the library."

"And?" asked the English teacher.

"Oh, he was fascinated. Of course, he had trouble with the current idioms and references to events since 1600, but I helped out. Poor fellow. I don't think he ever expected to get so much attention for his works. He kept saying, 'God have mercy!'"

The scientist paused for a minute. "Then I told him that we even give college courses in Shakespeare."

"I teach a course like that," said the English teacher.

"I know," said Welch. "I enrolled him in your evening course called 'Introduction to Shakespeare.' I never saw a man more eager than poor Bill to find out what people thought of him. He worked hard in the course, too."

"William Shakespeare was one of my students?" Robertson cried. He couldn't believe it. It was impossible. Or was it? He was beginning to recall a bald man with a strange way of talking. . . .

"I didn't enroll him under his real name, of course," said Dr. Welch. "Never mind what name he used. It was a mistake, that's all. A big mistake. Poor fellow."

"Why was it a mistake?" asked Robertson. "What happened?"

"I had to send him back to his own time," said Welch sadly. "The disgrace was more than he could take."

"What disgrace are you talking about?" asked the English teacher in a hoarse whisper.

Dr. Welch looked at him. "What disgrace? Why my dear man, you *flunked* him!"

READING COMPREHENSION

Summarizing. Choose the best phrase to complete each sentence. Then write the complete statements on your paper.

1. Welch told Robertson that he could _____ (visit the land of the dead, create a universal mind, bring people from the past into the present).

2. Welch thought that Shakespeare would like visiting our time because _____ (Shakespeare had a flexible mind, Newton agreed to travel with him, Shakespeare always loved to travel).

3. Shakespeare returned to his own time because he _____ (was lonely, failed a course in Shakespearean literature, couldn't get used to modern life).

Interpreting. Write the answer to each question on your paper.

1. Why didn't the scientists whom Dr. Welch brought back to life want to stay in the modern world for long?

2. What were Scott Robertson's impressions of the William Shakespeare who was enrolled in his course?

3. How did Shakespeare react when Dr. Welch told him how famous he had become since his death?

For Thinking and Discussing.

1. How do you think Shakespeare could flunk a course on his own writings?

2. What does *immortal* mean in this story?

UNDERSTANDING LITERATURE

Imagery and Humor. Imagery helps create a vivid picture in the reader's mind. Sometimes imagery can also make you laugh. In "The Immortal Bard," Asimov uses language to reveal the feelings of Robertson, the English teacher. The way Robertson's emotions change, as he learns more and more of Shakespeare's visits to modern times, adds humor to this story.

Read each excerpt below. Then, on your paper, write complete sentences that describe the impression — the feeling — that each suggests to the reader.

1. "'WHAT?' yelled Robertson. . . . 'Did you say you brought back William Shakespeare?'"

   The reader gets the impression that the teacher feels _____.

2. "'William Shakespeare was one of my students?' Robertson cried."

   The reader gets the impression that the teacher feels _____.

3. "It was impossible. Or was it? [Robertson] was beginning to recall a bald man with a strange way of talking. . . ."

   The reader gets the impression that the teacher feels _____.

WRITING

Imagine you are Shakespeare. Write a letter to Dr. Welch, explaining why you want to return to your own time. Use imagery and humor to help him understand.

Blackie,
the Electric Rembrandt

by Thom Gunn

We watched through the shop-front while
Blackie draws stars — an equal

concentration on his and
the youngster's faces. The hand

is steady and accurate;
but the boy does not see it

for his eyes follow the point
that touches (quick, dark movement!)

a virginal arm beneath
his rolled sleeve: he holds his breath.

. . . Now that it is finished, he
hands a few bills to Blackie

and leaves with a bandage on
his arm, under which gleam ten

stars, hanging in a blue thick
cluster. Now he is starlike.

---

1. What kind of artist is Blackie? Why do you
think he is called "the Electric Rembrandt"?
2. How would you describe the way in which
Blackie works? What lines in the poem tell
you?

Section Review

VOCABULARY

Multiple Meanings. Sometimes a word can have more than one meaning. What the word means, then, depends on the way it is used. For example, the word *current* can mean "the amount of an electrical charge in a circuit." *Current* can also mean "modern or belonging to the present time." Isaac Asimov used the word *current* to describe the present time period in his story about time travel.

On your paper, write the correct meaning of each italicized word below.

1. Pygmalion was fashioning an *object* so lovely that even he was beginning to *feel* admiration for it.
   object a. thing
   b. disagree
   feel a. touch with the hands or the skin
   b. an emotional reaction

2. One face looks out from all his *canvases.*
   canvases a. material on which oil paintings are made
   b. surveys of public opinion on given subjects

3. On this day, they *deck* Aphrodite's altar with roses.
   deck a. to cover with finery
   b. a platform on a ship

READING

Drawing Conclusions. When you read a selection, the author sometimes tells you directly what he or she wants you to know. In other cases, you have to put together the details and draw your own conclusions.

Read the exercises below. Select the best choice to complete the last statement in each exercise. Then write the entire sentence on your paper.

1. In Lin Yutang's story, Meilan lost the husband she loved, and her only child died. She spent the remaining years of her life in a convent, speaking to no one. You can draw the conclusion that Meilan _____.
   a. retreated from life because she had suffered such terrible sorrow
   b. was waiting for her husband to come back to her
   c. had really wanted to become an artist herself

2. In "The Immortal Bard," Shakespeare is transported from the 1600's to the present. He is one of the finest English writers who ever lived. Yet the English professor gave him a failing grade in a course based on Shakespeare's own work. From this, you can conclude that _____.
   a. the English professor had a better understanding of Shakespeare's literature than Shakespeare did
   b. Shakespeare was too homesick to concentrate on studies
   c. the English professor did not really understand Shakespeare's literature

WRITING

A Description. A written description uses words to create an object, scene, or event in the reader's mind. A good description revolves around a single main idea and involves the reader in what he or she is reading. Using vivid words and phrases to express descriptive details helps make a description come alive. Using words that appeal to the five senses — sight, sound, taste, touch, and smell — helps to create an image that seems real to those who read it.

Step 1: Set Your Goal

A topic for description should be one you are interested in and know well. It may be either something from your own experience or something imaginary that seems real to you. The more familiar you are with your topic, the more vividly you will be able to re-create it in words, and the better your description will be.

Use the stories in this section to come up with a topic for description. Here are some suggestions for you to consider:

- [ ] the mansion Meilan grew up in
- [ ] the jade goddess Chang Po made for the empress
- [ ] the laugher
- [ ] Pygmalion's statue
- [ ] Mehetabel's quilt
- [ ] Shakespeare's reaction to the 20th century

Once you have chosen a topic, you need to decide on your purpose for describing it. You can determine your purpose by thinking about the overall impression or feeling you want your description to create. For example, you may want your reader to feel as if he or she is seeing and experiencing an object or event exactly as you did. Or you might want your description to convey a certain emotion, such as happiness, fear, horror, sadness, or anger. Your purpose for writing will, to some extent, determine the kinds of words and phrases you use in your description.

Step 2: Make a Plan

Begin planning your description by writing a main-idea sentence that states your overall impression of your topic. Then list details that support the main idea. For example, in "The Jade Goddess," the main-idea sentence that introduces a description of Chang Po and Meilan's elopement is, "Reckless with despair, the girl and the boy planned to elope." Details that support the main idea include

- [ ] the couple escaped in the evening
- [ ] they left through the back of the garden
- [ ] an old servant saw them
- [ ] the servant held Meilan
- [ ] Chang hit the servant
- [ ] the servant fell down lifeless

Each detail supports the overall impression made in the main-idea sentence.

Once you have listed the details you want to include in your description, you need to organize them. If you are describing an event, you may want to organize the details in time order or order of importance. If you are describing a place, you may want to use spatial order. When you use spatial order, you guide the reader from one place to another. For example, in describing an artist's studio, you might start with the canvas the artist is working on and then describe the surrounding objects in the room. Organize your list of details in the way that best conveys the overall impression you want to make.

Step 3: Write a First Draft

As you write your first draft, remember it is not meant to be a perfect piece of writing. Writing a first draft allows you to turn your notes into sentences and arrange your sentences into paragraphs. Write freely and get your ideas down on paper. Use the following checklist as a guide:

- ☐ Keep your main idea in mind as you write.
- ☐ Use your list of details as a guide, but feel free to make changes.
- ☐ Try to use as many sensory and descriptive words as possible.

Step 4: Revise

As you revise, think about how you can make your description more vivid. Remember, you want to appeal to your readers' senses. Ask yourself if you can see, hear, touch, taste, or smell each detail. Try to use more specific nouns and verbs in place of general ones. Also, add adjectives and adverbs where you think they will help make a clearer impression.

When you have finished your revision, reread it. Will it leave the reader with the right impression, or are there other changes you still need to make? When you have made all the changes you feel are necessary, proofread your description for mistakes in grammar, spelling, and punctuation. Then make a neat, final copy.

QUIZ

The following is a quiz for Section 4. Write the answers in complete sentences on your paper.

Reading Comprehension

1. In "The Jade Goddess," why did Meilan warn Chang Po never to carve jade again?

2. What did Leonardo da Vinci like about being an artist?

3. Why did Pygmalion decide to sculpt a statue of a woman?

4. In "The Bedquilt," how did Mehetabel's family feel about her before she made the quilt?

5. In "The Immortal Bard," why did Welch think that Shakespeare would adjust well to modern life?

Understanding Literature

6. In "The Jade Goddess," what do the two statues of the goddess of mercy symbolize?

7. What is ironic about the way "The Laugher" earns his living?

8. What explanation is offered in "Pygmalion" for the name of the island of Paphos?

9. How does the character of Mehetabel change from the beginning to the end of "The Bedquilt"?

10. What is surprising about the ending of "The Immortal Bard"?

ACTIVITIES

Word Attack

1. In "The Jade Goddess," you read that the servant lay limp and lifeless on the ground after Chang Po hit him. The word *lifeless* is made up of the base word *life* and the suffix *-less*. In this case, the suffix *-less* means "lacking" or "without." The word *lifeless*, therefore, means "lacking or without life."

   Add the suffix *-less* to each of the base words below. Then use each new word in a sentence of your own.

home	child	friend
thought	sleep	blame
help	taste	hope

2. In "The Laugher," you learned that the narrator laughed in accordance with the director's requirements. The word *accordance* is made up of the base word *accord* and the suffix *-ance*. The suffix *-ance* is used to change verbs and adjectives into nouns. In this case, it means "the state, quality, or condition of." The word *accordance*, then, means "the state of being in accord or agreement."

   Write five words that end with the suffix *-ance*. Then use each word in a sentence. Refer to a dictionary if you need help.

Speaking and Listening

1. With a classmate, act out the story "The Immortal Bard." One of you should take the part of Dr. Phineas Welch, and the other should take the part of Scott Robertson. Use the dialogue in the story, and try to convey the feeling of the piece by the way you say your lines. Be prepared to present the story to the class.

2. Choose one of the poems in the section—"In an Artist's Studio" or "Blackie, the Electric Rembrandt"— for an oral reading. Practice reading the poem aloud until you feel you have captured the right mood. Then present the poem to the class.

Researching

1. In "The Bedquilt," making a quilt changed Mehetabel's life. Do some research on quilts. What is a quilt? How are they made? Where did they originate? What part have quilts played in American history and culture? Be prepared to share your information with the class.

2. The story "Pygmalion" is a famous Greek myth. Locate a book of Greek myths in the library, and choose one that interests you. Rewrite the myth in your own words. Be prepared to share the myth with the class.

Creating. Heinrich Böll used vivid language to describe "The Laugher." Write a paragraph in which you describe another unusual artist, such as "The Crier," "The Sneezer," or "The Whistler." Tell how the artist performs this art form and how he or she feels about the work.

DISCOVERY

*To see a world in a grain of sand
And a heaven in a wild flower,
Hold Infinity in the palm of your hand
And Eternity in an hour.*

— William Blake
England

The Enigma of Time
Giorgio de Chirico (1888-1978)
Private Collection
Courtesy Scala/Art Resource

Discovery

Discoveries are an important part of growing. They can happen as the result of a long or difficult experience—or flash on you in an instant. In reading about the discoveries made by writers or the characters they invent, you may discover something new about yourself.

Self-Discovery

A frightening experience can teach you a lot about yourself and your life. Writers often describe how a difficult experience reveals something new to a character.

We make many discoveries in childhood that we remember our whole lives. In the short story "Dinner for Monsieur Martin," a young girl living in the Swiss mountains must do an odd and frightening thing—enter a room containing a huge, powerful bear. In facing the dangerous animal alone, the young girl learns something important about fear—a lesson she tries to teach to her son later in life.

As adults, we continue to make discoveries in difficult times. Wartime can reveal many truths. In facing the possibility of death, and in choosing between your own needs and those of your country, you can learn a lot about yourself. A story by Ilse Aichinger, "The Opened Order," is set during a war. The reader is not sure what war is being fought, what country the

main character is defending, or even what his name is. But this story could happen to any soldier in any war. In a story such as this, the reader shares the narrator's experiences, fears, and discoveries.

A New Light

Something previously hidden can tell a lot about the real nature of a friendship, once it is finally revealed. We can have friendships with animals as well as with people. "A Secret for Two" by Quentin Reynolds is about the friendship between an old man and his horse. At first, nothing unusual happens in the story. A milkman, with the help of his horse, faithfully does his job for 30 years. Then a secret is revealed that shows how special their relationship was.

As we grow up, we make many discoveries that change the way we see the world and that make us more mature. Writers all over the world have been inspired to write about the revelations that turn a child into an adult.

In "Father and I" by Par Lagerkvist, a boy and his father take a walk in the countryside, something they often do on beautiful Sunday afternoons. Nothing is different this day except that they stay out a little later than usual. But as it grows dark, the boy's feelings about the things around him start to change. His father

Detail of **Cat and Spider,** *Toko, ca. 1868–1911*

tells him not to be afraid. And then something happens, or rather, almost happens. One event shows the boy that his father does not know everything and will not always be able to protect him. Suddenly he realizes that life is a vast unknown, which he must face alone.

The relationship between parent and child is often the source of discoveries. In "Frame of Mind," an amusing story by Sam F. Ciulla, a son is perplexed. How does his father always manage to come out on top, even when he does things about which he knows nothing? When the son discovers the answer, it is not what he expects. He learns an important lesson about the power of respect, confidence, and trust.

Perhaps the most entertaining kind of discovery is the kind that is found in a mystery story. In "Madame Sara," a police surgeon and a detective work together to solve a mystery that surrounds one crime and to prevent another crime from taking place.

Reporter Henry Cooper is eager to discover "The Secret" hidden on a colonized Moon of the future. What he uncovers seems like good news until he realizes the implications of sharing his discovery with fellow humans back on Earth.

In reading this section, you will share the discoveries of many real and imaginary people. If you read carefully, you may experience some revelations of your own.

Dinner for Monsieur Martin

by Georges Surdez

Georges Surdez was born in Switzerland. He later moved to the United States, where, in Brooklyn, New York, he died in 1949. But his homeland is the setting for this story. In it, a young girl must serve dinner to a very unusual guest.

When I was a boy and frightened in new surroundings, my mother did not scold me. She took my plight seriously and told me a story to illustrate an important point about fear, which I never forgot. Even today, I have use for that story on occasions.

"Here you are," she started quietly, "afraid of everything — afraid of other boys, afraid to go upstairs in the dark, afraid of strange dogs. Afraid of a lot of things you are not even sure you should be afraid of. What would you do if you had to go into a room with a bear?"

"I wouldn't go," I told her.

"I did," she informed me.

"*Maman!* With a bear in the room, you. . . ?"

She had done that and she told me all about it. She was about 14 years old at the time, living in a village in the Swiss Jura. Her father owned a sizable farm and was quite hospitable. A wandering showman, whom Mother called a Bohemian, came through with a performing bear and gave an open-air exhibition.

That bear was as shaggy and massive as a self-respecting bear can be. Being in a French-speaking region, he was called Monsieur Martin while performing, although his master called him Tonio in private. He could do a lot of tricks, dance to the sounds of the accordion, march in step with a beating drum, salute the flag of the Helvetic confederation.[1]

The showman told of his great strength and ferocity. Monsieur Martin, it seemed, had a quick temper and tolerated no fooling. To guard against a hasty reaction, the man had him rigged with a stout collar, a chain, a heavy leather muzzle. During his performance, he would growl and snarl and his master would push him back to his proper place with a stout stick.

That night, my grandfather invited the Bohemian to stay at the farm, and the

---

1. Helvetic confederation: the Swiss nation

bear was placed in a shed near the stable. Of course, as amusement was scarce in the mountains, neighbors dropped in to talk with the foreigner.

There was plenty of wine, and some local liquors distilled from plums and cherries, which boast some fame in the region.

The Bohemian was an amazing fellow, who told odd yarns with an odder accent, and played his accordion like an expert. He could sing in any language you suggested—German, French, Italian, Russian — and had even picked up some patois[2] ballads.

It was about 10 o'clock that an unusual tumult broke out — loud grunts, the sound of planking being pounded, accompanied before very long by the neighing of horses and the plaints of disturbed cows. "Don't worry," the Bohemian said, "it's my Tonio. You people have been so nice to me I forgot to feed him, and he is making a fuss."

My mother's father was ashamed that even a bear should be hungry under his roof. He beckoned to my mother, who had kept in a corner so that she would not be noticed and sent to bed, and told her to go and feed the animal.

My grandmother protested mildly, but when she was reminded that the bear was in an enclosure and chained solidly, she smiled at my mother and nodded for her to do as ordered.

"What does he eat?" Mother asked.

"Oh, anything. Vegetables, cabbages, carrots, bread, cooked meat," the show-man said. "Mix them together, like for your pigs. Give him a lot; he has a fine appetite."

So my mother went to the stove — it was in the same room — and made up a paté.[3] She took her time about mixing the stuff, wondering whether it would be more dangerous to protest to her father or to go in with the bear. She picked the bear.

As she crossed the courtyard, leaving the sounds of laughter and singing behind, she could hear the bear clamoring for food. He quieted the moment the latch clicked under her hand. She had taken along a storm lantern, and when she entered the shed, she suspended it on a hook just outside the door.

The bear looked her over as keenly as she looked him over, and grumbled something under his breath. Then he vanished behind the planking. My mother heard him snuffling — he knew where the opening to the manger was. She stood there, her heart pounding, for a time, then braced herself, walked the six or seven feet to the partition, and slid a plank aside. As she shoved the pan through the opening, she saw two paws with long, rasping claws seize the utensil and drag it inside.

She was afraid, but she was even more curious. She found a crack between the planks and put her eye to it. Then her heart nearly stopped beating.

The bear had a stout collar, to which a chain was attached. But the chain was not fastened to anything! It was looped around his neck! And it was obvious, from his great bulk and evident strength, that had

2. *patois*: regional dialect of a language (French)

3. *paté*: a fine-grained meat-loaf; often with vegetables added (French)

263

he really wished to, he could have beaten the partition to splinters, knocked down the door, and made his escape.

But he had been satisfied with merely making a lot of noise! That demonstration of self-control reassured her.

Meanwhile, the bear had shoved the pan into a corner and was standing there, peering over his shoulder at the exact spot where she stood behind the partition. He knew very well that she had not gone away, that she was watching him. He would sniff over the food, then turn to snuffle and grunt in an annoyed tone.

Of course, Mother thought then, he can't eat because of his muzzle. I'll go back and tell the man.

But before she had time to act, the bear squatted, licked the food tentatively. Then, very calmly, he brought up both forepaws, slid the heavy muzzle from his nose, pushed it above his eyes, and began to eat.

"You understand," my mother concluded. "That bear just quietly pushed that muzzle up like an old lady pushing her spectacles up to her forehead. I knew that my father had guessed the truth, that I had been afraid for nothing, that the stories the man told about Monsieur Martin, the fits of anger, were all make-believe, to make the show more interesting. After that, I never was afraid of anything until I found out whether there was anything to be afraid of."

READING COMPREHENSION

Summarizing. Choose the best phrase to complete each sentence. Then write the complete statements on your paper.

1. The mother told the boy the story _____ (to frighten him, to impress him with her bravery, to teach him a lesson about fear).

2. During a performance, Monsieur Martin would _____ (growl and snarl and act vicious, act gentle and kind, walk a tightrope).

3. When the boy's mother went to feed the bear, she found that he was _____ (vicious, not chained to anything, frightened of her).

4. The girl's father had known that _____ (their daughter was brave, the bear was safely caged, the bear was harmless).

Interpreting. Write the answer to each question on your paper.

1. Why did the showman lie about the bear's temperament?

2. Which actions showed that the girl was brave?

3. What did the boy learn about fear from his mother's story?

For Thinking and Discussing. Do you think the boy's grandparents were right in testing their daughter's courage as they did? Why or why not?

UNDERSTANDING LITERATURE

Mood. The *mood* of a story is the feeling it creates. For example, the mood of the following sentence is one of danger and fear: "The howling wind lashed the trees over the girl's head, and black clouds blocked the moon's light. The girl stood trembling and alone on the dark path."

Read the following excerpts from "Dinner for Monsieur Martin." Select the best choice to complete each sentence. Then write the completed sentence on your paper.

1. "'Here you are,' she started quietly, 'afraid of everything—afraid of other boys, afraid to go upstairs in the dark, afraid of strange dogs.'" The mood of this sentence is _____.
   fright   calm   humor

2. The bear "had been satisfied with merely making a lot of noise! That demonstration of self-control reassured her." The mood of this sentence is _____.
   panic   matter-of-fact   great danger

3. "After that, I never was afraid of anything until I found out whether there was anything to be afraid of." How is this statement of theme similar to the mood of the story?

WRITING

Rewrite one paragraph of the story using words that create a strong mood of fear and danger. Or write an original paragraph creating the same mood.

The Opened Order

by Ilse Aichinger

Ilse Aichinger was born in Vienna, Austria, in 1921. World War II broke out while she was in her teens. Because she was partly Jewish, the Nazis forced her to work in a factory for several years. Soon after the war, she published a novel reflecting her experiences in Nazi-occupied Austria. Since then, she has mainly written radio plays and short stories. As you will see, her stories can end with a shock.

No instructions had come from headquarters for a long time, and it looked as if they were going to stay there for the winter. In the fields all around, the last berries were falling from the bushes and rotting in the moss. Sentries sat forlornly in the treetops and watched the falling shadows.

The enemy lay beyond the river and did not attack. Instead, the shadows grew longer every evening, and every morning the mist clung stubbornly to the hollows. Among the young volunteers of the defending army there were some who resented this kind of warfare. They had made up their minds to attack without orders, if need be, before the snow came.

When, therefore, one of them was ordered one morning to take a message to headquarters, he had an uncomfortable feeling of foreboding. Careless though they seemed in other matters, he knew that they would stand no nonsense in the event of mutiny.

Some questions that were put to him after he had delivered his message reminded him of an interrogation and increased his uneasiness. He found it all the more surprising therefore when, after a long wait, he was given an order in a sealed envelope, with instructions to get back to his unit with it before nightfall.

He was told to take the shorter way, which was shown to him on the map. To his displeasure, a man was detailed to go with him. Through the open window, he could see the beginning of the road he had to take. After crossing the clearing, it disappeared wantonly between the hazel bushes. He was warned again to take extreme care, and then sent off.

It was soon after midday. Clouds drifted across the sun and grazing cattle wandered over the grass and vanished unconcernedly into the thickets. The road was bad, and in places almost impassable because of encroachment by undergrowth. As soon as the driver put on a little speed, branches started hitting them in the face.

Every now and again, they emerged from between the tree trunks into open fields, which gave them a better view, and also enabled a better view to be had of them. They crossed them as quickly as possible. The driver bounced the vehicle over the roots of trees, and every now and then glanced back at the man with the order as if to make sure that his load was all right. This made him angry, and convinced him of his superiors' mistrust.

What had his message contained? He had heard that early that morning one of the distant posts had observed movement on the other side of the river. But such rumors were continually in circulation, and it was possible that they were invented by the staff to keep the troops quiet. But it was equally possible that sending him to deliver the message had been a subterfuge, and the confidence shown in him was sheer dissimulation.

If his message had contained something unexpected, it would emerge from the contents of the order that he was taking back. He said to himself that it would be better to find out what it said now, while they were traveling in an area under enemy observation. When he was asked why he had broken the seal, he could give some explanation. He felt the envelope in his pocket and fingered the seal. The itch to open it mounted like a fever within him.

To gain time, he asked the driver to change places with him. Driving calmed him. They had been driving through the woods for hours. In places, the track was covered with rubble where obstacles had been built, and from this it was evident that they were nearing their destination. This proximity filled the man with indifference. Perhaps it would prevent him from breaking the seal.

He drove on calmly and confidently. At a spot where the track suddenly curved and plunged downward in a suicidal manner, they escaped without harm. But immediately afterward, the vehicle came to a halt in the middle of a mud patch.

The engine had failed, and the cries of the birds made the quiet deeper than ever. Ferns grew all around. They dragged the vehicle out of the mud. The driver set about finding out the cause of the trouble. While he was lying underneath the vehicle, the man hesitated no further, but broke open the envelope, scarcely bothering even to preserve the seal. He leaned over the vehicle and read the order, which said that *he was to be shot!*

He managed to put it back in his breast pocket before the driver scrambled out and announced that everything was now in order. The driver asked whether he should drive on. Yes, he should. While he bent over the starting-handle, the man wondered whether to shoot him now or while he was driving. He had no doubt that his driver was an escort.

The track broadened out, as if it repented of its sudden plunge downward, and started gently mounting. "The soul of suicide, carried by angels," the man

quoted to himself. What surprised him was the trouble that was being taken with him.

The driver turned and said: "We shall have a quiet night." This sounded like the sheerest irony. But their closeness to their destination seemed to make him talkative, and he went on, without waiting for an answer. "That is, if we get there safely." The man took his revolver from its holster.

It was so dark in the wood that one might have supposed that night had already fallen. "When I was a boy," the driver said, "I used to have to walk home from school through the woods. I always used to sing."

They reached the last clearing unexpectedly quickly. He decided to kill the driver as soon as they had crossed it, because there the wood grew thick again before it opened out upon reaching the hamlet where his unit lay.

The man rested his revolver on his knees. When the first shot rang out, he had the impression that he had fired prematurely, against his will. But if his companion had been hit, his ghost must have had great presence of mind, because it accelerated and drove on.

It took a relatively long time to discover that it was not the driver, but he himself who had been hit. His arm sagged, and he dropped his revolver. More shots rang out before they reached the cover of the wood, but they all missed.

The ghost in front turned his cheerful face toward him. "We were lucky to get across," he said. "That field was under observation."

"Stop," the man exclaimed.

"Not here," the driver answered. "We had better go a little deeper into the wood."

"I've been hit," the man said in desperation.

The driver drove on a little way without looking around, and then stopped. He managed to staunch the flow of blood and tie up the wound. Then he said the only comforting thing he could think of. "We're nearly there."

A wounded man condemned to death, the man said to himself. "Wait!" he said aloud.

"Is anything else the matter?" the driver said impatiently.

"The order," the man said, and felt in his breast pocket. At the moment of his deepest despair, he read its contents in a new light. The order said the bearer was to be shot, but mentioned no names.

"Take it," he said. "My coat is covered in blood." If his companion refused to take it, it would put the matter beyond doubt.

After a moment's silence, he felt the envelope being taken from his hand. "All right," said the driver.

The last half hour passed in silence. Time and distance had turned into wolves devouring each other.

The unit was quartered in a hamlet of five farmhouses, of which three had been burned out in earlier skirmishes. The place was surrounded by forest, the grass had been trampled down, and vehicles and guns were standing about. Barbed wire marked off the area from the surrounding forest.

When the sentry asked him his business

the driver said he had a wounded man with him and had brought an order.

While the wounded man tried to sit up, he thought to himself that this place was no more of a jail than any other place in the wide world. They were to be regarded as points of departure rather than of arrival. He heard a voice asking: "Is he conscious?" and kept his eyes shut. It was important to gain time. When they lifted him out of the vehicle, he hung limply in their arms.

They carried him into one of the houses across a yard in the middle of which was a well. Two dogs snuffed about him. The wound hurt. They laid him on a bench in a room on the ground floor. The windows were open, and there was no light. "You look after him," the driver said. "I mustn't lose any more time."

The man expected them to come and dress his wound, but when he opened his eyes, he found himself alone. Perhaps they had gone to fetch the first-aid kit.

There was a lively coming and going in the house, the sound of voices and footsteps and doors being slammed. But all this contained its own peculiar hush and increased the surrounding silence, as the shrieking of the birds had done.

What is all this about? the man said to himself and, after a few more minutes in which no one appeared, he started considering the possibility of immediate flight. A number of rifles were in the room. He would tell the sentry he had been ordered back to headquarters with another message. He had the necessary papers.

He tried to sit up, but was surprised to find how great was the weakness which he thought he had been shamming. Impatiently he put his feet down and tried to get up but found that he could not stand. He sat down again, and stubbornly tried a second time.

In doing so, he tore open the emergency dressing that the driver had put on his wound, and it started bleeding again. It opened with the vehemence of a hidden wish. He felt the blood seeping through his shirt and wetting the wood of the bench on which he had sunk back.

Through the window, he saw the sky over the whitewashed farmhouse wall. He heard the noise of hooves. The horses were being put back in their stable. There was more activity in the house than ever. It grew noisier and noisier. Something unexpected must have happened. He pulled himself up to the window, but collapsed again, and he called out, but no one heard. He had been forgotten.

As he lay there, the revolt seething inside him yielded to a desperate cheerfulness. It struck him that bleeding to death was like escaping through a bolted door, bypassing all sentries.

As he had wished for action for its own sake, and not for the sake of his country's defense, the sentence that was being fulfilled on him was right. As he was sick of inaction on the frontier, it meant release.

Shots rang out in the distance. He opened his eyes and remembered. Handing the order to the driver had been stupid and useless. While he lay there bleeding to death, they were leading the man to execution among the debris of the burned-out farmhouses. Perhaps they had already bound his eyes, and only his mouth was

still half open with surprise, and they were presenting, aiming, and. . . .

When he came round, he felt his wound had been dressed. He thought it an unnecessary service carried out by the angels for a man who had bled to death, an act of mercy performed too late. "So we meet again!" he said to the driver who was bending over him. Only when he noticed that an officer from the staff was standing at the foot of his bed did he realize with horror that he was not dead.

"The order!" he said. "What happened to the order?"

"It was damaged by the round that hit you," the officer answered, "but it was still legible."

"I should have delivered it myself," he said.

"We got here just in time," the driver interrupted. "The enemy has started a general assault."

"It was the news we were waiting for," the officer remarked as he turned to go. At the door, he turned again and, just for the sake of saying something, added:

"It's just as well you didn't know the wording of the message. We had an extraordinary code-phrase for the beginning of the operation."

READING COMPREHENSION

Summarizing. Choose the best phrase to complete each sentence. Then write the complete statements on your paper.

1. The volunteer soldiers were thinking about _____ (joining the enemy, attacking without orders, deserting the army).

2. The young man was shot just before he _____ (delivered the order, tried to shoot the driver, tried to escape).

3. The young man gave the driver the order so that _____ (the driver could read it, it would be delivered safely, the driver would be shot in his place).

4. The young soldier almost died from _____ (a shot from the firing squad, bleeding, suicide).

5. The order was _____ (really a coded message, a trick to fool the enemy, destroyed by the bullet).

Interpreting. Write the answer to each question on your paper.

1. What did the order actually mean?

2. Who shot the soldier?

3. Why did the soldier believe that his superiors might want to execute him?

For Thinking and Discussing. Near the end of the story, the soldier thought that he deserved to die. Why did he feel this way?

UNDERSTANDING LITERATURE

Mood and Character. The *mood* of a story is the feeling it creates. When the events of a story are told from the viewpoint of one *character*, the mood of the story reflects this character's state of mind.

In "The Opened Order," the events of the story are told to us through the viewpoint of the young soldier. The key to the soldier's state of mind is in the second paragraph:

Among the young volunteers of the defending army, there were some who resented this kind of warfare. They had made up their minds to attack without orders, if need be, before the snow came.

1. Which of the following emotions did the young soldier feel as a result of his mutinous ideas: pride, guilt, nervousness, fear, security, suspicion, confusion, calm? Write the correct choices on your paper.

2. Look back through the story and find three sentences that reflect the young soldier's emotional state. Write them on your paper.

WRITING

Rewrite the opening paragraph of the story from the viewpoint of a soldier who feels proud about delivering the order. Use details and words that help the reader understand the soldier's feelings. Try to create a mood that will reflect the soldier's state of mind.

A Secret for Two

by Quentin Reynolds

*In this story, set in Montreal, Quebec, in Canada, everyone
on Prince Edward Street knows that Joseph and Pierre are
quite a team. But not until someone makes a surprising
discovery do people realize just how close this friendship is.*

Montreal is a very large city but, like
all large cities, it has some very small
streets. Streets, for instance, like Prince
Edward Street, which is only four blocks
long, ending in a cul-de-sac.[1] No one knew
Prince Edward Street as well as did Pierre
Dupin, for Pierre had delivered milk to
the families on the street for 30 years now.

During the past 15 years, the horse that
drew the milk wagon used by Pierre was
a large white horse named Joseph. In
Montreal, especially in that part of Montreal that is very French, the animals, like
children, are often given the names of
saints. When the big white horse first came
to the Provinçale Milk Company, he didn't
have a name. They told Pierre that he
could use the white horse henceforth.
Pierre stroked the softness of the horse's
neck, he stroked the sheen of its splendid
belly, and he looked into the eyes of the
horse.

"That is a kind horse, a gentle and a
faithful horse," Pierre said, "and I can see
a beautiful spirit shining out of the eyes

of the horse. I will name him after good
St. Joseph, who was also kind and gentle
and faithful and had a beautiful spirit."

Within a year, Joseph knew the milk
route as well as Pierre. Pierre used to boast
that he didn't need reins — he never
touched them. Each morning, Pierre arrived at the stables of the Provinçale Milk
Company at five o'clock. The wagon would
be loaded and Joseph hitched to it. Pierre
would call, "Bonjour, vieil ami,"[2] as he
climbed into his seat and Joseph would
turn his head and the other drivers would
smile and say that the horse would smile
at Pierre. Then Jacques, the foreman, would
say, "All right, Pierre, go on," and Pierre
would call softly to Joseph, "Avance, mon
ami,"[3] and this splendid combination would
stalk proudly down the street.

The wagon, without any direction from
Pierre, would roll three blocks down St.
Catherine Street; then turn right two blocks
along Roslyn Avenue; then left, for that
was Prince Edward Street. The horse would

---

1. *cul-de-sac:* a dead-end (French)

2. *"Bonjour, vieil ami":* "Hello, my old friend." (French)
3. *"Avance, mon ami":* "Go on, my friend." (French)

273

stop at the first house, allow Pierre perhaps 30 seconds to get down from his seat and put a bottle of milk at the front door and would then go on, skipping two houses and stopping at the third. And so they went, down the street. Then Joseph, still without any direction from Pierre, would turn around and come back along the other side. Yes, Joseph was a smart horse.

Pierre would boast at the stable of Joseph's skill. "I never touch the reins. He knows just where to stop. Why, a blind man could handle my route with Joseph pulling the wagon."

So it went on for years — always the same. Pierre and Joseph both grew old together, but gradually, not suddenly. Pierre's huge walrus mustache was pure white now and Joseph didn't lift his knees so high or raise his head quite as much. Jacques, the foreman of the stables, never noticed that they were both getting old until Pierre appeared one day carrying a heavy walking stick.

"Hey, Pierre," Jacques laughed. "Maybe you got the gout, hey?"

"Mais oui,[4] Jacques," Pierre said uncertainly. "One grows old. One's legs get tired."

"You should teach the horse to carry the milk to the front door for you," Jacques told him. "He does everything else."

Pierre knew every one of the 40 families he served on Prince Edward Street. The cooks knew that Pierre could neither read nor write, so instead of following the usual custom of leaving a note in an empty

bottle if an additional quart of milk was needed they would sing out when they heard the rumble of his wagon wheels over the cobbled street, "Bring an extra quart this morning, Pierre."

Pierre had a remarkable memory. When he arrived at the stable, he'd always remember to tell Jacques, "The Parquins took an extra quart this morning; the Lemoines bought a pint of cream."

Jacques would note these things in a little book he always carried. Most of the drivers had to make out the weekly bills and collect the money, but Jacques, liking Pierre, had always excused him from this task. All Pierre had to do was to arrive at

---

4. *"Mais oui, Jacques"*: "Certainly, Jacques." (French)

five in the morning, walk to his wagon, which was always in the same spot at the curb, and deliver his milk. He returned some two hours later, got stiffly from his seat, called a cheery "Au 'voir"[5] to Jacques, and then limped slowly down the street.

One morning, the president of the Provinçale Milk Company came to inspect the early morning deliveries. Jacques pointed Pierre out to him and said, "Watch how he talks to that horse. See how the horse listens and how he turns his head toward Pierre? See the look in that horse's eyes? You know, I think those two share a secret. I have often noticed it. It is as though they both sometimes chuckle at us as they go off on their route. Pierre is a good man, Monsieur President, but he gets old. Would it be too bold for me to suggest that he be retired and be given perhaps a small pension?" he added anxiously.

"But of course," the president laughed. "I know his record. He has been on this route now for thirty years and never once has there been a complaint. Tell him it is time he rested. His salary will go on just the same."

But Pierre refused to retire. He was panic-stricken at the thought of not driving

---

5. *"Au 'voir"*: "Good-bye." (French)

Joseph every day. "We are two old men," he said to Jacques. "Let us wear out together. When Joseph is ready to retire — then I, too, will quit."

Jacques, who was a kind man, understood. There was something about Pierre and Joseph that made a man smile tenderly. It was as though each drew some hidden strength from the other. When Pierre was sitting in his seat, and when Joseph was hitched to the wagon, neither seemed old. But when they finished their work, then Pierre would limp down the street slowly, seeming very old indeed, and the horse's head would drop and he would walk very wearily to his stall.

Then one morning, Jacques had dreadful news for Pierre when he arrived. It was a cold morning and still pitch-dark. The air was like iced wine that morning and the snow, which had fallen during the night, glistened like a million diamonds piled together.

Jacques said, "Pierre, your horse, Joseph, did not wake this morning. He was very old, Pierre, he was twenty-five, and that is like seventy-five for a man."

"Yes," Pierre said, slowly. "Yes. I am seventy-five. And I cannot see Joseph again."

"Of course you can," Jacques soothed. "He is over in his stall, looking very peaceful. Go over and see him."

Pierre took one step forward, then turned. "No . . . no . . . you don't understand, Jacques."

Jacques clapped him on the shoulder. "We'll find another horse just as good as Joseph. Why, in a month you'll teach him to know your route as well as Joseph did. We'll — "

The look in Pierre's eyes stopped him. For years, Pierre had worn a heavy cap, the peak of which came low over his eyes, keeping the bitter morning wind out of them. Now Jacques looked into Pierre's eyes and he saw something that startled him. He saw a dead, lifeless look in them. The eyes were mirroring the grief that was in Pierre's heart and his soul. It was as though his heart and soul had died.

"Take today off, Pierre," Jacques said, but already Pierre was hobbling off down the street, and had one been near one would have seen tears streaming down his cheeks and have heard half-smothered sobs. Pierre walked to the corner and stepped into the street. There was a warning yell from the driver of a huge truck that was coming fast and there was the scream of brakes, but Pierre apparently heard neither.

Five minutes later, an ambulance driver said, "He's dead. Was killed instantly."

Jacques and several of the milk-wagon drivers had arrived and they looked down at the still figure.

"I couldn't help it," the driver of the truck protested, "he walked right into my truck. He never saw it, I guess. Why, he walked into it as though he was blind."

The ambulance doctor bent down. "Blind? Of course the man was blind. See those cataracts? This man has been blind for many years." He turned to Jacques. "You say he worked for you? Didn't you know he was blind?"

"No . . . no . . ." Jacques said, softly. "None of us knew. Only one knew — a friend of his named Joseph. . . . It was a secret, I think, just between those two."

READING COMPREHENSION

Summarizing. Choose the best phrase to complete each sentence. Then write the complete statements on your paper.

1. The most remarkable thing about Joseph was that he _____ (knew exactly where to go without any direction from Pierre, followed orders better than any other horse in Montreal, was patient).

2. Although Pierre had become old and tired, he refused to retire until _____ (he got a pension, Joseph was ready to retire, he couldn't see anymore).

3. The dreadful news that Pierre learned one morning was that _____ (he must retire, the milk company was closed, Joseph had died).

4. At the end of the story, we learned that _____ (Joseph had been Pierre's eyes, Pierre could not live without his job, Pierre and Joseph were heroes).

Interpreting. Write the answer to each question on your paper.

1. Why did Pierre not read notes or make out bills as part of his job?

2. What hint were we given in the story that Pierre might be blind?

3. Why did Pierre refuse to retire?

For Thinking and Discussing. Why did Pierre keep his blindness a secret? Do you think he was right to do so? Explain why or why not.

UNDERSTANDING LITERATURE

Setting. The "where" and "when" of a story is its *setting*. The setting provides the background through which the characters and the action move. Setting plays an important part in the story "A Secret for Two." The author gives a detailed description of the story's locale. He provides specific information about the main character's occupation, the streets on his milk route, and his daily routine. In short, he creates a very strong "sense of place" for his story's action.

Refer to the story to answer the following questions. Write the answers on your paper.

1. What is the geographic location, the "where," of the story? Give a specific example of a sentence from the story that tells you where the story is set.

2. What is the approximate time period of the story? Write a sentence from the story that gives you a clue to its time.

3. What is everyday life like for the main character? Write a sentence from the story that describes his way of living.

4. How does the setting — the time and place — add to the effectiveness of the story?

WRITING

Write a detailed description of a setting you are familiar with. Use details that tell the time and place you are describing.

Father and I

by Par Lagerkvist

The Swedish writer Par Lagerkvist received the Nobel Prize for literature in 1951. Much of his poetry and prose expresses a sense of despair, a feeling that the modern world is a dark and unknowable place. In this story, you will read about one step in the forming of the writer's attitude toward life.

When I was 10, Father took me by the hand one Sunday afternoon. We were to go out into the woods and listen to the birds singing. Waving good-bye to Mother, we set off briskly in the warm sunshine. We were sound, sensible people, Father and I, brought up with nature and used to it. There was nothing to make a fuss about. It was just that it was Sunday afternoon and Father was free. We walked along the railway line. People were not allowed to go there as a rule, but Father worked on the railway and so he had a right to. By doing this we could get straight into the woods, too, without going a roundabout way.

Soon the bird-song began and all the rest. The hum goes on all around you as soon as you enter a wood. The ground was white with wildflowers. The birches had just come out into leaf, and the spruces had fresh shoots. There were scents on all sides. Underfoot, the mossy earth lay steaming in the sun. There was noise and movement everywhere. Bumblebees came out of their holes, midges swarmed wherever it was marshy, and birds darted out of the bushes to catch them and back again as quickly.

All at once, a train came rushing along and we had to go down onto the embankment. Father hailed the engine driver with two fingers to his Sunday hat. The driver saluted and extended his hand. It all happened quickly. Then on we went. Everything smelled, grease and meadow-sweet, tar and heather by turns. The rails glinted in the sun. On either side of the line were telegraph poles, which sang as you passed them. Yes, it was a lovely day. The sky was quite clear. Not a cloud to be seen. There couldn't be any, either, on a day like this, from what Father said.

After awhile, we came to a field of oats to the right of the line, where a farmer we knew had a clearing. The oats had come up close and even. Father scanned them with an expert eye and I could see he was satisfied. I knew very little about such things, having been born in a town. Then we came to the bridge over a stream, which most of the time had no water to speak of but which now was in full spate. We held hands so as not to fall down between the planks. Soon we came to a cottage surrounded by greenery, apple trees and gooseberry bushes. We called in to see the owners and were offered milk. We saw their pig and hens, and their fruit trees in blossom; then we went on. We wanted to get to the river, for it was more beautiful there than anywhere else. It flowed past where Father had lived as a child. We usually liked to come as far as this before we turned back, and today, too, we got there after a good walk. It was near the next station, but we didn't go so far. Father just looked to see that the flag signal was right — he thought of everything.

We stopped by the river, which murmured in the hot sun, broad and friendly. The shady trees hung along the banks and were reflected in the backwater. It was all fresh and light here; a soft breeze was blowing off the small lakes higher up. We climbed down the slope and walked a little way along the bank, Father pointing out the spots for fishing. He had sat here on the stones as a boy, waiting for perch all day long. We hung about on the bank for a good while. We threw pebbles into the water to see who could throw farthest. We were both cheerful, Father and I. At last we felt tired and set off for home.

It was beginning to get dark. The woods were changed — it wasn't dark there yet, but almost. We quickened our steps. Mother would be getting anxious and waiting with supper. She was always afraid something was going to happen. But it hadn't. It had been a lovely day, nothing had happened that shouldn't.

The twilight deepened. The trees were so funny. They stood listening to every step we took. Under one of them was a glowworm. It lay down there in the dark staring at us. I squeezed Father's hand, but he didn't see the strange glow, just walked on. Now it was quite dark. We came to the bridge over the stream. It roared down there in the depths, horribly, as though it wanted to swallow us up. The pit yawned below us. We trod carefully on the planks, holding each other tightly by the hand so as not to fall in.

We went on. Father was so calm as he walked there in the darkness, with even strides, not speaking. I couldn't understand how he could be so calm when it was so murky. I looked all around me in fear. Nothing but darkness everywhere. I hardly dared take a deep breath. The embankment sloped steeply down, as though into pits black as night. The telegraph poles rose, ghostly, to the sky. Inside them was a hollow rumble, as though someone were talking deep down in the earth, and the white porcelain caps sat huddled fearfully together listening to it. It was all horrible. Nothing was right, nothing real. It was all so weird.

Hugging close to Father, I whispered, "Father, why is it so horrible when it's dark?"

"No, my boy, it's not horrible," he said, taking me by the hand.

"Yes, Father, it is."

"No, my child, you mustn't think that."

I felt so lonely, forsaken. It was so strange that only I was afraid, not Father, that we didn't think the same. And strange that what he said didn't help me and stop me from being afraid.

Railroad Tracks, *Oscar Bluemner, ca 1867–1931*

We walked in silence, each with his own thoughts. My heart contracted, as though the darkness had got in and was beginning to squeeze it.

Then we suddenly heard a mighty roar behind us! We were awakened out of our thoughts in alarm. Father pulled me down onto the embankment, down into the pit. He held me there. Then the train tore past, a black train. All the lights in the carriages were out, and it was going at frantic speed. What sort of train was it? There wasn't one due now! We gazed at it in terror. The fire blazed in the huge engine as they shoveled in coal; sparks whirled out into the night. It was terrible. The driver stood there in the light of the fire. He was pale, motionless, as though turned to stone. Father didn't recognize him. He didn't know who he was. The man just stared straight ahead, rushing into the darkness, far into the darkness that had no end.

Beside myself with dread, I stood there panting. I gazed after the furious vision. It was swallowed up by the night. Father took me up onto the line; we hurried home. He said, "Strange, what train was that? And I didn't recognize the driver." Then we walked on in silence.

But my whole body was shaking. It was for me, for my sake. I sensed what it meant. It was the fear and worry that was to come, the unknown. It was all that Father knew nothing about, that he wouldn't be able to protect me against. That was how this world, this life, would be for me. It was not like Father's, where everything was secure and certain. It wasn't a real world, a real life. It just hurtled, blazing, into a darkness that had no end.

READING COMPREHENSION

Summarizing. Choose the best phrase to complete each sentence. Then write the complete statements on your paper.

1. The boy's father seemed _____ (calm and strong, afraid and insecure, reckless).

2. When the boy began to feel afraid, his father _____ (was able to calm him, told him not to be afraid, was annoyed with him).

3. The train that came by at night was _____ (mysterious and completely unexpected, full of vacationers whom the boy's father knew, the regularly scheduled train).

4. The boy realized that _____ (his father was ignorant, he would be like his father someday, there were some things no one could protect him against).

Interpreting. Write the answer to each question on your paper.

1. What emotions did the boy feel in the daylight part of the walk?

2. How did the boy feel when darkness fell?

3. How did the boy view his relationship with his father at the beginning of the story and at the end?

For Thinking and Discussing. Why will the boy's life probably be very different from that of his father?

UNDERSTANDING LITERATURE

Mood and Setting. A story's *mood* is the feeling it creates in the reader. A story's *setting* is its physical background. Often these two elements interact in a story.

In "Father and I," a father and son take a walk on a bright, sunny day and return later in the gathering darkness. The story has two strong and contrasting moods: that of the daylight part of the walk and that of the nighttime part. The setting of each part is the same; however, the moods are very different.

1. The list below contains descriptions of the story's setting. Make two columns on your paper. Label one "Daylight," the other "Nighttime." Write each sentence below in the proper column.
   a. "The ground was white with wildflowers."
   b. "The rails glinted in the sun."
   c. "The telegraph poles rose, ghostly, to the sky."
   d. "The embankment sloped steeply down, as though into pits black as night."

2. Describe the mood of the daylight descriptions.

3. Describe the mood of the nighttime descriptions.

WRITING

Describe the nighttime part of the walk from the father's viewpoint. As you describe the setting, create a mood that shows the father's feelings.

Frame of Mind

by Sam F. Ciulla

Sometimes words stand for a lot more than they say. What do the words frame of mind *mean to you? In this story, a boy finally finds out that they mean something very special to his father; at the same time, he makes a discovery that is a step on the road to adulthood.*

Sometimes my father scares me. He can tackle something he knows nothing about, and nine times out of ten, it will come out all right. It's pure luck, of course, but try convincing him.

"Frame of Mind," he says. "Just believe you can do a thing, and you'll do it."

"Anything?" I asked. "What about brain surgery?"

"Oh, now, don't be foolish," my mother says. "Something like that takes years of practice."

"Step aside," my father says to me. "You're blocking the screen. How can I see the wrestlers with you blocking the screen?"

"Never mind the screen," I answer. "Someday your luck will run out. Then see what good your Frame of Mind will do."

Believe me, I am not just being a smart aleck. It so happens that I have actually tried Frame of Mind myself.

The first time was the year I went all out to pass the civics final. I *had* to go all out, on account of I had not cracked a book all year. I really crammed, and all the time I was cramming I was concentrating on Frame of Mind. Just believe you can do a thing — sure. I made the lowest score in the history of Franklin High.

"Thirty-three percent," I said, showing my father the report card. "There's your Frame of Mind for you."

He put it on the table without looking at it. "You have to reach a certain age and understanding," he explained. "That's the key to Frame of Mind."

"Yeah? What does a guy do in the meantime?"

"Maybe you should study. Some kids learn a lot that way."

That was my first experience with Frame of Mind. My latest one was for a promotion at the Austin Clothing Store. Jim Watson had more experience and a slightly better sales record. Me, I had Frame of Mind. Jim Watson got the job.

Did this convince my father? It did not. To convince him, something had to happen. To him, I mean. Something did hap-

283

pen, too, at the Austin Clothing Store. My father works there, too.

What happened was that Mr. Austin paid good money for a clever Easter window display. It's all set up and we're about to draw the curtain when we discover the display lights won't work. Mr. Austin looks like he is strangling. He is probably thinking of the customers that could go right by his store in the time it will take him to get hold of an electrician.

This is when my father comes on the scene. "Is something the matter?" he says.

"Oh, hello, Louis," Mr. Austin says.

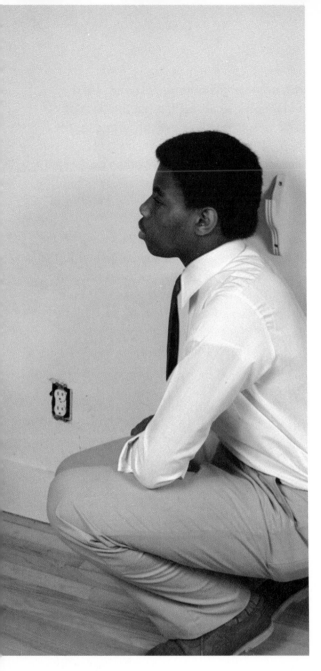

He calls my father "Louis." Me, Joe Conklin — one of his best salesmen — he hardly knows. My father, a stock clerk, he calls "Louis." "These darned lights won't work."

"H'mm, I see," my father says. "Maybe I can be of service." From inside his pocket comes a screwdriver.

Mr. Austin looks at him. "Can you really help us, Louis?"

"No, he cannot," I volunteer. "You think he's Thomas Edison or something?" I do not intend to say that. It just slips out.

"Young man, I was addressing your father," Mr. Austin says, giving me a cold hard look. "When I *want* sarcastic comments, I will ask for them."

"That's right," my father — my own flesh and blood — chimes in. "Mind your manners, Joey."

He turns and steps carefully around a manikin. He spies an electric-duct opening and starts to insert the screwdriver.

"Don't touch that!" I yell. "You'll be electrocuted!"

My father touches it. He is not electrocuted. The display lights go on. Mr. Austin stops getting red in the face. He smiles.

That evening my father explains Conklin's Principle of Frame of Mind as applied to display lighting.

"Frame of Mind, baloney," I object. "That had nothing to do with it."

"Step aside," my father says. "You're blocking the screen."

What happened next was that the big safe in Mr. Austin's office got jammed shut with all our paychecks in it. This was just before a weekend. The end of the month. Gloom. Despair.

From nowhere comes my father. "Is something the matter?" he says.

Suddenly I get this strange feeling that I have already lived through this. "It's this darned safe, Louis," Mr. Austin is saying. "It won't open."

"H'mm, I see," my father says. "Maybe I can be of service."

"Can you really help us, Louis?" Mr. Austin inquires.

I start to say no, he cannot, but I stop myself. I have had enough of Mr. Austin's cold hard looks. If my father wants to be a clown, that's his business.

"Mr. Austin," my father says, "what is the combination of this safe?"

Mr. Austin whispers the combination in my father's ear. He does so without hesitating. My father has a strange power over people.

Armed with the combination, he starts twirling the knob. I say to myself: Watch that safe door spring open — that old Conklin luck. But we wait and nothing happens.

"The tumblers are jobbled," he says at last. "The internal pin is unbalanced." As you can see, he doesn't know the first thing about office safes.

"Call the manufacturer," Mr. Austin orders.

Everyone groans. The manufacturer is way out in Chicago.

"Mr. Austin, wait a minute. I'm not finished yet," my father says. Already he is concentrating on the safe again, but this time it's a real production. First, he rolls up his sleeves. Then he rubs the tips of his fingers on his shirt front, no doubt to make them more sensitive. He begins twirling the knob, very slowly. And talk about ham — he even puts his ear to the safe door, to catch the telltale click of the tumblers!

I look around the room to see who is laughing. No one is laughing — not one person. I can't believe it. I look again. Still, no one is laughing. Not only are they not laughing at my father, but they actually think he's going to open up that safe for them. I can see it in their faces. It's fantastic: grown men and women standing hypnotized, *expecting* that safe door to open. And while they stand there, the safe door opens.

That evening my father and I are watching television. That is, *he* is watching television. Me, I'm just letting different thoughts float through my mind. Finally, my father speaks. "Go ahead, say it," he remarks. "Get it over with."

"Say what?" I inquire.

"Say it was luck, my opening the safe today."

"OK," I reply. "I'll say it: Maybe it was luck. But maybe it was something else, too."

Then I tell him what I saw in the faces of those people in Mr. Austin's office. To describe it I use words like *confidence* and *trust* and *respect*.

"That's the key to Frame of Mind," I conclude. "It won't help a high school kid make up a year of loafing, and it won't get a guy promoted over someone who deserves it more. The key to Frame of Mind is you have got to use it to help others, like you do. Otherwise it will not work."

My father just stares at me. I suspect he is thinking maybe I have reached a certain age and understanding. However, this is not what he says.

"Step aside," is what he says. "You're blocking the screen. How can I see the wrestlers with you blocking the screen?"

READING COMPREHENSION

Summarizing. Choose the best phrase to complete each sentence. Then write the complete statements on your paper.

1. Frame of Mind didn't help the son pass a test because he _____ (didn't believe in it, was too nervous, hadn't studied enough).

2. The father worked in a clothing store as _____ (a stock clerk, a salesman, an electrician).

3. Mr. Austin and the store employees reacted to the father with _____ (disbelief in his powers, nervousness, respect and trust).

4. The key to Frame of Mind is _____ (using it to help others, using it selfishly, luck).

5. By the end of the story, the son felt _____ (scorn for his father, envious of his father, respect for his father).

Interpreting. Write the answer to each question on your paper.

1. What was the son's attitude toward his father at the beginning of the story?

2. Why did Mr. Austin tell the father the safe combination without hesitating?

3. What lesson about life did the son learn?

For Thinking and Discussing. Do the father and son have good communication? Explain why or why not.

UNDERSTANDING LITERATURE

Mood and Point of View. The *mood* of a story is the feeling that the author conveys to the reader. The mood is very clear when a story is written from the *first-person point of view*. Sam F. Ciulla wrote the story "Frame of Mind" from the first-person point of view. The narrator reveals his attitude, or Frame of Mind, to us through the way he tells his story. The mood of the story matches his attitude toward life.

Answer the following questions about the story.

1. Is the mood of the story humorous or serious? How do the kinds of problems described by the narrator affect the mood of the story?

2. Read the following passage from the last part of the story and answer the question below.

The key to Frame of Mind is you have got to use it to help others, like you do. Otherwise it will not work.

How have the emotional attitude of the narrator and the mood of the story changed from the start of the story?

WRITING

Retell the story briefly from the father's point of view. What was he trying to teach his son? How did he finally succeed? Show how the father's mood and attitude toward his son changed from the beginning to the end of the story.

Madame Sara

by Lillie Meade and Robert Eustace

Lillie Meade was an author, and Robert Eustace was a scientist. Together, they created some of England's earliest and cleverest mystery stories. "Madame Sara" involves a crime so carefully constructed that it takes a scientist and a detective to solve it. Although this story was written nearly 100 years ago, it still presents a challenge to readers.

Everyone in England has heard of Werner's Agency. It's a detective agency that investigates the finances of business firms. Of this agency, I, Dixon Druce, was appointed manager. Since then, I have met odd people and seen strange sights. People do curious things for money in this world.

It so happened that my business took me to Madeira. I left the island on the 14th of the month. We sailed on a lovely night. The strains of the band in the public gardens came floating across the bay through the warm, balmy air. Then the engine bells rang to "full speed ahead." I bid farewell to the fairest island on earth; I turned to the smoking-room in order to light my cigar.

"Do you want a match, sir?"

The voice came from a slender, young-looking man. Before I could reply, he had struck one and held it out to me.

"Excuse me," he said, as he tossed it overboard, "but surely you are Dixon Druce?"

"I am, sir," I said, glancing keenly back at him, "but you have the advantage of me."

"Don't you know me?" he responded. "Jack Selby, Hayward's House, Harrow, 1879."

"By jove! So it is," I cried.

Our hands met in a warm clasp, and a moment later I found myself sitting close to my old school friend. I had not seen him from the moment when I said good-bye to Harrow School 20 years ago. He was a boy of 14 then, but nevertheless, I recognized him. He gave me a quick sketch of his history.

"My father left me plenty of money," he said, "and The Meadows, our old family place, is now mine. I have a taste for natural history. That taste took me two years ago to South America. I have had my share of strange adventures, and have collected valuable specimens. I am now on my way home from Para, on the Amazon. I came by a boat to Madeira and changed there to the Castle Line. But why all this talk about myself?" he added. "What about you, old chap? Are you settled down with a wife and kiddies of your own? Is that dream of your school days fulfilled, and are you the owner of the best private laboratory in London?"

"As to the laboratory," I said, with a smile, "you must come and see it. For the rest, I am unmarried. Are you?"

"I was married the day before I left Para, and my wife is on board with me."

"Capital," I answered. "Let me hear all about it."

"You shall. Her maiden name was Dallas; Beatrice Dallas. She is just 20 now. Her father was an Englishman and her mother a Spaniard. Neither parent is living. She has an elder sister, Edith, nearly 30 years of age, unmarried, who is on board with us. There is also a stepbrother, considerably older than either Edith or Beatrice. I met my wife last year in Para, and at once fell in love. I am the happiest man on earth. It goes without saying that I think her beautiful. She is also very well off. The story of her wealth is a curious one. Her uncle on the mother's side was an extremely wealthy Spaniard. He made an enormous fortune in Brazil. He owned several diamond mines. But it is supposed that his wealth turned his brain. At any rate, it seems to have done so as far as the disposal of his money went. He divided the yearly profits and interest between his nephew and his two nieces, but declared that the property itself should never be split up. He has left the whole of it to that one of the three who should survive the others. A perfectly insane arrangement."

"Very insane," I echoed. "What was he worth?"

"Over two million sterling."

"By jove!" I cried. "What a sum! But what about the half brother?"

"He must be over 40 years of age. I have never seen him. His sisters won't speak to him or have anything to do with him. I understand that he is a great gambler; I am further told that he is at present in England. One of the first things I must do when I get home is to find him out. He has to sign certain papers, for we shan't be able to put things straight until we get his whereabouts. Sometime ago, my wife and Edith heard that he was ill. Dead or alive, we must know all about him, and as quickly as possible."

I made no answer, and he continued:

"I'll introduce you to my wife and sister-in-law tomorrow. Beatrice is quite a child compared to Edith, who treats her almost like a mother. Bee is a little beauty. Edith is handsome, too, although I sometimes think she is as vain as a peacock. By the way, Druce, this brings me to another part of my story. The sisters know someone on board who is one of the most remarkable women that I have ever met. She goes by the name of Madame Sara, and knows London well. In fact, she has a shop in the Strand. What she has been doing in Brazil I do not know. She keeps all her affairs strictly private. But you will be amazed when I tell you what her calling is."

"What?" I asked.

"A professional beautifier. She claims to restore youth to those who consult her. She also declares that she can make quite ugly people handsome. There is no doubt that she is very clever. She knows a little bit of everything. She has wonderful recipes for medicines, surgery, and dentistry. She is a most lovely woman herself. She is very fair, with blue eyes, an innocent, childlike manner, and wavy gold hair. She says that she is very much older than she appears. She looks about 25. She seems to have traveled all over the world. Her father was Italian and her mother Indian. This woman deals in all sorts of curious secrets, but mainly in cosmetics. Her shop in the Strand could, I fancy, tell many a strange history. It is a fact that she occasionally performs small surgical operations. There is not a dentist in London who can compete with her. Edith Dallas is devoted to her."

"You give a very brilliant account of this woman," I said. "You must introduce me tomorrow."

"I will," answered Jack with a smile. "I should like your opinion of her. I am right glad I have met you, Druce. It is like old times. When we get to England, then you must come and see us. But I am afraid before I give myself up to mere pleasure I must find my brother-in-law, Henry Joachim Silva."

"If you have any difficulty, let me know," I said. "I can find almost any man in England, dead or alive."

I then gave Selby a short account of my own business.

"Well," he said. "You are the very man we want."

The next morning after breakfast Jack introduced me to his wife and sister-in-law. We had been chatting about five minutes when I saw coming down the deck a slight, rather small woman, wearing a big sun hat.

"Ah, Madame," cried Selby, "here you are. I had the luck to meet an old friend on board — Mr. Dixon Druce. I have been telling him all about you. Druce, this lady is Madame Sara."

She bowed gracefully and then looked at me earnestly. I had seldom seen a more lovely woman. Her eyes were penetrating and clever, and yet she had the innocent gaze of a child.

As we sat chatting lightly, I felt that she took an interest in me greater than might be expected upon an ordinary introduction. By slow degrees, she so turned the conversation as to leave Selby and his wife and sister out. Then as they moved away, she came a little nearer, and said in a low voice:

"I am very glad we have met, and yet how odd this meeting is! Was it really accidental?"

"I do not understand you," I answered.

"I know who you are," she said lightly. "You are the manager of Werner's agency. Its business is to know the private affairs of those people who would rather keep their own secrets. Now, Mr. Druce, I am going to be frank with you. I own a small shop in the Strand — a perfumery shop. Behind those innocent-looking doors I conduct the business that brings me in my living. Have you, Mr. Druce, any objection to my continuing to make a livelihood in perfectly innocent ways?"

"None whatever," I answered. "You puzzle me."

"I want you to pay my shop a visit

when you come to London. I have been away for three or four months. I do wonders for my clients, and they pay me well. I hold some secrets that I cannot tell to anyone. I have obtained them partly from the Indians and partly from the natives of Brazil. I have lately been in Para to find new ways to help my clients."

"And your trade is —?" I said, looking at her with amusement and some surprise.

"I am a beautifier," she said lightly. She looked at me with a smile. "Understand that my calling is quite an open one, but I do hold secrets. I should advise you, Mr. Druce, not to interfere with them."

The childlike expression faded from her face as she uttered the last words. There was a challenge in her tone. She turned away after a few moments and I rejoined my friends.

"You have been talking to Madame Sara, Mr. Druce," said Mrs. Selby. "Don't you think she is lovely?"

"She is one of the most beautiful women I have ever seen," I answered, "but there seems to be a mystery about her."

"Oh, indeed there is," said Edith Dallas.

"No one knows her age," said Mrs. Selby, "but I will tell you a curious fact, which, perhaps, you will not believe. She was bridesmaid at my mother's wedding 30 years ago. She declares that she never changes, and has no fear of old age."

"You mean that seriously?" I cried. "But surely it is impossible."

"Her name is on the register. My mother knew her well. She was mysterious then. I think my mother got on to her power, but of that I am not certain. Anyhow, Edith and I adore her, don't we, Edie?"

She laid her hand affectionately on her sister's arm. Edith Dallas did not speak, but her face was careworn. After a time she said slowly:

"Madame Sara is uncanny and terrible."

I felt now that this woman was a distinct mystery. That she was interested in me I did not doubt, perhaps because she was afraid of me.

The rest of the voyage passed pleasantly enough. The more I saw of Mrs. Selby and her sister, the more I liked them. They were quiet, simple, and straightforward. I felt sure that they were both as good as gold.

We parted at Waterloo, Jack and his wife and her sister going to Jack's house in Eaton Square, I returning to my quarters in St. John's Wood. I had a house there, with a long garden, at the bottom of which was my laboratory. The laboratory was the pride of my life. There I spent all my spare time, making experiments. I lived in hopes of doing great things some day. Werner's Agency was not to be the end of my career. Nevertheless, it interested me thoroughly, and I was not sorry to get back to my business.

The next day, just before I started to go to my office, Jack Selby was announced.

"I want you to help me," he said. "I have been trying to get information about my brother-in-law. But there is no such person in any of the directories. Can you help me?"

I said I could and would if he would leave the matter in my hands.

"With pleasure," he replied. Neither Edith nor Bee can get money with any regularity until the man is found. I cannot imagine why he hides himself."

"I will advertise in the newspapers," I said, "and ask anyone who can give information to communicate with me at my office. I will also give instructions to all the branches of my firm to keep their eyes open for any news. You may be quite certain that in a week or two we shall know about him."

Selby appeared cheered. Then, having begged of me to call upon his wife and her sister as soon as possible, took his leave.

On that very day, advertisements were drawn up and sent to several newspapers and agents. But week after week passed without the slightest result. Selby got very fidgety at the delay. He insisted on my coming, whenever I had time, to his house.

I was glad to do so. As to Madame Sara, I could not get her out of my head. One day, Mrs. Selby said to me:

"Have you ever been to see Madame? I know she would like to show you her shop."

"I did promise to call upon her," I answered, "but have not had time to do so yet."

"Will you come with me tomorrow?" asked Edith Dallas suddenly.

She turned red as she spoke. The worried, uneasy expression became more marked on her face. I had noticed for some time that she had been looking both nervous and depressed. I had first observed this on board the ship, but, as time went on, instead of lessening it grew worse. Her face, for so young a woman, was haggard. She jumped at each sound. Madame Sara's name was never spoken in her presence without her showing great emotion.

"Will you come with me?" she said, with great eagerness.

I immediately promised. The next day, about eleven o'clock, Edith Dallas and I found ourselves at Madame Sara's shop. In the windows of the shop were pyramids of perfume bottles. We stepped out of the cab and went indoors. Inside the shop were a couple of steps, which led to a door of solid mahogany.

Edith touched an electric bell. The door was immediately opened by a smartly dressed page-boy. He looked at Miss Dallas as if he knew her very well, and said:

"Madame is within, and is expecting you, miss."

He ushered us both into a quiet looking room. He left us, closing the door. Edith turned to me.

"Do you know where we are?" she asked.

"We are standing at present in a small room just behind Madame Sara's shop," I answered. "Why are you so excited, Miss Dallas? What is the matter with you?"

"We are on the threshold of a magician's cave," Edith said. "We shall soon be face-to-face with the most marvelous woman in the whole of London. There is no one like her."

"And you — fear her?" I said, dropping my voice to a whisper.

She started, stepped back, and with great difficulty calmed herself. At that moment, the page-boy returned to conduct us through to Madame herself.

"Ah!" she said, with a smile. "This is delightful. You have kept your word, Edith, and I am greatly obliged to you. I will now show Mr. Druce some of the mysteries of my trade. But understand, sir," she added, "that I shall not tell you any of my real secrets; but as you would like to know something about me you shall."

"How can you tell I should like to know about you?" I asked.

She said: "Knowledge is power. Don't refuse what I am willing to give. Edith, you will not object to waiting here while I show Mr. Druce through the rooms. First observe this room, Mr. Druce. It is lighted only from the roof. When the door shuts, it automatically locks itself, so that any intrusion is impossible. This is my private office — a faint odor of perfume pervades the room. This is a hot day, but the room itself is cool. What do you think of it all?"

I made no answer. She walked to the other end and motioned to me to accompany her. There stood a polished oak square table. On the table lay stoppered bottles full of strange medicines, mirrors, brushes, sprays, sponges, delicate needle-pointed instruments of bright steel, tiny lancets, and forceps. Facing this table was a chair, like those used by dentists. Above the chair hung electric lights in powerful reflectors, and lenses like bull's-eye lanterns. Another chair, supported on a glass pedestal, was kept there, Madame Sara informed me, for administering static electricity.

Madame took me into another room. Here were strange medicines, dentists' chairs, wooden operating table, and chloroform and ether apparatus. When I had looked at everything, she turned to me.

"Now you know," she said. "I am a doctor — perhaps a quack. These are my secrets. By means of these I live and flourish."

She turned her back on me and walked into the other room with the light, springy step of youth. Edith Dallas, white as a ghost, was waiting for us.

"You have done your duty, my child," said Madame. "Mr. Druce has seen just what I want him to see. I am very much obliged to you both. We shall meet tonight at Lady Farringdon's party. Until then, farewell."

When we got into the street and were driving back again to Eaton Square, I turned to Edith.

"Many things puzzle me about your friend," I said, "but perhaps none more than this. By what possible means can a woman shopkeeper obtain the invitation to some of the best houses in London? Why does society open her doors to this woman, Miss Dallas?"

"I cannot quite tell you," was her reply. "I only know the fact that, wherever she goes, she is welcomed and treated with consideration. Wherever she fails to appear, there is a universally expressed feeling of regret."

I had also been invited to Lady Farringdon's reception that evening, and I went there in a state of great curiosity. There was no doubt that Madame interested me. I was not sure of her. Beyond doubt there was a mystery attached to her.

I arrived early, and was standing in the crush near the head of the staircase when Madame Sara was announced. She wore the richest white satin and quantities of diamonds. I saw her hostess bend toward her and talk eagerly. I noticed Madame's reply and the pleased expression that crossed Lady Farringdon's face. A few minutes later, a man sat down before the grand piano. He played and Madame Sara began to sing. Her voice was sweet and low. It was the sort of voice that penetrates to the heart. There was an instant pause in the gay chatter. She sang amidst perfect silence. When the song had come to an end, there followed great applause. I was just turning to say something to my nearest neighbor when I observed Edith Dallas. Her eyes met mine. She laid her hand on my sleeve.

"The room is hot," she said. "Take me out on the balcony."

I did so. It was comparatively cool in the open.

"I must not lose sight of her," she said suddenly.

"Of whom?" I asked, somewhat astonished at her words.

"Of Sara."

"She is there," I said. "You can see her from where you stand."

We happened to be alone. I came a little closer.

"Why are you afraid of her?" I asked.

"Are you sure that we shall not be heard?" was her answer.

"She terrifies me," were her next words.

"I will not betray your confidence, Miss Dallas. Will you not trust me? You ought to give me a reason for your fears."

"I cannot — I dare not; I have said far too much already. Don't keep me, Mr. Druce. She must not find us together."

As she spoke, she pushed her way through the crowd, and before I could stop her was standing by Madame Sara's side.

The reception in Portland Place was, I remember, on the 26th of July. Two days later, the Selbys were to give their final party before leaving for the country. I was, of course, invited to be present, and Madame was also there. She had never been dressed more splendidly, nor had she ever before looked younger or more beautiful. Wherever she went, all eyes followed her. As a rule, her dress was simple, but tonight she chose a costume of many colors that glittered with gems. Her golden hair was studded with diamonds. Round her neck, she wore turquoise and diamonds mixed.

There were many other women in the room, but not the fairest had a chance beside Madame. It was not mere beauty. It was charm — charm that carries all before it.

I saw Miss Dallas, looking slim and tall and pale, standing at a little distance. I made my way to her side. Before I had time to speak, she bent toward me.

"Is she not divine?" she whispered. "She bewilders and delights everyone. She is taking London by storm."

"Then you are not afraid of her tonight?" I said.

"I fear her more than ever. She has cast a spell over me. But listen, she is going to sing."

I had not forgotten the song that Madame had sung at the Farringdons'. I stood still to listen. There was a complete hush in the room. Her voice floated over the heads of the guests in a dreamy Spanish song. Edith told me that it was a slumber song. Madame boasted of her power of putting almost anyone to sleep who listened to her rendering of it.

"She has many patients who suffer from insomnia," whispered Edith. "She generally cures them with that song, and that alone. Ah! We must not talk. She will hear us."

Before I could reply, Selby came hurrying up. He had not noticed Edith. He caught me by the arm.

"Come just for a minute to this window, Dixon," he said. "I must speak to you. I suppose you have no news with regard to my brother-in-law?"

"Not a word," I answered.

"To tell you the truth, I am getting

terribly put out over the matter. We cannot settle any of our money affairs because this man chooses to avoid us. My wife's lawyer wired to Brazil yesterday, but even his bankers do not know anything about him."

"The whole thing is a question of time," was my answer. "When are you off to Hampshire?"

"On Saturday."

As Selby said the last words, he looked around him, then he dropped his voice.

"I want to say something else. The more I see —" he nodded toward Madame Sara — "the less I like her. Edith is getting into a very strange state. Have you not noticed it? And the worst of it is my wife is also infected. I suppose it is that dodge of the woman's for patching people up and making them beautiful. Doubtless the temptation is overpowering in the case of a plain woman, but Beatrice is beautiful herself and young. What can she have to do with cosmetics and complexion pills?"

"You don't mean to tell me that your wife has consulted Madame Sara as a doctor?"

"Not exactly, but she has gone to her about her teeth. She complained of a toothache lately, and Edith is constantly going to her for one thing or another."

As Jack said the last words, he went over to speak to someone else, and before I could leave the seclusion of the window, I saw Edith Dallas and Madame Sara talking together. I could not help overhearing the following words:

"Don't come to me tomorrow. Get into the country as soon as you can. It is far and away the best thing to do."

As Madame spoke, she turned swiftly and caught my eyes. She bowed. The peculiar look, the sort of challenge she had given me before, flashed over her face. It made me uncomfortable, and during the night that followed, I could not get it out of my head. I remembered what Selby had said about his wife and her money affairs. Beyond doubt he had married into a mystery — a mystery that Madame knew all about. There was a very big money interest, and strange things happen when millions are concerned.

The next morning, I had just risen and was sitting at breakfast when a note was handed to me. It came by special messenger. It was marked "Urgent." I tore it open. These were its contents:

My dear Druce, A terrible blow has fallen on us. My sister-in-law, Edith, was taken suddenly ill this morning at breakfast. The nearest doctor was sent for, but he could do nothing. She died half an hour ago. Do come and see me. If you know any very clever specialist, bring him with you. My wife is in shock. Yours, Jack Selby.

I read the note twice before I could realize what it meant. Then I rushed out and, hailing the first cab I met, said to the man, "Drive to No. 192, Victoria Street, as quickly as you can."

Here lived a certain Mr. Eric Vandeleur, an old friend of mine. He was the police surgeon for the Westminster district, which included Eaton Square. No shrewder or sharper fellow existed than Vandeleur.

"Halloa!" Vandeleur cried. "I haven't seen you for ages. Do you want me?"

"Yes, very urgently," I answered. "Are you busy?"

"Head over ears, my dear chap. I cannot give you even a moment now, but
perhaps later on. I have to go to Eaton
Square like the wind, but come along
with me, if you like, and tell me on the
way."

"Capital," I cried. "The thing has been
reported then? You are going to Mr.
Selby's, No. 34a; then I am going with
you."

He looked at me in amazement.

"But the case has only just been reported. What can you possibly know about
it?"

"Everything. Let us take this cab, and
I will tell you as we go along."

As we drove to Eaton Square, I quickly
explained the situation.

"The thing promises to be serious," he
replied, as I finished, "but I can do nothing
until after the autopsy. Here we are, and
there is my man waiting for me; he has
been smart."

On the steps at Selby's stood an official-looking man in uniform, who saluted.

"Coroner's officer," explained Vandeleur.

We entered the silent, darkened house. Selby was standing in the hall. He came to meet us. I introduced him to Vandeleur, and he at once led us into the dining room. There we found Dr. Osborne, whom Selby had called in when Edith became ill. Dr. Osborne looked worried.

"I will have a chat with you in a few minutes, Dr. Osborne," Vandeleur said, "but first I must get Mr. Selby's report. Will you please tell me, sir, exactly what occurred?"

"Certainly," he answered. "We had a party here last night. My sister-in-law did not go to bed until early morning. She was in bad spirits, but otherwise in her usual health. My wife went into her room after she was in bed, and told me later on that she had found Edith in hysterics. She could not get her to explain anything. We both talked about taking her to the country without delay. Indeed, our intention was to get off this afternoon."

"Well?" said Vandeleur.

"We had breakfast about half-past nine, and Miss Dallas came down, looking well and apparently in good spirits. She ate with appetite, and, as it happened, she and my wife both ate the same food. The meal had nearly come to an end when she jumped up from the table. Then she uttered a sharp cry, turned very pale, pressed her hand to her side, and ran out of the room. My wife immediately followed her. She came back again in a minute or two, and said that Edith was in violent pain. She

begged of me to send for a doctor. Dr. Osborne lives just round the corner. He came at once. But Edith died almost immediately after his arrival."

"You were in the room?" asked Vandeleur, turning to Osborne.

"Yes," he replied. "She was conscious to the last moment, and died suddenly."

"Did she tell you anything?"

"No, except to assure me that she had not eaten any food that day until she had come down to breakfast. After the death occurred, I sent immediately to report the case. I locked the door of the room where the poor woman's body is. Then I saw also that nobody touched anything on this table."

Vandeleur rang the bell and a servant appeared. He gave quick orders. The entire remains of the meal were collected and taken charge of, and then he and the coroner's officer went upstairs.

When we were alone, Selby sank into a chair. His face was quite drawn and haggard.

"It is the horrible suddenness of the thing," he cried. "As to Beatrice, I don't believe she will ever be the same again. She was deeply attached to Edith. Edith was nearly 10 years her senior, and always acted the part of mother to her. This is a sad beginning to our life. I can scarcely think."

I remained with him a little longer, and then, as Vandeleur did not return, went back to my own house. There I could settle to nothing, and when Vandeleur rang me up on the telephone about six o'clock I hurried off to his rooms. As soon as I arrived, I saw that Selby was with him, and the expression on both their faces told me the truth.

"This is a bad business," said Vandeleur. "Miss Dallas has died from swallowing poison. An exhaustive analysis and examination have been made, and a powerful poison has been found. This is strange enough, but how it has been administered is a puzzle. It certainly was not in the remains of the breakfast, and we have her dying evidence that she took nothing else. Now, a poison with such strength would take effect quickly. She was quite well when she came to breakfast, and the poison began to work toward the close of the meal. But how did she get it? This question, however, I shall deal with later on. The more immediate point is this: The situation is a serious one. We may almost exclude the idea of suicide. We must, therefore, call it murder. This harmless, innocent lady is struck down by the hand of an assassin. For such an act, there must have been some powerful motive. The person who designed and executed it must be a criminal of great scientific ability. Mr. Selby has been telling me the exact financial position of the poor lady, and also of his own young wife. The disappearance of the stepbrother is strange. Knowing, as we do, that between him and two million sterling there stood two lives — *one is taken!*"

A deadly sensation of cold seized me as Vandeleur uttered these last words. I glanced at Selby. His face was colorless. He looked as though he saw something that terrified him.

"What happened once may happen again," continued Vandeleur. "We are in the presence of a great mystery. I advise you, Mr. Selby, to guard your wife with the utmost care."

"Mercy on us!" Selby muttered. "Tell me, Mr. Vandeleur, what I must do."

"You must be guided by me," said Vandeleur. "I shall place a detective in your household immediately. Don't be alarmed; he will come to you in plain clothes. He will simply act as a servant. Nevertheless, nothing can be done to your wife without his knowledge. As to you, Druce," he continued, turning to me, "the police are doing all they can to find this man Silva. I ask you to help them with your big agency, and to begin at once. Leave your friend to me. Wire instantly if you hear news."

"You may rely on me," I said, and a moment later, I had left the room.

As I walked rapidly down the street, the thought of Madame Sara came back to me. And yet what could Madame Sara have to do with the present mystery?

The thought had scarcely crossed my mind before I heard a clatter alongside the curb. I turned around and saw an open carriage, drawn by a pair of horses, standing there. I also heard my own name. I turned. Bending out of the carriage was Madame Sara.

"I saw you going by, Mr. Druce. I have only just heard the news about poor Edith Dallas. I am terribly shocked and upset. I have been to the house, but they would not admit me. Have you heard what was the cause of her death?"

Madame's blue eyes filled with tears as she spoke.

"I am not at liberty to tell what I have heard, Madame," I answered. "I am officially connected with the affair."

Her eyes narrowed. The brimming tears dried as though by magic. Her glance became scornful.

"Thank you," she answered, "your reply tells me that she did not die naturally. How terrible! But I must not keep you. Can I drive you anywhere?"

"No, thank you."

"Good-bye, then."

She made a sign to the coachman and, as the carriage rolled away, turned to look at me. Her face wore the defiant expression I had seen more than once. Could she be connected with the murder? I felt certain she was. Yet I had no reason to think so — none.

To find Henry Joachim Silva was now my main thought. My staff had instructions to make every possible inquiry and offer large money rewards. Branches of other agencies throughout Brazil were communicated with by cable. All the Scotland Yard channels were used. Still there was no result. The newspaper took up the case. There were paragraphs in most of them with regard to the missing stepbrother and the mysterious death of Edith Dallas. Then someone got hold of the story of the will. This was detailed with many additions for the benefit of the public. At the inquest, the jury returned the following verdict:

"We find that Miss Edith died from poison of unknown name. By whom or how administered there is no evidence."

This unsatisfactory state of things was destined to change quite suddenly. On the 6th of August, as I was seated in my office, a note was brought me by a private messenger. It was as follows:

Norfolk Hotel, Strand
Dear Sir — I have just arrived in London from Brazil. I have seen your advertisements. I was about to place one myself in order to find my sisters. I am quite ill and unable to leave my room. Can you come to see me at the earliest possible moment?
Yours, Henry Joachim Silva

I quickly sent two telegrams, one to Selby and the other to Vandeleur. I begged of them to be with me, without fail, as soon as possible.

So the man had never been in England at all. The situation was more bewildering than ever. One thing, at least, was probable — Edith Dallas' death was not due to her stepbrother.

Soon after half-past six, Selby arrived, and Vandeleur walked in ten minutes later. I told them what had occurred and showed them the letter. In half an hour's time, we reached the hotel. We were shown into a room on the first floor by Silva's private servant. Resting in an armchair, as we entered, sat a man. His face was terribly thin. The eyes and cheeks were so sunken that the face had almost the appearance of a skull. He made no effort to rise when we entered. He glanced from one of us to the other with the utmost astonishment. I at once introduced myself and explained who we were. He then waved his hand for his man to retire.

"You have heard the news, of course, Mr. Silva?" I said.

"News! What?" He glanced up to me and seemed to read something in my face. He started back in his chair.

"Good heavens," he replied. "Do you mean my sisters? Tell me, quickly, are they alive?"

"Your elder sister died on the 29th of July, and there is every reason to believe that her death was caused by foul play."

As I uttered these words, the change that passed over his face was fearful to witness. He did not speak, but remained motionless. His clawlike hands clutched the arms of the chair. His eyes were fixed and staring, as though they would start from their hollow sockets; the color of his skin was like clay. I heard Selby breathe quickly behind me, and Vandeleur stepped

toward the man and laid his hand on his shoulder.

"Tell us what you know of this matter," he said sharply.

Recovering himself with an effort, the invalid began in a tremulous voice:

"Listen closely, for you must act quickly. I am indirectly responsible for this fearful thing. My life has been a wild and wasted one, and now I am dying. The doctors tell me I cannot live a month. Eighteen months ago I was in Rio. I was living fast and gambled heavily. Among my fellow gamblers was a man much older than myself. His name was Jose Aranjo. He was, if anything, a greater gambler than I. One night, we played alone. The stakes ran high until they reached a big figure. By daylight, I had lost to him nearly $200,000. I could not pay a twentieth part of that sum. This man knew my financial position, and, in addition to a sum of $5,000 paid down, I gave him a note. I must have been mad to do so. The note said this — it was duly witnessed and attested by a lawyer — that, in the event of my surviving my two sisters and inheriting my uncle's wealth, half a million should go to Jose Aranjo. I felt the chances of my inheriting the money were small. Immediately after the completion of the document, this man left Rio. Then I heard a great deal about him that I had not previously known. He was partly Indian, partly Italian. He had spent many years of his life amongst the Indians. I heard also that he was as cruel as he was clever. He knew secrets of poisoning unknown to the West. I thought a great deal about this. I realized that by signing that document I had placed the lives of my two sisters between him and a fortune. I came to Para six weeks ago. There I learned that one of my sisters was married and that both had gone to England. Ill as I was, I followed them in order to warn them. I also wanted to arrange matters with you, Mr. Selby."

"One moment, sir," I broke in suddenly. "Do you happen to be aware if this man, Jose Aranjo, knew a woman calling herself Madame Sara?"

"Knew her?" cried Silva. "Very well indeed, and so, for that matter, did I. Aranjo and Madame Sara were the best friends, and constantly met. She called herself a professional beautifier. She had secrets for the pursuing of her trade unknown even to Aranjo."

"Good heavens!" I cried. "And the woman is now in London. She returned here with Mrs. Selby and Miss Dallas. Edith was very much influenced by her. There is no doubt in my mind that Sara is guilty. I have suspected her for some time, but I could not find a motive. Now the motive appears. You surely can have her arrested?"

Vandeleur made no reply. He gave me a strange look, then he turned to Selby.

"Has your wife also consulted Madame Sara?" he asked sharply.

"Yes, she went to her once about her teeth, but has not been to the shop since Edith's death. I begged of her not to see the woman, and she promised me faithfully she would not do so."

"Has she any medicines or lotions given to her by Madame Sara — does she follow any line of treatment advised by her?"

"No, I am certain on that point."

"Very well. I will see your wife tonight in order to ask her some questions. You must both leave town at once. Go to your country house and settle there. I am quite serious when I say that Mrs. Selby is in the utmost danger until after the death of her brother. We must leave you now, Mr. Silva. All business affairs must wait for the present. It is absolutely necessary that Mrs. Selby should leave London at once. Good night, sir. I shall give myself the pleasure of calling on you tomorrow morning."

We took leave of the sick man. As soon as we got into the street, Vandeleur stopped.

"I must leave it to you, Selby," he said, "to explain everything to your wife. The time for immediate action has arrived, and she is a brave and sensible woman. From this moment, you must watch all the foods and liquids that she takes. She must never be out of your sight or out of the sight of some other trustworthy companion."

"I shall, of course, watch my wife myself," said Selby. "But the thing is enough to drive one mad."

"I will go with you to the country, Selby," I said suddenly.

"Ah!" cried Vandeleur. "That is the best thing possible, and what I wanted to propose. Go, all of you, by an early train tomorrow."

"Then I will be off home at once to make arrangements," I said. "I will meet you, Selby, at Waterloo for the first train to Cronsmoor tomorrow."

As I was turning away, Vandeleur caught my arm.

"I am glad you are going with them," he said. "I shall write to you tonight.

Never be without a loaded revolver. Good night."

By 6:15 the next morning, Selby, his wife, and I were in a reserved, locked, first-class compartment, speeding rapidly west. The servants and Mrs. Selby's own special maid were in a separate carriage. Selby's face showed signs of a sleepless night. Yet, Mrs. Selby's face was calm.

By half-past nine, we arrived at the old home of the Selbys, nestling amid its oaks and elms. Everything was done to make the homecoming of the bride as cheerful as circumstances would permit. But a gloom, impossible to lift, overshadowed Selby himself.

The following morning, I received a letter from Vandeleur. It was very short, and once more impressed on me the necessity of caution. He said that two physicians had examined Silva. The verdict was that he could not live a month. Until his death, precautions must be strictly observed.

The day was cloudless. After breakfast, the butler brought me a telegram. I tore it open; it was from Vandeleur.

"Prohibit all food until I arrive. Am coming down," were the words. There was no doubt that something strange had happened. Vandeleur coming down so suddenly must mean a final clearing up of the mystery. All at once the sound of wheels and of horses galloping struck on my ears. The gates were swung open and Vandeleur, in an open carriage, dashed through them. Before I could recover from my surprise, he was out of the vehicle and at my side. He carried a small black bag in his hand.

"I came down by special train," he said, speaking quickly. "There is not a moment to lose. Come at once. Is Mrs. Selby all right?"

"What do you mean?" I replied. "Of course she is. Do you suppose that she is in danger?"

"Deadly," was his answer. "Come."

We dashed up to the house together. Selby, who had heard our steps, came to meet us.

"Mr. Vandeleur," he cried. "What is it? How did you come?"

"By special train, Mr. Selby. And I want to see your wife at once. It will be necessary to perform a small operation."

"Operation!" he exclaimed.

"Yes, at once."

We made our way through the hall and into the morning-room. Mrs. Selby was busily reading and answering letters. She started up when she saw Vandeleur and uttered an exclamation of surprise.

"What has happened?" she asked.

Vandeleur went up to her and took her hand.

"Do not be alarmed," he said, "for I have come to put all your fears to rest. Now, please, listen to me. When you visited Madame Sara with your sister, did you go for medical advice?"

The color rushed into her face.

"One of my teeth ached." she answered. "I went to her about that. She is a most wonderful dentist. She examined it, and found that it required filling. She got an assistant, a Brazilian, I think, to do it."

"And your tooth has been comfortable ever since?"

"Yes, quite. She had one of Edith's filled at the same time."

"Will you kindly sit down and show me which was the tooth into which the filling was put?"

She did so.

"This was the one," she said, pointing with her finger to one in the lower jaw. "What do you mean? Is there anything wrong?"

Vandeleur examined the tooth long and carefully. There was a sudden rapid movement of his hand, and a sharp cry from Mrs. Selby. He had pulled the tooth with one wrench. The suddenness of the whole thing, startling as it was, was not so strange as his next movement.

"Send Mrs. Selby's maid to her," he said, turning to her husband; "then come, both of you, into the next room."

The maid was summoned. Poor Mrs. Selby had sunk back in her chair, terrified and half fainting. A moment later Selby joined us in the dining room.

"That's right," said Vandeleur, "close the door, will you?"

He opened his black bag and brought out several instruments. With one he removed the filling from the tooth. It was quite soft and came away easily. Then from the bag he produced a small guinea pig, which he asked me to hold. He pressed the sharp instrument into the tooth and, opening the animal's mouth, placed the point on the tongue. The effect was instantaneous. The little head fell onto one of my hands—the guinea pig was dead. Vandeleur was white as a sheet. He hurried up to Selby and wrung his hand.

"Thank heaven!" he said. "I've been in time, but only just. Your wife is safe. This stopping would hardly have held another hour. I have been thinking all night over the mystery of your sister-in-law's death, and how the poison could have been administered. Suddenly the coincidence of both sisters having had their teeth filled struck me as remarkable. Like a flash, the solution came to me. The more I considered it, the more I felt that I was right. The poison is very strong, so violent in its deadly proportions that the amount that would go into a tooth would cause almost instant death. The poison has been kept in by a wax stopping, certain to come out within a month, probably earlier, and most probably during the chewing of food. The person would die either immediately or after a very few minutes. No one would connect a visit to the dentist with a death a month afterward."

What followed can be told in a very few words. Madame Sara was arrested on suspicion. She appeared before the court, looking innocent and beautiful. She denied nothing, but declared that the poison must have been put into the tooth by one of the two Brazilians whom she had lately hired to help her with her dentistry. She had her suspicions with regard to these men soon afterward. She had fired them. She believed that they were in the pay of Jose Aranjo, but she could not tell anything for certain. Thus Madame escaped conviction. I was certain that she was guilty. But there was not a shadow of real proof. A month later, Silva died, and Mr. and Mrs. Selby are now double millionaires.

READING COMPREHENSION

Summarizing. Choose the best phrase to complete each sentence. Then write the complete statements on your paper.

1. Dixon Druce worked as _____ (a professional beautifier, the manager of a detective agency, a police surgeon).

2. Madame Sara used her own medicines and treatments to _____ (make her clients appear young, predict the future, help Druce in his laboratory).

3. Madame Sara probably told Druce all about herself because she wanted him to _____ (stop her from killing Edith, know that she was clever enough to outwit him, become her assistant).

4. Selby's brother-in-law was _____ (an accomplice to Edith's murder, very sick and dying, never found).

5. The mystery surrounding the poison was solved by _____ (Dixon Druce, Selby, Dr. Vandeleur).

6. Dr. Vandeleur pulled out Mrs. Selby's tooth to _____ (save her from being poisoned, save her a trip to the dentist, keep her from visiting Madame Sara).

7. Madame Sara was not found guilty of murder because she looked so innocent and _____ (she begged the judge for mercy, she said her assistants must have poisoned Edith, no one could prove she had known Edith Dallas).

Interpreting. Write the answer to each question on your paper.

1. What made Druce realize that Silva could not have killed Edith?

2. Why didn't Edith Dallas stop seeing Madame Sara if she was afraid of her?

3. What clever precaution kept Madame Sara from being found guilty?

For Thinking and Discussing.

1. Did the story end the way you expected? Explain why or why not.

2. What clues did Druce miss that Dr. Vandeleur picked up?

UNDERSTANDING LITERATURE

Setting in a Detective Story. The *setting* of a story is the place and the time in which the story takes place. In some stories, all the action takes place in one setting. In other stories, the setting varies, and the action takes place at different times and places. "Madame Sara" is a mystery story that begins in South America and ends in England. *Where* and *when* specific events occurred are very important in solving the mystery in this story.

Make three columns on your paper, one with the heading "South America, 18 months ago"; one with the heading "Sara's Shop, before July 28"; and one with the heading "Selby's house, after July

28." Write each event below under the correct heading.

1. Henry Silva said that he had seen Jose Aranjo and Sara together and that Aranjo and Sara were close friends.

2. Beatrice and Edith had Madame Sara put fillings in their teeth.

3. Edith Dallas died after eating breakfast, but the food had not been poisoned.

4. Silva signed a note saying half a million would be paid to Aranjo if Silva outlived his sisters.

5. Madame Sara showed Druce her strange medicines and medical equipment.

6. Vandeleur learned that someone wanted to poison Beatrice Selby.

Now use the lists you've just completed and other details from "Madame Sara" to explain the following:

7. Who murdered Edith?

8. Why was the murder committed?

9. How was the murder committed?

WRITING

Write a report of the crime from Vandeleur's scientific point of view. Describe the setting, and tell exactly *where* and *when* the first crime occurred. Then tell *where* and *when* the second crime almost occurred and how it was avoided.

The Secret

by Arthur C. Clarke

Arthur C. Clarke takes us to the Moon. In this science-fiction tale, people live and work happily on the Moon. Reporter Henry Cooper is on the trail of an exciting revelation. Unfortunately, he is not so delighted once he uncovers the truth.

Henry Cooper had been on the Moon for almost two weeks before he discovered that something was wrong. At first it was only an ill-defined suspicion, the sort of hunch that a hardheaded science reporter would not take too seriously. He had come here, after all, at the United Nations Space Administration's own request. UNSA had always been hot on public relations — especially just before budget time, when an overcrowded world was screaming for more roads and schools and sea farms, and complaining about the billions being poured into space.

So here he was, doing the lunar circuit for the second time, and beaming back two thousand words of copy a day. Although the novelty had worn off, there still remained the wonder and mystery of a world as big as Africa, thoroughly mapped, yet almost completely unexplored. A stone's throw away from the pressure domes, the labs, the spaceports, was a yawning emptiness that would challenge men for centuries to come.

Some parts of the Moon were almost too familiar, of course. Who had not seen that dusty scar in the Mare Imbrium, with its gleaming metal pylon and the plaque that announced in the three official languages of Earth:

ON THIS SPOT
AT 2001 UT
13 SEPTEMBER 1959
THE FIRST MAN-MADE OBJECT
REACHED ANOTHER WORLD

Cooper had visited the grave of Lunik II — and the more famous tomb of the men who had come after it. But these things belonged to the past; already, like Columbus and the Wright brothers, they were receding into history. What concerned him now was the future.

When he had landed at Archimedes Spaceport, the Chief Administrator had been obviously glad to see him, and had shown a personal interest in his tour. Transportation, accommodations, and official guide were all arranged. He could

307

go anywhere he liked, ask any questions he pleased. UNSA trusted him, for his stories had always been accurate, his attitude friendly. Yet the tour had gone sour; he did not know why, but he was going to find out.

He reached for the phone and said: "Operator? Please get me the Police Department. I want to speak to the Inspector General."

Presumably Chandra Coomaraswamy possessed a uniform, but Cooper had never seen him wearing it. They met, as arranged, at the entrance to the little park that was Plato City's chief pride and joy. At this time in the morning of the artificial twenty-four-hour "day" it was almost deserted, and they could talk without interruption.

As they walked along the narrow gravel paths, they chatted about old times, the friends they had known at college together, the latest developments in interplanetary politics. They had reached the middle of the park, under the exact center of the great blue-painted dome, when Cooper came to the point.

"You know everything that's happening on the Moon, Chandra," he said. "And you know that I'm here to do a series for UNSA — hope to make a book out of it when I get back to Earth. So why should people be trying to hide things from me?"

It was impossible to hurry Chandra. He always took his time to answer questions, and his few words escaped with difficulty around the stem of his hand-carved Bavarian pipe.

"What people?" he asked at length.

"You've really no idea?"

The Inspector General shook his head.

"Not the faintest," he answered; and Cooper knew that he was telling the truth. Chandra might be silent, but he would not lie.

"I was afraid you'd say that. Well, if you don't know any more than I do, here's the only clue I have — and it frightens me. Medical Research is trying to keep me at arm's length."

"Hmm," replied Chandra, taking his pipe from his mouth and looking at it thoughtfully.

"Is that all you have to say?"

"You haven't given me much to work on. Remember, I'm only a cop; I lack your vivid journalistic imagination."

"All I can tell you is that the higher I get in Medical Research, the colder the atmosphere becomes. Last time I was here, everyone was very friendly, and gave me some fine stories. But now, I can't even meet the Director. He's always too busy, or on the other side of the Moon. Anyway, what sort of man is he?"

"Dr. Hastings? Prickly little character. Very competent, but not easy to work with."

"What could he be trying to hide?"

"Knowing you, I'm sure you have some interesting theories."

"Oh, I thought of narcotics, and fraud, and political conspiracies — but they don't make sense, in these days. So what's left scares the life out of me."

Chandra's eyebrows signaled a silent question mark.

"Interplanetary plague," said Cooper bluntly.

"I thought that was impossible."

"Yes — I've written articles myself proving that the life forms on other planets have such alien chemistries that they can't react with us, and that all our microbes and bugs took millions of years to adapt to our bodies. But I've always wondered if it was true. Suppose a ship has come back from Mars, say, with something *really* vicious — and the doctors can't cope with it?"

There was a long silence. Then Chandra said: "I'll start investigating. I don't like it either, for here's an item you probably don't know. There were three nervous breakdowns in the Medical Division last month — and that's very, very unusual."

He glanced at his watch, then at the false sky, which seemed so distant, yet which was only two hundred feet above their heads.

"We'd better get moving," he said. "The morning shower's due in five minutes."

The call came two weeks later, in the middle of the night — the real lunar night. By Plato City time, it was Sunday morning.

"Henry? Chandra here. Can you meet me in half an hour at air lock five? Good — I'll see you."

This was it, Cooper knew. Air lock five meant that they were going outside the dome. Chandra had found something.

The presence of the police driver restricted conversation as the tractor moved away from the city along the road roughly bulldozed across the ash and pumice. Low in the south, Earth was almost full, casting a brilliant blue-green light over the infernal landscape. However hard one tried, Cooper told himself, it was difficult to make the Moon appear glamorous. But nature guards her greatest secrets well; to such places men must come to find them.

The multiple domes of the city dropped below the sharply curved horizon. Presently, the tractor turned aside from the main road to follow a scarcely visible trail. Ten minutes later, Cooper saw a single glittering hemisphere ahead of them, standing on an isolated ridge of rock. Another vehicle, bearing a red cross, was parked beside the entrance. It seemed that they were not the only visitors.

Nor were they unexpected. As they drew up to the dome, the flexible tube of the air-lock coupling groped out toward them and snapped into place against their tractor's outer hull. There was a brief hissing as pressure equalized. Then Cooper followed Chandra into the building.

The air-lock operator led them along curving corridors and radial passageways toward the center of the dome. Sometimes they caught glimpses of laboratories, scientific instruments, computers — all perfectly ordinary, and all deserted on this Sunday morning. They must have reached the heart of the building, Cooper told himself when their guide ushered them into a large circular chamber and shut the door softly behind them.

It was a small zoo. All around them were cages, tanks, jars containing a wide selection of the fauna and flora of Earth.

Waiting at its center was a short, gray-haired man, looking very worried, and very unhappy.

"Dr. Hastings," said Coomaraswamy, "meet Mr. Cooper." The Inspector General turned to his companion and added, "I've convinced the Doctor that there's only one way to keep you quiet — and that's to tell you everything."

"Frankly," said Hastings, "I'm not sure if I care anymore." His voice was unsteady, barely under control, and Cooper thought, Hello! There's another breakdown on the way.

The scientist wasted no time on such formalities as shaking hands. He walked to one of the cages, took out a small bundle of fur, and held it toward Cooper.

"Do you know what this is?" he asked abruptly.

"Of course. A hamster — the commonest lab animal."

"Yes," said Hastings. "A perfectly ordinary golden hamster. Except that this one is five years old — like all the others in this cage."

"Well? What's old about that?"

"Oh, nothing, nothing at all . . . except for the trifling fact that hamsters live for only two years. And we have some here that are getting on for ten."

For a moment no one spoke, but the room was not silent. It was full of rustlings and slitherings and scratchings, of faint whimpers and tiny animal cries. Then Cooper whispered: "You've found a way of prolonging life!"

"No," retorted Hastings. "We've not found it. The Moon has given it to us . . . as we might have expected, if we'd looked in front of our noses."

He seemed to have gained control over his emotions — as if he was once more the pure scientist, fascinated by a discovery for its own sake and heedless of its implications.

"On Earth," he said, "we spend our whole lives fighting gravity. It wears down our muscles, pulls our stomachs out of shape. In seventy years, how many tons of blood does the heart lift through how many miles? And all that work, all that strain is reduced to a sixth here on the Moon, where a one-hundred-and-eighty-pound human weighs only thirty pounds."

"I see," said Cooper. "Ten years for a hamster — and how long for a man?"

"It's not a simple law," answered Hastings. "It varies with the size and the spe-cies. Even a month ago, we weren't certain. But now we're quite sure of this: on the Moon, the span of human life will be at least two hundred years."

"And you've been trying to keep it secret!"

"You fool! Don't you understand?"

"Take it easy, Doctor — take it easy," said Chandra softly.

With an obvious effort of will, Hastings got control of himself again. He began to speak with such icy calm that his words sank like freezing raindrops into Cooper's mind.

"Think of them up there," he said, pointing to the roof, to the invisible Earth, whose looming presence no one on the Moon could ever forget. "Six billion of them, packing all the continents to the edges — and now crowding over into the sea beds. And here —" he pointed to the ground — "only a hundred thousand of *us,* on an almost empty world. But a world where we need miracles of technology and engineering merely to exist, where a man with an I.Q. of only a hundred and fifty can't even get a job.

"And now we find that we can live for two hundred years. Imagine how they're going to react to *that* news! This is your problem now, Mister Journalist; you've asked for it, and you've got it. Tell me this, please — I'd really be interested to know — *just how are you going to break it to them?*"

He waited and waited. Cooper opened his mouth, then closed it again, unable to think of anything to say.

In the far corner of the room, a baby monkey started to cry.

READING COMPREHENSION

Summarizing. Choose the best phrase to complete each sentence. Then write the complete statements on your paper.

1. Henry Cooper was a _____ (police officer, science reporter, doctor).

2. Cooper began to get suspicious when _____ (Chandra Coomaraswamy said he didn't know anything, the Chief Administrator gave him a cold welcome, Medical Research kept putting him off).

3. Dr. Hastings had discovered _____ (an interplanetary plague, that all animals and humans will have a much longer life span on the Moon, the existence of a political conspiracy).

Interpreting. Write the answer to each question on your paper.

1. Why had the United Nations Space Administration sent Henry Cooper to the Moon?

2. What were some of the changes that had occurred on Earth and on the Moon since the present time?

3. Why did Dr. Hastings agree to tell Cooper everything?

4. What problem would be created if the people on Earth found out the secret?

For Thinking and Discussing. If you were Henry Cooper, would you report the news to the people on Earth? Explain why or why not.

UNDERSTANDING LITERATURE

Setting in a Science-Fiction Story. The setting of a science-fiction story plays an important part in the plot. Many science-fiction stories take place in the future, in a setting that is much more advanced than the present. In order to understand this type of story, it is important to pay attention to the details of the setting that the writer presents. The story's futuristic elements are essential to the story.

Below are some questions about the setting in "The Secret." Write the answer to each question on your paper.

1. How is the Earth described in "The Secret"? How is the description of the Earth related to the plot of the story?

2. In what ways was the Moon developed? How was it undeveloped?

3. Why was Plato City made up of domed buildings? What other details of the setting are related to the Moon's atmosphere?

4. Why couldn't millions of people from Earth come to live on the Moon?

WRITING

Imagine you are living sometime in the future. Write a description of a typical classroom. Give details about what the classroom looks like and what equipment is used. Include the date and place in your description.

Section Review

Prefixes and Suffixes. A base word is a word to which affixes can be added. The two main kinds of affixes are *prefixes* and *suffixes*. A prefix is added to the beginning of a base word; a suffix is added to the end. Prefixes and suffixes change the meaning of the base word. For example, the prefix *dis-* means "not," or "lack of." When you *disagree* with someone, you do not agree.

Study the meanings of the prefixes and suffixes that follow. Then read each sentence. On your paper, write each italicized word and its meaning. Some words may have both a prefix and a suffix.

Prefixes	Suffixes
im-, in-, un- = not	*-able* = able to
over- = too	*-ful* = full of
pre- = before	*-less* = without
	-ly = in a way

1. The road was *impassable* in many places.
2. He realized he had spoken *prematurely*.
3. There was a *lifeless* look in his eyes.
4. What he said didn't stop me from being *fearful*.
5. He felt *indirectly* responsible for what had happened.
6. The Earth was an *overcrowded* world screaming for more roads and schools.
7. Most of the moon was *unexplored*.

Significant Detail. Every story has many details. Some details help to make the setting or characters seem more real. But a story also has a number of details that are important, or significant, to the story's development and meaning. Significant details are different from other details in that they are essential to the sense of the story. A writer states them directly, but a careful reading of the story is necessary in order to understand them.

Below are sentences containing details from three of the selections in this section. Choose the one sentence from each group that contains a significant detail. On your paper, write the sentence and explain its significance.

1. "The Opened Order"
   a. He was told to take the shorter way, which was shown to him on the map.
   b. He . . . read the order, which said that *he was to be shot!*
   c. The last half hour passed in silence.

2. "A Secret for Two"
   a. Pierre . . . delivered milk.
   b. Pierre had a remarkable memory.
   c. Pierre "has been blind for five years."

3. "Dinner for Monsieur Martin"
   a. Her father owned a sizable farm and was quite hospitable.
   b. She found a crack between the planks and put her eye to it.
   c. That bear just quietly pushed that muzzle up. . . .

WRITING

A Firsthand Report. A firsthand report is based on direct experience. It is written by someone who was an eyewitness to an event and carefully observed what happened. There are two kinds of firsthand reports. In an *objective* firsthand report, the writer states only the facts. In a *subjective* firsthand report, the writer includes his or her feelings and opinions.

Step 1: Set Your Goal

A topic for a firsthand report should be one you have witnessed. You should be able to write about the events you actually saw. For this writing activity, imagine you were there and choose one of the following topics for a firsthand report:

1. You witnessed the girl's meeting with the bear in "Dinner for Monsieur Martin." Write an objective report describing what happened and how the showman's secret was discovered.

2. You witnessed the death of Pierre Dupin described in "A Secret for Two." Write a subjective report in which you describe what you saw and how you felt about it.

3. You attended the trial of Sara that was briefly described in "Madame Sara." Write an objective report in which you describe what happened at the trial.

4. As a reporter in "The Secret," you were assigned to go to Plato City and see what it was like. Write a subjective report to send back to Earth about what you saw there and what your opinions and feelings about it were.

Step 2: Make a Plan

Gathering information for a firsthand report consists of taking notes about what you observe and interviewing people at the scene. When you take notes for a firsthand report, jot down only the most important details. Your notes should include answers to these questions: *Who? What? When? Where? Why?* and *How?*

Suppose, for example, you have chosen to report on the death of Edith Dallas in "Madame Sara." You might plan your report with questions similar to the following:

1. What was the event? What was the cause?

2. Who was with her when she died?

3. When did she die?

4. Where did she die?

5. Why was murder suspected?

6. How did others react to her death?

Write down questions that you want answered about the event. Then, use your imagination and the information in the story to answer the questions you have listed. You may want to include direct quotations in your report, so be sure to write down a few of the characters' responses word for word.

Step 3: Write a First Draft

If you are writing an objective firsthand report, concentrate on listing the facts in your first draft. Answer the major *Who? What? When? Where? Why?* and *How?* questions in the first paragraph. In the following paragraphs, include less important facts and details that support the information in the first paragraph. Be careful not to include any opinions you might have about the event you have "witnessed."

If you are writing a subjective firsthand report, concentrate on setting the scene, rather than listing the facts. Try to capture the feeling of the event in the first paragraph. Write the report in the first person so the reader will know that you are presenting your point of view. Use words and phrases that let the reader know your reaction to the event.

Step 4: Revise

If you are working on an objective report, ask yourself these questions as you revise:

☐ Have I answered the *Who? What? When? Where? Why?* and *How?* questions?

☐ Have I put the most important information in the first paragraph?

☐ Have I included only the facts, leaving out my opinions and feelings?

If your report is subjective, ask yourself these questions:

☐ Have I captured the feeling of the event?

☐ Have I written in the first person?

☐ Have I included my own opinions and feelings about the event?

When you have finished revising your report, proofread it carefully for errors. Then make a neat, final copy.

QUIZ

The following is a quiz for Section 5. Write the answers in complete sentences on your paper.

Reading Comprehension

1. In "Dinner for Monsieur Martin," what was the truth about the performing bear's nature?

2. In "The Opened Order," why was the young soldier suspicious about the contents of the order?

3. In "A Secret for Two," what secret was shared between which two characters?

4. In "Frame of Mind," what did the son discover about the difference between luck and frame of mind?

5. In "The Secret," what was the discovery that Dr. Hastings stumbled upon?

Understanding Literature

6. In "Dinner for Monsieur Martin" and "Father and I," two young boys learned something about fear. Describe what each learned.

7. What details did "The Opened Order" present about the setting of the story? How did this affect the story's impact on the reader?

8. In "A Secret for Two," how did the time at which the story took place affect an important part of the plot?

9. From whose point of view was "Madame Sara" told? How did this affect the reader's knowledge of how and why events occurred?

10. In "The Secret," why was the setting of the story essential to the plot?

ACTIVITIES

Word Attack. The soldier in "The Opened Order" had a feeling of foreboding when he was ordered to take a message to headquarters. The word *foreboding* is made up of the base word *bode* and the prefix *fore-*. The prefix *fore-* in this case means "coming beforehand." *Bode* means "to be an omen or sign of." Foreboding is "a feeling beforehand that something bad is going to happen."

The prefix *fore-* can also mean "the front or first part." Add *fore-* to each of the following base words. Then use the resulting words in sentences of your own.

doom   see   stall
deck   mast   warn

Speaking and Listening

1. Imagine that you are a TV or radio newscaster. Select one of the following topics for a news story to present to the class. You may wish to make some notes to follow as you present your report.

   a. Report on the shooting of the young officer in "The Opened Order."

   b. Present a human-interest story on Pierre Dupin in "A Secret for Two."

   c. Report on how Louis Conklin opened the safe in "Frame of Mind."

2. In "Dinner for Monsieur Martin," a mother told her young son a story about her own childhood. Think of a story from your childhood and prepare to tell it to the class. Hold your listeners' attention by making the story as interesting as you can.

Researching

1. "Madame Sara" had several locations that you may not be familiar with. Refer to the story to find the general location of the places listed below. Then use encyclopedias, atlases, travel books, and other resources to find out what you can about each.

   Para   Waterloo
   Madeira   Hampshire
   the Strand   Cronsmoor

2. "The Secret" takes place in a city built on the Moon. Do some research to find out how feasible such a city is. What would one look like? How many years is it likely to be before there really is a lunar city? What are the problems of developing such a city? Write a report to share with the class.

Creating

1. In "Father and I," setting was used to create a strong mood. Think of some experience that you have had in which the physical setting played an important part in creating the emotional mood you felt. Write two or three paragraphs describing the experience. Choose details of the setting that had emotional significance for you. Describe how you were affected by them.

2. Plato City is only vaguely described in "The Secret." Draw a picture of what you think Plato City looked like. Base your illustration on the description in the story, but fill in the details using your imagination.

SECTION 6

LOVE

*My lady carries love within her eyes
All that she looks on is made pleasanter.*

— Dante Alighieri
Italy

The Offering of the Heart
Fifteenth Century Arras Tapestry
Cluny Museum, Paris
Courtesy Art Resource

Love

Every time it happens, love is a new experience. And writers have always wanted to share their feelings about it. But millions of people have written about love, and it is no longer enough just to say, "I love you." Each writer must find a new way to express these thoughts and emotions.

Transforming the World

Falling in love makes the whole world seem different. In Milton Kaplan's story "Feels Like Spring," you read the thoughts that pass through the mind of a young man riding the subway to work. Charmed by a young woman who rides his train every morning but whom he has never met, he imagines how they might accidentally meet and how, gradually, their friendship might turn into love. The possibility of romance makes the screeching of the subway sound, to him, like singing birds. Kaplan tells you that, no matter what season it is, the weather is always wonderful when you're in love.

Another View

A play from Spain, *A Sunny Morning,* looks at love from a more distant point of view. The play reminds you that beautiful young lovers grow old. It tells you that

even though people often think they will die if they lose the one they love, that usually doesn't happen. Eventually, disappointed lovers find new people to love, and continue their lives.

Poetry of Love

Love poetry has a long history in every language. In some cultures, there have been special ways, even rules, for expressing these feelings. In Japan and China, writing poems was such an important part of courtship that people in love often took poetry lessons. In Europe during the Middle Ages, lovers expressed their feelings in song. In the Middle East, love was regarded as such a delicate subject that poets could never express their feelings directly. Instead they used symbols, words that conveyed what the poet was expressing but that actually referred to something quite different—using "the moon" to mean "my lover's face," for example.

How does a poet find an original way to describe falling in love? Many poets use unusual comparisons. In "New Face," the modern American poet Alice Walker uses a comparison and a natural flow of words to express the mixed-up emotions of falling in love. In "Sonnet 43," a famous British poet, Elizabeth Barrett Browning, counts the many kinds of love, both

Detail of **Rubens and His First Wife in the Honeysuckle Arbour,** *Peter Paul Rubens, ca. 1610.*

peaceful and passionate. W. B. Yeats, an Irish poet, wrote "He Wishes for the Cloths of Heaven" in 1899, when he was a young man. Yet the feelings that Yeats expresses are very similar to those in Walker's modern poem.

The intense joy of being in love is matched by the pain and disappointment that occur when love ends. Poets have often written as expressively about these sorrows as they have about the joys of love. In "Of the Numberless Steps," Akiko Yosano, a Japanese poet, uses just a few words to create an image of a woman's feelings at the end of a relationship with a man. Like Yosano, the Russian poet Andrei Voznesensky uses symbols and comparisons in his poem "First Ice." In this poem, ice stands for the feeling of

being hurt by someone you love. In "Tonight I Can Write" by the Chilean poet Pablo Neruda, everything—the night, the stars, someone singing—seems sad to one who has lost love.

The Most Complex Emotion

Perhaps poetry, more than any other literary form, can express the joys, the sorrows, and the complexities of love. In her novel *Jane Eyre*, the 19th-century author Charlotte Brontë created one of the most unusual and suspenseful love stories ever written. The story adaptation of *Jane Eyre* that ends this section will allow you to experience one character's view of the sometimes wonderful, sometimes terrible feelings that are part of being in love.

321

Feels Like Spring

by Milton Kaplan

Milton Kaplan, a native New Yorker, was born in 1910. Besides writing poems, stories, and essays, he has taught English to high school students. You will see that he well understands the way a young man's imagination works.

I stop at the corner drugstore for a breakfast of doughnuts and coffee. I eat fast because I'm a little late, and then I race to the subway station and gallop down the steps to catch my usual train. I hold onto the strap and make believe I'm reading my newspaper, but I keep glancing at the people crowded in round me. They're the same ones I see every day. They know me and I know them, but we don't smile. We're strangers thrown together accidentally.

I listen to them talk about their troubles and their friends, and I wish I had someone to talk to, someone to break the monotony of the long subway ride.

As we approach the 175th Street station, I begin to get tense again. She usually gets into the train at this station. She slips in gracefully, not pushing or shoving like the rest, and she squeezes into a little space, clinging to the pole and holding onto an office envelope that probably contains her lunch. She never carries a newspaper or a book; I guess there isn't

much sense in trying to read when you're mashed like that.

There's a fresh outdoor look about her, and I figure she must live in New Jersey. The Jersey crowd gets in at that stop. She has a sweet face with that scrubbed look that doesn't need powder or rouge. She never wears make-up except for lipstick. And her wavy hair is natural, just a nice light brown, the color of poplar leaves when they turn in the fall. And all she does is hold onto the pole and think her thoughts, her eyes clear blue and warm.

I always like to watch her, but I have to be careful; I'm afraid she'll get sore and move away if she catches me at it, and then I won't have anyone, because she's my only real friend, even if she doesn't know it. I'm all alone in New York City, and I guess I'm kind of shy and don't make friends easily. The fellows in the bank are all right but they have their own lives to lead. Besides, I can't ask anyone to come up to a furnished room; so they go their way and I go mine.

The city is getting me. It's too big and noisy—too many people for a fellow who's all by himself. I can't seem to get used to it. I'm used to the quiet of a small New Hampshire farm, but there isn't any future on a New Hampshire farm any more; so after I was discharged from the Navy, I applied for this position in the bank and got it. I suppose it's a good break, but I'm kind of lonesome.

As I ride along, swaying to the motion of the car, I like to imagine that I'm friends with her. Sometimes I'm even tempted to smile at her, not in a fresh way, but just friendly-like, and say something like, "Nice morning, isn't it?" But I'm scared. She might think I'm one of those wise guys and she'd freeze up and look right through me as if I didn't exist, and then the next morning she wouldn't be there any more and I'd have no one to think about. I keep dreaming that maybe someday I'll get to know her. You know, in a casual way.

Like maybe she'd be coming through the door and someone would push her and she'd brush against me and she'd say quickly, "Oh, I beg your pardon," and I'd lift my hat politely and answer, "That's perfectly all right," and I'd smile to show her that I meant it. Then she'd smile back at me and say, "Nice day, isn't it?" and I'd say, "Feels like spring." And we wouldn't say anything more, but when she'd be ready to get off at 34th Street, she'd wave her finger a little at me and say, "Good-bye," and I'd tip my hat again.

The next morning when she'd come in, she'd see me and say, "Hello," or maybe "Good morning," and I'd answer and add something like, "Violets ought to be coming up soon" — something like that to show her I really knew a little about spring. No wisecracks, because I wouldn't want her to think that I was one of those smooth-talking guys who pick up girls in the subway.

And, after a while, we'd get a little friendlier and start talking about things like the weather or the news, and one day she'd say, "Isn't it funny. Here we are talking every day and we don't even know each other's names." And I'd stand up straight and tip my hat and say, "I'd like you to meet Mr. Thomas Pearse," and she'd say very seriously, "How do you do, Mr. Pearse. I want you to meet Miss Elizabeth Altemose." She'd be wearing those clean white gloves girls wear in the spring, and the other people around us would smile because people in the subway are so close to you that they just can't help sharing a little of your life.

"Thomas," she'd say, as if she were trying out the sound of it.

"What?" I'd ask.

"I can't possibly call you Thomas," she'd say. "It's so formal."

"My friends call me Tommy," I'd tell her.

"And mine call me Betty."

And that's the way it would be. Maybe after a while I'd mention the name of a good movie that was playing at the Music Hall and suggest if she weren't doing anything in particular —

And she would come right out with, "Oh, I'd love it." I'd knock off a little

earlier and meet her where she worked, and we would go out to dinner somewhere. I'd ask some of the men at the bank for the name of a good restaurant. And I would talk to her and tell her about New Hampshire and maybe mention how lonesome I got, and if it's a really nice place and it's quiet and cozy, maybe I'd tell her how shy I was, and she'd be listening with shining eyes and she'd clasp her hands and lean over the table until I could smell the fragrance of her hair and she'd whisper,

"I'm shy, too." Then we'd both lean back and smile secretly, and we'd eat without saying much because, after all, what's there to say after that?

We'd go to the Music Hall and I'd get reserved seats and we'd sit there, relaxed, enjoying the movie. Some time during the picture, in an exciting part, maybe her hand would brush against mine, or maybe I'd be shifting my position and my hand would touch hers accidentally, but she wouldn't take it away and I'd hold it, and

George Washington Bridge with the Hudson River flowing dark and mysterious below us, and then we'd be in New Jersey and we'd see the lights of small homes and we'd stop in one of those little towns, Englewood, Leonia, Ridgewood — I looked them up on a map, wondering which one was hers — and she'd invite me in but I'd say it was too late and then she'd turn to me and say, "Then you must promise to come for dinner this Sunday," and I'd promise and then —

The train is slowing down and the people are bracing themselves automatically for the stop. It's the 175th Street station. There's a big crowd waiting to get in. I look out anxiously for her, but I don't see her anywhere and my heart sinks, and just then I catch a glimpse of her, way over at the side. She's wearing a new hat with little flowers on it. The door opens and the people start pushing in. She's caught in the rush and there's nothing she can do about it. She bangs into me and she grabs the strap I'm holding and hangs on to it for her life.

"I beg your pardon," she gasps.

My hand is pinned down and I can't tip my hat, but I answer politely, "That's all right."

The doors close and the train begins to move. She has to hold on to my strap; there isn't any other place for her.

"Nice day, isn't it?" she says.

The train swings around a turn and the wheels squealing on the rails sound like the birds singing in New Hampshire. My heart is pounding like mad.

"Feels like spring," I say.

there I'd be in the middle of eight million people but I wouldn't be alone any more; I'd be out with my girl.

And afterward, I'd take her home. She wouldn't want me to travel all the way out. "I live in New Jersey," she'd say. "It's very nice of you to offer to take me home but I couldn't ask you to make a long trip like that. Don't worry, I'll be all right." But I'd take her arm and say, "Come on. I want to take you home. I like New Jersey." And we'd take the bus across the

325

READING COMPREHENSION

Summarizing. Choose the best phrase to complete each sentence. Then write the complete statements on your paper.

1. Thomas was originally from _____ (a small town in New Jersey, New York City, a farm in New Hampshire).

2. Thomas was attracted to the young woman because she _____ (looked like a sweet country girl, was sophisticated, talked to him every morning).

3. In Thomas's fantasy, the young woman _____ (married him, went out on a date with him, thought he was fresh).

4. In their real conversation, the girl _____ (repeated the words in Thomas's fantasy conversation, said hello, acted unfriendly).

Interpreting. Write the answer to each question on your paper.

1. Why was Thomas lonely?

2. Why was Thomas afraid to start a conversation with the girl?

3. Why did the train wheels sound like "birds singing in New Hampshire" to Thomas at the end of the story?

For Thinking and Discussing.

1. What do you think will happen to Thomas and the young woman after the end of the story?

2. Why do you think this story was set in the springtime?

UNDERSTANDING LITERATURE

Point of View and Style. A writer uses his or her own *style* to tell a story. Style determines how the author uses words to present the subject matter, the plot, the characters — everything that makes up the story. The story "Feels Like Spring" is told from the first-person point of view. *First-person* means that the writer uses the pronoun *I* to tell the story through one character. This character is the speaker or narrator, and describes his or her own feelings and thoughts. The reader "sees" the setting and the other characters only through the speaker's eyes.

A first-person point of view allows us a close look into the mind of one character. But it limits our knowledge of other characters and events.

Write the answers to the following questions on your paper.

1. Do you think the first-person point of view is effective for the subject matter of "Feels Like Spring"?

2. How does knowing only Thomas's thoughts make the reader interested in what happens after the story has ended?

WRITING

The other important character in the story is the young woman. Use your imagination to develop her character. Then write one or two paragraphs describing the subway ride from her point of view.

A Sunny Morning

by Sarafin and Joaquin Alvarez Quintero
translated by Lucretia Xavier Floyd

What happens when two lovers meet — half a century after they parted? A few things may have changed, as you will see in this funny play by two Spanish writers.

CHARACTERS

Doña Laura
Petra, her maid
Don Gonzalo
Juanito, his servant

A sunny morning in a corner of a park in Madrid, Spain. Autumn. A bench at one side.

Doña Laura, a handsome, bright-eyed, white-haired lady of about 70, enters, leaning upon the arm of her maid, Petra. In her free hand, she carries a parasol, which serves also as a cane.

Doña Laura: I am so glad to be here. I feared my seat would be occupied. What a beautiful morning!

Petra: The sun is hot.

Doña Laura: Yes, you are only 20. *(She sits down on the bench.)* Oh, I feel more tired today than usual. *(Noticing Petra, who seems impatient.)* Go, if you wish to chat with your guard.

Petra: He is not mine, señora; he belongs to the park.

Doña Laura: He belongs more to you than he does to the park. Go find him, but remain within calling distance.

Petra: I see him over there waiting for me.

Doña Laura: Do not remain more than 10 minutes.

Petra: Very well, señora. *(Walks away.)*

Doña Laura: Wait a moment.

Petra: What does the señora wish?

Doña Laura: Give me the bread crumbs.

Petra: I don't know what is the matter with me.

Doña Laura: *(smiling):* I do. Your head is where your heart is — with the guard.

Petra: Here, señora. *(She hands Doña Laura a small bag, and leaves.)*

Doña Laura: Adios. *(Glances toward trees.)* Here they come! They know just when to expect me. *(She rises, walks toward the pigeons, and throws them three handfuls of bread crumbs.)* These are for the liveliest, these for the greedy ones, and these for the little ones. *(Laughs. She returns to her seat and, with a pleased expression, watches the pigeons feeding.)*

(Enter Don Gonzalo and Juanito. Don

327

Gonzalo is a gentleman of 70, gouty and impatient. He leans upon Juanito's arm and drags his feet somewhat as he walks.)

Don Gonzalo: Idling their time away! They should be saying Mass.

Juanito: You can sit here, señor. There is only a lady. *Doña Laura turns her head and listens.)*

Don Gonzalo: I won't, Juanito. I want a bench to myself.

Juanito: But there is none.

Don Gonzalo: That one over there is mine.

Juanito: There are three priests sitting there.

Don Gonzalo: Rout them out. Have they gone?

Juanito: No, indeed. They are talking.

Don Gonzalo: Just as if they were glued to the seat. No hope of their leaving. Come this way, Juanito. *(They walk toward the birds.)*

Doña Laura *(with irritation):* Look out!

Don Gonzalo: Are you speaking to me, señora?

Doña Laura: Yes, to you.

Don Gonzalo: What do you wish?

Doña Laura: You have scared away the birds who were feeding on my crumbs.

Don Gonzalo: What do I care about the birds?

Doña Laura: But I do.

Don Gonzalo: This is a public park.

Doña Laura: Then why do you complain that the priests have taken your bench?

Don Gonzalo: Señora, we have not met. I cannot imagine why you take the liberty of addressing me. Come, Juanito. *(Both go out.)*

Doña Laura: What an ill-natured old man! Why must people get so fussy and cross when they reach a certain age? *(Looking off toward the right.)* I am glad. He lost that bench, too. Serves him right for scaring the birds. He is furious. Yes, yes; find a seat if you can. Poor man! He is wiping the perspiration from his face. Here he comes. A carriage would not raise more dust than his feet.

(Enter Don Gonzalo and Juanito.)

Don Gonzalo: Have the priests gone yet, Juanito?

Juanito: No, indeed, señor. They are still there.

Don Gonzalo: The authorities should place more benches here for these sunny mornings. Well, I suppose I must resign myself and sit on the bench with the old lady.

(Muttering to himself, he sits at the extreme end of Doña Laura's bench and looks at her indignantly. He touches his hat as he greets her.) Good morning.

Doña Laura: What, you here again?

Don Gonzalo: I repeat that we have not met.

Doña Laura: I was responding to your salute.

Don Gonzalo: "Good morning" should be answered by "good morning," and that is all you should have said.

Doña Laura: You should have asked permission to sit on this bench, which is mine.

Don Gonzalo: The benches here are public property.

Doña Laura: Why, you said the one the priests have was yours.

Don Gonzalo: Very well, very well. I have nothing more to say. *(Between his teeth.)*

Senile old lady! She ought to be at home knitting and counting her beads.

Doña Laura: Don't grumble any more. I'm not going to leave just to please you.

Don Gonzalo (*brushing the dust from his shoes with his handkerchief*): If the ground were sprinkled a little, it would be an improvement.

Doña Laura: Do you use your handkerchief as a shoe brush?

Don Gonzalo: Why not?

Doña Laura: Do you use your shoe brush as a handkerchief?

Don Gonzalo: What right have you to criticize my actions?

Doña Laura: A neighbor's right.

Don Gonzalo: Juanito, my book. I do not care to listen to nonsense.

Doña Laura: You are very polite.

Don Gonzalo: Pardon me, señora, but never interfere with what does not concern you.

Doña Laura: I generally say what I think.

Don Gonzalo: And more to the same effect. Give me the book, Juanito.

Juanito: Here, señor. (*Juanito takes a book from his pocket, hands it to Don Gonzalo, then exits. Don Gonzalo, casting indignant glances at Doña Laura, puts on an enormous pair of glasses, takes from his pocket a reading-glass, adjusts both to suit him, and opens his book.*)

Doña Laura: I thought you were taking out a telescope.

Don Gonzalo: Very well, señora, please allow me to read. Enough conversation.

Doña Laura: Well, you be quiet, then.

Don Gonzalo: But first I shall take a pinch of snuff. (*Takes out snuffbox.*) Will you have some? (*Offers box to Doña Laura.*)

Doña Laura: If it is good.

Don Gonzalo: It is of the finest. You will like it.

Doña Laura: (*taking a pinch of snuff*): It clears my head.

Don Gonzalo: And mine.

Doña Laura: Do you sneeze?

Don Gonzalo: Yes, señora, three times.

Doña Laura: And so do I. What a coincidence!

(*After taking the snuff, they await the sneeze, both anxiously, and sneeze alternately three times each.*)

Don Gonzalo: There, I feel better.

Doña Laura: So do I. (*aside.*) The snuff has made peace between us.

Don Gonzalo: You will excuse me if I read aloud?

Doña Laura: Read as loud as you please; you will not disturb me.

Don Gonzalo (*reading*): All love is sad, but sad as it is, it is the best thing that we know."

Doña Laura: Ah!

Don Gonzalo: There are some beautiful poems in this book. Here. "Twenty years pass. He returns."

Doña Laura: You cannot imagine how it affects me to see you reading with all those glasses.

Don Gonzalo: Can you read without any?

Doña Laura: Certainly.

Don Gonzalo: At your age? You're jesting.

Doña Laura: Pass me the book then. (*She takes the book and reads aloud.*) "Twenty years pass. He returns.

And each, beholding the other,
    exclaims —
Can it be that this is he?
Heavens, is it she?"
(*Doña Laura returns the book.*)

Don Gonzalo: Indeed, I envy you your wonderful eyesight.

Doña Laura (*aside.*): I know every word by heart.

Don Gonzalo: I am fond of good verses, very fond. I even composed some in my youth.

Doña Laura: Good ones?

Don Gonzalo: Of all kinds. I was a great friend of the poet Zorilla. I first met Zorilla in America.

Doña Laura: Why, have you been to America?

Don Gonzalo: Several times. The first time I went I was only six years old.

Doña Laura: You must have gone with Columbus!

Don Gonzalo (*laughing*): Not quite as bad as that. I am old, I admit, but I did not know Ferdinand and Isabella. (*They both laugh.*) I am a native of Valencia.

Doña Laura: You are?

Don Gonzalo: I was brought up there and there I spent my early youth. Have you ever visited that city?

Doña Laura: Yes, señor. Not far from Valencia there was a villa that, if still there, should retain memories of me. I spent several seasons there. It was many, many years ago. It was near the sea, hidden away among lemon and orange trees. They called it — let me see, what did they call it — Maricela.

Don Gonzalo (*startled*): Maricela?

Doña Laura: Maricela. Is the name familiar to you?

Don Gonzalo: Yes, very familiar. If my memory serves me right, for we forget as we grow old, there lived in that villa the most beautiful woman I have ever seen, and I assure you I have seen many. Let me see — what was her name? Laura — Laura — Laura Llorente.

Doña Laura (*startled*): Laura Llorente?

Don Gonzalo: Yes. (*They look at each other intently.*)

Doña Laura (*recovering herself*): She was my best friend.

Don Gonzalo: How strange!

Doña Laura: It is strange. She was called "The Silver Maiden."

Don Gonzalo: Precisely. "The Silver Maiden." By that name, she was known in that locality. I seem to see her as if she were before me now, at the window with the red roses. Do you remember that window?

Doña Laura: Yes, I remember. It was the window of her room.

Don Gonzalo: She spent many hours there. I mean, in my day.

Doña Laura (*sighing*): And in mine, too.

Don Gonzalo: She was ideal. Fair as a lily, jet black hair and black eyes, with an uncommonly sweet expression. She to cast a radiance wherever she was. Her figure was beautiful, perfect. "What forms of sovereign beauty God models in human clay!" She was a dream.

Doña Laura (*aside*): If you only knew that dream was by your side, you would realize what dreams come to. (*Aloud.*) She was unlucky and had a sad love affair.

Don Gonzalo: Very sad. *(They look at each other.)*

Doña Laura: Did you hear of it?

Don Gonzalo: Yes.

Doña Laura: The ways of Providence are strange. *(Aside.)* Gonzalo!

Don Gonzalo: The gallant lover, in the same affair —

Doña Laura: Ah, the duel?

Don Gonzalo: Precisely, the duel. The gallant lover was — my cousin, of whom I was very fond.

Doña Laura: Oh, yes, a cousin? My friend told me in one of her letters the story of that affair, which was truly romantic. He, your cousin, passed by on horseback every morning down the rose path under her window, and tossed up to her balcony a bouquet of flowers, which she caught.

Don Gonzalo: And later in the afternoon, the gallant horseman would return by the same path and catch the bouquet of flowers she would toss him. Am I right?

Doña Laura: Yes. They wanted to marry her to a merchant whom she would not have.

Don Gonzalo: And one night, when my cousin waited under her window to hear her sing, this other person presented himself unexpectedly.

Doña Laura: And insulted your cousin.

Don Gonzalo: There was a quarrel.

Doña Laura: And later a duel.

Don Gonzalo: Yes, at sunrise, on the beach, and the merchant was badly wounded. My cousin had to conceal himself for a few days and later to flee.

Doña Laura: You seem to know the story well.

Don Gonzalo: And so do you.

Doña Laura: I have explained that a friend repeated it to me.

Don Gonzalo: As my cousin did to me. *(Aside.)* This is Laura!

Doña Laura *(aside.):* Why tell him? He does not suspect.

Don Gonzalo *(aside.):* She is entirely innocent.

Doña Laura: And was it you, by any chance, who advised your cousin to forget Laura?

Don Gonzalo: Why, my cousin never forgot her!

Doña Laura: How do you account, then, for his conduct?

Don Gonzalo: I will tell you. The young man took refuge in my house, fearful of the consequences of a duel with a person highly regarded in that locality. From my home, he went to Seville, then came to Madrid. He wrote Laura many letters, some of them in verse. But undoubtedly they were intercepted by her parents, for she never answered at all. Gonzalo then, in despair, believing his love lost to him forever, joined the army, went to Africa, and there, in a trench, met a glorious death, grasping the flag of Spain and whispering the name of his beloved Laura —

Doña Laura *(aside.)* What a terrible lie!

Don Gonzalo *(aside.)* I could not have killed myself more gloriously.

Doña Laura: You must have been very upset by the calamity.

Don Gonzalo: Yes, indeed, señora. As if he were my brother. I imagine, though, on the contrary, that Laura in a short time was chasing butterflies in her garden, indifferent to regret.

Doña Laura: No, señor, no!

Don Gonzalo: It is woman's way.

Doña Laura: Even if it were women's way, "The Silver Maiden" was not of that disposition. My friend awaited news for days, months, a year, and no letter came. One afternoon, just at sunset, as the first stars were appearing, she was seen to leave the house. With quickening steps, she made her way toward the beach, the beach where her beloved had risked his life. She wrote his name on the sand, then sat down upon a rock, her gaze fixed on the horizon. The waves murmured their song and slowly crept up to the rock where the maiden sat. The tide rose with a boom and swept her out to sea.

Don Gonzalo: Good heavens!

Doña Laura: The fishermen along that coastline who often tell the story affirm that it was a long, long time before the ocean's waves washed away that name written on the sand.

Don Gonzalo *(aside):* She lies worse than I do.

Doña Laura: Poor Laura!

Don Gonzalo: Poor Gonzalo!

Doña Laura *(aside):* I will not tell him that I married two years later.

Don Gonzalo *(aside):* In three months, I ran off to Paris with a ballet dancer.

Doña Laura: Fate is curious. Here are you and I, complete strangers, met by chance, discussing the romance of old friends of long ago! We have been talking as if we were old friends.

Don Gonzalo: Yes, it is curious, considering the ill-natured beginning of our conversation.

Doña Laura: You scared away the birds.

Don Gonzalo: I was unreasonable, perhaps.

Doña Laura: Yes. That was evident. (*Sweetly.*) Are you coming again tomorrow?

Don Gonzalo: Most certainly, if it is a sunny morning. And not only will I not scare away the birds, but I will bring a few crumbs.

Doña Laura: Thank you very much. Birds are grateful and repay attention. I wonder where my maid is? Petra! (*Signals for her maid.*)

Don Gonzalo (*aside, looking at Laura, whose back is turned*): No, no, I will not reveal myself. I am ugly now. Better that she recall the gallant horseman who passed daily beneath her window, tossing flowers.

Doña Laura: Here she comes.

Don Gonzalo: That Juanito! He plays havoc with the nursemaids. (*Looks right and signals with his hand.*)

Doña Laura (*aside, looking at Gonzalo, whose back is turned*): No, I am too sadly changed. It is better he should remember me as the black-eyed girl, tossing flowers as he passed among the roses in the garden.

(*Juanito enters from one side, Petra from the other. She has a bunch of violets in her hand.*)

Doña Laura: Well, Petra! At last!

Don Gonzalo: Juanito, you are late.

Petra: (*to Doña Laura*): The guard gave me these violets for you, señora.

Doña Laura: How very nice! Thank him for me. They are fragrant. (*As she takes the violets from her maid, a few loose ones fall on the ground.*)

Don Gonzalo: My dear lady, this has been a great honor and a great pleasure.

Doña Laura: It has also been a pleasure to me.

Don Gonzalo: Good-bye until tomorrow.

Doña Laura: Until tomorrow.

Don Gonzalo: If it is sunny.

Doña Laura: A sunny morning. Will you go to your bench?

Don Gonzalo: No, I will come to this — if you do not object?

Doña Laura: This bench is at your disposal.

Don Gonzalo: And I will surely bring the crumbs.

Doña Laura: Tomorrow, then?

Don Gonzalo: Tomorrow!

(*Laura walks away, supported by her maid. Gonzalo, before leaving with Juanito, trembling and with a great effort stoops to pick up the violets Laura dropped. Just then, Laura turns her head and sees him picking up the flowers.*)

Juanito: What are you doing, señor?

Don Gonzalo: Juanito, wait —

Doña Laura (*aside*): Yes, it is he!

Don Gonzalo (*aside*): It is she, and no mistake.

(*Doña Laura and Don Gonzalo wave farewell.*)

Doña Laura: "Can it be that this is he?"

Don Gonzalo: "Heavens, is it she?"

(*They smile once more, as if she were again at the window and he below in the rose garden, and then disappear upon the arms of their servants.*)

READING COMPREHENSION

Summarizing. Choose the best phrase to complete each sentence. Then write the complete statements on your paper.

1. Don Gonzalo came to Doña Laura's bench because _____ (his usual bench was occupied, he thought he remembered her, he wanted to make friends).

2. Doña Laura did not admit the truth, so that Gonzalo would not _____ (go away, know that she had married another, be disappointed by the way she had changed).

3. Laura and Gonzalo did not marry because _____ (he was too poor, her parents disapproved, she went to America).

4. At the end of the play, _____ (both admitted their true identities, both planned to marry, each thought the other did not know the truth).

Interpreting. Write the answer to each question on your paper.

1. Why was the young Gonzalo forced to flee Valencia?

2. How did each lover recover after both "true loves" came to an end?

3. Why did Doña Laura and Don Gonzalo agree to meet again?

For Thinking and Discussing. Do you think Doña Laura and Don Gonzalo will ever reveal the truth to each other? Use details from the play to explain your answer.

UNDERSTANDING LITERATURE

Style in a Play. *Style* involves the words, ideas, form, and techniques that the author chooses to use. The play form allows an author to create dialogue for several characters, each with his or her own way of speaking and reacting. An *aside* is a form of dialogue that is directed to the audience. The Quinteros use *asides* to have Laura and Gonzalo reveal things to the audience while concealing the information from each other.

Below are some lines from "A Sunny Morning." On your paper, tell which are lines the characters share with each other. Tell which lines are asides.

1. "If you only knew that dream was by your side, you would realize what dreams come to."

2. "She was unlucky and had a sad love affair."

3. "This is Laura!"

The authors use asides to create *ironic humor*. Ironic humor occurs when something happens contrary to what the characters or readers expect or wish.

☐ On your paper, explain the ironic humor in this play.

WRITING

The servants speak very politely to their grouchy employers. Rewrite the lines of one servant, adding an aside that reveals what the servant really thinks.

Three Poems About Love

Here are three poems by well-known poets who write in the English language. As you read them, consider how Walker, Yeats, and Barrett Browning create images and rhyme to share their feelings about love.

New Face

by Alice Walker

I have learned not to worry about love,
but to honor its coming
with all my heart.
To examine the dark mysteries
of the blood
with headless heed and
swirl,
to know the rush of feelings
swift and flowing
as water.

The source appears to be
some inexhaustible
spring
within our twin and triple
selves;
the new face I turn up
to you
no one else on earth
has ever
seen.

---

1. Does the author seem to enjoy falling in love? What lines in the poem hint at this?

2. How does the author indicate that love is confusing, yet exciting?

3. Does the author feel that we may act differently with people we love? What does she mean by "our twin and triple selves"?

4. What is the meaning of the poem's title?

The Letter, *Mary Cassatt, 1891*

Sonnet 43

by Elizabeth Barrett Browning

How do I love thee? Let me count the
　　ways.
I love thee to the depth and breadth and
　　height
My soul can reach, when feeling out of
　　sight
For the ends of Being and ideal Grace.
I love thee to the level of every day's
Most quiet need, by sun and candlelight.
I love thee freely, as men strive for
　　Right;

I love thee purely, as they turn from
　　Praise.
I love thee with the passion put to use
In my old griefs, and with my
　　childhood's faith.
I love thee with a love I seemed to lose
With my lost saints — I love thee with
　　the breath,
Smiles, tears, of all my life! — and, if
　　God choose,
I shall but love thee better after death.

---

1.   Why do you think the poet chose to count the ways she loved her husband?

2.   In Elizabeth Barrett Browning's "Sonnet 43," how does she say death will affect her love?

3.   Although this poem is about love, the comparisons that the poet chooses suggest her view about other things that are also important to people. Find three examples of such comparisons in the poem.

He Wishes for the Cloths of Heaven

by William Butler Yeats

Had I the heavens' embroidered cloths,
Enwrought with golden and silver light,
The blue and the dim and the dark
    cloths
Of night and light and the half light,
I would spread the cloths under your
    feet:
but I, being poor, have only my dreams;
I have spread my dreams under your
    feet;
Tread softly because you tread on my
    dreams.

---

1. What image does Yeats create with his description of the "heavens' embroidered cloths"?

2. What does Yeats mean by the line "I have spread my dreams under your feet"?

Fulfillment, *Gustav Klimpt, 1909*

340

READING COMPREHENSION

Summarizing. Choose the best phrase to complete each sentence. Then write the complete statements on your paper.

1. Alice Walker called her poem "New Face" because she believes _____ (she would be happier if she looked different, many people are two-faced, each new love is different).

2. When Elizabeth Barrett Browning wrote "I love thee with the breath, smiles, tears, of all my life!" she meant that _____ (she loved him completely, she had loved him since childhood, their romance was stormy).

3. Yeats wrote "tread softly, because you tread upon my dreams." He meant that he _____ (had had a nightmare, feared being hurt or rejected, believed love is soft and gentle).

Interpreting. Write the answer to each question on your paper.

1. The poet is too poor to give his love "the cloths of heaven." What did he offer her instead?

2. What are some of the words and phrases Browning used to indicate the extent of her love?

3. What do "the cloths of heaven" represent in Yeats's poem?

For Thinking and Discussing. Discuss how the poems are alike and different. In your answer, consider the ideas expressed and the choice of language and imagery.

UNDERSTANDING LITERATURE

Elements of Style in Poetry. Although rhyme is not found in all poems, it is often used to create order and add a musical quality. Two words *rhyme* when they end with the same sound. Two lines *rhyme* when they end with rhyming words. The pattern of a poem's rhyme is its *rhyme scheme*. Look at "Sonnet 43."

1. On your paper, write the last words of the first eight lines of the poem. What pattern do you hear in the rhymes?

There is a shorthand to describe a poem's rhyme scheme. Letters stand for each different end sound, starting with *a* for the first end sound, *b* for the second, *c* for the third, and so on. The rhyme scheme of the first four lines of "Sonnet 43" is:

a	*b*	*b*	*a*
(ways)	(height)	(sight)	(grace)

"Sonnet 43" is a classic form of poetry called a *sonnet*. A sonnet contains 14 lines, each of about equal length. The rhyme scheme is: *abba abba cd cd cd*

2. Look back at the poem "He Wishes for the Cloths of Heaven." Its rhyme scheme is *abab cdcd*. What is unusual about the words that end each line?

WRITING

Write a five-line poem with an *abbab* rhyme scheme. In your poem, describe the beginning of an important experience.

Three Poems About Disappointment in Love

Here are three poems that were originally written in other languages. Akiko Yosano wrote in Japanese, Andrei Voznesensky in Russian, and Pablo Neruda in Spanish.

The actual images used by poets do not always carry the same message in another language. When these poems were translated into English, the translators could not always use the English version of the original words. They were, also, not able to keep the exact form of the poems. But they have chosen English words that carry the feeling of the original, and make it possible for the reader to share the emotions that the poets are describing. And these emotions are the same in people everywhere.

Of the Numberless Steps

by Akiko Yosano

Of the numberless steps
  Up to my heart,
He climbed perhaps
  Only two or three.

1. Who is the "he" in the poem? What do you think his relationship was to the poet?

2. Why do you think the poet chose to say so little about this person and her feelings about him?

Young Woman in a Pensive Mood, *Torii Kotondo, 1929*

First Ice

by Andrei Voznesensky

A girl freezes in a telephone booth.
In her droughty overcoat, she hides
A face all smeared
In tears and lipstick.

She breathes on her thin palms.
Her fingers are icicles. She wears
     earrings.

She'll have to walk home alone, alone,
Along the ice-bound street.

First ice. The very first time.
The first ice of telephone phrases.

Frozen tears glisten on her cheeks —
The first ice of human hurt.

1. Why do you think the girl is crying? What do you think her phone conversation was about?

2. What is the weather like outside the phone booth? How does the weather match the mood the girl is in?

3. Where in the poem does the word *ice* refer to actual ice? Where does it stand for a different kind of coldness?

Tonight I Can Write

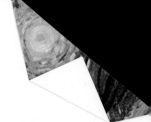

by Pablo Neruda
translated by W.S. Merwin

Tonight I can write the saddest lines.

Write, for example, "The night is
    shattered
and the blue stars shiver in the
    distance."

The night wind revolves in the sky and
    sings.

Tonight I can write the saddest lines.
I loved her, and sometimes she loved me
    too.

Through nights like this one I held her
    in my arms.
I kissed her again and again under the
    endless sky.

She loved me, sometimes I loved her too.
How could one not have loved her great
    still eyes.

Tonight I can write the saddest lines.
To think that I do not have her. To feel
    that I have lost her.

To hear the immense night, still more
    immense without her.

And the verse falls to the soul like dew
    to the pasture.

What does it matter that my love could
    not keep her.
The night is shattered and she is not
    with me.

This is all. In the distance someone is
    singing. In the distance.
My soul is not satisfied that it has lost
    her.

My sight searches for her as though to
    go to her.
My heart looks for her, and she is not
    with me.

The same night whitening the same
    trees.
We, of that time, are no longer the
    same.

I no longer love her, that's certain, but
    how I loved her.
My voice tried to find the wind to touch
    her hearing.

The Starry Night, *Vincent van Gogh, 1889*

Another's. She will be another's. Like
my kisses before.
Her voice, her bright body. Her infinite
eyes.

I no longer love her, that's certain, but
maybe I love her.
Love is so short, forgetting is so long.

Because through nights like this one I
held her in my arms
my soul is not satisfied that it has lost
her.

Though this be the last pain that she
makes me suffer
and these the last verses that I write for
her.

---

1. Why does the poet say "Tonight I can
write the saddest lines"?

2. Do you believe the narrator no longer
loves the woman he's describing? Explain why
or why not.

READING COMPREHENSION

Summarizing. Choose the best phrase to complete each sentence. Then write the complete statements on your paper.

1. Akiko Yosano's poem suggests that _____ (she was heartbroken, her romance never went far, she was not able to love).

2. In "First Ice," the girl had just _____ (talked to someone on the telephone, met a new boyfriend, learned of a friend's death).

3. In "Tonight I Can Write," Pablo Neruda wrote "Love is so short, forgetting is so long." He meant _____ (love is easily forgotten, it's hard to forget someone you once loved, love never lasts long).

Interpreting. Write the answer to each question on your paper.

1. How did the young girl in "First Ice" feel after the telephone conversation?

2. What does the phrase "numberless steps up to my heart" reveal about the poet's attitude toward love?

3. In which of the poems might the person still be in love with his or her lost love?

For Thinking and Discussing. Which poem in this section creates the strongest emotion in you, the reader? What techniques did the poet use to express his or her feelings?

UNDERSTANDING LITERATURE

Repetition in Poetry. Not every poem rhymes. Poets can also use other elements, such as repetition (the repeating of words, phrases, or lines) to help create order and form within a poem. Repetition also allows the poet to emphasize certain images and ideas that are important in the poem.

The third stanza of "First Ice" reads:

> "She'll have to walk home alone, alone,
> Along the ice-bound street."

By repeating the word *alone*, the poet emphasizes how alone the girl feels.

In the last two stanzas of this poem, the phrase *first ice* appears three times. This repetition emphasizes how surprising and painful disappointment in love can be the first time it occurs.

1. Look back at the poem "Tonight I Can Write." On your paper, write the line that is repeated several times in this poem. Explain how this repetition contributes to the reader's understanding of the poem's ideas and mood.

2. Look at the final two lines of Neruda's poem. Which significant word appears twice? On your paper, explain why the poet chose to repeat this word.

WRITING

Look at Akiko Yosano's poem. Modify this poem, using repetition to emphasize important ideas in the poem, or use repetition in an original poem about a disappointing experience.

Jane Eyre

based on the novel by Charlotte Brontë

In 1847, Charlotte Brontë completed her novel Jane Eyre. *She called Jane "a heroine as small and plain as myself." In this book, Brontë so skillfully combined her own experiences about life and love with the creation of interesting characters and mysterious situations that* Jane Eyre *is still widely read today. Here is your opportunity to join the millions of readers who have breathlessly followed 18-year-old Jane Eyre in her search for love and happiness.*

My parents died when I was very young. I do not even remember them. My mother's kind brother was to raise me, but he, too, died. I was left in the hands of his wife, who had no love for me. Again and again, she reminded me that I was a plain, penniless orphan. When I was old enough, she sent me away to boarding school, a school for orphans. I spent eight years there.

They were learning years, and at 18, I, Jane Eyre, was ready to strike out on my own. I had secured the position of governess to a lively child at Thornfield Hall. Yes, I was still plain, still a lonely orphan, but now I had real responsibilities, and the respect that came with such a job.

I liked the child, Adele, very much, and the housekeeper, Mrs. Fairfax, was pleasant, if dull, company. I was a little disappointed that the master of the house was never there, and that each day was like the next. I was restless and felt the need for something more in my life.

One cold January day, I set out alone to mail a letter two miles away. I enjoyed the walk and lingered to watch the sun set. Suddenly I heard the commotion of a horse coming along the icy road, and stepped aside. First a large dog ran past, and then a huge horse with a rider. Right before me, they slid on the icy road. Man and horse were down.

"Are you hurt? Can I help?" I asked.

"Stand aside," the man ordered, pulling himself up with difficulty. He was dark, perhaps 35 years old, stern and rough, and certainly not handsome.

If he had accepted my help, I would have thought no more of him, but his roughness and his frown appealed to me.

"Let me help you," I offered.

He looked at me. "You should be home. Where are you from?"

"Thornfield Hall," I answered.

"Do you know the whereabouts of Mr. Rochester, the master?"

"No, I don't know him or where he is."

His eyes ran over my simple dress. "Who are you? A servant?"

"I am the governess."

"Ah!" he said, and then winced with pain. He allowed me to help him limp to his horse and hand him his whip.

"Thank you," he said gruffly. "Now get home." He bounded away and vanished with his dog into the woods.

A small incident, but it made the day different from others. I thought of my lonely little room and lingered in the darkness outside the gloomy house.

When I finally went inside, I heard voices in Mrs. Fairfax's room, and there I found the dog who had run alongside the horseman.

"Whose dog is this?" I asked.

"Mr. Rochester's. He has returned home with a sprained ankle. The doctor is with him now."

So! The horseman was my master!

The next day, I could not control Adele's excitement. She was a restless student and wanted only to see her guardian, Mr. Rochester.

We were finally sent for in the evening, and he did not even look up as we entered the room. "Be seated," he said.

When Adele begged for a present, he searched my face with dark, piercing eyes. Did I expect a gift as well? I assured him I did not. He then began to question me about my background and my family. I told him I had neither home nor relatives who would have me. He ordered me to play the piano, and then said I played like any other school girl. I was amused and interested in this gruff man. Then he abruptly dismissed us.

Mrs. Fairfax had told me little about Mr. Rochester, yet I sensed there was a great deal to know.

I had little contact with him, except if he called for me with Adele. When we passed in the hall or on the stairs, I could never be sure if he would nod coldly or smile at me. He was so changeable.

One evening, he called us to the dining room where he gave Adele a gift, sent her off, and insisted I join him and sit exactly where he ordered.

This particular evening, he seemed less gloomy, with a smile on his lips and a sparkle to his eyes.

"Do you think I'm handsome, Miss Eyre?" he asked.

"No, sir," I answered too quickly.

"My word! And what are my faults?" Can you tell me?"

"I'm sorry. I didn't mean to say that. It's just that looks are not important."

He laughed and stood near the fireplace, his overall shape as equally unattractive as his face. But I liked him and his easy confidence.

"Do you wonder about Adele and why she is with me?"

"It's my position to teach her, that's all."

"Years ago, I lived in Paris. While there, I often visited Adele's mother, a music hall dancer. Recently I learned that she had died and her daughter had no one to care for her. I then arranged to become Adele's guardian."

"Knowing this," he asked, "do you wish to stay on, teaching the child of a silly French dancer?"

"Of course. It's no fault of hers. I will love her even more."

He seemed satisfied, and I was dismissed.

That night, I lay awake thinking of Mr. Rochester and how his moodiness seemed to be the result of some cruel fate. I could tell that beneath his tangle of misery there was an excellent man.

Suddenly I heard steps in the hall and then a horrible low laugh near my door. "Who's there?" I called, and I heard footsteps go up to the third floor. Was it Grace Poole, the odd servant who lived up there?

I opened my door with a trembling hand, surprised to see a cloud of smoke coming from Mr. Rochester's room. I flew to him to discover his bed on fire and Mr. Rochester in a sound sleep.

"Wake up!" I cried. I threw a basin of water on the bed.

"Is there a flood?" he cried, at last awake.

"No, sir, a fire. It's out now."

"Who did this?"

I told him about the laughter and the footsteps on the stair. Gravely he told me to wait in his room, and he left. When he came back he was pale. "Did you see anyone?" he asked.

"No, but I think it was Grace Poole's laugh."

"Just so," he said. "I will take care of this. Speak to no one about it."

"Good night then, sir," I said.

But he was reluctant for me to leave. "You saved my life. I knew when I first saw you that you would be good for me." He held my hand and would not let go until I said I was cold.

I was awake all night, feeling uneasy, tossed between trouble and joy.

I met Grace Poole the next morning. She was calm and without emotion. I was tense under her gaze. She spoke casually of the fire, and suggested I bolt my door against robbers.

All day, I waited to be called to Mr. Rochester. I wanted to ask why Grace Poole had not been dismissed. I wanted to be in his presence and look upon him. But there was no call, and in the evening, I learned from Mrs. Fairfax that he had gone to a party and was not expected back for a week.

She spoke of his friends and the lovely, rich ladies he knew. How foolish I had been to dream that such a man could waste a thought on a plain, dreary governess. I forced myself to push him from my mind.

Ten days passed without a word from him. I kept telling myself to be grateful that I worked for him and to expect nothing more. Soon there was word of his return. He was bringing the party home with him, and the bedrooms were to be prepared.

In the excitement of preparing, I watched Grace Poole as she spent one hour a day with her fellow servants and spent the rest of the time in the oaken chamber of the

third floor. I seemed to be the only one who thought her habits queer. Once I heard two maids talking about how able and how well paid she was. They stopped talking when they saw me.

Soon Adele and I watched the party arrive from our window. There were carriages and horsemen, and riding beside Mr. Rochester was a lady in a gleaming purple riding habit.

The servants forgot us that night, and we were not called to dinner. So I went myself and prepared plates for us.

"What beautiful ladies!" Adele cried as

she peeked through the door.

"Be patient," I said. "Mr. Rochester will call for you soon, and then you will meet everyone."

But he didn't call for us until the next evening. Mrs. Fairfax told us to wait in the drawing room. Adele was very excited and eager. I sat in a window seat, hoping to disappear into the draperies.

We watched the party enter the room. The ladies were richly and elegantly dressed. The woman whom we had seen riding with Mr. Rochester was with him. Her name was Blanche Ingram. She was graceful, clever, and self-assured.

The women fussed over Adele, calling her a puppet and a love. I was glad they ignored me. As for myself, I could not take my eyes off my master. He made me love him without looking at me. Oh, I had never intended to love him at all!

The women talked about Adele and asked Mr. Rochester why she wasn't in a school. Right before me, they discussed all the wretched governesses they had ever known. Blanche Ingram was especially rude. Someone whispered in her ear, apparently reminding her that I was present, and she said, "It may do her good to hear this."

Soon they tired of this, and Miss Ingram coaxed Mr. Rochester to the piano where they sang together. I wanted to leave, but my master had a fine voice. When the song was over, I slipped out, and he came after me.

"How are you?" he asked.

"I am very well, sir."

"What is wrong?" He looked closely at me. Could he see my tears?

"I am tired, sir."

He paused. "I expect you to appear every evening in the drawing room with Adele, as long as my visitors stay."

"Yes, sir."

He seemed to want to say more, but he turned abruptly and left me.

The following days at Thornfield Hall were full of excitement and partying. The gloom and sadness were gone, and in its place were music, entertainment, and life. I remained in the background, taking care of Adele and watching the activities. I could not stop loving my master now, but he never noticed me.

Soon I was certain that he would marry Blanche Ingram. He didn't appear to love her, but he accepted her attentions. She was always at his side. I looked for his faults, which had been so apparent once before, but now I saw nothing but goodness.

One rainy afternoon, he was called away on business. The activities quieted because of his absence and the rain. It would have been an empty day except for two visitors. The first was a Mr. Mason, whom I did not like. He was unsettling and odd. He had come to visit Mr. Rochester and was allowed to wait by the fire.

The second visitor was a gypsy woman who came to tell our fortunes. Each of the ladies went, out of curiosity and boredom, to see her in the kitchen. Blanche Ingram returned, looking disappointed and gloomy. The others returned laughing about how much the gypsy knew.

Then the gypsy called for the remaining lady — me. She was sitting by the fire in the kitchen, shrouded and covered. I waited.

"Why don't you tremble?" she asked.

"I am not cold."

"Why don't you turn pale?"

"I'm not sick."

"Why didn't you come right away?"

"I'm not silly."

"You are cold, sick, and silly."

"Prove it," I said.

"You are cold because you are alone, sick because you resist your feelings, and silly because you don't go to meet happiness."

"You could say that about anyone."

"Not everyone."

"You must know of us through the servants."

"I *do* know Grace Poole, but she tells me nothing."

The gypsy asked questions about the others, especially about Miss Ingram and Mr. Rochester. She let me know that she had told Miss Ingram that Mr. Rochester had little money. Did I think they were to marry soon?

"I have come for *my* fortune, no one else's," I said. Suddenly I noticed the gypsy's hand. It was my master's.

"Mr. Rochester, it is you!"

"I fooled the others but not you."

"How strange! How unfair!"

"Do you forgive me, Jane?"

I was confused. "May I leave now?"

"No, sit. Tell me what they are saying in there."

"They're discussing the gypsy, and — oh . . . there is a visitor, a Mr. Mason."

Mr. Rochester froze, and he grippped my hand. "Mason?" He staggered. "Oh, how I wish I were somewhere far away with you, my little friend."

"Can I help you, sir?"

"Jane, would you leave me if everyone turned against me?"

"No, sir, I would stay."

"Go ask Mr. Mason to come to me." He released my hand.

"Yes, sir."

That night in bed, I heard my master talking cheerfully with Mr. Mason. I felt at ease and slept soundly . . . until the scream.

My heart pounded as I listened in horror to cries for help and footsteps running up the third-floor stairs. I put on my clothes and rushed to the hall where all the guests stood, dazed and terrified. "What is it? What's happened?"

"It's all right. It's all right." Mr. Rochester entered the hall from the stairway. "A servant had a nightmare, that's all. Go back to your warm beds."

I returned to my room, but I did not go to bed. That was not a nightmare. The scream was in the room above me. Things quieted, and much later there was a tap on my door.

"Jane?" It was Mr. Rochester. "Come help me, and be very quiet."

He led me to the upper floor where he locked a side door on a snarling, laughing noise that I took to be Grace Poole. On the bed lay Mr. Mason, pale and covered with blood.

"Jane, tend to him while I go get a doctor. Stay with him, and don't speak to each other. Remember, no conversation." He left, locking the door behind him.

What was all this about? What were those noises behind the door? And what did Mr. Mason have to do with any of this? Mr. Mason moaned and looked ready to die. "She bit me, she bit me," he murmured.

Mr. Rochester returned with a doctor, who bandaged Mr. Mason and gave him medication. Mr. Mason was forced to his feet and to the stable where he was put on a horse and sent off with the doctor. Before Mr. Mason left he turned to my master. "Take care of her —" and then he wept.

When they were gone, I turned to go inside, but Mr. Rochester asked me to go into the garden with him.

"Are you all right, Jane?"

"Now will you fire Grace Poole?" I asked.

"No, Jane. Forget her. The danger is over. If only Mr. Mason would leave England, I would be safe."

"Mr. Mason doesn't seem like he could hurt you, sir."

"He could destroy me with one careless word."

I sat beside him on a small bench while he talked vaguely about guilt, his past mistakes, and peace of mind. He held my

hand. "Dear Jane, do you curse me?"

"Never, sir."

"Will you watch with me again?"

"Whenever you need me."

"The night before my wedding, I will not be able to sleep. Will you keep me company?"

"Yes, sir."

He looked deep into my eyes. "My bride is lovely."

I thought of Miss Ingram and ached inside. "Yes, sir, she is."

The next day, I was called downstairs by a messenger from Gateshead, the home of my aunt, Mrs. Reed, where I had spent my childhood. It had been eight years since I had seen Mrs. Reed or her children.

"I have bad news," the messenger said. "Mr. John died last week and his mother, Mrs. Reed, has had a stroke. She is dying, and she asks to see you."

"Me? She never wanted me near her."

"Please, she calls for you."

"All right. Let me get ready and tell my master."

I found Mr. Rochester playing billiards with Miss Ingram and asked him for a leave of absence. He was reluctant to let me leave and led me from the room. "You said you had no relatives."

"None that want me. It is a surprise to me that my dead uncle's wife calls for me, but I must go."

"Promise you won't stay for more than a week."

"I can't promise that."

"At least promise you'll return."

"But soon you'll be married and won't need me anymore. Maybe —"

"I insist you return. I will help you get another job, if necessary."

"All right. I promise to come back. Farewell."

"That's all ?" he asked. "Farewell? No handshake, or —"

The dinner bell rang, and suddenly he left me. I didn't see him again, and I left the next morning.

I returned to my childhood home, to the place where I had never been loved. I returned to the bedside of the one who had loved me least, to a room where I had been punished many times. My early terrors reclaimed me as I bent over her.

"Is this Jane Eyre?" she asked faintly.

"Yes, how are you, dear aunt?"

She appeared forgetful and restless. "I must tell you —"

"What?" I leaned close to hear her words.

"I must tell you two things. One, a broken vow. I vowed to raise you as my own. I promised my husband, your uncle, that I would love you. And I never did."

I knew that. "Why?" I asked.

"My husband adored your mother, his only sister. I hated her and you."

I waited. There was nothing to say.

"The other thing," she murmured. "Bring me the letter from my drawer. You have an uncle, John Eyre, who is wealthy and wishes to adopt you." The letter was three years old.

"Why didn't you tell me sooner?"

"And see you raised in ease and comfort? You hateful child!" She was becoming upset, and I soothed her the best I could.

Mrs. Reed died soon after in her sleep, and after helping with the arrangements, I left without shedding a tear.

I returned to Thornfield Hall with mixed feelings. I felt as if I were returning home, even though Mrs. Fairfax had written to me about wedding preparations. I knew I wanted to be with Mr. Rochester for the little time we had left.

I walked the last mile of my journey and came upon my master in the garden. "Jane! Where have you been?" he cried.

"My aunt is dead, sir."

"And you've come home."

How glad I was to see him, and how my heart filled when he called Thornfield my home. Oh, that it were! I hesitated, and looked at him.

"Mr. Rochester, wherever you are is my home, my *only* home." And I rushed off to the house.

For the next two weeks, life went on. There were no signs of a coming wedding, nor trips to Ingram Park to visit his future bride. He seemed totally at ease, and never had I loved him so well.

One lovely evening after Adele was asleep, I went out to the garden and found

Mr. Rochester there. I tried to excuse myself, but he insisted I stay with him.

"Do you like living here, Jane?"

"Yes, indeed," I told him.

"And Adele? You seem fond of her."

"She's a lovely child, sir."

"Then you'll be sad to leave?"

"Must I leave?"

"Yes, when I'm married, I'll no longer need a governess."

"May I stay here until I find a new position?"

"Of course, and I will help you. I know of a teaching job in Ireland."

Ireland! So far from my beloved. My eyes filled with tears. "It's so far."

"Far from what?" he asked.

"From you," I said before I could stop myself.

"So why do you leave?"

"Because of Miss Ingram, your bride."

"Miss Ingram is not the bride I want, Jane." He reached out to me and held me in his grasp. His lips pressed against mine.

"You're making fun of me," I said, struggling to get away, but he held me fast.

"I want *you* to be my wife, Jane. You are my bride. Do you doubt me?"

"Entirely."

"Jane, trust me. I knew I loved you the moment I first saw you. I wanted you to return my affection. I pretended an interest in Blanche Ingram only to attract your attention."

I couldn't believe my ears. "Do you truly love me?"

"I swear it."

My face felt hot; my heart raced. "Then, sir, I will marry you."

He was joyous. He held me, kissed me, and promised happiness. We sat in the darkness and the moon was suddenly in shadow. A stormy wind began to whip the trees. We went inside and parted with a tender kiss.

The next morning, when I awoke, I saw that the very tree we had sat under in the garden had been split by lightning during the night.

We began to make plans, but I insisted that I would continue as Adele's governess until we were married. He wanted to give me the family jewels and to buy me beautiful clothes, but I knew such things would make me uncomfortable.

Mrs. Fairfax was shocked by our announcement, and her skepticism brought tears to my eyes. Seeing how upset I was, she said she was sorry, and that she hoped I was not too young to know what I was doing.

Life went on happily for me in the next weeks, and the wedding day drew near. I even wrote a letter to my newly discovered uncle to tell him of my coming marriage.

Soon my gown and veil were ready, and plans had been made for our honeymoon. But two nights before the wedding, something terrible happened. I had been sleeping and dreaming restless dreams when I awoke to find my room lit and a woman before my mirror. My blood crept cold through my veins.

"It must have been one of the servants," Mr. Rochester told me.

"No. I had never seen such a woman before. She was tall with long, dark hair, and she put on my veil, and I saw her face — a ghastly face with red eyes, swollen purple lips, black eyebrows — "

"What did she do?" he demanded.

"She tore my veil in two and then stood over my bed staring at me."

Mr. Rochester's grip tightened around me. "And then?"

"I fainted from terror, and when I came to, she was gone."

"Ah, a dream, that is all."

"But my veil! In the morning, I found it torn in two."

He drew in his breath and after some moments said, "No doubt it was that strange Grace Poole. In your sleepiness, she seemed different. After we are married a year, I will tell you why I keep her in my house. Will you accept this for now?"

There seemed to be no other explanation, so I nodded.

"Tonight sleep in Adele's room."

I spent the night in her room, but I didn't sleep. I held her and wondered what my future held.

We rushed to the church early the next morning. Mr. Rochester was impatient and had rushed me there without receiving the good wishes of the servants. There were only the two of us; but as we flew up the church steps, I noticed two shadowed figures in the churchyard.

As we knelt before the priest to be married, I heard footsteps enter behind us. The priest explained matrimony and then asked if there was any reason we should not be joined together. He paused and a voice rose in the church.

"This marriage cannot go on."

"Why?" asked the priest.

Mr. Rochester gripped my hand. His face was like marble.

"Because Mr. Rochester is married, and his wife is living."

I felt faint. My master's face was colorless. The two men stepped forward.

"I am Briggs, a lawyer, and this is Mr. Mason, the true wife's brother and also acquaintance of John Eyre. Mr. Eyre is this bride's uncle, and he had received word of the wedding."

Mr. Rochester shook beside me; whether with fury or despair, I don't know. "Good God!" he cried.

"Remember you are in church, sir," the priest warned. "Are you certain the wife is still alive?" he asked the men.

"Yes," Mr. Mason answered.

"Enough!" shouted Mr. Rochester. "There will be no wedding, for I am married. But to a madwoman, a maniac, an idiot! Come with me and meet her."

We all left the church and went to Thornfield Hall. I was stunned and followed silently.

We entered the hall and climbed the stairs to the third floor. "You know this place, Mason," he said coldly. "She bit and stabbed you here."

He unlocked the door, and we entered to find Grace Poole cooking, and at the far end of the room a beast or human being on all fours, growling. The woman stood and cried out, the very monster who had torn my veil.

"She sees you, sir!" shouted Grace Poole. "Watch out!"

The woman sprang at Mr. Rochester, biting and clawing. He overwhelmed her with his strength and bound her to a chair.

"My wife, gentlemen," he announced. "And you have just seen her loving embrace."

We all withdrew in shame and horror. I went to my room and began to undress. I didn't mourn or cry. I felt dead and calm. I packed away my wedding dress and sat down to think. Once again, I was alone, Jane Eyre, a cold, solitary girl. All was lost, and I felt overcome by floods of sadness.

The next morning, I knew I must leave

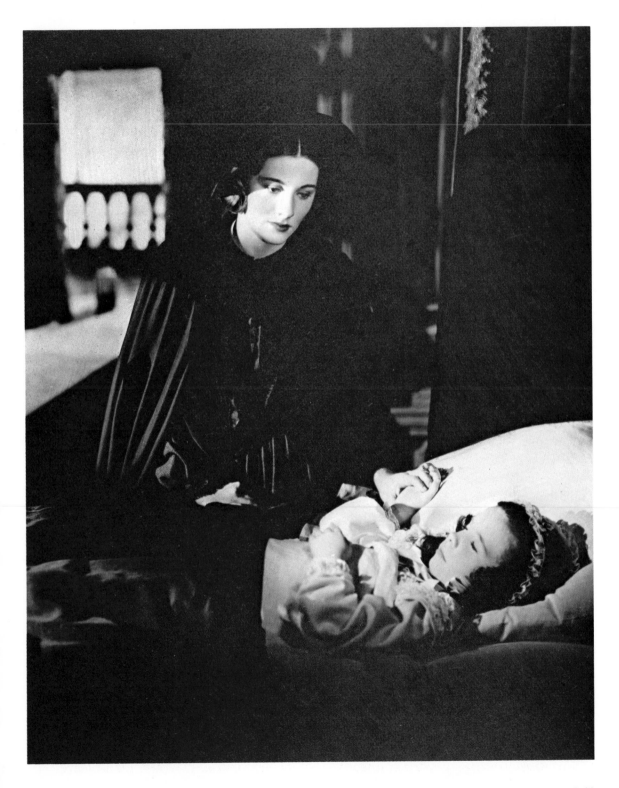

Thornfield Hall at once, and when I left my room, I found Mr. Rochester sitting in a chair by my door.

"You don't weep, Jane. No sobs, no bitterness. No passion. Will you ever forgive me?"

In my heart, I did forgive him, for he was so sad. Yet I said nothing. He tried to kiss me, and I pulled away.

"Can you go on, my love, as Adele's governess and be like stone and ice to me? We love each other."

"All is changed," I answered steadily. "I must leave."

"Why, my love, why?"

"You are married."

"Married? It is not a marriage. I was tricked into marrying her. No one told me that this terrible madness ran in her family. She was beautiful, charming, and destined to be shut up as a lunatic, like her mother and her uncle. Others knew, but no one told me. When she became mad, I chose to place her in safety and comfort, and to shelter her in secret. Grace Poole has been her keeper for 10 years. And then I roamed aimlessly over Europe looking for happiness. Then I found you! You are a joy that has entered my life, an unexpected delight. Pledge your fidelity to me, Jane."

I was silent.

"Jane! Will you leave me?"

"Yes."

"My life will be over if you leave."

"You will forget me before I forget you," I said.

I ran from the room and heard him sob behind me. "God bless you, my master," I whispered. "I love you, and farewell."

I left Thornfield Hall early the next morning without saying good-bye to anyone. I dared not go to my Uncle John's. I was afraid Mr. Rochester might look for me there. I took a road I have never taken before. It was summer, and I slept on the ground at night, desperate and alone.

Finally, feeling totally hopeless, I began going from door to door in a little village, begging for work or a bit of food. With my last bit of strength, I knocked at the door of a minister, St. John Rivers. He took pity on me and invited me in. I stood, sick and trembling, in his bright kitchen and met his sisters, Diana and Mary. They fed me and asked questions I would not answer. Then their servant prepared a warm, dry bed for me, and I slept for three days, unaware of time.

St. John and his sisters were kind to me, accepting that I would not tell them of my previous life and hardships. Once they knew I was an educated gentlewoman, St. John secured a position for me as teacher in the village. I was grateful to have both work and people who became like sisters and a brother to me. I could have gone on like that forever, holding back my longing for my darling master, except that St. John began to eye me strangely.

As homely as Mr. Rochester was, St. John was handsome and noble. He was young, tall and slender, with a classic face. His eyes were blue, and his hair was fair and soft. He was a religious man and had decided to go to India as a missionary, and he had also decided I would go with him, as his wife!

"St. John, nothing holds me here, and perhaps I would consider going to India, although I do believe I would be a martyr and die under such awful conditions. However, I would go as your sister, not as your wife."

"I need a wife," he stated intensely.

"That is not me. I'm not suited to be your mate. You do not love me."

"But you *are* suited. You are suited for work, not for love. I can tell."

I knew my life would be miserable with him, and the fire of my nature would never burn freely.

But he did not let up. I was very lonely, having been gone from Thornfield a full year. My life had little meaning. St. John would not allow me to go to India with him as anything but his wife, and there seemed to be nothing else for me. He was a good man, and maybe there would never be love in my life after all.

St. John used all his talents on me — guilt, religious fire, God, the angels — and just as I was about to give in one evening, weakened and at the point of tears, I had an odd experience. A sharp electrical shock shook my body.

"Jane! Jane! Jane!" I heard the beloved voice of Mr. Rochester call me in pain and urgency.

"I'm coming! I'm coming!" I cried. "Where are you?" I ran to the garden where the hills and the moorlands were silent. I knew what I had to do.

The next morning, I left for Thornfield.

The distance took 36 hours to travel, and I felt like a messenger-pigeon flying home.

How fast I walked the last mile of my journey! I ran to see my woods, my house, my home. But I stopped suddenly before the great mansion. I looked with joy, but saw a blackened ruin. Before me was the shell of a burned-out house with a silence of death about it.

I approached and wandered through the shattered walls. The fire had happened long ago. All was lost. And where was my master?

I hurried back to the inn in the village. Was Mr. Rochester dead, lost to me forever?

"Is Mr. Rochester living at Thornfield Hall?" I asked the owner of the inn, as if I knew nothing.

"No, ma'am. You must be a stranger here. No one is living there. It's in ruins. There was a terrible fire. I saw it myself."

"How did it happen?"

He lowered his voice. "There was a lunatic in the house. It turned out she was Mr. Rochester's wife, but he had hired a governess —"

"But the fire," I interrupted. "What about the fire?"

"I'm coming to that. Well, it seems he fell in love with the governess. The servants said they never saw such love. Anyway, it turns out the governess ran away, and Mr. Rochester searched all over for her, and then shut himself up like a hermit."

"He was there when the fire broke out?"

"Yes, indeed. He tried to rescue his mad wife as she stood on the roof, shouting and raving. They say she started the fire.

She jumped to her death."

"And Mr. Rochester?"

"He's alive, but he was injured and lost his sight and his hand. He is forever blind and crippled."

"Where is he now?" I asked.

"At Ferndean, 30 miles away."

"Can I hire a coach from you?" I asked. "I want to be taken to Ferndean immediately."

The house at Ferndean was secluded and desolate, and I stood at the gate. The door opened and a figure stood in the twilight — my master and no other! I held my breath and watched him. He blindly held out his one good hand to feel for rain and then returned into the house.

Now I went to the house and knocked. I was greeted by a servant who remembered me and acted as if she were seeing a ghost.

"I don't think he'll talk to you," she said. "He refuses everyone. But I'll tell him you're here." She was carrying a tray with a glass of water.

"Here," I said. "Give me the tray. I will carry it to him." My heart struck my ribs loud and fast as I entered his parlor.

"Give me the water, Mary," he said, turning to the sound of my footsteps.

"Mary is in the kitchen," I said.

"Who is this?" he demanded.

"Here is your water, sir."

"Who is it? Who speaks?"

"I've come home, sir."

"Great God! Jane Eyre! What sweet madness has seized me?"

"No madness. You have a sound and strong mind."

He groped for me, and I gave him my hand.

"Her very fingers!" he cried. "If so, there must be more of her." He blindly seized my arm, my shoulder, and gathered me to him.

"She is all here," I said. "Her heart, too. I am so glad to be near you again."

"Jane Eyre! Jane Eyre!" was all he said.

"I will never leave you again." I pressed my lips to his eyes and his brow. "I will be your housekeeper, your nurse, your companion — whatever you need."

"But I am a ghastly sight, Jane, aren't I?"

"You were never much to look at, Mr. Rochester, and now there's the danger of making too much of you and loving you too much."

"Oh, you are indeed here, my skylark. Stay with me. Do not fly away or vanish. All the sunshine I can feel is in your presence. Jane, will you marry me?"

"Yes, sir."

"Me, a poor blind man?"

"Yes."

"A cripple?"

"Most definitely, sir. To be your wife is, for me, to be as happy as I can be on earth."

Then he stretched out his hand to be led. I took his dear hand and held it a moment to my lips, and then let it pass around my shoulders.

I married him and went on to live a blessed life. He later regained enough sight in one eye to see his dark-haired son put into his arms. And we have always been thankful that God tempered His judgment with lasting mercy.

READING COMPREHENSION

Summarizing. Choose the best phrase to complete each sentence. Then write the complete statements on your paper.

1. Jane Eyre first came to Thornfield Hall to _____ (nurse her sick aunt, work as a governess, marry Mr. Rochester).

2. Jane Eyre and Mr. Rochester were kept from marrying when _____ (Jane Eyre had to go to India to do missionary work, Mr. Mason revealed that Mr. Rochester was already married, Mr. Rochester went to Paris).

3. When Jane Eyre returned to find Mr. Rochester, he was _____ (blind and crippled, wealthy, living at Thornfield).

Interpreting. Write the answer to each question on your paper.

1. Who actually was the madwoman in the tower?

2. What qualities in Jane Eyre's character and personality might have attracted Mr. Rochester to her?

3. Why was Mr. Rochester happier at the end of the story in spite of his disabilities than when he was rich and the master of a large estate?

For Thinking and Discussing. Describe Charlotte Brontë's attitude toward love as revealed in *Jane Eyre*. What qualities would she advise someone to look for in a marriage partner? Base your answer on the events, descriptions, and characters in the story.

UNDERSTANDING LITERATURE

Style. The *style* of a story or novel includes the language the author uses as well as the way the author tells the story. In *Jane Eyre*, the author writes in the style of a gothic romance. This kind of fiction has several characteristic elements:

1. The story is usually told from the first-person point of view of the main character. The choice of words and the sentence structure reflect this character's way of speaking and thinking.

2. The plot of the story includes many suspenseful elements, usually about a mystery or a secret.

3. The plot is usually complicated by romances that do not progress smoothly.

Write the answers to the following questions on your paper.

1. From whose point of view is *Jane Eyre* told?

2. What is one mystery or secret that is revealed in this story?

3. What romantic relationships are part of the plot?

WRITING

Choose an exciting incident from *Jane Eyre*, such as when she saves Mr. Rochester from the fire or learns he is already married. Rewrite it in a few paragraphs. Use a style that reflects your own way of speaking and your own attitudes.

Section Review

Simile, Metaphor, and Personification. A *simile* is a comparison between two things that uses the word *like* or *as*. "A Sunny Morning" contains this simile: She was "fair as a lily." The beauty of the young Laura is compared to that of a flower.

A *metaphor* is a comparison that does not use the word *like* or *as*. For example, W. B. Yeats wrote of "the heavens' embroidered cloths/Enwrought with golden and silver light." This is a metaphor for the beauty of the sky.

Personification is the description of an object, animal, or idea as though it were human. When Pablo Neruda wrote "the blue stars shiver in the distance," he used a metaphor that compares the cold-looking stars to shivering people.

Read the sentences below. On your paper, label each as a *metaphor* or *simile*. If the comparison is also *personification*, write this word as well. Then tell in your own words what the writer is saying.

1. ". . . the wheels squealing on the rails sound like the birds singing in New Hampshire."

2. "The waves murmured their song . . ."

3. "Tread softly because you tread on my dreams."

4. "Her fingers are icicles."

READING

Making Inferences. You will find that the author sometimes does not express something directly. Rather, the author *suggests* something. When you decide what the author is suggesting, you make *inferences*. Inferences are guesses based on information the author gives you.

Read the following exercises. Select the best choice to complete the last sentence in each exercise. Then write the entire sentence on your paper.

1. In "Feels Like Spring," Milton Kaplan describes a lonely young man who had moved to a big city. The young man saw the same people every day, but no one spoke to him. From this, you can infer that Kaplan believes that people in big cities _____.
   a. feel awkward about making conversation
   b. lead very busy lives
   c. are not very friendly to newcomers

2. In "New Face," Alice Walker says that she has "learned not to worry about love, but to honor its coming. . . ." You could infer that she _____.
   a. is a very carefree person
   b. had been in love before
   c. worries too much

3. In *Jane Eyre*, Jane was raised by an aunt who disliked her. Jane rejected St. John because he did not love her. You could infer that _____.
   a. Jane wanted to be loved
   b. Jane would never care for anyone
   c. Jane was a cold, unfeeling person

WRITING

An Autobiographical Narrative. An autobiographical narrative is a story someone writes about his or her own personal experiences. When you write an autobiographical narrative, you are telling part of your life story. Your story will have more meaning for the reader if you also tell how you felt about the experience.

Step 1: Set Your Goal

Since an autobiographical narrative is a story about yourself, there's nothing to look up. Search your memory for a topic based on your real-life experiences. The topic you choose should be important and interesting, but it doesn't have to be extraordinary. The following questions may help you decide on a topic.

- [ ] Have you ever discovered that you could do something that you had thought you couldn't do?
- [ ] Have you ever had an experience that was frightening at first but turned out all right in the end?
- [ ] Have you ever been in an embarrassing situation that taught you something or later turned out to be funny?

There may be many purposes for writing an autobiographical narrative. For example, you may want to share some new insight you have gained or make a point. You may simply want to entertain your readers by sharing a funny experience. Or, you may want to show how an event changed your life.

Look over the topic you have chosen and think about the point of your story. Ask yourself why the event was important to you and why the story is worth sharing. Write one sentence stating your purpose in telling the story.

Step 2: Make a Plan

In order for your narrative to become a real story, it must have a plot. A plot is made up of four basic elements — *action, conflict, climax,* and *resolution.* The action of a story is made up of what the characters do and what happens to them.

The conflict, or problem, in a story is the struggle between two opposing forces. In *Jane Eyre,* the conflict is between what Jane and Mr. Rochester felt for each other and the circumstances that prevented them from expressing their feelings.

The climax is the turning point in the story, at which the most important event occurs and the outcome seems inevitable. In *Jane Eyre,* the climax occurs when Jane hears Mr. Rochester's voice calling to her and she decides to return to him.

The resolution is the ending of the story. It shows the result of what happened at the climax. In *Jane Eyre,* the resolution occurs when Jane and Mr. Rochester agree to get married.

Like any story, an autobiographical narrative should have a beginning, a middle, and an end. The beginning introduces the characters, establishes the setting, explains the situation, and sets up the conflict. The middle tells what happened, bringing the action to the highest point, or climax. The end tells what the situation was like after the action was over. It brings the story to a satisfying close.

Prepare a plot outline for your story. List all the events that might be part of your story. Be sure there are events for each element of the plot. Then go over your list and group the events according to those that belong in the beginning, the middle, and the end of the story. Finally, number the events in chronological order.

Step 3: Write a First Draft

A story is more than a list of events. A well-written story has details that make the story seem real to the reader. Refer to your plot outline as you write. Use specific verbs, nouns, adjectives, and adverbs to make your descriptions vivid. Include dialogue to give your readers the sense that they're hearing live action.

Step 4: Revise

When you revise your first draft, imagine that you are reading the story for the first time. Use the following checklist to help you revise:

- ☐ Does your story have a plot that is easy to follow?
- ☐ Is there a conflict, a climax, and a resolution?
- ☐ Did you use descriptive details and dialogue to make your story come alive?

When you have finished revising your story, proofread it for errors and then make a neat, final copy.

QUIZ

The following is a quiz for Section 6. Write the answers in complete sentences on your paper.

Reading Comprehension

1. How did the narrator in "Feels Like Spring" travel to work?

2. What secret were Doña Laura and Don Gonzalo trying to keep from each other? Were they successful?

3. How does the poem "New Face" let you know that Alice Walker believes that love changes people?

4. What has made the speaker in Pablo Neruda's poem so sad?

5. Why did Jane Eyre leave Thornfield Hall? Why did she return?

Understanding Literature

6. From whose point of view is the story "Feels Like Spring" told? How does this affect the author's choice of language used in the story?

7. In "A Sunny Morning," what techniques do the authors use to let the reader or audience learn about the characters?

8. What standard poetic form did Elizabeth Barrett Browning use to write a love poem to her husband? How are rhyme and repetition important to the style of the poem?

9. Is the poem "First Ice" written in the first or third person? How does the choice of point of view affect the language and mood of the poem?

10. What is ironic about the ending of *Jane Eyre*?

ACTIVITIES

Word Attack. Each entry word in a dictionary is followed by its phonetic respelling. In a phonetic respelling, each sound is represented by a letter-symbol or diacritical mark. Letter-symbols are used to indicate different consonant sounds. For example, the letter *c* in *cinder* is represented by the letter *s* because the *c* sounds like an *s*. Diacritical marks are used to indicate different vowel sounds. There are many different diacritical marks, but the two most common are a straight line or a small curve over the vowel. For example, a straight line over the letter *ō* indicates that the vowel sound should be pronounced like the *o* in *go*. A curved line over the letter *ŏ* means that the vowel sound should be pronounced like the *o* in *top*.

All dictionaries have a pronunciation key that shows what each letter-symbol or diacritical mark means. If you forget what sound a particular letter-symbol or diacritical mark represents, you can check it in the pronunciation key.

Use a dictionary to write the phonetic respelling for each word below. Then check the pronunciation key to see if you are pronouncing each word correctly.

acquaint	drought	infinite
affirm	embroider	monotony
authority	exhaust	vaguely

Speaking and Listening

1. Choose a partner and continue the story "A Sunny Morning." Decide on the dialogue Doña Laura and Don Gonzalo will have at their next meeting. Will they confess their secrets to each other? If they do, what will happen? Present your scene to the class.

2. Select one of the following poems from this section and prepare to present an interpretive reading of it. An interpretive reading is one in which you convey or interpret the meaning of a poem in the way you say the words and phrases.

   "New Face"
   "Sonnet 43"
   "He Wishes for the Cloths of Heaven"
   "First Ice"

Researching. The story "Feels Like Spring" takes place in New York City. Draw a map of New York City (Manhattan) and include the major streets and avenues. Draw symbols on the map to locate the places mentioned in the story — 34th Street, 175th Street, Radio City Music Hall, and the George Washington Bridge. If possible, find the route of the subway line Thomas took and indicate it on your map.

Creating

1. Rewrite the last part of "Feels Like Spring" as a dialogue for a play. Use asides to help the audience know what Thomas and the other people on the train are thinking.

2. In a letter or poem, write about love from Jane Eyre's point of view. Direct your feelings and thoughts to Mr. Rochester.

SURVIVAL

We were sawing firewood when we picked up an elm log and gave a cry of amazement. It was a full year since we had chopped down the tree—and yet this elm log had not given up. A fresh green shoot had sprouted from it, promising a thick, leafy branch or even a whole new elm tree.

— Alexander Solzhenitsyn
Soviet Union

The Old Tulip Tree, Long Island
Ernest Lawson (1873-1939)
Hunter Museum of Art, Chattanooga
Gift of the Benwood Foundation

Survival

Before people learned to speak or write, they had to learn to stay alive. Knowing how to survive is still necessary in the modern world. A story can show you how to win against forces you may encounter in your own life. Some works of literature tell you that, to survive, you sometimes have to fight forces in yourself.

Learning from Nature

In nature, only strong and resourceful species survive. By observing the way things work in nature, people can often learn important lessons about survival. Sometimes these simple truths are more valuable than scientific knowledge.

"Feathered Friend," a short story by Arthur C. Clarke, is set in the future, on a space station floating far from Earth. When something goes wrong, sophisticated safety devices fail to warn the crew. But a pet bird provides the clue that saves the crew members' lives. Clarke shows that, no matter what amazing advances we make in science and technology, we will never escape the basic rules of nature.

Birds teach a lesson of survival in another work you will read. In "The Woman Who Had No Eye for Small Details," a short story by William Maxwell, a woman living alone in the country feeds hundreds of wild birds. When she has to go away for a while, she fears the birds will die during the harsh winter. In observing the birds, tiny and frail as they seem, the woman realizes something important about people. Although everyone must face death and sorrow at some time, life, with all the joys and surprises it has to offer, does go on.

Beating Death

In some stories, especially legends and folktales, events happen that are impossible in real life. But these stories can still tell us something about the real world.

"The Cow-Tail Switch" is a folktale from West Africa that takes place in a culture where people must hunt animals to survive. One day, a hunter is killed by a leopard. Years later, his sons go looking for him, find his bones, and use magic powers to bring their father back to life.

To beat death, we cannot use magic. But magic has nothing to do with the lesson of the story. Before the father could be brought back to life, his sons had to care enough to look for him. Even special powers do no good until someone decides to use them—which is a moral for every place and time.

"The Last Dive" is a very realistic story about a man's struggle against the forces of nature. A diver has to fight for his life

Bison with Two Arrows, *Cave of Niaux, France*

against sharks and other dangers of the sea. Will he outwit the forces that threaten him? Or has he risked his life once too often? Man's wits are pitted against the unpredictability of nature in this exciting story.

Keeping Afloat

"First Lesson," a poem by Philip Booth, is also about more than immediate survival. The words are those of a father who is teaching his young daughter to swim. When he tells her how to make "the long thrash to your island," he is actually telling her how to reach her goals as she makes her way through life. In this poem, the sea has another, deeper meaning—it is a *metaphor* for life.

The next story in this section is adapted from Alexandre Dumas' novel *The Count of Monte Cristo*. A man who has been imprisoned through the scheming of his enemies must use his wits and bravery to escape. But before he can escape, he must prevent himself from sinking to a state in which he no longer wants to live.

The final selection is "The Washwoman" by Isaac Bashevis Singer. This is a sensitive, sad tale about an old woman the author remembers from his youth in Poland. Somehow her sense of duty enables her to carry on . . . just long enough.

Many of the stories ahead remind us that inner forces can be as dangerous as outer ones. Sometimes, survival means winning a battle with yourself.

Feathered Friend

by Arthur C. Clarke

Arthur C. Clarke has written dozens of science-fiction stories, one of which was made into the movie 2001: A Space Odyssey. He has also written nonfiction books on space and has made important contributions to aerospace technology. Born in England in 1917, he now lives on the remote island of Sri Lanka, where he cannot even get television reception. But he is still in touch with the world; the story you will read says as much about the present as it says about the future.

To the best of my knowledge, there's never been a regulation that forbids one to keep pets in a space station. No one ever thought it was necessary — and even had such a rule existed, I am quite certain that Sven Olsen would have ignored it.

With a name like that, you will picture Sven at once as a six-foot-six Nordic giant, built like a bull and with a voice to match. Had this been so, his chances of getting a job in space would have been very slim; actually he was a wiry little fellow, like most of the early spacers, and managed to qualify easily for the 150-pound bonus that kept so many of us on a reducing diet.

Sven was one of our best construction men, and excelled at the tricky and specialized work of collecting assorted girders as they floated around in free fall, making them do the slow-motion, three-dimensional ballet that would get them into their right positions, and fusing the pieces together when they were precisely dovetailed into the intended pattern. I never tired of watching him and his gang as the station grew under their hands like a giant jigsaw puzzle; it was a skilled and difficult job, for a space suit is not the most convenient of garbs in which to work. However, Sven's team had one great advantage over the construction gangs you see putting up skyscrapers down on Earth. They could step back and admire their handiwork without being abruptly parted from it by gravity. . . .

Don't ask me why Sven wanted a pet, or why he chose the one he did. I'm not a psychologist, but I must admit that his selection was very sensible. Claribel weighed practically nothing, her food requirements were infinitesimal — and she was not worried, as most animals would have been, by the absence of gravity.

I first became aware that Claribel was aboard when I was sitting in the little cubbyhole laughingly called my office, checking through my lists of technical stores to decide what items we'd be running out of next. When I heard the musical whistle beside my ear, I assumed that it had come over the station intercom, and waited for an announcement to follow. It didn't; instead, there was a long and involved pattern of melody that made me look up with such a start that I forgot all about the angle beam just behind my head. When the stars had ceased to explode before my eyes, I had my first view of Claribel.

She was a small yellow canary, hanging in the air as motionless as a hummingbird — and with much less effort, for her wings were quietly folded along her sides. We stared at each other for a minute; then, before I had quite recovered my wits, she did a curious kind of backward loop I'm sure no earthbound canary had ever managed, and departed with a few leisurely flicks. It was quite obvious that she'd already learned how to operate in the absence of gravity, and did not believe in doing unnecessary work.

Sven didn't confess to her ownership for several days, and by that time it no longer mattered, because Claribel was a general pet. He had smuggled her up on the last ferry from Earth, when he came back from leave — partly, he claimed, out of sheer scientific curiosity. He wanted to see just how a bird would operate when it had no weight but could still use its wings.

Claribel thrived and grew fat. On the whole, we had little trouble concealing our unauthorized guest when VIP's from Earth came visiting. A space station has more hiding places than you can count; the only problem was that Claribel got rather noisy when she was upset, and we sometimes had to think fast to explain the curious peeps and whistles that came from ventilating shafts and storage bulkheads. There were a couple of narrow escapes — but then who would dream of looking for a canary in a space station?

We were now on 12-hour watches, which was not as bad as it sounds, since you need little sleep in space. Although of course there is no "day" and "night" when you are floating in permanent sunlight, it was still convenient to stick to the terms. Certainly when I woke up that "morning," it felt like six A.M. on Earth. I had a nagging headache, and vague memories of fitful, disturbed dreams. It took me ages to undo my bunk straps, and I was still only half awake when I joined the remainder of the duty crew in the mess. Breakfast was unusually quiet, and there was one seat vacant.

"Where's Sven?" I asked, not very much caring.

"He's looking for Claribel," someone answered. "Says he can't find her anywhere. She usually wakes him up."

Before I could retort that she usually woke me up, too, Sven came in through the doorway, and we could see at once that something was wrong. He slowly opened his hand, and there lay a tiny bundle of yellow feathers, with two clenched claws sticking pathetically up into the air.

"What happened?" we asked, all equally distressed.

"I don't know," said Sven mournfully.

"I just found her like this."

"Let's have a look at her," said Jock Duncan, our cook-doctor-dietitian. We all waited in hushed silience while he held Claribel against his ear in an attempt to detect any heartbeat.

Presently he shook his head. "I can't hear anything, but that doesn't prove she's dead. I've never listened to a canary's heart," he added rather apologetically.

"Give her a shot of oxygen," suggested somebody, pointing to the green banded emergency cylinder in its recess beside the door. Everyone agreed that this was an excellent idea, and Claribel was tucked snugly into a face mask that was large enough to serve as a complete oxygen tent for her.

For the last few minutes, something had been tugging at my memory. My mind seemed to be very sluggish that morning, as if I was still unable to cast off the burden of sleep. I felt that I could do with some of that oxygen — but before I could reach the mask, understanding exploded in my brain. I whirled on the duty engineer and said urgently:

"Jim! There's something wrong with the air! That's why Claribel's passed out. I've just remembered that miners used to carry canaries down to warn them of gas."

"Nonsense!" said Jim. "The alarms would have gone off. We've got duplicate circuits, operating independently."

"Er — the second alarm circuit isn't connected up yet," his assistant reminded him. That shook Jim; he left without a word, while we stood arguing and passing the oxygen bottle around like a pipe of peace.

He came back 10 minutes later with a sheepish expression. It was one of those accidents that couldn't possibly happen; we'd had one of our rare eclipses by Earth's shadow that night; part of the air purifier had frozen up, and the single alarm in the circuit had failed to go off. Half a million dollars' worth of chemical and electronic engineering had let us down completely. Without Claribel, we should soon have been slightly dead.

So now, if you visit any space station, don't be surprised if you hear an inexplicable snatch of bird song. There's no need to be alarmed: on the contrary, in fact — it will mean that you're being doubly safeguarded, at practically no extra expense.

To our delighted surprise, she revived at once. Beaming broadly, Sven removed the mask, and she hopped onto his finger. She gave her series of "Come to the cookhouse, boys" trills — then promptly keeled over again.

"I don't get it," lamented Sven. "What's wrong with her? She's never done this before."

READING COMPREHENSION

Summarizing.   Choose the best phrase to complete each sentence. Then write the complete statements on your paper.

1. The canary was in the space station because she _____ (had flown in, was smuggled aboard, was part of a scientific experiment).

2. Claribel thrived at the space station in spite of the _____ (lack of food, loneliness, absence of gravity).

3. Claribel was revived by _____ (a little food, an operation on her lungs, a breath of oxygen).

4. The air supply was damaged by _____ (a rare eclipse, an enemy spaceship, Claribel's careless flying).

Interpreting.   Write the answer to each question on your paper.

1. What did the narrator remember that helped him figure out what had happened to Claribel?

2. What might have happened if Claribel had not been on board the space station?

3. How did Claribel's presence make the station more pleasant for humans?

For Thinking and Discussing.   What would you add to or take away from the story "Feathered Friend" to make it a more accurate and realistic view of what a space station of the future would probably be like?

UNDERSTANDING LITERATURE

Character in Science Fiction.   Every story has a plot, characters, and a setting. In a science-fiction story, at least one of these must be based on scientific theory. In "Feathered Friend," scientific information is combined with information about *character*—how people of any time or place react to problems.

Make two columns on your paper. Label one "Character" and the other "Science." In the first, list the statements below that reveal character. In the second, list those that are based on scientific theory. Some entries may belong in both columns.

1. Sven and his team preferred working in space to working on Earth.

2. Sven wanted a pet, and he brought a canary on board.

3. The canary did well in space because it weighed little, ate little, and didn't mind the absence of gravity.

4. The narrator missed Claribel's songs when the bird was unable to sing.

5. Canaries were used to warn miners about problems with the air supply.

6. An eclipse had caused part of the air purifier to freeze.

WRITING

Make up four new details describing Sven Olsen. Two of the details should contain scientific information, and two should be about character.

The Woman Who Had No Eye for Small Details

by William Maxwell

William Maxwell was born in Illinois in 1908. Although he lived in New York and was an editor for The New Yorker *magazine for over 40 years, he has always felt like a Midwesterner. He is the author of several novels and many short stories. A number of his stories, including this one, resemble fairy tales. Like all good fairy tales, it contains a lesson.*

Once upon a time, there was a woman who had no eye for those small details that most women love to spend their time on — curtains and doilies, and the chairs arranged so, and the rugs so, and a small picture here, and a large mirror there. She did not bother with all this because, in the first place, she lived alone and had no one but herself to please, and, anyway, she was not interested in material objects. So her house was rather bare, and, to tell the truth, not very comfortable.

She lived very much in her mind, which fed upon books, and what she herself thought about what they said. She was not a homely woman. She had good bones and beautiful heavy hair, which was very long, and which she wore in a braided crown around her head. But no man had ever courted her, and at her present age, she did not expect this to happen. If some man had looked at her with interest, she would not have noticed it, and this would, of course, have been enough to discourage further attentions.

Her house was the last house on a narrow dirt road, deep in the country, and if she heard the sound of a horse and buggy or a wagon, it was somebody coming to see her, which didn't often happen. She kept peculiar hours, and ate when she was hungry. The mirror over the dressing table was sometimes shocked at her appearance, but since she almost never looked in it, she was not aware of the wisps of hair that needed pinning up, the eyes clouded by absentmindedness, the sweater with a button missing, worn over a dress that belonged in the ragbag. A blind man put down in her cottage would have thought there were two people; not one, living in it, for she talked to herself a great deal.

Birds in great number nested in the holes of her apple trees and in the ivy that covered her stone chimney. Their cheeping, chirping sounds were the background of all that went on in her mind. Often she caught sight of them just as they were disappearing, and was not sure whether she had seen a bird or only seen its flight. It was so like the way certain thoughts again and again escaped her just as she reached out for them.

When the ground was covered with snow, the birds closed in around the house and were at the feeding stations all day long. Even the big birds came — the lovely, gentle mourning doves, and the pheasants, out of the woods, and partridge, and quail. In bitter weather, when the wind was like iron, she put pans of warm water out for them, and, in a corner sheltered from the wind, kept a path of ground swept bare, since they wouldn't use the feeders. And at times, she was as occupied — or so she told herself — as if she were bringing up a large family of children, like her sister.

Her sister's children were as lively as the birds, and even noisier, and they were a great pleasure to the woman who lived all alone, when she went to visit them. She played cards with them, and let them read to her, and listened to all that they had to say, which their mother was too busy to do. While she was there, she was utterly at their disposal, so they loved her, and didn't notice the wisps of hair that needed pinning up, or that there was a button missing from her sweater, or the

fact that her dress was ready for the ragbag.

Looking around, she thought how, though her sister's house was small and the furniture shabby, everything her eye fell upon was there because it served some purpose or because somebody loved it. The pillows were just right against your

back, the colors cheerful, the general effect of crowdedness reflected the busy life of the family. Their house was them, in a way hers was not. Her house, to be her, would have had to be made of pine boughs or have been high up on some cliff. The actual house sheltered her, and that was all that could be said of it.

Her nieces and nephews would have been happy to have her stay with them forever, but she always said, "I have to get back to my little house," in the tone of voice grown-ups use when they don't intend to discuss something.

"Your house won't run off," her sister would say. "Why do you worry about it

so? I don't see why you don't make us a real visit."

"Another time," the woman said, and went on putting her clothes in her suitcase. The real reason that she could not stay longer she did not tell them, because she knew they would not take it seriously: She could not bear the thought of the birds coming to the feeders and finding nothing but dust and chaff where they were accustomed to find food. So home she went, promising to come back soon, and never out-staying her welcome.

But no woman — no man, either — is allowed to live completely in her mind, or in books, or with only the birds for company. One day when she opened her mailbox, which was with a cluster of other mailboxes at a crossroads a quarter of a mile away, there was a letter from her sister. She put it in her pocket, thinking that she knew what was in it. Her sister's letters were, as a rule, complaining. Her life was hard. Her handsome, easygoing, no-good husband had deserted her, she supported herself and the children by fine sewing. She worried about the children, because they were growing up without a father. And though they were not perfect, their faults loomed larger in her eyes than they perhaps needed to. In any case, she was tired and overworked and had no one else to complain to.

Hours later, the woman remembered that she had not read the letter, which turned out to be only three lines long: "I am very sick and the doctor says I must go to the hospital and there is no one to look after the children. Please come as soon as you can get here."

All the time the woman was packing, she kept thinking now about her poor sister and now about the poor birds. For it was the middle of the winter, there was deep snow on the ground, and the wind crept even into the house, through the crack under the door, through closed windows. She filled the feeders to overflowing with seeds and suet, and sprinkled cracked corn on the ground, knowing that in two days' time it would all be gone. It was snowing again when she locked the door behind her and started off, with her old suitcase, to the nearest farmhouse. She would have to ask the farmer to hitch up his horse and sleigh and drive her to the station in the village, where she could take a train to the place where her sister lived. Fluffed out with cold, the birds sat and watched her go.

When she came back, she was not alone. The farmer's sleigh was full of children with sober, pale faces. They climbed down without a word and stood looking at their new home. The woman had left at the beginning of February, and it was now nearly the end of March. The snow on the roof, melting, had made heavy cornices of ice along the eaves, and the ice, melting, had made long thin icicles. The woman got down, and thanked the farmer, and stood looking around, to see if there were any birds. The trees were empty, there was no sound in the ivy, and the cold wind went right through her.

"Come, children," she said, as she

searched through her purse for her door key. "Let us go in out of the cold. You can help me build a fire."

Inside it seemed even colder, but the stoves soon made a difference. She was so busy feeding the children and warming their beds that she scarcely had time to go to the door and throw out a handful of seed on the snow. No birds came. The next day, she swept a bare place in the sheltered corner, and put out corn for the pheasants and quail, and filled the feeders. But she did all this with a heavy heart, knowing that it was to no purpose. And her sister's death had been a great tragedy and she did not see how she could fill her sister's place in the children's hearts or do for them what their mother had done. The corn on the ground, the sunflower seeds in the feeders were untouched when night fell.

Inside the house, there was the same unnatural quiet. The woman did not talk to herself, because she was not alone. The children said, "Yes, please," and "No, thank you," and politely looked at the books she gave them to read, and helped set the table, and brought in wood and water, but she could see that they were waiting for only one thing — to go home. And there was no home for them to go to now but here. They did not quarrel with one another, as they used to, or ask her riddles, or beg her to play Old Maid with them. In the face of disaster, they were patient. They could have walked on air and passed through solid walls. They looked as if they could read her mind, but theirs were no longer open to her. Though they cried at home, they did not cry here — at least not where she could see them. In their beds at night, she had no doubt.

The next morning, exhausted, she overslept, and when she came into the kitchen, the children crowded at the window. Something outside occupied their attention, so they could hardly answer when she said good morning to them.

"Your birds have come back," the oldest nephew said.

"Oh surely not!" she cried, and hurried to the window. On the ground outside, in the midst of all the whiteness and brightness, it was like a party. The cardinals, the chickadees, the sparrows, the juncos, the nuthatches, the jays were waiting their turn at the feeders, pecking at the corn in the sheltered place, leaving footprints in the snow. Somehow, mysteriously, deep in the woods perhaps, they had managed without her help. They had survived. And were chirping and cheeping.

"We got our own breakfast," the children said. Though they didn't yet know it, they would survive also.

The tears began to flow down her cheeks, and the children came and put their arms around her. "So silly of me," she said, wiping her eyes with her handkerchief, only to have to do it again. "I thought they were all — I didn't think they'd survive the cold, with nobody to feed them, for so long." Then more tears, which kept her from going on. When she could speak, she said, "I know it's not — I know you're not happy here the way you were at home." She waited until she could speak

more evenly. "The house is not very comfortable, I know. I'm different from your mother. But I loved her, and if you will let me, I will look after you the best I can. We'll look after each other."

Their faces did not change. She was not even sure that they heard what she had said. Or if they heard but didn't understand it. Together, they carried warm water in pans; they swept off a new place for the quail; they hung suet in bags from the branches of the hemlock. They got out the bird book, and from that, they moved on to other tasks, and the house was never quite so sad again. Little by little it changed. It took on the look of that other house, where everywhere about you there were traces of what someone was doing, as sharp and clear and interesting as the footprints of the birds in the snow.

READING COMPREHENSION

Summarizing. Choose the best phrase to complete each sentence. Then write the complete statements on your paper.

1. The woman's house was bare and uncomfortable because she was _____ (always tired, very poor, not interested in material things).

2. The woman's nephews and nieces liked her because she _____ (paid attention to them, brought them presents, was very beautiful).

3. The children came to live with their aunt when their mother _____ (remarried, died, became too poor to feed them).

Interpreting. Write the answer to each question on your paper.

1. Why would a blind man have thought that more than one person lived in the woman's house?

2. What details indicate that the woman was careless about her appearance?

3. Why were the birds so important to the woman?

4. How did the wild birds bring the woman and the children closer together?

For Thinking and Discussing.

1. What kind of survival do you think this story is about?

2. How did the children change the woman's life?

UNDERSTANDING LITERATURE

Characterization. The purpose of a story determines to what extent a character is developed. "The Woman Who Had No Eye for Small Details" is the study of a woman's character; the woman is fully described, or "round," rather than briefly described, or "flat."

The author describes both the way the woman's mind works and her outward appearance. In fact, her appearance and actions are closely related to her feelings and thoughts.

The first (numbered) list below contains descriptions of the woman's physical appearance or actions. The second (lettered) list describes her personality and feelings. Match the items in the two lists, and write the answers on your paper.

1. Her house was rather bare.

2. She was not aware of the wisps of hair that needed pinning up.

3. She talked to herself a great deal.

a. She lived very much in her mind.

b. She lived alone and had no one but herself to please.

c. She was not interested in material objects.

WRITING

Try to imagine the thoughts of one of the woman's nieces or nephews after his or her mother has died. Write a paragraph in the first person, describing how he or she feels about living in a new home.

Forefathers

by Birago Diop

Listen more often to things rather than
    beings.
Hear the fire's voice,
Hear the voice of water.
In the wind hear the sobbing of the
    trees.
It is our forefathers breathing.

The dead are not gone forever.
They are in the paling shadows
And in the darkening shadows.
The dead are not beneath the ground,
They are in the rustling tree,
In the murmuring wood,
In the still water,
In the flowing water,
In the lonely place, in the crowd;
The dead are not dead.

Listen more often to things rather than
    beings.
Hear the fire's voice.
Hear the voice of water.

In the wind hear the sobbing of the
    trees.
It is the breathing of our forefathers
Who are not gone, not beneath the
    ground,
Not dead.

The dead are not gone forever.
They are in a woman's breast,
A child's crying, a glowing ember.
The dead are not beneath the earth,
They are in the flickering fire,
In the weeping plant, the groaning rock,
The wooded place, the home.
The dead are not dead.

Listen more often to things rather than
    beings.
Hear the fire's voice,
Hear the voice of water.
In the wind hear the sobbing trees.
It is the breath of our forefathers.

---

1. What do you think the poet means when he says, "the dead are not dead"?

2. What is your opinion of the poet's ideas about the dead? How would these ideas change a person's outlook on life?

3. How might some of the poet's ideas be true in a scientific sense? In an emotional sense?

4. The poet comes from the African nation of Senegal. Would he have written the same poem if he had grown up in a large American city? Explain.

*Luba–*Kirwebe Mask *from Zaire*

The Cow-Tail Switch

by Harold Courlander and George Herzog

Born in Indiana in 1908, Harold Courlander has traveled all over the world collecting folktales from many lands. He has published books of tales from African, Asian, Caribbean, and American Indian cultures. "The Cow-Tail Switch," a West African folktale recorded by George Herzog, is the title story in a collection of West African folktales compiled by Harold Courlander.

Near the edge of the Liberian rain forest, on a hill overlooking the Cavally River, was the village of Kundi. Its rice and cassava fields spread in all directions. Cattle grazed in the grassland near the river. Smoke from the fires in the round grass houses seeped through the palm-leaf roofs, and from a distance these faint columns of smoke seemed to hover over the village. Men and boys fished in the river with nets, and women pounded grain in wooden mortars in front of the houses.

In this village, with his wife and many children, lived a hunter by the name of Ogaloussa.

One morning, Ogaloussa took his weapons down from the wall of his house and went into the forest to hunt. His wife and his children went to tend their fields, and drove their cattle out to graze. The day passed, and they ate their evening meal of manioc and fish. Darkness came, but Ogaloussa didn't return.

Another day went by, and still Ogaloussa didn't come back. They talked about it and wondered what could have detained him. A week passed, then a month. Sometimes Ogaloussa's sons mentioned that he hadn't come home. The family cared for the crops, and the sons hunted for game, but after a while, they no longer talked about Ogaloussa's disappearance.

Then, one day, another son was born to Ogaloussa's wife. His name was Puli. Puli grew older. He began to sit up and crawl. The time came when Puli began to talk, and the first thing he said was, "Where is my father?"

The other sons looked across the rice-fields.

"Yes," one of them said. "Where is Father?"

"He should have returned long ago," another one said.

"Something must have happened. We ought to look for him," a third son said.

"He went into the forest, but where will we find him?" another one asked.

"I saw him go," one of them said. "He

388

went that way, across the river. Let us follow the trail and search for him."

So the sons took their weapons and started out to look for Ogaloussa. When they were deep among the great trees and vines of the forest, they lost the trail. They searched in the forest until one of them found the trail again. They followed it until they lost the way once more, and then another son found the trail. It was dark in the forest, and many times they became lost. Each time, another son found the way. At last, they came to a clearing among the trees, and there on the ground, scattered about, lay Ogaloussa's bones and his rusted weapons. They knew then that Ogaloussa had been killed in the hunt.

One of the sons stepped forward and said, "I know how to put a dead person's bones together." He gathered all of Ogaloussa's bones and put them together, each in its right place.

Another son said, "I have knowledge, too. I know how to cover the skeleton with sinews and flesh." He went to work, and he covered Ogaloussa's bones with sinews and flesh.

A third son said, "I have the power to put blood into a body." He went forward and put blood into Ogaloussa's veins, and then he stepped aside.

Another of the sons said, "I can put breath into a body." He did his work, and when he was through, they saw Ogaloussa's chest rise and fall.

"I can give the power of movement to a body," another of them said. He put the power of movement into his father's body, and Ogaloussa sat up and opened his eyes.

"I can give him the power of speech," another son said. He gave the body the power of speech, and then he stepped back.

Ogaloussa looked around him. He stood up.

"Where are my weapons?" he asked.

They picked up his rusted weapons from the grass where they lay and gave them to him. They then returned the way they had come, through the forest and the rice fields, until they had arrived once more in the village.

Ogaloussa went into his house. His wife prepared a bath for him and he bathed. She prepared food for him and he ate. Four days he remained in the house, and on the fifth day, he came out and shaved his head, because this was what people did when they came back from the land of the dead.

Afterward he killed a cow for a great feast. He took the cow's tail and braided it. He decorated it with beads and cowry shells and bits of shiny metal. It was a beautiful thing. Ogaloussa carried it with him to important affairs. When there was a dance or an important ceremony, he always had it with him. The people of the village thought it was the most beautiful cow-tail switch they had ever seen.

Soon there was a celebration in the village because Ogaloussa had returned from the dead. The people dressed in their best clothes, the musicians brought out their instruments, and a big dance began. The drummers beat their drums and the women sang. The people drank much palm wine. Everyone was happy.

Ogaloussa carried his cow-tail switch, and everyone admired it. Some of the men

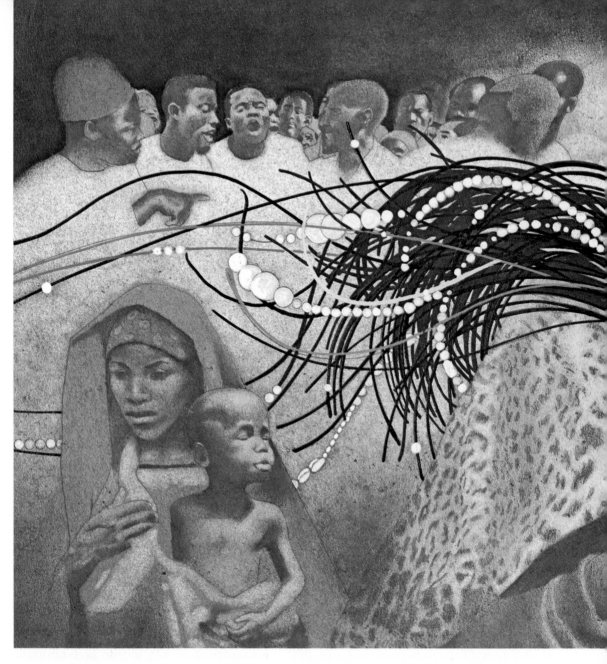

grew bold and came forward to Ogaloussa and asked for the cow-tail switch, but Ogaloussa kept it in his hand. Now and then, there was a clamor and much confusion, as many people asked for it at once. The women and children begged for it, too, but Ogaloussa refused them all.

Finally he stood up to talk. The dancing stopped and people came close to hear what Ogaloussa had to say.

"A long time ago, I went into the forest," Ogaloussa said. "While I was hunting, I was killed by a leopard. Then my sons came for me. They brought me back from the land of the dead to my village. I will give this cow-tail switch to

one of my sons. Each of them has done something to bring me back from the dead, but I have only one cow-tail to give. I shall give it to the one who did the most to bring me home."

So an argument started.

"He will give it to me!" one of the sons said. "It was I who did the most, for I found the forest trail when it was lost!"

"No, he will give it to me!" another son said. "It was I who put his bones together!"

"It was I who covered his bones with flesh!" another said. "He will give it to me."

"It was I who gave him the power of movement!" another son said. "I deserve it most!"

Another son said it was he who should have the switch, because he had put blood into Ogaloussa's veins. Another claimed it because he had put breath in the body. Each of the sons argued his right to possess the wonderful cow-tail switch.

Before long, not only the sons but the other people of the village were talking. Some of them argued that the son who had put blood into Ogaloussa's veins should get the switch, others that the one who had given Ogaloussa breath should get it. Some of them believed that all of the sons had done equal things, and that they should share it. They argued back and forth this way until Ogaloussa asked them to be quiet.

"To this son I will give the cow-tail switch, for I owe the most to him," Ogaloussa said.

He came forward and bent low and handed it to Puli, the little boy who had been born while Ogaloussa was in the forest.

The people of the village remembered then that the child's first words had been, "Where is my father?" They knew that Ogaloussa was right.

For it was a saying among them that a man is not really dead until he is forgotten.

READING COMPREHENSION

Summarizing. Choose the best phrase to complete each sentence. Then write the complete statements on your paper.

1. Ogaloussa's sons went to search for him _____ (the day he disappeared, a week after he disappeared, many months after he disappeared).

2. The sons brought Ogaloussa back to life by _____ (taking him to the hospital, making sacrifices, using magic).

3. Ogaloussa gave the cow-tail switch to _____ (his youngest son, the son who found his trail, his wife).

4. According to the story, a man is not really dead until he is _____ (buried, forgotten, no longer breathing).

Interpreting. Write the answer to each question on your paper.

1. What began the sons' search for their father?

2. Why was the cow-tail switch important to the people of the village?

3. Which events in the story were unrealistic or impossible?

For Thinking and Discussing

1. Why do you think the older sons did *not* search for the father when he first disappeared?

2. For you personally, what is the meaning of the saying, "A man is not really dead until he is forgotten"?

UNDERSTANDING LITERATURE

Symbol as a Key to Character. A symbol is something that has a meaning of its own but also stands for something larger than itself. For example, when a grandfather's pocketwatch is handed down from father to son, it may symbolize the love and respect people have for each other. A writer may use a symbol to add to the reader's understanding of a character.

The main symbol in "The Cow-Tail Switch" is Ogaloussa's cow-tail switch.

Below are several statements from the story. Answer the questions after each.

1. "'I will give this cow-tail switch to one of my sons . . . to the one who did the most to bring me home.'" What did the switch symbolize for Ogaloussa?

2. "Each of the sons argued his right to possess the wonderful cow-tail switch." What did the switch symbolize for the older sons? Why didn't they get it?

3. "'To this son I will give the cow-tail switch, for I owe the most to him,' Ogaloussa said. He . . . bent low and handed it to Puli." What does Puli's possession of the switch suggest about his character? About the story's theme?

WRITING

Choose something that symbolizes the United States, such as the Statue of Liberty, the bald eagle, or the American cowboy. Write a paragraph telling how it stands for the United States.

The Last Dive

by Dal Stivens

Dal Stivens, born in 1911 in Australia, is a painter as well as a writer. It may not surprise you to learn that he is also an expert on natural history; you will feel that you are many fathoms under the sea when you read this vivid story.

Bill Prentice walked in his stiff diving suit over the sea floor of Torres Strait. He was at the northern tip of the Australian continent. Thirty fathoms over Bill's curling red hair — and 60 feet forward of him on the blinding blue waters — lay a pearling boat. He was linked to it by the tubes of his air-pipe and lifeline.

In the slack tide, the boat was drifting slowly, towing Bill along the edge of Calico Reef in a search for pearl shell. Helen, his wife; Jack Harris, his partner; and four aborigines were aboard the ship.

Bill went lightly, easily, in the inflated suit. He heard at the back of his mind the urr-umph-grumph of the air-pump, which protected him from the great pressure of the water. His lead-soled boots kicked a fine trail of grit behind him.

Up from the depths, the coral of the reef grew in many forms. There were the spiked branches Bill knew as stag horns. There were nobby, brain-shaped clusters in black, curly clumps. There were shapes like pagodas and cathedrals, castles, trees, and mushrooms.

But here, where Bill walked, the only color was a murky blue. The Diver's Graveyard, he told himself. Then, ahead, he caught the gleam of something shining in the mud. It was small, a half-circle in shape. As Bill went forward, it blinked and disappeared.

Bill went to the spot, knelt on his left knee, and groped in the mud for the oyster. A mist grew under his fingers, floated between his rubber-covered legs, and spread out in a faint veil around him.

He found the plate-sized shell, glad to see that it was the more valuable gold-lip or true mother-of-pearl. He put it with the six others in the netting bag. "Shopping for security," he told himself, jiggling the bag. "For the capital to buy the farm."

He caught the hot, rubbery smell of his diving suit. He put his right hand to the valve of his helmet and released a small burst of air from his suit. "Too much air has been getting down your legs while you daydream," he thought.

He felt the outside pressure of the water squeezing the suit close round his legs. A shoal of dark fish emptied itself out of a crack in the wall and then poured itself back.

393

Here in this deep water, he did a shift of half an hour on the bottom. He would be brought back by stages, taking nearly an hour. "No point in taking risks. Least of all now. It creeps up on you silently, this paralysis. No diver's death in deep water for me. Not now."

He saw in his mind's eye the rows of white gravestones on the slope at Darney Island with the names in Japanese characters. The names of 60 men who had died in these waters from the bends.

"Let's call it a day," Jack had said at breakfast that morning. His lean face had been serious, his voice anxious. "We've cleaned up big on the reef. We've got enough now, man. Seven thousand pounds' worth."

Bill had looked at Jack and then at Helen, with her amber hair, laughing eyes, and long golden legs below the bright red shorts.

Bill said, "There's another half-ton of shell left — it'd be a shame not to pick that up. It'll buy something for the farm." He laughed. "Besides, we've come so far —"

Seven thousand miles, in fact, for the risk of riches. They had been stationed in these waters during the war and learned of the fabulous beds of shell in the depths off Calico Reef. Few divers dared to go for them now.

He stood up from the table on the deck, holding his cup of coffee. "I'm OK," he added. "I'm a bit tensed up, but the deep water does that." He didn't add, "And because it's nearly over, the whole 15 weeks of going into the sea."

On the sea floor, Bill Prentice signaled for them to take up his basket of shell. He saw it pulled up out of sight, until his helmet cut off his view.

Then he saw the shark. It came slowly toward him, head on. It stopped 12 feet off, only its gill slats moving. It was hanging four feet off the seabed. It appeared to be a tiger shark, about 12 feet long.

Bill waited for the shark to leave. "You're the guy who stole my lunch," he said to it. "You stole my white-fish."

Earlier that day, Bill had speared two long white-fish for lunch. He brought them up with him, breaking the water 20 feet from the boat. He saw Helen, slim, her hair gold in the sunlight, and Jack, waving to him and pulling in the air-pipe. Tommy, one of the aborigines, gathering up the lifeline.

Helen's face had changed suddenly, and her lips were moving quickly. He could hear nothing. Jack was pointing to the water.

Something bumped Bill's legs and swung him round. The spear was nearly torn from his grasp. Peering through the glass, he saw the white flash of a huge belly. He was pulled fast to the boat and then he was dragged onto the deck.

He felt no alarm about the shark now. He knew them to be cowardly, nervous creatures for the main part. The only danger lay in breaking the surface near one. Then it might rush a diver, mistaking him for a shoal of fish.

He opened the valve on his helmet. Silvery bubbles came out. The shark turned

VOTH

tail and swam rapidly away, stirring up the fine mud.

He was groping for shell when something solid struck him in the back and shoved him forward for a couple of feet. He straightened up and tried to move away. The creature stalked and butted him.

Its head was four feet across. Its eyes, large as plums, goggled at him. Its mouth gaped, and its huge, thick lips seemed to mumble. He realized then that this was not a shark, but a grouper, the 800-pound terror of the reefs. Groupers were short-sighted, slow, but fearless, not to be frightened as sharks were.

It barged slowly up to his chest, nibbling at the cords that held his two 40-pound lead ballast weights. Bill thrust his hands behind his back. He recalled stories of divers whose hands and arms had been nibbled away.

With relief, he watched the grouper drift back four feet. He put his hands deep into the folds of his suit, under his armpits. The grouper watched, like an old bull, his gills lifting and showing two huge troughs. Then the grouper came on, mouth working, and bumped him hard. Bill had to give way, nearly losing his balance.

"You can't scare them away," they told him at Darney. "You get out of there. Go up 30 or 40 feet if you can. They're short-sighted."

"This is some fine spot," he told himself. "If I try to close the valve to go up 30 feet, he'll nibble my hand off. Maybe he'll nibble my head off, too. He's big enough."

The grouper bumped the helmet again, this time on the top.

"Do that again, and you'll bust the valve off," Bill said to the fish. "Come down away from my air-line."

He sighed with some relief as the black mass dropped suddenly to his chest level. Large fleshy lips fumbled at his waist. Slowly it sank, inch by inch, to his thighs, with its belly on the mud.

"Now!" Bill's mind whispered. Cloaked in the mist, he shot his right hand and closed the valve. The suit filled rapidly. He signaled on his lifeline for Jack to take him up.

He soared then off the ocean bed like an actor on a wire. His feet whisked swiftly clean of the grouper. Thirty feet from the sea floor, he signaled Jack to stop the ascent. Must stop here, his mind warned. He moved his hand to open his valve and was puzzled to find his arm moving with deadly slowness. His head swam.

He knew no more until he was on the ladder at the surface. Jack and Helen were undoing the screws of his helmet glass. His suit was weirdly puffed out, like a toad fish.

He heard Jack saying, his face gravely troubled, "You burst right out of the water! What was it?"

He saw Helen smiling. "Good girl," he thought. "You're scared and so am I." He tried to tell about the grouper, but his tongue felt huge and clammy in his mouth. He tried to grip the ladder and his fingers wouldn't close. He became aware of fiery pains in his joints and limbs and the ache in his head.

"A grouper!" he got out. "I went up and passed out."

"You'll have to go back, Bill!" he heard Jack saying.

He nodded. Helen was helping Jack hold him on the ladder. He was dizzy and the sky was trying to stand on its side. He put out all his strength to fix his eyes on Helen's face. He saw the tears in the corners of her eyes and the tremor of the muscles in her throat.

Then quick fingers were wiping his glass and closing it. He heard Jack shout to the men and shortly after a roar from the depths. They had lowered a charge of dynamite and exploded it to scare off the grouper.

Then in a mist of pain as the flames licked more cruelly through his arms and legs, he heard the mutter of the pump. He was going down. Then it was black and quiet.

He came to on the seabed, not knowing at first why he was there nor how long he had been out. The pains had almost gone but his arms and legs would not obey him.

"I have a chance," he told himself. He tried to figure how long he had been out. He'd know when Jack started to move him. Five minutes on the sea bottom before going up slowly was the pattern. That was so the pressure gauge on the pump dropped only a pound a minute. It would be 80 minutes or more, with stops in the water, before he saw the sunlight and breathed the open air.

"If I have any luck, I might get out of this," he told himself. "I have to get out of it. A cripple can't work a farm." Then he felt himself going up very, very slowly. That would give his blood time to clear itself of the nitrogen bubbles that had formed in it as in a newly opened pop bottle.

Just two hours later, Bill was hanging 12 feet below the boat. The pains were gone, except for a headache. "Another 10 minutes and I'll know for sure," he said to himself. "You'll know when you try to walk on the deck."

He felt bored and reminded himself that he'd better try to enjoy what was going to be his last dive ever. It was a wise man who took a broad hint: The grouper and Calico Reef had handed him as broad a hint as they could.

They'd get out with what they had — 30 tons of shell worth $100,000 and pearls worth $10,000. Helen was going to have a well-to-do husband and one who wasn't a cripple, if his luck held. Far out on his left, he saw the dim shadow of the reef, and looking forward and up, he saw clearly the broad hull of the boat.

Then he looked ahead and saw the tiger shark. He thought he recognized it — the one he had scared away earlier that day. Ages ago.

"I see your game," Bill's voice said inside his head. "You've told yourself that here's a good fellow. He spears a fish and I take it from him. Maybe if I hang around, he'll spear another fish for me."

He opened the left sleeve of his suit and shot a stream of bubbles at the shark. He clapped his naked hands deep into the folds of his suit under the armpits.

The shark backed four feet and swung slowly in the water as though it was tied at its head.

"Off with you!" Bill unloosed more bubbles. The shark flashed into life. His tail cracked the water and he shot away to the right.

"Good riddance. It's just as well not to have you about when Jack pulls me to the top."

He felt better now. He swung himself around to the right. Caution made him try to see the shark safely away. He saw no sign of him, but a thought stirred in his head: He could not see directly above his head or below his legs. This worried him. Suppose the shark was below him now?

Suddenly the shark was there again, swimming sideways at his eye level, and followed by two others. The three of them circled him twice and then all of them froze to a loglike stop ahead of him.

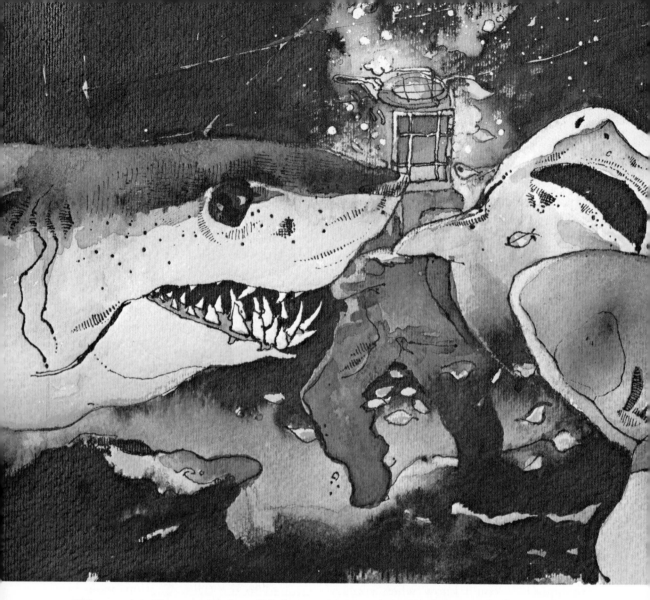

"Blast you! Clear out!" he told them angrily. There was less than five minutes to go. If they were around then, they would rush him. Unless, of course, Jack and the others on the boat saw them in time.

The sharks veered off a little. But almost immediately they came back. He released a longer burst of bubbles and the sharks left him — or at least his range of vision.

He waited. He thought about that last day with Helen before they sailed. They'd sat on the hillside watching the river twisting and throwing back the sunlight. He had shot four mallards that day. But he had not picked up the last one, though he'd hit it square.

He could see the barnacle-clustered bottom of the boat. Three sucker fish had attached themselves to the fishing line that Jack had thrown over the side.

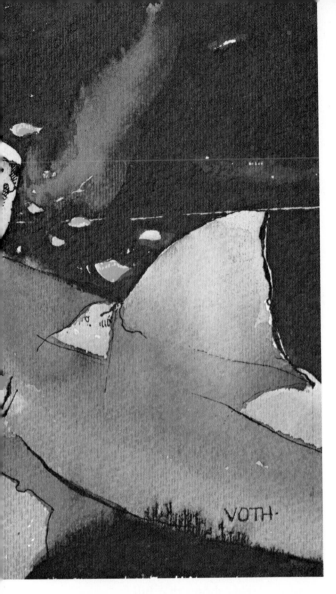
VOTH.

No one on the boat seemed to have noticed anything wrong.

Once again he opened his valve, but this time the sharks did not move. "They are unusually bold, or hungry, or both," he thought. "Well, it won't be long now."

Any minute now, Jack would haul him up. Then there would be a fierce rush at him and it would be all over. It occurred to him that he had found the reason for the sharks' boldness. Some of the blood of the white-fish must have got on his suit and they could smell it.

He fingered the hilt of the knife in his belt. His mind sought a way to defeat these brutes. For some reason, too, he found himself recalling the lost mallard.

That mallard had been flying high but he had hit it. It climbed and climbed and then fell down to earth. Out of somewhere, a hawk flashed and followed it as it tumbled in a flurry of failing wings.

The sharks closed in now, looming large and threatening with cold, unblinking eyes. "Like hawks!" His mind ran, taking fire. There was his only chance!

He felt the lifeline tightening and knew that Jack was bringing him up. He knew what he had to do. He tugged out his knife as he went up and slashed and slashed at the cords of his ballast. The weights fell away from him and sank fast. He saw the sharks diving down on them, like the hawk after the mallard.

Freed of the ballast, he was coming up fast.

He broke in a spray of bubbles out of the water. He waved wildly to Jack and the men, trying to tell them with gestures of his deadly peril.

Swiftly, but with what seemed to him terrifying slowness, they hauled him to the boat's side and helped him up, just as one of the sharks swirled up. He shouldered the water just where Bill's feet had been seconds before.

Later he got up and strode about the deck with his arms around Helen. He heard himself talking some foolishness to her and Jack about never shooting a hawk on that farm they were going to buy.

399

READING COMPREHENSION

Summarizing. Choose the best phrase to complete each sentence. Then write the complete statements on your paper.

1. Bill was making money to buy _____ (his own fishing boat, a farm, mother-of-pearl shells).

2. Bill surfaced too fast the first time _____ (because he was in a hurry, to escape the grouper, to escape a shark).

3. Bill was lowered into the sea the second time to _____ (gather more pearls, spear fish for food, clear his blood of nitrogen bubbles).

4. Bill fooled the sharks by remembering _____ (a war-time experience, a duck-hunting experience, his wife Helen on the boat).

Interpreting. Write the answer to each question on your paper.

1. What had the divers who were buried on Darney Island died from?

2. Why are grouper fish often more dangerous than sharks?

3. Why must divers surface slowly from the depths of the ocean?

4. How did Bill save himself from the sharks?

For Thinking and Discussing. What qualities did Bill Prentice have that made him a survivor? Give examples of each quality. Do you think his goal was worth the risks he took?

UNDERSTANDING LITERATURE

Indirect Characterization. An author can indirectly describe a character through actions or thoughts: "Max Ratchett liked to kick little dogs." In "The Last Dive," the author reveals the character of Bill Prentice in an indirect way.

Select the best choice of character traits to complete each statement below. Then write the entire sentence on your paper.

1. "He knew [sharks] to be cowardly, nervous creatures for the main part." This shows that Bill is _____.
   a. nervous
   b. calm
   c. cowardly

2. "Bill thrust his hands behind his back. He recalled stories of divers whose hands and arms had been nibbled away." This shows that Bill is _____.
   a. selfish
   b. hungry
   c. quick-thinking

3. "'If I have any luck, I might get out of this,' he told himself. 'I have to get out of it.'" This shows that Bill is _____.
   a. lucky
   b. scared
   c. determined

WRITING

Write a paragraph describing how either Helen or Jack felt while Bill was down for his second dive. Use the character's thoughts, feelings, and actions to show what his or her personality is like.

First Lesson

by Philip Booth

Lie back, daughter, let your head
be tipped back in the cup of my hand.
Gently, and I will hold you. Spread
your arms wide, lie out on the stream
and look high at the gulls. A dead-
man's float is face down. You will dive
and swim soon enough where this
      tidewater

ebbs to the sea. Daughter, believe
me, when you tire on the long thrash
to your island, lie up, and survive.
As you float now, where I held you
and let go, remember when fear
cramps your heart what I told you:
lie gently and wide to the light-year
stars, lie back, and the sea will hold you.

1. Who is the speaker in the poem? Who is he addressing?

2. The young girl is being taught an actual first lesson in what skill?

3. In this poem, the poet uses the lesson as a metaphor for something larger. Explain what it is.

4. What is the father telling his daughter about survival in life?

The Count of Monte Cristo

an excerpt based on the novel by Alexandre Dumas

The French novelist and playwright Alexandre Dumas wrote
more than 300 books. He is famous as a writer of adventure
and romance; The Count of Monte Cristo *is as gripping
today as it was when it was published in 1844.*

To the happiest day of my life!" cried
Edmond Dantès. He drained his wine glass
in one swallow and hurled it into the
fireplace.

"To Monsieur and the future Madam
Dantès!" echoed the wedding guests. Thirty
glasses smashed into atoms against the
iron grating.

"More wine!" shouted Edmond, reeling
slightly and giggling.

"And more glasses," laughed Mercédès.
"But I warn you, Edmond, try that with
our crystal and you'll sleep in the barn!"

The guests roared their approval. "She'll
tame you, all right, Edmond, and it's about
time!"

Edmond made an exaggerated bow while
the group teased him good-naturedly. Then
he snatched up a sugar pastry and popped
it into his mouth. "Eat!" he yelled, spray-
ing crumbs. "It's a wedding!"

The musicians struck up a waltz, and
several couples crushed into the center of
the crowded room. Edmond winked at
Mercédès, who had been captured as a
partner by an old man in green satin pants.
She blew him a kiss and was twirled into
the colorful flowing mob.

"So tell me, Edmond," said the uncle
of a friend, whom Edmond didn't know.
"Do you plan to give up the sea now that
you will soon have a wife?"

Edmond turned to the stranger and
clapped him on the back. "Well, it's like
this," he began as the two walked arm in
arm toward a tray of little meat cakes.

But that was as far as Edmond ever got.
All at once, the door crashed open. Two
armed guards in full uniform burst into
the room.

Everyone froze. The music stopped. A
thick silence rolled over the guests like a
fog that comes in from the sea.

"Monsieur Edmond Dantès!" announced the taller guard. "You are hereby
ordered to come with us!" His words were
gunshots.

The crowd stared, mute and gaping and

unmoving. The guard drew his pistol and waved it threateningly. The people drew back.

"What's the meaning of this?" thundered Edmond, pushing his way into the center of the room. "What right have you to come barreling in here?"

The second guard grabbed Edmond by the wrist. "You're under arrest," he barked. "Come along."

Edmond jerked his arm away. Instantly he heard the click of the guards' pistols. His breath caught in his throat, but he held his eyes steady. "And just what am I supposed to be guilty of?"

"You have been sneaking information to the Bonapartists," replied the second guard.

Edmond blinked, shocked at the outrage.

"Treason," said the first guard. "Now move it out." He shoved the barrel of the pistol into Edmond's ribs. "Don't make me get blood all over those fancy wedding clothes."

Monsieur Villefort twirled a jeweled ring on his right hand and studied the prisoner. He smiled in an oily way.

"Naturally, Monsieur, you believe you are innocent," he lisped.

"Naturally, Monsieur, I am," retorted Edmond.

Villefort leered. "Save it, Dantès. There is no way out of this." He smoothed the lace edging of his sleeve. "You have perhaps heard a little something about the infamous Chateau d'If?"

"It's a prison," replied Edmond calmly.

"Shame on you, Monsieur Dantès. You do not do it justice. The Chateau is a fortress. It rises like a festering boil on a small island off the coast of Marseilles. The black waters around it effectively swallow the foolhardy who think they can escape. But some, perhaps prefer them to the Chateau. The rats, I am told, are quite bothersome. Guard!"

The door opened wide, and an officer appeared.

"Take this prisoner to the Chateau d'If," ordered Villefort. "The dungeon should suit him quite nicely, I think."

"Yes, Monsieur le Deputy."

Villefort smirked confidently. "Enjoy your stay, Monsieur Dantès. I assure you it will be a long one."

Edmond could no longer recall how long he had been in prison. The days and months had melted together until they formed a shapeless lump that was simply the past.

Villefort and several others had engineered Edmond's imprisonment to hide their own treasonous activities. With time to do nothing but think, Edmond had long ago realized that he had been framed, and framed royally. He could, in fact, point his finger at those who were responsible. But with no hope of release, the only ones who would ever know the truth were the squealing red-eyed rats that scurried across Edmond's chest as he slept.

Then one day, as Edmond lay staring at the ceiling, a small section of the floor suddenly gave way. Edmond jumped at the loud down-rush of dirt and stones, and then jumped again when a head popped up from the hole.

"Darn! This isn't the outside!" grumbled the head. "I missed it! How did I miss it?"

"Monsieur?" said Edmond, leaning forward cautiously.

The man inched himself up until he could rest his elbows on the floor. "A tunnel," he said. "Dug it myself." He held out his hand. "My name is Abbé Faria. I am pleased to meet you."

Faria's escape route had taken a wrong turn somewhere. The tunnel brought the

pressed a little knife he had made into Edmond's hand. "You take this," he whispered. "You are young. Perhaps it will help you to find your own way out."

From that moment on, Edmond and Faria became great friends. They met daily, exchanging stories and secrets and dreams. Faria taught Edmond mathematics, drawing the signs and symbols in the dirt floor with his finger. Edmond learned history, and then, slowly, to speak Italian, in which Faria was fluent. But in the seventh year of their friendship, Edmond saw that the old man was dying.

Faria could no longer crawl through the tunnel to Edmond's cell. His eyes were sunken. His breathing became shallow and labored. His body was as frail as a dried leaf. Edmond sat beside his dear friend, choking back the tears that welled up inside him.

"Edmond!" rasped the old man.

"Don't try to talk."

"No, no. I must." His throat rattled. "Listen. There is a great fortune on the Isle of Monte Cristo. A treasure." A spasm of coughing wracked his chest, and Edmond waited, his heart breaking, while Faria fenced with Death.

"You will be rich, Edmond. The Isle of Monte Cristo. Make your escape and recover the treasure." His eyelids fluttered. "May God go with my friend Edmond Dantès —"

Death had parried and thrust and won the match.

old man to Edmond's cell instead of beyond the Chateau's walls.

"Ah, well," he said, brushing himself off. "So it is not to be. To begin again would be foolish. This gray head would never live to see a tunnel finished." He

Edmond could not pull his eyes away from the rough cloth sack that held the body of his friend. The loss of Faria had drained him of all feelings. There was nothing left anymore. He fingered Faria's knife and thought of his own escape. It would be swift and sure. It would release him from the pain of living.

A fly buzzed past Edmond's ear, and he swatted at it angrily. The fly shot off and lighted on the window ledge. Edmond watched it clean its tiny wings, take a few steps, stop, and then escape to the freedom beyond the bars.

"Yes!" Edmond cried suddenly, grabbing the knife.

He shoved Death back and slashed the top of the cloth sack.

"I will go in Faria's place," he breathed. "They will take me instead."

He slipped Faria's frail body out and dressed it in his own clothes. He arranged it in a sleeping position under his blanket, lowered the eyelids, and then wriggled into the shroud, sewing the top from the inside. Later he would use Faria's knife to cut the cloth and dig his way up through the earth that covered his grave.

Edmond lay motionless, his heart thundering like cannon fire, waiting for the fall of night and the two guards who would carry him to freedom.

"I thought this old guy would be a lot lighter," said a voice.

Edmond stiffened.

"Naw, I hear they get heavier when they're dead."

There was a shuffle of feet and then Edmond was off the floor and moving. Suddenly he met a rush of cold air and realized he was outside. He could hear the crunch of the guards' shoes on the hard ground and the roar of the waves breaking against the shoreline.

"Set him down. I'll be right back."

Edmond felt himself lowered, and then something was pressing against his ankles. He dared not move even a fraction to learn what it was.

"Hurry it up," hissed the voice at his feet.

"Keep your shirt on!" came the reply. "I got one." The voice drew nearer. It was out of breath. "Here. Tie this rock to his legs. Guaranteed he'll drop to the bottom of the sea."

Edmond's heart nearly shot through his chest. There would be no earthen grave! They were doing it the easy way!

"Grab a hold," said the first voice, and Edmond was in the air.

"On three. One . . . two . . . THREE!"

And suddenly, Edmond was flung sideways out over the jagged crags, like a sack of rotting garbage tossed into the sea. He hit the water feet first and plunged straight down as the heavy stone weight drove swiftly and steadily for the bottom.

Frenzied, Edmond stabbed at the cloth sack with his knife, ripping and slashing at the strong fibers. In seconds, he was through and writhing like a trapped eel to get at the ropes that held his ankles. His lungs were bursting. He needed air! He sawed feverishly at the ropes. At last, the strands began to give way under the blade.

Every muscle had gone beyond its limits. His brain fought wildly against his body's need for oxygen, against the craving to draw in something, anything, even if it

had to be the cold and blackened water all around him.

And then suddenly the ropes fell away. Edmond rocketed to the surface. His head and shoulders broke the water in an explosion of foam. He grabbed greedily for air, choking and grasping and breathing like some prehistoric sea beast.

His knife was gone, he was naked and freezing, but far in the distance he could see the stony walls of the Chateau d'If. A small wave broke against his lips, and for the first time in 14 years, Edmond Dantès knew the taste of freedom.

READING COMPREHENSION

Summarizing. Choose the best phrase to complete each sentence. Then write the complete statements on your paper.

1. Edmond Dantès was arrested because he _____ (was a political traitor, was framed by powerful men, planned to marry his enemy's daughter).

2. Edmond Dantès met Abbé Faria _____ (when Faria dug a tunnel to Dantès' cell, in the prison schoolhouse, when they were taken to prison together).

3. Edmond escaped from the prison by _____ (digging a tunnel to the outside, climbing down the prison walls, taking the place of a dead man).

4. Edmond almost died by _____ (drowning, being buried alive, starvation).

Interpreting. Write the answer to each question on your paper.

1. What was Edmond supposed to be guilty of?

2. In what ways did Abbé Faria help Edmond?

3. What did Edmond consider doing with Faria's knife before he thought of climbing into the shroud?

For Thinking and Discussing. Which character represents evil in the story? Which represents good? Explain your answer.

UNDERSTANDING LITERATURE

Characterization and Word Choice. An author paints a strong picture of a character through a few carefully chosen words. A word has a general meaning, and it also may have an emotional shade of meaning; for example, "The sergeant *snarled* his orders." The word *snarled* means "spoke," but it also implies a harsh, angry way of speaking. By using the word, the author tells us that the character is harsh.

In *The Count of Monte Cristo*, the characters are either good or evil. The author creates an immediate impression of them by using descriptive words that have a strong emotional impact. Below are descriptions of Monsieur Villefort. Explain the effect of each italicized word or phrase. Use a dictionary, if necessary.

1. "He smiled *in an oily way*."
2. "Villefort *leered*."
3. "Villefort *smirked* confidently."

Now describe your general impression of Monsieur Villefort.

WRITING

Imagine that a cruel prison guard comes to give Edmond a meal. In one paragraph, describe the guard and his actions. Reveal the guard's character, using carefully chosen descriptive words. Try to make an emotional impact with your description. You may include dialogue, but you should let your description of his appearance and actions do most of the work of showing the guard's evil nature.

The Washwoman

by Isaac Bashevis Singer

She is old, she is alone, and she is poor. She is the wash-woman—a poignant figure in Isaac Bashevis Singer's memory. Presented simply and honestly, she evokes more admiration than pity as we watch her struggle, and wonder at the source of her strength.

Our home had little contact with Gentiles. The only Gentile in the building was the janitor. Fridays he would come for a tip, his "Friday money." He remained standing at the door, took off his hat, and my mother gave him six groschen.

Besides the janitor there were also the Gentile washwomen who came to the house to fetch our laundry. My story is about one of these.

She was a small woman, old and wrinkled. When she started washing for us, she was already past seventy. Most Jewish women of her age were sickly, weak, broken in body. All the old women in our street had bent backs and leaned on sticks when they walked. But this washwoman, small and thin as she was, possessed a strength that came from generations of peasant forebears. Mother would count out to her a bundle of laundry that had accumulated over several weeks. She would lift the unwieldy pack, load it on her narrow shoulders, and carry it the long way home. She lived on Krochmalna Street, too, but at the other end, near the Wola section. It must have been a walk of an hour and a half.

She would bring the laundry back about two weeks later. My mother had never been so pleased with any washwoman. Every piece of linen sparkled like polished silver. Every piece was neatly ironed. Yet she charged no more than the others. She was a real find. Mother always had her money ready, because it was too far for the old woman to come a second time.

Laundering was not easy in those days. The old woman had no faucet where she lived, but had to bring in the water from a pump. For the linens to come out so clean, they had to be scrubbed thoroughly in a washtub, rinsed with washing soda, soaked, boiled in an enormous pot, starched, then ironed. Every piece was handled ten times or more. And the drying! It could not be done outside because thieves would steal the laundry. The wrung-out wash had to be carried up to the attic and hung on clotheslines. In the winter it would become as brittle as glass and almost break when touched. And there was always a to-do with other housewives and washwomen who wanted the attic clotheslines for their own use. Only God knows all the old woman had to endure each time she did a wash!

She could have begged at the church door or entered a home for the penniless and aged. But there was in her a certain pride and love of labor with which many Gentiles have been blessed. The old woman did not want to become a burden, and so bore her burden.

The woman had a son who was rich. I no longer remember what sort of business he had. He was ashamed of his mother, the washwoman, and never came to see her. Nor did he ever give her a groschen. The old woman told this without rancor. One day the son was married. It seemed that he had made a good match. The wedding took place in a church. The son had not invited the old mother to his wedding, but she went to the church and waited at the steps to see her son lead the "young lady" to the altar. . . .

The story of the faithless son left a deep impression on my mother. She talked about it for weeks and months. It was an insult not only to the old woman but to the entire institution of motherhood. Mother would argue, "Nu, does it pay to make sacrifices for children? The mother uses up her last strength, and he does not even know the meaning of loyalty."

And she would drop dark hints that she was not certain of her own children: Who knows what they would do some day? This, however, did not prevent her from dedicating her life to us. If there was any delicacy in the house, she would put it aside for the children and invent all sorts of excuses and reasons why she herself did not want to taste it. . . .

That winter was a harsh one. The streets were in the grip of a bitter cold. No matter how much we heated our stove, the windows were covered with frostwork and decorated with icicles. The newspapers reported that people were dying of the cold. Coal became dear. The winter had become so severe that parents stopped sending children to cheder, and even the Polish schools were closed.

On one such day the washwoman, now nearly eighty years old, came to our house. A good deal of laundry had accumulated during the past weeks. Mother gave her a pot of tea to warm herself, as well as some bread. The old woman sat on a kitchen chair trembling and shaking, and warmed her hands against the teapot. Her fingers were gnarled from work, and perhaps from arthritis, too. Her fingernails were strangely white. These hands spoke of the stubbornness of mankind, of the will to work not only as one's strength permits but beyond the limits of one's power. Mother counted and wrote down the list: men's undershirts, women's vests, long-legged drawers, bloomers, petticoats, shifts, featherbed covers, pillowcases, shawls, and the men's fringed garments. Yes, the Gentile woman washed these holy garments as well.

The bundle was big, bigger than usual. When the woman placed it on her shoulders, it covered her completely. At first she swayed, as though she were about to fall under the load. But an inner obstinacy

seemed to call out: No, you may not fall. A donkey may permit himself to fall under his burden, but not a human being, the crown of creation.

It was fearful to watch the old woman staggering out with the enormous pack, out into the frost, where the snow was dry as salt and the air was filled with dusty white whirlwinds, like goblins dancing in the cold. Would the old woman ever reach Wola?

She disappeared, and Mother sighed and prayed for her.

Usually the woman brought back the wash after two or, at most, three weeks. But three weeks passed, then four and five, and nothing was heard of the old woman. We remained without linens. The cold had become even more intense. The telephone wires were now as thick as ropes. The branches of the trees looked like glass. So much snow had fallen that the streets had become uneven. Sleds were able to glide down many streets as on the slopes of a hill. Kind-hearted people lit fires in the streets for vagrants to warm themselves and roast potatoes in, if they had any to roast.

For us the washwoman's absence was a catastrophe. We needed the laundry. We did not even know the woman's address. It seemed certain that she had collapsed, died. Mother declared she had had a pre-monition, as the old woman left our house that last time, that we would never see our things again. She found some old torn shirts and washed and mended them. We mourned, both for the laundry and for the old, toil-worn woman who had grown close to us through the years she had served us so faithfully.

More than two months passed. The frost had subsided, and then a new frost had come, a new wave of cold. One evening, while Mother was sitting near the kerosene lamp mending a shirt, the door opened and a small puff of steam, followed by a gigantic bundle, entered the room. I ran toward the old woman and helped her unload her pack. She was even thinner now, more bent. Her face had become more gaunt. Her head shook from side to side as though she were saying no. She could not utter a clear word, but mumbled something with her sunken mouth and pale lips.

After the old woman had recovered somewhat, she told us that she had been ill, very ill. Just what her illness was, I cannot remember. She had been so sick that someone called a doctor, and the doctor had sent for a priest. Someone had informed the son, and he had contributed money for a coffin and for the funeral. But the Almighty had not yet wanted to take this pain-racked soul to Himself. She began to feel better, she became well, and as soon as she was able to stand on her feet once more, she resumed her washing. Not just ours, but the wash of several other families, too.

"I could not rest easy in my bed because of the wash," the old woman explained. "The wash would not let me die."

"With the help of God you will live to be a hundred and twenty," said my mother, as a benedictum.

"God forbid! What good would such a long life be? The work becomes harder and harder . . . my strength is leaving me. . . . I do not want to be a burden on anyone!" The old woman muttered and crossed herself, and raised her eyes toward heaven.

Fortunately there was some money in the house and Mother counted out what she owed. I had a strange feeling: the coins in the old woman's washed-out hands seemed to become as worn and clean and pious as she herself was. She blew on the coins and tied them in a kerchief. Then she left, promising to return in a few weeks for a new load.

But she never came back. The wash she had returned was her last effort on this earth. She had been driven by an indomitable will to return the property to its rightful owners, to fulfill the task she had undertaken.

And now at last her body, which had long been no more than a shard supported only by the force of honesty and duty, had fallen. Her soul passed into those spheres where all holy souls meet, regardless of the roles they played on this earth, in whatever tongue, of whatever creed. I cannot imagine paradise without this Gentile washwoman. I cannot even conceive of a world where there is no reward for such effort.

READING COMPREHENSION

Summarizing. Choose the best phrase to complete each sentence. Then write the complete statements on your paper.

1. Singer's mother always gave her laundry to the same washwoman because she _____ (charged less than the others, was old and needed the money, did a perfect job for a fair price).

2. The washwoman did not beg at the church or enter a home for the poor because she _____ (didn't want to be a burden to anyone, had a rich son, had an easy job).

3. When weeks passed and the washwoman did not return, the family thought the old woman had _____ (stolen their laundry, moved away, died).

Interpreting. Write the answer to each question on your paper.

1. What was difficult about the washwoman's job?

2. How did Singer's mother feel about the washwoman's son? Why?

3. What did the washwoman mean when she said, "The wash would not let me die"?

For Thinking and Discussing. Singer said: "I cannot imagine paradise without this Gentile washwoman. I cannot even conceive of a world where there is no reward for such effort." What did he mean? Do you feel the same way?

UNDERSTANDING LITERATURE

Character Motivation. The reason why a character acts a certain way is called the *character's motivation*. Sometimes a character's motivation is explained directly in the story. Other times motivation is implied. You can figure out why a character acted a certain way because his or her behavior fits what you know about the character's personality or past actions.

Below are some actions of the characters in "The Washwoman." On your paper, explain the motivation of each act. Then indicate whether the motivation is *stated* or *implied* in the story.

1. The washwoman continued to work despite her old age.

2. The washwoman's son did not invite his mother to his wedding.

3. Singer's mother would put aside delicacies for her children and invent reasons why she did not want them.

4. Singer's mother gave the washwoman some tea and bread.

5. The washwoman recovered from her illness and resumed her washing.

WRITING

Choose a character from one of the other selections in this section. Describe this character's behavior in a particular situation in the story. Then write a paragraph explaining why you think this person behaved as he or she did.

Section Review

VOCABULARY

Context Clues in a Paragraph. The *context* of a particular word is derived from the groups of words that precede it and follow it in a sentence or paragraph. The meaning of a particular word in a sentence or paragraph is affected by the meanings of the words around it. A reader may use context clues, or clues from the surrounding words, to figure out the meaning of an unknown word.

The following paragraphs are from selections in this section. As you read each one, use context clues to figure out the meanings of the italicized words. Then match each italicized word with the word from the list below that has the same meaning. Write each italicized word and its meaning on your paper.

1. "*Frenzied*, Edmond stabbed at the cloth sack with his knife, ripping and slashing at the strong fibers. In seconds, he was through and *writhing* like a trapped eel to get at the ropes that held his ankles."
2. "Mother would count out to her a bundle of laundry that had *accumulated* over several weeks. She would lift the *unwieldy* pack, . . . and carry it the long way home."

| crazed | clumsy | gathered |
| climb | fall | twisting |

READING

Cause and Effect. Cause-and-effect relationships play an important role in the stories that authors write. A *cause* is a reason. It is the answer to the question: Why did this happen? An *effect* is a result. A result is the answer to the question: What will happen because of this?

In "The Cow-Tail Switch," one such relationship involved Puli: Puli thought about his father (cause); therefore, he received the cow-tail switch (result).

Below are pairs of sentences based on the selections in this section. One sentence in each pair states a cause. The other sentence states its effect. Make two columns on your paper. Label one "Cause" and the other "Effect." Write each sentence in the correct column on your paper.

1. **a.** The canary was revived by a breath of oxygen.
   b. The space worker realized the station's air supply system was not working properly.

2. **a.** The woman didn't like to leave her house for long.
   b. The woman worried that the birds could not survive without her.

3. **a.** Nitrogen bubbles had formed in Bill's blood.
   b. Bill surfaced from the water too quickly.

4. **a.** Lie back and float face up.
   b. The sea will hold you.

5. **a.** She did the laundry despite her age.
   b. She didn't want to be a burden.

WRITING

An Explanation. An explanation tells how or why something happened. The information in an explanation is made up of a series of steps that are arranged in the order in which things occurred. The steps should be written clearly and simply so that someone reading the explanation for the first time can understand it easily.

Step 1: Set Your Goal

The topic you choose for an explanation should be one you know well. It would be very difficult to explain something to someone if you didn't understand the explanation yourself. You should also think about who your audience will be. Are they classmates? Do they know much about your topic? Are they people who are familiar with what you are explaining? When you write an explanation, knowing who your audience is will help you decide which words to explain and how detailed the steps should be.

Select one of the topics below for an explanation:

1. Explain how the crew in "Feathered Friend" discovered that something was wrong with their air supply.

2. Explain how Ogaloussa's sons brought him back to life. Begin with Puli's asking, "Where is my father?" and end with Ogaloussa's return to the village.

Step 2: Make a Plan

To plan your explanation, decide what information you will want to include. Think about your topic and what you are explaining. Recall each step and jot it down as it comes to mind. Refer to the story to be sure you have included all of the important information.

For example, suppose you were going to write an explanation of how Edmond Dantès in "The Count of Monte Cristo" managed to escape from the Chateau d'If. Your list of steps might look like this:

1. Placed Faria's body in his own bed

2. Sewed himself into Faria's shroud (Tell how.)

3. Stayed perfectly still when the prison guards came to remove the body

4. Was dumped into the water

5. Escaped from drowning by freeing himself from the sack (Tell how.)

6. Found himself at sea, away from the chateau

In order for an explanation to make sense, the steps or details must be organized carefully. Each step must lead to the next in a logical order, usually the order in which things took place. Think about what happened first, second, third, and so on. Make sure your steps are listed in the correct sequence. This is the order in which you will present them in your explanation.

Step 3: Write a First Draft

Now that you have an organized list of steps, you can begin writing the first draft of your explanation. As you write your first draft, put your organized steps into sentences but don't worry about choosing the best words or writing perfectly. You will be able to improve your writing when you revise.

Begin your explanation with an opening sentence that tells your readers what it is that you are explaining. Then briefly describe the characters involved and their situations. End your explanation with a closing sentence that sums up what you were explaining. For example, an explanation of Dantès' escape might end with, "That is how Edmond Dantès regained his freedom after 14 years in prison."

Step 4: Revise

If possible, set your explanation aside for a day or two. That way you will be able to come back to it with a fresh eye. As you read over your first draft, try to picture each step as it is explained. Are the steps in logical order? Should you add or take out a step? Does your explanation make sense? Here is a checklist to help you:

☐ Does the explanation begin by telling what I am going to explain and briefly describing the characters and their situations?

☐ Are the steps in the right order? Have I used sequence words such as *first*, *second*, *next*, *then*, and *finally* to make the meaning clear?

☐ Are my sentences clearly written and to the point so that my readers can easily understand what I am saying?

☐ Does my explanation end with a sentence or two that sums up?

When you finish revising, proofread your explanation for errors in spelling, capitalization, punctuation, grammar, and usage. Then make a neat, final copy.

QUIZ

The following is a quiz for Section 7. Write the answers in complete sentences on your paper.

Reading Comprehension

1. In "Feathered Friend," how did Claribel's status change from the beginning of the story to the end?

2. In "The Last Dive," why was Bill more frightened by the grouper than by the shark?

3. In "The Cow-Tail Switch," what magical event occurred?

4. In "The Count of Monte Cristo," why was Dantès sent to the chateau?

5. In "The Washwoman," why did the washwoman recover from her illness only to die a short while later?

Understanding Literature

6. Name two selections in this section that treat survival after death. How do the authors view death?

7. Compare Bill Prentice in "The Last Dive" with Edmond Dantès in "The Count of Monte Cristo." What characteristics did they share?

8. On what scientific concept is "Feathered Friend" based?

9. In "The Woman Who Had No Eye for Small Details," how were the birds used as a symbol of survival?

10. What two things were compared in the metaphor of "First Lesson"?

ACTIVITIES

Word Attack. Every word is made up of parts called *syllables*. Every syllable contains a single vowel sound. Some words have only one vowel sound and, therefore, have only one syllable. Other words may have several vowel sounds and can be divided into several syllables. For example, look at the following words:

dive   wa·ter   ni·tro·gen

The word *dive* has one vowel sound ($\bar{\imath}$) and only one syllable. The word *water* has two vowel sounds ($\hat{o}$) and (∂) and can be divided into two syllables. The word *nitrogen* has three vowel sounds ($\bar{\imath}$, ∂, ∂) and can be divided into three syllables.

The following words are from "The Last Dive." Write each word as you pronounce it and draw a line between each of its syllables. Then check a dictionary to see if you were correct.

aborigine	partner	recognize
barnacle	dynamite	tremor
disappear	paralysis	valuable

Speaking and Listening

1. With several classmates, read the poem "Forefathers" aloud in unison. Choose one member of your group to be the leader and set the pace and rhythm of the poem. As you practice, think about words and phrases you may want to emphasize. Are there places where pauses would make the poem more dramatic? Try to create a dramatic mood in the way you read the poem.

2. Imagine that you are presenting a TV or radio news report about the events that occurred in "Feathered Friend." Your report must be about three minutes long. What details would be most important to include? How would you begin the report to catch your listeners' attention? How would you conclude it? Time the report as you practice. Be prepared to present your "news item" to the class.

Researching. In "The Last Dive," Bill suffered from the bends when he came to the surface too quickly. Do some research to find out what the bends are. What causes them? What are the symptoms? How dangerous are they? How can they be avoided? Be prepared to present your findings to the class.

Creating

1. Using "The Last Dive" and "The Count of Monte Cristo" as examples, write a brief character sketch of a person in a survival situation. The person could be in physical danger, such as a person who is drowning; or the person could be facing an emotional crisis, such as a young person at a parent's funeral. Describe the character in an indirect way. Record his or her thoughts and actions.

2. "The Cow-Tail Switch" is a written version of an African folktale. The story illustrates the message that a man is not really dead until he is forgotten. Write a message or "moral" that you think is important in people's lives today. Give an example of a situation that illustrates your message.

CHOICES

Above all learn when to say Yes.
Many say Yes without understanding.
Many are not asked, and many
Say Yes to falsehood. Therefore
Above all learn when to say Yes.

— Bertolt Brecht
Germany

The Engagement
Lucas Van Leyden (1494-1533)
Museum of Fine Arts, Antwerp
Courtesy Scala/Art Resource

Choices

In literature, as in life, people are constantly faced with choices. Some choices are relatively unimportant; others can change your life, even cause your death.

Deciding What Is Most Important

Stories often deal with many different choices. Chekov's story "The Bet" begins with an argument over which is a fairer way to punish a criminal—life imprisonment or the death penalty. To prove his point, one man bets another that he can remain in prison for 15 years without asking to be released. If he wins, his friend must pay him a large sum of money. The bet is carried out. As the years go by, the friend begins to fear that he will, in fact, have to pay. Should he kill the prisoner rather than lose all his money?

But during his imprisonment, the prisoner realizes that whether or not you are behind bars is not one of life's more important choices. The real choice lies in deciding what values will guide your life.

Putting Others First

What would you do if you had to choose between saving another person's life or losing your own? In "The Man in the Water," Roger Rosenblatt has written a true account of the choice one person made. During a plane crash, an unknown man chose to save others instead of himself. In making this choice, Rosenblatt says, this man gave something to everyone who saw or read of his deed. None of us is really sure what we would do in such a situation. In choosing to put himself last, this nameless man demonstrated the possibility of heroism in all of us.

Rosenblatt's essay is about something that happened recently; however, a play from ancient Greece shows that people have been pondering the same choices for over 2,000 years. In Euripides' *Iphigenia,* the gods demand the sacrifice of a woman before they will help the Greek army. The woman, Iphigenia, decides to die rather than allow the defeat of her country and the death of thousands of soldiers. In the end, she is rewarded in an unusual way for her choice.

Choosing How to Live

Nations as well as individuals must make choices. In "Return to India," Santha Rama Rau compares her native country to the Soviet Union, which she had recently visited. Rau shows that a people can choose freedom or repression, openness or suspicion. The choices are not simple. To Rau, comfort is not enough if it is gained at the expense of spiritual satisfaction. Even order is a bad thing if it means, as it can, the loss of beauty.

Another writer who valued beauty was

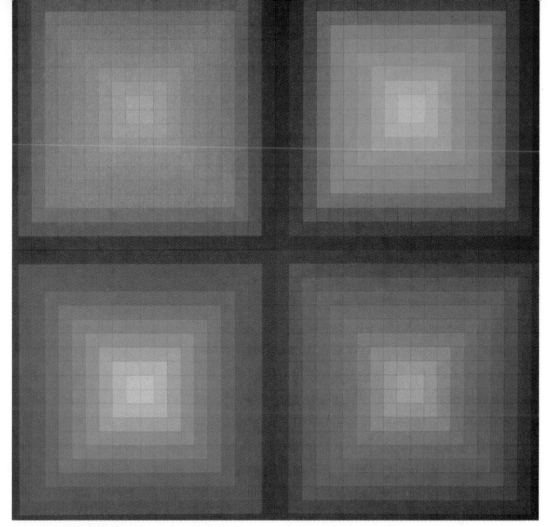

Arcturus II, *Victor Vasarely, 1966*

the British poet A. E. Housman. "Loveliest of Trees" is probably his best-known work. The poem, describing blossoming cherry trees, says that life is too short to miss a single beautiful spring. Housman has reminded many readers that, no matter what way of life one chooses, it is important to make time to enjoy the beauty around us.

"With All Flags Flying" is a story by Anne Tyler. An old man must choose between finishing his life in a senior citizens' residence or in the comfortable home of his daughter, among family. No one in the man's family can understand his decision, and it is not an easy one for him to make. But the old man sees the end of his life as a battle with death. He knows he must lose, but he is determined to die with dignity. Tyler's message is clear: Choosing the way you are going to lose, and sticking to it, can be more important than winning.

The last selection is "Just Lather, That's All" by Hernando Téllez. What will the barber decide to do when he finds his enemy's life is in his hands? As is often true, his choice will affect his own life as well as the lives of others.

The Bet

by Anton Chekov

Anton Chekov, born in Russia in 1860, is famous for his short stories and plays. He had originally planned to be a doctor; he began writing stories for magazines in order to earn some extra money. He died of tuberculosis at the age of 44, but during his short life he completed some of Russian literature's finest works.

It was a dark autumn night. The old banker was pacing from corner to corner of his study. He recalled the party he had given 15 years before. There were many clever people at the party. Among other things, they talked of capital punishment. The guests for the most part did not like capital punishment. Some of them thought that capital punishment should be replaced by life imprisonment.

"I don't agree with you," said the host. "I myself have experienced neither capital punishment nor life imprisonment. But in my opinion, capital punishment is more moral and more humane than imprisonment. Execution kills instantly, life imprisonment kills by degrees. Who is more humane, one who kills you in a few seconds or one who draws the life out of you slowly for years?"

"They're both equally wrong," remarked one of the guests, "because their purpose is the same, to take away life. It is not right to take away that which cannot be given back."

Among the company was a young lawyer. On being asked his opinion, he said:

"Capital punishment and life imprisonment are equally wrong. But if I were offered the choice between them, I would certainly choose the second. It's better to live somehow than not to live at all."

This led to a lively discussion. The banker suddenly lost his temper. He banged his fist on the table. He turned to the young lawyer and cried out:

"It's a lie. I bet you two million you wouldn't stay in a cell even for five years."

"If you mean it seriously," replied the lawyer, "then I bet I'll stay not for five but fifteen."

"Fifteen! Done!" cried the banker. "Gentlemen, I stake two million."

"Agreed. You stake two million, I my freedom," said the lawyer.

So this wild, ridiculous bet came to pass. The banker, who at that time had too many millions to count, was beside

himself with joy. During supper he said to the lawyer jokingly:

"Come to your senses before it's too late. Two million is nothing to me. You stand to lose three or four of the best years of your life. I say three or four, because you'll never stick it out any longer. The idea that you have the right to free yourself at any moment will poison the whole of your life in the cell. I pity you."

And now the banker, pacing from corner to corner, recalled all this. He asked himself:

"Why did I make this bet? What's the good? The lawyer loses 15 years of his life, and I throw away two million. Will it convince people that capital punishment is worse or better than life imprisonment? No, no! All stuff and rubbish. On my part, it was the whim of a well-fed man. The lawyer's was pure greed for gold."

He remembered further what happened after the evening party. It was decided that the lawyer must be jailed under the strictest observation. The jail was set up in a garden wing of the banker's house. It was agreed that during the period he would be deprived of the right to go out. He would not see people, hear human voices, or receive letters and newspapers. He was permitted to have a musical instrument, to read books, and to write letters. By the agreement, he could communicate, but only in silence, with the outside world through a little window especially constructed for this purpose. Everything necessary, books, music, he could receive in any amount by sending a note through the window. The agreement provided for all details. It stated that the lawyer was to remain exactly 15 years from 12 o'clock of November 14, 1870, to 12 o'clock of November 14, 1885. The least attempt on his part to violate the conditions freed the banker from the obligation to pay him the two million.

During the first year of imprisonment, the lawyer told in his short notes of terrible loneliness and boredom. From his wing, day and night came the sound of the piano. During the first year, the lawyer was sent books of a light character: love stories, stories of crime and fantasy, comedies, and so on.

In the second year, the piano was heard no longer. The lawyer asked only for classic literature. In the fifth year, music was heard again. Those who watched him said that during the whole of that year he was only eating, drinking, and lying on his bed. He yawned often and talked angrily to himself. He did not read. Sometimes at night he would sit down to write. He would write for a long time and tear it all up in the morning. More than once, he was heard to weep.

In the second half of the sixth year, the prisoner began to study languages, philosophy, and history. He fell on these subjects so hungrily that the banker hardly had time to get books enough for him. In the space of four years, about 600 books were bought at his request. It was while that passion lasted that the banker received the following letter from the prisoner: "My dear jailer, I am writing these lines in six languages. Show them to experts. Let them read them. If they do not find one single mistake, have a gun fired off in the garden. By the noise, I shall know that my efforts have not been in vain. The geniuses of all ages and countries speak in different languages. Yet in them all burns the same flame. Oh, if you knew my happiness now that I can understand them!" The prisoner's desire was fulfilled. Two shots were fired in the garden by the banker's order.

After the tenth year, the lawyer read only the New Testament. The banker found it strange that a man who in four years had mastered 600 learned volumes should have spent nearly a year in reading one book. After he finished the New Testament, he read the history of religions.

During the last two years, the prisoner read an extraordinary amount. First he read the natural sciences. Next he would read Byron or Shakespeare. Notes would come from him in which he asked to be sent at the same time a book on chemistry, a textbook of medicine, a novel, and a work on philosophy. He read as though he were swimming in the sea among pieces of wreckage. In his desire to save his life, he was eagerly grasping one piece after another.

The banker recalled all this, and thought: "Tomorrow at 12 o'clock, he receives his freedom. Under the agreement, I shall have to pay him two million. If I pay, it's all over with me. I am ruined forever. . . ."

Fifteen years before, he had too many millions to count. But now he was afraid to ask himself which he had more of, money or debts. Gambling on the stock exchange and reckless spending had grad- ually brought his business to decay. The fearless, self-confident, proud man of business had become an ordinary banker. He trembled at every rise and fall in the market.

"That cursed bet," murmured the old man. He clutched his head in despair. . . . "Why didn't the man die? He's only 40 years old. He will take away my last cent. He will enjoy life, and I will look on like an envious beggar. I'll hear the same words from him every day: 'I thank you for my happy life. Let me help you.' No, it's too much! The only escape from bankruptcy and disgrace . . . is that the man should die."

The clock had just struck three. The banker was listening. In the house, everyone was asleep. One could hear only the frozen trees whining outside the windows. Silently he took out the key of the door that had not been opened for 15 years. He put on his overcoat, and went out of the house. The garden was dark and cold. It was raining. A damp, penetrating wind howled in the garden and gave the trees no rest. Though he strained his eyes, the banker could see neither the ground, nor the white statues, nor the garden wing, nor the trees. Approaching the garden wing, he called the watchman twice. There was no answer. Evidently the watchman had taken shelter from the bad weather and was now asleep somewhere in the kitchen or the greenhouse.

"If I have the courage to fulfill my intention," thought the old man, "the suspicion will fall on the watchman first of all."

In the darkness, he groped for the steps and the door, and entered the hall of the garden wing, then poked his way into a narrow passage and struck a match. Not a soul was there. Someone's bed, with no bedclothes on it, stood there, and an iron stove loomed dark in the corner. The seals on the door that led into the prisoner's room were unbroken.

When the match went out, the old man, trembling, peeped into the little window.

In the prisoner's room, a candle was burning dimly. The prisoner himself sat by the table. Only his back, the hair on his head, and his hands were visible. Open books lay on the table, the two chairs, the floor.

Five minutes passed. The prisoner never once stirred. Fifteen years' confinement had taught him to sit motionless. The banker tapped on the window with his finger. The prisoner made no movement in reply. Then the banker cautiously tore the seals from the door. He put the key into the lock. The door creaked. The banker expected to hear a cry of surprise and the sound of steps. Three minutes passed, and it was as quiet inside as it had been before. He made up his mind to enter.

Before the table sat a man, unlike an ordinary human being. It was a skeleton, with tight-drawn skin, with long curly hair and a shaggy beard. The color of his face was of an earthy shade; the cheeks were sunken; the back long and narrow. The hand upon which he leaned his hairy head was so skinny that it was painful to look upon. His hair was already turning gray. No one who glanced at his face would have believed that he was only 40 years old. Before his bent head lay a sheet of paper. He had been writing a letter.

"Poor devil," thought the banker, "he's asleep and probably seeing millions in his dreams. I have only to take and throw this half-dead thing on the bed, and smother him with the pillow. The most careful examination will find no trace of unnatural death. But first, let me read what he has written here."

The banker took the sheet from the table and read:

Tomorrow at 12 o'clock midnight, I shall win my freedom and the right to mix with people. But before I leave this room and see the sun, I think it necessary to say a few words to you. I declare to you that I despise freedom, life, health, and all that your books call the blessings of the world.

For 15 years, I have studied earthly life. True, I saw neither the earth nor the people. But in your books, I drank, sang songs, hunted deer in the forests, loved women. . . . And beautiful women, created by the magic of your poets' genius, visited me by night and whispered to me wonderful tales, which made my head swim. In your books, I climbed the mountains and I saw from there how the sun rose in the morning and, in the evening, touched the sky, the ocean, and the mountain ridges with a purple gold. I saw from there how above me lightnings glimmered through the clouds. I saw green forests, fields, rivers, lakes, cities. In your books, I cast myself into bottomless pits, worked miracles, burned cities to the ground, preached new religions, conquered whole countries. . . .

Your books gave me wisdom. All that human thought created in the centuries is compressed to a little lump in my skull. I know that I am cleverer than you all.

And I despise your books. I despise all worldly blessings and wisdom. Everything is as false and misleading as a mirage. Though you be proud and wise and beautiful, death will wipe you from the face of the earth.

You are mad, and gone the wrong way. You take falsehood for truth and ugliness for beauty. You would marvel if suddenly apple and orange trees should bear frogs and lizards instead of fruit. So do I marvel at you, who have traded heaven for earth. I do not want to understand you.

That I may show you my contempt for your way of life, I no longer want the two million of which I once dreamed as of paradise. That I may lose my right to them, I shall come out from here five minutes before the agreed end of my term. Thus shall I break the agreement.

When he had read, the banker put the sheet on the table. He kissed the head of the strange man, and began to weep. He went out of the prison. Never at any other time, not even after his terrible losses on the exchange, had he felt such contempt for himself as now. Coming home, he lay down on his bed, but he could not sleep.

The next morning, the poor watchman came running to him. He told him that they had seen the prisoner who lived in the wing climb through the window into the garden. He had gone to the gate and disappeared. The banker instantly went with his servants to the wing and established the escape of his prisoner. To avoid unnecessary rumors, he took the prisoner's letter from the table. When he got home he locked it in his safe.

READING COMPREHENSION

Summarizing. Choose the best phrase to complete each sentence. Then write the complete statements on your paper.

1. The bet was made during an argument about _____ (capital punishment, religion, political candidates).

2. The prisoner spent most of his time _____ (eating, reading books, playing the piano).

3. Fifteen years later, the banker _____ (believed in capital punishment, couldn't afford to pay the money, feared that the lawyer might kill him).

4. The lawyer lost the bet because _____ (he willingly left the prison too soon, he died before the time was up, the banker tricked him).

Interpreting. Write the answer to each question on your paper.

1. What did the banker intend to do to the prisoner on the night of his release?

2. What kept the banker from carrying out his plan?

3. Why did the prisoner choose to leave before winning the bet?

For Thinking and Discussing.

1. After reading this story, which do you think is more humane — capital punishment or life imprisonment? Explain your answer.

2. In your opinion, who really won the bet — the banker or the lawyer?

UNDERSTANDING LITERATURE

Theme. The central idea in a literary work is called the *theme*. A theme is usually a general idea about life. An author may state a theme directly. More often, the theme is presented indirectly, through the characters' thoughts and actions.

In "The Bet," the theme is developed by a comparison of the values of the banker and the young lawyer. An important theme in this story is that the value of human life cannot be measured in money. Answer the following questions in order to understand the development of the story's theme.

1. "It's better to live somehow than not to live at all." Who is the speaker? What is his view of life?

2. "Why did I make this bet? . . . The lawyer loses 15 years of his life, and I throw away two million." Who is the speaker? What does he value most?

3. "The geniuses of all ages and countries speak in different languages. Yet in them all burns the same flame. Oh, if you knew my happiness now. . . ." Whose views are expressed? What does he value?

4. Who has changed most by the end of the story — the lawyer or the banker?

WRITING

Imagine that you are the banker at the end of the story. Write a letter to the lawyer describing how you feel about the bet and what it has taught you about life.

Loveliest of Trees

by A. E. Housman

Loveliest of trees, the cherry now
Is hung with bloom along the bough,
And stands about the woodland ride,
Wearing white for Eastertide.

Now, of my threescore years and ten,
Twenty will not come again,
And take from seventy springs a score,
It only leaves me fifty more.

And since to look at things in bloom
Fifty springs are little room,
About the woodlands I will go
To see the cherry hung with snow.

1. In the second stanza, the poet describes his present age and the age to which he expects to live. What are these ages? (Note: A score equals twenty years.)

2. What meaning does a blooming cherry tree have in the poet's life?

3. Describe the poet's general attitude toward life.

The Man in the Water

by Roger Rosenblatt

Roger Rosenblatt writes for newspapers and magazines about literature and current events. In this essay, he comments on a tragedy that occurred in 1982 in Washington, D.C. You may have already heard of this unknown man, but Rosenblatt will make you think about this modern hero's choice in a new way.

Last Wednesday, the elements, indifferent as ever, brought down Flight 90. And on that same afternoon, human nature — groping and flailing in mysteries of its own — rose to the occasion.

Of the four acknowledged heroes of the event, three are able to account for their behavior. Donald Usher and Eugene Windsor, a park helicopter team, risked their lives every time they dipped the skids into the water to pick up survivors. On television, side by side in bright blue jumpsuits, they described their courage as all in the line of duty. Lenny Skutnik, a 28-year-old employee of the Congressional Budget Office, said: "It's something I never thought I would do" — referring to his jumping into the water to drag an injured woman to shore. Skutnik added

that "somebody had to go in the water," delivering every hero's line that is no less admirable for its repetitions. In fact, nobody had to go into the water. That somebody actually did so is part of the reason this particular tragedy sticks in the mind.

But the person most responsible for the emotional impact of the disaster is the one known at first simply as "the man in the water." (Balding, probably in his 50's, an extravagant mustache.) He was seen clinging with five other survivors to the tail section of the airplane. This man was described by Usher and Windsor as appearing alert and in control. Every time they lowered a lifeline and flotation ring to him, he passed it on to another of the passengers. "In a mass casualty, you'll find

people like him," said Windsor. "But I've never seen one with that commitment."

When the helicopter came back for him, the man had gone under. His selflessness was one reason the story held national attention; his anonymity, another. The fact that he went unidentified invested him with a universal character. For a while he was Everyman, and thus proof (as if one needed it) that no man is ordinary.

Still, he could never have imagined such a capacity in himself. Only minutes before his character was tested, he was sitting in the ordinary plane among the ordinary passengers, dutifully listening to the stewardess telling him to fasten his seat belt and saying something about the "no smoking sign." So our man relaxed with the others, some of whom would owe their lives to him. Perhaps he started to read, or to doze, or to regret some harsh remarks made in the office that morning. Then suddenly, he knew that trip would not be ordinary. Like every other person on that flight, he was desperate to live, which makes his final act so stunning.

For at some moment in the water, he must have realized that he would not live if he continued to hand over the rope and ring to others. He *had* to know it, no matter how gradual the effect of the cold. In his judgment, he had no choice. When the helicopter took off with what was to be the last survivor, he watched everything in the world move away from him, and he deliberately let it happen.

Yet there was something else about the man that kept our thoughts on him, and that keeps our thoughts on him still. He was *there,* in the essential, classic circumstance. Man in nature. The man in the water. For its part, nature cared nothing about the passengers. Our man, on the other hand, cared totally. So the timeless battle commenced in the Potomac. For as long as that man could last, they went at each other, nature and man.

Since it was he who lost the fight, we ought to come again to the conclusion that people are powerless in the world. In reality, we believe the reverse, and it takes the act of the man in the water to remind us of our true feelings in this matter. It is not to say that everyone would have acted as he did, or as Usher, Windsor, and Skutnik. Yet whatever moved these men to challenge death on behalf of their fellows is not peculiar to them. Everyone feels the possibility in himself or herself. That is the abiding wonder of the story. That is why we would not let go of it. If the man in the water gave a lifeline to the people gasping for survival, he was likewise giving a lifeline to those who observed him.

The odd thing is that we do not even really believe that the man in the water lost his fight. "Everything in nature contains all the powers of nature," said Emerson. Exactly. So the man in the water had his own natural powers. He could not make ice storms, or freeze the water until it froze the blood. But he could hand life over to a stranger, and that is a power of nature, too. The man in the water pitted himself against an implacable, impersonal enemy; he fought it with charity; and he held it to a standoff. He was the best we can do.

READING COMPREHENSION

Summarizing. Choose the best phrase to complete each sentence. Then write the complete statements on your paper.

1. The plane crash was due to _____ (a hijacker, bad weather, a pilot's error).

2. The greatest hero of the essay was _____ (a passenger on the plane, the plane's pilot, the author).

3. The man in the water died because _____ (the helicopter couldn't find him, he jumped from a bridge to save a passenger, he passed the lifeline to others).

Interpreting. Write the answer to each question on your paper.

1. How did Usher, Windsor, and Skutnik act heroically?

2. Why was the man in the water the most heroic of all?

3. How was this incident of heroism an example of "man battling against nature" and winning?

4. What did the man in the water demonstrate about human nature?

For Thinking and Discussing

1. How do you feel about the man in the water?

2. Do you think you could, or would, make the choice that the man in the water did?

UNDERSTANDING LITERATURE

Theme in an Essay. A *theme* is a general truth about people or life that an author wants to communicate to his or her readers.

Roger Rosenblatt's "The Man in the Water" is an essay inspired by a real event. A newspaper article would have covered the event in a factual way, without a theme or message. This essay contains statements both of fact and of theme.

Identify each quote below as a "statement of fact" or a "statement of theme."

1. "This man was described by Usher and Windsor as appearing alert and in control."

2. "Every time they lowered a lifeline and flotation ring to him, he passed it on to another of the passengers."

3. "For a while he was Everyman, and thus proof . . . that no man is ordinary."

4. "Only minutes before . . . he was sitting in the ordinary plane among the ordinary passengers. . . ."

5. "The odd thing is that we do not even really believe that the man in the water lost his fight."

6. "The man in the water pitted himself against an implacable, impersonal enemy. . . . He was the best we can do."

WRITING

Imagine that you are the man in the water. Explain the choices you face. Tell why you chose to behave as you did.

Iphigenia

based on the play by Euripides

Although the Greek writer Euripides lived from about 480 to 405 B.C., the characters he created are so human that we can still understand their thoughts and decisions today. In Iphigenia, *as in all his plays, a character has a difficult choice to make.*

CHARACTERS

Agamemnon (ag-uh-MEM-nahn), King of Argos, a Greek city-state
Menelaus (men-uh-LAY-us), King of Sparta, Agamemnon's brother
Clytemnestra (kly-tem-NES-tra), wife of Agamemnon
Iphigenia (if-i-jen-I-a), eldest daughter of Agamemnon and Clytemnestra
Achilles (uh-KILL-ees), leader of a troop of soldiers called the Myrmidons
An Old Servant
A Messenger
A Chorus of Women*
Orestes (o-RES-tees), brother of Iphigenia

The seaport town of Aulis, in Greece. Armies from many of the Greek city-states, each with its leader, are encamped here, preparing to sail for Troy. Their purpose is revenge: Paris, the Prince of Troy, has stolen Helen, the wife of Menelaus, and taken her with him to Troy. Now all of Menelaus' allies have joined forces to help him punish the Trojans and recapture his wife.

Although each of the Greek armies has its military chief, all of them recognize one supreme commander: He is Agamemnon, the brother of the wronged Menelaus. As the story unfolds, it becomes clear that the Greeks should have sailed for Troy long before this, and that Agamemnon is responsible for the delay.

The action begins outside Agamemnon's tent. His old servant, whom he has sent on an errand, is seen struggling with Menelaus.

---

* Plays in ancient Greece normally used a speaking chorus that provided background information, described off-stage actions, gave plot summaries, etc.

Menelaus: Take your hands off me, old man! Don't you know who I am?

Old Servant: I know you, King Menelaus — but king or no king, you have no right to steal my master's letter!

Menelaus: Your master is a traitor! This letter could destroy the Greeks!

Old Servant: That is not my business — give me back the letter!

Menelaus: I will not! Let go of me! I'll have you beheaded for this!

Old Servant: Help, King Agamemnon, help! Your letter has been stolen.

Agamemnon (coming from tent): What's all this shouting? Menelaus! My brother fighting with my servant! Have you lost both your dignity and your mind?

Menelaus: Look me in the face, Agamemnon — meet my eyes if you can.

Agamemnon: What do you mean? Why should I be afraid to look at you?

Menelaus: Look at this letter — are you not ashamed to have written it?

Agamemnon: Ashamed? You are the one who should hang your head. That letter was on its way to my wife, and you broke the seal and read it.

Menelaus: And shall I show it to the army, too? Are you proud of it?

Agamemnon: Proud that I have come to my senses at last — yes, I *am* proud! I have changed since you came and begged me to do that terrible thing!

Menelaus: You've changed, all right. You change and veer with every wind.

Agamemnon: Perhaps I do, but I don't need advice from a cruel and vicious brother.

Menelaus: I'm not surprised to see you prove again that you are weak and contemptible — yes, and treacherous, too. You give your sacred word and then go back on it — over and over again. More than a dozen years ago, you made a vow to the goddess Artemis, but you have not kept it.

Agamemnon: You know what keeping it would have meant. I promised her the most beautiful thing born in that year — and it was my daughter, my Iphigenia! How could I sacrifice my baby, my first child?

Menelaus: A vow is a vow — and your vows are a king's vows. Now we are at war. The honor of Greece demands that we sail to Troy and avenge the insult that Prince Paris has given me!

Agamemnon: And get your wife back for you.

Menelaus: Paris didn't steal only my wife when he took Helen — he took the honor of all the Greeks! The army is ready to sail and make Troy pay, but, because of you, the goddess Artemis won't give us a wind. Here we sit, becalmed on a beach where no waves break, because you refuse to keep your promise to her! The prophet Calchas has told us she will not send the wind until you keep that promise — but you run true to form! When you wanted to become general of the army, you were all smiles, everyone's friend, willing to promise anything. Then, when you got into power, you forgot everyone who had helped you. A few days ago, when you were afraid you'd lose your command because we couldn't sail, you promised to send for Iphigenia — you invented this

marriage to Achilles, to get her mother to send her here. Now you have written this vile letter saying she's not to come! Oh, this is like you. But it's Greece I mourn for. Greece will be humiliated before the world. Her enemies will laugh at her!

Agamemnon: Stop, Menelaus — think. Why are you raging at me? What do you want — your lovely wife? I can't help you. You couldn't keep her when you had her. You are insane even to want her back. A man is well rid of such a dishonorable woman. Why should I suffer for you? Yes, I *have* changed my mind. Why should my child die to save your pride?

Menelaus: Agamemnon, I am your brother.

Agamemnon: A true brother would not ask me to bring death and ruin on my own family!

Menelaus: And Greece — you refuse to help *her?*

Agamemnon: If Greece demands this murder, she is mad — and you are too.

Menelaus: You are a traitor to your family and your country! *(With sarcasm.)* Take care of your scepter, King! I'll find another way.

(Enter messenger.)

Messenger *(to Agamemnon):* They're here, sire — the queen, Clytemnestra, and Princess Iphigenia are here! They've brought the baby prince, Orestes, too! They've just stopped to have something to eat outside the camp. The whole army knows they're on the way, and, sire, there's all kinds of talk making the rounds. Some people say she's not going to be married at all, but given to Artemis. *(More cheerfully.)* Well — if she *is* going to be married, shouldn't somebody go out to meet her? Shouldn't we have music?

Agamemnon: Thank you for bringing this news. We'll take care of everything. *(Exit messenger.)* Clytemnestra! I should have known she'd come! What have the gods done to me? How can I face my wife? She thinks her daughter is to be married, and instead, the child's to be murdered. And oh, my little girl! What will *she* say to me?

Menelaus: Give me your hand.

Agamemnon: You have won. It must be done — you heard him — the army knows.

Menelaus: No. It shall *not* be done. I can't torture you like this. I can't ask you to kill your child for me. You're right — why should that poor girl die to win back Helen for me? There are other women. Disband the army. Tell them to go home. Forget everything I said. I was wrong. I see now that love and pity are more important than a prophecy *or* a promise.

Agamemnon: Thank you, Menelaus — but it's too late. I must do it.

Menelaus: Why? No one will force you now.

Agamemnon: The army will force me.

Menelaus: Send her back to Argos secretly — she can be smuggled out of the camp.

Agamemnon: Calchas will tell them the prophecy — we can't hide that. And Odysseus, their hero, knows it, too. He'll incite the men to kill us both, and they'll sacrifice the girl. There's nothing we can do . . . except . . . Menelaus, go to the army and ask them to keep it from Clytemnestra. A mother must not know her child is going to be married to Death.

(Exit Menelaus. Iphigenia runs in, followed by Clytemnestra.)

Iphigenia: Father, oh, Father, I'm so glad to see you! It's been so long.

Agamemnon: Long for me, too.

Iphigenia: But — what's wrong? You're not glad to see me! Your eyes are so sad.

Agamemnon: I *am* glad to see you. I'm sad for your sake —

Iphigenia: What do you mean? Because you're going to war and I won't see you for so long? I wish I could go with you!

Agamemnon: You are going somewhere else. *(Bitterly.)* But you won't forget me.

Iphigenia: Where am I going? Is Mother going too?

Agamemnon: No, you must go alone, without either of us.

Iphigenia: Father — do you mean that I'm going to have my own home?

Agamemnon: You mustn't ask such questions — you know that.

Iphigenia: Well, conquer Troy and hurry back to us!

Agamemnon: I have a sacrifice to offer before I go.

Iphigenia: Oh, shall I lead the dances around the altar?

Agamemnon *(in pain):* Oh, you are so happy, and so innocent! Go to the tent, my dear — kiss me and go — you'll be away so long! Oh, dear little face — lovely, shining hair — I can't say any more — I mustn't touch you — go in. *(Iphigenia exits.)* Forgive me, Clytemnestra, if I seem too — upset — at giving our Iphigenia to Achilles. It's a fine match, but fathers don't like to lose their little girls.

Clytemnestra: All girls must marry. Achilles will be a fine son-in-law. When had you planned to hold the wedding?

Agamemnon: When the moon is full.

Clytemnestra: And the marriage feast — you're going to have that afterward?

Agamemnon: When I have sacrificed to the gods.

Clytemnestra: You mean you haven't killed the victim for the goddess yet?

Agamemnon: I will — I must. Clytemnestra, there is one thing. I want to give the bride away alone. I do not want you at the ceremony.

Clytemnestra: What? You don't want me at my own daughter's marriage? Where do you expect me to go?

Agamemnon: Back to Argos, to take care of our other daughters.

Clytemnestra: This is unheard of! Why? Why shouldn't I go to my own child's wedding — why?

Agamemnon: Because it is my wish.

Clytemnestra: Oh! Well, we'll see about that! I suggest you mind your own business and leave things like this to me! *(Goes angrily into tent.)*

Agamemnon: She will not go! Oh, how I twist the truth and plot against the child I love! I tell myself it is for Greece — the goddess must be pleased — but how can I bear it? *(Enters tent.)*

Chorus: Troy must fall, and Paris must be the cause. That was predicted when the prince was born. His fearful father left him to a shepherd, and he grew up tending sheep, not knowing he was a prince. How could a simple shepherd make Troy fall? Three goddesses came to Paris in the fields, and asked him to tell which one of them was fairest. He chose the Goddess of Love, and she, to thank him, gave him a charm that would win him the love of the world's most beautiful woman. That was Helen, wife of King Menelaus. Paris, restored, a Trojan prince once more, journeyed to Greece and made her fall in love. He took her back to Troy to live with him. Now the Greeks have gathered under their fair-haired kings to sail and conquer. The prophecy that Paris would bring destruction on his country approaches consummation. But first the ships must sail — and ships need wind. And Artemis will not release the wind until the promised sacrifice is made. Now, that murder must be done by a weeping father, when the moon is full. We, women of Aulis, have come to see. Even the tears of a king cannot wash destiny away. Troy must fall, and Paris must be the cause.

(Achilles enters.)

Achilles: Agamemnon! Where are you, General? It's Achilles — come out and talk to me! My men are restless, waiting for this wind that never comes. If something isn't done soon, they'll forget about Troy and go home.

Clytemnestra: I hear you, Achilles, and I am glad to see you.

Achilles: A woman? And a magnificent one! Who are you? What are you doing in a camp?

Clytemnestra: I am Clytemnestra, Agamemnon's wife. Give me your hand. I wish you many years of happy marriage!

Achilles: I cannot clasp a queen's hand. I have no right —

Clytemnestra: Even when you are going to marry my daughter?

Achilles: Marry your daughter, my lady? I don't understand.

Clytemnestra: I know it must be strange to hear such words from someone you have never met before.

Achilles: Madam, I have not asked to marry your daughter. Nor has King Agamemnon ever mentioned it to me.

Clytemnestra: What? What do you mean?

Achilles: We both have reason to wonder what this means.

Clytemnestra: Has my husband made a fool of me? This is humiliating.

Achilles: Someone has obviously played a joke on us. But let's forget it; it's not important.

Clytemnestra: Please go — I can't look at you.

Achilles: I am embarrassed too, my lady. I'll go into the tent and ask your husband what he meant by this.

Old Servant *(entering):* Wait — wait, Achilles! Wait, my queen, wait!

Clytemnestra: It's my old servant. What is it? What do you want?

Old Servant: Are you alone? Can anyone overhear us?

Achilles: Don't be afraid.

Clytemnestra: You know you can trust *me*. Speak, old man!

Old Servant: Lady — he's going to kill her! He's going to kill your child — his child!

Clytemnestra: You're out of your mind, old man!

Old Servant: I saw the knife — he's sharpening it now.

Clytemnestra: You're telling a horror story — or is my husband insane?

Old Servant: He's sane enough, my lady. It's the prophet. He says it must be done so the ships can sail to Troy and bring Helen back.

Clytemnestra: Oh! Oh! My child! For Helen's sake, my little girl must die?

Old Servant: Yes, my lady. He's going to sacrifice her to Artemis.

Clytemnestra: Then it was a lie, his story about a marriage?

Old Servant: Yes, just to get her here.

Clytemnestra: Achilles, do you hear? They used your name to lure my child to her death.

Achilles: A despicable trick.

Clytemnestra: Oh, Achilles, help me! I'm on my knees to you — have pity on the girl I dressed in a wedding gown for you. Your name brought her here — don't desert her!

Achilles: This is tyranny! I will not serve a leader who could commit this crime! Don't be afraid, my lady. I won't let them sacrifice your child. She came here trusting me — I would be a murderer if I let her die. Calm yourself. If anyone touches so much as the hem of her robe, he'll face my sword.

Clytemnestra: You are a brave and noble man. I have no way to thank you.

Achilles: If I do not keep my promise, I shall die. But, lady, let us try to persuade the king to change his mind.

Clytemnestra: He is a coward. He is afraid of the army.

Achilles: Plead with him, anyway. If he listens, there will be no need for me. If he will not listen — I will be waiting.

Clytemnestra: I will beg him. The gods — (*Bitterly.*) if there are any gods — will bless you for your help!

(*Achilles and Clytemnestra go out slowly.*)

Chorus: Troy must fall, and Paris must be the cause. And so a knife is sharpened for a bride.

Clytemnestra (*re-entering after a pause*): Where is my husband? I've told my poor child how her father loves her — what he plans to do! I can still hear her crying. Ah, here comes the murderer now!

Agamemnon: Good; my queen. I'm glad

you're here. Call the bride out of the tent. Everything is ready for the marriage.

Clymnestra (*bitterly*): How smoothly you talk! (*Calls into tent.*) Come, Iphigenia! Your father wants you, dear. (*Iphigenia enters.*) Here is your daughter, sire, as you asked. She can't speak for sobbing — and I will tell you why.

Agamemnon: Why are you crying, little

girl? No smile for me? Why are you hiding your sweet face? Why do you both look so sad?

Clytemnestra: Answer the question I am going to ask you — tell the truth.

Agamemnon: Ask whatever you like.

Clytemnestra: Your daughter — your own daughter and mine — you plan to kill her, don't you?

Agamemnon: You dare to ask me that? What are you implying?

Clytemnestra: Answer the question, my lord. Answer the question.

Agamemnon: Oh, terrible day!

Clytemnestra: For her and for me — for all of us.

Agamemnon: You know. Someone has told you.

Clytemnestra: I know everything. Don't bother to deny it.

Agamemnon: I will not lie — my grief is too deep for that.

Clytemnestra: I never loved you — you forced me to marry you. But I was a faithful wife. I gave you three daughters and a son, and now you want to rob me of my eldest child! And why? To bring back Helen. You're willing to trade your own child for that worthless woman! If you do it, how can I stay home while you are in Troy, and look at my daughter's empty room, and think, "Your father killed you, my child, killed you himself!" Do you expect me to welcome you when you come back? You'll get a welcome — the welcome you deserve! Don't drive me to murder, too! If you kill your child, how can you pray to the gods? What can you ask? With what can they reward you, who has killed his own child?

Iphigenia: Father, I don't know what to say to you — I can only cry. Please let me live! I love the sun — don't send me to a dark grave! When I was a little girl, you used to say you'd see me a happy wife, married to a good husband — and I'd say I'd always want you as my guest. I remember the gifts you gave me, how I'd sit on your lap. . . . But you've forgotten it all. You want me to die. Please have mercy. I have nothing to do with Helen's love — why should she end everything for me? Father, look at me — kiss me just once more. Let me take that memory to the grave with me, if I must die. Listen — my baby brother Orestes is crying. Even he understands how wrong this is. Life is so sweet! No one wants to die whose mind is whole. The worst life is better than the proudest death.

Agamemnon: I know what mercy is. I am not insane. I love my children. The thing I have to do is terrible — but not to do it is also terrible. If I refuse what Artemis asks and the ships can never sail, the Trojans will invade Greece and kill your sisters, and you, too. I must save Greece, whatever it costs me. We live to guard our country's freedom.

Clytemnestra: We make fools of the gods if we suppose they can love murderers. If you were a man, you'd make Menelaus give his own daughter for Helen! Why should Helen come home and find her child, while I, a decent woman, must lose mine? Am I wrong? Answer. We cannot let foreigners rule us.

(He leaves.)

Clytemnestra: Oh, my little girl! You must die! Your father has thrown you into the jaws of death.

Iphigenia: Mother, oh, Mother! The daylight is dead; the light of the sun is gone. I once saw Helen — her face was death. We are all children of sorrow!

Clytemnestra: There is still hope, child. Look! Our friend Achilles has come back with a company of soldiers.

(Achilles enters.)

Iphigenia: I must hide. I can't meet him. That story about the marriage — I'm ashamed.

Clytemnestra: There's no time for such foolishness! Stay here. What is it, Achilles?

Achilles: The news is bad. The army is screaming for your daughter's murder.

Clytemnestra: Is no one taking her part?

Achilles: I tried, and they stoned me for it.

Clytemnestra: What about your own men?

Achilles: They were the first to turn against me.

Clytemnestra: My darling, we are lost!

Achilles: They said I was lovesick. They laughed at me.

Clytemnestra: What did you say?

Achilles: I said, "You cannot kill my bride!"

Clytemnestra: A brave answer.

Achilles: I was shouted down. But I will save her yet.

Clytemnestra: How can you? You are only one man against an army.

Achilles: You see this handful of men-at-arms behind me? They will fight.

Clytemnestra: Then there is hope.

Achilles: She will not be sacrificed while I still live.

Clytemnestra: Are they coming here to seize her?

Achilles: Ten thousand of them — Odysseus is leading them. But I'll keep him off.

Clytemnestra: Will he — drag her to the altar against her will?

Achilles: Yes. He will.

Clytemnestra: What can I do?

Achilles: Hold her — hold her fast.

Clytemnestra: If it will save her, she is safe forever!

Achilles: It may soon be the only thing left to do.

Iphigenia: Mother, let me speak. It's no use being angry with my father; there's no use fighting when we know we can't win. Thank your friend for his bravery and his kindness, but don't let him fight the army. It won't help us, and he will only die. I have been thinking — listen to me, please. I have made a choice, my own free choice. I have chosen death. *(Achilles and Clytemnestra gasp.)* I have been a coward — but I'm over that now. Honor is the important thing to me now. Oh, Mother, say that I'm right! My country needs me — I can make the fleet sail; I can conquer Troy. My death will save the women of my people — they will bless my name — I will be called "the woman who set Greece free"! Life is not so sweet that I can shrink from my duty. When you gave a child to a Greek king, you gave her for Greece's sake, not your own. Think! Thousands of soldiers are on fire to serve their country, to die for her honor. Is my one poor life to stand in their way? Could we pretend that was right? Could we call it justice? And, Mother, how can we let our friend Achilles die fighting his own men for me? The goddess needs my blood; how can I refuse? No — take me. Conquer Troy. Victory for my country shall be my husband, and my children, and my fame.

Achilles: I would have been the proudest man on earth to have you as my wife! Greece and you are well matched. Now that I see what kind of woman you are, I want you for my own! Let me fight for you.

Iphigenia: Helen's face has caused enough battles and enough murders. Don't die because of me, and don't kill any more. Let me save Greece if I can.

Achilles: You are glorious! But when you stand at the altar, your thoughts may not be the same. My men and I will go and station ourselves around it. When the sharp steel comes toward your throat, if you suddenly know you do *not* want to die, I will not let it happen. *(He exits.)*

Iphigenia: Mother, don't cry. Promise to do something for me. Don't cut your hair or wear black clothes.

Clytemnestra: I must not mourn?

Iphigenia: There is no reason — I am happy. I am giving my life for Greece.

Clytemnestra: What shall I tell your sisters?

Iphigenia: Oh, don't let them wear black either. Tell them good-bye for me. And Orestes — take care of him for me. Bring him up to be a fine man.

Clytemnestra: Hold him. Look at him just once more.

Iphigenia *(to the baby):* Little darling, you gave me all the help you could. And, Mother, don't hate my father. He offered me to Greece against his will.

Clytemnestra: By treachery! He is not worthy to be a king!

Iphigenia: I must go now. If I don't, they'll come and drag me to the altar.

Clytemnestra: I'll go beside you —

Iphigenia: No, Mother; stay here. It's easier for us both that way.

Clytemnestra: Oh, don't leave me! *(She collapses.)*

Iphigenia: She has fainted. It's better that way. I won't shed a single tear! Sing — sing the song of my destiny! Sing to Artemis! Let all the Greeks hear the glad sound of it! Call my father to the altar. Today I will bring victory and salvation to my country! Follow me — I am the taker of Troy! Dear sunlight, good-bye. Good-bye! *(She leaves.)*

Chorus: There goes the conqueror of Troy. Oh, Artemis, her blood is a rich gift for you! Send the wind. Send our Greeks like a flood to drown that treacherous town! *(Messenger enters.)*

Messenger: Queen Clytemnestra — oh, my queen, my queen! Come out and hear the wonderful thing that has happened!

Clytemnestra *(coming from tent):* What is wonderful enough to interrupt my grief?

Messenger: My lady — it was a miracle! Your daughter is alive. She was not sacrificed — she is with the gods!

Clytemnestra: What are you saying? What kind of joke is this?

Messenger: I saw it, lady. She stood there at the altar, brave and proud, willing to die for Greece. Her father sobbed and had to hold his cape to catch his tears. They said the prayers. The priest raised the knife — and suddenly, Iphigenia was not there!

Clytemnestra: Not there? Where was she, then?

Messenger: The gods had taken her. Where she had been standing there was a deer — and the altar was red with deer's blood, not with hers. The gods save souls they love. She is immortal!

Clytemnestra: I can't believe this story.

Agamemnon *(entering):* But it is true. Our daughter is with the gods. And this very day, the army will be at sea. Go home, my queen. I will send word from Troy.

Chorus: Go to war with joy, oh king! Bring back to us rich spoils from captured Troy!

READING COMPREHENSION

Summarizing. Choose the best phrase to complete each sentence. Then write the complete statements on your paper.

1. The Greeks were at war with Troy because _____ (Paris had taken Helen, Iphigenia was sacrificed, Menelaus was hungry for power).

2. Agamemnon had to sacrifice Iphigenia because _____ (he had stolen Menelaus's wife, she had wronged the gods, he had made a promise to Artemis).

3. Iphigenia arrived at the camp thinking she was to be _____ (sacrificed, honored, married).

4. Iphigenia went to the sacrificial altar _____ (by her own free will, after Achilles married her, under arrest by the soldiers).

Interpreting. Write the answer to each question on your paper.

1. Why did Iphigenia decide to be a willing sacrifice?

2. Who would probably win the war — the Greeks or the Trojans? Explain why.

3. Why did the women of the chorus call Iphigenia "the conqueror of Troy"?

For Thinking and Discussing. Which characters do you admire? Which characters do you think were not admirable? Explain why.

UNDERSTANDING LITERATURE

Theme and Culture. The great literature of the world deals with themes that are universal. But any work of literature is also the product of its author's *culture*. Culture includes the shared beliefs, values, and traditions of any group of people.

For the ancient Greeks, the gods they worshiped were powerful and demanding. To go against the will of the gods was to tempt fate and bring destruction upon oneself and one's country. The Greeks also believed in the power of prophecies, that it would be foolish to try to change the outcome of a prophecy.

To understand the theme of *Iphigenia* better, answer the following questions. Refer to the play if necessary.

1. Why was Agamemnon expected to sacrifice Iphigenia?

2. What problems did the Greeks face because Agamemnon had not yet sacrificed Iphigenia?

3. It was prophesied that Paris would bring destruction to Troy. How was this prophecy coming true?

4. What happened to Iphigenia when she gave herself as a sacrifice? Why was she honored by the gods?

WRITING

Write one or two paragraphs telling how Iphigenia's sacrifice reflected the values she believed in — the values of ancient Greek culture.

Return to India

by Santha Rama Rau

Santha Rama Rau was born in India in 1923, but was educated in England and the United States. Perhaps her varied background helps explain her ability to make a culture come alive to readers of every nationality. In this selection, you may come to understand both the Soviet Union and the writer's native India more clearly.

During the three months that my husband and I and our small son were in the Soviet Union, we lost count of the number of times Russians asked us, "Don't you think our life here is good?"

"Yes, very good," we always replied, politely refraining from adding "for the Russians."

Inevitably the point would be pressed a little further. Life in the Soviet Union was not only good, we would be assured, but was getting better every day. Certainly on the evidence of the past few years, this was no more than the truth. Usually after this kind of opening exchange, the Russians we met proved to be very curious about life in America, my husband's country, and the questions ranged from the price of nylons to American intentions for nuclear war. Sometimes they even showed a faint interest in my country, India.

On one such occasion, I had a brief conversation with a Russian acquaintance that I was to remember much later with quite a different feeling. A young man, noticing across a restaurant that I wore a sari[1], came over to the table where my husband and I were sitting. "*Hindi-Russki bhai-bhai!*" he announced proudly — a phrase Russians learned when Prime Minister Nehru visited their country, a phrase they love to use. It means, in Hindi, "Indians and Russians are brothers."

"*Hindi-Russki bhai-bhai,*" I replied dutifully, and then, after the usual opening formalities, he started to ask me — or rather, to tell me — about life in India.

With my husband interpreting for us, he remarked, "The Indian people are very poor."

"Yes, they are."

"I have seen photographs. They have few clothes and many have no shoes."

"That's true."

"Most of them are uneducated."

"Yes."

---

1. sari: a loose, flowing, draped garment worn by women in India.

448

"Many beggars on the streets."

"Yes."

"It must be very difficult to live in such a country."

"No —" I began, suddenly feeling homesick.

But the young man was finished with the subject of India. "In Russia we have a very good life."

After our stay in Russia, I returned with my son to visit my family in India. We flew from Uzbekistan in the far south of Russia, over the magnificent expanse of the Himalayas, to New Delhi. The plane arrived after dark. By the time we reached my uncle's house, it was quite late and we were too tired to do much talking or to pay much attention to our surroundings.

The next morning, with my first glimpse of the newspapers, I was sharply aware not so much that I was in India as that I was out of Russia. One paragraph was enough to convince me. It ran, as I remember, something like this: "Yesterday the Prime Minister opened the debate in parliament[2] on the second five-year plan with a two-hour speech in his usual diffuse style." I read, and reread, and reread the words "his usual diffuse style," remembering the admiring tone of all Russian newspapers toward all Russian leaders — the ones in favor, that is.

This was small enough as an incident, but during the first day, a number of moments — equally minor — began to acquire a collective force. I had offered to help

---

2. parliament: the national legislature, which makes the laws of India.

with the household shopping, partly because I enjoy bazaars and partly because I wanted to show my son a little of the city. We started in the fruit market, which I'm afraid my Russian friends would have found hopelessly disorganized. No orderly lines, no rationing, no fixed prices, no stern-faced women with string shopping bags waiting in line, dutifully reading signs saying, "Drink fruit juices. They are good for you."

silver jewelry, brilliant silks and cottons, or painted wooden toys. The vendors who can't afford a stall sit on the sidewalk outside the market, their baskets stacked behind them, their wives in vivid cotton saris crouching in the shade. In front of them are spread carpets of scarlet chilies drying in the sun, small hills of saffron, tumeric, coriander, ginger, cinnamon — all the magical names from the old days of the spice trade with the Indies. With a worn stone mortar and pestle, the vendor or his wife will grind your spices for you, blending them according to your particular taste, and weigh them in tiny brass scales strung on twine and balanced delicately in one hand. In all transactions, you receive a pleasantly individual attention — nothing standardized.

The vegetable and fruit and flower merchants are surrounded by baskets of purple eggplant, green peppers, strings of tiny silvery onions, heads of bitter Indian spinach, and a dozen Indian vegetables for which I don't even know the English names. I had forgotten about the profusion of fruit in India — it is only during the brief, intense summer that you see much variety of fruit in Moscow. In Russia, as winter approaches, all vegetables except for potatoes and the pervasive cabbage in soup seem to disappear from the menus.

My son was enjoying himself, pouncing on the stacks of bananas — unobtainable in Russia — regarding with some suspicion the papayas and chikus, which he had not remembered from his last stay in India. He prodded a pile of the tiny, sharp Indian limes to see if they would collapse, an action for which he would have been

To me, an Indian bazaar is a source of endless delight and excitement. It is usually a series of plain wooden stalls on which are piled, with unconcious artistry, brightly colored fruits, vegetables, spices, gleaming

severely reprimanded in Russia. I was reminded of the evening when we had run into an official of the Ministry of Culture in the lobby of the Metropole, our hotel in Moscow. He had come to the hotel to buy a lemon. It seemed like an extraordinary place for such an item, but there were too few lemons in the winter, so they were saved for the tourists and the foreigners and could only be obtained, if you were lucky, at an Intourist hotel.

Flowers. This was something I missed very much in Russia, where flowers are a real luxury. I can remember standing at a street corner in Russia, astonished by the sight of a flower-woman sitting in the middle of a splash of color in those gray streets. The Russians stopped to look, too. Not many of them bought the flowers — too costly — but a surprising number paused in the rush to get home from offices, factories, and shops in the shadowy autumn twilight just to feast for a moment on the rare color of a few stiff bunches of chrysanthemums on a street corner.

All around us, in Delhi, there were flowers. Yes, it is a tropical country, and yes, the climate makes this possible — but there was a personal pride and feminine joy in the country women who tucked a marigold casually into their hair, who wove roses into small hoops to wear more formally around the knot of hair on the back of the head. I realized then that I had missed all this in Russia; the pleasure of women being women, a sense of decoration and unquestioned right of anyone to the small, cheap luxuries and gaieties.

But most impressive — to me, anyway — are the people in an Indian bazaar. First of all, there is the inquisitiveness that often embarrassed foreigners. When you are engaged on an errand as simple as buying potatoes, in the course of the transaction your vendor may well ask you any variety of what my American friends would call personal questions. How old are you? How many children do you have? Only one? (A shake of the head.) Better hurry and have another before you are too old. Where do you live? Is your mother-in-law alive? Inevitably I made the comparison with Russia, where this kind of passing, interested exchange (between Russians) is so suspect. The right to express ordinary human curiosity about a fellow countryman came to seem like a privilege.

Meanwhile, the routine of bargaining would be going on, and the whole performance would be mixed with jokes and cracks and comments. Next to me, a man, bargaining for tangerines, remarked to the old woman standing behind the stall, "Clearly you believe in the soak-the-rich program." This was the popular description of India's new taxation policy. The woman, amused, replied dryly, "Give me your income and I will gladly pay your taxes." And so it went. It was all very Indian, or rather, un-Russian.

We finished our shopping and hired a boy to carry our purchases out of the bazaar — another small, cheap luxury.

On our way out of the market, we passed the familiar barrage of beggars on the sidewalk and, as usual, gave them the small change left from shopping. Even my son noticed the contrast to Moscow. "Why are they asking for money, Mummy?"

"Because they are poor, darling."

"Why are they poor, Mummy?"

"India is a poor country, darling. Too many people and not enough food."

"We could give them some of our fruit."

"Well, that's what we've done in another way. We've given them some money to buy whatever they choose."

Then I was left wondering, as so often in the past, about the ethics of begging and giving. It is easy to win approval from foreigners by criticizing two elements of Indian life — the caste structure[3] and begging for a livelihood. The best that can be said about either of them is that it is gradually disappearing. However, it would be less than honest to pretend that social ills are all that is involved in either system. The goals in the Hindu view of life are not the same as those of Russia or the Western world. Indeed, India's highest caste, the Brahmans, are traditionally sworn to poverty. Ambition, getting ahead, comfort, success are obstacles, not aims, in the Hindu concept of a good life. Enlightenment is reached, if it is reached, when you have detached yourself from worldly considerations and emotional drives of any sort, so it is not surprising that many of India's most respected "holy men" are, in fact, beggars, or perhaps live on contributions from strangers, admirers, casual visitors.

What in the West is almost always a degrading occupation can, in India, be a high achievement. Not, of course, that all beggars beg for religious reasons. Many are simply poor, or sick, or unemployed,

or seeking a little extra income. If, to a Westerner, they are an embarrassment or raise guilts about his own privileged life, to an Asian they are more likely to prompt a down-to-earth recognition of conditions as they are and an urge to contribute in a small way to a social responsibility. This is combined with the knowledge that there is no society, including the Russian, in which privilege is unknown. Money, birth, education, accomplishment, something makes a class (or caste) structure. The Hindu view is not to rise to a higher level of privilege but to rise beyond the concern with privilege and levels altogether. It is hard enough to explain this attitude to a sympathetic, philosophic Westerner; it is impossible to describe to the average Russian, to whom spiritual values seem to be mysterious, unacceptable, or discredited.

Could the Indian government, like the Russian or the Chinese, abolish beggars with a sweeping compulsory measure? I suppose it could. Would the cost in undemocratic forcefulness be too high? I think it might. We are committed to raising the standard of living in India, but by different methods, at a different pace — a pace designed to preserve other important aspects of our life. Although a number of these thoughts occurred to me that day at the bazaar, luckily I hadn't the time to try to explain many of them to my son because he was thirsty and was more concerned with demanding a lemonade of the sort he had liked in Russia. We stopped at a nearby coffeehouse.

An Indian coffeehouse, like an Indian bazaar, has its own peculiar atmosphere. It is a cheerful, comfortable place in

---

3. Caste system: the Hindu system of assigning a person, from birth, to a social and economic class.

which to dawdle, encounter friends, talk, discuss, gossip. Students make fiery speeches to each other; women meet for a break in a morning's shopping; idlers stop by for a rest, to watch the world go by, to pick up a chance colleague. The actual drinking of coffee is the least important part of the whole affair. Looking around at the animated groups of uninhibited talkers at the tables, I couldn't help thinking that this particular sort of place doesn't exist in Moscow. There one can find restaurants (mostly rather expensive by any standard), or "Parks of Culture and Rest," or hotel dining rooms, and several varieties of bar ranging from the *pivnaya,* where as a rule you can't even sit down, where women are seldom seen, and where the customers walk to the bar, order a drink, down it, and leave, all within the space of five minutes, to the *stolovoye,* which is considered more refined, more suitable for women, and where ordinary vodka is not served, though wines and brandy are brought to your table. But India is not a drinking country, even in areas where there is no ban on alcohol. The sight of drunks being thrown out of restaurants with the offhand ruthlessness that the Russians employ for such occasions is extremely rare in India.

Indians meet in public places for sociability, and though poor housing contributes, as it does in Russia, to the life of cafes and restaurants and street corners, still Indians do not meet for the dedicated purpose of getting drunk. They are incurable talkers. At the coffeehouse, I found myself once again cozy and amused in the endless stream of comments, criticism,

scandal, anecdote, and analysis that accompanies one's days in any Indian society. I like the idea that one can be interested, amused, or disapproving of the activities or remarks of one's neighbors, friends, and acquaintances, or of political figures, college professors, taxi drivers, and artists. I like the idea that one's concern, malicious or pleasant, in one's fellow countrymen cannot lead to their political harassment.

Listening that morning in the coffeehouse to the flurry of debate that rose from the students' tables about the latest political controversy, mixed with the social chitchat of the ladies or the shop talk of secretaries, office workers, and clerks, I thought of the sad, sly exchanges we had shared with our Russian acquaintances. I remembered the way conversation with a Russian in a restaurant would stop cold whenever a waiter came to the table or strangers walked by. At first, I was astonished to find that Russians are much more willing to talk than I had expected, that people will come up to you in parks, restaurants, on the street, drawn by curiosity to a foreigner, eager to ask and answer questions. But we soon learned, after hearing some deeply intimate confidences from Russians we scarcely knew, that our relations with them were very much in the nature of a shipboard romance. It can be intimate because it is so brief. "I can talk to you frankly," one of our friends said, not wistfully, merely as a statement of fact, "because you are in Moscow only a short time. Soon you will go and we will never meet again."

I remembered a waiter at the Metropole Hotel who had seen us so often in the dining room that one day he drifted over to our table to ask us in muttered conversation and scribbled notes about foreign writers. In return for whatever information we could give him, he told us about his favorite poet, Valery Bryusov. We had never heard of him, and then learned that he was banned in the Soviet Union. "You see," the waiter whispered, "he is a symbolist." In the rowdy air of the coffeehouse, it seemed incredible that there were places where poetry, even symbolist poetry, was considered too dangerous for the fragile human intellect.

After those early days in India, both the novelty of being home and the continual contrasts with Russia began to wear thin. Soon I slipped back into the slow pace and familiar daily life of India. My son no longer noticed beggars. I no longer thought of a trip to the bazaar or the coffeehouse as an occasion. I even remembered the cold blue evenings of Moscow with some fondness as the Indian climate warmed up to its early spring. But once during that time, I thought of my trip to Moscow, and of India as a nation, with a shock of rediscovery. It was during the Independence Day parade that takes place in New Delhi every January 26.

It is an immense celebration, and villagers from all the surrounding areas of the city had been walking into the town or arriving in their bullock carts for days before. As the day grew closer, all the open spaces of New Delhi were gradually filled with impromptu camps. Carts were unhitched, oxen grazed in the parks, the evening air was filled with the haze of open-air cooking fires for the scanty dinners of the travelers. On the streets, you saw everywhere the brilliantly colored full ankle-length skirts and jackets of the village women. Each footstep (yes, barefoot, I would have had to admit to my Russian acquaintance) was emphasized by the metallic clink of silver anklets or toe rings. If a small child was hitched into a more comfortable position on his mother's hip, the sound of silver bracelets would accompany the movement. The fathers, proudly carrying sons to see the city's sights or carefully washing their oxen at a public fountain, were less decorative but good-humored and ready for a festival. The streets were full of color and excitement and nobody checked the wanderings of the villagers as they looked around the capital.

In Russia, you need a permit to travel even within the country, an identity card and an official permit before you may stay at a hotel. For most non-Moscovites, the only way to get to Moscow is to come, as a reward for outstanding service, on a brief "workers' tour" or as a member of some delegation. Chekov's yearning phrase "To Moscow, to Moscow[4]. . . ." has just as intense a meaning now.

The day of the parade brought thousands of villagers and citizens of Delhi to the parade route, lining the roads in a dense, active crowd of mothers, fathers, children, babies, donkeys, oxen. Many families had their lunches tied up in pieces of cloth. Children clutched balloons or candy sticks. Little stalls selling nuts, tea, sweets, and fruit sprang up everywhere. I was lucky enough to have a seat on one of the bleachers outside the president's house where the procession started, and next to me was an old man in a worn khaki sweater and army trousers. A faded patch on his arm said "Engineers." He was obviously a veteran, obviously now retired, and obviously he had never been higher in rank than sergeant.

When the procession began with the arrival of the Indian president, the old man stood up to get a better view. All the pomp and ceremony from India's days of British rule surrounded the president — the outriders, the cavalry escort, the great coach drawn by matched horses, guarded by lancers. Out of the coach stepped a small thin man in a brown *achkan* (the Indian jacket), narrow trousers wrinkled at the ankles, a Gandhi cap on his head. He looked embarrassed by the flashy display that surrounded him. Smiling shyly, he brought his hands together in a *namaskar,* the Indian greeting, and hurried to his place on the reviewing platform. This in no way discouraged the old man next to me. He raised his hands in a *namaskar* above the heads of the people around him. With tears streaming down his face, he yelled (apparently convinced that the president could hear him), *"Namaste ji! Jai Hind!"* and continued with such fervor that the rest of us near him suddenly found ourselves joining in a tribute from an Indian who had spent all his life in the British Army to an Indian who represented, at last, the fact that all this and India itself belonged to all of us.

---

4. In a play *The Three Sisters* by the Russian writer Anton Chekov, this line is said often by the characters, who yearn to go to Moscow but never do.

READING COMPREHENSION

Summarizing. Choose the best phrase to complete each sentence. Then write the complete statements on your paper.

1. The Russians the author met viewed India as _____ (a wonderful place to live, a poor and backward country, an ally of America).

2. The author saw life in India as _____ (much more restricted than life in the Soviet Union, freer and more interesting than life in Russia, poor and depressing).

3. The author's visit to India made her feel _____ (embarrassed by its poverty, homesick for America, proud of its culture).

Interpreting. Write the answer to each question on your paper.

1. What parts of Russian life did the author dislike?

2. What aspects of Indian life did the author praise?

3. Why is begging in India not always a degrading occupation?

For Thinking and Discussing.

1. How did the Russians speak of their country to the author? Did she think they were honest? Explain.

2. Why are many writers censored in the Soviet Union? What is your opinion of such censorship?

UNDERSTANDING LITERATURE

Theme: Comparison and Contrast. A writer may present a theme indirectly though *comparison* and *contrast*. The writer provides information about two subjects; in so doing, the writer implies his or her views on the subject. In "Return to India," Rama Rau contrasts life in the Soviet Union with life in India.

The statements in the numbered list below describe India. Match each with a statement about the Soviet Union from the lettered list. On your paper, write the pairs of statements and what each comparison suggests.

1. "An Indian coffeehouse . . . is a cheerful, comfortable place in which to dawdle, . . . discuss, gossip."

2. "To me, an Indian bazaar is a source of endless delight and excitement."

3. "The day of the parade brought thousands . . . to the parade route. . . ."

a. "In Russia, you need a permit to travel even within the country."

b. ". . . conversation with a Russian in a restaurant would stop cold whenever a waiter came to the table. . . ."

c. Russian stores had ". . . orderly lines, rationing, fixed prices, and stern-faced women . . . waiting in line."

WRITING

In two paragraphs, compare an Indian market with a U.S. supermarket. Be sure to include details in your comparison.

With All Flags Flying

by Anne Tyler

Anne Tyler was born in Minneapolis in 1941. She has published several novels as well as numerous short stories. Her writing often deals with loneliness. In this story, an old man chooses to be lonely. After you have read the story, see if you can understand why.

Weakness was what got him in the end. He had been expecting something more definite — chest pains, a stroke, arthritis — but it was only weakness that put a finish to his living alone. A numbness in his head, an airy feeling when he walked. A wateriness in his bones that made it an effort to pick up his coffee cup in the morning. He waited some days for it to go away, but it never did. And meanwhile, the dust piled up in corners, the refrigerator wheezed and creaked for want of defrosting. Weeds grew around his rosebushes.

He was awake and dressed at six o'clock on a Saturday morning, with the patchwork quilt pulled up neatly over the mattress. From the kitchen cabinet, he took a hunk of bread and two Fig Newtons, which he dropped into a paper bag. He was wearing a brown suit that he had bought on sale in 1944, a white T-shirt, and copper-toed work boots. These and his other set of underwear, which he put in the paper bag along with a razor, were all the clothes he took with him. Then he rolled down the top of the bag and stuck it under his arm, and stood in the middle of the kitchen staring around him for a moment.

The house had only two rooms, but he owned it — the last scrap of the farm that he had sold off years ago. It stood in a hollow of dying trees beside a superhighway in Baltimore County. All it held was a few sticks of furniture, a change of clothes, a skillet, and a set of dishes. Also, odds and ends, which disturbed him. If his inventory were complete, he would have to include six clothespins, a salt and pepper shaker, a broken-toothed comb, a cheap ballpoint pen — oh, on and on, past logical numbers. Why should he be so cluttered? He was 82 years old. He had grown from an infant owning nothing to a family man with a wife, five children, everyday and Sunday china, and a thousand appurtenances, down at last to solitary old age and the bare essentials again, but not bare enough to suit him. Only what he needed surrounded him. Was it possible he needed so much?

459

Now he had the brown paper bag; that was all. It was the one satisfaction in a day he had been dreading for years.

He left the house without another glance, heading up the steep bank toward the superhighway. The bank was covered with small, crawling weeds planted especially by young men with scientific training in how to prevent soil erosion. Twice his knees buckled. He had to sit and rest, bracing himself against the slope of the bank. The scientific weeds, seen from close up, looked straggly and gnarled. He sifted dry earth through his fingers without thinking, concentrating only on steadying his breath and calming the twitching muscles in his legs.

Once on the superhighway, which was fairly level, he could walk for longer stretches of time. He kept his head down and his fingers clenched tight upon the paper bag, which was growing limp and damp now. Sweat rolled down the back of his neck, fell in drops from his temples. When he had been walking maybe half an hour, he had to sit down again for a rest. A black motorcycle buzzed up from behind and stopped a few feet away from him. The driver was young and shabby, with hair so long that it drizzled out beneath the back of his helmet.

"Give you a lift, if you like," he said. "You going somewhere?"

"Just into Baltimore."

"Hop on."

He shifted the paper bag to the space beneath his arm, put on the white helmet he was handed, and climbed on behind the driver. For safety, he took a clutch of the boy's shirt, tightly at first, and then more loosely when he saw there was no danger. Except for the helmet, he was perfectly comfortable. He felt his face cooling and stiffening in the wind, his body learning to lean gracefully with the tilt of the motorcycle as it swooped from lane to lane. It was a fine way to spend his last free day.

Half an hour later, they were on the outskirts of Baltimore, stopped at the first traffic light. The boy turned his head and shouted, "Whereabouts did you plan on going?"

"I'm visiting my daughter, on Belvedere near Charles Street."

"I'll drop you off, then," the boy said. "I'm passing right by there."

The light changed, the motor roared. Now that they were in traffic, he felt more conspicuous, but not in a bad way. People in their automobiles seemed sealed in, overprotected; men in large trucks must envy the way the motorcycle looped in and out, hornetlike, stripped to the bare essentials of a motor and two wheels. By tugs at the boy's shirt and single words shouted into the wind, he directed him to his daughter's house, but he was sorry to have the ride over so quickly.

His daughter had married a salesman and lived in a plain, square, stone house that the old man approved of. There were sneakers and a football in the front yard, signs of a large, happy family. A bicycle lay in the driveway. The motorcycle stopped just inches from it. "Here we are," the boy said.

"Well, I surely do thank you."

He climbed off, fearing for one second

that his legs would give way beneath him and spoil everything that had gone before. But no, they held steady. He took off the helmet and handed it to the boy, who waved and roared off. It was a really magnificent roar, ear-dazzling. He turned toward the house, beaming in spite of himself, with his head feeling cool and light now that the helmet was gone. And there was his daughter on the front porch, laughing. "Daddy, what on earth?" she said. "Have you turned into a teeny-bopper?" Whatever that was. She came rushing down the steps to hug him — a plump, happy-looking woman in an apron. She was getting on toward 50 now. Her hands were like her mother's, swollen, and veined. Gray had started dusting her hair.

"You never told us," she said. "Did you ride all this way on a motorcycle? Oh, why didn't you find a telephone and call? I would have come. How long can you stay for?"

"Now . . ." he said, starting toward the house. He was thinking of the best way to put it. "I came to a decision. I won't be living alone any more. I want to go to an old folks' home. That's what I *want*," he said, stopping on the grass so she would be sure to get it clear. "I don't want to live with you — I want an old folks' home." Then he was afraid he had worded it too strongly. "It's nice *visiting* you, of course," he said.

"Why, Daddy, you know we always asked you to come and live with us."

"I know that, but I decided on an old folks' home."

"We couldn't do that. We won't even talk about it."

"Clara, my mind is made up."

Then, in the doorway, a new thought hit her, and she suddenly turned around. "Are you sick?" she said. "You always said you would live alone as long as health allowed."

"I'm not up to that any more," he said.

"What is it? Are you having some kind of pain?"

"I just decided, that's all," he said. "What I *will* rely on you for is the arrangements with the home. I know it's a trouble."

"We'll talk about that later," Clara said. And she firmed the corners of her mouth exactly the way her mother used to do when she hadn't won an argument but wasn't planning to lose it yet either.

In the kitchen, he had a glass of milk, good and cold, and the hunk of bread and the two Fig Newtons from his paper bag. Clara wanted to make him a big breakfast, but there was no sense wasting what he had brought. He munched on the dry bread and washed it down with milk, meanwhile staring at the Fig Newtons, which lay on the smoothed-out bag. They were the worse for their ride — squashed and pathetic-looking, the edges worn down and crumbling. They seemed to have come from somewhere long ago and far away. "Here, now we've got cookies I baked only yesterday," Clara said; but he said, "No, no," and ate the Fig Newtons, whose warmth on his tongue filled him with a vague, sad feeling deeper than homesickness. "In my house," he said, "I left things a little messy. I hate to ask it of you, but I didn't manage to straighten up any."

"Don't even think about it," Clara said. "I'll take out a suitcase tomorrow and clean everything up. I'll bring it all back."

"I don't want it."

"Don't want any of it? But Daddy —"

He didn't try explaining it to her. He finished his lunch in silence and then let her lead him upstairs to the guest room.

Clara had five boys and a girl, the oldest 20. During the morning, as they passed one by one through the house on their way to other places, they heard of his arrival and trooped up to see him. They were fine children, all of them, but it was the girl he enjoyed the most, Francie. She was only 13, too young yet to know how to hide what she felt. And what she felt was always about love, it seemed: whom she just loved, who she hoped loved her back. Who was just a darling. Had 13-year-olds been so aware of love in the old days? He didn't know and didn't care; all he had to do with Francie was sit smiling in an armchair and listen. There was a new boy in the neighborhood who walked his English sheepdog past her yard every morning, looking toward her house. Was it because of her, or did the dog just like to go that way? When he telephoned her brother Donnie, was he hoping for her to answer? And when she did answer, did he want to talk a minute or to have her hand the receiver straight to Donnie? But what would she say to him, anyway? Oh, all her questions had to do with where she might find love, and everything she said made the old man wince and love her more. She left in the middle of a sentence, knocking against a doorknob as she flew from the room, an unlovable-looking tangle of blond hair and braces and scrapes and Band-Aids. After she was gone, the room seemed too empty, as if she had accidentally torn part of it away in her flight.

Getting into an old folks' home was hard. Not only because of lack of good homes, high expenses, waiting lists; it was harder yet to talk his family into letting him go. His son-in-law argued with him every evening, his round, kind face anxious and questioning across the supper table. "Is it that you think you're not welcome here? You are, you know. You were one of the reasons we bought this big house."

His grandchildren, when they talked to him, had a kind of urgency in their voices, as if they were trying to impress him with their acceptance of him. His other daughters called long distance from all across the country and begged him to come to them if he wouldn't stay with Clara. They had room or they would make room; he had no idea what homes for the aged were like these days. To all of them, he gave the same answer: "I've made my decision." He was proud of them asking, though. All his children had turned out so well, every last one of them. They were good, strong women with happy families, and they had never given him a moment's worry. He had felt luckier than he had a right to be. He had felt lucky all his life, dangerously lucky, cursed by luck; it had seemed some disaster must be waiting to even things up. But the luck had held. When his wife died, it was at a late age, sparing her the pain she would have had to face, and his life had continued in its steady, reasonable pattern with no more sorrow than any other man's. His final lot was to weaken, to crumble, and to die — only a secret disaster, not the one he had been expecting.

He walked two blocks daily, fighting off the weakness. He shelled peas for Clara, and mended little household articles — which gave him an excuse to sit. Nobody noticed how he arranged to climb the stairs only once a day, at bedtime. When he had empty time, he chose a chair without rockers, one that would not be a symbol of age and weariness and lack of work. He rose every morning at six and stayed in his room a full hour, giving his legs enough warning to face the day ahead. Never once did he disgrace himself by falling down in front of people. He dropped nothing more important than a spoon or a fork.

Meanwhile the wheels were turning; his name was on a waiting list. Not that that meant anything, Clara said. "When it comes right down to driving you out there, I just won't let you go," she told him. "But I'm hoping you won't carry things that far. Daddy, won't you put a stop to this foolishness?"

He hardly listened. He had chosen long ago what kind of old age he would have; everyone does. Most, he thought, were weak and chose to be loved at any cost. He had seen women turn soft and sad, anxious to please, and had watched with pity and impatience their losing battles. And he had once known a schoolteacher, no weakling at all, who said straight out that, when she grew old, she would finally

eat all she wanted and grow fat without worry. He admired that — a simple plan, dependent upon no one. "I'll sit in an armchair," she had said, "with a lady's magazine in my lap and a box of homemade fudge on the lampstand. I'll get as fat as I like and nobody will give a hang." The schoolteacher was thin and pale, with

the kind of stooped, sloping figure that was popular at the time. He had lost track of her long ago, but he liked to think that she had kept her word. He imagined her 50 years later, cozy and fat in a puffy chair, with one hand moving constantly between her mouth and the candy plate. If she had died young or changed her mind or put off her eating until another decade, he didn't want to hear about it.

Clara cried all the way to the home. She was the one who was driving; it made him nervous. One of her hands on the steering wheel held a balled-up tissue, which she had stopped using. She let tears run unchecked down her face, and drove jerkily, with a great deal of brake-slamming and gear-gnashing.

"Clara, I wish you wouldn't take on so," he told her. "There's no need to be sad over me."

"I'm not sad so much as mad," Clara said. "I feel like this is something you're doing to me, just throwing away what I give. Oh, why do you have to be so stubborn? It's still not too late to change your mind."

The old man kept silent. On his right sat Francie, chewing a thumbnail and scowling out the window, her usual self except for the unexplainable presence of her other hand in his, tight as wire. Periodically she muttered a number; she was counting red convertibles, and had been for days. When she reached a hundred, the next boy she saw would be her true love.

He figured that was probably the reason she had come on this trip — a greater exposure to red convertibles.

Whatever happened to DeSotos? Didn't there used to be a car called a roadster?

They parked in the U-shaped driveway in front of the home, under the shade of a poplar tree. If he had had his way, he would have arrived by motorcycle, but he made the best of it — picked up his underwear sack from between his feet, climbed the front steps ramrod-straight. They were met by a smiling woman in blue who had to check his name on a file and ask more questions. He made sure to give all the answers himself, overriding Clara when necessary. Meanwhile, Francie spun on one squeaky sneaker-heel and examined the hall, a cavernous, polished square with old fashioned parlors on either side of it. A few old people were on the plush couches, and a nurse sat idle beside a lady in a wheelchair.

They went up a creaking elevator to the second floor and down a long, dark corridor deadened by carpeting. The lady in blue, still carrying a sheaf of files, knocked at number 213. Then she flung the door open on a narrow green room flooded with sunlight.

"Mr. Pond," she said, "this is Mr. Carpenter. I hope you'll get on well together."

Mr. Pond was one of those men who run to fat and baldness in old age. He sat in a rocking chair with a gilt-edged Bible on his knees.

"How-do," he said. "Mighty nice to meet you."

They shook hands cautiously, with the women ringing them like mothers asking their children to play nicely with each other. "Ordinarily I sleep in the bed by the window," said Mr. Pond, "but I don't hold it in much importance. You can take your pick."

"Anything will do," the old man said.

Clara was dry-eyed now. She looked frightened.

"You'd best be getting on back now," he told her. "Don't you worry about me. I'll let you know," he said, suddenly generous now that he had won, "if there is anything I need."

Clara nodded and kissed his cheek. Francie kept her face turned away, but she hugged him tightly, and then she looked up at him as she stepped back.

Her eyebrows were tilted as if she were about to ask him one of her questions. Was it her the boy with the sheepdog came for? Did he care when she answered the telephone?

They left, shutting the door with a gentle click. The old man made a great business out of settling his underwear and razor in a bureau drawer, smoothing out the paper bag and folding it, placing it in the next drawer down.

"Didn't bring much," said Mr. Pond, one thumb marking his page in the Bible.

"I don't need much."

"Go on—take the bed by the window. You'll feel better after a while."

"I *wanted* to come," the old man said.

"That there window is a front one. If you look out, you can see your folks leave."

He slid between the bed and the window and looked out. No reason not to. Clara and Francie were just climbing into the car, the sun on the tops of their heads. Clara was blowing her nose with a dot of tissue.

"*Now* they cry," said Mr. Pond, although he had not risen to look out himself. "Later they'll buy themselves a milkshake to celebrate."

"I wanted to come. I made them bring me."

"And so they did. *I* didn't want to come. My son wanted to put me here — his wife was expecting. And so he did. It all works out the same in the end."

"Well, I could have stayed with one of my daughters," the old man said. "But I'm not like some I have known. Hanging around making burdens of themselves, hoping to be loved. Not me."

"If you don't care about being loved," said Mr. Pond, "how come it would bother you to be a burden?"

Then he opened the Bible again, at the place where his thumb had been all the time and went back to reading.

The old man sat on the edge of the bed, watching the tail of Clara's car flash as sharp and hard as a jewel around the bend of the road. Then, with nobody to watch that mattered, he let his shoulders slump and eased himself out of his suit coat, which he folded over the foot of the bed. He slid his suspenders down and let them dangle at his waist. He took off his copper-toed work boots and set them on the floor neatly, side by side. And although it was only noon, he lay down full-length on top of the bedspread. Whiskery lines ran across the plaster of the ceiling high above him. There was a crackling sound in the mattress when he moved; it must be covered with something waterproof.

The tiredness in his head was as vague and restless as anger; the weakness in his knees made him feel as if he had just finished some exhausting exercise. He lay watching the plaster cracks settle themselves into pictures, listening to the silent, neuter voice in his mind form the words he had grown accustomed to hearing now: Let me not give in at the end. Let me continue gracefully until the moment of my defeat. Let Lollie Simpson be alive somewhere even as I lie on my bed; let her be eating homemade fudge in an overstuffed armchair and growing fatter and fatter and fatter.

READING COMPREHENSION

Summarizing. Choose the best phrase to complete each sentence. Then write the complete statements on your paper.

1. The old man gave up living by himself because of _____ (loneliness, weakness, chest pains).

2. The old man told Clara of his decision to _____ (live with her, live with another of his daughters, go to an old folks' home).

3. The old man admired the schoolteacher, Lollie Simpson, because _____ (she decided to stop teaching, she planned to do as she liked in her old age, she went to an old folks' home).

4. Above all, the man valued his _____ (family life, independence, physical strength).

Interpreting. Write the answer to each question on your paper.

1. How did the old man's family feel about his decision to go to a nursing home?

2. What were the reasons for the old man's decision?

3. Why did the old man think of Lollie Simpson at the end of the story?

For Thinking and Discussing

1. How is this portrait different from society's stereotype of old people?

2. Do you think the man made the right choice? Why or why not?

UNDERSTANDING LITERATURE

Theme and Character. In some stories, the *theme* is developed through a central *character*. In "With All Flags Flying," the old man is the central character. To understand the story's theme, you must understand the man's character.

The quotes below each reveal something about the character of the old man. Choose the correct personality traits from those listed and write them on your paper.

1. "Never once did he disgrace himself by falling down in front of people."
   healthy   dependent   proud

2. "'I came to a decision. . . . I want to go to an old folks' home. That's what I *want*.'"
   determined   cautious   unsure

3. "Let me not give in at the end. Let me continue gracefully until the moment of my defeat."
   foolish   strong   fearful

4. Using the list of character traits you have written down, explain the meaning of the following quote: "He had chosen long ago what kind of old age he would have; everyone does."

WRITING

Write two one-paragraph letters. One letter should be from Francie to her grandfather in the nursing home; the other, from him to Francie in reply. Use your knowledge of the characters to decide what each would say about the grandfather's choice.

Just Lather, That's All

by Hernando Téllez

Outwardly, he is just a man in a barber's chair, getting a shave. But the undercurrents are so strong and violent, you may need a seat belt to remain in your chair as you read along.

He said nothing when he entered. I was passing the best of my razors back and forth on a strop. When I recognized him I started to tremble. But he didn't notice. Hoping to conceal my emotion, I continued sharpening the razor. I tested it on the meat of my thumb, and then held it up to the light. At that moment he took off the bullet-studded belt that his gun holster dangled from. He hung it up on a wall hook and placed his military cap over it. Then he turned to me, loosening the knot of his tie, and said, "It's unbearably hot. Give me a shave." He sat down in the chair.

I estimated he had a four-day beard. These were the four days taken up by the latest expedition in search of our troops. His face seemed reddened, burned by the sun. Carefully, I began to prepare the soap. I cut off a few slices, dropped them into the cup, mixed in a bit of warm water, and began to stir with the brush. Immediately the foam began to rise. "The other boys in the group should have this much beard, too," he said. I continued stirring the lather.

"But we did all right, you know. We got the main ones. We brought back some dead, and we've got some others still alive. But pretty soon they'll all be dead."

"How many did you catch?" I asked.

"Fourteen. We had to go pretty deep into the woods to find them. But we'll get even. Not one of them comes out of this alive, not one." He leaned back on the chair when he saw me with the lather-covered brush in my hand. I still had to put the sheet on him. No doubt about it, I was upset. I took a sheet out of a drawer and knotted it around my customer's neck. He wouldn't stop talking, He probably thought I was in sympathy with his party.

"The town must have learned a lesson from what we did the other day," he said.

"Yes," I replied, securing the knot at his dark, sweaty neck.

"That was a fine show, eh?"

"Very good," I answered, turning back

for the brush. The man closed his eyes with a gesture of fatigue and sat waiting for the cool caress of the soap. I had never had him so close to me. The day he ordered the whole town to file into the patio of the school to see the four rebels hanging there, I came face-to-face with him for an instant. But the sight of the mutilated bodies kept me from noticing the face of the man who had directed it all, the face I was now about to take into my hands. It was not an unpleasant face, certainly. And the beard, which made him seem a bit older than he was, didn't suit him badly at all. His name was Torres. Captain Torres. A man of imagination, because who else would have thought of hanging the naked rebels and then holding target practice on their bodies?

I began to apply the first layer of soap. With his eyes closed, he continued. "Without any effort I could go straight to sleep," he said, "but there's plenty to do this afternoon." I stopped the lathering and asked with a feigned lack of interest: "A firing squad?" "Something like that, but a little slower." I got on with the job of lathering his beard. My hands started trembling again. The man could not possibly realize it, and this was in my favor. But I would have preferred that he hadn't come. It was likely that many of our faction had seen him enter. And an enemy under one's roof imposes certain conditions. I would be obliged to shave that beard like any other one, carefully, gently, like that of any customer, taking pains to see that no single pore emitted a drop of blood. I had to be careful that the little tufts of hair did not lead the blade astray.

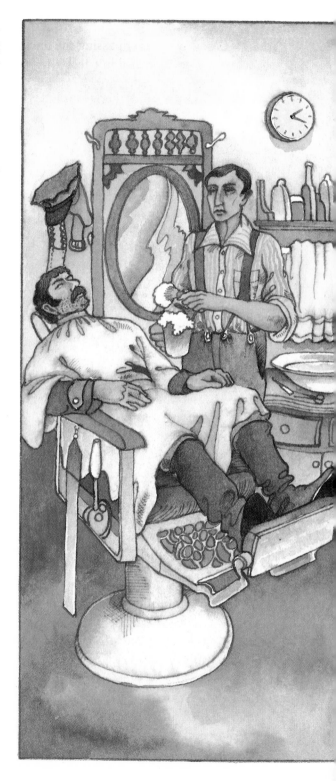

I had to see that his skin ended up clean, soft, and healthy, so that passing the back of my hand over it I couldn't feel a hair. Yes, I was secretly a rebel, but I was also a conscientious barber, and proud of the preciseness of my profession. And this four days' growth of beard was a fitting challenge.

I took the razor, opened up the two protective arms, exposed the blade, and began the job, from one of the sideburns downward. The razor responded beautifully. His beard was inflexible and hard, not too long, but thick. Bit by bit the skin emerged. The razor rasped along, making its customary sound as fluffs of lather mixed with bits of hair gathered along the blade. I paused a moment to clean it, then took up the strop again to sharpen the razor, because I'm a barber who does things properly. The man, who had kept his eyes closed, opened them now, removed one of his hands from under the sheet, felt the spot on his face where the soap had been cleared off, and said, "Come to the school today at six o'clock." "The same thing as the other day?" I asked, horrified. "It could be better," he replied. "What do you plan to do?" "I don't know yet. But we'll amuse ourselves." Once more he leaned back and closed his eyes. I approached him with the razor poised. "Do you plan to punish them all?" I ventured timidly.

"All."

The soap was drying on his face. I had to hurry. In the mirror I looked toward the street. It was the same as ever: the grocery store with two or three customers in it. Then I glanced at the clock: two-twenty in the afternoon. The razor continued on its downward stroke. Now from the other sideburn down. He had a thick, blue beard. He should have let it grow like some poets or priests do. It would suit him well. A lot of people wouldn't recognize him. That would be much to his benefit, I thought, as I attempted to cover the neck area smoothly. There, for sure, the razor had to be handled masterfully, since the hair, although softer, grew into little swirls. He had a curly beard. One of the tiny pores could be opened up and issue forth its pearl of blood. A good barber such as I prides himself on never allowing this to happen to a client. And this was a first-class client. How many of us had he ordered shot? How many of us had he ordered mutilated? It was better not to think about it. Torres did not know that I was his enemy. He did not know it nor did the rest. It was a secret shared by very few, precisely so that I could inform the revolutionaries of what Torres was doing in the town and of what he was planning each time he undertook a rebel-hunting excursion. So it was going to be very difficult to explain that I had him right in my hands and let him go peacefully — alive and shaved.

The beard was now almost completely gone. He seemed younger, less burdened by years than when he had arrived. I suppose this always happens with men who visit barbershops. Under the stroke of my razor, Torres was being rejuvenated — rejuvenated because I am a good barber, the best in the town, if I may say so. I dab a little more lather here, under his chin, on his Adam's apple, on this big vein. How hot it is getting! Torres must be sweating as much as I. But he is not afraid. He is a calm man, who is not even thinking about what he is going to do with the prisoners this afternoon. On the other hand, I, with this razor in my hand, stroking and restroking this skin, trying to keep blood from oozing from these pores, can't even think clearly. Curse him for coming, because I'm a revolutionary and not a murderer. And how easy it would be to kill him. And he deserves it. Does he? No! What the devil! No one deserves to have someone else make the sacrifice of becoming a murderer. What do you gain by it? Nothing. Others come along and still others, and the first ones kill the second ones, and they the next ones, and it goes on like this until everything is a sea of blood. I could cut this throat just so, zip! zip! I wouldn't give him time to complain, and since he has his eyes closed he wouldn't see the glistening knife blade or my glistening eyes. But I'm trembling like a real murderer. Out of his neck a gush of blood would spout onto the sheet, on the chair, on my hands, on the floor. I would have to close the door. And the blood would keep inching along the floor, warm, ineradicable, uncontainable, until it reached the street, like a little scarlet stream. I'm sure that one solid stroke, one deep incision would prevent any pain. He wouldn't suffer. But what would I do with the body? Where would I hide it? I would have to flee, leaving all I have behind, and take refuge far away, far, far away. But they would follow until they found me. "Captain Torres's murderer. He slit his throat while he was shaving him — a coward." And then on the other side: "The avenger of us all. A name to remember. [And here they would mention my name.] He was the town barber. No one knew he was defending our cause."

And what of all this? Murderer or hero? My destiny depends on the edge of this blade. I can turn my hand a bit more, press a little harder on the razor, and sink it in. The skin would give way like silk, like rubber, like the strop. There is nothing more tender than human skin and the blood is always there, ready to pour forth. A blade like this doesn't fail. It is my best. But I don't want to be a murderer, no sir. You came to me for a shave. And I perform my work honorably. . . . I don't want blood on my hands. Just lather, that's all. You are an executioner and I am only a barber. Each person has his own place in the scheme of things. That's right. His own place.

Now his chin had been stroked clean and smooth. The man sat up and looked into the mirror. He rubbed his hands over his skin and felt it fresh, like new.

"Thanks," he said. He went to the hanger for his belt, pistol, and cap. I must have been very pale; my shirt felt soaked. Torres finished adjusting the buckle, and straightened his pistol in the holster. From his pants pocket he took out several coins to pay me for my services. And he began to head toward the door. In the doorway he paused for a moment, and turning to me he said:

"They told me that you'd kill me. I came to find out. But killing isn't easy. You can take my word for it." And he headed on down the street.

READING COMPREHENSION

Summarizing. Choose the best phrase to complete each sentence. Then write the complete statements on your paper.

1. When Captain Torres came into the shop, the barber was _____ (pleased, calm, nervous).

2. The barber helped the rebels by _____ (finding out about Torres' plans, fighting Torres' men, finally killing Torres).

3. At the end of the story, Captain Torres revealed that he _____ (had come to kill the barber, knew that the barber was a revolutionary, had decided to join the rebels).

Interpreting. Write the answer to each question on your paper.

1. How did the barber show that he took pride in his work?

2. Why was the barber upset when Captain Torres told him about catching the rebels?

3. Why did the barber wish Captain Torres hadn't come for a shave?

4. What stopped the barber from killing Captain Torres?

For Thinking and Discussing. How do you think the barber felt when Captain Torres said: "They told me that you'd kill me"? What did Captain Torres reveal about himself by coming to the barber?

UNDERSTANDING LITERATURE

Theme and Character. A writer often develops a story's theme through the main character. By focusing on the character's thoughts, words, and actions, the reader understands that this character's life is meant to illustrate an idea or message about life in general.

In "Just Lather, That's All," the theme is expressed through the barber's way of looking at life. The theme is stated directly when the barber says: "Each person has his own place in the scheme of things."

Below are some other statements from the story. On your paper, write the statements that point to the story's theme.

1. "Yes, I was secretly a rebel, but I was also a conscientious barber, and proud of the preciseness of my profession."

2. "No one deserves to have someone else make the sacrifice of becoming a murderer."

3. "He is a calm man, who is not even thinking about what he is going to do this afternoon."

4. "I don't want blood on my hands. Just lather, that's all."

5. "'But killing isn't easy. You can take my word for it.'"

WRITING

Write a paragraph in which you either attack or defend the story's theme. Illustrate your point with examples.

Section Review

VOCABULARY

Connotation and Denotation. Every word in a story, poem, or play can be important. A word may have two kinds of meanings: a denotative, objective meaning and a connotative meaning with emotional overtones. For example, the words *bad* and *vicious* both denote something that is not good, but the word *vicious* has a more negative meaning than *bad*. A writer would choose the word *vicious* to make an emotional impact on the reader. A word with a strong emotional connotation can help a writer make an image more vivid or a character more real.

The numbered sentences below are from the selections in this section. On your paper, answer the following questions about each italicized word or phrase. Use a dictionary, if necessary. What is the word's denotative, or objective, meaning? What is the word's connotative, or emotional, meaning?

1. "The old banker was *pacing* from corner to corner of his study."
2. "Now you have written this *vile* letter saying she's not to come!"
3. "I had forgotten about the *profusion* of fruit in India. . . ."
4. "He kept his head down and his fingers *clenched* tight upon the paper bag."

READING

Fact and Opinion. It is important to be able to recognize the difference between fact and opinion in what you read. A *fact* is a statement that can be proven to be true. Here is an example of a fact: "Santha Rama Rau was born in India." An *opinion* is a statement of an individual's personal views or feelings. Here is an example of an opinion: "The Soviet Union has a better form of government than India."

The following statements are from or about the selections you have read in this section. Identify each statement as either a fact or an opinion. Write your answers on your paper.

1. Capital punishment is more moral and humane than life imprisonment.
2. Cherry trees in blossom are the loveliest of all trees.
3. The man in the water risked his life in order to save the lives of others.
4. The passengers who survived the crash of Flight 90 were selfish and uncaring about their fellow passengers.
5. *Iphigenia* is a play that takes place in ancient Greece.
6. There are many flowers in India because it is a tropical country with a warm climate.
7. A nursing home is the best place for old people.
8. Many nations have been torn by civil war.

474

WRITING

An Opinion. An opinion is an expression of a person's feelings and beliefs. Whenever you say you like or dislike something, you are expressing your opinion, or point of view. Sometimes your opinions agree with the views of others, and sometimes they are different. A respected opinion is one that is well thought out. Someone who gives an opinion without providing reasons to back it up is not likely to be taken very seriously.

Step 1: Set Your Goal

The topic you choose for an opinion paper should be one you are interested in and feel strongly about. Your readers won't take your opinion seriously if you don't take it seriously yourself. You should be familiar enough with the topic to be able to provide several good reasons to support your point of view.

Choose one of the following topics for an opinion paper:

1. Think about how Agamemnon planned to sacrifice his daughter in *Iphigenia*. Tell why you agree or disagree with his willingness to sacrifice her and with the way he planned to get her to come to the sacrificial altar.

2. Think about why the old man in "With All Flags Flying" decided to live in a home. Tell why you agree or disagree with his choice.

3. Tell why you agree or disagree with the way the barber handled the situation with Captain Torres in "Just Lather, That's All."

Once you have chosen a topic, focus your opinion by writing a clear and concise statement of your point of view. For example, if you were writing about Santha Rama Rau's essay "Return to India," you might focus your opinion with the following statement: I agree (or disagree) with the author that India is a better place to live than Russia.

Step 2: Make a Plan

Begin gathering information for your paper by jotting down your reasons for having your opinion. Then write down facts or examples that support your reasons. Refer to the selection, if necessary, to find details that support your opinion. Also, think about the objections or counterarguments your readers might make. Make a list of the objections you think might be raised, and then write your response to each.

Next, look over your list of reasons and decide which are the strongest. Eliminate any reasons that do not present your point of view convincingly. Rewrite your list of reasons in the order of their importance, with the most important point either first or last. That is, arrange the points in either descending or ascending order of importance.

Step 3: Write a First Draft

As you write your first draft, use your list of reasons as a guide, and ask yourself the following questions: Why do I have the opinions I have? What effect do I want to have on my readers? What attitudes and reactions do I want my readers to have? Begin your paper with an introduction that states your opinion and provides the reader with any background information you think necessary. Then present your reasons, and give facts and examples that support your opinion. Raise possible objections, and give your response to each. End your paper with a conclusion that restates your opinion.

Step 4: Revise

The revise stage gives you a chance to take a critical look at what you have written and decide whether or not you have achieved your goal. If possible, set your paper aside for a few days before you begin working on it again. It is easier to spot changes you should make after some time has passed. Refer to the following checklist as you revise:

☐ Do your ideas flow logically from one to the other?

☐ Does each idea support your opinion?

☐ Have you used the best possible words to express your thoughts?

☐ Did you begin with an introductory paragraph that clearly states your opinion?

☐ Did you end with a concluding paragraph that restates your point of view?

After you have revised the content, sentence structure, and organization of your work, proofread it carefully for errors in spelling, grammar, and punctuation. Then make a final copy.

QUIZ

The following is a quiz for Section 8. Write the answers in complete sentences on your paper.

Reading Comprehension

1. In "The Bet," what were the terms of the lawyer's imprisonment?

2. Who were the four heroes of the plane crash described in "The Man in the Water"?

3. Which two main characters other than Agamemnon wanted to save Iphigenia's life in *Iphigenia*? What were their reasons?

4. In "Return to India," what were two examples the author gave of censorship in the Soviet Union?

5. In "With All Flags Flying," how was the man's roommate in the nursing home different from him?

Understanding Literature

6. Describe how the themes of "The Man in the Water" and *Iphigenia* were similar.

7. Describe the theme of "Loveliest of Trees."

8. What method did the author of "Return to India" use to express her views?

9. What did the old man in "With All Flags Flying" gain by making his choice to go to an old folk's home? What did he lose?

10. What was the conflict that the barber in "Just Lather, That's All" had to face? How did he finally resolve his conflict?

ACTIVITIES

Word Attack. In "The Man in the Water," you read, "The man in the water pitted himself against an implacable, impersonal enemy. . . ." The words *implacable* and *impersonal* both begin with the prefix *im-*, meaning "not." The word *implacable* means "not placable," or "not able to be calmed." *Impersonal* means "not personal." List five other words with the prefix *im-*, and write the meaning of each. Then use each word in a sentence of your own. Use a dictionary if you need help.

Speaking and Listening

1. "The Bet" opens with the old banker recalling a party he had given 15 years ago. The people at the party had argued the issue of capital punishment versus life imprisonment. Choose a partner with whom to debate this issue. One of you should argue for capital punishment. The other should argue against capital punishment and for life imprisonment. Take some time to prepare your arguments. Then present a short debate for the class.

2. In Greek tragedy, the chorus provides background information, describes offstage action, gives plot summaries, and so forth. The role of the chorus is usually performed by several people speaking in unison. Get together with several classmates and practice reading the part of the chorus in the play *Iphigenia*. Be prepared to present your reading to the class.

Researching

1. The play *Iphigenia* was written about 2,500 years ago by the Greek writer Euripides. Do some research to find out what we know about this great writer. Where was he born? What do we know about his life? How many plays did he write? How many were tragedies? What are the names of some of his plays? How were his plays different from other Greek tragedies of the time? What useful purpose did his plays perform? Be prepared to present your findings to the class.

2. In the story "Return to India," the author Santha Rama Rau talks fondly about the country of her birth. India is a very ancient country with a history that dates back at least 4,500 years. Do some research on the history of India. What were its earliest origins? When was its "Golden Age"? Who have been its invaders over the centuries? When did the British colonize India? When did it gain its independence? Who were some important figures in India's history? Write up your findings in a report to share with the class.

Creating. Choose an elderly person you know. Describe the person in several paragraphs. Write about the person's character and present situation in life. Use your knowledge of the person's past and his or her attitudes toward life to create an individual portrait of the person, like the portrait of the man in "With All Flags Flying."

THE UNKNOWN

There was a Door to which I found no Key;
There was a Veil through which I might not see.

—Omar Khayyam
Persia

Form and Light, Motive in Western New Jersey
Oscar Bluemner (1867-1938)
Hunter Museum of Art, Chattanooga
Gift of the Benwood Foundation

The Unknown

Writers have always been fascinated by the feelings and experiences that can't be explained. Sometimes their stories try to analyze these mysteries. At other times, their stories make you see something ordinary in a new and mysterious light. Sometimes, in tales of the unknown, writers are just trying to scare you.

Mysterious Appearances

Many reports exist of ghostly appearances, "people" who aren't really there. Do these things really happen? Whether they do or don't, tales about ghosts and spirits are found all over the world. In these stories, the teller is always careful to create *suspense* (the excitement of knowing there is a secret; the nervous curiosity that keeps you turning the pages).

Charles Dickens, one of the most popular British writers, probably knew and understood his society better than anyone else. But sometimes he explored areas that no one can know or understand. In his story "The Signal-Man," a ghostly figure appears on the railroad tracks again and again. Each time it appears, some disaster occurs. When the ghost appears once more, suspense is created. You know there is danger on the tracks. But what danger? And to whom? You may not be able to sleep after you finish this eerie tale.

The Future

The future has interested many writers. In the 19th century, Jules Verne and H. G. Wells started a new form of literature we call science fiction. Science-fiction stories stretch our imaginations to another time—and sometimes they make us think about present-day life in a new way.

Herbert Goldstone's story "Virtuoso" tells about a robot that can learn anything explained to it. But aren't some things impossible to explain? How would you explain music to a robot? This story asks you to think not only about the possibilities of the future, but also about the meaning of something we live with every day. Which is really more remarkable—a robot that can learn anything, or music's ability to affect our feelings? Perhaps, after all, some of life's most basic things really are the most mysterious.

A story from Italy entitled "Mirrors" also makes us look at something ordinary in a new way. What really happens when you look in a mirror? Could you lose your reflection if you turned away too quickly? Be careful the next time you glance in a shop window as you pass.

The Greatest Unknown

Death is one of life's deepest mysteries. For centuries, writers have intrigued and

The Nightwind, *Charles Burchfield, 1918*

frightened readers with their attempts to understand death.

In many old folktales, death appears in the form of a person who takes victims away. This old theme occurs in a modern story written in the simple style of one of these ancient tales: The events in W. Somerset Maugham's story "An Appointment in Samarra" are not realistic; they are fantasy, clearly the product of human imagination. Yet this fable points out one of the truths of real life—none of us, no matter what we do, can escape death.

Another story about death, "The Vam-

pire" by Jan Neruda, begins in a very ordinary way, describing pleasant events and beautiful places. This is part of Neruda's plan to scare you. Because of the calm tone of the story's beginning, the ending comes as a greater shock. But writers have always known that many readers love a shock, a chill, the thrill of the unknown.

The final selection is a gentle poem by a man who has created worlds of fantasy: J. R. R. Tolkien. "The Old Walking Song" is about enchanting possibilities and unknown places.

The Signal-Man

by Charles Dickens

Charles Dickens, born in 1812 to a hard, unhappy child-hood, grew up to become a highly successful and widely loved novelist. He wrote David Copperfield, Oliver Twist, *and many other long novels full of comedy, suffering, and comment on social conditions of his time. As you will see, he could also spin a chilling ghost story.*

"Halloa! Below there!"

When the signal-man heard my call to him, he was standing at the door of his box. The flag in his hand was furled around its short pole. He could not have doubted from where my voice came. Yet, instead of looking up to where I stood, he turned around and looked down the Line. There was something odd in his manner of doing so. It was odd enough for me to notice, even though I was high above him. The glow of an angry sunset was so strong that I had shaded my eyes with my hand before I saw him at all.

"Halloa! Below!"

From looking down the Line, he turned around again. He raised his eyes and saw my figure high above him.

"Is there any path by which I can come down and speak to you?"

He looked up at me without replying. I looked down at him without pressing him too soon for an answer. Just then the earth and air vibrated and an oncoming rush caused me to start back as though it had force to draw me down. A rapid train had passed. When it was skimming away over the landscape, I looked down again. I saw him refurling the flag he had shown while the train went by.

I repeated my question. After a pause, he motioned with his rolled-up flag toward a point on my level. I called down to him, "All right!" and made for that point. There I found a rough zigzag path notched out, which I followed.

When I came down low enough to see him again, I saw that he was standing between the rails on the way by which the train had passed. He looked as if he were waiting for me to appear. He had his left hand at his chin, and that left elbow rested on his right hand, crossed over his breast. His attitude was one of such expectation and watchfulness that I stopped a moment, wondering at it.

I went on my downward way. When I drew nearer to him, I saw that he was a dark man, with a dark beard and rather heavy eyebrows. His post was lonely and dismal. On either side was a dripping-wet wall of jagged stone. The only view was a strip of sky. In one direction, one sees only the winding tracks. In the other direction is a gloomy red light, and the gloomier entrance to a black tunnel. So little sunlight ever found its way to this spot that it had an earthy, deadly smell. So much cold wind rushed through it that it struck chill to me. I felt as if I had left the natural world.

Before he stirred, I was near enough to him to have touched him. Not even then removing his eyes from mine, he stepped back one step, and lifted his hand.

"This must be a lonesome post," I said. "A visitor is a rarity, I should suppose. I hope I am not an unwelcome rarity." Thus I spoke to him. But something in the man frightened me.

He looked toward the red light near the tunnel's mouth. He looked all about it, as if something were missing from it. Then he looked at me.

"That light is part of your charge, isn't it?" I asked.

He answered in a low voice, "Don't you know it is?"

The monstrous thought came into my mind — that this was a spirit, not a man. I stepped back. But in making the action, I saw fear in his eyes. This put the monstrous thought to flight.

"You look at me," I said, forcing a smile, "as if you were afraid of me."

"I was doubtful," he answered, "whether I had seen you before."

"Where?"

He pointed to the red light he had looked at.

"There?" I said.

He replied but without sound, "Yes."

"My good fellow, what should I do there? However, be that as it may, I never was there."

His manner cleared, like my own. He replied to my remarks with readiness, and in well-chosen words. Had he much to do there? To change that signal, to trim those lights, and to turn this iron handle now and then, was all he had to do. Regarding those many long and lonely hours, he could only say he had grown used to it.

He took me into his box, where there was a fire, a desk for a book in which he had to make certain entries, a telegraph, and an electric bell, which called him now and then. He seemed to have been well educated. He said he had been a student; but he had run wild, gone down, and never risen again. He had no complaint to offer about that. He had made his bed, and he lay upon it. It was far too late to make another.

He spoke in a quiet manner, with his attention divided between me and the fire. He was several times interrupted by the little bell. Then he read off messages, and sent replies. Once he had to stand outside the door, and display a flag as a train passed. In doing his job, he was remarkably exact and alert. He broke off his speech at a syllable, and remained silent until what he had to do was done.

I should have set this man down as one of the safest men in this job. Yet twice he broke off, turned his face toward the little bell when it did NOT ring. Then he opened the door of the hut, and looked out toward the red light near the mouth of the tunnel.

On both of these instances, he came back to the fire with an odd air about him.

Said I, when I rose to leave him, "You almost make me think that I have met with a contented man."

"I believe I used to be so," he said, in a low voice in which he had first spoken; "but I am troubled, sir, I am troubled."

"With what? What is your trouble?"

"It is very difficult to say, sir. It is very, very difficult to speak of. If ever you make me another visit, I will try to tell you."

"But I intend to make you another visit. Say, when shall it be?"

"I go off early in the morning, and I shall be on again at 10 tomorrow night, sir."

"I will come at 11."

He thanked me, and went out the door with me. "I'll show my white light, sir," he said in his peculiar low voice, "till you have found the way up. When you have found it, don't call out! And when you are at the top, don't call out!"

His manner seemed to make the place colder to me, but I said no more than, "Very well."

"And when you come down tomorrow night, don't call out! Let me ask you a parting question. What made you cry, 'Halloa! Below there!' tonight?"

"Heaven knows," said I. "I cried something to that effect —"

"Not to that effect, sir. Those were the very words. I know them well."

"Yes, those were the very words. I said them, no doubt, because I saw you below."

"For no other reason?"

"What other reason could I possibly have?"

"You had no feeling that they were conveyed to you in any supernatural way?"

"No."

He wished me good night, and held up his light. I walked by the side of the line of rails. (I had the unpleasant feeling that a train was coming behind me.) Finally I found the path. It was easier to go up than to go down, and I got back to my inn without any trouble.

Punctual to my appointment, I placed my foot on the first notch of the zigzag next night, as the distant clocks were striking 11. He was waiting for me at the bottom, with his white light on.

"I have not called out," I said as we came close. "May I speak now?"

"By all means, sir." With that, we walked side by side to his box, entered it, closed the door, and sat down by the fire.

"I have made up my mind, sir," he began, "that you shall not have to ask me twice what troubles me. I took you for someone else yesterday evening. That troubles me."

"That mistake?"

"No. That — someone else."

"Who is it?"

"I don't know."

"Like me?"

"I don't know. I never saw the face. The left arm is across the face, and the right arm is waved — violently waved. This way."

I followed his action with my eyes. The action of an arm that seemed to say, "For God's sake, clear the way!"

"One moonlit night," said the man, "I was sitting here, when I heard a voice cry,

'Halloa! Below there!' I started up, looked from that door. I saw this — someone standing by the red light near the tunnel. He was waving as I just showed you. The voice seemed hoarse with shouting. It cried, 'Look out! Look out!' And then again, 'Halloa! Below there! Look out!' I caught up my lamp, turned it on red, and ran toward the figure, calling, 'What's wrong? What has happened? Where?' It just stood — just outside the blackness of the tunnel. I came so close upon it that I wondered at its keeping the sleeve across its eyes. I ran right up at it and had my hand stretched out to pull the sleeve away, when it was gone."

"Into the tunnel?" said I.

"No. I ran on into the tunnel, 500 yards. I stopped, and held my lamp above my head. I saw nothing but wet stains stealing down the walls and trickling through the arch. I ran out again faster than I had run in, and looked all around. I telegraphed both ways, 'An alarm has been given. Is anything wrong?' The answer came back, both ways, 'All well.' "

I tried to show him how his eyes could have been fooled. "As to an imaginary cry," said I, "do but listen for a moment to the wind in this valley while we speak so low, and to the wild harp it makes of the telegraph wires."

That was all very well, he said, and he ought to know something of the wind and the wires — he who so often passed long winter nights there, alone and watching. He begged that he had not finished.

He slowly added these words, touching my arm. "Within six hours after the — appearance, a terrible accident happened on this Line. Within 10 hours, the dead and wounded were brought through the tunnel over the spot where the figure had stood."

A disagreeable shudder crept over me, but I did my best against it. It was not to be denied, I remarked, that such coincidences did continually occur.

He again begged that he had not finished.

I apologized for interrupting.

"This," he said, again laying his hand upon my arm, and glancing over his shoulder with hollow eyes, "was just a year ago. Six or seven months passed, and I had recovered from the surprise and shock. Then one morning, as the day was breaking — I, standing at the door, looked toward the red light, and saw the ghost again." He stopped, with a fixed look at me.

"Did it cry out?"

"No. It was silent."

"Did it wave its arm?"

"No. It leaned against the shaft of the light, with both hands before the face. Like this."

Once more, I followed his action with my eyes. It was an action of mourning. I have seen such an attitude in stone figures on tombs.

"Did you go up to it?"

"I came in and sat down, partly to collect my thoughts, partly because it had turned me faint. When I went to the door again, daylight was above me, and the ghost was gone."

"But nothing followed? Nothing came of this?"

"That very day, as a train came out of

the tunnel, I noticed, at a window on my side, what looked like a disturbance and — something waved. I saw it just in time to signal the driver, 'Stop!' He shut off, and put his brake on. But the train drifted past here 150 yards or more. I ran after it. As I went along, I heard terrible screams and cries. A beautiful young lady had died suddenly in one of the compartments. She was brought in here, and laid down on this floor between us."

I could think of nothing to say. My mouth was very dry. The wind and the wires took up the story with a long, lamenting wail.

He resumed. "Now, sir, mark this, and judge how my mind is troubled. The ghost came back a week ago. Ever since, it has been there, now and again, by fits and starts."

"At the light?"

"At the danger-light."

"What does it seem to do?"

He repeated that former action of, 'For God's sake, clear the way!'

Then he went on: "I have no peace or rest for it. It calls to me, 'Below there! Look out! Look out!' It stands waving to me. It rings my little bell — "

I caught at that. "Did it ring your bell yesterday evening when I was here, and you went to the door?"

"Twice."

"Why, see," said I, "how your imagination misleads you. My eyes were on the bell, and my ears were open to the bell, and if I am a living man, it did NOT ring at those times."

He shook his head. "I have never made a mistake as to that yet, sir. I have never confused the ghost's ring with the man's. The ghost's ring is a strange vibration. The bell does not stir to the eye. I don't wonder that you failed to hear it. But I heard it."

"And did the ghost seem to be there when you looked out?"

"It WAS there."

"Both times?"

He repeated firmly, "Both times."

"Will you come to the door with me and look for it now?"

He bit his under lip, as though he were somewhat unwilling, but got up. I opened the door, and stood on the step, while he stood in the doorway. There was the danger-light. There was the dismal mouth of the tunnel. There were the high, wet stone walls of the cutting. There were the stars above them.

"Do you see it?" I asked him.

"No," he answered. "It is not there."

"Agreed," said I.

We went in again. I shut the door, and we resumed our seats. "By this time, you will fully understand, sir," he said, "what troubles me so dreadfully. What does the ghost mean?"

I was not sure, I told him, that I did fully understand.

"What is its warning against?" he said. "What is the danger? Where is the danger? There is danger overhanging somewhere on the Line. It is not to be doubted this third time, after what has gone before. But surely this is a cruel haunting of me. What can I do?"

He pulled out his handkerchief, and wiped the drops from his heated forehead.

"If I telegraph — Danger, on either side

of me, or on both, I can give no reason for it," he went on, wiping the palms of his hands. "I should get into trouble, and do no good. They would think I was mad. This is the way it would work — Message: 'Danger! Take care!' Answer: 'What — Danger? Where?' Message: 'Don't know. But for God's sake, take care!' They would displace me. What else could they do?"

His pain of mind was most pitiable to see. It was the mental torture of a conscientious man.

"When it first stood under the danger-light," he went on, "why not tell me where that accident was to happen — if it must happen? Why not tell me how it could be avoided — if it could be avoided? When on the second coming it hid its face, why not tell me, instead, 'She is going to die. Let them keep her at home'? If it came, on those occasions, only to show me that its warnings were true, and so to prepare me for the third, why not warn me plainly now? And I, Lord help me! A mere poor signal-man on this lonely station! Why not go to somebody with credit to be believed, and power to act?"

For the poor man's sake, as well as for the public's safety, I felt that what I had to do for the time was to compose his mind. Therefore, I set aside all question of reality and unreality between us. I told him that at least he understood his duty, though he did not understand these — appearances. In this effort, I succeeded far better than in the attempt to reason him out of his belief. He became calm. His tasks were beginning to make larger demands on his attention. I left him at two

in the morning. I had offered to stay through the night, but he would not hear of it.

That I more than once looked back at the red light as I went up the pathway, I

see no reason to hide. That I did not like the two sequences of the accident and the dead girl, I see no reason to hide that either.

But what ran most in my thoughts was the consideration of how I ought to act, knowing all this. I had proved the man to be intelligent, alert, and exact. But how long might he remain so, in his state of mind? Though in a low position, still he held a most important trust. Would I like to stake my own life on the chances of his continuing to do his job with precision?

I felt that it would be wrong to tell his superiors in the company, without first proposing a middle course to him. I thought of offering to accompany him to the wisest doctor for an opinion. A change in his time of duty would come the next night, he told me. He would be off an hour or two after sunrise, and on again soon after sunset. I had planned to return then.

Next evening was a lovely evening. I walked out early to enjoy it. The sun was not yet quite down when I reached the path near the top of the deep cutting. I would extend my walk for an hour, I said to myself. Half an hour on and half an hour back, then it would be time to go to my signal-man's box.

Before starting my walk, I stepped to the brink and looked down. I cannot describe the chill that seized me when, close at the mouth of the tunnel, I saw the appearance of a man, with his left sleeve across his eyes, passionately waving his right arm.

The nameless horror passed in a moment. I saw that this appearance of a man was a man indeed. He seemed to be rehearsing the gesture to a little group of other men. The danger-light was not yet lighted. Against its shaft, a little low hut had been made of some wood and cloth. It looked no bigger than a bed.

I had a terrible sense that something was wrong. I felt a flashing fear that an accident had happened because I left the man there, and didn't try to have someone oversee or correct what he did. Then I went down the path with all the speed I could make.

"What is the matter?" I asked the men.

"Signal-man killed this morning, sir."

"Not the man belonging to that box?"

"Yes, sir."

"You will recognize him, sir, if you knew him," said the man who spoke for the others, "for his face is quite composed."

"Oh, how did this happen?" I asked, turning from one to another.

"He was struck by an engine, sir. No man in England knew his work better. But somehow he was not clear of the outer rail. It was just at broad day. He had struck the light, and had the lamp in his hand. As the engine came out of the tunnel, his back was toward the train — and he was hit. The man who drove the engine can show you how it happened. Show the gentleman, Tom."

The man who wore rough dark clothes stepped back to his former place at the mouth of the tunnel.

"Coming round the curve in the tunnel, sir," he said, "I saw him at the end. There was no time to check speed, and I knew him to be very careful. He didn't seem to hear the whistle, so I shut it off when we were running down upon him. Instead I called to him as loud as I could call."

"What did you say?"

"I said, 'Below there! Look out! For God's sake, clear the way!'"

I started.

"Ah! It was a dreadful time, sir. I never stopped calling to him. I put this arm before my eyes not to see. I waved this arm to the last. But it was no use."

READING COMPREHENSION

Summarizing. Choose the best phrase to complete each sentence. Then write the complete statements on your paper.

1. After the ghost's first appearance, there was a _____ (terrible train accident, violent storm, murder committed).

2. After the ghost's second appearance, _____ (another train was wrecked, a young woman died on the train, the train's conductor jumped onto the tracks).

3. The signal-man died when he _____ (saw the ghost again, tried to save a dying passenger, was struck by a train).

Interpreting. Write the answer to each question on your paper.

1. Who did the signal-man think the narrator was when he first saw him?

2. What was troubling the mind of the signal-man?

3. Did the narrator ever see the ghost?

4. How did the ghost predict the signal-man's accidental death?

For Thinking and Discussing.

1. What possible logical explanation can you give for the events in the story?

2. How might the signal-man have been saved?

UNDERSTANDING LITERATURE

Suspense. *Suspense* is a state of anticipation, uncertainty, and curiosity about the outcome of a story. Writers build suspense in their descriptions of the setting, characters, and action.

Read the following quotes. Identify each on your paper as a description of (a) character, (b) setting, or (c) action. Then explain how each builds suspense.

1. "So little sunlight ever found its way to this spot that it had an earthy, deadly smell. So much cold wind rushed through it that it struck chill to me."

2. "The monstrous thought came into my mind — that this was a spirit, not a man. I stepped back. But in making the action, I saw fear in his eyes."

3. "Within six hours after the — appearance, a terrible accident happened on this Line. Within 10 hours, the dead and wounded were brought through the tunnel over the spot where the figure had stood."

4. "'But surely this is a cruel haunting of me. What can I do?' He pulled out his handkerchief, and wiped the drops from his heated forehead."

WRITING

Continue the story by having the ghost appear to the narrator and predict the narrator's death. Create a suspenseful mood in your story.

Virtuoso

by Herbert Goldstone

In this story about the unknown world of the future, Herbert Goldstone asks: Could a robot become a better musician than a human being?

"**S**ir?"

The maestro continued to play, not looking up from the keys.

"Yes, Rollo?"

"Sir, I was wondering if you would explain this machine to me."

The maestro stopped playing, his thin body stiffly relaxed on the bench. His long fingers floated off the keyboard.

"Machine?" He turned and smiled at the robot. "Do you mean the piano, Rollo?"

"This machine that produces varying sounds. I would like some information about it, its operation and purpose. It is not included in my reference data."

The maestro lit a cigarette. He preferred to do it himself. One of his first orders to Rollo, when the robot was delivered two days before, had been to ignore his built-in instructions on the subject.

"I'd hardly call a piano a machine, Rollo," he smiled, "although technically you are correct. It is actually, I suppose, a machine designed to produce sounds."

"I learned that much by observation," Rollo replied in a brassy baritone that no longer sent tiny shivers up the maestro's spine. "Wires of different thickness struck by felt-covered hammers."

"A very cold-blooded description of one of man's nobler works," the maestro remarked dryly. "You make Mozart and Chopin mere laboratory technicians."

"Mozart? Chopin?" The hard metal sphere that was Rollo's head shone. Its immediate surface was unbroken except for two vision lenses. "The terms are not included in my memory banks."

"No, not yours, Rollo," the maestro said softly. "Mozart and Chopin are not for vacuum tubes and fuses and copper wire. They are for flesh and blood and human tears."

"I do not understand," Rollo droned.

"Well," the maestro said, smoke curling lazily from his nostrils, "Mozart and Chopin are composers. Composers are humans who design sound patterns that can be played by the piano or by other instruments.

"Sometimes these instruments, as we call them, are played, or operated, individually; sometimes in groups — orchestras, we call them — and the sounds blend together, they harmonize. That is, they have an orderly, mathematical relationship to each other which results in . . ."

The maestro threw up his hands.

"I never imagined," he chuckled, "that I would some day struggle so hard to explain music to a robot!"

"Music?"

"Yes, Rollo. The sounds produced by this machine and others of the same category are called music."

"What is the purpose of music, sir?"

"Purpose?"

The maestro crushed the cigarette in an ashtray. He turned to the keyboard of the concert grand and flexed his fingers briefly.

"Listen, Rollo."

The maestro's fingers glided and wove the opening bars of "Clair de Lune," slender and delicate as spider silk. Rollo stood rigid. The fluorescent light over the music rack cast a bluish jeweled sheen over his towering bulk, and shimmered in his amber vision lenses.

The maestro drew his hands back from the keys and the subtle thread of melody melted into silence.

"Claude Debussy," the maestro said. "One of our mechanics of an era long past. He designed that succession of tones many years ago. What do you think of it?"

Rollo did not answer at once.

"The sounds were well formed," he replied finally. "They did not jar my auditory senses as some do."

The maestro laughed. "Rollo, you may not realize it, but you're a wonderful critic."

"This music, then," Rollo droned. "Its purpose is to give pleasure to humans?"

"Exactly," the maestro said. "Sounds well formed, that do not jar the auditory senses as some do. Marvelous! It should be carved in marble over the entrance of New Carnegie Hall."

"I do not understand. Why should my definition —?"

The maestro waved a hand. "No matter, Rollo. No matter."

"Sir?"

"Yes, Rollo?"

"Those sheets of paper you sometimes place before you on the piano. They are the plans of the composer indicating which sounds are to be produced by the piano and in what order?"

"Just so. We call each sound a note; combinations of notes we call chords."

"Each dot, then, indicates a sound to be made?"

"Perfectly correct, my man of metal."

Rollo stared straight ahead. The maestro felt a peculiar sense of wheels turning within that metal sphere.

"Sir, I have scanned my memory banks and find no specific or implied instructions against it. I should like to be taught how to produce these notes on the piano. I request that you feed the necessary information into my memory banks."

The maestro peered at him, amazed. A slow grin traveled across his face.

"Done!" he exclaimed. "It's been many years since I've had pupils. But I have the feeling that you, Rollo, will prove a most fascinating student. To teach music to metal and machinery. . . . I accept the challenge gladly!"

He rose, touched the cool power of Rollo's arm.

"Sit down here, my Rolleindex Personal Robot, Model M-e. We shall start Bee-

thoven spinning in his grave — or make musical history."

More than an hour later, the maestro yawned and looked at his watch.

"It's late," he spoke into the end of the yawn. "These old eyes are not tireless like yours, my friend." He touched Rollo's shoulder. "You have the complete fundamentals of musical notation in your memory banks, Rollo. That's a good night's lesson, particularly when I recall how long it took me to acquire the same amount of information. Tomorrow we'll attempt to

put those awesome fingers of yours to work."

He stretched. "I'm going to bed," he said. "Will you lock up and put out the lights?"

Rollo rose from the bench. "Yes, sir," he droned. "I have a request."

"What can I do for my star pupil?"

"May I attempt to create some sounds with the keyboard tonight? I will do so very softly so as not to disturb you."

"Tonight? Aren't you —?" Then the maestro smiled. "You must pardon me, Rollo. It's still a bit difficult for me to realize that sleep has no meaning for you."

He hesitated, rubbing his chin. "Well, I suppose a good teacher should not discourage impatience to learn. All right, Rollo, but please be careful." He patted the polished mahogany. "This piano and I have been together for many years. I'd hate to see its teeth knocked out by those sledgehammer fingers of yours. Lightly, my friend, very lightly."

"Yes, sir."

The maestro fell asleep with a faint smile on his lips, dimly aware of the shy, tentative notes that Rollo was coaxing forth.

Then gray fog closed in and he was in that half-world where reality is dreamlike and dreams are real. It was soft and feathery and lavender clouds and sounds were rolling and washing across his mind in flowing waves.

Where? The mist drew back a bit and he was in red velvet and deep and the music swelled and broke over him.

He smiled.

My recording. Thank you, thank —

The maestro snapped erect, threw the covers aside.

He sat on the edge of the bed, listening.

He groped for his robe in the darkness, shoved bony feet into his slippers.

He crept, trembling uncontrollably, to the door of his studio and stood there, thin and brittle in the robe.

The light over the music rack was an eerie island in the brown shadows of the studio. Rollo sat at the keyboard, inhuman, rigid, twin lenses focused somewhere off into the shadows.

The massive feet working the pedals, arms and hands flashing and glinting — they were living entities, separate, somehow, from the machined perfection of his body.

The music rack was empty.

A copy of Beethoven's "Appassionata" lay closed on the bench. It had been, the maestro remembered, in a pile of sheet music on the piano.

Rollo was playing it.

He was creating it, breathing it, drawing it through silver flame.

Time became meaningless, suspended in midair.

The maestro didn't realize he was weeping until Rollo finished the sonata.

The robot turned to look at the maestro. "The sounds," he droned. "They pleased you?"

The maestro's lips quivered. "Yes, Rollo," he replied at last. "They pleased me." He fought the lump in his throat.

He picked up the music in fingers that shook.

"This," he murmured. "Already?"

"It has been added to my store of data," Rollo replied. "I applied the principles you explained to me to these plans. It was not very difficult."

The maestro swallowed as he tried to speak. "It was not very difficult," he repeated softly.

The old man sank down slowly onto the bench next to Rollo, stared silently at the robot as though seeing him for the first time.

Rollo got to his feet.

The maestro let his fingers rest on the keys, strangely foreign now.

"Music!" he breathed. "I may have heard it that way in my soul. I know Beethoven did!"

He looked up at the robot, a growing excitement in his face.

"Rollo," he said, his voice straining to remain calm. "You and I have some work to do tomorrow on your memory banks."

Sleep did not come again that night.

He strode briskly into the studio the next morning. Rollo was vacuuming the carpet.

"Well, are you ready for work, Rollo?" he asked. "We have a lot to do, you and I. I have such plans for you, Rollo — great plans!"

Rollo, for once, did not reply.

"I have asked them all to come here this afternoon," the maestro went on. "Conductors, concert pianists, composers, my manager. All the giants of music, Rollo. Wait until they hear you play."

Rollo switched off the vacuum and stood quietly.

"You'll play for them right here this afternoon." The maestro's voice was high-pitched, breathless. "The 'Appassionata' again, I think. Yes, that's it. I must see their faces!

"Then we'll arrange a recital to introduce you to the public and the critics and then a major concerto with one of the big orchestras. We'll have it telecast around the world, Rollo. It can be arranged.

"Think of it, Rollo, just think of it! The greatest piano virtuoso of all time . . . a robot! It's completely fantastic and completely wonderful. I feel like an explorer at the edge of a new world."

He walked feverishly back and forth.

"Then recordings, of course. My entire repertoire, Rollo, and more. So much more!"

"Sir?"

The maestro's face shone as he looked up at him. "Yes, Rollo?"

"In my built-in instructions, I have the option of rejecting any action that I consider harmful to my owner," the robot's words were precise, carefully selected. "Last night you wept. That is one of the signs I am instructed to consider in making my decisions."

The maestro gripped Rollo's thick, superbly molded arm.

"Rollo, you don't understand. That was for the moment. It was silly of me, childish!"

"I beg your pardon, sir, but I must refuse to approach the piano again."

The maestro stared at him, unbelieving, pleading.

"Rollo, you can't! The world must hear you!"

"No, sir." The amber lenses almost seemed to soften.

"The piano is not a machine," that powerful inhuman voice droned. "To me, yes. I can translate the notes into sounds at a glance. From only a few, I am able to grasp at once the composer's conception. It is easy for me."

Rollo towered magnificently over the maestro's bent form.

"I can also grasp," the brassy monotone rolled through the studio, "that this . . . music is not for robots. It is for people. To me, it is easy, yes. . . . It was not meant to be easy."

READING COMPREHENSION

Summarizing. Choose the best phrase to complete each sentence. Then write the complete statements on your paper.

1. Rollo understood the piano as a _____ (toy, machine, source of beautiful music).

2. For the maestro, music was meant to _____ (be difficult, show orderly sound patterns, give pleasure to humans).

3. After hearing Rollo play, the maestro _____ (sent him back to the factory, planned a great musical career for him, forbade him to play again).

4. Rollo refused to continue playing the piano because he _____ (had become bored by it, considered it harmful to his owner, knew he was a failure).

Interpreting. Write the answer to each question on your paper.

1. Why did the maestro agree to teach Rollo to play the piano?

2. Why did the maestro cry when he heard Rollo play?

3. How did Rollo interpret the maestro's tears?

For Thinking and Discussing.

1. What thoughts do you think the maestro had after hearing Rollo play?

2. At the end of the story, Rollo states that music is not for robots but for people, because music is not meant to be easy. What did he mean?

UNDERSTANDING LITERATURE

Surprise Ending. A *surprise ending* is a conclusion to a story that is unpredictable from the events that have gone before it. However, a surprise ending has to make sense in relation to the development of the story's plot.

In "Virtuoso," we are surprised by Rollo's success as a pianist. However, the author constructed the plot in such a way that this outcome also seems logical.

Write the correct answers for each question below on your paper.

1. Which of the facts below suggest that Rollo would fail as a pianist? Which suggest that he would learn quickly and well?
   a. He wanted to practice.
   b. He viewed the piano as a machine.
   c. He was made of clumsy metal.
   d. He was curious to learn.
   e. He had powerful memory banks.

2. Which of the following statements explain the second plot surprise: Rollo's refusal to play the piano anymore?
   a. He had human emotions after all.
   b. His built-in instructions included not harming his owner.
   c. He was bored by the piano quickly.

WRITING

Write the surprise ending of the story in the form of an entry that Rollo might make into his memory banks. Write it in a way that a robot might write.

Mirrors

by Massimo Bontempelli

*Born in Como, Italy, Massimo Bontempelli (1878–1960)
wrote many short stories. This tale of fantasy and imagination may cause you to take a second look at some of the
objects you use every day.*

Talking of mirrors, I must tell of another experience. I know I shall be accused of abusing this theme, but be patient, my friend. I would rather not have one think that I spend most of my life before a mirror. On the contrary, it is because I so seldom use this baffling object that it still creates for me the strange illusions it denies to those who use it too often.

About eight days ago, just before noon, my landlady woke me up with a telegram. It was from Vienna. It was addressed to me, to me alone, and it was correctly addressed. This is what it said: "Leaving for Rome day after tomorrow Stop Arrivederci* Stop Massimo."

I was in Vienna two months ago, for 15 days. I tried to recall all the people I had met during those 15 days. There was an old Hungarian friend of mine called Tibor. Some others were named Fritz, Richard, and John. I could think of no other Massimo in Vienna but myself.

There was just one conclusion and it was a clear one. Since I was the only Massimo I could think of in Vienna, the Massimo who sent me the telegram was myself.

Therefore, it was my telegram.

"I understand!" I shouted.

But the reader, on the other hand, cannot as yet have understood.

I shall explain. But before I do so, it is necessary that I tell my reader of some of the other experiences I have had about telegrams. One example is enough. I was arranging my things in my room one day when I noticed that my umbrella was gone. I looked for it everywhere. More than once I looked for it in the corner where I usually kept it, but in vain. I finally resigned myself to the loss and went about my business. We lose greater things in life than an umbrella.

---

* *Arrivederci*: See you soon (Italian)

The False Mirror, *René Magritte, 1928*

I had almost forgotten it when, two days later, I received the following telegram: "Shall arrive tonight Stop Umbrella."

I gave it a little thought and slept peacefully that night. The following morning, the first thing to attract my attention was my umbrella. Sure enough, there it was, in the very corner where I had looked for it many times.

Of course, I know quite well that one usually finds a lost article in the very place where one has looked for it many times before. And there is really no use talking about it. But to have a lost article announce its return by telegram, that is unusual.

At this point, we must go back a bit.

Two months ago in Vienna, I was standing before a mirror fixing my tie. I was getting ready to take my train back to Rome. There were riots going on throughout the city at the time.

As I have said, I was standing before a mirror fixing my tie. Suddenly a great explosion shook the house. It smashed my mirror into bits.

I realized it was a bomb. I went on

fixing my tie without the mirror. When I was through, I took my bag, drove to the station, and left. A few days later, I was in Rome. It was late at night, so I immediately went to bed.

The next morning, I stood before the mirror with my shaving brush in one hand and a towel in the other. To my great surprise, I saw nothing there. To be exact, everything was there but me. I could see the soap-soaked brush dangling to and fro, and a towel equally agitated, as if it had suddenly gone mad in the empty space. But I, I was not to be seen. Neither my face nor my image was there.

Realizing at once what had happened, I broke into laughter.

All those who use a mirror must have noticed that the moment they pull themselves from it, they feel a bit uneasy. There is a little jerk in the parting. Well, this results from the very light effort we all make when tearing ourselves away, when withdrawing the image that is there.

Now this is exactly what happened to me on that day in Vienna. My mirror broke so instantly, it was smashed and destroyed so suddenly, that I was not quick enough to withdraw my image. I wasn't able to pull it back before it disappeared.

Naturally, since I was in a hurry, I paid little attention to the incident at the time. I first realized what had happened when I faced a mirror here in Rome two days later.

And so, for these past two months, I have been without my image. It was annoying at first, especially for my tie and beard. But I learned to get along without it. As for my beard, I shaved it to my ear.

I took the mirror down from its usual place and put it away in my trunk.

The only thing I had to be very careful about was not to have anyone see me standing before any of the mirrors along the streets, in the cafes, or in the homes of others. People are easily surprised, you know. They would want to know why and how, and then I would need to explain.

For this reason, though the loss itself wasn't serious, I was happy to receive that telegram eight days ago. I understood at once that the telegram had been sent to me by my own image so that I might be informed of its homecoming.

Naturally, I did not hasten to look at myself in the mirror. Not at all. I did not want to give my image the satisfaction of knowing that I care very much about it. It must not think that I have been waiting, that I cannot do without it. Since it left Vienna eight days ago, it should have reached here at least four days ago. But I did not show myself until yesterday. It was only yesterday that I took the mirror out. I put it in its usual place in the bathroom without even looking at it. Then calmly and indifferently, I adjusted my collar and tie and took a look. There I was. There was my image unchanged. I had had a vague fear that I might find it a little disturbed. It might have been angry because I didn't miss it. It might have been tired from the long trip and its many experiences. Instead it seemed to be okay, as calm and as indifferent as its owner.

READING COMPREHENSION

Summarizing. Choose the best phrase to complete each sentence. Then write the complete statements on your paper.

1. The narrator received a telegram from Vienna from _____ (his twin brother, a friend named Massimo, his mirror image).

2. The article that disappeared and sent a telegram before returning was _____ (a mirror, an umbrella, a book).

3. The narrator's mirror image disappeared because _____ (it disliked his looks, it remained in the mirror in Vienna, he was really dead).

Interpreting. Write the answer to each question on your paper.

1. How did the narrator react when he first realized that his image was not reflected in his mirror?

2. Why did the narrator not hurry to look at himself in the mirror when he knew his image had returned?

3. What was the "vague fear" concerning his image to which the narrator refers at the end of the story?

For Thinking and Discussing

1. Which events in this story are unlike anything that could happen in real life? When did you first become aware that this story wasn't realistic?

2. What emotional mood did the author want to create?

UNDERSTANDING LITERATURE

Suspense and Plot. The story "Mirrors" tells of strange and illogical happenings. The author presents these events to us in a calm, matter-of-fact manner.

The story develops its *suspense* through its *plot* rather than its mood. As the action develops, our curiosity and anticipation build — as does the story's suspense.

The plot is arranged in three anecdotes — short, humorous stories. Each follows the same pattern. Answer the following questions on your paper.

1. What sent the narrator the first telegram? Why was this telegram sent?

2. What did the narrator do after receiving the first telegram?

3. The only explanation the narrator offers for these strange experiences comes in the first paragraph:

   I would rather not have one think that I spend most of my life before a mirror. On the contrary, it is because I so seldom use this baffling object that it still creates for me the strange illusions it denies to those who use it too often.

   What strange idea is the narrator suggesting in this quote?

WRITING

Write an additional anecdote for this story using the same form and style as the author. Describe some missing thing that announces its coming return by telegram.

An Appointment in Samarra

by W. Somerset Maugham

The British writer W. Somerset Maugham, born in 1874, produced many novels, short stories, and plays. He loved to travel, and often set his stories in exotic places. This is a fable — a story with a moral; it is short but its impact is powerful.

502

Death speaks:

There was a merchant in Baghdad who sent his servant to market to buy provisions and in a little while the servant came back, white and trembling, and said, "Master, just now when I was in the marketplace I was jostled by a woman in the crowd and when I turned I saw it was Death that jostled me. She looked at me and made a threatening gesture; now, lend me your horse and I will run away from this city and avoid my fate. I will go to Samarra and there Death will not find me." The merchant lent him his horse, and he dug his spurs in its flanks and as fast as the horse could gallop he went.

Then the merchant went down to the marketplace and he saw me standing in the crowd and he came to me and said, "Why did you make a threatening gesture to my servant when you saw him this morning?"

"That was not a threatening gesture," I said, "it was only a start of surprise. I was astonished to see him in Baghdad, for I have an appointment with him tonight in Samarra."

503

READING COMPREHENSION

Summarizing. Choose the best phrase to complete each sentence. Then write the complete statements on your paper.

1. Death appeared in _____ (a graveyard, the merchant's house, the marketplace).

2. The servant said that Death looked at him and _____ (laughed, made a threatening gesture, shook her head).

3. To escape Death, the servant fled to _____ (Samarra, Baghdad, the desert).

4. Death told the merchant that the servant had _____ (outwitted her, surprised her, tricked her).

Interpreting. Write the answer to each question on your paper.

1. Who was the narrator of the story?

2. Why did the servant flee from the city of Baghdad?

3. What happened to the servant at the end of the story?

For Thinking and Discussing.

1. Why does the ending of the story have such a strong impact?

2. Did you think the servant would succeed in running away from Death? Why or why not?

3. What creates the instant mood of suspense in this story?

UNDERSTANDING LITERATURE

Suspense and Surprise Ending. A *surprise ending* is an unexpected conclusion to a story. It develops logically, however, from earlier events in the plot.

"An Appointment in Samarra" combines suspense and a surprise ending in a short but powerful story.

Write the answers to the following questions on your paper.

1. What are the first two words in the story? What emotional effect did these words have on you when you read them?

2. How would you feel about the idea of meeting Death?

3. How did the servant plan to outsmart Death?

4. Did you think he would succeed in running away from Death?

5. Which of the following statements best sums up the meaning of the story's surprise ending?
   a. Death can be outwitted.
   b. If you are unlucky, Death will find you.
   c. There is no escaping Death.

WRITING

Write a short description of the scene between the servant and Death that night in Samarra. Your description should reflect surprise on the part of the servant at meeting Death in Samarra.

The Vampire

by Jan Neruda

Jan Neruda was an important 19th-century Czech author. A versatile writer, he produced novels, poetry, criticism, and plays as well as short stories. But his stories were especially popular, and after you read "The Vampire," you will understand why. We usually think of a vampire as a creature that sucks people's blood. But Neruda's tale shows that the word can have a wider meaning.

The excursion steamer brought us from Constantinople to the shore of the island of Prinkipo and we disembarked. The number of passengers was not large. There was one Polish family, a father, a mother, a daughter and her bridegroom, and then we two. Oh, yes, I must not forget that when we were already on the wooden bridge that crosses the Golden Horn to Constantinople, a Greek, a rather youthful man, joined us. He was probably an artist, judging by the portfolio he carried under his arm. Long black locks floated to his shoulders. His face was pale, and his black eyes were deeply set. In the first moment, he interested me, especially for his obligingness and for his knowledge of local conditions. But he talked too much, and I then turned away from him.

All the more agreeable was the Polish family. The father and mother were good-natured, fine people. The lover was a handsome young fellow, of direct and refined manners. They had come to Prin-

kipo to spend the summer months for the sake of the daughter, who was slightly ailing. The beautiful pale girl was either just recovering from a severe illness or else a serious disease was just fastening its hold upon her. She leaned upon her lover when she walked. Very often she sat down to rest. A frequent dry little cough interrupted her whispers. Whenever she coughed, her escort would pause in their walk. He always cast upon her a glance of sympathetic suffering. She would look back at him as if she would say: "It is nothing. I am happy!" They believed in health and happiness.

On the recommendation of the Greek, who left us immediately at the pier, the family went to a hotel on the hill. The hotel-keeper was a Frenchman. His entire building was equipped comfortably and artistically, according to the French style.

We breakfasted together. When the noon heat had ceased somewhat, we all betook ourselves to the heights. There in the grove

of pines, we would refresh ourselves with the view. We found a suitable spot and settled ourselves. Then the Greek appeared again. He greeted us lightly. Then he looked about and seated himself only a few steps from us. He opened his portfolio and began to sketch.

"I think he purposely sits with his back to the rocks so that we can't look at his sketch," I said.

"We don't have to," said the young Pole. "We have enough before us to look at." After a while, he added, "It seems to me he's sketching us in as a sort of background. Well — let him!"

We truly did have enough to gaze at. There is not a more beautiful or more happy corner in the world than that very Prinkipo! If I could live a month of my life there, I would be happy for the memory of it for the rest of my days! I shall never forget even that one day spent at Prinkipo.

The air was as clear as a diamond. At the right, beyond the sea, projected the brown hills. To the left, in the distance, stood the purple coasts of Europe. Chalki, one of the neighboring islands, rose with its cypress forests into the peaceful heights like a sorrowful dream.

The Sea of Marmara was but slightly ruffled and played in all colors like a sparkling jewel. In the distance, the sun was as white as milk, then rosy, between the two islands a glowing orange, and below us it was beautifully greenish blue, like a transparent sapphire. Nowhere were there any large ships — only two small craft flying the British flag sped along the shore. Trustful dolphins darted in and out among them. Through the blue heavens, now and then, calm eagles winged their way, measuring the space between two continents.

The entire slope below us was covered with blossoming roses. Their fragrance filled the air. From the coffeehouse near the sea, music was carried up to us through the clear air.

The effect was enchanting. We all sat silent and enjoyed completely this picture of paradise. The young Polish girl lay on the grass with her head supported on the shoulder of her lover. Her delicate face was slightly tinged with soft color. Her blue eyes suddenly gushed tears. The lover understood, bent down, and kissed tear after tear. Her mother also was moved to tears. I — even I — felt a strange twinge.

"Here mind and body both must get well," whispered the girl. "How happy a land this is!"

"God knows I haven't any enemies, but if I had, I would forgive them here!" said the father in a trembling voice.

And again we became silent. We were all in such a wonderful mood — so unspeakably sweet it all was! Each felt for himself a whole world of happiness. Each one would have shared his happiness with the whole world. All felt the same — and so no one disturbed another. We had scarcely even noticed that the Greek, after an hour or so, had left.

Finally, after several hours, the mother reminded us it was time to go. We arose and walked down toward the hotel with the easy steps of carefree children. We sat down in the hotel under the handsome awning.

Suddenly we heard below the sounds of quarreling. Our Greek was wrangling with the hotel-keeper. For the entertainment of it, we listened.

The amusement did not last long. "If I didn't have other guests," growled the hotel-keeper, and climbed the steps toward us.

"I beg you to tell me, sir," asked the young Pole of the hotel-keeper, "who is that gentleman? What's his name?"

"Eh — who knows what the fellow's name is?" grumbled the hotel-keeper, and he gazed angrily downward. "We call him the vampire."

"An artist?"

"Fine trade! He sketches only corpses. Just as soon as someone dies, that very day, he has a picture of the dead one completed. That fellow paints them beforehand — and he never makes a mistake — just like a vulture!"

The old Polish woman shrieked. In her arms lay her daughter pale as chalk. She had fainted.

In one bound the lover had leaped down the steps. With one hand he seized the Greek, and with the other reached for the portfolio.

We ran down after him. Both men were rolling in the sand. The contents of the portfolio were scattered all about. On one sheet, sketched with a crayon, was the head of the young Polish girl. Her eyes were closed and there was a wreath of myrtle on her brow.

READING COMPREHENSION

Summarizing. Choose the best phrase to complete each sentence. Then write the complete statements on your paper.

1. The family went to Prinkipo _____ (to improve the daughter's health, to inspect property, to study the landscape).

2. The young woman _____ (complained about her illness, pretended to feel better than she did, recovered).

3. The vampire was the _____ (bridegroom, hotel-keeper's brother, artist).

4. The artist had drawn a picture of the _____ (beautiful landscape, young Polish girl, the hotel-keeper).

Interpreting. Write the answer to each question on your paper.

1. How had the artist drawn the young girl?

2. Why was the artist called "the vampire"?

3. Why was the family upset to hear this news about the artist?

For Thinking and Discussing.

1. What do you think will happen to the daughter? What clues in the story led you to your conclusion?

2. What is the story's mood when the family is on the mountain? What is the mood at the end of the story? Explain the contrast.

UNDERSTANDING LITERATURE

Foreshadowing. *Foreshadowing* consists of the suggestions and clues that an author puts in a story to hint at the story's conclusion. In a story of suspense, these foreshadowing clues build a sense of anticipation and uncertainty.

The story "The Vampire" uses foreshadowing to alert the reader to its dreadful outcome. Most of the story, however, is narrated in a calm, peaceful mood.

Answer the questions below to understand better the use of foreshadowing in "The Vampire."

1. How is the story's title itself a foreshadowing clue to the reader? What did it suggest to you?

2. On your paper, write the description of the young artist given in the first paragraph. What does this description suggest about the character?

3. Find a description of the young Polish girl in the second paragraph that suggests some sad outcome for her. Write it on your paper.

4. How does the hotel-keeper describe the artist's sketches? What idea does his description suggest to the family and the narrator?

5. What event does the entire story foreshadow, but is not told to the reader?

WRITING

Write a final paragraph for this story, describing what you think will happen to the young Polish girl.

The Old Walking Song

by J. R. R. Tolkien

The Road goes ever on and on
  Down from the door where it began.
Now far ahead the Road has gone,
  And I must follow, if I can,
Pursuing it with eager feet,
  Until it joins some larger way
Where many paths and errands meet.
  And whither then? I cannot say.

1. What does the speaker mean when he says "And whither then?" Why doesn't the speaker know what he will do?

2. How might the Road be a symbol for life? What might the poet be saying about the paths we take and the choices we make in life?

Section Review

Shades of Meaning. A word has not only a general meaning, but also a *shade of meaning*. For example, the words *bad*, *wicked*, and *vicious* all have the same general meaning. But *wicked* has a more negative meaning than *bad*, and *vicious* has the most negative and frightening shade of meaning of all.

Choosing a word with the correct shade of meaning can help a writer to make an image more vivid or a character more real.

Below are some lines from the selections in this section. On your paper, write the answer to the question that follows each.

1. "A disagreeable *shudder* crept over me, but I did my best against it." Why did the author use *shudder* instead of *feeling*?

2. "The maestro *snapped* erect, threw the covers aside." Why did the author use *snapped* instead of *sat up*?

3. "Suddenly a great explosion shook the house. It *smashed* my mirror into bits." Why did the author use *smashed* instead of *broke*?

4. "I was *astonished* to see him in Baghdad, for I have an appointment with him tonight in Samarra." Why did the author use *astonished* instead of *surprised*?

Critical Reading. As you read a piece of literature, you develop an understanding of what the author thinks is important and of what the characters are like. In other words, you begin to understand the values of the author and the characters. Developing this understanding is part of reading critically.

Look at the following statements. Decide which of the characters listed below might have said each one. On your paper, write the name of the character and a short explanation of your choice.

Characters

- [ ] The signal-man ("The Signal-Man")
- [ ] The maestro ("Virtuoso")
- [ ] The young Polish man ("The Vampire")
- [ ] Massimo ("Mirrors")
- [ ] The servant ("An Appointment in Samarra")

1. The beauty of beautiful music cannot be explained scientifically.

2. There are few things in life serious enough to get upset about; I prefer to laugh at the strange things that happen in life.

3. I love my fiancée very much and would do almost anything to help her get well.

4. There are spirits that know more than we do about our own fate.

5. If you think fast enough and run quickly enough, you can avoid trouble.

WRITING

A Review. A review evaluates and gives an opinion about such things as books, movies, plays, and music. A review usually includes a good or bad recommendation that helps people decide whether or not to read the book, see the movie, and so forth.

A reviewer's evaluation is based on his or her personal standards, or set of ideas about what makes something good or bad. Two people may have different standards by which they judge the same thing. For example, you may like a book because of the way the author develops his or her characters. Someone else may like it because of the way its plot is developed. Your opinion of the book is the same, but your reasons are different.

Step 1: Set Your Goal

Now it's time to try being a reviewer. Your task is to review one of the stories in this section, and to make a recommendation about it for others. Choose a story you liked very much or not at all. Having a strong opinion about something makes it easier to find things to say.

Step 2: Make a Plan

In order to gather information for your review, decide which elements to evaluate and what your standards are. In a review of a story, the main elements to consider are plot, characters, setting, mood, and the author's purpose. The questions in the checklist below reflect the standards upon which you may judge these different elements. As you reread the story, ask yourself these questions and make a list of your responses.

Plot

- ☐ Is the plot well constructed?
- ☐ Does each incident have a purpose?
- ☐ Does each incident grow out of what comes before and lead to what comes next?
- ☐ Is each incident related to the story's main idea or theme?

Characters

- ☐ How did the author reveal characters?
- ☐ Are the characters' actions and dialogue believable?

Setting and Mood

- ☐ Is the story's setting well chosen and well described?
- ☐ What mood is the author trying to create: suspenseful, humorous, mysterious?
- ☐ Is the mood suitable for the story?

Author's Purpose

- ☐ What is the author's purpose in telling the story?
- ☐ For what audience is the story most suitable? Why?

Step 3: Write a First Draft

Before you begin to write your first draft, remember that a review is more than just a statement of your opinions. You must be able to support your opinions with examples that illustrate the points you are trying to make. For example, if you believed the author was particularly good at creating a mood, you might provide a line or two from the story to illustrate this point.

Begin your first draft with an opening statement that expresses your overall opinion, and includes the title of the selection and the name of the author. For example:

> *The Blessing Way* by Tony Hillerman is an action-packed mystery that will keep you in suspense until the very end.

Refer to the checklist and your list of responses as you write your review. Write one paragraph for each category of questions. Remember to support your evaluation with specific examples from the story. End your review with a sentence that tells why you would or would not recommend this selection to other readers.

Step 4: Revise

If possible, wait a day or two before you revise your paper. Then read it over carefully, looking for ways to make it clearer and more effective. Use the following checklist as a guide:

☐ Did I begin by clearly identifying what I'm reviewing and by stating my overall opinion about it?

☐ Have I written one paragraph to cover each of the factors I considered?

☐ Have I made clear exactly how the story I am reviewing does or does not live up to my standards?

☐ Have I used specific examples to support my opinions?

☐ Have I concluded my review with a statement that tells whether or not I would recommend the story to others?

After you have revised your review, proofread it for mistakes in grammar, punctuation, and spelling. Finally, type your paper or copy it over neatly.

The following is a quiz for Section 9. Write the answers in complete sentences on your paper.

Reading Comprehension

1. In "The Signal-Man," why did the signal-man react so fearfully when he first saw the narrator?

2. Compare the maestro's description of music with the description made by Rollo, the robot, in "Virtuoso."

3. In "Mirrors," why did the narrator's image disappear for a while?

4. Who was the narrator of the story in "An Appointment in Samarra"?

5. In "The Vampire," what sort of picture had the artist sketched of the young Polish girl?

Understanding Literature

6. In "The Signal-Man," what two incidents foreshadowed the signal-man's death?

7. In "Virtuoso," why might Rollo's skill at the piano be called ironic?

8. In "Mirrors," what explanation did the narrator give for his strange experience with mirrors?

9. What theme, or meaning, does the surprise ending of "An Appointment in Samarra" suggest?

10. Why do you think the author of "The Vampire" chose this particular title for the story?

ACTIVITIES

Word Attack. In "Virtuoso," you read that a composer is someone who creates a musical piece. The word *composer* comes from the Latin word *com-*, meaning "together," and the Middle French word *poser*, meaning "to place or put." A composer creates music by putting together various notes. List five other words that include the word part *com-*, *-pos-*, or both, and write the meaning of each. Use a dictionary if you need help.

Speaking and Listening

1. Each of the stories in this section creates a particular mood that adds to the suspense and mystery. Select one of the stories and try to establish its mood in your own words. Imagine that you are introducing the story for a radio or television show. Your introduction must set the mood for your audience. Be prepared to present your introduction orally to the class.

2. "The Old Walking Song" by J. R. R. Tolkien is from the book *The Fellowship of the Ring*, one of a series of books about the Hobbits. The Hobbits are imaginary, gnomelike creatures who have a world and language of their own, and who often sing songs. Locate one of Tolkien's books about the Hobbits and find a song-poem you like. Prepare to read it to the class.

Researching

1. In "Virtuoso," several famous composers were mentioned: Chopin, Mozart, Debussy, and Beethoven. Choose one for the subject of a short biography. Research facts about the composer, including where and when he lived and his achievements.

2. Many horror stories have been written about vampires. Do some research about the myth of the vampire. Just exactly what is a vampire supposed to be? What are the characteristics of a vampire? How are they destroyed? Where did the myth originate? How has it been popularized?

Creating

1. The author of the story "Mirrors" creates strange and haunting possibilities from commonplace incidents. There are, in fact, many odd and unexplainable things that happen in everyday life. For example, you may receive a telephone call from someone you have just thought about. Or, you may have known that someone was coming to visit you before they actually arrived. Write a story like one of the anecdotes in "Mirrors" in which you create bizarre circumstances and explanations based on an everyday event.

2. Using "An Appointment in Samarra" as an example, write a short, tightly constructed story that has a surprise ending. Develop your plot by thinking of a situation in which a character's assumptions are reversed. Keep your character and your reader in the dark until the very end when you write the surprise climax.

AMBITION

If you never assume importance,
you never lose it.

—Lao Tzu
China

The K'ang-hsi Emperor's Second Tour of the South:
Scroll No. 3, Detail No. 2
Wang Hui (1632-1717)
Metropolitan Museum of Art
The Dillon Fund Gift

Ambition

Ambition—the desire to do, have, or own something—has been the theme of many of the world's poets and storytellers. Some of the greatest heroes of literature, and some of the most evil villains, are driven by some powerful desire. Ambition can drive people on to greatness—or can destroy them.

A Dream Saved

A dream can be the one thing that keeps you going. It can even give you the strength to do something impossible. But what happens when a dream starts to die? In "Trumpet Man," a short story by Lucy Cundiff, a jazz trumpet player who once dreamed of greatness realizes that he is a failure. He is a mediocre, unsuccessful musician without much talent. Losing hope, he begins to play even more poorly. Even the desire to go on living is slipping away. But the trumpet player gets one last chance to prove himself. Is it too late—or can he still hang on to his dream? This story shows that it takes more than talent to make a person great.

Wanting Too Much

The desire for land has motivated people since the beginning of time. This desire has led to the discovery of new continents, the building of nations, and the loss of life in wars. Land has always stood for wealth and power. But wanting too much of anything can lead to disaster.

How much is too much? In a simple tale by Leo Tolstoy entitled "How Much Land Does a Man Need?" the chief of a Russian mountain tribe has the answer. A visitor wants to buy land from the chief. But the visitor is greedy; he tries to take too much. However, he ends up with exactly as much land as he needs, which may be considerably less than you think.

Trickery

Another story about people and land comes from Brazil. In "The Farm Magnate," a landowner no longer wants his land; he wants to sell it. Moreira's farm produces nothing and keeps him in continual debt. But who will buy such poor land? Overcome by greed, Moreira and his family try to trick a potential buyer into taking the land. But they get what they deserve when they are tricked in return. Sometimes land is harder to get rid of than it is to get.

Ambition doesn't always lead to either disaster or greatness—it can lead to comedy. In Oscar Wilde's famous play *The Importance of Being Earnest,* Jack Worthing's ambition is to marry Gwendolen Fairfax. But for reasons that you will discover, Jack has tricked Gwendolen

Icarus, *Paper Sculpture, Peter Di George, 1965*

into believing that his name is actually Ernest. When Jack tries to reveal his real name, he discovers that, unfortunately, Gwendolen's ambition is to marry a man named Ernest. Oscar Wilde makes fun of British society in this witty play. But eventually, everyone gets what he or she wants.

Remnants of a Dream

The desire for power can lead to the conquering of nations and the building of new empires. But even mighty empires do not last forever. In "Ozymandias," a poem by Percy Bysshe Shelley, a traveler tells of finding the ruins of the statue of a king, perhaps the last traces of a city in the midst of the desert. Inscribed on the statue are words that tell of a tyrant's great pride and lust for power. But now, the tyrant's domains have crumbled into dust.

Yet even in the emptiness of the desert, a sense of the ruler's power is still felt by the traveler. A tyrant's dream, like any other, can be hard to destroy completely. Immortalized by art or literature, some dreams never die.

While many clamor for notoriety, some people prefer to remain safely on the sidelines. This seems to be Emily Dickinson's message in "I'm Nobody!"—the poem that wraps up a section about ambition with a celebration of anonymity.

Trumpet Man

by Lucy Cundiff

When Dan Daly comes to the big city, he realizes that his ambitions are unrealistic. But someone who loves him still believes in him. Will Dan give up his dream?

At 2 A.M., the last car pulled away from the gravel parking space in front of Griffin's Lively Slipper Club. The neon slippers that capered back and forth across the big sign at the edge of the highway winked for the last time and turned into dull, twisted tubes. For a moment the smaller sign below it — FEATURING DAN DALY AND HIS DANCING FIVE — remained lighted, and then it, too, went dark. Across the prairie came the faint, mournful whistle of a train; the tires of a car whined on the highway, then all was still.

In the club, Dan Daly stepped down from the bandstand and walked wearily toward the rear exit. In the dim lights of the dining room, he could pass for a man in his middle 30s; but under the raw bulb of the back hallway, he looked 10 years older. His tall, thin figure sagged a little. His face was gray and tired.

He had his hand on the knob of the rear door when he heard Griffin call to him. Dan turned and waited, his eyes expressionless as he tried to keep his dislike from showing.

Griffin was in a mean mood. Business hadn't been good that night. As the man came up to him, Dan decided that Griffin had been his own best customer at the bar. Dan watched him uneasily, fighting the sick feeling in the pit of his stomach.

Griffin stopped in front of Dan and looked him up and down before he spoke. The slow, measuring stare was deliberately insulting. Then he said, "I'm paying for a six-piece band, Daly. I intend to have a six-piece band."

Dan knew what Griffin was driving at, but he kept his temper under control. He said evenly, "Pete'll be back next week. The doctor says he'll be able to play again by Monday."

Griffin scowled. "I'm not talking about Pete."

Dan knew he wasn't, but he said nothing. Instead he swung the door open, but Griffin called after him, "Your contract's got two months to run, Daly, but don't think I can't break it if you don't live up to the terms."

Dan closed the door behind him and stood there, drawing the cool night air into his sore lungs, giving himself time to let the hot, sick anger inside of him wash away. Across the gravel, he could see the trailer with a light burning in the kitchen where Molly would be waiting for him.

In the glow that still fanned out from the club's rear windows, he could see the sign on the side of the trailer — DAN DALY AND HIS DANCING FIVE. Once when the trailer had been new, before the gilt had begun to peel from the trumpet above his name, the sign had meant something. Not much, he admitted honestly, as he walked toward it, but there had been a Dancing Five then. A solid working outfit. No brilliance, but steady and reliable. Benny, his pianist, was the only one left out of the original group.

There was an out, of course. He could hire a man to replace him on trumpet, let Benny go, and take over on piano himself. But he knew he couldn't do it. Benny was old. They'd played together for years. Benny was like Dan. He was a musician. He didn't know anything else. Sure, you could say, "Well, stop being a musician." To Dan, it was like telling a horse to stop being a horse.

He rubbed his face as he neared the trailer, as if to rub off the discouragement he knew must be there. In the kitchen, Molly was sitting by the table. As he pushed open the door, she felt the coffee-pot.

She called out cheerfully, "Still good and hot, Dan, and I made some rolls this afternoon before you woke up."

She smiled at him as he sat down. She pushed the sleeves of her robe up and rested her elbows on the table. It was a familiar pose. How many nights had they finished like this, with Molly sitting across from him in her night clothes, her soft, round face scrubbed clean and still shining

a little from the soap, her black hair taken down and hanging in two braids over her shoulders, her blue eyes still alert as she waited, willing to talk over the night's work, if he felt like it.

Years and years and years of this, and she could still look at him with that air of bright hope. "Molly, Molly," he thought, "how can you do it?"

He went along for months, sometimes even for years, taking her faith and cheerfulness for granted, until there'd come a moment like this one — a moment when his nerves were rubbed raw and quivering, and he'd suddenly see her as a person, know what she had meant to him and know that her dreams hadn't come true any more than his own. Yet she could still lift that small chin and smile.

She pushed the rolls toward him again, but when he shook his head, she said, "You're too tired to eat, honey. You work harder when Pete's out. You get to bed and I'll rinse the dishes."

He didn't argue, though he usually helped her. He got into bed and presently he felt Molly slip in softly beside him. He lay quietly, so that she'd think he was asleep, and soon he knew by the sound of her even breathing that she was.

Dan lay back on the pillow and tried to burrow into the comfort of his dream, but the comfort wouldn't come. He no longer believed in his dream. It had changed in its direction through the years, its fiction shaped by his failures and defeats, but always there had been an inner dream to sustain him.

When he and Molly had been young in Mercerville, the dream had been shining

and complete. It was polished by Molly's admiration and propped up by his own knowledge that he was the best trumpeter for miles around. The trouble was that there weren't many trumpeters *around*. You didn't have to be very good to beat what there was. Maybe he should have stayed in Mercerville.

Chicago was drawing the musicians in those days the way flypaper draws flies. So Dan went. He lined up a job the first week he was there, and the balloon he was carrying in place of a head got a little bigger.

Then one night after they got through, one of the other men in the band asked him if he'd like to go over to The Swamp, where some of the boys from the various bands were holding a jam session.

He went, taking his trumpet with him, thinking maybe he'd sit in if they were good enough. He never took it out of the case. When the door opened and he heard that horn, he slid into a chair as if his bones were made of jelly.

He never moved until it was over. He never moved and he never took his eyes off the man who was playing the horn. It took him a while to realize that it wasn't a trumpet, but a cornet.

The man sat there in his tux, his hair slicked back from a middle part, tipping a glass up now and then when he wasn't playing. Then he'd bring that cornet up and you'd forget there was anyone else in the room.

It ended eventually, and Dan walked all the way back to his room, hardly knowing what he was doing. It was sleeting, and at one point he stopped in the street and stood there, bareheaded in the sleet, his coat open, and said, like a prayer, "If I could just play with him — just once." Not play as well as he did. Dan knew there wasn't anyone who could.

He lay down on the bed in his room without taking off his wet clothes, and because he was very young and had suddenly come to grips with his own stature, he cried. He knew that he'd never be more than just an average trumpet player.

But because he was young, too, he went back to his trumpet in the morning. He was a better bandman after that, because he wasn't set on showing everyone how good he was. He played pretty regularly, and in one of the good years, he went back to Mercerville and got Molly.

He didn't see that splendid horn in action again, and one night, when he was playing in Kansas City, the word went around on the stand that death had silenced that golden horn forever. There wasn't a man who didn't feel it, no matter what instrument he played, but Dan felt it the way you feel when one of your own — the flower, the best, the brightest in your family — dies.

He didn't have trouble getting bookings in those early years. Not with the top bands, but he worked steadily because he was known as capable and reliable.

Then the bottom seemed to fall out of everything. Big bands got fewer. Juke boxes were driving the combos out of the small places. Molly was pregnant and Dan decided to quit the road. They settled down and he decided to teach. He hated the teaching. The only bright spots were the one-night gigs he got to do now and then. But Molly was happy, and when the boy was born, Dan's dreams began to take another shape. Maybe the boy would have what Dan had never had.

It was about this time that he wrote "Molly's Tune." He heard her one day, and he rushed out to the kitchen, all excited. What was that thing she was singing? Molly lifted her hands out of the soapsuds and stared at him, puzzled. She looked around as if to make sure he was talking to her. Sing? Why, he knew that she couldn't sing a note. Oh, that noise she was making? She laughed then, and even her laughter had something of the same sound in it. Why, that — that was just some sounds she made when she felt happy inside.

Dan almost drove Molly to tears trying to get her to go through it often enough for him to get it down, until he realized that she meant exactly what she said. She made those sounds only when she was happy. After that, he didn't ask her, but he'd listen for them when she was bathing the baby or cooking or something. He'd wait, listening for those slightly off-pitch notes that eventually became "Molly's Tune."

He was elated when he finished it. He couldn't put all the notes down for the trumpet solo the way he heard them in his head, but a good man on a horn would know what to do with it. Molly and he dreamed about what they'd do with the money, but he couldn't get it published. Nobody wanted it. Molly's happy little chirps remained black and silent on the printed sheets.

Their savings were just about gone when Dan got a chance to go out on the road. They talked it over and he went by himself. He was in Phoenix when the telegram came. Although he sat on the edge of the seat in the plane, pushing it every mile as it flew through the night, he knew he was going to be too late. Knew it even before he raced down the hospital corridor toward that closed door.

They buried the boy in Mercerville beside Dan's parents. He went back to Phoenix with Molly beside him — a white-faced Molly who looked as if she would never smile again. After a long time, he woke up one day to hear those chirping little sounds in the kitchenette. He played better that night than he had played in years.

It was shortly after that that he got his own group together. Molly and he had a new dream. If they could save enough, they'd open a little place of their own — a clean place with good food, no juke boxes, and music that was just for listening. A place where the boys from the bands could come and jam when they felt like jamming.

A place of their own. On his pillow, now, Dan closed his eyes and smothered a groan. They had never been farther from it.

Molly and Dan went over to the club about eight-thirty. She took her usual place, and Dan turned on the lights at the stand and began sorting music. The band didn't start to play until nine o'clock.

The rest of the boys filed onto the stand and Benny took his place at the piano.

The room was beginning to fill now, and as the band slid into their first number, Dan saw Griffin watching him. Then he forgot him in his efforts to keep his lip from rolling. He saw Benny's eyes over the top of the grand, wise and full of sympathy. Benny was taking it easy, swinging lightly from one number to another, a medley of old tunes that Dan could have played in his sleep. Dan kept his trumpet going through the choruses, but when they took a break, he almost staggered as they walked off the stand. His lungs ached from the breath he couldn't release into his horn. He was dizzy from the pressure in his head.

Dan was thinking. "If Griffin would just stay away from me, I'd be all right. I'd forget the trumpet and just let it out." But in his heart, he knew it wasn't true. It wasn't just Griffin standing there watching him; it was all the years out there in the shadows; it was the night in the sleet, the fly-specked teaching sign in the window, that race down the hospital corridor toward that closed door. Places like the Lively Slipper merging into one another like a row of boxes as far as he could see into the distance — all of the years, getting into the muscles of his mouth, blocking his breath and making his lip tremble and roll.

He didn't see Griffin at all during their next set, and he kept his trumpet on his lap. He felt a little more relaxed when they came back on the stand again. Most of the tables were filled now.

He saw a group of men in sports clothes come in. Griffin was with them. As they sat down, Griffin shot a look at the band-stand and then said something to the group and they all laughed. Dan felt cold. Was Griffin bargaining with a group to replace him? There was something about the way Griffin was hovering over them that made Dan certain. He swung around to see if Molly had noticed, but she wasn't at her table. He searched the crowd until he saw her standing at the entrance, talking to the hostess. The girl was whispering to Molly behind her stack of menus, her eyes straying constantly to the group at the table.

Molly turned and started toward the bandstand, and Dan knew that something was up. He hated the fact that Molly had to learn about it this way. The boys were going along nicely, following Benny's rhythm. Dan laid his trumpet down and walked to the edge of the stand.

Molly's eyes were almost black with excitement. "Dan!" she cried. "Dan! You know who just came in? Teddy Armister! Their bus broke down and it's in a garage up the road. Teddy Armister!"

Dan stared at her, not taking it in. Realizing at first only that this wasn't a band to replace him. Teddy was big time — the biggest. He'd never play in a place like the Lively Slipper. His band got more money for a one-night stand than Dan's outfit could pick up in a year.

The relief made him feel stupid. Molly said quickly, "Dan, it's your big chance!"

His thoughts moved thickly. Surely she didn't think — surely even Molly, with all her faith, didn't think that Teddy was going to think Dan was so hot he'd want to sign him up — even Molly —

She grasped his arm and shook it. "The

tune, Dan, the tune! You always said if you could just get some big band to listen to it and like it and put it over for you —"

Dan shook his head slowly from side to side. "I — I can't, Molly! I — "

Her grip on his sleeve tightened. "You've got to, Dan — you've just got to! It's our last chance! It's — " Then her face smoothed out and she smiled her old, easy smile, "Sure you can, Danny honey, for Molly's sake." She turned then and walked away.

Dan stood looking down at the place where she had stood, aware that the band was going on and on, that Benny was taking them through more numbers than they usually played in a set, giving Dan time.

He turned back to the stand and said to Benny, "OK. Take 10."

The boys filed off the stand, and Dan stayed, aware that the floor was empty, that Molly was watching him. He went to the case where he kept his extra arrangements, and he moved stiffly, like an old man.

Numbly he put an arrangement on each man's rack, burying it under four others. Maybe when Teddy got some of Griff's lousy food, he'd have enough of the place and leave. Maybe the bus would be fixed before they got to "Molly's Tune" — "Molly's Tune" with its trumpet choruses, the ones on paper and the ones that weren't even written down, that existed only in Dan's head. He stared down at the simple melodic line — a line that a man could grab hold of and take out of this world if

he played that kind of a horn, but Dan didn't. Even in his best days, he'd never been able to play "Molly's Tune" the way it should be played.

He left the stand and went past the boys in the hallway and on out into the night. He felt the night. He felt the air drying the sweat on his forehead. "I can't," he whispered into the darkness. "God help me, I can't."

He stumbled like a blind man as he came back onto the stand. He told the boys. He saw Benny look at him. The rest of them didn't. They'd all gone through the piece once or twice. He always had a new outfit rehearse it, because sometimes Molly sat in on rehearsals, and he didn't want her to know that he'd lost faith in the thing years ago. He knew that none of them thought much of it, but he also knew that they'd never heard the trumpet part played.

When the band started in again, the group over at Teddy's table looked at them, but not for long. They were soon back in a huddle of their own conversation, even before the dancers filled the floor and Dan could no longer see their table. He looked at Molly. She was sitting there, her eyes full of excitement, looking like a kid expecting to see Santa Claus come down the chimney at any minute.

And then it was time. Benny slid into it slow and easy, and Molly rested her cheek against her hand and looked at Dan with all her love in her eyes. Dan wiped the mouthpiece of his trumpet. The perspiration was running down his forehead, fogging his sight.

Then someone slid into Pete's empty chair and said in a soft voice, "I'll sit in on this one with you."

They rose as one man. Dan saw the shining blur as the other horn came up; he heard the words, "Take it easy going in and then we'll break it up." He looked out and saw Armister still at his table.

Dan closed his eyes, brought his horn to his mouth, and stiffened his lip. It stayed stiff. No roll, no curl, but Dan wasn't even aware of it. He only knew that he was following the other's lead, a smoky line of notes like skywriting against the blackness of his underlids. They curled and soared, true and clear, going up and up and curling over and coming down, easy at first, clear as a chime, then pushing on and on and out. Something inside his head kept saying, "I can't. I can't."

And suddenly the words were lost too, and there was nothing but the touch of the horn against his lips, nothing but the golden patterns against his eyelids, nothing but the trail the other man was laying down for him to dance on — as solid as a brick highway. You couldn't wander off it; you couldn't fall off. It rode under you there, carrying you right up to the stars, and beyond that to where the stars paled and you were out there somewhere, swinging into space.

"Molly," the trumpet blew, "Molly, this is for you. This is my love — like this — solid and pure, and nothing can take it away."

Things were happening out in front of the stand now, but Dan didn't know it. The men at the table were standing up now, standing on chairs, so they could look over the heads of the dancers at the stand. On the stand, things were happening, too. Benny was keeping the rhythm going — a solid beat — reaching beyond himself, as if to catch those shining notes on his flying fingers when they came tumbling down.

Then suddenly it was over. Dan brought his trumpet down and ran the back of his hand across his mouth. He was still rocking inside. The people in front of him were just a mist.

Who started the applause he didn't know, but Molly said later that it was the great Teddy himself who began pounding on the table. The men started it, and the dancers kept it up. Most of them didn't even know what they'd heard; they just sensed that they'd lived through something it wasn't the privilege of many to live

through. They crowded around the stand. The men in the band looked at Dan as if he were a stranger.

He shook his head to clear it and turned and stared at Pete's empty chair. He said in a half whisper, "Where did he go?"

The words were drowned in the jumping and shouting out in front, and it was just as well, for even as he said the words, Dan knew. "Sweet heaven and earth," he whispered. And the way he said them, the words were filled with prayerful awe. They washed out the lean years, and laid a firm foundation of unforgettable memory. No one but Dan Daly would ever know it, but he'd really played with the master of the golden cornet. He'd really done it at last! And then he saw Molly coming toward him with tears running down her face.

There probably isn't anyone who hasn't heard "Molly's Tune" by now. There wasn't a juke box in the country that didn't carry Teddy Armister's recording of it. Teddy rounded up a man to write some lyrics, sort of sweet and catchy. It went like wildfire. Hit the Top Ten and stayed there for months. But no one has ever heard it played the way it was played that night. Sometimes when the boys come down to the little place in the Fifties — Molly's Place that "Molly's Tune" paid for — sometimes when they jam, they take a try at it, and sometimes they almost make it, but not quite. Dan knows that they never will. Dan knows that the horn that played that tune that night was the one that death had silenced 20 years before.

READING COMPREHENSION

Summarizing. Choose the best phrase to complete each sentence. Then write the complete statements on your paper.

1. Dan's ability as a trumpet player was _____ (poor, outstanding, average).

2. "Molly's Tune" was a melody that _____ (Dan heard on the radio one day, Molly hummed when she was happy, the famous cornet player had written).

3. The great cornet player helped Dan play "Molly's Tune" by _____ (joining him in a duet, accompanying him on the piano, inspiring Dan through Dan's memories).

4. Dan and Molly achieved their dream of _____ (getting rich, traveling from club to club, opening a jazz club of their own).

Interpreting. Write the answer to each question on your paper.

1. What replaced the big bands in many places?

2. Why was Dan so affected by hearing the cornet player?

3. What gave Dan the courage to play "Molly's Tune" in front of Teddy Armister?

For Thinking and Discussing. Dan always had a dream. What was his dream and how did it change? Why are such dreams important to people?

UNDERSTANDING LITERATURE

Irony and Plot. The plot of a story is the series of events that leads to its conclusion. *Irony* occurs when what seems to be true and what really is true are opposites. A writer usually builds the action of a plot in a way that leads the reader to expect certain conclusions. If the action of the plot suddenly turns so that the outcome is the opposite of the expected, it has an ironic twist. "Trumpet Man" contains this sort of ironic twist.

Read each statement about the story. On your paper, answer the questions.

1. Dan wrote "Molly's Tune" and tried to get it published, but he was turned down again and again. What is the expected outcome of this situation? What actually happened?

2. Dan and Molly dreamed of having a place of their own, but their lack of money made the dream seem impossible. What would be the expected outcome? What actually happened?

3. Dan knew he would never be able to play "Molly's Tune" in front of Teddy Armister. He thought he would fail. What would be the expected outcome? What actually happened?

WRITING

Write a description of the scene in which Dan plays "Molly's Tune" from Molly's point of view. Did she expect him to be a success? Show her feelings and thoughts as she listens to him play.

How Much Land Does a Man Need?

based on the story by Leo Tolstoy

The great 19th-century Russian novelist Leo Tolstoy also wrote plays, essays, and short stories. Tolstoy thought and wrote a great deal about right and wrong, about values. He often used satire to point out what he felt was ridiculous or wrong about society and about people's behavior. Through his writing, he tried to bring about changes that he felt would improve life. His writings often had a moral; this story is an example.

Pakhom and the old chief stood at the top of the hill. They looked out at the rich land. It all belonged to the Bashkirs.

"How much do you want for your land?" Pakhom asked.

"We have only one price," the old chief answered. "A thousand dollars a day."

Pakhom could not understand. He had come to buy land by the acre.

"How can you measure land by the day?" Pakhom asked.

"You may have as much land as you can walk around in a day," the old chief answered.

Pakhom was surprised. "Look," he said, "a day's walking is a lot of land."

The old chief laughed. "It's all yours!" he said. "There is just one condition. You must leave from this hill at sunrise. If you are not back at sunset, your money is lost."

"How will you know where I walk?" Pakhom asked.

"Well, we will stand on this hill and wait while you walk around the land. You take a shovel with you and dig holes to show where you've walked. Pile the dirt high. All the land you walk around is yours, as long as you're back here on the hill at sunset."

Pakhom was very happy. This land would be the best that he had ever owned.

That night, Pakhom stayed in the tent of the old chief. But Pakhom was so excited that he could hardly sleep. He had traveled 500 miles to see the land of the Bashkirs. Tomorrow he would own a large part of it. He stayed awake planning what he would do with it. And finally, just before dawn, he drifted off to sleep.

When he woke, he saw the dawn through the open door of the tent. The sky was already turning white. "I must wake up the people," he thought. "It's time to go." Pakhom got up and woke his hired hand, who was asleep in the wagon outside. Then they woke the old chief.

"If we're going, let's go," Pakhom said. "It's time."

The Bashkirs got together, climbed on horseback and into wagons, and went to the hill. Meanwhile, Pakhom took a shovel and set off with his hired hand in his own wagon. They arrived at the hill just as day was breaking. The Bashkirs climbed out of their wagons, slid down from their horses, and got together in a group. The old chief came up to Pakhom and pointed to the land.

"There," he said. "Everything the eye can see is ours. Take your pick."

Pakhom's eyes glowed. It was all grassland, level as the palm of the hand.

The elder took off his cap and put it on the ground.

"That," he said, "will be the marker. Leave from here; return here. Whatever you walk around will be yours."

Pakhom drew out his money and placed it on the cap in front of the old chief. Then he took off his cap and his outer coat, put a bag of bread inside his jacket, took the shovel from his hired hand, and got set to go. He thought and thought over which way to take — it was good everywhere. He was thinking, "It's all the same. I'll head toward the sunrise." He turned to face the sun and waited for it to come up. "I must lose no time," he thought. "And walking's easier while it's still cold." As soon as the sun's rays came up, Pakhom put the shovel over his shoulder and started off across the land.

He walked neither quickly nor slowly. He covered a mile, stopped, dug a hole, and piled the dirt up so it could be seen. He walked farther. He covered still more ground, dug still another pit.

Pakhom looked back. He could see the hill and the people standing there. Pakhom guessed that he had covered about three miles. It was getting warmer; he took off his jacket, flung it over his shoulder, and went on. He covered another three miles. It was warm. He looked at the sun — already breakfast time.

"One leg finished," thought Pakhom. "But there are three more to go; it's too early to turn around yet. I'll just take my boots off." He sat down, took them off, stuck them in his belt, and went on. Walking became easier. He thought, "I'll just cover about three more miles, then start turning left. This is a very nice spot, too good to leave out. The farther away it is, the better it gets." He walked straight on. When he looked around, he could hardly see the hill. The people looked like black ants.

"Well," thought Pakhom, "I've taken enough on this side; I must turn. Besides, I've been sweating — I'm thirsty." He stopped, dug a bigger hole, and stacked the earth. He had a drink from his water flask. Then he turned sharply to the left. On and on he went; the grass grew taller and the day became hot. Pakhom began to feel tired; he looked at the sun — it was already lunch time. He stopped, sat on the ground, ate bread and drank water, but did not lie down. "Lie down and you'll fall asleep," he thought. After a while, he walked on. Walking was easy at first. Eating had increased his strength. But it had become very hot and he was becoming sleepy. Still he went on, thinking, "An hour of suffering for a lifetime of living."

He walked a long way in this direction, too. Then, after digging a hole and turning a second corner, Pakhom looked back at the hill. It was hardly visible — 12 miles away. "Well," thought Pakhom, "I've taken long sides; I must take this one shorter."

As he walked the third side, he walked faster. He looked at the sun — it was already late afternoon, and he had only covered a mile on the third side of the square. And it was still 12 miles to the starting point. "No," he thought, "I'll have a lopsided place, but I must go straight back so I'll arrive in time. I'll not take any more. There's lots of land already." Pakhom shoveled out a hole as quickly as he could and turned straight toward the hill.

As Pakhom walked toward the hill, he began having difficulties. He was perspiring, and his bare legs were cut and bruised

and were beginning to fail him. He wanted to rest but could not — otherwise he would not arrive before sunset. The sun would not wait; it continued sinking, sinking. "Ah," he thought, "if only I haven't made a mistake and taken too much! What if I don't make it?" He looked ahead at the hill and looked at the sun. The starting point was far away, and the sun was getting close to the horizon.

So Pakhom went on with difficulty; he kept walking faster and faster. He walked, walked — and was still far away; he broke into a run. He threw off his jacket, dropped his boots and water flask; he kept only his shovel to lean on. "Ah," he thought, "I've been too greedy; I've ruined the whole thing; I won't get there by sundown." And fear shortened his breath even more. Pakhom ran; his shirt and trousers clung to his body with sweat; his mouth was dry. A hammer beat in his heart, and his legs no longer seemed to belong to his body — they were collapsing under him. Pakhom began to worry about dying of strain.

He was afraid of dying, but unable to stop. "I've run so far," he thought. "I'd be a fool to stop now." He ran and ran, and was very close when he heard a screeching — the Bashkirs were shrieking at him — and his heart became even more inflamed by their cries. Pakhom pressed forward with his remaining strength, but the sun was already reaching the horizon; and, slipping behind a cloud, it became large, red, and bloody.

Pakhom was not far from the starting point. He could see the people waving at him, urging him on. He saw the cap on the ground and the money on it; and he saw the old chief sitting on the ground, laughing, holding his sides with his hands. "There is plenty of land," he thought, "if it please God to let me live on it. Oh, I've ruined myself," he thought. "I won't make it."

The sun had touched the earth and began to slip behind the horizon, which cut it into an arc. Pakhom used all of his remaining strength, driving his body forward so that his legs could barely move fast enough to keep him from falling. Just as Pakhom ran up to the base of the hill it suddenly became dark. The sun had set. He sighed. "My work has fallen through," he thought. He was about to stop when he heard the Bashkirs still shrieking. And he remembered that though it looked from below as if the sun had set, it would still be shining on top of the hill. It was still light there. As Pakhom reached the top, he saw the old chief sitting in front of the cap, laughing, holding his sides with his hands. Pakhom groaned; his legs gave way, and he fell, his hands touching the cap.

"Aiee, good man!" cried the old chief. "You have gotten plenty of land!"

Pakhom's hired hand ran to lift him, but the blood was flowing from Pakhom's mouth and he lay dead.

The hired hand took the shovel and dug Pakhom a grave just long enough to reach from his feet to his head — six feet in all — and buried him.

READING COMPREHENSION

Summarizing. Choose the best phrase to complete each sentence. Then write the complete statements on your paper.

1. A thousand dollars was the price of _____ (an acre of the Bashkirs' land, all of the land, all the land a man could walk in a day).

2. Pakhom had to be back on the hill at _____ (sunrise, noon, sunset).

3. If Pakhom didn't get back in time, he would lose _____ (his dignity and self-respect, the land and his money, his life).

4. Pakhom died because of his _____ (hard work, greed, anger).

Interpreting. Write the answer to each question on your paper.

1. What kind of land did the Bashkirs offer for sale?

2. What did Pakhom do in the late afternoon to shorten his trip?

3. Why were the Bashkirs willing to offer their land at such an inexpensive price?

4. What is the answer to the question in the title of the story: How much land does a man need?

For Thinking and Discussing. What sort of person is a modern-day equivalent of Pakhom? What might his or her goals be? How might he or she make a fatal mistake?

UNDERSTANDING LITERATURE

Satire. *Satire* is a form of literature in which an author criticizes a human shortcoming by making it look ridiculous. Writers who use satire have a serious purpose. They are trying to correct what they see as wrong or ridiculous in human behavior. They want their readers to change their own ridiculous behavior.

A writer of satire usually has very strong beliefs of his or her own. This was true of the author of "How Much Land Does a Man Need?" Tolstoy thought that people could find true happiness not through wealth but through spiritual ideas and good deeds.

To understand this story better, answer these questions on your paper.

1. What was Pakhom's greatest desire?

2. What mistake did Pakhom make in walking off his piece of land?

3. What character trait did Pakhom possess that caused him to make this mistake?

4. What was Pakhom's punishment?

5. How was the end of the story ironic, the opposite of Pakhom's intentions?

WRITING

Describe Tolstoy's purpose in writing this story. What was he ridiculing about human nature? What lesson was he trying to teach?

Ozymandias

by Percy Bysshe Shelley

The Questioner of the Sphinx, *Elihu Vedder, 1863*

I met a traveller from an antique land,

Who said: Two vast and trunkless legs of stone

Stand in the desert. Near them, on the sand,

Half sunk, a shattered visage lies, whose frown

And wrinkled lip and sneer of cold command

Tell that its sculptor well those passions read,

Which yet survive stamped on these lifeless things

The hand that mocked them, and the heart that fed:

And on the pedestal these words appear:

"My name is Ozymandias, King of Kings:

Look on my works, ye Mighty, and despair!"

Nothing beside remains. Round the decay

Of that colossal wreck, boundless and bare

The lone and level sands stretch far away.

---

1. What was the character of Ozymandias that the sculptor captured so well in stone?

2. What is the setting of this poem?

3. What was the meaning of the words that Ozymandias had carved in his statue? What do they reveal about how Ozymandias viewed himself?

4. The last three lines of the poem express its theme. What is the poet's attitude toward Ozymandias and ambition?

The Farm Magnate

by Monteiro Lobato

Everyone in Moreira's family wants something. His wife wants a big house in the city. His daughter wants a piano — and a husband. But they try to get what they want by trickery. All the tricksters are tricked in this tale from Brazil.

The Corn Stalk was probably the worst farm in Brazil. It had already ruined three owners. The latest owner, David Moreira de Souza, acquired it on an installment plan. He was convinced then that it was a bonanza. But there he was, dragging along under the burden of debt, scratching his head in despair.

The coffee trees would be bare year in, year out. Lashed by hail or blighted by frosts, their yield never filled a good-sized basket.

The pasture grounds had become a camping ground of ants who shared the field with deadly weeds. Any animal that set foot there was soon a skeleton covered with insects, a most pitiful sight to see.

Exhausted, dry soil showed through underbrush and sparse wild cane. The sugarcane grew no thicker than a reed, producing cane so hard that it passed whole through the mill.

The roads were left half-laid. Fences lay on the ground. Farmhands' quarters had shaky, leaky roofs over ugly rooms. Even the manor house was decaying. Loose sections of plaster, rotting floors, windows without panes, cracked walls. . . . It was doubtful that there was anything whole in the place.

Within this crumbling frame lived Moreira, the owner, whose worries made him scratch the top of his gray head a hundred times a day. His wife, poor Doña Izaura, had a face marked with years of hard toil. Zico, their eldest, was a good-for-nothing son. If not asleep, he did nothing but pursue unsuccessful romances.

Zilda, the daughter, was about 18. She was a nice girl, but sentimental beyond reason. All she did was read love stories and build castles in the air.

The one way out of this situation was to sell this dismal farm. It wasn't easy, however, to get hold of a big enough fool. Quite a few would-be buyers had already been lured by artful ads. No one had made an offer.

"I wouldn't have it as a gift," they grumbled to themselves.

Moreira's dizzy brain, after so much scratching, came up with a wily plan. Why not set plants from the rich neighboring soil in one or two places where visitors might look! The rascal did even more. In a certain hollow, he stuck a stick of garlic imported from red earth. Then he fertilized the coffee trees along the road, enough to cover up the other bare trees. The old man then concealed the sterile soil under a screen of rich sifted earth.

One day, he received a letter from his agent announcing a new buyer. "Play up to this fellow," the agent said, "for he'll fall. His name is Pedro Trancoso. He's very rich, very young, very talkative, and wants to run a farm for the fun of it. Everything depends on how well you can fool him."

Moreira got ready for the job. First of all he told all his hands to be at their posts and know what to say. They must answer all questions in such a way that the dismal farm was transformed into a marvel of fertility. Buyers usually suspected what owners said and were in the habit of secretly questioning the help. Here, if this happened, and it always did happen, dialogues of this sort would take place:

"Does it ever freeze here?"

"Sometimes, and only in bad years."

"Peas pretty good?"

"Only this year, I planted five quarts and I gathered 50 bushels. You just ought to see them!"

"Are the cattle troubled with ticks?"

"Bah! One now and then. But there's no better place for breeding. No bad weeds in the pastures. It's a pity the poor owner hasn't the strength he needs, for this would be a model estate!"

After training the hands, the family discussed the preparations for receiving their guest. The revival of their dying hopes filled everybody with happiness.

"Something tells me that this time the deal will go through," said the good-for-nothing son. Then he announced that he was going to need some money to set himself up in business.

The wife wanted a house in the city. For a long time, she had had an eye on one, a nice house for moderately rich people. Zilda asked for a piano, and crates and more crates of novels.

That night, they went to bed happy. Early the next day, they sent to the city for some food for their guest — butter, cheese, cookies. There was some hesitancy about the butter.

"It's really not worth the trouble," grumbled the wife. "It means three thousand *reis*. I'd rather buy goods that I need so much with that money."

"We've got to do it, old girl. Sometimes one little detail will clinch the deal. Butter is grease and grease oils the wheels."

The butter won out.

While they were waiting for these things, Doña Izaura got busy with the house, sweeping, dusting, and arranging things. She cooked the fattest of the bony chickens and a lame little suckling pig. She was making dough for pastry when:

"Here he comes!" shouted Moreira from the window where he had been posted since early morning. He was as nervous as could be, scanning the road with an

537

old pair of binoculars. Without leaving his observation post, he kept describing the details that he could make out.

"He's young. . . . Well dressed. . . . Panama hat. . . ."

At last, the guest arrived and presented his card. Pedro Trancoso de Carvalhaes Fagundes. Fine appearance. The air of one who has plenty of money. Younger and far more refined than any buyer who had thus far visited the estate.

He told a number of tales with the ease of one who is absolutely at home in the world. He related his trip, the incidents on the way — a tiny, long-tailed monkey that he had seen hanging from a branch.

After Moreira and Trancoso had gone into the sitting room, Zico glued his ear against the keyhole. From this strategic point, he whispered to the women who were busy arranging the table whatever he managed to catch of the conversation. Then he excitedly told his sister, "He's a bachelor, Zilda!"

Unable to hide her feelings, Zilda dropped the knives and forks and disappeared. A half hour later, she returned, wearing her best dress. There were two round spots on her cheeks.

Trancoso managed to enchant the whole family. Zilda received compliments such as she had never dreamed of, and they set her heart fluttering. Similar praise was meted out to everything — the chicken stew, the pie, even the drinking water. Doña Izaura was filled with joy. The praise of her cooking had won her heart.

Buyers, as a rule, ran down everything and had eyes only for the defects. Not

Trancoso. He praised things to the skies. When he was shown the camouflaged spots, he exclaimed, "This is extraordinary!"

Seeing the garlic, he was beside himself with surprise. "This is simply marvelous! Never did I imagine that I would find such a plant in these parts!" He even plucked off a leaf, which he put in his notebook as a souvenir.

Trancoso continued his sweet-talking until night.

What a night that was! One would have thought that the angel of happiness had spread glittering wings over that sad household. Zilda saw the realization of all the love stories she had read. Doña Izaura had visions of marrying her off to a wealthy magnate. Moreira dreamed that his debts were paid and money filled his pockets. Zico pictured himself a merchant. He was loaning goods to Tudinha's family, until the man, won over by kindness, gave Zico his daughter to marry.

Only Trancoso slept like a rock, unvisited by dream or nightmare. It's great to be rich!

The next day, Trancoso visited the rest of the estate — the coffee trees and the pastures. He started talking about improvements. Meanwhile, Moreira had decided to ask 40 *contos* for the Corn Stalk. As Trancoso's enthusiasm continued, the owner thought it would be a good idea to raise the price. After the scene of the garlic shoot, he made up his mind to ask 45. After seeing the cattle, he had raised the amount to 50. On the way back from the coffee trees, he went up to 60. When at last the great question was asked, the old man replied in a firm voice:

"Seventy-five," and he awaited the answer. He was ready for a storm of objections. To his surprise, however, Trancoso found the price reasonable.

"Why, that's not bad at all," he replied. "It's a lower figure than I had expected."

The old rascal bit his lip and tried to remedy his error.

"Seventy-five, yes, but . . . not including the cattle."

"Oh, certainly," responded Trancoso.

". . . nor the pigs, either."

"Of course."

". . . nor the furniture."

"Quite natural."

Moreira gasped. There was nothing more to exclude. He called himself stupid. Why hadn't he asked 80?

His wife, when told of the situation, called him an idiot.

"But, woman, even 40 would have been a fortune!"

"Then 80 would have been twice as good. Don't make excuses. I never yet saw a Moreira who wasn't a blockhead. It's in the blood. You're not to blame."

For a moment, they were both sullen. Then their mood changed by their eagerness to build castles in the air with this unexpected windfall.

Zico took advantage of the situation to clinch the promise of the money he needed.

Doña Izaura changed her mind about their new home. She had thought of another one now — Eusebio Leite's house on the street through which all the processions passed.

"But that costs 12 *contos*," protested the husband.

"Yes, but it's much better than that other hovel. It's well laid out. The only thing I don't like about it is the bedroom. . . . Too dark."

"We can put in a skylight."

"Then the garden needs repairs."

Into the wee hours, they were busy restoring the house. As they were sleepily putting the finishing touches, Zico knocked at the door.

"Three *contos* won't be enough. I must have five."

The father, between two yawns, agreed to six.

And Zilda? She was sailing the high seas of a fairy tale.

Let her sail on.

The day when the genial buyer had to leave came at last. Trancoso said his farewells. He was indeed sorry that he could not prolong so delightful a stay. He had important matters to handle elsewhere. The deal was as good as settled. He would give his answer within a week.

So he left, taking with him a package of eggs. He liked the breed of the hens they raised there very much. He also took a little sack of *caras*, which he was so fond of eating.

He took, in addition, an excellent souvenir: the best horse on the farm. He had praised the animal so highly during their rides. When he offered to buy it, Moreira felt honor-bound to give it as a gift.

The family was honored that such a wealthy man would take such humble gifts. And thus, even after he had left, the wealthy young man filled the thoughts of the household for a whole week.

But the week passed without bringing the eagerly awaited reply. Then another. And still another. Moreira, a little worried, wrote to him. No reply. He recalled a friend who lived in the same city, and sent him a letter. He asked him to ask Trancoso for his decision. As for the price, he would come down a trifle.

His friend replied without delay:

Dear Moreira:
Either I am mistaken or you have been taken in. There isn't any wealthy man here by that name. There is a Trancosinho, a scamp who deceives folks who don't know him. At times, he pretends to be a farm buyer. He spends a week at the home of the owner. He eats and drinks of the very best — and then, when everything is just about settled, he skips out. He's done this a hundred times, always changing the scene of his activities. The rascal likes a change of diet. I won't bother telling him about your offer. Imagine that good-for-nothing buying a farm!

Moreira collapsed into a chair, utterly crushed, the letter dropping from his fingers. Then blood rushed to his face and his eyes blazed.

"The dirty dog!"

The four hopes of the household came tumbling down with a crash. The daughter was in tears, the mother was furious, and the two men raged. Zico declared that he would find the rascal and smash his face.

"Patience, my boy. The world goes round. One fine day, I'll come across the thief. Then I'll square accounts."

Poor air castles! They were transformed into gloomy, abandoned ruins. Doña Izaura mourned her cakes, her butter, her chickens. As for Zilda, the disaster was like a hurricane roaring through a flourishing garden. All the tragic passages of the novels she had read passed through her mind's eye. In every instance, she was the victim.

The tale would have ended here if not for an unexpected turn of events.

Fortune willed that the rascal, Trancosinho, should win 50 *contos* in the lottery. Don't laugh. Why shouldn't it have been Trancoso? Luck is blind — and he had the right number in his pocket! He won the 50 *contos* — the most money he had ever laid hands on.

It took him weeks to get over his surprise. Then he decided to become a land owner. He would buy a farm.

He ran mentally over the list of all he had visited during years of wanderings. He finally settled upon the Corn Stalk. The determining factor was, above all, the recollection of the girl and the old lady's cakes. He planned to let his father-in-law manage the farm. He will live a life of ease, lulled by Zilda's love and his mother-in-law's cooking.

So he wrote to Moreira announcing his return to close the deal.

When that letter reached the Corn Stalk, there were roars of rage mingled with howls of vengeance.

"At last!" cried the old man. "The rascal liked the feast and is coming back for more. But this time, I'll ruin his appetite. See if I don't!" he said, rubbing his palms.

A flash of hope passed over Zilda's heart. But she did not dare say a word for fear of her father and brother who were plotting a terrible settlement. She hoped for a miracle.

The great day arrived. Trancoso burst in upon the estate on the horse given to him by Moreira. The old man came out to welcome him, his arms behind his back. The amiable rascal burst into greetings:

"My dear, dear Moreira! At last the day has come. I am ready to take over your estate at once."

Moreira was trembling with anger. He waited for the scoundrel to dismount. Trancoso released the reins and came toward him, all smiles, with open arms. Then the old man drew from under his coat a whip and started lashing away at him.

"So you want a farm, do you? Here, here's your farm. Thief!" and slash, slash, fell the whip tails.

The poor young man, dazed by this unexpected attack, rushed to his horse and threw himself blindly on it. Zico sailed into him with all the anger of a brother-in-law-that-might-have-been.

Doña Izaura set the dogs upon him.

The ill-fated farm magnate, cornered like a fox, dug the spurs into his horse. He fled beneath a shower of insults — and stones. As he cleared the gateway he could hear the old lady shouting, "Cake gobbler! This is your last trick, egg robber, yam thief!"

And Zilda?

Behind the window, her eyes burned out with weeping. The sad lass saw the gallant prince of her dream disappear forever in clouds of dust.

542

READING COMPREHENSION

Summarizing. Choose the best phrase to complete each sentence. Then write the complete statements on your paper.

1. Moreira hoped to sell the farm by _____ (fooling a rich buyer, improving the property, selling the farm for less than it was worth).

2. Zilda, the daughter, had dreams of _____ (living in the city, owning the farm herself, marrying Trancoso).

3. Trancoso was really _____ (an impostor, a Brazilian prince, a rich landowner).

4. On his second visit, Trancoso's aim was to _____ (trick Moreira again, buy the farm, steal another horse from Moreira).

Interpreting. Write the answer to each question on your paper.

1. What did each family member expect to gain from Trancoso's purchase of the farm?

2. The wife said, "I never yet saw a Moreira who wasn't a blockhead." How does this apply to each member of the family?

3. What ironic event occurred at the end of the story?

For Thinking and Discussing. Do you think Moreira and Trancoso both got what they deserved at the end of the story? Why or why not?

UNDERSTANDING LITERATURE

Satire and Irony. In *satire*, a writer criticizes a human shortcoming by making it look ridiculous. Irony is a favorite weapon of the satirist. By turning the tables on a foolish character, a writer makes him look even more ridiculous.

Read the statements below. Answer the questions that follow on your paper.

1. In "The Farm Magnate," the author presents us with a cast of ridiculous characters, and he does not hide his scorn for them. Find two statements that describe the Moreira family in a critical way. Write them on your paper.

2. The first ironic twist in the story came when the buyer left the farm, promising to be in touch. Moreira never heard from him again. What did they learn about the buyer?

3. When the scoundrel Trancoso won a fortune in a lottery, he made a decision that was a joke on him. What did Trancoso want to do with his money?

4. The author ends the story with a second ironic twist, Moreira again being the target of his satire. What was the second ironic incident in the story?

WRITING

Continue the story by describing some misfortune that came to Trancoso and his money. Write your description from a satiric point of view.

The Importance of Being Earnest

adapted from the play by Oscar Wilde

Oscar Wilde was born in 1854 in Ireland and was educated at Oxford. He is famous for the wit and satire of his plays and stories. The Importance of Being Earnest *is one of his best and funniest works.*

CHARACTERS

Jack Worthing
Lane, a manservant
Algernon Moncrieff
Lady Augusta Bracknell
Gwendolen Fairfax
Miss Prism, a governess
Cecily Cardew
Dr. Chasuble, a minister
Merriman, a butler

Scene One

Jack: Half Moon Street, West, driver. Algernon Moncrieff's home. (*He arrives at Algernon's home.*)

Lane (*announcing, in typical butler fashion*): Mr. Ernest Worthing. (*Enter Jack. Lane exits.*)

Algernon (*a young, pleasant man with a brisk way of speaking*): How are you, my dear Ernest? What brings you up to town?

Jack: Oh, pleasure, pleasure! What else should bring one anywhere?

Algernon: Where have you been since last Thursday?

Jack: In the country.

Algernon: What on earth do you do there?

Jack: When one is in town, one amuses oneself. When one is in the country, one amuses other people. It is excessively boring.

Algernon: And who are the people you amuse?

Jack (*airily*): Oh, neighbors, neighbors.

Algernon: Are they nice, your neighbors?

Jack: Perfectly horrible. Never speak to one of them.

Algernon: How immensely you must amuse them!

Jack: But why all these cups, Algy? Are you expecting someone to tea?

Algernon: Merely Aunt Augusta and Gwendolen.

Jack (*pleased*): How perfectly delightful!

Algernon: I'm afraid Aunt Augusta won't quite approve of your being here.

Jack: Oh? May I ask why?

Algernon: My dear fellow, the way you flirt with Gwendolen is perfectly disgraceful. It's almost as bad as the way Gwendolen flirts with you.

Jack: But I'm in love with Gwendolen. I've come up to town expressly to propose to her.

Algernon: I thought you had come up for pleasure. I call that business!

Jack: How utterly unromantic you are!

Algernon: I really don't see anything romantic in proposing. Oh, it's very romantic to be in love. But there's nothing romantic in a definite proposal. Besides, I don't give my consent.

Jack: Your consent?

Algernon: My dear fellow, Gwendolen is my first cousin. And before I allow you to marry her, you will have to clear up the whole question of Cecily. *(He rings bell.)*

Jack: Cecily? What do you mean, Algy, by Cecily? I don't know anyone of the name of Cecily.

Lane *(enters):* You rang, sir?

Algernon: Yes, Lane. Bring me the cigarette case Mr. Worthing left in the smoking room the last time he dined here.

Lane: Yes, sir.

Jack: Do you mean to say you have had my cigarette case all the time? I've been frantic over it. I was very nearly offering a reward.

Algernon: Well, I wish you would offer one. I happen to need cash!

Jack: There is no good offering a reward now that the thing has been found.

Lane: The cigarette case, sir. *(Algernon takes it at once. Lane exits.)*

Algernon: No matter if you should offer a reward, for I see now that I look at the inscription, that it isn't yours at all.

Jack: Of course it's mine.

Algernon: But this case is a present from someone named Cecily, and you said that you didn't know anyone of that name.

Jack: Well, if you want to know, Cecily happens to be my aunt.

Algernon: Then why does she call you her uncle? Here's the inscription: "From little Cecily, with her fondest love to her dear Uncle Jack." Besides, your name isn't Jack at all; it's Ernest.

Jack: It isn't Ernest; it's Jack.

Algernon: But your name has always been Ernest!

Jack: Well, my name is Ernest in town and Jack in the country, and the cigarette case was given to me in the country.

Algernon: Will you kindly explain yourself?

Jack: Give me my cigarette case first. Thank you. Now listen closely to what I am about to say. Old Mr. Thomas Cardew, who adopted me when I was a little boy, made me in his will guardian to his granddaughter, Miss Cecily Cardew. Cecily, who addresses me as her uncle, lives at my place in the country under the charge of her admirable governess, Miss Prism.

Algernon: Where is this place in the country?

Jack: That is nothing to you, dear boy. You are not going to be invited.

Algernon: Now go on. Why are you Ernest in town and Jack in the country?

Jack: In order to be a good guardian to Cecily, I must adopt a high moral tone regarding everything while I am in the country. This becomes rather boring at times, and so in order to get up to town, I have always pretended to have a younger brother by the name of Ernest, who lives in the Albany, and gets into the most dreadful scrapes. That, my dear Algy, is the whole truth pure and simple.

Algernon: The truth is rarely pure and never simple!

Lane *(enters to announce):* Lady Bracknell and Miss Fairfax. *(Turns and exits.)*

Lady Bracknell *(enters; a fatuous woman):* Good afternoon, dear Algernon. I hope you are behaving very well.

Algernon: I'm feeling very well, Aunt Augusta.

Lady Bracknell: That's not quite the same thing. Ah, Mr. Worthing, good afternoon.

Algernon: How are you today, Gwendolen?

Gwendolen *(a coy, almost too-sweet girl):* How do I look?

Jack: You're quite perfect, Miss Fairfax.

Lady Bracknell: While I think of it, Algernon, have you the music you promised to give me for my little musicale this evening?

Algernon: I've laid the music out on the piano. You can pick out those selections you prefer. If you'll kindly come into the next room for a moment . . .

Lady Bracknell: Thank you, Algernon. It is very thoughtful of you. I'm sure the program will be delightful. After all, you have such excellent taste. *(They exit.)*

Jack *(falteringly):* Charming day it has been, Miss Fairfax.

Gwendolen: Oh, oh yes.

Jack: I would like to take advantage of Lady Bracknell's absence . . .

Gwendolen: I would advise you to do so. Mamma has a way of coming back into a room so suddenly!

Jack *(nervously):* Miss Fairfax, ever since I met you, I have admired you more than any girl . . . I have ever met since . . . I met you.

Gwendolen: Yes, I am quite aware of that fact. And even before I met you, I must confess, I was far from indifferent to you. We live, as you know, in an age of ideals. My ideal has always been to love someone of the name of Ernest. There is something in that name that inspires confidence. The moment Algernon told me that he had a friend called Ernest, I knew that I was destined to love you.

Jack: But you don't really mean to say that you couldn't love me if my name wasn't Ernest? Supposing it were something else.

Gwendolen: Like what?

Jack: Well . . . like Jack.

Gwendolen: Jack? No, there is very little music in the name of Jack, if any at all, indeed. It produces no vibrations. The only really safe name is Ernest.

Jack: Gwendolen, I must get christened at once — I mean, we must get married at once.

Gwendolen: But you haven't proposed to me yet.

Jack: Well, may I propose to you now?

Gwendolen: I think it would be an admirable opportunity. And I'll spare you any possible disappointment, Mr. Worthing. It's only fair to tell you that I am fully determined to accept you.

Jack: Gwendolen!

Gwendolen: Yes, Mr. Worthing? What have you to say to me?

Jack: Gwendolen, will you marry me?

Gwendolen: Of course I will, darling.

Really, how long you took!

Lady Bracknell *(entering angrily):* Mr. Worthing! Rise, sir, from your knees. Such a position is most unbecoming.

Gwendolen: Mamma! I am engaged to Mr. Worthing.

Lady Bracknell: Well, in that event, sir, I have a few questions to put to you. Gwendolen, you will wait for me below in the carriage.

Gwendolen: Mamma!

Lady Bracknell: In the carriage, Gwendolen!

Gwendolen: Yes, Mamma. *(She exits.)*

Lady Bracknell: How old are you, Mr. Worthing?

Jack: Twenty-nine.

Lady Bracknell: A very good age to be married at. Now to your parents.

Jack: I have lost both my parents.

Lady Bracknell: Both? That seems like carelessness. Who was your father? **Jack:** I'm afraid I really don't know. The fact is, Lady Bracknell, I was . . . well, found. In the cloakroom of a train station by a gentleman named Mr. Thomas Cardew. He gave me the name of Worthing because he happened to have a ticket to Worthing in his pocket. Yes, I was found, Lady Bracknell, in a large, black handbag.

Lady Bracknell (indignant): I'm sure that you can hardly consider that a proper basis for recognition in society.

Jack: May I ask, then, what you would advise me to do?

Lady Bracknell: I would strongly urge you, sir, to try to acquire some relations as soon as possible. You can hardly imagine that I would allow my only daughter to marry into a cloakroom, and form an alliance with a parcel! Good morning, Mr. Worthing! (She exits.)

Jack (calling out): It's all right, Algy. You can come out now.

Algernon (enters): Didn't it go off all right, old boy? You don't mean to say that Gwendolen refused you!

Jack: Oh, Gwendolen is as right as a trivet. Her mother is unbearable.

Algernon: Did you tell Gwendolen the truth about Ernest?

Jack: My dear fellow, the truth isn't the sort of thing one tells a nice young lady like Gwendolen. I plan to get rid of Ernest by the end of the week; he shall die of a chill — in Paris.

Lane (enters and announces): Miss Fairfax.

Algernon: Gwendolen, upon my word!

Gwendolen: Mamma has just told me all, Ernest. I may never meet you again in town. However, if you'll give me your country address . . .

Jack (in a stage whisper): I don't want Algy to know, but it's the Manor House, Woolton, Hertfordshire.

Gwendolen: What is it again? I can't hear!

Algernon: He said he didn't want me to hear, but it's the Manor House, Woolton, Hertfordshire.

Jack *(outraged):* Oh, bother, Algy! Come along, Gwendolen, I'll escort you to the door.

Algernon *(pleasantly):* Good-bye, Cousin Gwendolen. Good-bye, Ernest. *(Calling off.)* Oh, Lane. Tomorrow I'm going visiting — to Mr. Worthing's country home.

Lane: Yes, sir.

Algernon: I shall probably not be back till Monday. Pack my full dress and my summer suit. Oh, I hope tomorrow will be a fine day, Lane.

Lane: It never is, sir. It never is!

Scene Two

Garden at the Manor House.

Miss Prism *(a prim, proper voice, calling):* Cecily! Cecily! Ah, so you're here in the garden. Put away that diary and come to your German lesson. You know your Uncle Jack put particular stress on your German lesson before he left for town yesterday. I really don't see why you waste your time on a diary, when you could be spending it on your German lesson.

Cecily *(a sweet, but affected, girl):* I keep a diary in order to enter the wonderful secrets of my life.

Miss Prism: But memory is the diary that we all carry about with us.

Cecily: I believe it's memory that is responsible for those horrible three-volume novels everyone reads nowadays.

Miss Prism: Do not speak slightingly of the three-volume novel. I wrote one myself in earlier days. Alas, I lost the manuscript once, and so I was never able to finish it.

Cecily: That is a shame, Miss Prism. But look, I see dear Dr. Chasuble coming up through the garden.

Miss Prism *(sighing):* Ah, Dr. Chasuble. This is indeed a pleasure.

Dr. Chasuble *(an elderly minister):* Has Mr. Worthing returned from town yet?

Miss Prism: No, we don't expect him till Monday.

Dr. Chasuble: Well then, I'll be on my way. Would you care to walk a way with me, Miss Prism?

Miss Prism *(sighing):* Gladly. Now study your German, Cecily! *(They exit.)*

Cecily *(annoyed):* Oh, horrid, horrid, horrid German!

Merriman *(entering):* Excuse me, Miss Cardew. Mr. Ernest Worthing is calling.

Cecily *(delighted):* Mr. Ernest Worthing! Uncle Jack's wicked brother! How exciting! Send him out, please, Merriman.

Algernon *(enters):* You must be my little cousin Cecily, I'm sure!

Cecily: And you are Uncle Jack's brother, my cousin Ernest, my wicked cousin Ernest. I don't understand how you happen to be here. Uncle Jack won't be back till Monday afternoon.

Algernon: What a shame that I must leave, then, on Monday morning.

Cecily: It would be better if you could wait for him, I think. He is anxious to talk to you about emigrating. He said he's sending you to Australia. I shouldn't wonder that he does — you do look awfully pale.

Algernon: I expect it's because I'm so awfully hungry.

Cecily: How thoughtless of me! Won't you come in for tea?

Algernon: Thank you. You know, cousin

Cecily, you're the prettiest girl I ever saw.

Cecily: Miss Prism says that all good looks are a trap.

Algernon: They are a trap — one every sensible man wants to be caught in!

Cecily: Oh, I don't think I would care to catch a sensible man! I shouldn't know what to talk to him about! *(They pass into the house. Miss Prism and Dr. Chasuble return.)*

Jack *(enters):* Ah, Miss Prism! Dr. Chasuble!

Miss Prism: Mr. Worthing! Why, we didn't expect you back till Monday! But — are you in mourning?

Jack: My poor brother.

Dr. Chasuble: Still leading his shameful, wicked life?

Jack *(mournfully):* Alas, he is leading no life at all. He's dead — of a chill, in Paris.

Dr. Chasuble: My sympathies, sir. I shall mention this in Sunday's sermon.

Jack: Ah, that reminds me. I should like to be christened, Dr. Chasuble. This afternoon, if convenient.

Dr. Chasuble: But you have never been christened before?

Jack: I don't know. At any rate, I should like to be christened this afternoon. Will half-past-five do?

Cecily *(entering):* Uncle Jack! How nice to see you back. Who do you think is in the dining room? Your brother Ernest. He arrived half an hour ago. And what do you think? He has already proposed marriage to me. Of course, I have accepted him. And he's promised to be wicked no more, but to change his ways.

Miss Prism: But Mr. Worthing's brother Ernest is dead, Cecily.

Algernon *(enters):* I am no such thing, Miss Prism. *(With warmth.)* Dear brother Jack!

Jack *(astonished):* Algernon! *(Catching himself.)* I mean, Ernest!

Dr. Chasuble: I think it is so touching to see this family reunion. Come, Cecily, Miss Prism; we shall leave them alone.

Cecily: Do forgive each other — please! *(Cecily, Miss Prism, and Dr. Chasuble exit.)*

Jack: Algy, you young scoundrel. You must leave at once.

Algernon: Don't be silly, Jack. I'm engaged to Cecily, and I'm staying.

Jack *(calling):* Merriman, send for the dogcart. Mr. Ernest is leaving.

Algernon *(calling):* Never mind, Merriman. He's decided to stay after all.

Jack: He hasn't!

Algernon: He has.

Jack: Oh, no he hasn't!

Algernon: Oh, yes he has!

Jack *(after a pause):* Ohhhhh, what's the use?

Scene Three

Manor House.

Merriman *(announcing):* Miss Gwendolen Fairfax.

Cecily: Pray let me introduce myself. I am Cecily Cardew.

Gwendolen: How do you do, Miss Cardew? I am Gwendolen Fairfax.

Cecily: How do you do?

Gwendolen: Are you on a visit here at Mr. Worthing's country home?

Cecily: Why no, I am Mr. Worthing's ward.

Gwendolen: His ward! He never told me that he had a ward. Though I must say, I'm not jealous. Ernest is so dependable!

Cecily: Oh, it is not Mr. Ernest Worthing who is my guardian. It is his elder brother — Jack. Oh no, Mr. Ernest is not my guardian — indeed, soon I shall be his. You see, Mr. Ernest and I are engaged.

Gwendolen *(with controlled coolness):* My darling Cecily, I thing there must be some error. Mr. Ernest Worthing is engaged to me.

Cecily: My dearest Gwendolen, it is you who are mistaken. Ernest proposed to me just 15 minutes ago.

Gwendolen: It is certainly quite curious; he asked me to be his wife yesterday afternoon at 5:30. Therefore, I have the prior claim.

Cecily: I should say it was quite clear that he has changed his mind.

Gwendolen: But here he comes now. I'll ask him myself. Ernest, dear!

Jack *(enters):* Gwendolen, darling, this is a surprise.

Cecily: I knew there must be some mistake, Miss Fairfax. The gentleman whom you are now kissing is my dear guardian, Uncle Jack.

Gwendolen *(horrified):* Jack!

Cecily: Here comes Ernest now.

Algernon *(enters):* Well, whom have we here?

Cecily: May I ask, Ernest, if you are engaged to this young lady?

Algernon: To what young lady? Good heavens, Gwendolen!

Cecily: Yes, Ernest, to good heavens, Gwendolen.

Gwendolen: I knew there was an error, Miss Cardew. The gentleman you now embrace is my cousin, Mr. Algernon Moncrieff.

Cecily *(horrified):* Algernon!

Gwendolen: Well, then, if *you* are not Ernest, and if *you* are not Ernest — who on earth *is* Ernest?

Jack *(slow and hesitatingly):* Gwendolen — Cecily — it is very painful for me to say this, but I'm afraid the truth is — that there is no Ernest!

Merriman *(announces):* Lady Bracknell!

Algernon: Good lord, it's Aunt Augusta!

Gwendolen: Heavens, it's Mamma!

Lady Bracknell *(enters):* Mr. Worthing, why have you spirited off my daughter?

Gwendolen: He didn't spirit me off, Mamma. I came of my own free will. Mr. Worthing and I are engaged.

Lady Bracknell: You are no such thing. And Algernon, who is the girl around whose waist your left arm is twined?

Jack: Allow me to present my ward, Miss Cecily Cardew.

Algernon: Cecily and I are engaged.

Lady Bracknell: You are no such thing. There must be something strange in the air hereabouts. There seems to be a peculiar number of engagements!

Merriman *(announcing):* Dr. Chasuble and Miss Prism.

Dr. Chasuble *(enters):* About the christenings, gentlemen . . .

Gwendolen and Cecily: Christenings?

Dr. Chasuble: Yes, Mr. Jack Worthing is to be christened Ernest at 5:30; Mr. Ernest Worthing is to be christened — er, I don't know what — at 6:00.

Gwendolen: You were prepared to make this sacrifice for us?

Cecily: Darlings!

Dr. Chasuble: Well, about the christenings. Might they be postponed?

Jack: Whatever for?

Dr. Chasuble: Well, sir, the fact is — Miss Prism here and I have just become engaged!

Lady Bracknell: What's going on here? (*Suddenly shouting.*) Miss Prism!

Miss Prism: Lady Bracknell!!!

Lady Bracknell (*slowly and emphatically*): Miss Prism, where is that baby?

All: What?

Lady Bracknell: Twenty-eight years ago, Miss Prism, you left Lord Bracknell's house in charge of a baby carriage containing a baby of the male sex. You never returned. A few weeks later, the police discovered the carriage standing by itself in a remote corner of Bayswater. It was empty, except for the unfinished manuscript of a dreadful novel. Miss Prism! Where is that baby?

Miss Prism (*shamefully*): I don't know, I admit it. I only wish I did. The plain facts

are these. By mistake, I put the manuscript for a book I was writing into the carriage, and I put the baby into a large, black handbag that I had intended for the manuscript.

Jack (*urgently*): Where did you deposit the handbag?

Miss Prism: I left it in the cloakroom of one of the larger railway stations in London.

Jack: What railway station?

Miss Prism (*crushed*): Victoria. The Brighton Line.

Jack (*excitedly*): Excuse me, for one moment! (*He exits.*)

Lady Bracknell: I need not tell you, Miss Prism, I suppose, of the weeks — nay, years of anguish your error has caused?

Miss Prism (*sorrowful*): I can imagine, Lady Bracknell. I can imagine!

Lady Bracknell: Can you?

Jack *(enters):* Miss Prism. Is this the hand-bag? Examine it carefully before you speak! Is this the handbag?

Miss Prism *(calmly):* It seems to be mine. Yes, here are my initials on the clasp. Thank you so much for restoring it to me.

Jack: Miss Prism, more has been restored to you than the handbag. I am the baby that you placed in it.

Lady Bracknell: Mr. Worthing! Then you are the son of my dear dead sister, and therefore Algernon's elder brother.

Jack: Algy's elder brother! Then I have a brother after all. I always said I had a brother. Miss Prism, Dr. Chasuble, meet my unfortunate younger brother.

Gwendolen: My own! But what own are you? What is your real name, now that you have become someone else?

Jack: Good heavens! I almost forgot. Can you not love me but under that one name?

Gwendolen: Alas no. Cecily and I have both resolved to marry men by the name of Ernest.

Lady Bracknell: That's it. You were named after your father, Mr. Worthing; his name was General Ernest John Moncrieff!

Jack *(calmly):* I always told you my name was Ernest, didn't I, Gwendolen?

Gwendolen: Ernest, my own! I felt from the first you could have no other name.

Jack: Gwendolen, it is a terrible thing for a man to find out that all of his life he has been speaking nothing but the truth. Can you forgive me?

Gwendolen: I can. For I feel that you are sure to change.

Algernon: Do you forgive me too, Cecily?

Cecily: Yes, Algernon — if you promise to be rechristened Ernest tomorrow!

Algernon: I do, my love, I do. And now, may I kiss you?

Cecily: But of course!

Lady Bracknell *(taken aback):* My dear nephew, what has come over you?

Algernon: Why, Aunt Augusta, I've only just realized for the first time in my life, the vital importance of being earnest!

READING COMPREHENSION

Summarizing. Choose the best phrase to complete each sentence. Then write the complete statements on your paper.

1. Jack used the name Ernest when in _____ (trouble, town, the country).

2. Gwendolen and Cecily would only marry men _____ (who lived in town, named Ernest, who were rich).

3. Jack Worthing had been left in the Victoria train station as a baby by _____ (his mother, Lady Bracknell, Miss Prism).

4. Jack turned out to be _____ (Cecily's father, Algernon's older brother, Miss Prism's son).

Interpreting. Write the answer to each question on your paper.

1. Where had Miss Prism put the manuscript for the book she had been writing?

2. Why did Lady Bracknell object to Jack and Gwendolen's engagement?

3. What is the meaning of the pun, or play on words, in the title "The Importance of Being Earnest"?

For Thinking and Discussing.

1. What aspects of human nature do you think the author is making fun of in this play?

2. What kind of literature do you think the author was making fun of by writing this play?

UNDERSTANDING LITERATURE

Satire and Society. Laughter is one of the best weapons of a satirist. By making people laugh at a person or idea, the satirist makes his or her target look foolish and discredits it.

In "The Importance of Being Earnest," author Oscar Wilde uses humor to criticize the manners of the society of his time. Wilde lived in England during the late 1800's. At that time, society was governed by strict rules of conduct. People were expected to behave properly and to speak earnestly—with great sincerity and seriousness. In this play, Wilde makes the manners of his society look ridiculous through his satiric use of characters and plot.

To understand the point of Wilde's satire better, answer the following questions on your paper.

1. Which character in the play is the least earnest, or breaks the rules of society the most? What is the author's attitude toward him or her?

2. Which character best represents the rules of society in his or her words and behavior? What is the author's attitude toward him or her?

3. In what sort of society do you think Oscar Wilde would have wanted to live?

WRITING

In a paragraph, tell how Oscar Wilde made fun of romantic love in this play.

I'm Nobody!

by Emily Dickinson

I'm nobody! Who are you?
Are you nobody, too?
Then there's a pair of us — don't tell!
They'd banish us, you know.
How dreary to be somebody!
How public, like a frog
To tell your name the livelong day
To an admiring bog.

1. What would the speaker find "dreary"? What does she compare a "somebody" to? In what way are the two things alike?

2. What do you think are some advantages of being famous? What are some disadvantages?

Section Review

VOCABULARY

Context Clues in a Passage. The context of a word is found in the group of words that precede and follow it in a reading passage. The meaning of a particular word in a passage is always connected to the meanings of the words around it. A reader can use *context clues*, or clues from surrounding words, to guess at the meaning of an unknown word. The reader may also use context clues to understand what particular meaning a known word has in a specific context.

The following passage is from "The Farm Magnate." Using the context clues in the passage, write the meaning of the italicized words on your paper.

> The Corn Stalk was probably the worst farm in Brazil. It had already ruined three owners. The latest owner, David Moreira de Souza, *acquired* it on an installment plan. He was convinced then that it was a *bonanza*. But there he was, dragging along under the *burden* of debt, scratching his head in *despair*.
> The coffee trees would be bare year in, year out. *Lashed* by hail or *blighted* by frosts, their *yield* never filled a good-sized basket. . . .
> *Exhausted*, dry soil showed through underbrush and sparse wild cane. . . .
> The roads were left half-laid. Fences lay on the ground. Farmhands' *quarters* had shaky, leaky roofs over ugly rooms. Even the *manor* house was *decaying*.

READING

Cloze Exercise. As you become a better reader, you are able to anticipate what word, or what sort of word, you will read next in a passage. For example, what word belongs in the blank space in this sentence? "Pakhom dug into the rich soil with his _____ and threw it onto a high pile." The missing word is *shovel*. You were probably able to guess this word because of the meaning of the sentence and because you knew that the missing word was a noun.

Read the paragraphs below. On your paper, write the words that are missing.

"Trumpet Man"
Dan glanced nervously at the other members of the _____ on the stage with him. Then he raised his _____ to his lips. He began to _____ "Molly's Tune." He saw Molly watching him with a _____ of love on her face. Her love inspired him to play _____.

"How Much Land Does a Man Need?"
Pakhom saw the _____ sinking beneath the mountain. He began to _____ as fast as he could toward it. His legs were so _____ they could hardly carry him. He could hear the Bashkirs shrieking with _____. He ran _____ even though his heart felt ready to burst.

The Importance of Being Earnest
Jack asked Gwendolen to marry _____. Gwendolen said yes, because she had always wanted to marry a _____ named Ernest.

WRITING

A Persuasive Letter. In Section 8, you wrote an opinion and supported it with reasons. Sometimes expressing your opinion on a particular issue is not enough. You may want to convince others to share your views and perhaps act on your opinion. What could you do? You could write a persuasive letter.

How does persuasion differ from expressing an opinion? In writing persuasively, it is not enough to express your own opinion, although you will do so as strongly as you can. You must convince someone to see things your way. In doing so, it is important that you adopt a calm and reasonable attitude. A hysterical and unfriendly approach will only serve to alienate your reader. You must also present your point of view fairly and honestly. Nothing will damage a persuasive argument more than a lie or a half-truth. Demonstrate your knowledge of the subject by presenting convincing reasons why your point of view should be accepted.

Step 1: Set Your Goal

Choose one of the following topics for a persuasive letter:

1. In "Trumpet Man," Dan Daly sent copies of "Molly's Tune" to music publishers and performers long before the tune was actually published. Write a letter to a record company or a popular musician. Tell him or her about "Molly's Tune." Why is it a good song? Who would listen to it? What kind of musician should record it? Persuade your reader to produce the song.

2. Imagine you are Algernon or Cecily in *The Importance of Being Earnest*. If you choose to be Algy, tell why it is better to marry a man named Algy than one named Ernest. If you choose to be Cecily, write a letter persuading Algy to change his name. If you wish, your letter can follow the satiric style of Wilde's play.

3. Think of an ambition of your own, such as playing major league baseball, acting in a television show, or buying your own car. Write a letter to a person who can help you achieve your goal. Try to persuade that person to give you a chance to fulfill your ambition.

Step 2: Make a Plan

In order to make an effective persuasive argument, you need to consider *whom* you are trying to persuade. Ask yourself what the other person knows about the subject and what the other person's point of view is. This will help you choose the most convincing arguments. It will also help you set the right tone for your letter. For example, if you are trying to persuade a friend or relative, your tone would probably be more informal and personal than if you were trying to persuade a businessperson or official. To set the right tone, you must choose your words carefully as you tell your reader just why you feel your opinion is the right one.

To begin gathering ideas for your letter, make a list of reasons that might convince your reader of your point of view. Also, consider any arguments your reader might have against your opinion. Then respond

559

to these objections with convincing counter-arguments of your own. Use the right proportion of fact and emotional appeal to support your arguments.

Once you know what your arguments are going to be, you need to organize them in the order of their importance. You may begin with your most important point, or save your strongest argument for the end.

Step 3: Write a First Draft

Now that you have gathered your ideas and organized your arguments, it is time to write the first draft of your persuasive letter. As you begin writing, think about the following questions:

- ☐ What effect do I want my letter to have?
- ☐ What attitudes and reactions do I think my audience will have?
- ☐ How do I want my letter to "sound" to my audience?

Begin your letter with a clear statement of your point of view and your purpose. Then present your arguments in their order of importance. Don't forget to consider the point of view of your reader as you write. Keep the tone of your letter positive and calm. End the letter with a statement that leaves the matter open for discussion.

Step 4: Revise

As you revise your persuasive letter, you will have a chance to make your arguments even more convincing. When you feel that your letter is as persuasive as possible, proofread it carefully for mistakes in spelling, grammar, and punctuation. Then make a neat, final copy.

QUIZ

The following is a quiz for Section 10. Write the answers in complete sentences on your paper.

Reading Comprehension

1. In "Trumpet Man," where did Dan get the idea for "Molly's Tune"?

2. In "How Much Land Does a Man Need?," what mistakes did Pakhom make when he paced off his land?

3. What is the setting of the poem "Ozymandias"?

4. In "The Farm Magnate," what would Moreira have gained if Trancoso had bought the farm?

5. In *The Importance of Being Earnest,* what had Miss Prism done with Jack when he was a baby?

Understanding Literature

6. In "Trumpet Man," how did the author feel about her main character?

7. Compare the satire used by Leo Tolstoy in "How Much Land Does a Man Need?" to that of Monteiro Lobato in "The Farm Magnate."

8. What two ironic incidents occurred in "The Farm Magnate"?

9. Describe the plot twist that created an ironic surprise ending in *The Importance of Being Earnest.*

10. What statement does "I'm Nobody!" make about personal ambition?

ACTIVITIES

Word Attack. One of the most common vowel sounds in English is represented phonetically by an upside down *e* (ə), called a *schwa*. It sounds like a very light "uh" and is heard only in unaccented syllables. Each of the vowel letters can have the schwa sound, as in the following examples:

a in around	*o* in lesson
e in given	*u* in circus
i in pencil	

The following words from *The Importance of Being Earnest* have the schwa vowel sound. Write each word on a piece of paper. Underline the letter or letters that have the schwa sound. Then list five additional words with this sound.

horrible	approve	propose
consent	definite	happen
uncle	listen	adopt

Speaking and Listening

1. Choose a partner and practice reading the poem "Ozymandias." Each of you should alternate reading one line of the poem at a time. Practice your reading so that each line flows easily into the next. Try to capture the rhythm and mood of the poem as you read your lines. Be prepared to present your reading to the class.

2. Select one of the three scenes from *The Importance of Being Earnest* to act out in class. Be sure you have enough people to take each of the parts. Try to capture the sarcastic tone of Wilde's writing as you speak the lines.

Researching

1. "Trumpet Man" is about a musician who plays the trumpet. Most traditional musical instruments have long and interesting histories. Select one of the instruments below to research. Where did it originate? How long has it been in existence? How has the instrument changed over the years? Share your findings with the class.

piano	trumpet	violin
guitar	flute	harp

2. Select one of the following authors from this section and prepare a short biography about him or her. Share your report with the class.

Leo Tolstoy	Percy Bysshe Shelley
Oscar Wilde	Emily Dickinson

Creating

1. Irony is a reversal of expectations. Each of the selections in this section contains ironic events. Real life, as well as literature, has its ironic moments. In two or three paragraphs, describe some ironic event that has happened to you. Such an event would be an experience in which you expected one thing to happen and the opposite actually occurred.

2. Imagine that you are a casting director for the play *The Importance of Being Earnest*. Select one of the characters and write a description of how he or she should look and act. Base your description on the way Wilde presented the character in his play.

SHAKESPEARE'S MACBETH

All the world's a stage
And all the men and women merely players.
They have their exits and their entrances
And one man in his time plays many parts.

— William Shakespeare
England

Scene from "Macbeth"
Richard Cattermole (1800-1868)
The Folger Shakespeare Library

Shakespeare's Macbeth

Today a play is a hit if it runs for several months. But William Shakespeare's plays have been performed for almost 400 years. They were hits when they were first performed in London, England, and they have never stopped being popular. This section is made up of Shakespeare's play *Macbeth*. This play had a special meaning during Shakespeare's time, and it still remains one of his best-known works.

The Man and His Time

William Shakespeare was born in a small English town called Stratford-on-Avon, in 1564. He was attracted to the theater and, as a young adult, moved to London. There he joined a "fellowship of players" at the Globe theater. At first, he acted in small parts, but soon he began writing plays. By the time he died in 1616, Shakespeare had completed more than 36 plays and hundreds of poems.

By 1598, Shakespeare was known as England's greatest playwright. His theatrical company, the Chamberlain's Men, prospered and was often called upon to act at the court of Queen Elizabeth I. When Elizabeth died in 1603, her successor, King James I, took over the company.

King James took a great interest in Shakespeare's plays. In fact, the play *Macbeth*, written in 1606, was inspired by events in the life of James I. *Macbeth* takes place in Scotland during the 11th century and is based on real events from history. An important character in the play is the Scottish nobleman Banquo. King James I was from Scotland, and Banquo was his ancestor. In 1605, there was an attempt on the life of James I. This shocked the people of Shakespeare's day. They believed that killing a king was the most terrible crime possible. In *Macbeth*, the murder of a king leads to terrible consequences.

Shakespeare Today

What makes Shakespeare's drama endure? Shakespeare makes us experience and think about the problems of life. He examines questions of loyalty—to a family or to a king. He looks at the struggle between good and evil forces in people and in society. But he doesn't give simple answers. It isn't always easy to condemn his villains or to praise his heroes. He reminds us that a bad person may have good qualities, and a good person may have weak moments.

Shakespeare's plays are also carefully plotted. The stories involve many vivid characters in plots that are rich in surprising twists. He freely used magic, prophecies, witches, and the like, along with "real" characters and "real" situations. But still, somehow the action follows logically from this mix.

Shakespeare, further, presents his characters' thoughts and feelings in poetic rhythms and images. When Macbeth cannot sleep after murdering King Duncan, he doesn't say, "I can't sleep." He says, "I thought I heard a voice cry, 'Sleep no more! Macbeth has murdered sleep,' —innocent sleep, sleep that knits up the raveled sleeve of care. . . ."

Thunder and lightning, three witches, and a barren field—these set the scene for the tragedy of Macbeth. "Fair is foul, and foul is fair," the witches warn at the start of this tale of treachery and treason. King Duncan is the highest authority in Scotland. But Macbeth is ambitious; his wife's desire for him to achieve power is even greater than his own.

Shakespeare understood human psychology long before there were any psychologists. He shows us real men and women, loving, hating, suffering, and thinking. He knew the human heart so well that his characters seem like people we might know.

On the following pages, the characters of *Macbeth* are waiting for you to discover them.

Macbeth

based on the play by William Shakespeare

A great battle has just ended in Scotland. Two winning generals, Macbeth and Banquo, are returning home when they meet three witches. The witches tell Macbeth he will become Thane of Cawdor, and then King of Scotland. Banquo learns he will never be king but will father a line of kings. Soon, Macbeth is indeed named Thane of Cawdor. As he begins to believe the prophecy, his hunger to be king grows. Banquo fears the evil that the prophecy represents.

Soon, King Duncan visits Macbeth at his castle, Dunsinane. Macbeth will be king if he kills Duncan. Macbeth hesitates, but Lady Macbeth, his strong-willed wife, urges him on. "I have done the deed," he tells her, his hands red with blood, his mind full of torment. She calms him — but this crime leads to others. "Blood will have blood," as Macbeth learns.

Duncan's two sons, Donalbain and Malcolm, flee after Duncan's death, and Macbeth is crowned King. To protect his crown, he hires murderers to kill Banquo — and then is haunted by Banquo's ghost. Deep into evil, Macbeth visits the witches again and begs to know more of his future. They create terrible visions that tell Macbeth to beware of Macduff, who is eager to end Macbeth's bloody rule; that Macbeth will be king until "Birnam Wood to . . . Dunsinane shall come;" and that "none born of woman" can kill him. Macbeth learns that Macduff has left Scotland; he orders the murder of Macduff's family and earns a reputation for cruelty. Rebellion stirs in the kingdom.

At home, a troubled Lady Macbeth walks restlessly in her sleep, moaning as she tries to wash away her guilt. But she finds no peace and, at last, kills herself. Too late, Macbeth realizes how useless his struggles have been, as the prophecies come true in a series of ironic events.

CHARACTERS

First Witch
Second Witch
Third Witch
King Duncan of Scotland
Malcolm, Duncan's older son
Donalbain, Duncan's younger son
Lennox, a Scottish lord
Captain, in Duncan's army
Ross, a Scottish nobleman
Angus, a Scottish nobleman
Macbeth, Thane[1] of Glamis, a general in
    the Scottish Army
Banquo, a Scottish lord, also a general
Lady Macbeth, a Scottish noblewoman
Messenger
Fleance, Banquo's son
Macduff, Thane of Fife

First Murderer
Second Murderer
Lords of Scotland, who attend
    Macbeth's feast
First Vision, called forth by the Three
    Witches
Second Vision
Third Vision
Doctor
Maid-in-Waiting, to Lady Macbeth
Menteith, a Scottish nobleman
Siward, Earl of Northumberland,
    general of English forces opposing
    Macbeth
Seyton, an officer loyal to Macbeth
Young Siward, son of Northumberland

Act I

Scene One

A barren field in Scotland. Thunder and lightning. Three witches enter.

First Witch: When shall we three
    meet again —
In thunder, lightning, or in rain?
Second Witch: When the hurly-burly's
    done,
When the battle's lost and won.
Third Witch: That will be ere the set
    of sun.
First Witch: Where the place?
Second Witch: Upon the heath.
Third Witch: There to meet with
    Macbeth.

Three Witches: Fair is foul
    and foul is fair.
Hover through the fog and filthy air.
(They exit.)

Scene Two

A camp near Forres, Scotland. Enter King Duncan, Malcolm, Donalbain, and Lennox. They meet a captain, bleeding from wounds.

Duncan: What bloody man is that?
    Can he report
News of the revolt?
Malcolm: This captain
Fought like a good and hardy soldier
Against those who would take me
    captive. Speak, brave friend!

---

1. Thane: chief of a clan; nobleman

Tell the king what happened as you
    were leaving.
Captain: The merciless rebel
    Macdonwald
Had troops of hired soldiers at
    his command.
It seemed that Fortune smiled
    on his cause.
But brave Macbeth, waving his bloody
    sword,
Carved out a passage till he reached
    the knave.
He split him open, belly to jaw,
And set his head upon the fortress wall.
Duncan: Oh, valiant cousin Macbeth!
    Worthy gentleman!
Captain: Mark, King of Scotland, mark.
As soon as Macdonwald's men took to
    their heels,
The King of Norway, with fresh ranks
    of men,
Began a fresh assault.
Duncan: Did this not trouble
Our generals, Macbeth and Banquo?
Captain: As sparrows trouble eagles,
    or the hare the lion.
They doubled their attack upon the foe.
But I am faint. My gashes cry for help.
Duncan: As well your words honor you
    as your wounds.
Both sound of honor. Go, get him
    surgeons.
(*Ross and Angus enter.*)
Duncan: Who comes here?
Malcolm: The worthy Thane of Ross.
Ross: I am come from Fife, great king,
Where the King of Norway's banners
    fill the sky
And fan our people cold. Norway's
    king,

Assisted by that traitor,
    the Thane of Cawdor,
Began a fight. But brave Macbeth
    confronted him.
The victory fell to us.
Duncan: Great happiness!
Ross: Now Sweno, King of Norway,
    asks a treaty.
We would not allow the burial of his
    men
Until he paid us a ransom.
Duncan: No more the Thane of Cawdor
    shall deceive us.
We sentence him to death. Go now,
And with his former title greet Macbeth.
Ross: I'll see it done.
Duncan: What he has lost,
    noble Macbeth has won.

Scene Three

*A barren field near Forres. The three
witches enter.*

Third Witch: A drum! A drum!
    Macbeth does come.
Three Witches: The Weird Sisters,
    hand in hand,
Who travel fast on sea and land,
Thus do go about, about,
Three times to yours, and three to mine,
And three again, to make up nine.
Peace! The charm's wound up!
(*Macbeth and Banquo enter.*)

Macbeth: So fair and foul a day
    I have not seen.
Banquo: What are these,
So withered and so wild in what they
    wear?
They look not like the inhabitants
    of the earth,

And yet are on it. Do you live?
    Are you anything
That man may question? You seem
    to understand me,
For each her roughened finger lays
Upon her skinny lips. You should be
    women,
And yet your beards forbid me to
    interpret
That you are so.
Macbeth: Speak, if you can. What are
    you?
First Witch: All hail, Macbeth!
    Hail to you, Thane of Glamis!
Second Witch: All hail, Macbeth!
    Hail to you, Thane of Cawdor!
Third Witch: All hail, Macbeth,
    that shall be king hereafter!
Banquo: Good sir, why do you start
    and seem to fear
Things that sound so fair?

(To the witches.) To me you speak
    not.
If you can look into the seeds of time
And say which grain will grow
    and which will not,
Speak to me then, who neither beg nor
    fear
Your favors or your hate.
First Witch: Hail!
Second Witch: Hail!
Third Witch: Hail!
First Witch: Lesser than Macbeth,
    and greater.
Second Witch: Not so happy,
    yet much happier.
Third Witch: You shall father kings,
    though you yourself be none.
So all hail, Macbeth and Banquo!
Macbeth: Stay, you mysterious
    speakers, tell me more!
I know I am Thane of Glamis.

But how of Cawdor?
The Thane of Cawdor lives,
	a prosperous gentleman.
And to be king! That's no more possible
Than to be Cawdor. Say from where
You get this strange intelligence, or why
Upon his barren heath you stop us
With such prophecies. Speak, I
	command!

(*The witches vanish.*)

Banquo: The earth has bubbles,
	as the water has;
And these are of them. Where have they
	gone?
Macbeth: Into the air, and what
	seemed solid melted
As breath into the wind. I wish
	they had stayed!
Banquo: Were they really here,
	the things we speak about?
Or have we eaten some poisoned root
That takes the reason prisoner?
Macbeth: Your children shall be kings.
Banquo: You shall be king.
Macbeth: And Thane of Cawdor, too.
	Went it not so?
Banquo: The very tune and words.
	Who's here?

(*Ross and Angus enter.*)

Ross: The king has happily received,
	Macbeth,
The news of your success. Thick as hail
Came messengers, and every one did
	bear
Your praises in the kingdom's defense.
Angus: We're sent to give you
	our royal master's thanks.
Ross: And as a token of your
	well-earned honor,

He bade me, from him, call you
	Thane of Cawdor.
Hail, most worthy Thane. The title's
	yours.
Banquo (*to Macbeth*): What, can the
	devil speak true?
Macbeth: The Thane of Cawdor lives.
	Why do you dress me
In borrowed robes?
Angus: He who *was* the Thane
	lives yet,
But under sentence of death
	bears that life,
Which he deserves to lose. Treason,
Confessed by him and proved,
	has overthrown him.
Macbeth (*to himself*): Glamis and
	Thane of Cawdor! The greatest is
	to follow!
(*To Banquo.*) Do you not hope your
	children shall be kings,
When those that said I should be
	Thane of Cawdor
Promised the crown to them?
Banquo: That promise, if we trust it
All the way, may bring you to the crown
As it has made you Thane of Cawdor.
	But 'tis strange!
Often to win us over to their side,
The creatures of darkness tell us truths.
Macbeth (*to himself*): This
	supernatural promise cannot be
Both evil and good. If evil,
	why has it started
With the truth? I am Thane of Cawdor.
If good, why does the thought of
	what will come
Make my heart knock at my ribs?
Present fears are less than horrible
	imaginings.

I am shaken by what lives only in my
  mind.
If chance will make me king, why
  chance must crown me.
I shall not stir.
Banquo *(to himself):* New honors come
  upon him,
Like stiff new clothes that are not
  comfortable
Till they are worn a while.
Macbeth: Let us go to the king.
(Aside to Banquo.) Think upon what has
  happened. Another time,
When we have thought it over, let us
  speak
Freely to each other.
Banquo: Very gladly.
Macbeth: Till then, enough.
  Come, friends.

(They exit.)

Scene Four

*Inverness, Macbeth's castle. Lady Mac-
beth enters, alone, reading a letter.*

Lady Macbeth: "They met me on the
  day of my success. When I burned
  with desire to question them
  further, they vanished into the air.
  While I stood in wonder,
  messengers came from the king,
  who called me Thane of Cawdor.
  By that title, the Weird Sisters had
  already saluted me, and also with
  'Hail, king that shall be!' This I
  thought good to tell you, my
  dearest partner in greatness, that
  you might rejoice at the greatness
  promised you. Take it to your
  heart. Farewell."

Lady Macbeth *(speaking to Macbeth
  although he is not there):*
Glamis you are, and Cawdor, and shall
  be
What you are promised. Yet I fear
  your nature.
It is too full of the milk of
  human kindness
To do what must be done.
  You would be great—
Are not without ambition—but without
The wickedness it needs.
  You would seek the heights,
But want a blessing on it;
  would not play false,
And yet would wrongly win. Hurry to
  me
That I may pour my spirit in your ear
And talk away, with the courage
  of my tongue,
All that would keep you from
  the golden crown,
Which fate and the very spirits of the air
Seem to have given you.
(A messenger enters.)
Lady Macbeth: What message have
  you?
Messenger: The king comes here
  tonight.
Lady Macbeth: You're mad to say that!
Your master is with him—if this were
  so,
He would have told us so we might
  prepare.
Messenger: So please you, it is true.
  They're on the way.
*(Lady Macbeth waves him out. He
  exits.)*
Lady Macbeth: Great news! The raven
  himself is hoarse

That croaks the fatal entrance of
    Duncan
Into my castle. Oh, spirits, fill me full
From crown to toe with direst cruelty!
    Make thick my blood;
Stop my conscience, so no gentle doubts
Shake my dark purpose. Come, thick
    night,
Be dark, as the deepest smoke of hell,
That my keen knife won't see the wound
    it makes,
Nor heaven peep through the blanket
    of the dark
And cry, "Hold! Hold!"
(Macbeth enters.)
Lady Macbeth: Great Glamis!
    Worthy Cawdor!
Greater than both you will be hailed
    hereafter!
Your letters have carried me beyond
This unknowing present. Now I feel
The future in this moment.
Macbeth: My dearest love,
Duncan comes here tonight.
Lady Macbeth: When does he leave?
Macbeth: Tomorrow is his plan.
Lady Macbeth: Oh, never
Shall the sun see that tomorrow!
Your face, my thane, is as a book
    where men
May read strange matters. To hide
    your purpose,
Be the genial host. Bear welcome
    in your eye,
Your hand, your tongue. Look like
    the innocent flower,
But be the serpent under it.
    He that's coming
Must be provided for. You shall put
This night's great business in my hands.

This night shall bring power and
    greatness
To all our future nights and days.
Macbeth: We will speak further.
Lady Macbeth: Remember, look
    innocent.
    Leave all the rest to me.

Scene Five

Duncan has arrived at the castle and has been warmly greeted by Lady Macbeth. Later, Macbeth's servants prepare for a banquet. Macbeth enters.

Macbeth: If it's to be done,
    and finished when it is done,
Then it's best if it's done quickly.
    If our success
Was born with Duncan's death
    and that were all,
We would not think of heaven
    or hell to come.
But there is judgment *here*.
    The bloody deeds we do
Return to plague us. Justice may hold
    our poisoned cup
To our own lips. Duncan has double
    cause to trust me:
First, I am his kinsman and his subject.
    Then, I am his host,
Who should shut the door against
    his murderer,
Not bear the knife myself. Besides,
    this Duncan
Has been a humble, blameless king.
His virtues will plead like angels,
    trumpet-tongued,
Against the cursed way he meets his end.
I do not wish to do what I have
    planned.

My ambition is too high.

(*Lady Macbeth enters.*)

Macbeth: What news is there?

Lady Macbeth: He has almost supped.
Why did you leave the hall?

Macbeth: Has he asked for me?

Lady Macbeth: You know that he has.

Macbeth: We will proceed no further
in this business.

He has honored me of late, and I have
won

Golden opinions from all sorts of
people.

I want to keep them, while they
still shine,

Not cast them aside so soon.

Lady Macbeth: Was the hope drunk

In which you wrapped yourself? Has it
slept since?

And does it wake now to look so green
and pale

At what it sought so strongly?
From this time,

So shall I trust your love.
Are you afraid

To be the same in action and courage

As you are in desire? Do you crave
the highest,

And know yourself a coward in your
heart?

Macbeth: Peace, I pray!

I dare do all a man should rightly do.

One who dares do more is not a man.

Lady Macbeth: What beast was it, then,

That made you tell this plan of yours
to me?

When you dared do it, then you were a
man.

I have nursed a baby, and know how
tender

It is to love the babe I nourish.

I would, while it was smiling in my face,

Have plucked my nipple from
his toothless gums

And dashed his brains out,
had I so sworn as you

Have done to this.

Macbeth: If we should fail?

Lady Macbeth: We fail?

Screw your courage to the sticking
point,

And we'll not fail. When Duncan is
asleep,

I'll go and give his servants so much
wine,

Their minds will turn to smoke
and drift away.

Then, when in sleep they lie
drunk as if in death,

What cannot you and I perform
upon the unguarded Duncan?

His guards shall bear the guilt
of our great murder.

Macbeth: Bring forth men-children
only, for your strong spirit

Should only make up males! Will
everyone believe,

When we have marked the guards
with Duncan's blood

And used their daggers, that they have
done it?

Lady Macbeth: Who'll dare question it,
as we shall roar

Our grief and rage upon his death?

Macbeth: It is settled. I am ready.
Let us go.

False face must hide what the false
heart does know.

(*They exit.*)

READING COMPREHENSION

Summarizing. Choose the best phrase to complete each sentence. Then write the complete statements on your paper.

1. The three witches told Macbeth _____ (he would become Thane of Cawdor and then king, he would father kings, to kill the king).

2. Lady Macbeth wanted to kill King Duncan so that _____ (Scotland would be free, the war would be over, Macbeth would be king).

3. Macbeth hesitated to kill the king because _____ (King Duncan had just honored him, Duncan knew of the plan, Banquo warned him it was unwise).

Interpreting. Write the answer to each question on your paper.

1. Whom did Lady Macbeth plan to blame for the king's death?

2. How was Lady Macbeth's personality different from her husband's?

3. How did Lady Macbeth persuade her husband to go along with her plan to kill Duncan?

4. What did Macbeth mean when he said, "False face must hide what the false heart does know"?

For Thinking and Discussing. Do you think Macbeth will regret killing King Duncan? What clues in the story led you to have this opinion?

UNDERSTANDING LITERATURE

Plot. The *plot* of a play is the series of events in the play. The events occur in a particular order. The plot has a beginning, a middle, and an end.

Sometimes you find clues in the play that hint at what may happen later. These clues are called "foreshadowing."

In Act I of *Macbeth*, the order of events is very important. The scene in which Macbeth and Banquo speak with the Weird Sisters contains foreshadowing of what is to come later.

Read the following events carefully. Write them in the order in which they occur in Act I.

1. Ross and Angus inform Macbeth that he is Thane of Cawdor.

2. Lady Macbeth learns that King Duncan will arrive that night.

3. A captain tells King Duncan about Macbeth's bravery in battle.

4. Macbeth and his wife plot to kill the king.

5. The three witches tell Macbeth and Banquo of their futures.

WRITING

The Weird Sisters have given Macbeth clues to his future. How might the plot develop according to these foreshadowings? Write a paragraph developing the plot and describing what you think might happen next.

Act II

Scene One

The courtyard of Macbeth's castle. Banquo and Fleance enter.

Banquo: How goes the night, boy?
Fleance: The moon is down.
    I have not heard the clock.
Banquo: The moon goes down at 12.

(Macbeth enters.)

Banquo: Who's there?
Macbeth: A friend.
Banquo: What, sir, not yet at rest?
The king's in bed. *(Takes Macbeth
    aside.)*
I dreamed last night of the three Weird
    Sisters.
To you they have showed some truth.
Macbeth: I don't think of them.
Yet, when we find an hour free,
We should spend it in some words
    upon that business.
Banquo: I am at your service.
Macbeth: Until that time, sleep well!
Banquo: Thanks, sir, the same to you.

(Banquo and Fleance exit.)

Macbeth *(alone):* When all is ready,
    she will ring the bell.
(He stares into space.)
Is this a dagger that I see before me,
The handle toward my hand? Come,
    let me clutch you!
I have you not, and yet I see you still.
Are you only a dagger of the mind,
A false creation of my troubled brain?
I see you yet — in form as real

As this that I now draw. I see you still;
And on your blade and handle,
    gouts of blood,
Which were not there before.
    There's nothing here.
It is the bloody business I'm about
That makes me see you. Oh, firm
    and solid earth,
Hear not which way my footsteps go,
    for fear
The very stones will cry out where I am
And stop the horror that the time
    has come
For me to do. While I talk, he lives;
Words give cold breath to the heat
    of deeds. *(A bell rings.)*
I go, and it is done.
    Duncan, hear not the bell.
It summons you to heaven or to hell.
(He exits.)

Scene Two

A room in the castle. Lady Macbeth enters.

Lady Macbeth: That which has made
    them drunk has made me bold.
What has quenched them has given me
    fire. Listen!
It was the owl that shrieked.
    He's killing him now.
The doors are open, and the drunken
    guards
Keep watch with snores.
    I have drugged their wine.
Macbeth *(from inside):* Who's there?

Lady Macbeth: Oh, no. I am afraid they
   are awake,
And 'tis not done! To try and not
   succeed
Will ruin us. Listen!
   I placed their daggers ready.
He could not miss them.
   Had the king not resembled
My father as he slept,
   I would have killed him.
(Macbeth enters.)
Lady Macbeth: My husband!

Macbeth: I have done the deed.
    Did you not hear a noise?

Lady Macbeth: I heard the owl scream
    and the crickets cry.

Did you not speak?

Macbeth: When?

Lady Macbeth: Now.

Macbeth: As I came down the stairs?

Lady Macbeth: Yes.

Macbeth: Listen! Who sleeps in the
    second chamber?

Lady Macbeth: Donalbain, Duncan's
    son.

Macbeth (*Looking at his bloody
    hand):* This is a sorry sight.

Lady Macbeth: A foolish thought, to
    say a sorry sight.

Macbeth: One guard laughed in his
    sleep, and one cried, "Murder!"

They woke each other. I stood
    and heard them.

But they said their prayers
    and went back to sleep.

One cried, "God bless us!"
    and "Amen!" the other,

As if they'd seen me with these
    hangman's hands.

I could not say, "Amen," when they
    said, "God bless us!"

I needed blessing, but amen stuck in
    my throat.

Lady Macbeth: Do not think of it.
    It will make us mad.

Macbeth: I thought I heard a voice cry,
    "Sleep no more! Macbeth has
    murdered sleep"—
    innocent sleep,

Sleep that knits up the raveled
    sleeve of care.

Lady Macbeth: What do you mean?

Macbeth: Still it cried, "Sleep no
    more!" to all the house;

"Glamis has murdered sleep,
    and therefore Cawdor

Shall sleep no more! Macbeth shall
    sleep no more!"

Lady Macbeth: Who was it that cried
    that way? Worthy Thane,

Your mind is sick. Go get some water

And wash this filthy evidence
    from your hand.

Why did you bring these daggers
    from the place?

They must lie there. Go, carry them
    back, and smear

The sleepy guards with blood.

Macbeth: I'll go no more.

I am afraid to think what I have done.

I dare not look at it again.

Lady Macbeth: Weak of purpose!

Give me the daggers. The sleeping
    and the dead

Are just like pictures. 'Tis only
    a child's eye

That fears a painted devil.
    If Duncan bleeds,

I'll paint the faces of the guards
    with blood,

For they must seem guilty.

(*She exits. Knocking is heard.*)

Macbeth: Where is that knocking?

How is it with me, when every noise
    appalls me?

Will all great Neptune's[2] ocean
    wash this blood

Clean from my hand? No.

---

2. Neptune: god of the ocean in ancient Roman myth

My hand will stain
All the seas of the world
    with crimson blood
Making the green water red.

(Lady Macbeth enters.)

Lady Macbeth: My hands are of your
    color, but I shame
To wear a heart so pale.
(Knocking is heard.) I hear a knocking
At the south entry. Let us go
    to our chamber.
A little water clears us of this deed.
Get on your nightclothes,
    lest they come to get us
And find us awake. Don't lose yourself
In painful thoughts.
Macbeth: Knowing what I have done,
I would rather not know myself.
    (Knocking.)
Wake Duncan with your knocking!
    I wish you could!

(They exit.)

Scene Three

The castle hall. Macduff and Lennox enter.
Macduff speaks to a servant.

Macduff: Friend, is your master
    stirring?

(Macbeth enters.)

Macduff: Our knocking has awakened
    him. Here he comes.
Lennox: Good morrow, noble sir.
Macbeth: Good morrow, both.
Macduff: Is the king stirring,
    worthy Thane?
Macbeth: Not yet.

Macduff: He commanded me to call
    upon him at this hour.
Macbeth: I'll bring you to him.
Macduff: I will find my way. *(He exits.)*
Lennox: The night has been unruly.
    The place we stayed—
Our chimneys were blown down;
    and people say
Sobbing was heard in the air,
    strange screams of death,
And terrible prophecies of fire
    and confusion.
All night, the owl cried.
    Some say the earth
Shook with a fever.
Macbeth: 'Twas a rough night.

(Macduff enters.)

Macduff: Oh, horror, horror, horror!
    Tongue or heart
Cannot conceive or name it!
Macbeth and Lennox: What's the
    matter?
Macduff: Murder has broken open
    the temple of the Lord
And stole its life!
Macbeth: What is it you say?
Lennox: You mean his majesty?
Macduff: Go to the chamber. Do not
    make me speak.
See, and then speak yourselves.

(Macbeth and Lennox exit.)

Macduff: Awake! Awake!
Ring the alarm! Murder and treason!
Banquo and Donalbain! Malcolm!
    Awake!
Shake off your sleep, come,
    look on death itself!
Malcolm! Banquo! Ring the bell!

(Lady Macbeth enters.)

Lady Macbeth: What has happened,
That you should wake us all
    with such a cry?
Speak! Speak!
Macduff: Oh, gentle lady.
'Tis not for you to hear what I can
    speak!

(Banquo enters.)

Macduff: Oh, Banquo, Banquo!
    Our royal master's murdered!
Lady Macbeth: Woe! Alas!
    Not in our house!
Banquo: Too cruel anywhere.
    Macduff, I pray you,
Take back what you have said,
    and say it is not so.

*(Macbeth enters, with Lennox and
    Ross.)*

Macbeth: Had I but died an hour
    before this time,
I would be blessed.

(Malcolm and Donalbain enter.)

Donalbain: What is wrong?
Macbeth: The fountain of your blood
Is stopped. The very source of it
    is stopped.
Macduff: Your royal father's murdered.
Malcolm: Oh! By whom?
Lennox: His guards, it seems,
    have done it.
Their hands and faces were all
    smeared with blood;
So were their daggers, which we found
    unwiped
Upon their pillows.
Macbeth: I am sorry, but in my fury,
    I killed them.
Macduff: Why did you do that?

Macbeth: Who can be wise, shocked,
    calm, and furious,
Loyal, and unmoved, in the same
    moment?
No man. Here lay Duncan,
His silver skin laced with
    his golden blood:
There, the murderers,
    red with the color of their trade,
Their daggers dipped in blood.
    Who could hold back
That had a heart to love and in that
    heart
Courage to make his love known?

(Lady Macbeth faints.)

Banquo: Look to the lady.
Donalbain *(aside to Malcolm):* We have
    no time for talk.
Our fate may hide where we can't see it,
And rush and seize us. Let's go away.
Banquo: Look to the lady.

(Lady Macbeth is carried out.)

Banquo: Let us meet
And study this most bloody piece of work
To know it further.
Macbeth: Let us go at once
And meet in the hall together.

(All exit but Malcolm and Donalbain.)

Malcolm: Let us not go with them.
To show an unfelt sorrow is a duty
That the false man does easily.
I'll go to England.
Donalbain: To Ireland, I.
We shall be safer if we separate.
There's daggers in men's smiles.
Malcolm: Let us not stay.
    There is no mercy here.

(They exit.)

READING COMPREHENSION

Summarizing. Choose the best phrase to complete each sentence. Then write the complete statements on your paper.

1. After Macbeth killed Duncan, he felt _____ (fearful and guilty, relieved, triumphant).

2. Macbeth killed the guards in order to _____ (keep them from killing the king, seem like a hero to Lady Macbeth, keep them from telling the truth about the murder).

3. Malcolm and Donalbain went away because they _____ (felt that to stay was dangerous, feared they might kill Macbeth, felt guilty about lying).

Interpreting. Write the answer to each question on your paper.

1. Why couldn't Lady Macbeth kill King Duncan herself?

2. Why wouldn't Macbeth return the daggers to the place where the guards lay asleep?

3. What does Macbeth mean when he asks, "Will all great Neptune's ocean wash this blood clean from my hand?"

4. Why did Malcolm and Donalbain leave separately for different destinations?

For Thinking and Discussing. Do you think anyone suspected the real murderer? Why or why not?

UNDERSTANDING LITERATURE

Character. The *characters* in a play are the people who take part in the action. You learn about them through their actions, speech, and spoken thoughts.

In *Macbeth*, there are many important characters. By the end of Act II, you have learned several things about each character's personality.

Read each of the descriptions below. On your paper, indicate if the description is about Macbeth, Lady Macbeth, Banquo, or Malcolm.

1. was concerned about the truth of the Weird Sisters and dreamed of them

2. saw an imaginary dagger

3. would have killed the king if he had not looked like the person's father

4. became annoyed after the murder and accused the murderer of being weak

5. was haunted by the murder and feared the blood would not wash off

6. claimed to have killed the guards out of fury

7. left the country in order to avoid danger

WRITING

Choose one of the characters, Macbeth, Lady Macbeth, Malcolm, or Banquo, and find other descriptions of them in Act II. Write a paragraph about the character you chose, using the descriptions you found in the play.

Act III

Scene One

The Palace. Banquo enters, speaking his thoughts.

Banquo: You have it now —
    king, Cawdor, Glamis, all,
As the Weird Women promised. And I
    fear
You played most foully for it.
    Yet it was said
You would not father kings,
But I, myself, should be the ancestor
Of many kings. If truth does come
    from them
(their words came true for you,
    Macbeth),
May they not have told the truth to me
    as well?
May I not have hope? But hush, no
    more!

(Enter Macbeth, as king; Lady Macbeth, as queen; Lennox; Ross; other lords and attendants.)

Macbeth: Here's our chief guest.
Lady Macbeth: If he had been
    forgotten,
There would have been a gap
    in our great feast.
Macbeth: Tonight we hold
    a royal supper, sir.
I ask your presence.
Banquo: My duty is to follow your
    command.
Macbeth: We hear our blood-stained
    cousins now are lodged
In England and in Ireland, not
    confessing
Their father's murder, but spreading
strange stories. We will speak of that
Tomorrow. Does Fleance hunt with
    you?
Banquo: Yes, good lord.
Macbeth: Go, then.

(Banquo exits.)

Macbeth: We will stay alone
Till supper time. Till then, God be with
    you! *(Exit all but Macbeth and a
    servant.)* Bring in those men.

(Servant exits.)

Macbeth: To be king is nothing
If I am not safely king.
    Our fear of Banquo
Goes deep. In his royalty of nature
Reigns that which must be feared. None
Else do I fear. The sisters on the heath
Hailed him as father to a line of kings.
Upon my head, they placed a futureless
    crown
And put a barren scepter in my grip.
No son of mine, they said, would wear
    the crown.
If it be true, for Banquo's children
Have I destroyed my peace.
For them, the gracious Duncan
    have I murdered.
I have given my soul to the devil
To make them kings —
    the children of Banquo kings!
Who's there?

(A servant enters with two murderers.)

Macbeth: Go to the door and stay there
    till we call. *(Servant exits.)*

Macbeth: Was it not yesterday
we spoke together?

Murderers: It was, your highness.

Macbeth: Both of you know
Banquo is your enemy.

First Murderer: True, my lord.

Macbeth: So is he mine.
Each minute that he lives
Threatens my life. And though I could
use
My kingly power to sweep him from my
sight,
I must not, for certain friends,
both his and mine,
Would blame me if I openly struck him
down.
And so, I call on you.

Second Murderer: We shall, my lord,
Do what you command us.

Macbeth: It must be done today.
I'll tell you where to find him
within the hour.
Fleance, his son, will keep him company.
He, too, must meet the fate of that
dark hour.
Go, now, and wait until I come to you.
(Murderers exit.)
It is arranged. Banquo,
if your soul will go to heaven,
It must go there tonight! *(He exits.)*

Scene Two

*The great hall of the palace. A banquet is
set on tables. Macbeth enters, with Lady
Macbeth, Ross, Lennox, lords and attendants.*

Macbeth: You know your places. Sit
down, and hearty welcome.

Lords: Thanks to your majesty.

Lady Macbeth: My heart, too, says
welcome to all our friends.

*(The first murderer appears at the door.
Macbeth moves toward him.)*

Macbeth: There's blood upon your face.
Is he dispatched?

Murderer: My lord, his throat is cut.
But, most royal sir, Fleance
escaped.

Macbeth: But Banquo's gone?

Murderer: Ay, my lord. Safe in a ditch,
With 20 deep-cut gashes on his head;
The smallest would cause his death.

Macbeth: Thanks for that. Get you
gone.
Tomorrow you and I will speak again.

(Murderer exits.)

Lady Macbeth: My royal lord, you do
not give the toast.
Our guests will wish that they had
stayed at home.

*(The ghost of Banquo enters and sits in
Macbeth's place. Macbeth does not see
it.)*

Macbeth: A sweet reminder! Good
health! Good appetite!

Lennox: Come sit, your highness.

Macbeth: Where is our honored
Banquo?
I hope no accident has kept him from
us.

Ross: Please come, your highness.
Grace us with your royal company.

Macbeth: The table's full.

Lennox: Here is a place reserved, sir.

Macbeth: Where? *(He sees the ghost.)*

Lennox: Here, my good lord. What is it
that troubles your highness?

Macbeth: Which of you has done this?

Lords: What, my good lord?

Macbeth *(to Banquo's ghost):* You cannot say I did it! Never shake
Your gory locks at me!

Ross: Gentlemen, his highness is not well.

Lady Macbeth: Sit, worthy friends. My lord is often thus,
And has been from his youth. Pray, sit.
Within the moment, he will again be well.
But if you watch him, you shall offend him.
And make the fit last longer.
Eat, and do not look at him.
    (To Macbeth.) Are you a man?

Macbeth: Aye, and a bold one who dares look on that
Which might horrify the devil.

Lady Macbeth: Oh, foolishness!
This is an image made from your fear,
Like the dagger of empty air you said
Led you to Duncan. These fits of nervousness
Would suit a child telling fearful tales
Around his grandmother's fire.
    Shame upon you!
Why do you make such faces?
There's nothing there except an empty stool.

Macbeth: I pray you, look!
    (To the ghost.) How say you?
If you can nod, speak too.
Do graves send those we bury back to us?

(Ghost exits.)

Lady Macbeth: You are lost in this foolishness.

Macbeth: As I stand here, I saw him.

Lady Macbeth: Fie, for shame!

Macbeth: The time has been that, when the brain was gone,
The man would die! But now they rise again,
With 20 fatal murders on their heads,
And push us from our stools.

Lady Macbeth: My worthy lord, your friends are calling for you.

Macbeth: I forget myself. *(To the guests.)* Do not wonder at me, my most worthy friends.
I have a strange illness, which is nothing
To those that know me.
    Come, love and health to all!
Give me some wine. *(He sits at the table.)*

(The ghost enters again.)

Macbeth: I drink to the general joy of the whole table,
And to our dear friend, Banquo, whom we miss.
Would he were here! To all, and him, we drink!
To all! To all!

Lords: We are your men! Good health to all!

Macbeth *(to the ghost):* Go, go, and leave my sight! Let the earth hide you!
Your bones are drained, and your blood is cold!
No sight or knowledge is in those eyes.
That you glare with!

Lady Macbeth: Think of this, good lords,
As a thing that happens often.
    It has no meaning.

Macbeth: What a man may dare, I dare.
Approach! Take any shape but this,

And my firm nerves shall never tremble.
> Or be alive again

And dare me to a duel of swords.
If then I come forth trembling, call me
A baby. Go, horrible shadow!
Unreal mockery, go! *(The ghost exits.)*
> There.
> It is gone, I am a man again.

Lady Macbeth: You have spoiled the
banquet with this shocking
disorder.

Macbeth: Can such things come upon
us suddenly,
Like clouds in a summer sky,
> give no warning?

(To the others.) How can you look upon
such sights
And keep the natural color in your
cheeks
When mine are pale with fear?

Ross: What sights, my lord?

Lady Macbeth: I pray you, do not
speak.
> He grows worse and worse

Questioning enrages him.
> Please, good night.

Do not bother with polite good-byes,
> but go at once.

Lennox: Good night, and better health
attend his majesty!

Lady Macbeth: A kind good night to
all.

*(All but Macbeth and Lady Macbeth
exit.)*

Macbeth: It will have blood, they say.
> Blood will have blood.

Stones have been known to move
> and trees to speak.

Birds have formed strange signs in the
sky.

What is the time of night?
Lady Macbeth: It is almost morning.
Macbeth: Why do you think Macduff
does not come at my bidding?
Lady Macbeth: Did you send for him?
Macbeth: No, I'm told he will not

come. But I will send.
Tomorrow, early, I will go and find
   the Weird Sisters.
They shall say more. I intend to know
The worst that is to come.
    I have stepped so far

In blood, there is no turning back.
Lady Macbeth: You lack the sweetener
   of all natures, sleep.
Macbeth: Yes, come, we'll sleep.
    My visions come from the fear
Of one who is young in crime.

READING COMPREHENSION

Summarizing. Choose the best phrase to complete each sentence. Then write the complete statements on your paper.

1. Macbeth decided to have Banquo killed because he feared that _____ (Banquo might run away, Banquo's children would become kings, Banquo might kill Macbeth).

2. The murder plot failed in part because _____ (Banquo managed to escape, Fleance managed to escape, Banquo revealed the truth about Duncan's death before he died).

3. When Banquo's ghost sat at the banquet, _____ (everyone was frightened by it, only Lady Macbeth could see it, only Macbeth could see it).

Interpreting. Write the answer to each question on your paper.

1. Why did Macbeth want to have Fleance killed with his father, Banquo?

2. Whom did Macbeth blame for Duncan's murder?

3. How did Macbeth's behavior reflect his feelings about the murders he had committed?

4. How did Lady Macbeth try to cover up her husband's strange behavior at the banquet?

For Thinking and Discussing. Do you think Macbeth will continue to murder? Why or why not?

UNDERSTANDING LITERATURE

Conflict. Characters in a play usually face some sort of problem, or *conflict*. You learn about the characters by observing the ways in which they try to solve the conflict. Characters may face three types of conflict:

1. *People against people:* One character wants something and is opposed by another character.

2. *People against nature:* Characters are challenged by a natural force, such as flood or fire.

3. *People against themselves:* Characters must overcome a personal problem or make a personal decision.

The characters in *Macbeth* face certain conflicts. Read the descriptions of conflicts listed below. Then write whether each conflict is an example of people against people, people against nature, or people against themselves.

1. Macbeth tried to overcome his guilty conscience for killing Duncan.

2. Lady Macbeth urged her husband to be stronger and braver.

3. Fleance escaped from the murderers.

WRITING

Macbeth faced several different kinds of conflict during the play. Choose one of the situations in which he experienced conflict, and write a paragraph describing how he was or was not able to solve the problem.

Act IV

A cave with a boiling caldron in the center.
Thunder sounds. The three witches enter.

First Witch: Thrice[3] the striped cat
    has mewed.
Second Witch: Thrice, and once the
    hedgepig whined.
Third Witch: A harpy cries; 'tis time,
    'tis time.
First Witch: Round about the caldron
    go;
Poisoned cuttings in it throw.
Three Witches: Double, double,
    toil and trouble —
Fire burn, and caldron bubble.
Second Witch: Flesh from off a
    marshland snake
In the caldron boil and bake;
Eye of newt and toe of frog,
Wool of bat and tongue of dog,
Adder's tongue and blindworm's sting,
Lizard's leg and owlet's wing;
For a charm of powerful trouble,
Like a hell broth, boil and bubble.
Three Witches: Double, double,
    toil and trouble —
Fire burn and caldron bubble.
Second Witch: Cool it with a baboon's
    blood;
Then the charm is firm and good.
By the pricking of my thumbs,
Something wicked this way comes.
Open locks,
Whoever knocks!

(Macbeth enters.)

Macbeth: How now, you secret, dark,

and midnight hags?
What is it you do?
Three Witches: A deed without a name.
Macbeth: In the name of that which
    you believe —
However you come to know it, answer
    me.
First Witch: Speak.
Second Witch: Demand.
Third Witch: We'll answer.
First Witch: Say, would you rather
    hear it from our mouths
Or from our masters?
Macbeth: Call them! Let me see them.
First Witch: Pour in the blood
    of a sow that ate her young.
Grease scraped from a murderer's
    gallows, throw
Into the flame.
Three Witches: Come, high or low;
Yourself and your meaning quickly
    show!

(Thunder. The first vision appears, of a
head wearing a helmet.)

Macbeth: Tell me, unknown power —
First Witch: He knows your thoughts.
Hear his speech, but say nothing.
First Vision: Macbeth! Macbeth!
    Macbeth! Beware Macduff,
The Thane of Fife! Dismiss me.
    Enough. *(He disappears.)*
Macbeth: Whatever you are,
    for your good caution, thanks!
You have guessed my fear.
    But one word more —
First Witch: He will not be commanded.
    Here's another,

---

3. thrice: three times

More powerful than the first.

(Thunder. The second vision appears, a bloody child.)

Second Vision: Macbeth! Macbeth! Macbeth!

Macbeth: If I had three ears, I'd hear you.

Second Vision: Be bloody, bold, and firm; for none of woman born
Shall harm Macbeth. *(He disappears.)*

Macbeth: Then, live Macduff. What need I fear of you?
But yet, I'll make my safety doubly sure
And join my hand to fate.
Macduff shall not live!

(Thunder. The third vision appears, a child crowned, with a tree in his hand.)

Macbeth: What is this that rises like the child of a king
And wears upon his baby's brow the round
Symbol of royalty?

Three Witches: Listen, but do not speak to it.

Third Vision: Be lion-spirited, proud, and do not care
Who worries, who frets, or who opposes you.
Macbeth shall never be beaten until
Great Birnam Wood[4] to high Dunsinane Hill[5]
Shall come against him. *(He disappears.)*

Macbeth: That will never be.
Who can command the forest, or bid the tree

---

4. Birnam Wood: a forest near Dunsinane

5. Dunsinane Hill: the site of Macbeth's castle

Tear up his earth-bound root?
Sweet promises, good!
Till the wood of Birnam rise,
Macbeth shall live out all his life
and meet his death
From natural causes. Yet my heart
Throbs to know one thing. Tell me,
if your art
Can tell so much — shall Banquo's
children ever
Reign in his kingdom?
Three Witches: Seek to know no more.
Macbeth: I will be satisfied!
Deny me this,
And an eternal curse fall on you!
Let me know.
First Witch: Show!
Second Witch: Show!
Third Witch: Show!
Three Witches: Show his eyes,
and grieve his heart!
Come like shadows, and so depart!

(*Visions of crowned kings appear, one by
one, followed by Banquo. The eighth holds
a mirror.*)

Macbeth: You are too much like the
ghost of Banquo!
Your crown burns my eyeballs. Filthy
hags!
Why do you show me this? Will the line
Stretch out to the crack of doom?
I'll see no more. And yet, the eighth
appears, who bears a mirror,
Which shows me there are many more
to come.
Horrible sight! Now I see it is true;
For bloodied Banquo smiles at me
and points at them.

(*The visions disappear.*)

Macbeth: Is this so?
First Witch: Aye, sir, all this is so.
But why
Should Macbeth stand amazed?
Come sisters, let us
cheer his spirits, show
The best of the delights we know.

(*The witches dance, then disappear.*)

Macbeth: Where are they? Gone?
Let this evil hour
Stand cursed forever in the calendar!
Come in! Who is out there?

(*Lennox enters.*)

Lennox: What's your grace's will?
Macbeth: Did you see the Weird
Sisters?
Lennox: No, my lord.
Macbeth: Didn't they go by you?
Lennox: No indeed, my lord.
Macbeth: Infected be the air on which
they ride,
And cursed all those that trust them!
Lennox: I bring you word, my lord.
Macduff has fled to England.
Macbeth (*aside*): From this moment,
the first thought of my heart shall
be
The first acts of my hand. And even
now,
To crown my thoughts with acts,
be it thought and done!
The castle of Macduff I will surprise,
Seize Fife, and give the edge of the
sword
To his wife, his babe,
and all unfortunate souls
That have his blood in them! (*He exits.*)

READING COMPREHENSION

Summarizing. Choose the best phrase to complete each sentence. Then write the complete statements on your paper.

1. Macbeth visited the witches because _____ (he wanted to know his future, Lady Macbeth told him to, Banquo's ghost led him there).

2. One vision told Macbeth that he would not be harmed by _____ (Macduff, anyone born of a mother, Banquo's ghost).

3. Another vision told Macbeth that he would not be beaten until _____ (Macduff had died, he was an old man, a forest moved toward his castle).

4. Macbeth learned from Lennox that Macduff _____ (had fled to England, had seen the witches, planned to attack).

Interpreting. Write the answer to each question on your paper.

1. What were the witches doing before Macbeth arrived?

2. Why did the vision of the crowned kings upset Macbeth?

3. What reasons did Macbeth have for killing Macduff and his family?

For Thinking and Discussing. Do you think it was unnecessary for Macbeth to plot Macduff's death? Would he have been just as safe with Macduff alive? Explain.

UNDERSTANDING LITERATURE

Setting and Mood. The *setting* of a play is the time and place of the action and the general atmosphere. Sometimes the setting is not important. The events might have occurred at any place and time. But in other stories, setting is very important. It helps create a particular feeling, or *mood*.

The setting in *Macbeth* is very important. It helps create a dark and frightening mood in the story.

Read the details below from *Macbeth*. On your paper, write those details that help create a mood of fright or terror.

1. Three witches stand in a dark cave.

2. Malcolm is a son of Duncan.

3. There is thunder and lightning.

4. An owl screams at midnight.

5. Duncan admires Macbeth's bravery.

6. Lady Macbeth wishes to gain power.

7. Lennox cannot see the witches.

8. Macduff lives in a castle.

9. A fire burns and a caldron bubbles.

10. Banquo has several sons.

WRITING

The setting of Act IV creates an atmosphere of fear and terror. Find four more details that help to create the mood in Act IV.

Act V

Scene One

Macduff's wife and children have been murdered. In England, Malcolm and Macduff plan to lead an army to overthrow Macbeth. At Macbeth's castle, Dunsinane, Lady Macbeth's maid-in-waiting has called a doctor to watch the Lady's strange behavior during the night.

Doctor: I have watched with you two nights, but can find nothing to prove what you say.

Maid-in-Waiting: Ever since his majesty has been at war, I have seen her rise from her bed, unlock her desk, take out paper, fold it, write on it, read it. Then she seals it and returns to bed. Yet all this time she is fast asleep.

Doctor: Besides her walking, and the other things she does, what have you heard her say?

Maid-in-Waiting: That, sir, which I will not report.

Doctor: You must tell *me*.

Maid-in-Waiting: No, not you or anyone. I have no witness to confirm what I say.

(Lady Macbeth enters, with a candle.)

Maid-in-Waiting: Here she comes! See, she is fast asleep. Observe her. Stand close.

Doctor: How came she by that light?

Maid-in-Waiting: It was at her bedside. She has light by her all the time. It is her command.

Doctor: Her eyes are open.

Maid-in-Waiting: Aye, but their sense is shut.

Doctor: What is she doing now? Look how she rubs her hands.

Maid-in-Waiting: She does that often, seeming to wash her hands. I have known her to do this for a quarter of an hour.

Lady Macbeth: Yet here's a spot.

Doctor: Listen, she speaks.

Lady Macbeth: Out, damned spot! Out, I say! One. Two. Why then, it is time to do it. Hell is murky. What, my lord, a soldier and afraid? Why be afraid who knows it, when none can question our power? Yet who would have thought the old man had so much blood in him?

Doctor: *(to the Maid-in-Waiting):* Did you hear that?

Lady Macbeth: The Thane of Fife had a wife. Where is she now? What, will these hands never be clean? No more of that, my lord, no more of that! You spoil all with this trembling.

Maid-in-Waiting: She has spoken what she should not, I am sure of that! Heaven knows what she has known.

Lady Macbeth: Here's the smell of the blood still. All the perfumes of Arabia will not sweeten this little hand. Oh, oh, oh!

Doctor: What a sigh she gives! Her heart is very heavy.

Maid-in-Waiting: I would not have such a heart.

Doctor: This disease is beyond my knowledge. Yet I have known those who have walked in their sleep that died in a holy state in their beds.

Lady Macbeth: Wash your hands, put on your nightclothes, look not so pale! I tell you yet again, Banquo's buried. He cannot come out of his grave.

Doctor: Even so?

Lady Macbeth: To bed, to bed! There's knocking at the gate. Give me your hand! What's done cannot be undone. To bed, to bed, to bed! *(She exits.)*

Doctor: Will she go to bed now?

Maid-in-Waiting: At once.

Doctor: There are foul rumors everywhere. Unnatural deeds
Breed unnatural troubles. Infected minds
Tell their guilty secrets
    to their deaf pillows.
She needs a priest more than a
    physician.
Look after her. God, God, forgive us all!

(They exit.)

Scene Two

In the country, near Birnam Wood. Malcolm, Macduff, Siward, and their allies are preparing for battle to take the kingship from Macbeth. Macbeth is in his castle at Dunsinane.

Malcolm: Cousins, I hope the days are near at hand
When Scots can sleep in safety.

Menteith: We do not doubt it.

Siward: What wood is this before us?

Menteith: The wood of Birnam.

Malcolm: Let every soldier cut himself a bough
And bear it before him. In that way, we shall hide
The numbers in our army, and enemy lookouts
Will give a wrong report.

Soldiers: It shall be done.

Siward: We hear that the confident tyrant
Plans to stay in Dunsinane and wait,
Believing he can outlast our seige.

Malcolm: It is his only hope.
    Men of all sorts
Rebel against him. None serve him now,
But those with the hearts of slaves.

Siward: The time approaches for us to prove ourselves.
Only the battle will decide our cause.

(They exit.)

Scene Three

Inside the castle of Dunsinane. Macbeth enters with Seyton.

Macbeth: Hang out our banners from the castle walls.
Our castle's strength will mock a siege.
Let them lie there till hunger and fever eat them up.
If they were not strengthened by those who deserted us,
We could have met them fearlessly, beard to beard,
And beat them backward, home.

(There is a cry from another part of the castle.)

Macbeth: What is that noise?

Seyton: It is the cry of women, my good lord. *(He exits.)*

Macbeth: I have almost forgotten
 the taste of fear.
Once it would have chilled my blood
 to hear
A night-shriek, and the hair upon my
 head
Would at a horror story rise and creep.
I have swallowed so much horror now,
It is familiar to my murderous thoughts
And cannot shake me.

(Seyton enters.)

Macbeth: What was that cry?
Seyton: The queen, my lord, is dead.
Macbeth: She should have waited to
 die—
There would have been a time
 to hear such news.
Tomorrow, and tomorrow, and
 tomorrow
Creeps in this petty pace from day to
 day
To the last syllable of recorded time;
And all our yesterdays have lighted fools
The way to dusty death.
  Out, out, brief candle!
Life's but a walking shadow,
 a poor player
That struts and frets his hour
 upon the stage
And then is heard no more. It is a tale
Told by an idiot, full of sound and fury,
Signifying nothing.

(A messenger enters.)

Macbeth: You come to use your tongue.
 Quick, your story!
Messenger: Gracious lord,
I must report that which I know I saw,
But do not know how to do it.
Macbeth: Well, say it, sir!

Messenger: As I was standing watch
 upon the hill,
I looked toward Birnam,
 and it seemed to me
The woods began to move.
Macbeth: Liar and slave!
Messenger: Punish me as you wish,
 if it is not so.
Three miles off, you may see it coming.
I swear, the forest is moving.
Macbeth: If you speak false,
Upon the next tree you shall hang alive,
Till starvation claim you. If your speech
 is true,
I care not if you hang *me* there instead.
"Fear not, till Birnam Wood comes
 to Dunsinane!"
And now a wood comes toward
 Dunsinane. . . .
(To the others.)
If this he says he witnessed is really
 happening,
There is no way to flee nor to stay here.
I begin to be weary of the sun.
Ring the alarm bell! At least we'll die
With armor on our back!

(They exit.)

Scene Four

*Outside the castle of Dunsinane. Enter
Malcolm, Siward, Macduff, and their army,
holding boughs of trees in front of them.*

Malcolm: We are near enough.
 Throw down your leafy screens
And show yourselves as you are.
 You, worthy uncle,
Shall with my cousin, your most noble
 son,

Lead our first battle. Worthy Macduff
and I
Shall take on ourselves what else
there is to do,
According to our plan.
Siward: Fare you well.
We will test the tyrant's power tonight.
Let us be beaten, if we cannot fight.
Macduff: Let all our trumpets sound,
give them all breath,
The horns that call us out
to blood and death.

(They exit. Alarms ring out.)

Scene Five

The battlefield. Macbeth enters.

Macbeth: I cannot flee. I must fight
to the end.
But tell me, who is he who was not
born of woman?
Such a one am I to fear, or no one.

(Young Siward enters.)

Young Siward: What is your name?
Macbeth: My name's Macbeth.
Young Siward: The devil himself
could not pronounce a name
More hateful to my ear.
Macbeth: No, nor more frightening.
Young Siward: You lie, hated tyrant!
With my sword,
I'll prove the lie you speak.

(They fight. Young Siward is killed.)

Macbeth: You were born of woman.
Swords I smile at, weapons laugh to
scorn,
If they're raised by man
that's of a woman born.

(Macbeth exits. Macduff enters.)

Macduff: Tyrant, show your face!
If you are dead, and by no stroke of
mine,
My wife and children's ghost will
haunt me still.
I cannot strike at hired fighters.
Either I meet you, Macbeth, or I sheathe
My sword again. Let me find him,
Fortune!
I ask no more.

*(Macduff exits. Malcolm and Siward
enter.)*

Siward: This way, my lord. The castle
has surrendered.
The tyrant's people fight on both sides
at once.
The noble thanes do bravely in the war;
The day is almost yours.
There's little left to do.
Enter, sir, the castle.

(They exit.)

Scene Six

Another part of the field. Macbeth enters.

Macbeth: Should I fall on my sword
and kill myself?
As long as I have foes, I'd rather give
The wounds to them.

(Macduff enters.)

Macduff: Turn, hell-hound, turn!
Macbeth: Of all men living,
I have avoided you.
But stand back! My soul is
too much stained
With blood of yours already.
Macduff: I have no words.
My voice is in my sword,
you bloody villain!

(They fight.)

Macbeth: You waste your labor.
  I bear a charmed life,
Which will not yield to one of woman
  born.
Macduff: Forget your charm!
And let the evil angel whom you serve
Tell you Macduff was ripped from
  his mother's womb
Before her time.
Macbeth: Cursed be the tongue that
  tells me so,
For it has made of me a lesser man!
And let those friends who spoke with
  double tongue
Be trusted no more.
  I will not fight with you!
Macduff: Then yield, coward,
And live to be a show for all to gaze at!
We'll have your picture painted
  and hung out
On a pole, and under it the words:
"Here may you see the tyrant!"
Macbeth: I will not yield,
To kiss the ground before
  young Malcolm's feet
And to be laughed at by the mob,
  and cursed.
Though Birnam Wood has come to
  Dunsinane,
Yet I will fight to the last.
  Before my body
I lift my warlike shield.
Fight on, Macduff! And cursed be him
That first cries, "Hold — enough!"

*(They exit fighting. Siward, Ross, and
  Malcolm enter.)*

Ross: *(To Siward):* Your son, my lord,
  has paid a soldier's debt.

He only lived till he was just a man,
And then, when his courage was
  confirmed,
He died like a man.
Siward: Then he is dead?
Ross: Aye, carried off the field.
Siward: Did he die fighting?
Ross: He did.
Siward: Why, then he's God's soldier.
Had I as many sons as I have hairs,
I would not wish them to a fairer death.
So, God be with him.
  Here comes new comfort.
*(Macduff enters, carrying Macbeth's
  head.)*
Macduff *(to Malcolm):* Hail, King!
  For so you are.
Here is the tyrant's cursed head.
  The land is free.
Hail, King of Scotland!
All: Hail, King of Scotland!
Malcolm: We shall not wait to pay you
  for your love.
My thanes and kinsmen, from this hour
  on,
Be earls, an honored title unknown
  in Scotland.
Now we must call home our exiled
  friends
Who fled the snares and spies of
  tyranny,
And we must find the cruel followers
Of this dead butcher and his
  fiendlike queen.
Whatever else we're called to do,
  we will perform.
So thanks to all at once, and to each
  one,
Whom we invite to see us crowned at
  Scone.

READING COMPREHENSION

Summarizing. Choose the best phrase to complete each sentence. Then write the complete statements on your paper.

1. When Lady Macbeth sleepwalked, she tried to _____ (jump out of a castle window, kill herself with a dagger, wash away an imaginary spot of blood).

2. Malcolm's army sneaked up on Macbeth by _____ (hiding behind tree boughs, using an underground passage, traveling only at night).

3. At the end of the play, _____ (Macbeth killed Macduff, Macduff killed Macbeth, Macduff and Macbeth both died).

Interpreting. Write the answer to each question on your paper.

1. Why did the doctor say that Lady Macbeth needed a priest more than a physician?

2. Why did Malcolm and Macduff attack Macbeth's castle?

3. How did Macbeth feel about life after he heard the news of his wife's death?

For Thinking and Discussing.

1. In Act IV, the visions gave Macbeth three warnings. How did each warning come true in Act V?

2. How were Macbeth and his wife destroyed by their own evil actions?

UNDERSTANDING LITERATURE

Character Motivation. Each character in a play behaves in a certain way. By the end of the play, you should be able to understand why characters acted as they did. Their *motivation*, or reason for their actions, should be clear to you.

For example, in Act V of *Macbeth*, Lady Macbeth killed herself. Her motivation was that she was haunted by guilt about the murders that had occurred. She could no longer live with the truth, knowing what she and her husband had done.

Read the actions described in the list below. Then write what the character's motivation was for each of the actions.
1. King Duncan made Macbeth the Thane of Cawdor.
2. Lady Macbeth urged her husband to kill Duncan.
3. Lady Macbeth smeared blood on Duncan's guards.
4. Malcolm and Donalbain fled the country after Duncan's murder.
5. Macbeth had Banquo killed.
6. Macbeth returned to visit the witches.
7. Macduff killed Macbeth.

WRITING

At the end of the play, Macbeth had changed from a gentle man who resisted killing to a murderous tyrant. What motivation contributed to the changes in his actions? In a paragraph, describe how the motivation for his behavior changed from the beginning to the end of the play.

Section Review

VOCABULARY

Context Clues. Sometimes you find an unfamiliar word in a story. You might figure out the meaning of the word by its *context*, or the way the word is used in the sentence. For example:

> Macbeth fought against soldiers who wanted to take him *captive*.

Look how the word *captive* is used in the sentence. What would soldiers fighting against someone want to take? They might want a prisoner. The word *captive* means "prisoner."

Write the word after each sentence that means the same as the italicized word.

1. The witches made *prophecies* that Macbeth would be king someday.
   arguments   predictions   answers

2. Lady Macbeth urged her husband to hide his evil purpose by acting like a *genial* host to Duncan.
   rude   forgetful   friendly

3. Macbeth and his wife *craved* power so much that they were willing to commit murder for it.
   helped   disliked   desired

4. Macbeth became so disturbed after Duncan's murder that even slight noises *appalled* him.
   bored   upset   amused

READING

Cloze Exercise. Many reading tests use a special technique, called *cloze*, to measure comprehension. In a cloze comprehension test, words are omitted from a selection, and your job is to fill in the blanks. Each word you choose should make sense in the context of the selection. The other words give you clues that help you decide which word belongs in each blank.

Here are two incomplete sentences from *Macbeth*. Following each sentence are three words. On your paper, write the word that best completes the sentence.

1. "New honors come upon him, like stiff new clothes that are not comfortable till they are _____ a while."
   mended   worn   bought

2. "Are you only a dagger of the mind, a false creation of my troubled _____?"
   knife   ghost   brain

Below is a passage from *Macbeth*. Read it carefully. Then, on your paper, write the missing words. When you have finished, turn to page 577 and compare your words to the ones used in the play.

Lady Macbeth: Your mind is sick. Go get some _____ and wash this filthy evidence from your _____. Why did you _____ these daggers from the place? They must lie there. Go, carry them _____, and smear the sleepy guards with _____.

Macbeth: I'll go no more. I am _____ to think what I have _____. I dare not look at it _____.

A Speech. Speech writing differs from other kinds of writing in that a speech is meant to be heard, not read. However, when you write a speech, you follow the same four steps in the writing process. A speech is also like many other kinds of writing in that it has an introduction, a body, and a conclusion.

Step 1: Set Your Goal

When you give a speech, you want to capture your listeners' attention. People will listen if your speech is interesting and you present it well. To write an interesting speech, you must think carefully about your topic and what you want to say. Choose one of these topics for a speech:

☐ A speech for Duncan to give praising Macbeth for his courage and success in battle (Act I, Scene Two)

☐ A speech for Banquo to give in honor of the dead King Duncan (Act II, Scene Three)

☐ A speech for Malcolm to give to his allies as they prepare to advance on the castle of Dunsinane (Act V, Scene Two).

There are many purposes for giving a speech. You may want to describe or explain something. Or you may want to persuade your listeners to act in a certain way. For example, if you chose to write Malcolm's speech, your purpose might be to persuade the allies to follow you into battle. Or it might be to explain why the battle is important. Write a statement of purpose for your speech.

Step 2: Make a Plan

Begin gathering ideas for your speech by taking notes on the points you want to cover. Remember, you are writing a speech for a character in a play. Put yourself in the character's place. Think about the audience you are addressing, and make sure your points are appropriate.

Once you have identified the points you want to include in your speech, you need to organize them. How you organize them will depend on your purpose. For example, if you are writing to persuade, you may want to put your most important points first. If you are writing to describe, you may want to use natural order or chronological order. If you are explaining how to do something, you may want to organize the points to show how one thing leads to another.

Review your organized list of points once more to make sure they all relate to the main topic of your speech. Add or delete any points you think would strengthen or weaken your speech.

Step 3: Write a First Draft

Now that you have organized your notes, it is time to write the body of your speech. The body of your speech contains the message you, or your character, want to convey. Write your notes as sentences. You'll have time to revise later.

After you have finished the body of your speech, think about the introduction. Write something that will grab your listeners' attention and give them a clear idea of what your speech is about.

Write the conclusion of your speech last. Your conclusion should summarize the main idea of your speech and give your audience something to think about. Bear in mind that your conclusion will contain the last thought you will leave with your listeners.

Step 4: Revise

Like other kinds of writing, you should set your speech aside for a few days before you begin to revise it. As you revise, keep in mind that your speech is going to be heard, not read. Read it aloud several times to determine if it sounds natural and appropriate for the character for whom you are speaking. One sentence should flow easily into the next. If you find any sentences that sound awkward when spoken, rewrite them. Here is a checklist to refer to as you work on your revision:

☐ Will the introduction grab the audience's attention? Does it give a clear idea of the topic of the speech?

☐ Are all the points presented in the body of the speech?

☐ Does the conclusion summarize the main idea of the speech? Does it make the audience think?

☐ Does the speech sound natural when it is read aloud?

As a final step before you begin to rehearse your speech, correct any grammatical errors. Even though your audience won't be reading the speech, they will hear any mistakes in grammar. Also, correct errors in punctuation and spelling. It will be easier to make your speech sound natural if it is punctuated correctly. You will be less likely to mispronounce words if they are spelled correctly.

QUIZ

The following is a quiz for Section 11. Write the answers in complete sentences on your paper.

Reading Comprehension

1. In Act I, what made Macbeth decide to kill Duncan?

2. In Act II, how did Macbeth and his wife try to cover up the murder?

3. In Act III, how did Macbeth show that his conscience bothered him after Banquo's murder?

4. In Act IV, what did the three visions show Macbeth?

5. In Act V, how did Lady Macbeth show that her conscience bothered her about the murders?

Understanding Literature

6. *Macbeth* contains many instances of foreshadowing. What clues told you about events to come later?

7. What did you learn about Lady Macbeth through her actions, speech, and thoughts?

8. What conflicts did Macbeth face? Which were against other people? Against nature? Against himself?

9. What was Lady Macbeth's motivation for killing herself?

10. What was Macbeth's motivation in refusing to be taken alive?

ACTIVITIES

Word Attack. In Act V of *Macbeth*, the castle at Dunsinane is under siege. The vowel sound you hear in the word *siege* is the long *e* vowel sound. Usually when the letters *ie* are preceded and followed by a consonant, they stand for the long *e* vowel sound. Find five additional words in Act V that have the long *e* vowel sound spelled with the letters *ie*. Write the words on your paper.

Speaking and Listening

1. Choose one of the following scenes from *Macbeth* to act out for the class. Be sure you have one person to take each part before you begin rehearsing a reading of the scene. Refer to the stage directions for assistance as you try to catch the mood of your character.

   Act I, Scene Two

   Act I, Scene Five

   Act II, Scene One

   Act IV (entire act)

   Act V, Scene One

   Act V, Scene Three

   Act V, Scene Six

2. As *Macbeth* begins, three witches enter the stage to the background of thunder and lightning. Practice reading this first scene, bearing in mind that it sets the tone for the rest of the play. Take the part of all three witches, using different voices for each one. Be prepared to present your reading of the scene to the class.

Researching

1. Shakespeare loosely based his play on the life of the real Macbeth. Do some research to find out about the real Macbeth. How long ago did he live? What country did he come from? What was his station in life? What aspect of the real Macbeth's life did Shakespeare portray in his play? Was there a real Duncan and a real Malcolm in Macbeth's life? Compare the facts you find with those of your classmates.

2. Shakespeare lived and wrote during England's Elizabethan Age. Do some research to find out about this period of English history. Why was it called the Elizabethan Age? How long did it last? What were the living conditions like? What were some of the customs and beliefs of the period? What were the fashions? What part did the theater play in Elizabethan life? Be prepared to present your findings to the class.

Creating

1. Imagine that you are Macbeth or Lady Macbeth. Write a dialogue to describe what mistakes you have made and how you would change your life if you could go back and do things differently.

2. Prophecy is an important part of *Macbeth*. Write a short prophecy about the future of someone famous or someone you know. Then write a paragraph and tell how this person's life might change after he or she learns of the prophecy.

PRONUNCIATION KEY

ă	pat	j	judge	sh	dish, ship
ā	aid, fey, pay	k	cat, kick, pique	t	tight
â	air, care, wear	l	lid, needle	th	path, thin
ä	father	m	am, man, mum	*th*	bathe, this
b	bib	n	no, sudden	ŭ	cut, rough
ch	church	ng	thing	û	circle, firm, heard, term,
d	deed	ŏ	horrible, pot		turn, urge, word
ĕ	pet, pleasure	ō	go, hoarse, row, toe	v	cave, valve, vine
ē	be, bee, easy, leisure	ô	alter, caught, for, paw	w	with
f	fast, fife, off, phase, rough	oi	boy, noise, oil	y	yes
g	gag	ou	cow, out	yo͞o	abuse, use
h	hat	o͝o	took	z	rose, size, xylophone, zebra
hw	which	o͞o	boot, fruit	zh	garage, pleasure, vision
ĭ	pit	p	pop	ə	about, silent, pencil, lemon,
ī	by, guy, pie	r	roar		circus
î	dear, deer, fierce, mere	s	miss, sauce, see	ər	butter

PART OF SPEECH LABELS

n.	(noun)	*conj.*	(conjunction)
adj.	(adjective)	*prep.*	(preposition)
adv.	(adverb)	*v.*	(verb)
pron.	(pronoun)	*interj.*	(interjection)

The additional italicized labels below are used as needed to show inflected forms:

pl.	(plural)	*sing.* (singular)

STRESS

Primary stress ′
  bi · ol′o · gy | bī ŏl′əjē |
Secondary stress ′
  bi′o · log′i · cal | bī′ə lŏj′ĭ kəl |

In this glossary, definitions were chosen to show the meanings of the words as they are used in the selections. Unless otherwise indicated, entries based on © 1977 by Houghton Mifflin Company. Reprinted by permission from The American Heritage School Dictionary.

a·bid·ing | ə bī′ dĭng | *adj.* Long-lasting; permanent: *abiding love; abiding faith.*

ab·o·rig·i·ne | ăb′ ə rĭj′ ə nē | *n.* Any member of a group of people who are the first known to have lived in a given region.

a·cre | ā′ kər | *n.* A unit of area equal to 43,560 square feet or 4,840 square yards, used in measuring land.

ad·der | ăd′ ər | *n.* Any of several poisonous Old World snakes, especially the common viper of northern Europe and Asia.

af·flict | ə flĭkt′ | *v.* To cause distress to; cause to suffer; trouble greatly: *Mankind is afflicted with many ills.*

ag·i·tate | ăj′ ĭ tāt′ | *v.* **ag·i·tat·ed, ag·i·tat·ing.** To disturb; upset.

ail | āl | *v.* To be ill: *My mother is ailing.*

al·ly | ăl′ ī′ | *or* | ə lī′ | *n., pl.* **al·lies.** A person or country that is friendly toward another.

a·nat·o·my | ə năt′ə mē | *n.* The scientific study of the shape and structure of living things.

an·guish | ăng′ gwĭsh | *n.* A pain of the body or mind that causes agony; torment; torture. **an·guished** | ăng′ gwĭsht | *adj.* feeling, expressing, or caused by anguish: *anguished souls clinging to a sinking ship; a wounded elephant's anguished trumpeting.*

ap·pren·tice | ə prĕn′ tĭs | *n.* A person who works for another without pay in return for instruction in a craft or trade.

ap·pur·te·nance | ə pûr′ tnəns | *n.* **appurtenances.** Any equipment, such as clothing or tools, used for a specific purpose; gear.

arc | ärk | *n.* A portion of a curve, especially of a circle.

as·pi·ra·tion | ăs′ pə rā′ shən | *n.* A strong desire, as for the realization of an ambition, an ideal, etc.: *unsympathetic with the students' aspirations for involvement in determining the role of their schools.*

as·pire | ə spīr′ | *v.* **as·pired, as·pir·ing.** To have a great ambition; desire strongly: *aspire to become a good player; aspire to great knowledge.*

as·sured | ə shŏord′ | *adj.* Certain; guaranteed: *an assured success.*

au·di·to·ry | ô′ dĭ tôr′ ē | *or* | —tōr′ē | *adj.* Of hearing or the organs of hearing.

au·top·sy | ô′ tŏp′ sē | *or* | ô′ təp— | *n.* A medical examination of a dead human body, especially to determine the cause of death.

a·venge | ə věnj′ | *v.* **a·venged, a·veng·ing.** To take revenge for: *taking up arms to avenge an insult.*

balm·y | bä′ mē | *adj.* **balm·i·er, balm·i·est.** Mild and pleasant: *balmy, subtropical climates.*

bar·ren | băr′ ən | *adj.* Lacking or unable to produce growing plants or crops: *a barren desert; barren soil.*

blunt | blŭnt | *adj.* Abrupt and frank in manner.

browse | brouz | *v.* **browsed, brows·ing.** To feed on leaves, young shoots, twigs, and other plants.

ca·lam·i·ty | kə lăm′ ĭ tē | *n., pl.* **ca·lam·i·ties.** Something that causes great distress and suffering; a disaster.

can·vas | kăn′ vəs | *n.* **1.** A heavy, coarse cloth of cotton, hemp, or flax, used for making tents, sails, etc. **2.** An oil painting on canvas or a piece of canvas used to paint on.

cat·a·ract | kăt′ ə răkt′ | *n.* a condition in which the lens of an eye or the membrane that covers it turns cloudy, causing total or partial blindness.

ca·tas·tro·phe | kə tăs′ trə fē | *n.* A great and sudden calamity, such as an earthquake or flood.

caul·dron | kôl′ drən | *n.* A form of the word *caldron.* A large kettle for boiling.

cav·ern·ous | kăv′ ər nəs | *adj.* Resembling a cavern; huge, deep, and hollow.

chaff | chăf | *n.* Grain husks that have been separated from the seeds by threshing.

chan·de·lier | shăn′ də lĭr′ | *n.* A fixture that holds a number of light bulbs or candles and is suspended from a ceiling.

cir·cuit | sûr′ kĭt | *n.* **1. a.** A route or path that turns back to where it began. **b.** A journey made on such a path or route: *He made a circuit around the campground.* **2.** A periodic trip through a set of places, usually in a fixed order and in connection with one's work, such as that of a salesman.

clam·or | klăm′ ər | v. **clam·or·ing. 1.** To make a loud or strong demand. **2.** To make a loud, continuous, and usually confused noise: *The children clamored for ice cream.*

clench | klĕnch | v. To close (a hand or the teeth) tightly: *clench one's fist.*

com·mit·ment | kə mit′ mənt | n. A pledge or obligation, as to follow a certain course of action: *our treaty commitments to protect small nations; a commitment to work for peaceful change.*

com·pas·sion | kəm păsh′ ən | n. The feeling of sharing the suffering of another, together with a desire to give aid or show mercy.

con·ceive | kən sēv′ | v. **con·ceived, con·ceiv·ing.** To form or develop in the mind: *James Watt conceived the idea of the steam engine from watching a boiling kettle when he was a boy.*

con·cer·to | kən chĕr′ tō | n., pl. **con·cer·tos** or **con·cer·ti** | kən chĕr′ tē | A musical composition written for one or more solo instruments and an orchestra.

con·fine·ment | kən fīn′ mənt | n. A condition of being confined, i.e., restricted in movement or imprisoned.

con·firm | kən fûrm′ | v. **1.** To give moral strength to: *"confirm thy soul in self-control, thy liberty in law"* ("America the Beautiful"). **2.** To support or establish the validity of: *The news confirmed the rumors. Experiments confirmed the theory.*

con·so·la·tion | kŏn′ sə lā′ shən | n. Comfort during a time of disappointment or sorrow.

con·spic·u·ous | kən spĭk′ yōō əs | adj. Attracting attention; striking the eye: *a conspicuous error.*

con·spir·a·cy | kən spîr′ ə sē | n., pl. **con·spir·a·cies.** A secret plan to commit an unlawful act.

con·tempt | kən tĕmpt′ | n. A feeling that someone or something is inferior and undesirable: *to have contempt for a traitor.*

con·tra·ry | kŏn′ trĕr ē | adj. Completely different; opposed: *contrary points of view.*

çor·nice | kôr′ nĭs | n. The uppermost projection of stone or molding at the top of a wall or column.

cor·o·ner | kôr′ə nər | or | kŏr′— | n. A public official who investigates any death not clearly due to natural causes.

court·ly | kôrt′ lē | or | kōrt′— | adj. Suitable for a royal court; dignified, polite, etc.: *a courtly ceremony; courtly manners.*

coy | koi | adj. Pretending to be shy or modest so as to attract the interest of others.

crim·son | krĭm′ zən | or | —sən | n. A vivid purplish red. —adj. Vivid purplish red.

cut·ting | kŭt′ ĭng | n. **1.** Something made by cutting away at a larger whole, i.e., a record, a path. **2.** An excavation made through high ground in the construction of a road, railway, or the like.

da·is | dā′ ĭs | or | dās | n. A raised platform for a throne, a speaker, or a group of honored guests.

de·duce | dĭ dōōs′ | or | —dyōōs′ | v. **de·duced, de·duc·ing.** To reach (a conclusion) by reasoning.

des·o·late | dĕs′ə lĭt | adj. Lonely and sad; wretched; forlorn: *a child with a desolate air.*

des·pi·ca·ble | dĕs′ pĭ kə bəl | or | dĭ spĭk′ ə— | adj. Deserving contempt or disdain; vile: *a despicable person; a despicable act.*

des·tine | dĕs′ tĭn | v. **des·tined.** To determine beforehand, as if by some force or power over which one has no control: *a defeat that destined Theodore Roosevelt to political exile.*

dev·as·tate | dĕv′ ə stāt′ | v. **dev·as·tat·ed, dev·as·tat·ing.** To lay waste; ruin: *The storms devastated much of the county.* —**dev′as·tat′ing** adj.: *a devastating blow.*

de·vise | dĭ vīz′ | v. **de·vised, de·vis·ing.** To form or arrange in the mind; plan; invent; contrive.

dire | dīr | adj. **dir·er, dir·est.** Having dreadful or terrible consequences; disastrous: *a dire catastrophe.*

dis·ar·ray | dĭs ə rā′ | n. **1.** A state of disorder or confusion: *The mail lay in disarray on his desk.* **2.** Disordered or insufficient dress.

dis·band | dĭs bănd′ | v. To break up and separate: *disband an orchestra.*

dis·con·cert | dĭs′ kən sûrt′ | v. To upset the self-possession of; perturb.

dis·em·bark | dĭs′ ĕm **bärk′** | *v.* To go out or put ashore from a ship: *disembark in Boston; forbade the captain to disembark a single passenger.*

dis·sim·u·late | dĭ sĭm′ yə lāt | *v.* **dis·sim·u·lat·ed, dis·sim·u·lat·ing.** To hide one's true feelings or intentions; dissemble. —**dis·sim′u·la′ tion** *n.*

dis·suade | dĭ swād′ | *v.* **dis·suad·ed, dis·suad· ing.** To discourage or keep (someone) from a purpose or course of action: *His invitation dissuaded her from leaving early.* —**dis· sua′sion** | dĭ swā′ zhən | *n.*

ear·nest | ûr′ nĭst | *adj.* **1.** Showing or expressing deep, sincere feeling: *The king knelt in earnest prayer.* **2.** Serious and determined in purpose: *groups of earnest students.*

ec·stat·ic | ĕk **stăt′** ĭk | *adj.* In a state of ecstasy; enraptured: *He bounded about the room in ecstatic. delight.* —**ec·stat′i· cal·ly** *adv.*

ef·fu·sive | ĭ **fyoo′** sĭv | *adj.* Unrestrained or excessive in emotional expression; gushy: *an effusive display of gratitude.* —**ef·fu′ sive·ly** *adv.*

em·bank·ment | ĕm **băngk′** mənt | *n.* A mound of earth or stone built up to hold back water or to support a roadway.

en·croach | ĕn **krōch′** | *v.* To intrude or infringe upon the rights or property of another: *encroach on the fields of a neighboring farm.* —**en·croach′ment** *n.*

en·ti·ty | ĕn′ tĭ tē | *n., pl.* **en·ti·ties.** Something that exists and may be distinguished from other things: *American English and British English are often considered separate entities.*

ere | âr | *Archaic. prep.* Previous to; before.

er·u·dite | ĕr′ yoo dīt′ | *or* | ĕr oo— | *adj.* Having or marked by great knowledge or learning; learned: *an erudite book.*

e·ther | ē′ thər | *n.* The ether formed from ethanol, containing carbon, hydrogen, and oxygen in the proportions $C_4H_{10}O$. It evaporates easily, is very flammable, and is used as a solvent and in medicine as an anesthetic.

ex·al·ta·tion | ĕg′zôl **tā′** shən | *n.* The state or feeling of intense, often excessive exhilaration and well-being; rapture; elation.

ex·cur·sion | ĭk **skûr′** zhən | *n.* A short, brief journey, especially a tour made for pleasure with a group; an outing.

ex·haus·tive | ĭg **zŏs′** tĭv | *v.* Comprehensive; thorough: *exhaustive tests.*

fa·ce·tious | fə **sē′** shəs | *adj.* Meant to be funny; humorous: *a facetious remark.*

feign | fān | *v.* To give a false appearance of; pretend: *feign illness.*

fer·vor | **fûr′** vər | *n.* Intensity of emotion; fervency; ardor: *religious fervor.*

fi·del·i·ty | fĭ **děl′** ĭ tē | *or* | fī— | *n.* **1.** Faithfulness to a person, cause, etc.; loyalty: *the fidelity of a crew to a captain.*

fife | fīf | *n.* A small, high-pitched musical instrument similar to a flute, often used with drums to accompany military music.

fit·ful | **fit′** fəl | *adj.* Interrupted by or as if by fits: *fitful sleep.*

flail | flāl | *v.* To thresh or beat with or as if with a flail (a long wooden tool).

flank | flăngk | *n.* The fleshy part of the body between the ribs and the hip.

fore·bod·ing | fôr **bō′** dĭng | *or* | fōr— | *n.* An uneasy feeling that something bad is going to happen.

fun·da·men·tal | fŭn′ də **měn′** tl | *n.* Something that is an elemental or basic part of a system, as a principle or law; an essential: *the fundamentals of mathematics.*

gal·lant | **găl′** ənt | *adj.* **1.** Brave and noble; courageous; valorous: *a gallant knight; a gallant try.* **2.** | *also* gə **lănt′** | *or* | —**lănt′** | . Polite and attentive to women; chivalrous: *his gallant manner.*

gape | gāp | *or* | găp | *v.* **gaped, gap·ing.** To open wide: *Cracks gaped on the levee after the flood.* —**gap·ing** *adj.*: *a gaping hole; a gaping wound.*

gasp | găsp | *or* | gäsp | *v.* To inhale in a sudden, sharp way, as from shock or surprise: *The crowd gasped in amazement.*

ghet·to | **gĕt′**ō | *n.* A section or quarter in a European city to which Jews are or were restricted.

gor·y | **gôr′** ē | *or* | **gōr′** ē | *adj.* **gor·i·er, gor·i·est.** Covered with or characterized by blood; bloody: *a gory battle.*

gout | gout | *n.* **1.** A disease in which, as a result of faulty metabolism, hard deposits form in joints, especially of the big toe, causing arthritis. **2.** A mass of something wet or sticky.—**gout·y** | gou′ te | *adj.* Suffering from or affected by gout.

gran·deur | **grăn′** jər | *or* | —joor | *n.* Awe-inspiring greatness; splendor.

hag·gard | **hăg′** ərd | *adj.* Appearing worn and exhausted because of suffering, worry, etc.; gaunt: *a haggard face.*

hag·gle | **hăg′** əl | *v.* **hag·gled, hag·gling.** To bargain, as over the price of something.

har·ass·ment | ha **răs′** mənt | *n.* The act of bothering or tormenting with repeated interruptions, attacks, etc.

har·py | **här′** pē | *n., pl.* **har·pies. 1.** A hideous female monster. **2.** A nasty or greedy person.

heath | hēth | *n.* An open, uncultivated stretch of land covered with low-growing shrubs or plants such as heather.

hur·tle | **hûr′** tl | *v.* To move or cause to move with or as if with great speed: *He hurtled through the dust toward the highway.*

im·per·ti·nent | ĭm **pûr′**tn ənt | *adj.* Impudent; rude: *an impertinent manner.*

im·per·vi·ous | ĭm **pûr′** vē əs | *adj.* Not capable of being affected; immune: *He seemed impervious to fear.*

im·pla·ca·ble | ĭm **plā′** kə bal | *or* | —**plăk′ə**— | *adj.* Not easily calmed, pacified, or appeased: *an implacable fury; their implacable enemy.*

im·pli·ca·tion | ĭm′ plĭ **kā′** shən | *n.* The act of saying or conveying indirectly, or suggesting without stating: *The writer conveyed his idea by implication.*

im·promp·tu | ĭm **prŏmp′** tōō | *or* | —tyōō | *adj.* Not prepared beforehand; not rehearsed: *an impromptu lecture.*

in·con·gru·ous | ĭn **kŏng′** grōō əs | *adj.* Not consistent with what is logical, customary, or expected; inappropriate: *the incongruous cheerfulness of the executioner.*

in·dig·nant | ĭn **dĭg′** nənt | *adj.* Feeling or expressing righteous anger: *indignant over her remarks.*

in·fi·nite | **ĭn′** fə nĭt | *adj.* **1.** Greater in value than any specified number, however large: *an infinite number.* **2.** Having a measure that is infinite: *an infinite plane.* —**in·fi·nite·ly** *adv.*

in·fin·i·tes·i·mal | ĭn′ fĭn ĭ **tĕs′** ə məl | *adj.* Extremely small; minute: *Matter is made up of infinitesimal units called atoms.*

in·som·ni·a | ĭn **sŏm′** nē ə | *n.* Inability to sleep, especially when persistent.

in·ter·plan·e·tar·y | ĭn′tər **plăn′** ĭ tĕr′ē | *adj.* Between planets, especially of the solar system.

in·ter·ro·ga·tion | ĭn tĕr′ə **gā′** shən | *n.* The act of questioning closely, as under formal conditions: *the interrogation of suspects.*

in·ti·mate | **ĭn′** tə mĭt | *adj.* Very personal; close: *an intimate friend.*

in·tu·i·tion | ĭn′ tōō **ĭsh′** ən | *or* | —tyōō | *n.* The power of knowing or understanding something instantly, by instinct, without having to reason it out or to get proof.

jade | jād | *n.* Either of two minerals that are usually white or pale green and are used as gemstones and as materials from which art objects are carved.

jos·tle | **jŏs′** əl | *v.* **jos·tled, jos·tling.** To come into contact, crowd, or brush against: *Thousands of people were jostling in the square.*

jour·nal·is·tic | jûr′ nə **lĭs′** tĭk | *adj.* Of or typical of journalism (the gathering and presentation of news), or journalists (people employed in journalism, especially reporters or editors).

leg·a·cy | **lĕg′** ə sē | *n., pl.* **leg·a·cies.** Something passed on to those who come later in time; heritage: *a legacy of military strength.*

lyr·ics | **lĭr′** ĭks | *n.* The words of a song.

mag·is·trate | **măj′** ĭ strāt′ | *or* | —strĭt | *n.* A civil official with the authority to administer the law.

mag·nate | **măg′** nāt′ | *or* | —nĭt | *n.* A powerful and influential person, especially in business.

ma·li·cious | mə **lĭsh′** əs | *adj.* Having, showing, or motivated by malice; spiteful: *a malicious lie.*

marsh·y | **mär′** shē | *adj.* **marsh·i·er, marsh·i·est.** Wet and swampy like a marsh (an area of low-lying, wet land).

mas·sive | **măs′** ĭv | *adj.* Large; heavy and solid; bulky: *a massive elephant.*

med·ley | **měd′** lē | *n., pl.* **med·leys.** A musical arrangement that uses a series of melodies from different sources.

mir·age | mĭ **räzh′** | *n.* An optical illusion in which something that is not really there is seen.

mock·ing | **mŏk′** ĭng | *adj.* Making fun of, often by imitating or depicting in an insulting way; ridiculing: *mocking eyes and a laugh of contempt.**

mon·o·tone | **mŏn′** ə tōn′ | *n.* A succession of sounds or words uttered in a single tone of voice.

mor·tar | **môr′** tər | *n.* A bowl used to hold substances while they are crushed or ground with a pestle.

murk·y | **mûr′** kē | *adj.* **1.** Dark; gloomy. **2.** Not clear; foggy; hazy: *a murky day.* **3.** Cloudy and dark with sediment: *Pools of murky water dotted the swampy shore.*

mute | myo͞ot | *adj.* Refraining from speech; silent: *remained mute under questioning.*

ni·tro·gen | **nī′** trə jən | *n.* One of the elements, a colorless, odorless, tasteless gas that forms about four-fifths of the earth's atmosphere.

o·blique | ō **blēk′** | *adj.* Indirect or evasive; not straightforward: *an oblique question.*

oil·y | **oi′** lē | *adj.* Unpleasantly smooth, as in manner or behavior: *his oily, insincere compliments.*

o·pal | **ō′** pəl | *n.* A translucent mineral composed of a form of silica, having rainbow-like, iridescent colors and often used as a gem.

op·u·lence | **ŏp′** yə ləns | *n.* **1.** Great wealth. **2.** A great amount or supply; abundance.

os·ten·si·ble | ə **stěn′** sə bəl | *adj.* Seeming or stated to be such, but often not actively so; pretended: *His ostensible purpose was charity, his real goal popularity.* —**os·ten′ si·bly.** *adv.*

o·ver·bear·ing | ō vər **bâr′** ĭng | *adj.* Arrogant and domineering in manner: *an overbearing person.*

pac·i·fy·ing·ly | **păs′** ə fī yĭng′ lē | *adv.* **1.** Calmingly. **2.** In a manner intended to establish peace.

pa·go·da | pə **gō′** də | *n.* A many-storied Buddhist tower, usually built as a memorial or shrine.

pal·lor | **păl′** ər | *n.* Unhealthy paleness.

pang |păng | *n.* A brief, sharp feeling of strong emotion: *a pang of remorse.*

par·a·dise | **păr′** ə dīs′ | *or* | —dĭz′ | *n.* A perfect or ideal place: *a paradise for fishermen.*

parch | pärch | *v.* To make or become very dry, especially with intense heat: *A constant south wind parched the topsoil. The skin wrinkles and parches with age.* —**parch·ing.**

ped·es·tal | **pěd′** ĭ stəl | *n.* A support or base, as for a column or statue.

per·se·vere | pûr′ sə **vîr′** | *v.* **per·se·vered, per·se·ver·ing.** To hold to or persist in a course, belief, purpose, etc., in spite of opposition or discouragement: *Many religions have persevered even under the most serious persecution.*

pes·si·mist | **pěs′** ə mĭst | *n.* A person who takes the gloomiest possible view of a situation or of the world.

pi·ous | **pī′** əs | *adj.* Reverently and earnestly religious; devout: *a simple, pious people.*

plight | plīt | *n.* A serious condition or a situation of difficulty or peril.

port·fo·li·o | pôrt **fō′** lē ō′ | *or* | pōrt— | *n., pl.* **port·fo·li·os.** A portable case for holding loose papers, documents, etc.

pre·vail | prĭ **vāl′** | *v.* To be greater in strength and influence; triumph: *"The wrong shall fail, the right prevail."*

pri·or | **prī′** ər | *adj.* Preceding in time or order: *his prior employment.*

pro·fu·sion | prə **fyo͞o′** zhən | *n.* Great quantity or amount.

proph·e·sy | **prŏf′** ĭ sī′ | *v.* **proph·e·sied, proph·e·sy·ing, proph·e·sies.** To predict (what is to happen) solemnly or confidently.

prox·im·i·ty | prŏk sĭm′ ĭ tē | *n.* The quality or fact of being near; closeness.

quench | kwĕnch | *v.* To cool and satisfy: *quenched her thirst with a tall glass of ice-cold water.*

ran·cor | răng′kər | *n.* Bitter resentment; deep-seated ill will.

rap·ture | răp′ chər | *n.* Overwhelming delight; joy that carries one away; bliss.

rasp | răsp | *or* | räsp | *n.* A harsh, grating sound. —**rasp′ing** *adj.*: *a rasping voice.*

rav·eled | răv′ əld | *adj.* Separated into single, loose threads; frayed.

rav·en·ous·ly | răv′ə nəs lē | *adv.* With greedy eagerness for food; in extreme hunger: *The dog snatched the meat and ate ravenously.**

rec·ol·lec·tion | rĕk′ ə lĕk′ shən | *n.* **1.** The act or power of remembering. **2.** Something remembered.

reel | rēl | *v.* To stagger: *reeling out of the smoky room, half-suffocated.*

re·fined | rĭ fīnd′ | *adj.* Cultivated; elegant: *a refined young lady.*

re·frain | rĭ frān′ | *v.* To hold oneself back; forbear: *refrain from talking.*

re·furl | rē fûrl′ | *v* To roll up and fasten again (a flag, a sail) to a pole.

re·morse | rĭ môrs′ | *n.* Bitter regret or guilt for having done something harmful or unjust.

ren·der·ing | rĕn′ dər ĭng | *n.* Performance (of a musical composition, dramatic work, etc.).

rep·er·toire | rĕp′ ər twär′ | *or* | —twôr′ | *n.* All of the songs, plays, operas, or other works that a person or company is prepared to perform.

re·signed | rĭ zīnd′ | *adj.* Feeling or showing passive acceptance of or submission to an unpleasant fate: *a resigned look on his face.* —**re·sign′ed·ly** *adv.*

rev·e·la·tion | rĕv′ ə lā′ shən | *n.* Something revealed, especially something surprising.

rev·er·ie | rĕv′ ə rē | *n.* Abstracted thought; daydreaming: *lost in a reverie.*

ro·man·tic | rō măn′ tĭk | *adj.* Inclined to dream of adventure, heroism, or love.

rout | rout | *v.* To drive a force from a resting place: *routing cattle from the barn.*

ruth·less | rooth′ lĭs | *adj.* Showing no pity; cruel. —**ruth′less·ly** *adv.* —**ruth′less·ness** *n.*

sa·cred | sā′ krĭd | *adj.* Regarded or treated with special reverence as belonging to, coming from, or being associated with God or a divine being or power; holy: *a sacred place; a sacred book.*

scep·ter, also **sceptre** | sĕp′ tər | *n.* A staff held by a sovereign as a sign of authority.

sear | sîr | *v.* To scorch or burn the surface with or as if with heat.

se·nile | sē′ nīl′ | *or* | sĕn′ īl′ | *adj.* Of, showing, or characteristic of senility (the weakening or loss of a person's mental or physical abilities due to old age).

ser·vi·tude | sûr′ vĭ tood′ | *or* | —tyood′ | *n.* The state of being subject to another person's authority. —**ser·vi·tudes.** Acts in service to others; slavish or obligated activities.

sheep·ish | shē′ pĭsh | *adj.* Embarrassed and apologetic: *He peeled the bubble gum from his nose with a sheepish grin.*

shoot | shoot | *n.* A plant or plant part, such as a stem, leaf, or bud, that has just begun to grow, sprout, or develop.

shroud | shroud | *n.* A cloth used to wrap a body for burial.

siege | sēj | *n.* The surrounding and blockading of a town or fortress by an army bent on capturing it.

sig·ni·fy | sĭg′ nə fī′ | *v.* **sig·ni·fied, sig·ni·fy·ing, sig·ni·fies.** To serve as a sign of: *What does this monument signify?*

sin·ew | sĭn′ yoo | *n.* The connective tissue of which tendons are composed: *sometimes animal sinews are prepared and used as cords or threads.*

sin·is·ter | sĭn′ ĭ stər | *adj.* Suggesting an evil force or motive: *a dark, sinister man.*

skep·ti·cism | skĕp′ tĭ sĭz′ əm | *n.* A doubting or questioning state of mind.

so·ber | sō′ bər | *adj.* **1.** Serious or grave: *sober gray eyes.* **2.** Not gay; plain or subdued: *the sober light of a rainy morning.*

span | spăn | *n.* A period of time: *a span of four hours.*

spas·mod·ic | spăz mŏd′ ĭk | *adj.* Happening intermittently; fitful: *spasmodic attempts to climb the mountain.*

spate | spāt | *n.* A sudden flood, rush, or outpouring: *a spate of bad luck.*

spell | spĕl | *v.* To relieve (someone) from work temporarily by taking a turn.

spoils | spoilz | *n.* Goods or property seized from the loser of a military conflict.

spurn | spûrn | *v.* To reject or refuse with disdain; scorn.

steam·er | stē′ mər | *n.* A steamship.

stig·ma | stĭg′ mə | *n.* *pl.* **stig·mas** or **stig·ma·ta** | stĭg mä′ tə | or | stĭg′ mə tə | . A mark or reputation of shame, disgrace, etc.: *There should be no stigma attached to doing strenuous physical work.*

sub·mis·sive | səb mĭs′ ĭv | *adj.* Tending to submit readily; compliant: *a submissive personality.*

sub·ter·fuge | sŭb′ tər fyooj′ | *n.* An evasive tactic or trick.

su·et | soo′ ĭt | *n.* The hard, fatty tissue around the kidneys of cattle and sheep, used in cooking and in making tallow.

sus·tain | sə stān′ | *v.* To keep in being or in effect; maintain; prolong: *sustain an effort; sustain a note for four beats.*

tac·i·turn | tăs′ ĭ tûrn′ | *adj.* Habitually silent or uncommunicative: *a taciturn man.*

ten·ta·tive | tĕn′ tə tĭv | *adj.* Not certain or permanent; not definite: *tentative plans; a tentative production schedule.* **—ten·ta·tive·ly** *adv.*

thrice | thrīs | *adj.* Three times: *He was thrice named player of the year.*

toil | toil | *n.* Struggle; battle; a laborious effort.

trans·fix | trăns fĭks′ | *v.* To pierce through with or as if with a pointed weapon; impale.

treach·er·ous | trĕch′ ər əs | *adj.* **1.** Characterized by or manifesting treachery (a violation of trust). **2.** Likely to betray a trust.

trem·u·lous | trĕm′ yə ləs | *adj.* Vibrating or quivering; trembling: *speaking with a tremulous voice.*

trill | trĭl | *n.* A fluttering or tremulous sound, as that made by certain birds; a warble.

trunk | trŭngk | *n.* The main part of the body, not including the arms, legs, and head. **—trunk·less** *adj.:* without a trunk.

tu·mult | too′ məlt | *or* | tyoo′— | *n.* din and commotion of a great crowd.

tyr·an·ny | tîr′ ə nē | *n., pl.* **tyr·an·nies.** Absolute power, especially when exercised unjustly or cruelly.

ty·rant | tī′ rənt | *n.* A ruler who exercises power in a harsh, cruel manner; an oppressor.

un·checked | ŭn chekt′ | *adj.* Not stopped; not controlled.

u·ni·ver·sal | yoo′ nə vûr′ səl | *adj.* **1.** Extending to or affecting the whole world; worldwide: *universal peace.* **2.** Of, for, done by, or affecting all: *universal education.*

un·re·quit·ed | ŭn rē kwīt′ əd | *adj.* Not returned; not reciprocated: *unrequited love.*

un·wield·y | ŭn wēl′ dē | *adj.* Difficult to carry or handle because of shape or size; clumsy: *an unwieldy bundle.*

vague | vāg | *adj.* Not clearly expressed; lacking clarity: *a vague statement; a vague promise.*

venge·ance | vĕn′ jəns | *n.* The act of causing harm to another person in retribution for a wrong or injury.

vir·tu·o·so | vûr′ choo ō′ sō | *n., pl.* **vir·tu·o·sos.** A musical performer of unusual excellence or ability.

vis·age | vĭz′ ĭj | *n.* The face or facial expression of a person.

wan | wŏn | *adj.* **wan·ner, wan·nest.** Unnaturally pale, as from illness: *a wan face.*

wan·ton | wŏn′ tən | *adj.* Shameless and uncontrolled: *wanton treachery; wanton lawlessness.* **—wan′ton·ly** *adv.*

with·er | wĭth′ ər | *v.* To become or cause to become wasted, worn out, etc., as if by drying out: *old people withering in strange new surroundings.*

wrack | răk | *v.* To have a violent or shattering effect on: *Sobs wracked her body.*

wran·gle | răng′ gəl | *v.* **wran·gled, wran·gling.** To argue noisily and angrily; bicker.

Handbook
of Literature, Reading, Vocabulary, and Research Skills and Terms

The following pages contain information about skills and terms that you will find helpful as you read the selections in this book and other materials as well. The terms are arranged alphabetically, with a brief definition or explanation for each. Examples from this book are used, and the section where a term is taught is indicated.

act   A part of a play. Acts may be divided into *scenes*.

almanac   A book containing many facts. Almanacs are published every year so that the facts will be up-to-date. The subjects almanacs cover include government leaders of the world, sports records, weather records, awards like the Nobel Prize, and the size and population of different countries. The facts may be given in the form of lists and charts.

When to use an almanac.   Almanacs give facts, but they do not discuss or explain them. Use an almanac when you are looking for a particular name or date, especially if the information is too recent to be in an encyclopedia. For example, if you wanted to find out who won the Nobel Prize for literature in 1986, an almanac would be the best place to find the information.

How to use an almanac.   To find the topic you want in an almanac, look it up in the index. The *index* is a section at the back of the book that lists topics alphabetically. If you were looking for Nobel Prize winners, you would look under *n* for *Nobel*. The index would tell you what page or pages the information is on.

Use the newest almanac you can get to be sure of finding the most recent information.

alphabetical order   The order of the letters in the alphabet. To put words in alphabetical order, look at the first letter of each word first. If the first letters are the same, look at the second letters, and so on.

Many research materials are arranged in alphabetical order, including *card catalogs, dictionaries, encyclopedias,* and *indexes.*

Remember, if you are looking for a person's name in alphabetical order, look for the last name first. If you are looking for a book title, ignore the articles *a, an,* and *the.*

antonyms Words that have opposite meanings. *Up* and *down* are antonyms. [Section 2]

article A short, nonfiction work; not a made-up story. Articles appear in newspapers, magazines, and books. (See also news story.)

atlas A book of maps. Some atlases also give other geographical information, such as the products of various regions, countries, or states.

When to use an atlas. Use an atlas when you need information on a map, including directions, locations of particular places, and distances between places. For example, if you wanted to know how far Miami, Florida, is from Gainesville, Florida, you would use an atlas.

How to use an atlas. Most atlases have an *index,* a section at the back of the book where the places shown on the maps are arranged in alphabetical order. The indexes will usually tell you both the number of the map you need and the particular section of the map that shows the place you are looking for.

For example, if you look up *Gainesville, Florida,* in the index, you might see a notation like this after it: "42 E 4." You would turn to map number 42 in the atlas. You would see that the map is divided into squares. You would look along the top of the page until you found the square marked E. Then you would look along the side of

the page for the square marked 4. Where the two squares meet, in square E 4, you would find Gainesville.

author The writer of an article, a story, a play, a poem, or a book. If you know who wrote a book, you can find the book in the library by looking at the *author card* in the *card catalog.*

author card A card in the library's *card catalog* that has the author's name at the top. Author cards are arranged alphabetically by the author's last name. (See also catalog card.)

author's purpose The author's goal in writing. Authors may wish to *entertain* readers by making them laugh as in "The Immortal Bard" (page 249), or by scaring them as in "The Last Dive" (page 393). Or an author may want to give readers a serious message about life as in "The Cat Who Thought She Was a Dog and the Dog Who Thought He Was a Cat" (page 29), explain something to readers, or tell a true story about a person as in "The Elephant Man" (page 34). (See also theme.)

autobiography Someone's true account of his or her own life. An autobiography is usually written from the *first-person point of view,* using the pronouns *I* and *me.* It tells important events from the author's life and says how the author feels about those events. "Excerpt from the Diary of Anaïs Nin" (page 168) is an example of an autobiography.   [Section 6]

bibliography A list of writings. Many books contain lists of other books and articles on the same subject. Here is part of a bibliography from a book about zoos. Notice that the entries are arranged alphabetically by the authors' last names. After each author's name comes the title of the book, the place where it was published, the publisher, and the date:

Crandall, Lee S. *Management of Wild Mammals in Captivity.* Chicago: University of Chicago Press, 1964.

Elgin, Robert. *The Tiger Is My Brother.* New York: Morrow, 1980.

Bibliographies are usually at the end of a book, although sometimes short bibliographies are given at the end of each chapter.

By looking at a bibliography, you can find the authors and titles of other books that may give you more information about the subject you are interested in.

For a list of bibliographies, look up your subject in *The Bibliographic Index.* It will tell you which publications contain bibliographies on the subject.

biographical dictionary   A special dictionary that gives information about famous people. Some biographical dictionaries are *Webster's Biographical Dictionary,* which includes information about people from many nations; the *Dictionary of American Biography;* and *Who's Who in America,* which is revised every second year and includes only people living at the time of publication.

When to use a biographical dictionary. Use a biographical dictionary when you need brief, factual information about a famous person. Biographical dictionaries usually give information such as birth (and death) dates, birthplaces, and important accomplishments. Many biographical dictionaries do not include details about a person's life. You may be able to find more details in an *encyclopedia.* If there is a *biography,* or book about the person's life, it would contain the most information of all.

How to use a biographical dictionary.   If the person you are looking up became famous recently, make sure the biographical dictionary you are using is new enough to list him or her. Check to see whether the dictionary includes people from your person's country.

In most biographical dictionaries, people are listed in alphabetical order by their last names. If you wanted information about George Washington, you would look for *Washington, George.* However, if you wanted information about Queen Victoria, you would look for *Victoria.* People are not listed by their titles.

biography   A true story about a person's life written by another person. A book-length biography will give you a lot of information about a person. "The Elephant Man" (page 34) is a short biography.   [Section 1]

To find out whether your library has any biographies about the person you are interested in, look for the person's name in the *subject cards* in the *card catalog.* The person would be listed there in alphabetical order, last name first. On library shelves, biographies are arranged together, alphabetically by subject names.

Books in Print   A list of books that are available for purchase from publishers doing business in this country. *Books in Print* is published every year in three sets. One set lists books alphabetically by author; another set lists books alphabetically by title; and a third set, *The Subject Guide to Books in Print,* lists books alphabetically by subject.

Books in Print is excellent for finding out what books are available at regular bookstores. Remember, though, that there are millions of books that are no longer "in print" but that can still be found in libraries and second-hand bookstores.

call number   The *Dewey Decimal Classification* number. A number written on library books and at the upper left-hand corner of *catalog cards* to show where the books are placed on the library shelves.

card catalog   A large cabinet in the library whose drawers, called trays, contain filing cards listing all the books in the library. There are three types of *catalog cards:* author, title, and subject. All are usually combined in the cabinet in alphabetical order. Letters on the front of each drawer, or tray, show which section of the alphabet it contains. The trays themselves are placed in the

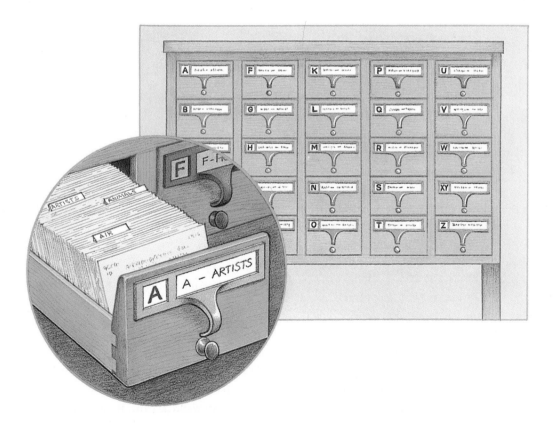

cabinet in alphabetical order, from top to bottom.

When to use the card catalog. Use the card catalog when you want to find out whether your library has a book whose title you know, or when you want to see what books your library has by a particular author or on a particular subject.

How to use the card catalog. See the next section, catalog card, for information on how to use the card catalog.

catalog card There are at least three cards in the *card catalog* for every nonfiction book in the library: an author card, a title card, and a subject card. Here is an example of an author card:

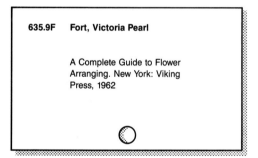

The top of this card tells you the author's name. Her name is Victoria Pearl Fort, but last names are listed first on catalog cards. Below the author's name are the title of the book, the place where it was published, the publisher's name, and the date of publication. At the top of the card is the call number that you should look for on the shelf in order to find the book: 635.9F. This card is called the *author card* because it has the author's name at the top.

The other two catalog cards contain the same information in a different order. Here is an example of a title card for the same book:

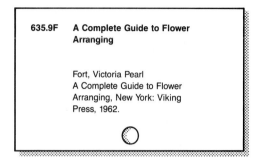

This is called a *title card* because it has the title at the top. Otherwise, the information is the same as on the author card.

Here is an example of a subject card:

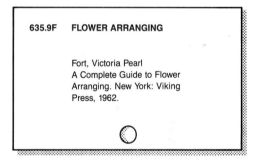

This is the *subject card* because it has the subject of the book at the top. If a book covers several subjects, it will have a separate subject card for each subject. Fiction books usually do not have subject cards.

When to use catalog cards. Use catalog cards to find out what books your library has and where they are located on the shelves.

How to use catalog cards. If you know the title of a book, you can look in the card catalog for the title card. Remember, all the cards are arranged in alphabetical order. If you were looking for *A Complete Guide to Flower Arranging,* you would look in the catalog drawer containing the letter *c* (for *Complete*), because the articles *a, an,* and *the* are ignored in alphabetizing titles. If you find the card, your library has the book. Note the call number given in the upper left-hand corner of the card. It will help you find the book on the shelves.

If you are looking for books by a particular author, look for author cards with that author's name. In this case, you would look in the *f* drawer for *Fort, Victoria Pearl.* There will be a separate card for each book the library has by that author. Make notes of the titles and call numbers.

If you are looking for books on a particular subject, look for subject cards. If you were interested in flower arranging, for example, you would look in the *f* drawer for cards with this heading. There will be a card for each book the library has on the subject. Note the titles, authors, and call numbers.

Now you can find the books on the library shelves. Look at the call numbers you wrote down. For the book we have been discussing, it is *635.9F.* This book would probably be on a shelf marked *635.* It would come after books with the call number *635.8.* (In a library, call numbers are marked on the side of the books, or *spines*.) The *F* in the call number is the initial of the author's name.

There are some exceptions to the rule. *Fiction* books are arranged on the shelves not by call number but alphabetically by the author's last name. *Biographies* are shelved together alphabetically by the sub-ject's name. *Reference books,* including *dictionaries* and *encyclopedias,* are kept on special shelves.

cause   Something that makes something else happen. (See also cause and effect.) [Section 7]

cause and effect   In some stories and some sentences, there is a cause-and-effect relationship. The *cause* is something that makes another thing happen. What happens is called the *effect.* In "The Necklace," (page 93), Madame Loisel lost her friend's necklace. The effect was that she and her husband borrowed money to buy a new necklace and lived in poverty for a number of years to pay off the loans.

Effects may have more than one cause. The Loisels' decision to lie to Madame Forestier about the necklace instead of telling her that it had been lost was another cause of the Loisels' poverty.

Think about cause-and-effect relationships as you read. Noticing clue words and phrases such as *because, since, so, so that, as a result of,* and *for this reason* will help you.   [Section 7]

character   A person or an animal in a story. (See also flat character and round character.)

characterization   The way an author informs readers about characters. *Direct characterization* is when the author describes the character directly. For example, an author might describe a character like this: "Sam hated parties. They always made him feel awkward and shy, and he never talked to anyone." *Indirect characterization* is when the author lets readers find out about a character through the character's own thoughts, speech, or actions. Sam might be described this way: "Sam spent most of the party standing by the refreshment table. When someone spilled lemonade on his pants, he said, 'I'm sorry.'"

Pay attention to the characters' thoughts, words, and actions when you read a story. They may be related to the message or *theme* that the author wants you to discover.   [Section 3]

chart   An orderly list of facts. Here is an example of a chart:

Noun	Adjective
Danger	Dangerous
Beauty	Beautiful
Remark	Remarkable

You can read this chart down or across. If you read down each column, you see a list of nouns and a list of adjectives. If you read across, you see which nouns and adjectives are similar.

climax   The highest point of action in a story. The climax is the same as the *turning point*.   [Section 2]

cloze exercise   A reading test in which words are left out of a selection and the reader is asked to fill in the blanks.   [Sections 10, 11]

compare   To say how two or more people or things are alike. Comparing often uses the words *like* or *as*. In "New Face" (page 336), the poet writes "the rush of feelings/ swift and flowing/as water." (See also comparison and contrast.)   [Section 3]

comparison and contrast   Comparison involves identifying how two people or things are alike. Contrast involves finding out how they are different. Comparisons add emphasis to reading and writing.

If you say that "New Face" (page 336) and "First Ice" (page 344) are both poems, you are making a comparison. If you say that "New Face" is about the joy of love, but "First Ice" is about the sadness of love, you are making a contrast.

In your writing, you will often be asked to compare and contrast two people or things; to say both how they are alike and how they differ.   [Section 3]

comparison of unlike things   See figurative language.

composition   See writing.   [Section 3]

compound word   A word made up of two or more smaller words. *Cowboy* is an example of a compound word. It is made up of the words *cow* and *boy*. Notice that the meaning of the compound word is different from the meaning of each word alone. [Section 1]

conclusion   1. The end of an article, a story, a play, a poem, or a book. 2. An opinion or judgment. To find out how to form opinions about stories and characters, see drawing conclusions.

conflict   A struggle or fight. Many selections contain conflict, because conflict helps make a story interesting. Readers want to find out who or what will win the struggle.

There are several types of conflict: (1) *Conflict of a person against another person or group.* For example, in "The Count of

Monte Cristo," (page 402) Edmond's conflict is with those who put him in jail. (2) *Conflict of a person against nature.* This type of conflict is found in "The Last Dive" (page 393). (3) *Inner conflict.* A person struggles with his or her own different feelings. Macbeth (page 566) has this type of conflict.   [Section 11]

contents   See table of contents.

context   The selection or part of a selection that contains a particular word or group of words. The context can affect the meaning of words or sentences. If you just read the sentence "Laura was hurt," you might think that Laura had been injured. However, if the sentence was in a story about someone refusing a present Laura had bought, you would know it meant she was insulted.   [Sections 1, 7, 10, 11]

context clues   Other words in a sentence, a paragraph, or lines of poetry that help you figure out the meaning of a word you do not know. Here is an example: "The teacher's *lucid* explanation helped the students understand." The explanation helped the students understand, so it must have been clear.   [Sections 1, 7, 10, 11]

contrast   To say how two or more people or things are different. (See also comparison and contrast.)   [Section 3]

copyright date   The date a book was published. The date is usually printed like this: ©1987. If you need up-to-date information, be sure the book was published recently.

critical reading   Making judgments about what you read. To read critically, you must try to find the author's message and under-

stand how the characters think and feel. You must read the author's descriptions and the characters' words and actions.

Here are some of the questions you might think about as you read critically: What is the *author's purpose,* and how well does he or she accomplish it?

In a story, does the *plot* make the message clear?

If *facts* are presented, are they correct?

Are the *characters* in a story believable? [Section 9]

decoding   Figuring out unfamiliar words from the sounds of the letters they contain. Knowing the sounds that different letters and groups of letters may make is important in decoding. Here are some examples:

a The letter *a* usually stands for the short *a* sound when it is followed by two consonants, as in *batter,* or by one consonant and no vowel, as in *tag. A* usually stands for the long *a* sound when it is followed by *i, y,* or a consonant and a vowel, as in *daily, day,* and *race.*

ch When the letters *ch* come together in a word, they may stand for the sounds at the beginning of *child.* That is the sound they always make when a *t* comes before the *ch,* as in *patch.* At other times, though, the letters *ch* together make a sound like *k,* as in *character.* If you are not sure which sound *ch* stands for, try saying the word both ways. See which way sounds like a word you know.

ea When the vowels *ea* come together, they usually stand for the long *e* sound, as in *teach.* However, sometimes they stand for the short e sound *thread*, the long a sound *great*, the vowel sound in *her*, *heard*, or the vowel sound in *here*, *beard*. If you are not sure which sound *ea* makes in a word you are reading, try pronouncing the word different ways until one pronunciation sounds like a word you know.

-ed Many words end with the suffix *-ed*. Sometimes the suffix is pronounced like a *t*, as in *skipped*. Sometimes it sounds like a *d*, as in *demanded*. At other times it stands for the *ed* sound, as in *batted*. If you know the base word, you can figure out which sound *-ed* has.

g The letter *g* usually stands for the sound at the beginning of *go*. However, when *g* is followed by an *e*, *i*, or *y*, it may make a *j* sound, as in *badge*, *giant*, or *gym*. Often when a *g* and an *h* come together, they are both silent, as in *night*.

i The letter *i* usually stands for the long *i* sound when it is followed by a consonant and then a vowel, as in *kite*. It usually stands for the short *i* sound when it is followed by two consonants, as in *kitten*, or by one consonant and no vowel, as in *him*. When *i* is followed by the letters *gh*, the *i* usually stands for the long *i* sound, as in *night*.

-ly Some words end with the suffix *-ly*. When the letters *-ly* come together at the end of a word, they make the sound *lee*, as in *slowly*.

-ous When the letters *-ous* come together at the end of a word, the suffix is usually pronounced like the word *us*. *Dangerous* is an example.

-tion Some words end with the suffix *-tion*. The letters *-tion* almost always make the sound *shun*, which rhymes with *run*. *Perfection* is an example.

y When the letter *y* comes at the beginning of the word, it usually stands for the sound you hear at the beginning of *yes*. When *y* comes at the end or in the middle of a word, it may stand for a vowel sound, as in *my*, *flying*, or *city*. When *y* comes after a vowel, it usually helps the vowel make a vowel sound, as in *say*, *joy*, or *saying*.

definition   The meaning of a word or term. Definitions are given in *dictionaries*.

description   A word picture of what someone or something is like. Authors include details about the person, place, or thing being described to help the readers form pictures in their minds.   [Section 4]

detail   A small piece of information. In a paragraph, the *main idea* tells what the paragraph is about, and the details give information to support or explain the main idea.

Sometimes important details are called *significant details*. *Significant* means "important" or "meaningful." For example, a significant detail in "Feathered Friend" (page 374) is that Claribel kept keeling over.   [Section 5]

Dewey Decimal Classification System   A system of arranging books according to their subject matter that was invented by Melvil Dewey. The subjects are divided into nine main classes and many sub-classes. The *call number* that is written on library books and *catalog cards* is the number the book is given in this system.

diagram A drawing that shows the parts of something or shows how something works.

dialect The way a character would speak in person. Spoken language is often different from standard written language. It is informal. It may contain expressions, slang, or pronunciations that are casual. (See also expressions.)

dialogue The conversation in a story or a play. The exact words the characters say. In a story, quotation marks point out the dialogue.

dictionary A book that lists words in alphabetical order and gives their meanings, pronunciations, and other information.

When to use a dictionary. Use a dictionary to find out any of the following things: the meaning of a word; how a word is spelled; how it is pronounced; where it is divided into syllables; where it comes from; synonyms (words that mean the same) and antonyms (opposites) for a word; the meanings of prefixes (word parts added to the beginning of a word) and the meanings of suffixes (word parts added to the ending of a word).

How to use a dictionary. Look up your word in alphabetical order. Guide words at the top of each dictionary page will tell you the first and last words contained on that page. Following a word are letters and symbols that tell you how to pronounce it. If you are not sure what the symbols stand for, turn to the pronunciation key at the beginning of the dictionary. That explains the meanings of the symbols.

direct characterization An author's direct description of a person or an animal in the story. The reader does not have to form an opinion about the character from his or her thoughts, speech, or actions, because the author says what the character is like. An example is in "The Elephant Man" (page 34), when the author writes that "He was a gentle, loving, lovable being, pleasant without a sour thought or unkind word for anyone." [Section 3]

drawing conclusions Making your own decisions about a story and its characters. The happenings and details in a story help you draw conclusions. For example, in "The Count of Monte Cristo" (page 402), when Faria dies, Edmond thinks of killing himself, from which you can conclude that Faria had been Edmond's only reason for continuing to live. [Section 4]

editorial An item in a newspaper or magazine that expresses the opinions or beliefs of the editors.

effect Something that happens as a result of a cause. (See also cause and effect.) [Section 7]

elements of plot The plot is the sequence, or order, of important events in a story or a play. The plot usually has four elements, or parts: (1) the *problem* that the characters face; (2) the *rising action* as the characters try to solve the problem; (3) the *turning point*, the highest point of the action, as the characters find a solution; and (4) the *resolution*, when readers learn how the solution affects the characters. (See also plot.) [Section 2]

encyclopedia A book or set of books containing information about many topics.

When to use an encyclopedia. Use an encyclopedia when you need a lot of information about a subject. For example, if you wanted to find out the history of libraries, the names of some famous modern libraries, and how libraries arrange their books, it would be a good idea to look up *library* in an encyclopedia.

How to use an encyclopedia. The articles in encyclopedias are arranged in alphabetical order. If the encyclopedia you are using is in more than one book or *volume*, be sure to look in the volume that includes the letter you are looking for.

entertain To give readers enjoyment by making them laugh or by scaring them. An *author's purpose* in writing may be to entertain readers.

essay A brief discussion of a particular subject or idea. [Section 8]

explain To state how or why something happens. An *author's purpose* may be to explain. [Section 7]

explanation An account of how or why something happens. When you write an explanation, help your readers understand by stating the events clearly and in the correct order. [Section 7]

expression A word or a group of words with a specific meaning; an idiom. For example, *hanging around* is an expression that means "waiting."

fact Something that can be proved or observed. For example, in "The Man in the Water" (page 432), the author says that Flight 90 was the flight that crashed. This is a fact that can be proved. You can look it up in newspapers of the time. The author also says that the real hero of the day was "the man in the water." This is a fact that was observed. [Section 8]

When you read, think about which statements are facts and which are *opinions* (ideas, beliefs, or feelings that cannot be proved).

fiction Made-up stories. Many of the stories in this book are fiction. Fiction that contains imaginary characters and events that are very much like people and happenings in real life is called *realistic fiction.* "The Laugher" (page 228) is an example of realistic fiction.

"The Cow-Tail Switch" (page 388) is not realistic fiction because it contains an event that could not happen in real life. [Section 1]

figurative language Words used in a fresh, new way to appeal to the imagination. The words take on more than their usual meanings.

Figurative language often compares two things that are not usually thought of as alike. Here are some examples:

The man's hair was as smooth as velvet. (The man's hair is compared to velvet.)

His voice was thunder. (His voice is compared to thunder.)

The clouds frowned at the earth. (The clouds' appearance is compared to a person's frown.) (See also *simile, metaphor,* and *personification.*)

first-person point of view Telling a story by using the pronouns *I* and *me.* Some stories told from the first-person point of view are *autobiographies,* or true accounts of a person's life. "Excerpt from the Diary of Anaïs Nin" (page 168) is an example. Other stories told in this way are *fiction*, or made-up stories, but the author pretends to be a character in the story and writes as if the events had happened to him or her. "Jane Eyre" (page 349) is an example.

finding facts   First decide what kind of fact you are looking for. For facts about words, you would look in a *dictionary*. For facts about places, you might use an *atlas*, an *encyclopedia*, or an *almanac*. For facts about people, you might use a *biography*, an *autobiography*, a *biographical dictionary*, an *encyclopedia*, or a *newspaper*. Sometimes you will want to read a *nonfiction* book to find facts. The *catalog cards* in the library's *card catalog* will tell you what books the library has and where to find them on the shelves.

flat character   A person in a story who is described only briefly. The author does not provide much information about the character. Sometimes that is because the character does not have a big part in the story. Other characters are more important. In "The Woman Who Had No Eye for Small Details" (page 379), the children are examples of this. At other times, even the main characters in a story are flat, because the author wants readers to concentrate on other things.

folktale   A story that has been handed down from generation to generation. Originally, folktales were spoken rather than written. Many folktales contain these elements:

They happened long ago and far away.

They contain unusual characters.

There is a *moral*, or lesson, to be learned from the story.   [Section 2]

foreshadowing   Clues in a story that hint at what is to happen at the end. In "Macbeth" (page 567), clues in the story hint of impending tragedy.   [Section 2]

form   The particular way in which an author chooses to write a story, an article, or a poem. For example, an author may choose to write a modern story as though it were an old folktale. Or an author may choose to write an article by stating the main idea and then giving examples that support it.

glossary   A list of important or hard words in a book, with their meanings. A glossary is usually at the end of a book. Not every book has a glossary.

graph   A drawing that shows how two kinds of information are related. There are several kinds of graphs. Here is a bar graph that shows average summer temperatures in Juneau, Alaska.

The two kinds of information that are related on this graph are the months, shown at the bottom of the graph, and the temperatures, shown at the left.

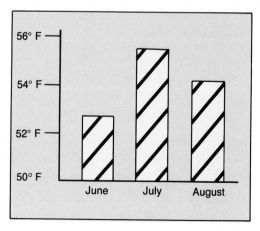

Here is a line graph that shows the same things:

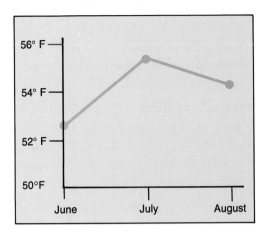

guide words   Words printed at the top of dictionary and encyclopedia pages to let you know the first and last words or topics on that page.

homophone   Words that sound alike but are spelled differently. The words *whole* and *hole* in the following sentences are homophones:

The whole family will be here.

Be careful you don't fall into the hole.

humor   The quality of being funny. An *author's purpose* or goal may be to entertain readers by making them laugh. In other cases, the author's main purpose may be to teach readers a message about life, but he or she uses humor to keep readers interested. In "The Immortal Bard" (page 249), the characters speak with humor. Through these characters, especially Robertson, the author gives the reader the message about how we sometimes only see things in our own, very narrow way.

Authors can create humor in several ways. They may use funny events or situations. They may use funny characters. They may use *word play*, such as nonsense words and words with double meanings. "The Importance of Being Earnest" (page 545) contains humorous characters and word play.

imagery   Words that appeal to the senses of sight, hearing, taste, touch, or smell. "The saw screeched through the wood," for example, is an image that appeals to the sense of hearing. Imagery is used in all forms of writing, but it is most common in poetry.   [Section 4]

index   A section at the back of a nonfiction book that lists the topics in the book in alphabetical order and tells what pages they are on. Use an index to see if facts you need are in the book.

Indexes in atlases usually give map numbers and sections instead of page numbers; see *atlas* to find out how to use this type of index. Indexes in newspapers are usually printed on the first page. They list sections and pages of regular features in the newspaper, such as the crossword puzzle.

indirect characterization   Instead of describing a character directly, the author tells about the character's thoughts, speech, and actions and leaves it up to the reader to decide what the person is like.

For example, in indirect characterization, an author would not say, "Ken was helpful." He or she might say, "When Ken had finished eating, he immediately cleared the table." Readers should be able to see for themselves that Ken was helpful.

inference A conclusion or guess based on the information presented. When you make an inference, you recognize clues the author gives as well as information he or she presents directly.

For example, in "With All Flags Flying" (page 459), when the old man first arrives at his daughter's house, she greets him with, "Did you ride all this way on a motorcycle? Oh, why didn't you find a telephone and call? I would have come. How long can you stay for?" You can infer from this, and especially from the use of the word "can," that the daughter cares very much for her father.   [Section 6]

inform To give readers information about some topic. An *author's purpose* may be to inform.

inner conflict A person's struggle with his or her own different feelings. If you love pizza but you are on a diet, you may have an inner conflict when you are offered a slice of pizza. (See also conflict.)

interview A meeting in order to get information from a person.

When to use an interview. Interviews are a good way of getting first-hand information from somebody with special experience or knowledge. For example, if you were interested in becoming a teacher, you might interview one of your teachers and ask about the advantages and disadvantages of teaching as a career.

How to interview. Before the interview, make a list of the questions you want to ask. Make an appointment for the interview, and tell the person what the purpose of the interview is. Ask permission to take notes. Notes will help you remember what the person said. If you have a recorder, you can use that instead of taking notes, but again you will need the person's permission. Ask permission to use the person's name if you are going to write about the interview or speak about it.

ironic turn of events When something happens that is different from what was expected. In "The Necklace" (page 93), Madame Loisel found out that the necklace was an imitation. [Section 10]

joint author A book with more than one author is said to have joint authors. There is an author card for each author in the *card catalog*.

journal 1. A diary. 2. A magazine, newspaper, or other work that is published every day, every week, or at other intervals.

judgment An opinion based on facts. Your own knowledge and experience help you make good judgments.   [Section 9]

legend A story handed down from earlier times that tries to explain how or why something in nature came to be. Every country and group of people has legends.

librarian A person who works in a library.

library 1. A collection of books and/or other materials. 2. The place where such a collection is kept. For information on finding books in a library, see catalog card.

library card A card that allows a person to borrow books from a library.

Library of Congress system A way of classifying and arranging books that is used in the National Library in Washington, D.C., and some other large libraries. The system is different from the *Dewey Decimal Classification System*, which is used in most school libraries.

magazine   A publication that contains stories, articles, pictures, and/or other features. Magazines are published weekly, monthly, or at other intervals.

main idea   The most important idea in a paragraph; the sentence that tells what the paragraph is about. The main idea may be at the beginning, the middle, or the end of a paragraph. In this paragraph from "Father and I" (page 278), the main idea is found in the first sentence: "I felt so lonely, forsaken. It was so strange that only I was afraid, not Father, that we didn't think the same. And strange that what he said didn't help me and stop me from being afraid." [Section 1]

map   A drawing or diagram of a place. Here is a map of California.

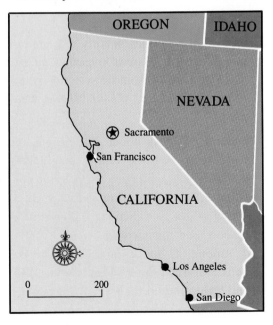

On the map, a special symbol stands for the capital city. You can tell that the capital of California is Sacramento.

Most maps contain a *compass rose* that shows directions. You can tell that San Diego is southeast of Sacramento.

The above map is called a *political map*. Political maps show divisions such as countries, states, and boundaries. There are other kinds of maps as well. For example, *physical maps* show physical features of the earth's surface, such as mountains and valleys.

For information about books of maps, see atlas.

meaning in poetry   Because poets often use words in special ways that appeal to your senses and allow you to form mental pictures, it is important to read the whole poem and examine all the words and ideas carefully so that you can understand the full meaning of the poem.   [Section 6]

message   An important idea about life that the author wants to tell readers. An author's purpose in writing may be to give readers such a message. (See also theme.) [Section 8]

metaphor   A comparison of two things that are not usually thought of as alike. Metaphors do not contain words such as *like* or *as*. Here is an example of a metaphor: "The football player's legs were tree trunks." The author does not mean the legs were really tree trunks. He or she is just comparing them to tree trunks.

Metaphors are a type of *figurative language*.   [Section 6]

mood   The strongest feeling or emotion in a work of literature. Plots, descriptions, conversations, and actions contribute to the mood. Examples of mood are *humor* and *suspense*.   [Section 5]

moral   A message or lesson about right and wrong. In some works, the moral is stated directly. In other works, readers can figure it out for themselves from the plot and the actions, thoughts, and speeches of the characters. Not every work has a moral.

multiple meaning of words   Some words have more than one meaning. From the context clues, or the way a word is used in a sentence, you can decide which meaning is correct. For example, *bat* can mean "a flying mammal" or "a stick." In the sentence "Joanne stepped up to the mound and lifted her bat," you can tell that *bat* means "a stick."   [Section 4]

mystery   A story or a play that contains a puzzle that the characters and the readers try to solve.   [Section 1]

myth   A story told by people in ancient times to explain life and nature. Many myths, including the Greek myths, are about gods and goddesses.

narration   Writing or speaking that tells a story.

narrative essay   See personal narrative essay.

narrative poem   A poem that tells a story. Like a story, a narrative poem has *characters* and a *plot* (a sequence of important events). The events occur in a particular order, or *sequence*. The poem has a beginning, a middle, and an end.   [Section 1]

narrator   A person who tells a story. Some stories, poems, and plays have a narrator who is a character in the work. For example, in "Feathered Friend" (page 374), the narrator is someone working on the space station.

newspaper   A paper that contains news, editorials (writings giving the editors' opinions), features, and that usually is published every day of the week.

When to use a newspaper.   Use a newspaper to find out about important recent happenings and about sports and entertainment events. Use newspaper advertisements to find out products for sale and jobs that are available.

How to use a newspaper.   Most newspapers have indexes on the front page that tell the sections and the pages of regular features, such as movie listings.

Libraries usually have old copies of newspapers. Sometimes they have been reduced in size and copied on film called *microfilm*. Libraries have special machines for viewing these films.

news story   A nonfiction story that appears in a newspaper or news magazine; an article. A news story should answer these questions: *Who? What? When? Where? Why? How?*

nonfiction   Writing about real people and real events. Articles, essays, biographies, and autobiographies are examples of nonfiction. Some nonfiction works such as encyclopedias and dictionaries, give information used for reference.

Among the nonfiction selections in this book are "The Painter's Hands" (page 232) and "The Man in the Water" (page 432).

notes   When you are doing research, it helps to take notes on what you read so that you will remember it. Write down the important information and the title, author, and page number of the book where you got it.

novel   A book-length piece of writing that tells a story. Novels are *fiction;* that is, they are made-up stories.

numbers   In alphabetical order, numbers appear as though they were spelled out. For example, if you were looking for a catalog card for a book title that started with *12,* you would look under *t* for *twelve.*

opinion   A statement about a person's ideas, beliefs, or feelings. Opinions cannot be proved true or false. Another person may have a different opinion. For example, in "The Man in the Water" (page 432), the author says, "Yet whatever moved these men to challenge death on behalf of their fellows is not peculiar to them. Everyone feels the possibility in himself or herself." This statement is an opinion. You may agree or disagree.

Authors often support their opinions with *facts* (statements that can be proved) that they hope will convince readers to share their beliefs.   [Section 8]

out-of-print book   A book that is no longer available for sale from the publisher or regular bookstores. You can often find out-of-print books in libraries or second-hand bookshops.

parts of a book   The front cover of a book gives the title and author and perhaps the person who did the pictures. The *spine* of the book is the side that shows on the li-brary shelves. The spine also gives the title and author. In libraries, the *call number* of the book is marked on the spine so that you can find the book on the shelf. Here is a picture of a book's spine:

Inside the book, one of the first pages is the *title page,* which again gives the title and author. Next to it is the *copyright page,* which tells when the book was published. If you need up-to-date facts, be sure the book was published recently.

Two parts of a book help you find out what topics are covered in the book. The *table of contents,* which is in the front of many books, lists all the chapters in the book. The *index,* which is at the back of many nonfiction books, is an alphabetical list of the topics in the book and the pages they are on. Use the table of contents to find out what broad subjects are covered in the book. Use the index to see whether facts you need are in the book.

A Complete Guide to Flower Arranging · Pearl

635.9F

periodical   A publication that comes out daily, weekly, monthly, or at other intervals. Magazines are periodicals.

personal narrative essay   A brief, nonfiction work in which an author expresses his or her own beliefs about a particular subject or idea.   [Sections 6, 8]

personification   Writing about a nonhuman thing as if it were human. For example, an author might say, "The wind grabbed at my coat." Personification really compares a nonhuman thing to a human being. In the example, the wind is compared to a person, who can grab a coat.

Personification is a type of *figurative language.*

persuasion   Convincing people to share your beliefs.

persuasive writing   Writing that tries to convince people to share the author's beliefs. The author usually states his or her opinions, or beliefs, and then supports them with facts, or true statements, and examples that may convince readers. [Section 10]

places   You can find information about places in *atlases, encyclopedias,* and *almanacs.*

play   Something written to be performed before an audience. A play may be divided into parts called *acts.* The acts are often divided into smaller parts called *scenes. Stage directions* tell the director or actors how the stage should look and how the characters should act, move, and speak.

Like stories, plays have plots, characterization, and settings. The *plot* is the sequence, or order, of important events. *Characterization* is the way an author informs the reader or the audience about the characters. In a play, you can learn about the characters through their speech and actions or through a narrator's descriptions. *Setting* is the time when and the place where the events of the story happen. The characters' speeches, the narrator's descriptions, and the stage directions all may give information about the setting.

Some plays in this book are *Iphigenia* (page 436), and *Macbeth* (page 566).

plot   The *sequence,* or order, of important events in a story, that makes a point or brings out a reaction in the reader. The plot has a beginning, a middle, and an end. The events are planned to get the reader interested and to show what the *theme,* or most important idea in the selection, is.

Usually the events that make up the plot can be divided into three elements, or parts:

1. *Rising action* is the part of the plot where a problem situation develops and the action builds up. In "Pygmalion" (page 234), Pygmalion carved a statue of a woman and fell in love with it.

2. The *turning point* is the highest point of the action. The characters find a way to solve the problem. In "Pygmalion," the statue came alive.

3. The *resolution* is the last part of the plot. The problem is solved, and readers learn how the characters react. In "Pygmalion," Pygmalion and Galatea got married. [Section 4]

poem   A written or spoken work with language chosen for its sound, beauty, and power to express feelings. (See also poetry.)

poet   The author of a poem.

poetry   Poems. Poetry looks and sounds different from other forms of writing. It looks different because poets arrange their words in lines instead of sentences and group these lines into stanzas instead of paragraphs. It sounds different because poets often use rhythm, rhyme, imagery, and figurative language.

Rhythm is the arrangement of the syllables in a line to make a particular sound pattern, or beat, as in music. You can hear the rhythm of a line of poetry best when you read it aloud. The punctuation and capitalization in a poem will help you decide when to pause and what to stress in order to hear the rhythm.

Rhyme is an element that many poems have. Two words rhyme when they end with the same sound: *cat, fat.* Two lines rhyme when they end with rhyming words. Here are rhyming lines from "Lady Clare" (page 59):

It was the time when lilies blow,
And clouds are highest up in air,
Lord Ronald brought a lily-white doe
To give his cousin, Lady Clare.

Imagery is language that appeals to the senses of sight, hearing, taste, touch, or smell.

Figurative language means words that are used in a new way to appeal to the imagination. Two things that do not seem alike may be compared. In "Loveliest of Trees" (page 430), for example, cherry blossoms are compared with snow.

There are other elements poets may use. For instance, *humor.*

The words and elements a poet chooses are part of the poet's *style.*

point of view The position from which a story is told. In the *first-person point of view,* an author tells a true story about his or her own life; or, in a made-up story, the author pretends to be one of the characters. The first-person point of view uses the pronouns *I* and *me* in telling the story. In the *third-person point of view,* the story-teller is not a character in the story. The author uses the pronouns *he, she,* and *they* to tell the story.

"Madame Sara" (page 288) is an example of a story told from the first-person point of view. "A Secret for Two" (page 273) is an example of a story told from the third-person point of view.   [Section 3]

predicting outcomes Guessing what will happen next in a story. You have a better chance of being right if you keep in mind what has already happened and what the characters are like.   [Section 2]

prefix A word part added to the beginning of a word. Each prefix has its own meaning. For example, the prefix *un-* means "not." If you add a prefix to a word, you change the meaning of the word. For example, *done* means finished. Add the prefix *un-* and you get *undone,* meaning "not finished."

If you do not know a word, look at the word parts. The meaning of each part can help you figure out the word.
[Sections 2, 5, 8, 9]

problem A difficult situation that the characters in a story have to solve. The problem is the first part of the *plot.* In "Pygmalion" (page 234), for example, the problem is that Pygmalion has fallen in love with a statue.   [Section 2]

prose Written work that is not poetry.

pun A humorous play on words, usually using a word or phrase with a double meaning.

publisher A person or company that prints and sells books, newspapers, magazines, and/or other written materials.

realistic fiction   Stories that contain made-up characters and events that are similar to people and happenings in real life. "With All Flags Flying" (page 459) is an example of realistic fiction.

Readers' Guide to Periodical Literature   A guide that comes out once or twice a month and lists recent magazine articles by their subjects. If you wanted to see what magazine articles had been written recently about whales, you would take a recent copy of the *Readers' Guide* and look under *w* for *whales*. If you wanted to read one of the listed articles, you might be able to borrow the magazine from the library. Large libraries have copies of many old and new magazines.

reference books   Books that are not meant to be read from cover to cover like a story but instead are used to look up particular facts. *Dictionaries, encyclopedias, atlases, almanacs,* and *biographical dictionaries* are important types of reference books.

Reference books are kept on special shelves in the library.

research   Investigation to find facts.

resolution   The last part of the *plot,* when the problem is solved, and you learn how the solution affects the characters. In "Pygmalion" (page 234), the resolution comes when Pygmalion and Galatea get married. [Section 2]

rhyme   An element found in many, though not all, poems. Words rhyme when they end with the same sound. Lines rhyme when they end with rhyming words.

rhythm   The arrangement of the syllables in a line of poetry so that they make a particular sound pattern, or beat, as in music. When you read poetry aloud, listen for the rhythm. The punctuation and capitalization in a poem will help you decide when to pause and what words to stress to make the rhythm clear.

rising action   The first part of a *plot.* The action builds up and a problem situation develops. In "Pygmalion" (page 234), the sculptor, who has always hated women, is overcome by the desire to carve a statue of a woman.   [Section 2]

root word   A word from which other words can be made. By adding a *prefix* to the beginning of a root word or a *suffix* to the end, you can change the word's meaning. For example, if you add the prefix *re-* to the root word *play,* you form the word *replay,* which means "play again." If you add the suffix *-ful* to the end of the root word, you get *playful,* which means "full of play" or "fun-loving."   [Sections 2, 5, 8]

round character   A character that is described fully. The author includes details that help you understand how the character thinks, acts, looks, and feels. The old man in "With All Flags Flying" (page 459) is a round character.   [Sections 3, 7]

scene   Part of a play. Plays are often divided into parts called *acts,* which, in turn, may be divided into smaller parts, the scenes.

sensory imagery   Words that appeal to the senses of sight, hearing, taste, touch, or smell.

sequence of events   The order in which events occur in a story or play. The events are put in a particular order, or sequence, so that the reader will understand what the story is about. The order of important events in a story makes up the *plot*.

setting   The time when and the place where the events of the story happen. You can tell what the setting is by looking for words or phrases that tell when and where.

Pay attention to time and place words throughout the selection, because the setting may change as the story or play goes on. For example, in "Sanctuary" (page 112), the setting shifts from an English village to London and back again. [Sections 9, 11]

short story   A brief work of *fiction* (made-up story).

significant detail   A small but important bit of information. (See also detail.) [Section 5]

simile   A comparison. Usually similes contain the word *like* or the word *as*. Examples of similes are "her hands were like ice" and "her hands were as cold as ice."   [Section 6]

speaking and listening   (See decoding.)

speech   A formal talk given in public before an audience. Speeches may present facts or opinions or both.   [Section 11]

spine   The part of a book that shows on the library shelf. The spine tells the book's title and author and, in a library, is marked with the book's *call number*.

stanza   A division of a poem that is longer than a line. Lines in poetry are grouped into stanzas in much the same way that sentences in other works are grouped into paragraphs.

The following stanza is part of the poem "Lady Clare" (page 59).

"He does not love me for my birth,
  Nor for my lands so broad and fair;
He loves me for my own true worth,
  And that is well," said Lady Clare.

stage directions   Directions in a play that tell the director or actors how the stage should look and how the characters are to act, move, and speak. Stage directions are not meant to be spoken out loud to the audience.

style   The words an author uses and the type of sentences he or she writes. For example, some authors use more *imagery*, or words that appeal to the senses, than other authors. Some authors write in short sentences, while others prefer to use long sentences. An author may change his or her style for different types of writing. In poetry, for instance, the author might use more imagery than when he or she was writing a nonfiction article.   [Section 6]

suffix   A word part added to the ending of a word. Each suffix has its own meaning. For example, the suffix *-less* means "without." If you add a suffix to a word, you change the meaning of the word. For example, *care* means "concern." Add the suffix *-less* and you get *careless*, which means "without concern."

If you do not know a word, look at the word parts. The meaning of each part can help you figure out the word. Here are some other examples of suffixes: *-ful*, "filled with"; and *-able*, "able." [Sections 2, 3, 4, 5, 8, 11]

subject card A card in the library's *card catalog* that has the subject at the top.

  The subject tells what the book is about. Subject cards are arranged alphabetically in the card catalog. *Fiction* books do not have subject cards. (For more information about subject cards, see catalog cards.)

summary A brief retelling of a story. A summary tells the main events. In order for people who have not read the story to understand it, the events should be in the correct order, or *sequence*.

surprise ending An ending that is different from what readers have been led to believe would happen. In most stories, the ending follows logically from the rest of the plot, or sequence of events. However, in stories with a surprise ending, the story takes an unexpected twist at the end.

  In "The Necklace" (page 93), the ending comes as a surprise both to the readers and to the characters in the story.   [Section 2]

suspense A quality that produces feelings of curiosity and tension in the reader, because the reader is not sure what will happen next. The suspense keeps you reading the story. The stories in Section 9 are written with suspense.   [Section 9]

synonyms Synonyms are words that have the same or almost the same meaning. *Try* and *attempt* are synonyms.   [Section 2]

symbol Something that stands for something else. For example, a heart may be a symbol of love. In "The Cat Who Thought She Was a Dog and the Dog WhoThought He Was a Cat" (page 29), the mirror symbolizes the loss of innocence.   [Section 7]

table of contents A section at the front of many books that lists all the chapters in the order in which they appear in the book. The table of contents tells you what broad subjects are covered in the book.

telephone directory A list of names, addresses, and telephone numbers.

theme The author's message; the most important idea in a written work. The *plot,* or sequence of important events in a story, helps to show what the theme is. So does the *characterization,* or what the author lets readers know or discover about the characters. Even if the author does not state the theme directly, you can figure out the message by thinking about the events in the story and the characters' thoughts, words, and actions.

  In some stories readers learn a lesson about life while laughing at the characters or the situations. The author uses humor to develop the theme. "The Cat Who Thought She Was a Dog and the Dog Who Thought He Was a Cat" (page 29) is an example of this. One theme of the story is that sometimes we're better off without the luxuries we desire so much.   [Sections 1, 8]

third-person point of view Telling a story by using the pronouns *he, she,* and *they*. Most *biographies,* or true accounts of another person's life, are written from the third-person point of view. "The Elephant Man" (page 34) is an example. Most (though not all) made-up stories are also written in a third-person point of view. (See also first-person point of view.)   [Section 3]

title card A card in the library's *card catalog* that has the book's title at the top.

Title cards are arranged alphabetically in the card catalog. The articles *a*, *an*, and *the* are ignored in alphabetizing the cards. (For more information about title cards, see catalog cards.)

title page   A page at the beginning of a book that gives the book's title and author.

turning point   The highest point of the action in a story. At the turning point, or climax, the characters finally find a way to solve the problem they have been facing. In "Pygmalion" (page 234), the turning point comes when the statue comes to life. [Section 2]

volume   1. A book. 2. One book in a set of books. 3. A group of issues of a magazine or other periodical.

word meaning   A definition. The best place to find the meaning of a word is in a dictionary. (See also context.) [Sections 1, 7, 10]

word origin   Where a word comes from. Most dictionaries include this information.

word parts   Root words, prefixes, and suffixes. A *root word* is a word from which other words can be made. A *prefix* is a word part added to the beginning of a word. A *suffix* is a word part added to the ending of a word. If you know the meaning of each word part, you can figure out the word.

For example, in the word *prepayable*, the prefix *pre-* means "before"; the root word *pay* means "to give money"; and the suffix *-able* means "able to be." By putting all these meanings together, you can see that *prepayable* means "able to be given money for, in advance." [Section 3]

word play   A humorous use of words. In order to be funny, authors sometimes use nonsense words and *puns*, or words with double meanings.

writing   These four steps will help you in your writing:

Step 1: Set Your Goal
Choose the topic that you will write about.

Step 2: Make a Plan
Plan what you are going to say. Often this involves making a list.

Step 3: Write a First Draft
Use your plan to write a first draft.

Step 4: Revise
Read what you have written. Make sure that it says what you want to say in a clear way. Correct any errors in spelling, grammar, and punctuation. Make a final, neat copy.

Here are the main writing assignments given in this book:

autobiographical narrative   For step 2, you list the details for each section of your narrative.   [Section 6]

composition   For step 2, you list all the facts and ideas that relate to your topic, gather information, and organize the information.   [Section 3]

description   For step 2, you list details that support the main idea and put them in order.   [Section 4]

explanation   For step 2, you list the steps that will be included and arrange them in a logical order.   [Section 7]

firsthand report   For step 2, you list the answers to who, what, when, where, how, and why questions.   [Section 5] *opinion*   For step 2, you list facts that support your opinion and arguments to counter possible objections.   [Section 8]

persuasive letter   For step 2, you list arguments that will convince your reader of your point of view.   [Section 10]

review   For step 2, you decide on your standards and choose examples to support them.   [Section 9]

story   For step 2, you describe the characters and the setting for the story, make a plot outline, and choose the point of view you will use.   [Section 2]

writing a speech   For step 2, you take notes on your topic and organize them.   [Section 11]

writing process   For step 2, you list the points you want to include.   [Section 1]

ACKNOWLEDGMENTS

Grateful acknowledgment is made to the following authors and publishers for the use of copyrighted materials. Every effort has been made to obtain permission to use previously published material. Any errors or omissions are unintentional.

Isaac Asimov for an adaptation of "The Immortal Bard" from *Earth Is Room Enough* by Isaac Asimov. Copyright © 1953 by Palmer Publications, Inc. Copyright renewed 1981 by Isaac Asimov.

Avon Books, a Division of The Hearst Corporation, for "The Speckled Band" from *Sir Arthur Conan Doyle's The Adventures of Sherlock Holmes* adapted from Catherine Edwards Sadler. Copyright © 1981 by Catherine Edwards Sadler.

The Bobbs-Merrill Company, Inc. for "Ooka and the Stolen Smell" from *Ooka the Wise: Tales of Old Japan.* Copyright © 1961 by I.G. Edmonds.

The Bodley Head for Canadian rights for "The Elm Log" from *Stories and Prose Poems* by Alexander Solzhenitsyn, translated by Michael Glenny.

Harold Courlander and George Herzog for "The Cow-Tail Switch" from *The Cow-Tail Switch and Other West African Stories* by Harold Courlander and George Herzog.

Crown Publishers, Inc. for "Forefathers" by Birago Diop in *An African Treasury* edited by Langston Hughes. Copyright © 1960 by Langston Hughes.

Joan Daves Agency for "Fear" by Gabriela Mistral from *Selected Poems of Gabriela Mistral*, translated by Doris Dana. Copyright © 1961, 1964, 1970, 1971 by Doris Dana.

Doubleday & Company, Inc. for excerpts from "Sheppey" by W. Somerset Maugham. Copyright 1933 by W. Somerset Maugham; "Marriage is a Private Affair" from *Girls At War and Other Stories* by Chinua Achebe. Copyright © 1972, 1973 by Chinua Achebe.

The Estate of Sir Arthur Conan Doyle for the adaptation of "The Speckled Band."

Faber and Faber Ltd. for "Blackie, the Electric Rembrandt" from *Moly and My Sad Captains* by Thom Gunn. Copyright © 1961, 1971, 1973 by Thom Gunn.

Farrar, Straus & Giroux, Inc. for "The Open Order" from *The Bound Man* by Ilse Aichinger, translated from the German by Eric Mosbacher. Copyright © 1956 by Ilse Aichinger; "Father and I" from *The Marriage Feast* by Par Lagerkvist, translated by Alan Blair. Copyright 1954 by Albert Bonniers Forlag; "The Elm Log" from *Stories and Prose Poems* by Alexander Solzhenitsyn. English translation copyright © 1970 by Michael Glenny; "The Cat Who Thought She Was a Dog and the Dog Who Thought He Was a Cat" from *Naftali the Story-Teller and His Horse, Sus* by Isaac Bashevis Singer. Copyright © 1973 by Isaac Bashevis Singer; "The Washwoman" from *A Day of Pleasure* by Isaac Bashevis Singer. Copyright © 1963, 1965, 1966, 1969 by Isaac Bashevis Singer; "Blackie, the Electric Rembrandt" from *Moly and My Sad Captains* by Thomas Gunn. Copyright © 1961, 1971, 1973 by Thom Gunn.

Everett C. Frost, Executive Producer of *The Spider's Web*, WGBH, Boston, for the adaptation of "Billy Budd," a radio play by Marvin Mandell, based on the story by Herman Melville. Copyright © 1984 by WGBH, Boston.

Herbert Goldstone for "Virtuoso." Copyright 1953 by Mercury Press, Inc. Reprinted from *The Magazine of Fantasy and Science Fiction.*

Harcourt Brace Jovanovich, Inc. for excerpts from *The Diary of Anaïs Nin, Volume V.* Copyright © 1974 by Anaïs Nin; "Feathered Friend" from *The Other Side of the Sky* by Arthur C. Clarke. Copyright © 1958 by Arthur C. Clarke; "The Secret" from *The Wind from the Sun: Stories from the Space Age* by Arthur C. Clarke. Copyright © 1962, 1963, 1964, 1965, 1967, 1970, 1971, 1972 by Arthur C. Clarke; "New Face" from *Revolutionary Petunias and Other Poems* by Alice Walker. Copyright © 1973 by Alice Walker.

Harold Ober Associates and Dodd, Mead & Co. for "Sanctuary" by Agatha Christie from *Double Sin and Other Stories* by Agatha Christie. Copyright 1954 by Agatha Christie. Copyright renewed 1982 by Rosalind Hicks; for Canadian rights for "Marriage is a Private Affair" from *Girls At War and Other Stories* by Chinua Achebe. Copyright © 1972, 1973 by Chinua Achebe.

Holt, Rinehart and Winston, Publishers for "The Bedquilt" from *Hillsboro People* by Dorothy Canfield Fisher. Copyright 1915 by Holt, Rinehart and Winston. Copyright 1943 by Dorothy Canfield Fisher; "Loveliest of trees, the cherry now" from "A Shropshire Lad" (Authorized Edition) from *The Collected Poems of A.E. Housman.* Copyright 1939, 1940, © 1965 by Holt, Rinehart and Winston. Copyright © 1967, 1968 by Robert E. Symons.

Houghton Mifflin Company and George Allen & Unwin Ltd. for "The Old Walking Song" from *The Fellowship of the Ring* by J.R.R. Tolkien. Copyright © 1965 by J.R.R. Tolkien.

Lysander Kemp for "Return Voyage" by Jorge Carrera Andrade, translated by Lysander Kemp, from *Modern European Poetry* edited by Willis Barnstone. Published by Bantam Books.

Alfred A. Knopf, Inc. for "The Woman Who Had No Eye for Small Details" from *The Old Man at the Railroad Crossing and Other Tales* by William Maxwell. Copyright © 1966 by William Maxwell; an adaptation of "The Necklace" from *The Collected Novels and Stories of Guy de Maupassant* by Guy de Maupassant, translated by Ernest Boyd. Copyright 1924 and renewed 1952 by Alfred A. Knopf, Inc.

McGraw-Hill Book Company for "The Laugher" from *18 Stories* by Heinrich Böll, translated from the German by Leila Vennewitz. Copyright © 1966 by Heinrich Böll.

ILLUSTRATION AND PHOTOGRAPHY CREDITS

Illustrations: pp. 21, 24-25, 27, 198-199, 203, 376-377, 538-539, 543, Lyle Miller; pp. 30-31, 102-103, 106-107, 530-531, Silvia Almeida; pp. 36, 40-41, 172-173, 176, 180-181, Paul Geiger; pp. 96-97, 99, 240-241, 245, 246, Sue Rother; pp. 113, 116, 120, 123, 126, Bradley Clark; pp. 154-155, Barbara Samuels; p. 165, Carla Bauer; pp. 218-219, 223, 390-391, 438, 442-443, Floyd Cooper; p. 229, Robert Steele; pp. 235, 324-325, Kathryn Yingling; pp. 250-251, Will Kefauver; p. 253, Brian Cody; p. 264, Rosekrans Hoffman; pp. 268, 271, 404-405, 407, Rick Porter; pp. 292, 297, 301, Gerry Hoover; pp. 308, 311, Tom Leonard; pp. 329, 332, 395, 398-399, Greg Voth; p. 411, Arieh Zeldich; pp. 423, 426-427, 470, 502-503, Arvis Stewart; pp. 460, 464-465, Tom Stoerle; pp. 484, 488-489, Konrad Hack; p. 494, Ron Hall; p. 506, Alberto Montano; pp. 520, 525, Ivan Powell.

Photography: p. 19, Yale University Art Gallery, New Haven; pp. 46-47, 51, 54-55, 186-187, 188, 192-193, 233, 274-275, 352, 358, 548-549, 553, 554-555, 565, 588-589, The Bettmann Archive; p. 60, The Cleveland Museum of Art, Ohio; pp. 65, 87, 355, 357, 361, Culver Pictures; pp. 71, 132, 137-138, 140-141, 569, 576, 584-585, 594, Movie Stills Archive; p. 91, Toledo Museum of Art, Ohio; pp. 151, 226, Saskia/Editorial Photocolor Archives; pp. 160-161, 261, 280-281, 338, 509, The Metropolitan Museum of Art, New York; pp. 166-167, Albert Moldaun/Woodfin Camp and Associates; p. 169, Freer Gallery of Art/Smithsonian Institution; p. 215, Bishop Hill Historic Site, Illinois; pp. 284-285, Barbara Kirk; p. 321, Scala/Editorial Photocolor Archives; p. 337, Richard Hutchings/Photo Researchers; p. 340, Osterreichisches Museum fur angerwandte Kunst, Vienna; p. 343, Ronin Gallery; p. 344, Carl Mydans/Black Star; pp. 346-347, 481, 499, Museum of Modern Art, New York; p. 373, Tom McHugh/Photo Researchers; pp. 380-381, Townsend P. Dickinson/Photo Researchers; p. 387, Marc and Evelyne Bernheim/Woodfin Camp and Associates; p. 401, Michal Heron/Woodfin Camp and Associates; p. 449, Paolo Koch/Photo Researchers; pp. 450-451, Mathias Oppersdorff/Photo Researchers; pp. 454-455, Leonard Wolfe/Photo Researchers; p. 517, Jack Daly; p. 384, Laura Riley/Bruce Coleman; p. 421, Hirshhorn Museum and Sculpture Garden/Smithsonian Institution; p. 433, Wide World Photos; p. 534, Museum of Fine Arts, Boston; pp. 430-431, Gene Ahrens/Bruce Coleman; p. 557, Whitney Museum of American Art, New York.